W9-CZS-884

BASEBALL BETWEEN THE WARS

A PICTORIAL TRIBUTE TO THE MEN WHO MADE THE GAME IN CHICAGO FROM 1909 TO 1947

BILL HAGEMAN

Contemporary Books

Chicago   New York   San Francisco   Lisbon   London   Madrid   Mexico City
Milan   New Delhi   San Juan   Seoul   Singapore   Sydney   Toronto

Brooklyn Dodgers catcher Al Lopez shows
the ump he held onto the ball after tagging
the Cubs' Kiki Cuyler at home during an
8–3 Cubs victory in May of 1935.

Library of Congress Cataloging-in-Publication Data

Hageman, Bill.
　　　Baseball between the wars : a pictorial tribute to the men who made the game
　　in Chicago from 1909 to 1947 / Bill Hageman.
　　　　　　p.　　cm.
　　　Includes index.
　　　ISBN 0-8092-9748-5 (acid-free paper)
　　　　　1.　Baseball—Illinois—Chicago—History—20th century.　　2.　Baseball—
　　Illinois—Chicago—History—20th century—Pictorial works.　　3. Chicago Cubs
　　(Baseball team)—History —20th century.　　4.　Chicago White Sox (Baseball
　　team)—History—20th century.　　I.　Title.

　　GV863.I32　H34　　2001
　　796.357′64′097731109041—dc21　　　　　　　　　　　　　　　00-48392

Contemporary Books

A Division of The **McGraw·Hill** *Companies*

1 2 3 4 5 6 7 8 9 0　KGP/KGP　0 9 8 7 6 5 4 3 2 1

ISBN 0-8092-9748-5

Interior design by Nick Panos
This book was set in Bembo
Printed and bound by Quebecor—Kingsport

Interior photos courtesy of The Chicago Tribune Company

McGraw-Hill books are available at special quantity discounts to use as premiums and
sales promotions, or for use in corporate training programs. For more information, please
write to the Director of Special Sales, Professional Publishing, McGraw-Hill, Two Penn
Plaza, New York, NY 10121-2298. Or contact your local bookstore.

This book is printed on acid-free paper.

In memory of Ellis Schwartz, a true baseball fan

PREFACE

CONTENTS

THE STORY OF THE *Chicago Tribune*'s glass negatives was always kind of a work-

place urban legend. Late one night about 15 years ago, in a conversation around

the sports copy desk, someone mentioned that there was a room in Tribune

Tower full of boxes of old baseball-related glass negatives.

PREFACE

Every few years, it seemed I'd hear something else about these negatives—most of them were cracked or broken; they weren't cataloged and no one knew exactly what was stored; the *Tribune* was going to hire a company to catalog the collection and was probably going to sell it; most of the collection had been thrown out years before and only a few hundred survived.

These additional tidbits kept my interest alive. Finally, three years ago I decided to make some inquiries. I discovered that, like most urban legends, the story of the glass negatives wasn't as mysterious as I'd been led to believe. There were indeed glass negatives in storage—hundreds of boxes of them, covering not only baseball, but all aspects of life in the first 40 years of the twentieth century—and most were cataloged to some degree. Some were cracked and some had deteriorated badly, but many were in fairly good condition. Most interesting to me, these photos hadn't been seen in print for 70 or 80 years.

My original idea was to republish some of the baseball images in book form. During a meeting at which I made my proposal, I was told about other material in storage—photos from the *Tribune* and papers the *Tribune* has owned over the years (the *Chicago American*, *Chicago Herald American*, and *Chicago Herald & Examiner*). These, I was told, would also be available to me, giving me thousands of images from which to choose.

After almost two years of looking at microfilm indexes, digging through boxes of negatives, and pulling photo files out of cabinets and off shelves, I have come up with almost 300 wonderful images.

This book would have remained just a dream without the help of a number of people. My sincere thanks to Rob Taylor and Caroline McCoy at Contemporary Books, who shepherded this project along. From the *Chicago Tribune* I want to acknowledge and thank the following people: Joe Leonard, who approved the project for the *Tribune* and gave me some much-appreciated early guidance; John Jansson, who granted me access to the archives and spent a lot of his time making sure photos and negatives got to the right people; Kemper Kirkpatrick, Rich Rott, and Larry Underwood, who led me into the dusty depths of Tribune Tower, showed me where everything was stored, and turned me loose; and the Photo Department's Don Bierman, who oversaw all the scanning of photos and negatives. Also, thanks to my family, Dona, Julie, Kelly, and Katie, for putting up with still more piles of my clutter around the house. Lastly, my thanks to the dozens of anonymous photographers who captured the images presented here. They witnessed history, and through their work, they preserved it for the rest of us to enjoy.

BASEBALL BETWEEN
THE WARS

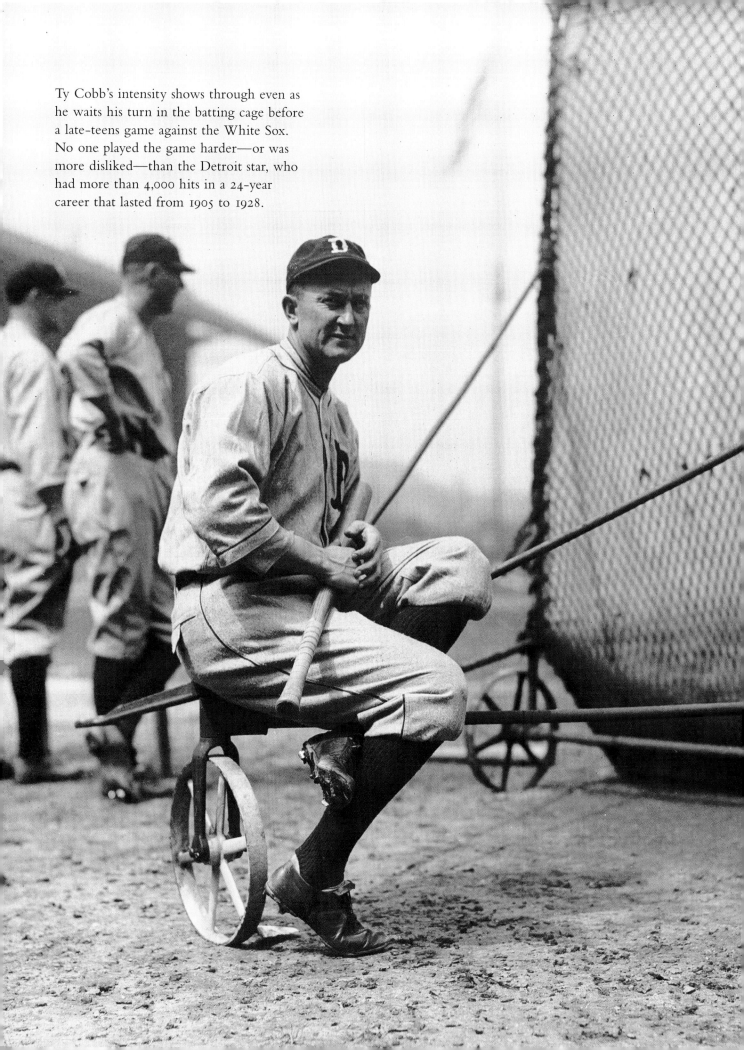

Ty Cobb's intensity shows through even as he waits his turn in the batting cage before a late-teens game against the White Sox. No one played the game harder—or was more disliked—than the Detroit star, who had more than 4,000 hits in a 24-year career that lasted from 1905 to 1928.

THEY HAD NICKNAMES LIKE Three Finger and the Georgia Peach, Hippo and the Flying Dutchman, the Crab and the Hitless Wonders. Largely unschooled and often crude, they were a raucous bunch who came from the nation's coal mines, farms, and dirty industrial cities. And America loved them.

THE DEAD-BALL ERA

With its roots in the British games of cricket, rounders, and town ball, baseball evolved into a professional sport during the last third of the nineteenth century. By the turn of the century, baseball had captured the interest and loyalty of Americans. Our national pastime had been established, and baseball's stars became our heroes.

Arguably, the greatest player in the early years was John Peter "Honus" Wagner. After leaving the Pennsylvania coal mines as a teenager, he became the National League's top player, batting .349 between 1900 and 1910, leading the league in hitting seven times, and carrying the Pittsburgh Pirates to pennants in 1903 and 1909.

Then there was Cobb, as despised as he was dazzling. Breaking in with the Tigers in 1905, he was the game's dominant hitter for a generation, chalking up 4,189 hits, a .366 lifetime batting average, a career .512 slugging average, and 10 American League batting championships. "There are a lot of things to remember about Cobb," former Sox great Ray Schalk once told the *Tribune*'s Dave Condon. "The most vivid, however, is . . . his determination. He'd see a player who could do something great, and he'd say to himself, 'I can do it better.'" With Cobb leading the way, and with a strong supporting cast that included

Sam Crawford, Davey Jones, Ed Killian, and Bill Donovan, the Tigers won AL pennants in 1907, '08, and '09.

The most dominant aspect of baseball in these years was pitching, due mainly to a combination of the dead ball and some legendary pitchers. Foremost among them was Christy Mathewson, the scholarly gentleman from Factoryville, Pennsylvania, who came to the New York Giants in 1900 and owned the decade. His accomplishments include winning 30 or more games four times; posting a cumulative 263–121 record from 1900 to 1910; leading the league in strikeouts five times, in shutouts four times, and in ERA three times; and helping manager John McGraw's Giants win two pennants. "When big things were at stake," Irving Vaughan wrote in the *Tribune*, "it was Matty who toiled. His right arm was the backbone of the Giants."

Chicago was not without its own talent during this dead-ball era, most of it on the mound. The Cubs boasted several of the game's top pitchers, including Mordecai "Three Finger" Brown. As a child Brown lost one finger in a farm accident and had two others broken and misshapen. As a result, he held the ball in a way that produced a devastating curve. He came to the Cubs in a trade with St. Louis before the 1904 season. He won 15 and 18 games in his first two campaigns, and then led Chicago to the World Series in a breakout 1906 season, which included 10 shutouts. The *Tribune* called him "a pitching wonder, greater than the great Mathewson, even at Christy's best." He won 20, 29, 27, and 25 games in his next four seasons, with ERAs of 1.39, 1.47, 1.31, and 1.86.

Another of Cubs manager Frank Selee's brilliant moves was signing pitcher Ed Reulbach off the Notre Dame campus in 1905. He won 18 games in his rookie season, then followed it with 19–4, 17–4, and 24–7 seasons.

Still another pitching mainstay at West Side Park was Orval Overall. The Cubs obtained him in a trade with Cincinnati in July 1906, and he promptly won 12 of 15 decisions to help them to the NL pennant.

There was no shortage of heroes on the South Side during this era, either. Again, that roster was dominated by pitchers. The best of them was Ed Walsh. One of baseball's great workhorses, Walsh came to the Sox in 1904, acquired sight-unseen for $750 by owner Charles Comiskey. His first two years were mediocre, but he blossomed in 1906 after mastering the spitball. Walsh won 17 games that year, followed by 24, 40, 15, 18, 27, and 27. He led the league in appearances five times and twice pitched more than 400 innings in a season.

Another South Side pitching star was Doc White. He broke in with Philadelphia in 1901 and came to the Sox two years later. From 1903 to 1910, he won 139 games for the South Siders, including an 18–6, 1.52 ERA season in 1906 and a league-leading 27 victories in 1907. As diverse as he was talented, Doc earned his nickname through his prebaseball work as a dentist. He also cowrote songs with famed writer Ring Lardner and designed the Sox uniforms worn when Comiskey Park was inaugurated in 1910.

It was players like these that made the first years of the twentieth century so memorable. The stage, however, had been set years earlier. The National League, born in 1876, was dominated in its first year by the Chicago White Stockings and their star pitcher Al Spalding. The White Stockings—known also as the Colts, Orphans, Spuds, and eventually the Cubs—dominated the early years of the new league and won pennants in 1876, '80, '82, '85, and '86. They then finished second or third in each of the next five seasons before sinking into mediocrity.

The 1900 season provided a turning point in baseball, not only in Chicago but across the country. On March 8, National League owners voted to eliminate unprofitable franchises in Baltimore, Cleveland, Washington, and Louisville, reducing the league to eight teams. Star players such as Wagner, McGraw, Buck Freeman, Joe McGinnity, and Fred Clarke were forced to find new homes. The elimination of the four franchises made dozens of players available and left several large territories without professional teams. The creation of the American League filled this gap.

Previously, the American League had been called the Western League. President Ban Johnson changed the name, encouraged his teams to sign some of the now-available talent, and put teams in three cities abandoned by the National League—Baltimore, Cleveland, and Washington. Most significant, though, was the move of Charles Comiskey's St. Paul, Minnesota, franchise to Chicago.

"For several years it has been the great ambition of the Western—now American—League to get a foothold in Chicago," reported the *Chicago Tribune* in a preview of the 1900 season. "They wanted the prestige of Chicago as a member of their circuit. That much is already accomplished, and the American League is reaping and will continue to reap its benefits."

Comiskey's White Sox—he took the name as a jab at Chicago's other team, now known as the Orphans—opened their season at a new 7,500-seat ballpark at 39th and Wentworth. "When the fans see the new grounds they will probably be surprised, for the park is one of the finest in the country," the *Tribune* reported.

Chicago fell in love with its new team, if only because the White Stockings showed themselves to be among the American League's best. The Orphans, on the other hand, tailed off and tied for fifth place in the National League race. "Another century is coming," the *Tribune* said of the Orphans, "and perhaps in that Chicago may win a pennant."

During their inaugural season, the White Stockings held off the Connie Mack-managed Milwaukee ball club to capture the first American League pennant. Encouraged by the success in Chicago and elsewhere, Johnson declared his American League a major league, an equal to the National League. He put teams in Philadelphia and Boston, in direct competition with the National League, and more than 100 former NL players moved to the upstart league for the 1901 season.

Soon it was quite obvious that the Chicago teams were equal in name only. The White Stockings repeated as American League champs, while the Orphans stumbled home sixth, 37½ games behind the Wagner-led Pittsburgh Pirates.

The Orphans' turnaround began with the naming of Selee as manager in 1902. He pieced together what would become a Hall of Fame infield by making catcher Frank Chance his first baseman, moving Joe Tinker from third to short, and acquiring Johnny Evers from the minors. The team climbed to fifth place that season, only one game under .500, but the foundation for their domination of the rest of the decade had already been laid.

Over on the South Side, Comiskey's ball club was the victim of the American League's success at raiding the National League for talent. Mack's Philadelphia A's, bolstered by the addition of former NL players such as Harry Davis, Rube Waddell, Lave Cross, and Socks Seybold, won the AL pennant in 1902 and '05. Boston, with NL refugees Cy Young, Bill Dineen, and Fred Parent leading the way, won in 1903 and '04. The New York Giants won consecutive National League pennants in 1904 and '05. With a pitching staff that was second to none, the Orphans were runners-up in 1904 and placed third in '05. In 1906, though, there would be no stopping them, as they began a winning streak of three consecutive National League pennants.

The 1906 season is memorable for a variety of reasons: the Orphans—who became the Cubs in 1907—went 116–36 to win the pennant by 20 games, Harry Steinfeldt (the answer to a great trivia question: who was the fourth and generally forgotten member of Chicago's immortal infield?) had a .327 batting average and 83 RBIs, the Cubs had a league-leading .262 batting average and .969 fielding percentage, and pitcher Three Finger Brown went 26–6 with a 1.04 ERA.

What made the season even more memorable was what was going on at 39th and Wentworth. The White Sox entered the month of August in fourth place with a 50–42 record, 8½ games in back of first-place Philadelphia. But manager Fielder Jones's boys came alive, winning 19 straight to put themselves in the driver's seat. "The Sox are the merriest bunch in the land tonight," the *Tribune* reported the day after they'd beaten Washington for their nineteenth in a row. "Jones and his lads have nothing but smiles."

"As for the world's championship," Jones told the *Tribune* on August 24, the day before the streak ended, "it will be played in Chicago, at least as far as we are concerned. Bet your bottom cent on that. And here is something more: Bet on the Sox to win the world's championship against the Spuds."

The Sox were true to their manager's word, beating out the New York Highlanders—later known as the Yankees—by three games. They won the championship with pitching and defense, for these White Sox were the original Hitless Wonders. Frank Isbell was their leading hitter at .279; Jones, who also played center field, led in homers with two (they had only six as a team); and the Sox were last in the league in batting (.230) and slugging (.286). Anchoring the pitching was Nick Altrock (21–12, 2.06), followed by Frank Owen (19–12, 2.33), Walsh (19–15, 1.88), and White (18–6, 1.52). Even with that staff, the punchless White Sox would be no match for Chance's powerful ball club. Or so the experts thought.

As usual, the experts were wrong. The White Sox used great pitching and just enough hitting to win the Series in six games. Walsh won two games, allowing only two earned runs and seven hits in 15 innings of work (he also had 17 strikeouts). "Maybe we'll get another whack at each other next year," Comiskey told Cubs owner Charles Murphy after the final game.

"That's right," Murphy answered. "I hope both clubs win again next year, and that we'll have another meeting next fall." Ninety-five years later, the world is still waiting.

The World Champions came back to earth in 1907, finishing third, 5½ games behind Cobb's powerful Tigers. It would be 10 years before they gave Comiskey another pennant, as they finished third in 1908, fourth in '09, and sixth in '10.

The Cubs, on the other hand, continued their dominance. They won 107 games in 1907 to capture their second consecutive pennant, this time by 17 games. Again the explanation was pitching: Brown was 20–6, Overall was 23–8, Reulbach was 17–4, Jack Pfeister was 15–9, and the staff ERA was a major-league best 1.73. Cobb and the Tigers were no match for these Cubs, who, after the teams played to a tie in Game 1, swept the next four games of the World Series.

The 1908 season is remembered for the greatest pennant race in National League history. In the end, the champion was decided not by a play that was made, but by one that wasn't. The Cubs, Giants, and Pirates engaged in a three-way race all season. The turning point came on September 23 at the Polo Grounds in New York. In the bottom of the ninth, with two out, Moose McCormick on third and Fred Merkle on first, Al Bridwell lined a clean single to center. McCormick trotted home with the apparent winning run, but Merkle stopped before reaching second and headed straight to the clubhouse. Quick-thinking Evers, in the midst of the celebrating New York mob, called for the ball, touched second, and then went to umpire Hank O'Day claiming a force on Merkle. O'Day agreed and, with the field overrun by fans, declared the game a 1–1 tie.

"There have been some complicated plays in baseball," wrote Charles Dryden in the next morning's *Tribune*, "but we do not recall one like this in a career of years of monkeying with the national pastime."

The regular season ended with the Cubs and Giants having identical 98–55 records, setting the stage for a one-day playoff October 8 in New York. The Cubs, with the pitching of Brown and the hitting of Tinker, beat Mathewson to advance to the World Series. There they again made short work of the Tigers, winning their second consecutive World Championship in five games and, as of this writing, their last.

The 1909 season belonged to Wagner's Pirates, who were wire-to-wire winners as the Cubs slipped to second despite winning 104 games. They rebounded in 1910, however, winning their third NL pennant in four years, but lost to Mack's A's in the World Series.

Although there wasn't much to cheer about on the South Side in the closing years of the first decade of the twentieth century, White Sox fans did have something to celebrate. On July 1, 1910, the Sox opened Comiskey Park, the "Baseball Palace of the World." Previewing the new ballpark, I. E. Sanborn wrote in the *Tribune*, "Today, with Charles A. Comiskey, noblest Roman of them all, as host, Chicago will christen as the new home of its White Sox, the greatest baseball plant in the world, not only in size, but in detail; one which combines every perfection of its predecessors in other cities and in which no expense has been spared to remove all imperfections of other plants of similar nature."

Over the next 80 years, Comiskey Park would see some of the greatest players and teams the sport has ever known. And in 1919, it was the sight of the game's biggest scandal.

Frank Chance, baseball's "Peerless Leader," warms up at the Cubs' West Side Park in 1908. Chance managed and played first base that season for the Cubs, who finished one game ahead of New York and Pittsburgh in the National League race and then beat Ty Cobb and Detroit in five games in the World Series. Chance teamed with Joe Tinker and Johnny Evers to form the most famous—though probably not the best—double-play combination of their time. Immortalized in verse by New York sportswriter Franklin P. Adams ("These are the saddest of possible words: Tinker to Evers to Chance"), all three entered the Hall of Fame in 1946.

"Doc" White came by his
nickname honestly: he was a
dentist. In addition to his
pitching skills—190 victories in
13 major-league seasons for the
White Sox and Phillies—he
was also a violinist, singer, and
songwriter. He later coached a
college team, owned a minor-
league franchise, and was a
traveling evangelist.

Pittsburgh's Honus Wagner was bow-legged and barrel-chested, hardly the prototype shortstop. But with his huge hands and surprising speed, he handled the position remarkably well. He was an even better hitter, winning eight National League batting titles and hitting .300 or better for 17 consecutive seasons.

Fielder Jones—that was his given name—was a solid outfielder for Brooklyn and the White Sox from 1896 to 1908. He also managed the "Hitless Wonders" of 1906 to their World Series victory over the heavily favored Cubs. Jones closed out his playing career with St. Louis of the Federal League in 1915.

Charles Comiskey, "The Old Roman,"
had an uneventful playing career in the
1880s, but became one of the most
important men in the game after
moving his Western League franchise
to Chicago as part of the new
American League.

Ban Johnson could be
stubborn and heavy-
handed, but he was just
what was needed to get
the upstart American
League off the ground in
1901. As league president,
he was arguably the most
powerful man in
baseball—until the arrival
of Kenesaw Mountain
Landis as baseball's first
commissioner.

Infielder Lee Tannehill spent 10 years
with the White Sox, never hitting
above .254. Defensively, though, he
was one of the best, a perfect fit for
the "Hitless Wonders" who won
with pitching and defense.

Ed Reulbach led the
National League in
winning percentage in
1906 (the year this
photo was taken),
1907, and 1908, all
pennant-winning
years for the Cubs.

Jim "Hippo" Vaughn—he got his nickname not from his size, but because he had a peculiar side-to-side gait when he ran—began his career in the American League in 1908 and came to the Cubs in 1913. He won 20 or more games five times and 19 games once for them in eight years. His greatest moment came in 1917, when he and Cincinnati's Fred Toney hooked up in a double no-hitter through nine innings. Vaughan eventually lost in the tenth on an error and misplayed grounder.

Walter Johnson began his career in 1907 in the dead-ball era and was still winning games more than 20 years later. His long arms and huge hands helped make him one of the most dominant pitchers the game has ever seen. He went 36–7 with a 1.09 ERA in 1913, the year these photos were taken, and won 416 games over 21 years for the Washington Senators. As gentlemanly as he was skillful, Johnson was a favorite of opponents, fans, and the press.

Josh Devore earned a reputation as an expert leadoff man for John McGraw's New York Giants. Walks and stolen bases were his specialty.

Two childhood farm accidents cost Mordecai Brown his index finger and left two other fingers badly misshapen. He soon realized that the gnarled hand allowed him to do wondrous things with a baseball, and he became one of the game's top pitchers in the first decade of the twentieth century. With a curveball second to none—Ty Cobb said it was the most devastating pitch he ever faced—Three Finger Brown won 239 games in a 14-year career.

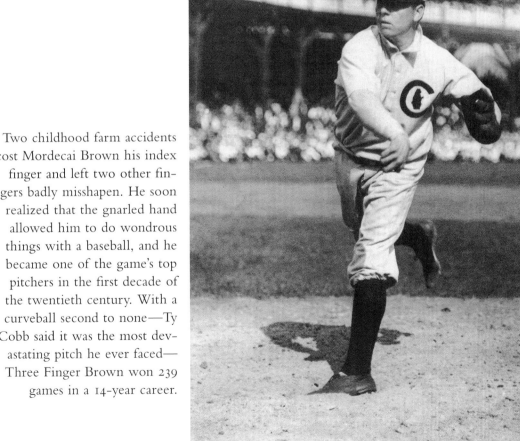

The sportswriter in the middle of this 1910 photo is William Veeck of the *Chicago American*. His frequent criticism of the Cubs in print later prompted owner William Wrigley to name him club president. Ten years later, Veeck was called to testify before a grand jury that was investigating the fixing of games, a probe that uncovered the Black Sox scandal.

Spitballer Ed Walsh was the workhorse for the White Sox staffs between 1907 and 1912. In five of those seasons, he led the league in appearances, and in four of them was tops in innings pitched. His 1908 season was one for the ages: 40 victories, 42 complete games, 6 saves, 464 innings pitched, and 269 strikeouts, all major-league leading figures.

Cubs owner Charles Weeghman and manager Fred Mitchell pc during the pennant-winning 1918 season. The Cubs had the misfortune of meeting the Boston Red Sox and their ace pitcher, Babe Ruth, in the World Series, with Ruth winning two games and the Red Sox beating the Cubs in six games.

By THE SECOND DECADE of the twentieth century, baseball had established itself as America's national game. As interest in the sport grew, so too did the number of new ballparks. Concrete and steel facilities were christened in Boston (Fenway Park, 1912, and Braves Field, 1915), Brooklyn (Ebbets Field, 1913), and Cincinnati (Crosley Field, 1912). Two new ballparks also opened in Chicago during this era: White Sox Park at 35th and Shields in 1910, and North Side Ball Park (later Weeghman Park and eventually Wrigley Field) at Clark and Addison in 1914.

GROWTH AND SCANDAL

This building boom not only reflected the public's interest in the game, but owners' interest in increased seating capacity. Combined attendance for the American and National Leagues climbed steadily, from 3.6 million in 1901 to 6.5 million in 1919, with only the arrival of the Federal League and World War I reversing the trend.

While stadiums were changing, the game itself didn't evolve much during these years. Rule changes were few and relatively minor—a foul bunt with two strikes became a strikeout, coaches on the sidelines were allowed to communicate with batters and baserunners, and batters had to touch all of the bases in order. Strategy still reflected the dead-ball era mentality of pitching, defense, and playing for one or two runs through use of the hit-and-run, bunts, and stolen bases.

But two things would eventually change the face of the game. The first was the introduction of a livelier, cork-centered ball in 1910. By the time it became standard, the dead-ball era would disappear and the long-ball era would be born. The second big event that forever changed baseball was the arrival of the Great Bambino.

It was announced in an eight-line story at the very bottom of the lead sports page in the July 10, 1914, *Chicago Tribune*: "President James J. Lannin of the Boston Americans today announced that he had purchased pitchers Ruth and Shore from the Baltimore club of the International league," the story read. "Catcher Egan also was included in the deal. Lannin said that the three players represented an outlay of more than $25,000 by the Boston club."

Babe Ruth had arrived in the American League, and baseball would never be the same.

Ruth was born in 1895, the son of a Baltimore saloonkeeper. He spent much of his youth at St. Mary's Industrial School, where orphans, delinquents, and children from broken homes or poor families could get an education. Ruth starred for St. Mary's baseball teams, and shortly after he turned 19, he signed a contract with the International League club in Baltimore. The deal with Boston came only a few months later, and Ruth made his big-league debut on July 11, 1914, pitching the Red Sox to a victory over Cleveland.

Harry Hooper, one of Ruth's teammates in those early days, later recalled the big, crude kid who came to Boston. "George was six feet two and weighed 198 pounds, all of it muscle," he once told author Lawrence S. Ritter. "He had a slim waist, huge biceps, no self-discipline, and not much education—not so very much different from a lot of other 19-year-old would-be ball players. Except for two things: he could eat more than anyone else, and he could hit a baseball further."

Ruth appeared in only five games for Boston that season, then blossomed into one of the top pitchers in the game over the next three years, going 18–8 in 1915, 23–12 in 1916, and 24–13 in 1917. But his batting skills—he hit .315, .272 and .325 in those first three full seasons, and he led the American League in home runs in '17 with 11—convinced Boston management it needed Ruth in the lineup on a daily basis. So, starting in 1918, he split his time between the mound and the outfield.

Despite Ruth's arrival on the scene and almost immediate stardom, the biggest name in the American League was still Ty Cobb. Between 1911 and 1920, the Georgia Peach won seven American League batting championships, including seasons of .420 in 1911 and .409 in 1912. He led the league in hits five times, in slugging four times, in stolen bases four times, and in runs three times.

He was also at the center of one of baseball's strangest controversies. On May 15, 1912, Cobb went into the stands during a game in New York and attacked a fan who had been heckling him. Cobb, quoted in the *Tribune*, said, "I tried to avoid the man, but when his language became too much for me to stand I lost my head."

American League President Ban Johnson suspended Cobb indefinitely, and Cobb's teammates responded by going on strike, refusing to take the field for a game on May 18 at Philadelphia. Seeking to avoid a $5,000 fine for a forfeit, Detroit management put together a makeshift team of college players, coaches, and sandlotters. The result was a 24–2 loss.

The walkout lasted only one game. The regulars returned, professing loyalty to owner Frank Navin, and were each fined $100 by the league. Cobb's suspension was lifted after 10 days, and he returned to the lineup on May 25.

Although Cobb went on to bat .409 in 1912, the real hitting star that season played his ball in Chicago. Henry Zimmerman—most called him "Heine," though he preferred "The Great Zim"—had a career year for the Cubs, hitting .372 with 207 hits, 41 doubles, 14 triples, 14 homers, 99 runs batted in, and 23 stolen bases.

Zimmerman's 1912 season reads like fiction. Coming out of spring training, Cubs player-manager Frank Chance had him penciled in as a utility man. But recurrent headaches, the result of years of beanings, forced Chance to end his playing career. Zimmerman took over as the Cubs' first baseman—he was later shifted to third—and hit safely in his first 23 games as a regular. He kept his average over .400 until the last week of July, and coasted to the NL batting championship.

Zimmerman was never able to replicate his career season. He had three more years with the Cubs, each less productive than the previous. He was traded to the New York Giants in 1916, and his career ended in 1919 when he was suspended by manager John McGraw, who learned that the Great Zim had offered a teammate $800 to throw a game.

Zimmerman's 1912 season was one of the few highlights for the Cubs during the early years of the decade. McGraw's Giants won the National League pennant in 1911, '12, and '13, while the Cubs finished second, third, and third those seasons.

The 1914 season was memorable on several accounts. One was the Miracle Braves from Boston, who spent much of the season in last place and were 10 games out of first in mid-July. They won 60 of their last 76 games, took the

National League pennant by 10½ games, and then swept Connie Mack's Philadelphia A's in four games in the World Series.

Bigger headlines in 1914 came from the birth of the rival Federal League, which put teams in Chicago, Baltimore, Brooklyn, Buffalo, Indianapolis, Kansas City, Pittsburgh, and St. Louis. The Feds weren't around long, but the league's impact on baseball was undeniable. For starters, several big names jumped to the Federal League, including Joe Tinker and Claude Hendrix (Chicago), Russ Ford and Hal Chase (Buffalo), Mordecai Brown and Fielder Jones (St. Louis), and Howie Camnitz (Pittsburgh). In addition, the added competition cut into the established league's attendance and profits and helped drive up player salaries to more reasonable levels.

The Federal League lasted only two seasons, but it left a legacy in Chicago that still stands today: Wrigley Field.

The Chicago Feds were owned by businessman Charles Weeghman, who built North Side Ball Park. As part of the agreement between American and National League owners and the Federal League, Weeghman was allowed to purchase the Cubs. He delivered a $500,000 check on January 20, 1916, to complete the deal.

"It was an epochal day in the history of the great American game in Chicago, and the happiest man of them all was Weeghman," wrote James Crusinberry in the next morning's *Tribune*. "It has been his ambition for years to own the Cubs, and when the final details of the sale had been completed he expressed his joy with admirable enthusiasm."

" 'This is the biggest day of my life,' he said. '. . . I hope we can restore the Cubs to the place they once held in the hearts of Chicago fans. I think we will have a great team this year to start our task.' "

Weeghman was in for a disappointment. The Cubs' new ballpark (and lack of competition for fans from the Feds) helped them double their attendance to more than 453,000 fans. But the Cubs staggered home a disappointing fifth, 19 games under .500.

It would be 1918 before the Cubs justified Weeghman's optimism. That year, led by a strong pitching staff anchored by Hippo Vaughn, Hendrix, and Lefty Tyler, they won the National League pennant by 10½ games in a season shortened by America's involvement in World War I.

The Cubs' reward was a date with Ruth and the Red Sox in the World Series.

The Series was dominated by pitching. Ruth outdueled Vaughn 1–0 in the opener. The Cubs bounced back to win Game 2 3–1. Vaughn was again the loser in Game 3 despite another stellar performance, losing 2–1 to Carl Mays. Ruth put Boston ahead 2–0 in Game 4 with a two-run triple in the fourth, and pitched shutout ball into the eighth, increasing his record of scoreless World Series innings to 29⅔. The Cubs tied the game briefly, but the Red Sox scored in the bottom of the eighth and won 3–2 for a 3–1 Series lead. Vaughn was finally able to win one the next day, blanking Boston 3–0 on five hits. But the Red Sox wrapped up the Series with a 2–1 victory in Game 6, Mays outdueling Tyler.

This World Series loss began a period of decline for the Cubs, who finished third in 1919 and sixth the following season, a slide that continued through the first half of the 1920s.

On the South Side of town, the White Sox weren't even a .500 ball club from 1911 to 1914, going 303–308 under managers Hugh Duffy and Nixey Callahan, and never finishing higher than fourth. Mack's Philadelphia A's won pennants in three of those four years, and Boston finished first in 1912, '15, and '16. By 1916, though, Comiskey had managed to put together a contender.

Taking advantage of Mack's payroll-reduction housecleaning after the 1914 season, Comiskey purchased star second baseman Eddie Collins, the cornerstone of Philadelphia's famed "$100,000 infield." Also during that off-season, he acquired outfielder Oscar "Happy" Felsch from the minors, and in August of 1915 traded for Cleveland outfielder Joe Jackson.

The 1916 team won 89 games and finished second, two games behind the Red Sox. Collins hit .308, Felsch .300, and Jackson .341 to provide the offense, while the Sox pitching, led by Ed Cicotte (15–7, 1.78 ERA), Lefty Williams (13–7, 2.89), and Red Faber (17–9, 2.02), was the best in the league.

It all came together for the White Sox in 1917. A major-league record 684,521 fans visited Comiskey Park and saw their heroes go 100–54—the franchise has never again equaled that winning percentage—and run away with the American League pennant.

Chicago's opponent in the World Series was John McGraw's Giants, easy winners in the National League. It promised to be an exciting Series.

"Nothing that happens should surprise the fans," wrote Irving E. Sanborn in the October 4, 1917, *Tribune*. "The White Sox may win the world's pennant in four straight games, the Giants may cop it in four straight, or it may go the limit, plus extra innings."

With Collins hitting .409, Jackson .304, and shortstop Buck Weaver .333, and Faber winning three times, the White Sox beat the Giants in six games for their second—and, to this day, last—World Series crown.

World War I cost the White Sox several key players in 1918, and the team finished the abbreviated season in sixth place at 57–67. The following year, with everyone having returned, the White Sox were able to take the American League lead in July and coast to the 1919 pennant. The stars for the Sox were Jackson (.351), Collins (.319), Cicotte (29–7, 1.82), and Williams (23–11, 2.64). The supporting cast included first baseman Chick Gandil (.290), shortstop Swede Risberg (.256), third baseman Buck Weaver (.296), centerfielder Felsch (.275), and backup infielder Fred McMullin (.294). Those last five, along with Cicotte, Jackson, and Williams, would leave a mark on the game that would never be forgotten.

The World Series pitted Chicago against the underdog Cincinnati Reds. Before Game 1, with "smart money" gamblers starting to bet heavily on the Reds, the first rumors of a fix surfaced. Cicotte's first pitch of the opening game hit the Reds' leadoff man, a prearranged message to gamblers that the fix was in. The Reds won the Series—expanded to best-of-nine by owners looking for extra revenue—in eight games. Cicotte, almost unbeatable during the regular season, lost his first two decisions before winning Game 7. Williams walked six batters in Game 2, the first of his three Series losses. Felsch batted just .182 and Risberg .080 in eight games.

Despite the rumors and suspicions, it would be almost a year before the scandal broke. It started with a trickle. On August 31, 1920, the Phillies were in Chicago. Cubs management was tipped off that there was heavy betting on the Phils and there were rumors that the game was fixed. Cubs starting pitcher Claude Hendrix was pulled and replaced by Grover Cleveland Alexander, who pitched well but still lost. (Hendrix, incidentally, was cut after the season and never pitched in the majors again.) In the following days, talk of more fixed games began to surface. The September 5 *Tribune* reported that in the past year, 26 major-leaguers had been suspected of being in league with gamblers.

A grand jury investigation was begun, and the scandal soon blossomed. New York Giants pitcher Rube Benton, former Giants Hal Chase and Heine Zimmerman, both of whom came under suspicion of throwing games in 1919 and were suspended by manager John McGraw, and former Cub Lee Magee were among those called as witnesses.

The page 1 headline in the September 23, 1920, *Tribune* told the story: "BARE FIXED WORLD SERIES." The accompanying story, by James Crusinberry, went on to report the testimony of Cubs infielder Buck Herzog, who laid out the details of the World Series fix.

"The last world series between the Chicago White Sox and the Cincinnati Reds was not on the square," assistant state's attorney Hartley L. Replogle told the *Tribune*. "From five to seven players on the White Sox were involved."

Eight players were eventually indicted: Cicotte, Jackson, McMullin, Felsch, Risberg, Williams, Weaver, and Gandil. When news of the indictments was announced on September 28, Comiskey immediately suspended all but Gandil, who had already quit baseball after the 1919 season.

The suspensions effectively eliminated the Sox from the 1920 pennant race. At the time, they were only two games out of first place and were, arguably, a better ball club than the 1919 American League champions. Less than a month after the indictments were announced, major-league owners named Kenesaw Mountain Landis, a U.S. district court judge, commissioner of baseball. Among his first acts in this role was the suspension of the eight players the following March, pending their trial.

The players went on trial in June 1921. Five weeks of legal maneuvering and testimony ended with a jury deliberation of only 2 hours and 47 minutes—and the acquittal of all eight players.

For Landis, however, that wasn't enough. "Regardless of the verdict of juries," he said in a statement issued the following day, "no player that throws a game, no player that entertains proposals or promises to throw a game, no player that sits in a conference with a bunch of crooked gamblers, where the ways and means of throwing games are discussed, and does not promptly tell his club about it, will ever play professional baseball."

The next day he banned the players for life. "The most scandalous chapter in the game's history is closed," he said. And the most glorious era was about to begin.

Bill Killifer was a good defensive catcher who came to the Cubs in a package deal with his batterymate, pitcher Grover Cleveland Alexander, for $55,000 just before World War I. He led National League catchers in fielding three times and closed out his 13-year career with the Cubs in 1921.

White Sox owner Charles Comiskey (right) visits with William "Kid" Gleason, manager of the ill-fated "Black Sox" team of 1919. Gleason managed the Sox for four more years after the scandal, compiling an overall managerial record of 392–364.

Red Killifer of the New York Giants shows his form before a game against the Cubs in 1916.

Wilbert Robinson—
"Uncle Robbie"—
managed Brooklyn for
18 seasons, compiling a
1,399–1,398 record and
winning pennants in 1916
and 1920. For many of
those years, the team was
known as the Robins, in
honor of its well-liked
manager.

For one season, 1912, there
was no better hitter in the
National League than
Heine Zimmerman. In his
first year as a regular, "The
Great Zim," as he liked to
be called, had 207 hits, 14
homers, and a .372 batting
average, all National
League bests. But his performance declined every
year after that, and his
career ended in 1919 when
he was suspended by the
New York Giants, allegedly
for trying to bribe team-
mates to throw games.

Babe Ruth, as a Boston Red Sox pitcher, waits in the on-deck circle at
Comiskey Park. Between 1914 and 1919, Ruth won 89 games for the Red
Sox. He also hit 45 homers during that time, including league-leading figures
of 11 in 1918 and 29 in 1919.

Chicago restaurateur Charles Weeghman passes a check for $500,000 to J. G. Wakefield of the Corn Exchange National Bank in January 1916, thereby taking over ownership of the Cubs. Weeghman had owned the Chicago Whales of the Federal League, and as part of the peace agreement that put the Feds out of business, he was allowed to buy the Cubs from Charles Taft. Weeghman, pictured with State Sen. Albert J. Olsen of Woodstock and a mascot after the deal was finalized, owned the Cubs only until 1921, when he sold controlling interest to William Wrigley.

Zach Wheat warms up at Cubs Park, as Wrigley Field was called in 1919, and strikes a serious pose at the ballpark in 1926. A line-drive hitter, Wheat spent 18 of his 19 major-league seasons playing left field for Brooklyn. He retired after the 1927 season with a .317 lifetime average and almost 2,900 hits.

Managers Hughie Jennings of Detroit (left) and Pants Rowland of the White Sox meet at home plate with umpires Silk O'Laughlin (right) and George Hildebrand before a 1916 game at Comiskey Park.

Oscar "Happy" Felsch limbers up at Comiskey Park in 1916. An outfielder and one of the players banned because of the Black Sox scandal, Felsch hit .300 or better in three of his six major-league seasons, including a career-high .338 in 1920, his final season.

Ed Cicotte passes a baseball to his daughter and wife at Military Day at Comiskey Park, August 23, 1917. It was Cicotte who let gamblers know the fix was in during Game 1 of the 1919 World Series when he hit the first batter he faced. Cicotte won 29 games during the regular season that year, but lost both Games 1 and 4 in the Series. He once explained he went along with the conspiracy to get enough money for security for his family. "I did it for the kiddies," he said.

Grover Cleveland Alexander lines up a shot in a Chicago pool hall during the early '20s. Alexander, one of baseball's greatest pitchers and most tragic figures, won 373 games over a 20-year career. He was coming off three consecutive 30-win seasons when he came to the Cubs in 1918. He went only 2–1 that season before going off to war. Alexander was never the same after he came back, as epilepsy, alcoholism, and shell shock took their toll. Still, he remained in the majors until 1930.

The most unfortunate victim of the Black Sox scandal may have been third baseman Buck Weaver. He knew the fix was in, but was reportedly threatened into silence by two of the conspirators. The fact that he hit .324 in the Series and that there was no evidence implicating him in the fix wasn't enough for Commissioner Kenesaw Mountain Landis, who banned him for life. Weaver regularly applied for reinstatement, but his pleas were all rejected.

Charles "Swede" Risberg watches the action from the White Sox dugout in 1920. A few weeks later, Risberg was indicted for his part in the Black Sox scandal. A shortstop of average skill, he was one of the leaders in the fix and, like the others, was banned for life despite being acquitted in court. He was the last survivor of the eight, dying in 1975.

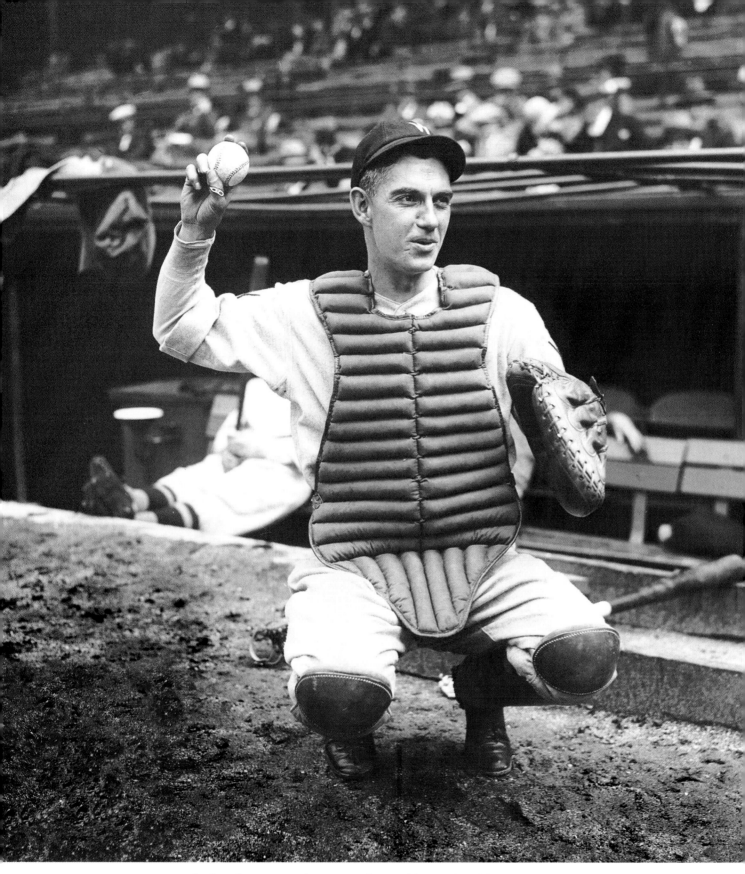

Only five feet nine and 150 pounds, Muddy Ruel still had a splendid 14-year major-league catching career with the Senators, Yankees, and Red Sox, among others. He also was the general manager for the Detroit Tigers and field manager for the St. Louis Browns, and later served as an assistant to Commissioner Happy Chandler.

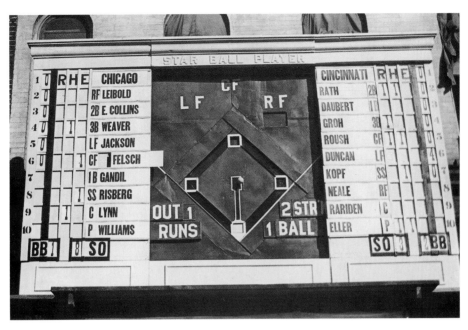

Before the Internet, before television, before radio, fans flocked to large scoreboards to follow World Series action. This one was reporting on the 1919 Series between the White Sox and Reds.

White Sox players are mobbed by happy fans as they leave the courthouse after they were acquitted of throwing the 1919 World Series.

This is the jury that heard the case against the eight White Sox players accused of throwing the 1919 World Series. It took them only two hours of deliberation on August 2, 1921, to find the players not guilty. Two days later, Commissioner Kenesaw Mountain Landis banned the players for life.

Dutch Ruether, who went 19–6 for the Cincinnati Reds during their pennant-winning 1919 season, waits to testify before the Black Sox grand jury.

Most people think of Miller Huggins as the manager of the great Yankee
ball clubs of the late '20s. But Huggins had a solid 13-year playing career for
the Cincinnati Reds and St. Louis Cardinals. He was one of the game's best
leadoff men, four times leading the National League in walks, and was just as
skilled as a second baseman, twice leading the league in assists and once in
putouts.

Roger Bresnahan, in a 1913 photo, made history in 1907 when he became the first catcher to wear shin guards in a game, while catching for the New York Giants. He came to the Cubs in 1913 after being fired as player-manager in St. Louis, and spent three years in Chicago.

Swede Risberg (left) and Happy Felsch (right) consult with attorney Ray Cannon at the Black Sox trial.

New York Giants pitcher Rube Benton waits to testify before the grand jury investigating the 1919 World Series. Benton testified that Cubs infielder Buck Herzog had offered him $800 to throw a game in 1919. It was later alleged that Benton had been tipped off about the Series fix and won $3,800.

Babe Ruth shares a laugh with White Sox pitcher Ed Cicotte before a Sox-Yankees game on August 1, 1920. Cicotte had the last laugh: Ruth was hitless with one walk in four trips to the plate and Cicotte blanked the Yankees on five hits 3–0.

Pitcher Claude Hendrix became a Cub in 1916 after the Federal League folded. His largely undistinguished five-year career with the Cubs came to an end in 1920 after he was accused of betting against his teammates in a game he was scheduled to pitch. A subsequent grand jury investigation led to the discovery of the 1919 World Series fix.

Author and humorist Ring Lardner was a member of the *Chicago Tribune* for eight years, from 1909 to 1911 and from 1913 to 1919. He started out as a baseball writer, then took over the "Wake of the News" column. In 1920 he moved to New York, where he gained fame as a novelist and playwright. Lardner died in 1933 at the age of 48.

By the time he came to the Cubs in 1919, the well-traveled Buck Herzog was at the end of a career that had seen him go from the Giants to the Braves to the Giants to the Reds to the Giants to the Braves, and finally to Chicago. While a Cub, he was accused of offering a teammate $800 to throw a game.

Charles Comiskey and his son, Louis, show off their catch for photographers.

As a 23-year-old prospect, Red Faber injured his
arm and took up the spitball. An intelligent
pitcher blessed with excellent control, he spent
his entire 20-year career with the White Sox,
winning 254 games. His best seasons were in
1921 and '22, when he went 25–15 and 21–17,
respectively, for seventh- and eighth-place
ball clubs.

Babe Ruth, manager Miller Huggins, and other Yankees argue with umpire Tommy Connolly after he called Ruth out on a controversial play. Ruth hit a long fly into the fringe of the crowd that had overflowed onto the field. Sox left-fielder Joe Jackson backed into the crowd, stumbled, and disappeared in the mob. He emerged with the ball, and Connolly ruled Jackson had held the ball "momentarily," and Ruth was out.

In his prime, Roger Peckinpaugh (in a 1920 photo) was the best shortstop in the American League. His career began with the Cleveland Indians in 1910, but he blossomed after being traded to the New York Yankees in 1913. His greatest season was 1919, when he had a 29-game hitting streak on his way to a .305 average. Traded to Washington after the 1921 season, he helped the Senators to the World Series in 1924 and '25.

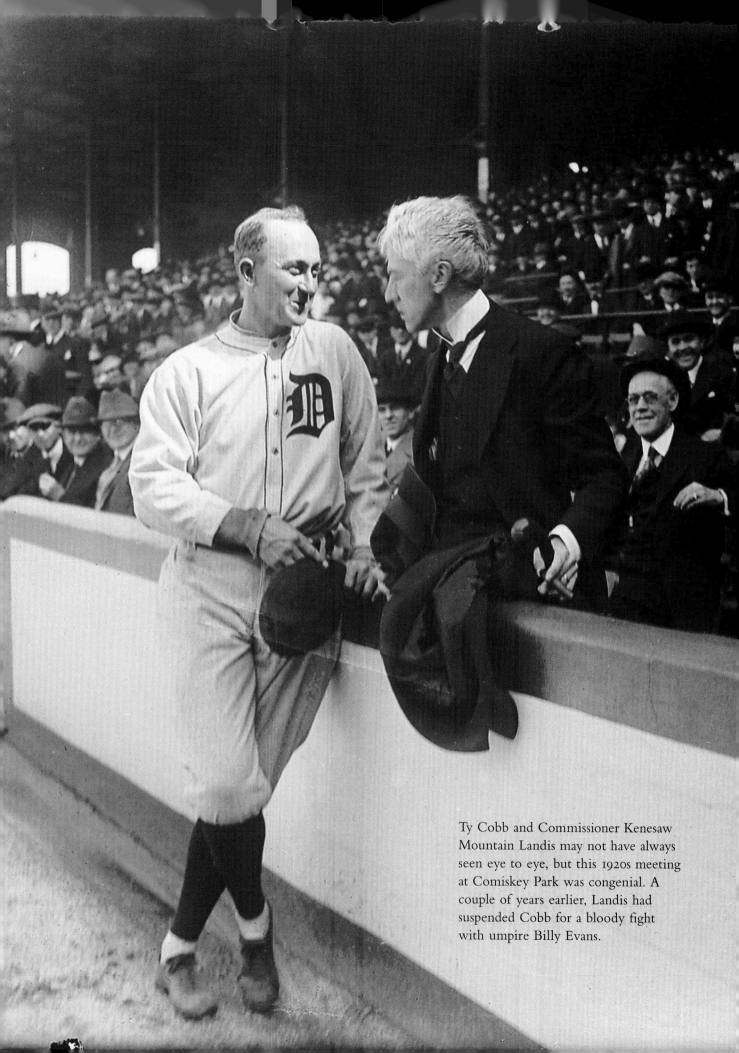

Ty Cobb and Commissioner Kenesaw Mountain Landis may not have always seen eye to eye, but this 1920s meeting at Comiskey Park was congenial. A couple of years earlier, Landis had suspended Cobb for a bloody fight with umpire Billy Evans.

THE NEWS BROKE IN THE PAPERS ON TUESDAY, January 6, 1920. Babe Ruth, baseball's home run king and its biggest drawing card, had been sold by the Boston Red Sox to the New York Yankees.

A WHOLE NEW BALL GAME

The deal, which had been made 10 days earlier and was kept secret, brought Red Sox owner Harry Frazee $425,000—$125,000 in cash and a loan of $300,000, which he needed to finance other ventures. Frazee tried to put a positive spin on the sale. "I sold Ruth for the best interests of the club," he told reporters. "The Babe was not an influence for good or for team play. He thought only of himself."

Maybe so, but this bad influence had led the Red Sox to three World Series titles in the previous five years. Not only that, but he was coming off of a tremendous season in which he had led the American League in home runs (29, almost three times his nearest rival), runs batted in (112), runs scored (103), and slugging average (.657). He also had a .322 batting average, and for good measure, he went 9–5 with a 2.97 ERA in 17 games as a pitcher.

The sale of Ruth was one in a series of deals that Frazee made with the Yankees to raise money; deals that, in retrospect, look pretty one-sided. Among the other players on the Boston-to-New York shuttle were Carl Mays, Waite Hoyt, Joe Bush, Joe Dugan, George Pipgras, and Herb Pennock, key parts in the building of the Yankee dynasty that started in the 1920s. Even the man largely responsible for building that dynasty, Ed Barrow, had been Frazee's manager in Boston before fleeing to the Yankees after the 1920 season. But the most prominent name was Ruth, and his coming to New York marked the biggest change the game had ever seen, and launched baseball into its golden age.

Ruth's arrival in New York coincided with the end of the dead-ball era and the birth of the long ball. The stage was set for this new era when owners voted to outlaw trick pitches such as the spitball and emery ball. Further, umpires were instructed to take dirty baseballs out of the game (balls that were scuffed were easier for pitchers to manipulate, as well as being harder for batters to see). The use of fresh baseballs, easier to see and hit and having a tendency to travel farther, led directly to an increase in home runs. And Ruth was just the man for these times.

In 1920 he hit 54 homers, shattering his year-old record of 29. How dominant was Ruth? His total of 54 was more than the total homers of 14 of the other 15 teams (only the Philadelphia Phillies, with 64, outhomered Ruth), and his nearest competitor in the home run race was St. Louis' George Sisler with 19. Ruth also led the league in runs batted in (137), slugging average (.847), runs scored (158), and walks (148), and batted .376.

"One might try to compare batting stars of the past with Ruth," wrote Ray Pearson in the *Chicago Tribune*, "but what's the use when the records show the number of homers that Babe has clouted in a single season? Lajoie was a great batsman in his day, so were Ed Delehanty, Cap Anson, Honus Wagner, and several others who shone in different years. They were great men at the plate, but they didn't compare with Ruth, evidence that is substantiated by the records and ball yards that are loaded to capacity, not to see the ball game so much as to see Babe smash one over the fence."

Indeed, attendance had rebounded from the shortened seasons of 1918 and 1919 with a record 9.1 million fans attending major league games in 1920. But after the Black Sox scandal broke late that season, fans started losing their faith in the game and attendance for 1921 was down by more than a half-million. Ruth was just what the game needed, a crowd-pleaser who could bring fans, hometown and otherwise, to their feet with one swing.

Other players, seeing how popular and well paid Ruth was because of his home runs, started abandoning what was left of the hit-and-run, play-for-one-run strategy and likewise began swinging for the fences. Home run totals started climbing in the American League—from 240 in 1919 to 525 in 1922. And the fans were won back, particularly in New York (Yankee attendance more than doubled from 619,164 in pre-Ruth 1919 to 1,289,422 in 1920).

The Roaring Twenties opened with the greatest, and in the end, darkest, season in American League history. Attendance was up, and three teams—Chicago, Cleveland, and New York—were in a tight pennant race. The turning point of the season came on August 17 when Ray Chapman, the Indians' well-liked and respected shortstop, died as a result of being hit in the head by a pitch from the Yankees' Carl Mays the day before. On the day of his death, Cleveland was a half-game ahead of Chicago and a game and a half ahead of New York. The Indians used Chapman's death as a rallying point, finishing two games ahead of the White Sox and three ahead of the Yankees in the American League race, then beating Brooklyn five games to two in the World Series.

The other shadow over the 1920 season was the exploding Black Sox scandal. When news of the fix broke in September, White Sox owner Charles Comiskey suspended the eight players who had been implicated, taking his team out of contention. The eventual lifetime bans of the players also effectively killed what had been a budding dynasty in Chicago. With the team gutted, Sox fans would have to wait until 1936 for the ball club to again finish as high as third.

Before the start of the 1921 season, owners named Judge Kenesaw Mountain Landis as the game's first commissioner. Landis, 54, had been a U.S. district judge in Chicago and had been the judge in the Federal League's court case against the American and National Leagues.

Once in office, Landis let it be known who was boss, though some of his decisions now seem arbitrary and unfair. Although the Black Sox players were cleared in court, he banned them from the game for life. Other players were also banned from baseball—Philadelphia's Eugene Paulette for associating with a gambler, New York's Benny Kauff for being implicated in a car-theft ring (he was acquitted), Cincinnati's Ray Fisher after he had taken a college coaching job and was later contacted by an "outlaw league." He suspended Ruth after the 1921 season for violating a rule that barred players from pennant-winning teams from participating in post–World Series barnstorming tours. Because of this, Ruth ended up missing the first six weeks of the 1922 season. The commissioner was determined to clean up baseball, even if it was only his version of it.

Baseball in the '20s wasn't just Babe Ruth, Ty Cobb, and the 16 major-league teams. There was another version of the game out there, being played by athletes deemed not qualified for the American or National Leagues because of the color of their skin.

Blacks and whites had played beside each other before the turn of the century, but some of baseball's big names, most notably Chicago White Stockings manager Cap Anson, led a segregation movement. Blacks, as a result, had their own teams, their own leagues, and their own stars.

In 1920, the Negro National League was founded by Rube Foster, a baseball innovator and showman who had run one of the nation's best black teams, the Leland Giants, out of a ballpark near 69th and Halsted in Chicago. Although there had been black teams and leagues dating to the late 1860s, Foster's Negro National League was the first to survive for any length of time (it lasted until 1931). Other leagues, stable and otherwise, popped up in the 1920s—the Southern Negro League, the Eastern Colored League, and the American Negro League, for example. Through the years, these leagues and others like them provided the stage for some of the best players ever to play the game—John Henry "Pop" Lloyd, Oscar Charleston, Martin Dihigo, and perhaps the greatest player of any race, Josh Gibson. They played in front of small crowds and big crowds, in small-town parks and sizeable stadiums, against each other and against white teams. They were largely ignored by the white press, but white ballplayers knew who they were.

Pittsburgh Pirates great Honus Wagner was once told that Lloyd was "the colored Wagner." Wagner said he was honored by the comparison, but that maybe he was "the white Lloyd." The New York Giants were on the verge of signing black pitcher George Stovey in 1888, but backed off in the face of protests. Years later Giants manager John McGraw reportedly told Foster, "If I had a bucket of whitewash that wouldn't wash off, you wouldn't have five players left tomorrow."

This from a man who had one of the best teams in the game. For the first three years of the 1920s, New York was the center of the baseball world as the Giants and Yankees each won their league's respective pennants in 1921, '22, and '23. McGraw's Giants, led by George Kelly, Frank Frisch, and Ross Youngs, won the Series in '21 and '22, with the Yankees getting revenge in '23.

The 1924 season proved to be a showcase for one of the game's most beloved figures, Walter Johnson. The 36-year-old right-hander, who had never been in postseason play, led the Washington Senators to their first American League pennant and first World Series title. He won 23 games, pitched six shutouts, and had a 2.72 earned run average, all American League bests.

Johnson started the season in incredible fashion, throwing four consecutive shutouts. The fourth came on May 23 against the visiting White Sox, who managed just one hit, a fourth-inning single by Harry Hooper. "The Sox of today were just as helpless against Johnson as the Sox of 1908 were when Walter was having a good day," wrote James Crusinberry in the *Tribune*. Johnson struck out 14, including 6 in a row at one point, tying the American League record.

In addition to Johnson's pitching, Washington had a powerful lineup led by Joe Judge (.324), Sam Rice (.334), and Goose Goslin (.344). The surprising Senators, who had finished fourth, 23½ games out of first just a year earlier, beat out the Yankees by two games. The National League champion again was McGraw's Giants, and the two teams staged a memorable Series.

Johnson lost the opener 4–3 in 12 innings despite striking out 12 Giants. The Senators came back to win Game 2 4–3 on a Roger Peckinpaugh single in the bottom of the ninth, but the Giants took Game 3. Washington tied the Series at two games apiece by winning Game 4 behind Goslin's four hits. Johnson was again a loser in Game 5, as Fred Lindstrom banged out four hits. The Senators tied the Series at three games each when Tom Zachary outdueled Art Nehf 2–1.

In Game 7, Washington got on the board with a run in the fourth, but New York scored three times in the sixth. The Senators came back in the bottom of the eighth, the tying runs scoring with two out when Bucky Harris's hard grounder to the left side of the infield hit a pebble and bounced over the head of third baseman Lindstrom.

Johnson came on in relief in the ninth. He had trouble in each of the four innings he worked: Frisch tripled in the ninth with one out, he gave up a lead-off walk in the tenth, and the first batters up in the eleventh and twelfth got hits. But each time, Johnson dramatically worked out of the jam. In the bottom of the twelfth, with one out, Muddy Ruel doubled down the third base line. One batter later, Earl McNeely hit a grounder toward third that incredibly again hit a pebble and bounded over the head of a helpless Lindstrom. Ruel came around to score the run that gave the Senators, and Johnson, their first World Series championship.

Washington made it to the World Series the next season as well, but there wouldn't be another fairy tale ending for Johnson. He won Game 1, holding the Pittsburgh Pirates to just five hits. The Pirates won Game 2, however, when Peckinpaugh, the league's MVP, made an eighth-inning error that was followed by a home run by Kiki Cuyler. Washington rebounded to win Game 3, and won Game 4 on a Johnson shutout, giving the Senators a three-games-to-one lead. But the Pirates won the next two games to force a Game 7. Johnson was staked to a four-run lead in the first inning, but Pittsburgh fought back and eventually beat Johnson 9–7 on Cuyler's two-run double in the bottom of the eighth.

Just as the 1924 and '25 seasons put Johnson in the spotlight, another of baseball's grand old men, Grover Cleveland Alexander, had his time in 1926.

Alexander—nicknamed "Pete"—had broken in with the Philadelphia Phillies in 1911, winning 28 games. He had three 30-win seasons in Philadelphia, and led the league in victories and ERA five times. He was traded to the Cubs in 1917 and, despite missing almost all of the next season because of service in World War I, won 128 games for the Cubs over the next 7½ seasons. On June 22, 1926, the Cubs sent Alexander to St. Louis on waivers (five days later he four-hit his former teammates). He went 9–7 in 33 games for the Cardinals, who beat out Cincinnati by two games for the National League pennant. Their World Series opponent would be New York, back in the Series after a two-year absence.

The teams split the first six games, with Alexander pitching complete-game victories in Games 2 and 6. In the deciding seventh game, the Cardinals had a 3–2 lead when the Yankees loaded the bases in the bottom of the seventh with two out. With slugger Tony Lazzeri coming up, Cardinals manager Rogers Hornsby brought in the 39-year-old Alexander, who just 24 hours earlier had pitched nine innings. Alexander's first pitch was a ball. The next, a curve for a strike. Lazzeri then lined a foul into the left-field seats. The next pitch was a curve over the outside corner that Lazzeri swung at and missed, retiring the side.

"There were only about 40,000 people at the game," Crusinberry reported in the October 11 *Tribune*, "but every one of them was screaming like mad at that moment. They stood up and yelled. They threw hats and yet this man was beating their heroes." Alexander finished the game to preserve the Cardinals' victory and clinch the team's first World Series.

The Yankees weren't down for long. They came back in 1927 with what many baseball historians consider the greatest team ever—the Murderers' Row lineup that included Ruth (60 homers, 158 runs scored, .772 slugging average), Lou Gehrig (.373 batting average, 47 homers, 175 RBIs), and Earle Combs (231 hits, .356 batting average). The pitching staff included Waite Hoyt (22–7, 2.63 ERA), Wilcy Moore (19–7, 13 saves, 2.28 ERA), Herb Pennock (19–8, 3.00 ERA), and Urban Shocker (18–6, 2.84 ERA). The Yankees went 110–44 (.714), winning the American League race by 19 games over second-place Philadelphia, then swept Pittsburgh in the World Series in four games.

The Yankees slipped to 101 wins in 1928 and finished only two games ahead of Connie Mack's resurgent Philadelphia ball club, but still needed four games to sweep to a second consecutive World Series title, this time beating St. Louis.

The 1929 season saw the Athletics—behind Jimmie Foxx, Al Simmons, Mickey Cochrane, Lefty Grove, and George Earnshaw—finally dethrone the Yankees and get to the World Series. Their opponent: the reborn Chicago Cubs.

William Wrigley had purchased control of the ball club in 1921. Through his first five seasons his team never finished higher than fourth, and hit bottom, literally, in 1925 with an eighth-place finish. But then the Cubs started rebuilding. Wrigley hired the relatively unknown Joe McCarthy as his manager in 1926. That same year they took advantage of an oversight by the New York Giants and drafted Hack Wilson from the Giants' Toledo farmclub. The Giants protested, but Commissioner Landis sided with the Cubs, leaving the five feet six, 195-pound slugger the property of Chicago.

Another piece of the puzzle fell into place on November 28, 1927, when Cubs president William Veeck traded infielder Earl "Sparky" Adams and outfielder Pete Scott to Pittsburgh for outfielder Kiki Cuyler, who had been relegated to part-time duty after a fallout with his manager. Cuyler came to Chicago with a career .336 batting average and was the National League's top base stealer.

The 1928 Cubs were contenders in the National League, winding up third, four games behind St. Louis. Then came the deal that put them over the top. On November 7, 1928, the Cubs sent $200,000 and five players to the Boston Braves for slugging second baseman Rogers Hornsby.

The greatest right-handed hitter baseball ever saw, Hornsby had hitting down to a science, with a perfect swing that sent line drives to all fields. He had led the National League with a .387 average in 1928, when he also served as the Braves' manager for the last 122 games (he was 39–83 and they finished a dismal seventh). How could Boston trade a player of that caliber, someone who had hit .377 over the past 10 years? Easy. The same way the Cardinals and Giants could trade him.

Hornsby's determination to succeed drove him, while also alienating management and teammates. He could be sarcastic or downright mean. He was frank, stubborn, and had a prickly personality, and he disliked authority figures. He was also the ultimate professional, dedicated to winning. He had spent 12 years in St. Louis before owner Sam Breadon could no longer take him and sent him to New York in 1927. Hornsby wore out his welcome there in only one season and was traded to the Braves. There were fewer personality conflicts in Boston, but the Cubs' package of money and players was too good for the Braves to pass up.

Upon hearing of his trade to the Cubs, Hornsby, in his usual frank way, predicted a pennant for 1929. "I feel that I can give the Cubs the punch that will put them over in next year's race," he told the *Tribune*. He was true to his word.

He turned in an MVP season—.380 batting average, 39 homers, 149 RBIs, and 156 runs scored—to lead the Cubs to the National League pennant. He got plenty of support from Cuyler (.360), Wilson (.345, 159 RBIs), and Riggs Stephenson (.362), while Pat Malone (22–10), Charlie Root (19–6), and Guy Bush (18–7) led the pitching staff.

The Cubs won the National League race by 10½ games, but ran into Mack's powerhouse Athletics in the World Series. Losing the first two games of the Series, they took Game 3 behind Bush's complete game and Cuyler's two-run single in the sixth. The Cubs were on the verge of tying the Series when they took an 8–0 lead into the bottom of the seventh in Game 4. But then came one of the most remarkable innings in baseball history, as the A's scored 10 runs. The biggest goat was Wilson, who lost two fly balls in the sun during the inning, one going for a single, the other for a three-run homer. Philadelphia went on to win 10–8, then wrapped up the Series in Game 5 by scoring three runs in the bottom of the ninth for a 3–2 victory.

Despite the way their season ended, the Cubs had reason to be optimistic about their future. The same couldn't be said on the other end of town, where the White Sox were a struggling team through the '20s. After their 1920 season ended with the breaking of the Black Sox scandal, Charles Comiskey's team sank quickly. The White Sox were 30 games under .500 in 1921, climbed to fifth place at 77–77 the next year, then finished seventh and eighth the following two seasons.

Heroes and highlights were few. Holdovers from the prescandal years included catcher Ray Schalk, second baseman Eddie Collins, and pitcher Red Faber. New faces such as Bibb Falk (1920), Willie Kamm (1923), Harry Hooper (1921), and Ted Lyons (1923) arrived on the scene and gave fans something to cheer, with Lyons, in fact, leading the American League in victories in 1925 and '27. But after 1920, the Sox were chronic also-rans. Despite a 1927 revamping of Comiskey Park to add an upper deck in the outfield, the Sox failed to draw even a half-million fans in 1928 and '29 when they finished fifth and seventh, 29 and 46 games out of first place.

Off the field there were problems as well. Pitcher Dickie Kerr, one of the untainted players in the 1919 World Series, signed with a semipro team in Texas after turning down a contract offer from Comiskey. Kerr, who was 53–33 in three years with the Sox, later faced some of his banished teammates in a game and found himself banned from baseball by Landis in 1922. The ban was lifted in 1925, but he managed to go only 0–1 in 12 games that year for the Sox.

Another problem player was Bill Cissell. A promising young infielder who came up with the Sox in 1928, he never developed into a star and was unable to deal with his lack of success. He started drinking and was traded, eventually dying at the age of 45.

In 1927 another kind of tragedy hit the team. Outfielder Johnny Mostil, who had become a regular in 1921 and who had batted a career-high .328 in 1926, tried to kill himself during spring training. Reportedly upset over the discovery of his affair with the wife of one of his teammates, he cut his wrists, throat, and chest in a hotel room. Mostil recovered from the injuries and returned to the team late in the season. He played two more years for the Sox before leaving baseball.

As dismal as the 1920s were on the South Side, things would get even worse before the team's luck turned around.

White Sox pitcher Ted Blankenship poses with his father before a late-'20s game at Comiskey Park. The elder Blankenship had another son, Homer, who also pitched briefly in the majors.

NO BETTING

Mike Cvengros had a 25–40 record in six major-league seasons, but managed to get to three World Series—in 1922 with the New York Giants, in 1927 with the Pittsburgh Pirates, and in 1929 with the Cubs. Here he's warming up in front of the Comiskey Park bleachers.

During the White Sox's lean years in the 1920s, Buck Crouse was the backup catcher to Ray Schalk and Moe Berg. He spent his entire eight-year major-league career with the Sox.

Virgil Cheevers—
nicknamed "Chief"—
went 26–27 for the
Cubs between 1920
and 1923.

Marty Krug holds the distinction of having a nine-year gap between his two
seasons in the majors. He broke in with the Boston Red Sox in 1912 and
finished his career with the Cubs in 1922, when this photo was taken, hitting
.276 in 127 games.

Wilbur Cooper was one of the top left-handers in the National League in the late teens and early '20s for the Pittsburgh Pirates. By the time he came to the Cubs in 1925, his best days were behind him, and he went 14–15 in two seasons in Chicago. He wound up his 15-year big-league career with 216 wins.

Harry Courtney was a lanky left-hander who played only part of one season, 1922, with the White Sox. He went 5–6 in 18 games for them in what would be his last year in the majors.

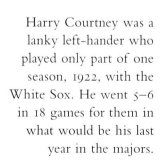

Boston Red Sox pitcher Bill Piercy earned the nickname "Wild Bill" for his propensity to walk hitters. He also pitched for the New York Yankees and wound up his career with the Cubs in 1926.

Cubs owner William Wrigley Jr. and Grover Cleveland Alexander and his wife, Aimee, wait to board a train in Chicago in the early '20s.

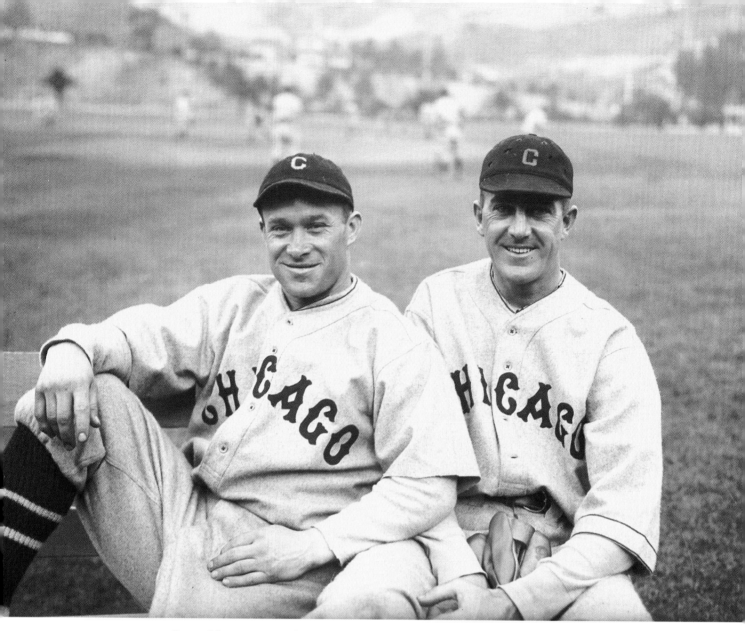

Second baseman Sparky Adams (left) and shortstop Jimmy Cooney anchored the Cubs infield in 1926. Their partnership didn't last long, as Cooney was sent to the Philadelphia Phillies during the 1927 season and Adams went to the Pittsburgh Pirates after it.

Swede Risberg, one of the ringleaders of the 1919 World Series fix, prepares to meet with Commissioner Kenesaw Mountain Landis in 1927 after charging that his Sox teammates paid the Detroit Tigers to throw a four-game series in 1917. His accusations— supported by another Black Sox conspirator, Chick Gandil—led Landis to hold a week of hearings.

Commissioner Landis leaves a January 1927 hearing at which he heard allegations that the White Sox, as a team, were involved in a fix in 1917. Landis found no basis for the charges and cleared all 21 players whom Risberg and Gandil had implicated.

James Evers, son of Cubs manager Johnny Evers, served as the team mascot during the 1921 season.

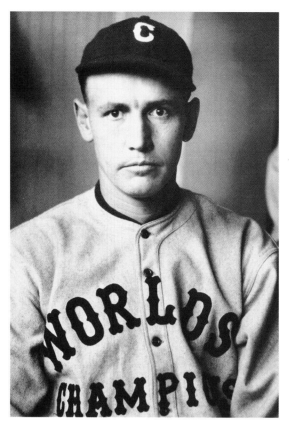

Joe Wood was one of the game's greatest pitchers in 1911 and 1912, winning 23 and 34 games for the Boston Red Sox. But arm troubles slowed him after that. Here he's a member of the world champion Cleveland Indians in 1920, his last season in the majors.

By today's standards, five feet eight, 155-pound Joe Judge would be too small to be a first baseman. But he was one of the best at the position, leading the American League in fielding five times and finishing his 20-year career with a .993 fielding percentage. He also could handle the bat, hitting .298 lifetime.

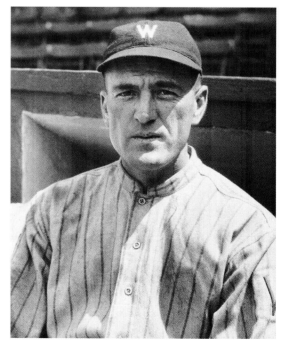

Cleveland Indians manager Tris Speaker poses with his mother at the 1920 World Series. The black armband is in memory of Indians shortstop Ray Chapman, who was killed by a pitch earlier in the season.

A headache forced Wally Pipp from the New York Yankees' lineup in a game in 1925 and turned him into the answer to a trivia question as the man who was replaced by Lou Gehrig. With Pipp out, Gehrig stepped in and played every game for the next 14 years. Pipp—a career .281 hitter and good first baseman—was traded to the Cincinnati Reds in 1926 and wound up his career two years later.

Sam Rice was a career .322 batter who had 2,987 hits—almost 2,300 of them singles—over 20 years, 19 of them with the Washington Senators. He's also remembered for one of his defensive plays. In the 1925 World Series, he tumbled into the right-field bleachers after catching a drive by Pittsburgh's Earl Smith. The question of whether he dropped the ball in the stands was asked for years, but he always refused to say.

Rice left a letter that was opened after his death in 1974, in which he described the play and asserted, "At no time did I lose possession of the ball."

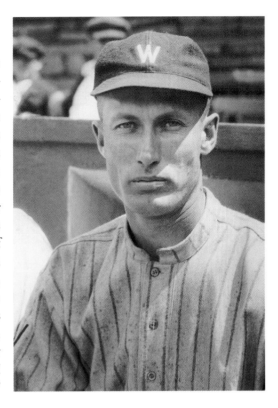

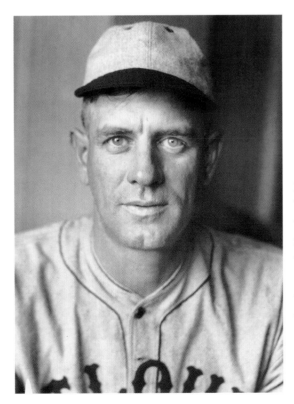

Lefty Leifield won 103 games between 1906 and 1911 for the Pittsburgh Pirates, including going 19–8 during their world championship 1909 season. But he developed a sore arm and won only 16 more games in a career that ended in 1920.

Bud Clancy was a decent backup first baseman for the White Sox in the 1920s. He spent a total of nine years in the majors and finished with a .281 career batting average.

George Gibson was the star catcher for the powerhouse Pittsburgh Pirate teams during the early years of the twentieth century. Never a big hitter—his best year was 1914 when he hit .285—he had a career .236 average over 14 seasons. He later had two three-year stints as manager of the Pirates, and served as manager for the final 26 games of the 1925 season for the last-place Cubs.

White Sox fans jam Comiskey Park for a July 1925 game against Washington. The Senators, behind pitcher Stanley Coveleski, beat the Sox 10–2. The 1925 season saw the Sox with their best record (79–75) and attendance (823,231) since 1920, before the Black Sox scandal broke. They finished fifth in the American League race.

In his only full season in the majors, Rip Wheeler went 3–6 with a 3.91 ERA for the 1924 Cubs.

Standing in the middle of
Michigan Avenue, White
Sox catcher Ray Schalk
catches a ball thrown
from the top of Tribune
Tower, a height estimated
at 460 feet. The May 11,
1925, publicity stunt was
witnessed by more than
10,000 people.

The Comiskey Park grandstand is packed for a 1928 game. Full houses were
rare that season, when the Sox drew less than a half-million fans and finished
fifth, 10 games under .500 and 29 games behind the first-place New York
Yankees.

Fun-loving Pat Malone was a mainstay on the Cubs pitching staff in the late '20s and early '30s. He led the National League in victories in 1929 (22) and '30 (20), and was a double-figure winner in each of his seven seasons in Chicago. He spent the final three years of his career with the Yankees, pitching largely in relief. He left baseball in 1939 and opened a tavern in Altoona, Pennsylvania, his hometown. He died in 1943 at the age of 41.

Art Nehf had a knack for getting to the World Series. He played for four teams during a 15-year career that started in 1915, and was on eight pennant winners: the Red Sox of 1915 and '18, the Giants of 1920, '21, '22, '23, and '24, and the Cubs of '29. He had a 184–120 career record.

With a half-dozen teammates watching and club president William Veeck at his side, Cubs slugger Hack Wilson signs on the dotted line. Manager Rogers Hornsby (second from left) may have been all smiles at this point, but he eventually tired of Wilson's off-field escapades and drinking and traded him after the 1931 season, just a year after Wilson had hit 56 home runs and driven in 190 runs.

Cubs teammates Riggs Stephenson (from left), Woody English, and Hack Wilson work on their golf game in the Cubs offices at Wrigley Field in 1929. They also found time to play some baseball that season, as Stephenson hit .362, English .276, and Wilson .345 and helping the Cubs win the National League pennant by 10½ games.

Dave Bancroft—nicknamed "Beauty"—was a picture-book shortstop for the New York Giants in the early '20s. Defensively, there was none better, and he was a leader on the field as well. He also developed into a good hitter, finishing above .300 five times during a 16-year National League career that took him to Philadelphia, New York, and Boston.

Tom Zachary may be best known as the pitcher who gave up Babe Ruth's sixtieth home run in 1927, but he had a solid 19-year major-league career that included 186 wins, two World Series victories for the Washington Senators in 1924, and a 12–0 mark for the New York Yankees in 1929.

Charles Root Jr., son of the Cubs pitcher, makes a new friend with the help of Cubs manager Charlie Grimm in May 1928.

Walter Johnson gets in a Comiskey Park workout with two of his children.

Billy Herman demonstrates his hitting skill—or maybe he's just working on his golf game—with teammate Wally Stephenson in 1935, the year Herman led the majors with 227 hits.

Twice during the 1929 season—the same year he was made White Sox captain—Art Shires got into fistfights with his manager, Lena Blackburn. Shires fancied himself a pugilist and boxed professionally during the off-season until Commissioner Kenesaw Mountain Landis intervened. After 2½ wild seasons with the Sox, Shires was traded to the Washington Senators, where he lasted for only half a season before being shipped to the Boston Braves. His career ended there in 1932.

Jim Bottomley broke in with the St. Louis Cardinals late in the 1922 season.
The following year, the young left-handed cleanup hitter batted .371.
Bottomley had a career .310 average with more than 2,300 hits over 16
seasons, and still holds the record for most RBIs in a game (12).

George Sisler started his career as
a pitcher, and a good one. But his
hitting skills made it imperative
for him to play every day, so he
was converted to a first baseman
and became one of the best in the
game. His batting skills were what
made him famous, however. He
had six 200-plus hit seasons,
including 257 in 1920, and he had
a lifetime .340 average, hitting
.420 in 1922.

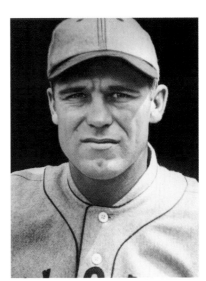

Willie Kamm came to the White Sox and settled in at third base for eight full seasons before being traded to the Cleveland Indians. A career .281 hitter, his real value was in the field. He led American League third basemen in fielding in six of his eight years in Chicago.

Burleigh Grimes (left) and Dazzy Vance were the aces of the Brooklyn Dodger pitching staff in the early '20s. Their best year was 1924, when Vance went 28–6 with a 2.16 ERA, and Grimes was 22–13, 3.82. That year, Brooklyn finished second, 1½ games behind the New York Giants.

Young Bill Veeck is flanked by his parents before hitting the road with the Cubs.

Dolf Luque—"The Pride of Havana"—was one of the first Cubans to star in the major leagues. In a 20-year career (1914–1935) spent mostly with the Cincinnati Reds, he won 194 games and had a 3.24 ERA. His best season was 1923, when he went 27–8 with six shutouts and a 1.93 ERA for the Reds.

Ty Cobb, player-manager of the Detroit Tigers, and Sox manager Kid Gleason meet at home plate before a 1923 contest at Comiskey Park. Detroit finished second, the Sox seventh that season.

Babe Ruth in his element: surrounded by kids during a personal appearance
on June 23, 1923.

Ray Grimes visits with his son, Oscar Ray Jr., before a Cubs game around 1921. Ray played first base for the Cubs, Red Sox, and Phillies. Oscar Jr. became a major-leaguer as well, putting in 12 seasons with the Indians, Yankees, and A's.

John McGraw watches his ball
club warm up before a game
at Wrigley Field. As a player
and manager, the fiery
McGraw would do anything
necessary to win. He was a
manager for 33 years, 30 of
them with the Giants, and
won nine National League
pennants and three World
Series.

Mark Koenig was the shortstop on the Yankee power-
houses of the late '20s. He led
the league in errors in 1926
and '27 and was eventually
replaced by Leo Durocher.
Koenig came to the Cubs in
August of 1932 and hit .353
down the stretch to help them
win the National League
pennant.

Two old friends—Eddie Collins and manager Connie Mack—relax in the Philadelphia A's dugout in 1932. Collins had been one of the stars on Mack's great teams that won American League pennants in 1910, '11, '13, and '14. When Mack broke up the team in 1915, Collins was sold to the White Sox, where he put in 12 more stellar seasons before coming back to the A's in 1927. He saw part-time playing duty over the next four years and became Mack's right-hand man in the dugout.

With his straw hat and business suit, Connie Mack was a fixture in the Philadelphia A's dugout for a half-century. He retired in 1950 at the age of 87. "I'm not quitting because I'm too old," he said after his last game. "I'm quitting because I think people want me to."

Hooks Wiltse broke into the majors with the New York Giants in 1904 by going 13–3. In 11 seasons with the Giants, he never had a losing record. His finest moment came on July 4, 1908, when he pitched a 10-inning no-hitter against the Philadelphia Phillies. He allowed only one baserunner in the game, a hit batsman in the ninth.

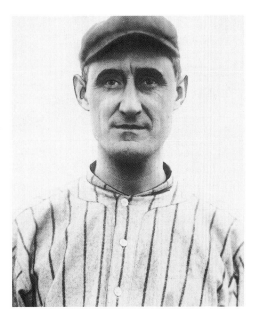

A packed house at Comiskey Park watches Babe Ruth take his cuts. The catcher is Ray Schalk; the umpire is Dick Nallin.

91

Chief Bender (left) and Eddie Collins watch the White Sox in a game against Philadelphia in 1925. Collins, the longtime Sox second baseman, was the playing manager for the team in 1924, '25, and '26. Bender joined Collins's coaching staff in '25 and spent three seasons with the team.

Comiskey Park underwent a major renovation before the 1927 season. New box seats were added and an enclosed grandstand was built in the outfield. The new upper deck accommodated an additioinal 23,200 fans.

Just a kid at heart, Babe Ruth plays with a balloon in the Comiskey Park outfield in the late '20s.

Charles Root Jr., son of
the Cubs pitcher, shows
his form in 1927.

Edd Roush broke in with the White Sox in 1913, but jumped to the Federal League the next season and later had his greatest years with the Cincinnati Reds. Using a 48-ounce bat, heaviest in the majors, he led the National League in hitting in 1917 (.341) and 1919 (.321). In the twilight of his career, he played for the New York Giants.

95

Never one to pass up a photo opportunity, Babe Ruth dons fire gear for photographers at Comiskey Park in 1928.

Herb Pennock was another
of those players traded by
the cash-strapped Red Sox
to the Yankees. A decent
pitcher with the A's and
Red Sox in the teens, he
became a big winner after
coming to the Yankees for
the 1923 season. His best
year was 1928, when he
was 17–6 with a 2.56 ERA
and five shutouts.

Heine Groh was as famous for his bat as for what he did with it. He used a bottle bat, with its thin handle and nontapered barrel, to collect more than 1,700 hits in a 16-year career with the Giants, Reds, and Pirates. Groh was an ideal leadoff man, capable of laying down a perfect bunt or getting on via a walk, and twice led the National League in on-base percentage.

Tempestuous Lefty Grove is considered by some to be the best left-handed pitcher ever to play the game. His 1931 season for the Philadelphia A's underscores that opinion: a 31–4 record, 2.06 ERA, 27 complete games, four shutouts, and 175 strikeouts, all league-leading marks. Grove won 20 or more games for seven consecutive seasons before being sold to the Boston Red Sox in another of Connie Mack's housecleanings. Faced with a sore arm and the loss of his fastball, Grove became a finesse pitcher and went 105–62 over the next eight seasons for Boston.

J. Louis Comiskey watches his White Sox practice. He took over the team after the death of his father in 1931, but despite his rebuilding efforts never saw the ball club finish higher than third. He died in 1939 at the age of 56.

Earle Combs was an outstanding leadoff man and centerfielder for the Yankees' Murderers' Row ball club in 1927. He led the American League with 231 hits that year and batted .356, starting a string of eight .300 seasons. Combs's career came to a premature end because of a skull fracture he suffered after crashing into an outfield wall in St. Louis in 1934. He tried a comeback in 1935, but played in only 89 games. He became a coach for the Yankees and later held the same position with the St. Louis Browns, Boston Red Sox, and Philadelphia Phillies.

Billy Sunday was a speedy outfielder for several National League teams from 1883 to 1890. He quit the game at age 28 to become an evangelist, and for the next 40 years crossed the nation preaching. He would often begin his sermons by running and sliding onto the stage, and would refer to his baseball past in his fire-and-brimstone speeches. Sunday and his wife, Helen, known as Ma Sunday, lived in Chicago. He died in 1935.

Crowds gather in Grant Park to follow the progress of the 1928 World Series between the St. Louis Cardinals and New York Yankees on a giant *Herald-Examiner* scoreboard.

Kid Gleason spent 22 years in the majors as a player and another five seasons as manager. His career managerial record was 392–364, not bad considering his last three ball clubs were largely gutted of talent by Commissioner Landis's banishment of eight players.

Former Sox catching great, now their manager, Ray Schalk watches his team in 1928. He managed them for two seasons, compiling a 102–125 record.

Guy Bush and his father, G. W. Bush of Shannon, Mississippi, pose for a family photo before Game 1 of the 1929 World Series at Wrigley Field. It was the first time the elder Bush attended a major-league game. His son was the only Cubs pitcher to win a game against the Philadelphia Athletics, who took the Series in five games.

Lena Blackburn had a 99–133 record in his two seasons as Sox manager (1928–29). He later became more famous for the mud he sold to baseball leagues around the country. Blackburn and his family dredged the mud from the New Jersey River, canned it, and sold it to the American, National, and International Leagues. Umpires used the mud to rub up new baseballs to take the sheen off them and make them less slippery.

Broadway's George M. Cohan and former Sox manager Nixey Callahan visit at Chicago's Blackstone Hotel in 1930.

Cubs slugger Hack Wilson
takes his son for a buggy
ride in January 1927.

Members of the 1930 Cubs pose in the dugout (from left): Charlie Grimm, Rogers Hornsby, Footsie Blair, Woody English, Billy Jurges, Clyde Beck, and Les Bell.

The main cogs in the Cubs' pennant-winning club of 1929—Hack Wilson, Charlie Grimm, Rogers Hornsby, and manager Joe McCarthy—look at Grimm's injured left hand in September of that year. He had broken a bone in his throwing hand in late August and didn't return to the lineup until October 1.

Banjo-playing, affable Charlie Grimm would do almost anything for a laugh. His temperament was the opposite of the man he replaced as Cubs manager, Rogers Hornsby. Grimm must have been doing something right. He was the manager the last four times the Cubs got to the World Series.

Cubs second baseman Rogers Hornsby and manager Joe McCarthy had
plenty to smile about in 1929. The Cubs traded for Hornsby in November
1928, figuring he could put them over the top. The plan worked as Hornsby
hit .380 to lead them to the National League pennant. The following year
was another story, though, as Hornsby missed most of the season with a
broken ankle. McCarthy quit and was replaced by Hornsby, and the Cubs
finished second, just two games behind the St. Louis Cardinals.

Lew Fonseca was a natural hitter whose career was cut short by injuries. His best season was 1929, when he hit a league-leading .369 for the Cleveland Indians. The next year he broke his arm and hit only .279 in 40 games. He came to the White Sox in 1931 and retired after the '33 season, a leg injury ending his career. Fonseca later pioneered the use of film as an instructional tool in baseball.

The Babe and his wife, Claire, at Comiskey Park. After their marriage in 1929, she did her best to tame his wild ways. She watched his diet, kept him away from hard liquor, and instituted a curfew. She also handled their finances and put him on an allowance.

THE 1930 SEASON WAS ONE FOR THE BOOKS, with hitters dominating the game as they never had before, and never have since. Leading the way was a most unlikely looking hero, the Cubs' Hack Wilson, who hit 56 home runs and drove in 190 runs. The Giants' Bill Terry had 254 hits and batted .401, the Yankees and Cardinals each scored more than 1,000 runs, 71 players and nine teams hit over .300 (the National League as a whole was at .303), and the weakest hitter in the Cardinals' starting lineup, centerfielder Taylor Douthit, batted .303.

THE GREATEST SHOW ON EARTH

Two examples of how offense ruled the game were the Cardinals' Showboat Fisher and Brooklyn's Babe Herman. About halfway through the season, Fisher was hitting .374—and he still got sent to the minors. And Herman hit .393; had 241 hits, including 48 doubles, 11 triples, and 35 homers; scored 143 runs; and drove in 130, but still didn't lead the league in any offensive category.

Into this slugging frenzy stepped the Cubs' Wilson. Standing only five feet six and weighing 190 pounds, he looked like an inverted triangle, with a bull neck, massive shoulders, and a huge chest that tapered down to a narrow waist and finished off with size 6 spikes. After a slow start, he spent 1930 terrorizing National League pitching. His August that year was one of the most remarkable months ever for a hitter—a .385 batting average, 13 home runs, and 53 runs batted in. Wilson's production helped the Cubs move into first on August 13, but they were passed a month later by the Cardinals, who wound up winning the pennant by two games. Late in the season owner William Wrigley announced that Rogers Hornsby, who had missed most of the season after breaking his ankle, would replace Joe McCarthy as manager for the upcoming season.

The Cardinals' opponent in the World Series was Connie Mack's Philadelphia Athletics, the defending World Series champs who had won the American League pennant by eight games over Washington. In this season of remarkable hitting, it was pitching that decided the Series, as George Earnshaw and the rest of the A's staff held the Cardinals to a .200 average.

Philadelphia dominated the American League race again in 1931. The Athletics won 107 games to finish 13½ games ahead of the Yankees. Leftfielder Al Simmons, with a league-leading .390 batting average, led the way. Other big contributors were catcher Mickey Cochrane, first baseman Jimmie Foxx, and pitchers Lefty Grove and Earnshaw. The A's opponent in the World Series was again St. Louis, making its fourth Series appearance in six years. Led by centerfielder Pepper Martin (12 hits, including four doubles and a home run, five RBIs, and five stolen bases), the Cardinals outlasted the A's in seven games in what would be Philadelphia's last World Series appearance for 40 years.

Two weeks after the end of the Series, baseball lost one of its pioneers when White Sox owner Charles Comiskey died at his summer home in Wisconsin at the age of 72. "The Old Roman," who had owned the franchise since its birth in 1901 and who had been forever shaken by the 1919 Black Sox scandal, had spent his final years as an absentee owner, seldom even coming out to the ballpark that bore his name.

Exactly three months later, Cubs owner William Wrigley Jr. died at the age of 70. The chewing gum magnate had been one of Charles Weeghman's partners when Weeghman purchased the Cubs after the death of the Federal League, and Wrigley eventually bought controlling interest in the team. The deaths of the two owners had little immediate impact on the fortunes of the teams. The White Sox were still in the midst of their postscandal decline, while the Cubs continued to be one of the top teams in the National League.

The White Sox finished next to last in 1929, '30, and '32 and were dead last in '31 and '34 before finally showing some signs of life. Attendance at Comiskey Park reflected the team's misery, as well as the deepening depression. Only 406,000 fans showed up in 1930, with numbers declining to 233,000 in '32 and 236,000 in '34.

The clouds did lift occasionally at Comiskey Park during the 1930s. One of the brightest moments came late in the 1930 season, when a 23-year-old rookie made his debut at shortstop. Luke Appling would spend 20 years in a White Sox uniform, becoming a Chicago icon as he banged out almost 3,000 hits and won two batting titles on his way to the Hall of Fame. He and Ted Lyons, who won 260 games for some truly poor Sox teams over 21 years, were the Sox mainstays during the decade.

On September 28, 1932, the White Sox took a giant step toward respectability when they purchased three of the Philadelphia Athletics' top players. A's owner Connie Mack, with the highest payroll in baseball history, and at the height of the depression, no less, sent Al Simmons, Mule Haas, and Jimmy Dykes to Chicago for $150,000. The impact was noticeable the following season. Simmons led the Sox in batting and runs batted in, Haas played a solid center field, and Dykes led American League third basemen in assists as the three helped Chicago climb to sixth place.

But the big news at Comiskey Park in 1933 occurred on July 6, when the first major-league All-Star Game was played. Conceived by *Chicago Tribune* sports editor Arch Ward, the game was to be a showcase for baseball's best. The lineups were a Who's Who of the game—Frisch, Klein, Waner, Terry, O'Doul, Traynor, Gehringer, Ruth, Gehrig, Cronin, and Dickey, to name a few. And the game lived up to expectations. With Babe Ruth hitting a two-run homer in the third inning and making a nice running catch on Chick Hafey's liner in the eighth, the American League won 4–2 in front of more than 47,000 fans.

"It was the most sportsmanlike crowd ever gathered for such an important event," the *Tribune*'s Harvey Woodruff wrote. "South siders shouted in approval and glee when some American leaguer produced a hit or a brilliant bit of fielding. North siders clamored when the hero was a National leaguer. Yet there was composite applause from the two elements for the various stars."

It was one of the few times cheers were heard at Comiskey Park in the 1930s. The Sox fell back to last place in 1934, when Dykes took over as manager. The following season, behind Appling, Simmons, and second-year man Zeke Bonura, the Sox finished in fifth place. The turnaround continued in 1936 and '37 with third-place finishes, the most success on the South Side since the ill-fated 1920 season. Simmons, who had slumped to .267 in 1935, was sold to Detroit before the '36 season, but he was hardly missed as Appling hit .388, Rip Radcliff .335, Bonura .330, and Jackie Hayes .312. The star of the pitching staff was Vern Kennedy (21–9). But despite finishing third, 11 games over .500, the Sox were still 20 games behind the first-place Yankees.

The story was much the same the following year. The Sox continued to improve, going 86–68, as Bonura hit .345, Radcliff .325, and Appling .317, and

25-year-old right-hander Monty Stratton went 15–5 with a 2.40 ERA and five shutouts. But the Yankees were again runaway winners in the AL pennant race.

The White Sox closed out the decade with sixth- and fourth-place finishes, and a couple of sad events that were becoming too commonplace for the franchise. Pitcher Stratton, who had posted a 15–9 record in 1938, was injured in a hunting accident and had his right leg amputated at the knee. He appeared in a Comiskey Park exhibition game in his honor the following season and was later hired on as a coach, but never returned to the majors (though he went 18–8 in the East Texas League in 1946). And for the second time in less than 10 years, the White Sox lost their owner. In July of 1939, owner J. Louis Comiskey died at the family resort in Wisconsin.

In contrast to the White Sox's struggles through most of the 1930s, the Cubs were enjoying the greatest decade in their history. The 1929 pennant was followed by a second-place finish in 1930 that cost manager Joe McCarthy his job and a third-place finish in 1931 under Rogers Hornsby.

The 1932 season brought another pennant, but not without some off-the-field episodes that made things interesting.

Fans were shocked when Hack Wilson, the slugging star of 1930, was traded after an injury-filled 1931 season. His homer production had dropped from 56 to 13, his RBI total from 190 to 61, and his average from .356 to .261. Worse for him, his fun-loving ways had angered Hornsby. Then in July, shortstop Billy Jurges was shot by a young woman in his hotel room. He recovered and finished the season, and the woman, a dancer, later returned to the stage billing herself as Violet "I Did It for Love" Valli.

Less than a month after the shooting, with the Cubs in second place, six games behind the Pittsburgh Pirates, manager Hornsby was fired and replaced by first baseman Charlie Grimm. At the press conference announcing the firing, reporters asked Cubs president Bill Veeck Sr. if there had been a falling out between the two. "There has been no quarrel, has there Rog?" he asked. Responded the ever-honest Hornsby with a laugh, "I guess we won't call it a quarrel. Only big differences of opinion about the ball club and the way it should be handled."

Grimm was the antithesis of Hornsby. A banjo-playing, camera-loving ham, he had broken in with the Philadelphia A's in 1916 and played for the St. Louis Cardinals and Pittsburgh Pirates early in his career. He joined the Cubs in 1925 and became their regular first baseman, averaging over .300 through his first seven seasons. His appointment as manager turned the Cubs' fortunes around.

They went 37–20 over the last two months of the season to pass the Pirates and win the National League pennant by four games.

Their opponent in the World Series was the powerhouse Yankees, led by Ruth (.341, 41 HRs, 137 RBIs), Lou Gehrig (.349, 34 HRs, 151 RBIs), Lefty Gomez (24–7), and Red Ruffing (18–7). There was also a subplot that would make this one of the most memorable World Series ever.

There was animosity between the teams because the Cubs had voted only a partial World Series share to former Yankee Mark Koenig, who had hit .353 in 33 games after coming to the Cubs in midseason. Ruth was further bothered when the Cubs refused to give ex-manager Hornsby any share of the World Series money. Ruth spent much of the first two games of the Series—both won easily by New York—taunting the Cubs from the Yankee dugout. "Sure I'm on 'em," he was quoted in the *Tribune* after the Yankees won Game 2. "I hope we beat 'em four straight. They gave Koenig and Hornsby a sour deal in their player cut. They're chiselers and I tell 'em so."

Ruth took his anger to a new level in Game 3. He hit two homers, the second of which has gone down in baseball lore as his "called shot." Facing Charlie Root, Ruth quickly fell behind 0–2. The Cubs bench, led by Guy Bush and Bob Smith, was letting him have it. Here's how the *Tribune*'s Irving Vaughan reported what happened next: "Babe listened to this and yelled back, apparently unannoyed: 'That's only two strikes, boys. I still have one coming,' he cried, meanwhile holding up two fingers. And when the next one came Ruth sent it to distant parts."

The holding up of the two fingers was misinterpreted by some fans as Ruth pointing to the bleachers, where the ball eventually landed, adding another chapter to the Babe Ruth legend. The Yankees won both that game and the next to wrap up the Series.

The Cubs finished third the following two seasons, then went to the Series again in 1935 after one of the most thrilling pennant races in history. On Labor Day, the defending champion Cardinals led New York by one game and the third-place Cubs by 1½. St. Louis had just returned from a long trip during which it won 24 of 29 games. And the schedule called for the Cardinals to play their next 30 games at home, where they already were 34–13 for the season. St. Louis wound up winning 19 of those 30 games but still couldn't match the Cubs, who won 21 games in a row and wrapped up the pennant in a double-header sweep of the Cardinals on September 27 in St. Louis. The World Series, however, was another story. After winning the opener on Lon Warneke's shutout, the Cubs dropped the next three games to Detroit, led by Hank Greenberg, Mickey Cochrane, and Schoolboy Rowe. Warneke kept them alive with another victory in Game 5, but the Tigers scored in the bottom of the ninth in Game 6 to become the world champions.

The Cubs were runners-up to New York the next two years, as manager Bill Terry got the Giants to two World Series only to have them lose both times to the Yankees. The big guns for the Giants were Mel Ott, who led the National League in homers both seasons, and Carl Hubbell, who led the league in pitching victories both years.

They continued their habit of winning a pennant every three years with another classic finish in 1938. The Pittsburgh Pirates had a seven-game lead on September 1, but then the Cubs staged a charge. By September 27, the lead was down to a game and a half and the Pirates were in Chicago for a three-game series. The Cubs won the opener behind a sore-armed Dizzy Dean—who was traded to the Cubs in April of '38—to move within a half-game. The next day turned out to be one of the greatest in franchise history. The Pirates led 5–3 but the Cubs tied the score in the eighth. Then in the bottom of the ninth, with two out and darkness falling, Gabby Hartnett sent one of Mace Brown's fastballs over the wall in left, the famous "Homer in the gloamin'," to put the Cubs in first with their ninth straight victory.

"You have seen them rush out to greet a hero after he touched the plate to terminate a great contest," Edward Burns reported in the *Tribune*. "Well you never saw nothin'. The mob started to gather around Gabby before he had reached first base. By the time he had rounded second he couldn't have been recognized in the mass of Cub players, frenzied fans and excited ushers but for that red face, which shone out even in the gray shadows."

The Cubs finished the sweep of the Pirates the next day and charged into the World Series, where they again faced the Yankees. The Series was all New York, though, as the Cubs were swept in four games in what would be their last postseason appearance for seven years.

Despite this win, these weren't the same old Yankees, as they were undergoing a changing of the guard. Before 1934, the Yankees had been Babe Ruth's team. But in '34, with his best years well behind him, the 40-year-old Bambino became a supporting player as teammate Lou Gehrig won the American League Triple Crown and established himself as the undisputed team leader. Ruth's Yankee career ended after that season and he retired in 1935 after a brief and unhappy stint with the Boston Braves.

Yet Gehrig was the main player in the Yankees spotlight for only three seasons. On May 2, 1939, slumping and bothered by general weakness, he took himself out of the lineup, ending a consecutive game streak of 2,130 games. In June, it was announced that Gehrig was suffering from amyotrophic lateral sclerosis—henceforth commonly known as Lou Gehrig's disease—which would claim his life two years later. And just as Gehrig had stepped in to replace Ruth in the eyes of Yankee fans, there was someone there to replace Gehrig.

Joseph Paul DiMaggio had broken in with the Yankees in 1936 and was an immediate sensation. He hit over .300 his first three seasons and established himself as one of the top defensive players in the game. His breakthrough season came in 1939, when he won the American League batting championship with a .381 average.

There was also another hitter who arrived on the scene in the American League that season. He hit .327 and drove in 145 runs for the Boston Red Sox. Not bad for a guy who was just 20 when the season began, and it was just a preview of what Ted Williams would do over the next two decades.

Frank Grube had two stints as a backup catcher for the White Sox, from 1931 to '33 and 1935 and '36. His most productive season was 1932, when he hit .282 and drove in 31 runs in 93 games.

Cubs trainer Andy Lotshaw gives catcher Zack Taylor's sprained thumb the once-over between games of a 1929 double-header. Lotshaw, a former standout minor-league ballplayer himself, spent more than 30 years as the team's trainer before retiring in 1952.

Clay Bryant came up to the Cubs
as a relief pitcher in 1935. His best
year, though, was the pennant-
winning season of 1938 when he
was used primarily as a starter and
went 19–11 with a league-leading
135 strikeouts.

American League President Ernest Barnard throws out the first pitch at Opening Day 1930 at Comiskey Park.

Cubs owner William Wrigley Jr., manager Rogers Hornsby, president William Veeck, and team officials William Walker and John Leys on November 14, 1931.

Les "Toots" Tietje came to the White Sox in 1933 and went 2–0. He stayed in Chicago another 2½ seasons before moving on to St. Louis, where he finished his career with the Browns in 1938.

The White Sox were the
last stop in the six-team,
22-year major-league
career of right-hander
Sam Jones. His best sea-
sons were with the
Boston Red Sox in 1918
(16–5, 2.25 ERA), New
York Yankees in 1923
(21–8), and Washington
Senators in 1928 (17–7).
In four years with the
White Sox, Jones was
36–46.

Ted Lyons was a great
pitcher who had the mis-
fortune of playing on some
very bad teams. He broke
into the game in 1923
when the White Sox were
still trying to rebuild after
the Black Sox scandal. He
pitched for the Sox for 21
seasons, with three years
off for the war, and ended
his career in 1946 at the
age of 45. Of those 21
seasons, the Sox finished
above .500 only six times.
Still, Lyons was able to
win 260 games.

White Sox pitchers Bump Hadley (left) and Sam Jones warm up in 1932. Hadley appeared in only three games for the Sox before being traded to the St. Louis Browns, where he went 13–20. Jones was 10–15 for the Sox in '32.

Cubs owner William Wrigley talks with his manager, Rogers Hornsby, before an April 1931 game. The hard-driving Hornsby led the Cubs to a third-place finish that season.

The mainstays of the 1933 Cub pitching staff—(from left) Pat Malone (10–14), Guy Bush (20–12), Lon Warneke (18–13), and Charlie Root (15–10)—strike a pose in spring training.

Vern Kennedy warms up in 1937. After an 0–2 rookie season in 1934, Kennedy went 11–11, 21–9, and 14–13 for the Sox before being sent to Detroit. He had one winning season there, going 12–9 in 1938, then never had another season of .500 or better in seven more years in the majors.

Luke Sewell was a solid, if unspectacular, catcher through 20 major-league seasons. His best year was with the Cleveland Indians in 1927, when he hit .294. He came to Chicago in 1935 and spent four years in a White Sox uniform.

Johnny Watwood (left) and Smead Jolley both changed their Sox from White to Red during the 1932 season, going from Chicago to Boston.

One Cub meets another as manager Charlie Grimm bottle feeds a bear cub at Wrigley Field in 1937.

Hank Osterbosch was the White Sox field announcer for a few years in the 1930s. He later became a police and fireman's uniform salesman.

Cubs field announcer Pat Pieper announces the lineup for a 1936 game at Wrigley Field. Pieper started out selling hot dogs and popcorn at West Side Park, and was the Cubs announcer for 59 years until his death in 1974.

Jimmie Foxx's nickname, "The Beast," came not from his disposition—he was likeable and gentle—but from the way he could hit a baseball. One of the game's greatest power hitters, he had a career .325 average with 534 home runs and 1,922 RBIs over 20 seasons. He was one of the few players to hit a baseball out of Comiskey Park.

A gaggle of press photographers records Dizzy Dean's every move as he warms up for the Cubs in 1938.

Don Hurst (left) and Chuck Klein await their turn in the batting cage at
Wrigley Field. The two former Philadelphia Phillies came to the Cubs in
1934. Klein hit .301, and Hurst, in his only season as a Cub, batted .199 in
limited duty.

Cubs pitcher Bill Lee
gets a few tips from
his son in 1938.

Bill Dickey, the first in a long line of great New York Yankee catchers, puts on his gear. Dickey spent 17 seasons behind the plate for the Yankees, four times leading American League catchers in fielding. He could also hit, retiring in 1946 with a .313 career average. Dickey also coached for the Yankees and was instrumental in turning Yogi Berra into a catcher early in Berra's career.

Cubs first baseman Phil Cavarretta plays catch with one of his wife's tea cups in the kitchen of their home in 1939.

Stan Hack had a 16-year major-league career, all with the Cubs. He was a lifetime .301 hitter who twice led the league in hits and twice led National League third basemen in fielding. But he was also known for something else: his ever-present smile. "I enjoy playing baseball, and this grin is just my way of showing it," he once said.

133

Vince was the oldest of the three DiMaggio brothers who played in the majors. Unlike Joe (Yankees) and Dom (Red Sox), who each spent his entire career with one team, Vince moved around. Here with the Boston Bees, he also played for the Reds, Pirates, Phillies, and Giants over a 10-year career.

Art Shires gets a few tips from Jimmy McKechnie, son of Boston Braves manager Bill McKechnie, in the on-deck circle in 1932.

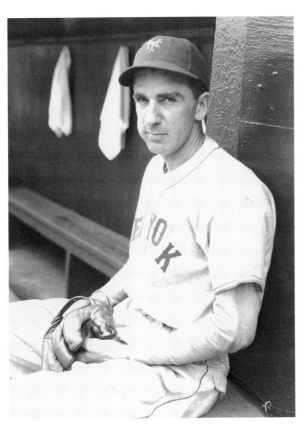

In both 1936 and '37 (pictured), left-hander Carl Hubbell led the National League in victories, helping the New York Giants to the pennant. In 1936, his second MVP season (the first was 1933), he was 26–6 with a 2.31 ERA.

Babe Ruth finds a bat to his liking before batting practice at Comiskey Park in September 1934. Once asked the secret of his hitting success, Ruth said, "All I can tell 'em is I pick a good [pitch] and sock it. I get back to the dugout and they ask me what it was I hit, and I tell 'em I don't know except it looked good."

A player can work up quite a hunger at the ballpark. When he couldn't sneak out of Comiskey Park during a game to grab a hot dog, Ruth would order out and have a sandwich brought to the bench.

Mel Ott shows his classic foot-in-the-bucket batting form—bat back, right foot lifted—as he awaits a pitch at Wrigley Field in the late '30s. Ott made his major-league debut at age 17 and hit .322 as a 19-year-old. Over his 22-year big-league career, spent entirely with the New York Giants, Ott hit 511 home runs and collected 2,876 hits.

Cubs manager Charlie Grimm visits with his wife, Lillian, and daughter, Mae Gene, before a 1932 game at Wrigley Field.

St. Louis Browns man-
ager Gabby Street
instructs his players
from the dugout at
Comiskey Park in 1938.
Street, a former catcher
with the Reds, Sena-
tors, and Yankees,
managed for six sea-
sons, twice winning
National League pen-
nants with the Cardi-
nals. In his one season
with the Browns, they
finished seventh with a
53–90 record.

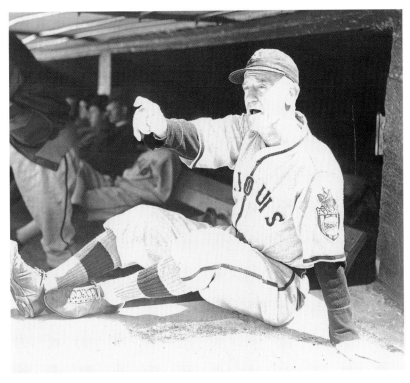

It's not difficult to see
why Babe Ruth was
such a favorite subject of
photographers. Give
him a prop, no matter
how odd, and he'd pose.

Babe Ruth shares some cookies with his biggest fans. Ruth, who spent much of his childhood at St. Mary's Industrial School in Baltimore, always found time for children.

The swing that revolutionized baseball. Ruth's hitting ushered in a new era in the 1920s, when the game was still reeling from the Black Sox scandal. The key to Ruth's hitting success, some experts say, was the way he generated power by rotating his hips. As Ruth followed through on his powerful swing, his hips would be facing foul territory.

Monty Stratton looks over his uniform upon his return to Comiskey Park for Monty Stratton Day in 1939. Stratton won 15 games in 1937 and 15 in '38, but a hunting accident in November 1938 forced the amputation of his right leg at the knee. He pitched just once more for the Sox, in a May 1939 exhibition against the Cubs, winning 4–1. Stratton never returned to the majors as a player, though he did serve as a coach for the Sox from 1939 to '41.

 Stratton is presented the keys to a new car by former teammate Tony Piet at pregame ceremonies on Monty Stratton Day in 1939. Watching are Sox manager Jimmy Dykes (left) and Cubs manager Gabby Hartnett.

Commissioner Landis chows down on a hot dog at Stratton Day.

Lou Gehrig shows the sweet swing that made him one of the game's great hitters. He was a lifetime .340 hitter. Among his personal bests: 220 hits and a .379 average in 1930, 49 home runs in 1934 and '36, 127 runs batted in in 1936, and a .458 on-base percentage in 1937.

Moe Berg (in a 1930 photo) was an average catcher for the White Sox and four other teams during his 15-year career. He achieved much more notoriety for his stint as a spy for the United States. Berg, who had a law degree and spoke several languages, spied on military installations during a major-league tour of Japan in the 1930s. He was also reportedly later involved in atomic bomb espionage.

Joe McCarthy, in a 1930 photo, spent five years as Cubs manager but quit at the end of the 1930 season after the team failed to repeat as NL pennant-winners. He wasn't out of work for long. The Yankees signed him for 1931, starting a string of 16 seasons during which he won eight American League pennants. He finished second four other times.

Commissioner Kenesaw Mountain Landis takes in a White Sox game with his granddaughter, Joanne, in 1931. Landis was a regular fixture at Sox games during his tenure as commissioner.

Cleveland Indians manager Roger Peckinpaugh and White Sox manager Donie Bush meet before the White Sox's 1931 home opener. The Sox were 10–2 winners.

Hughie Jennings was one of the most colorful men ever associated with the game. A career .311 hitter, he was best known for his success as manager of the Tigers, whom he led to American League pennants in 1907, '08, and '09. He verbally prodded his players, vocally harassed opponents, and incited crowds wherever he went.

Once the property of the Cubs, Luke Appling came to the White Sox in a cash transaction and made his major-league debut late in the 1930 season. Over 20 seasons he amassed 2,749 hits and twice led the American League in hitting. It was Appling's misfortune to play on perennial also-rans; the Sox never finished better than third during his playing career.

Luke Appling set major-
league records for games
played at shortstop and double plays, and American
League records for putouts
and assists (all later broken
by Luis Aparicio). He led
AL shortstops in assists seven
times and was always near
the top in putouts and
chances per game.

Rogers Hornsby, nursing a broken ankle, catches up on the news in the Cubs dugout in 1930. Hornsby had had one of the greatest seasons in Cub history in 1929—a .380 batting average, 47 doubles, 39 homers, and 149 RBIs—and led them to the World Series. Shortly before the end of the 1930 season, Hornsby replaced Joe McCarthy as Cubs manager. As player-manager in 1931, he hit .331 and led the Cubs to a third-place finish.

148

George Pipgras won 102 games over an 11-year career, most of it spent with the Yankees. His best season was 1928, when he won a league-high 24 games and had a 3.38 ERA.

Bob Shawkey took over as manager of the New York Yankees following the
death of Miller Huggins. He held the job for just one season, 1930, and the
Yankees slipped to third place. Still, Shawkey's spot in Yankee lore was
secure. He was the ace of the pitching staff in the 1920s, he won 20 or more
games four times, and he was the starting pitcher in the first game at Yankee
Stadium in 1923.

Manager Charlie Grimm (holding his hat) and his Cubs bid farewell to Chicago on their way to New York for the 1932 World Series. Other Cubs pictured are Bob Smith (far left), team president William Veeck (behind Grimm), Kiki Cuyler (in light suit), Woody English (behind Cuyler), Gabby Hartnett (in straw hat), Billy Herman, Guy Bush, and Rollie Hemsley. The ride back to Chicago wasn't as festive. The Yankees won both games in New York and went on to sweep the Cubs in four straight.

Catcher Zack Taylor came to the Cubs during the 1929 season, but as backup to Gabby Hartnett he saw limited action over the next four seasons. He appeared in 77 games from 1930–33 and didn't make an error.

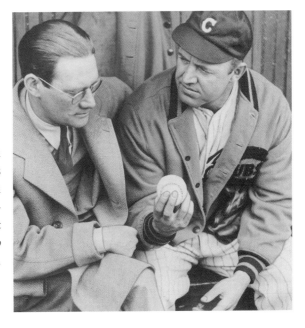

Cubs spitballer Burleigh Grimes discusses the ins and outs of pitching with sportswriter Jimmy Corcoran for a series that appeared in the *Chicago American* in 1932.

Gabby Hartnett (left) and Charlie Root do a pregame radio show on WGN before the Cubs' April 14, 1931, season opener at Wrigley Field.

A September 1931 charity game between the White Sox and Cubs at
Comiskey Park gave a couple of veteran pitchers, Red Faber and Charlie
Root, a chance to compare notes.

Former Cubs slugger Hack Wilson towels off in the Brooklyn Dodgers dugout during a 1932 game at Wrigley Field. Wilson, who was traded to Brooklyn after the 1931 season, went on to hit .297 for the Dodgers in '32.

Cubs pitcher Lon Warneke clowns with film comedian Joe E. Brown before the start of Game 4 of the 1932 World Series at Wrigley Field. Warneke relieved starter Guy Bush in the first inning of the game, which the Yankees won 13–6 to complete a Series sweep.

Babe and Claire Ruth relax in their room at the Edgewater Beach Hotel while in town for the 1932 World Series. Ruth hit .333 with two home runs in the four-game sweep.

154

The Dean brothers, Paul (left) and Dizzy, were a formidable 1–2 punch for the St. Louis Cardinals in the 1930s. In 1934, Dizzy was 30–7 and Paul was 19–11 as the Cardinals went to the World Series where they beat the Tigers in seven games.

Two keys to the Cubs' pennant-winning season of 1932 were team captain and third baseman Woody English (left) and right-fielder Kiki Cuyler. English hit .272 and Cuyler .291.

Cubs owner William Wrigley throws out the ceremonial first ball before a game at Wrigley Field.

Even in a new suit,
Babe Ruth looked
like he should be
playing ball.

The Babe takes
a few minutes
before heading to
the ballpark to
autograph a
briefcase full of
baseballs.

Waite Hoyt shows off his footwork at a Chicago nightclub with Gertrude (left) and Margie Green.

Al Schacht had a short and undistinguished major-league career between 1919 and 1921, but achieved fame and fortune as "The Clown Prince of Base-ball." Starting during his days as a coach for the Washington Senators, Schacht would don a beat-up coat and ratty jacket and do a comedy act. He performed at ballparks across the nation—here he's making a 1933 appearance at Comiskey Park—and entertained crowds at 25 World Series and 18 All-Star Games.

A car carrying Babe Ruth is mobbed by fans as he tries to make his way to Comiskey Park.

Detroit pitcher Schoolboy Rowe signs a baseball for 12-year-old Billy Cassidy before Game 5 of the 1934 World Series in St. Louis. Rowe had gone 24–8 for the Tigers that year, winning 16 consecutive decisions at one point. He followed 1934 with two 19-win seasons before arm troubles curtailed his career.

Connie Mack and John McGraw, opposing managers at the first All-Star Game, meet at home plate during pregame festivities.

As a hitter and behind the plate, catcher Mickey Cochrane was one of the best in the game, first with the Philadelphia Athletics—here he's with the A's in 1933—and later with the Detroit Tigers. Cochrane's career was cut short when he was hit in the head by a Bump Hadley fastball in 1937. Near death and in and out of a coma for more than a week, he recovered, but never played again.

Kiki (pronounced Kuy-kuy) Cuyler, sidelined by a broken leg, cheers on his Cub teammates in 1933. An outstanding outfielder and baserunner, Cuyler was traded to the Cubs by the Pittsburgh Pirates after a run-in with his manager. He spent eight seasons at Wrigley Field, his best being 1929 when he hit .360 to help the Cubs to the National League pennant. Cuyler finished his 18-year career with a .321 lifetime batting average.

Babe Ruth crosses the plate after hitting the first home run in All-Star Game history on July 6, 1933, at Comiskey Park. It was a two-run shot in the third inning and provided the winning margin in the American League's 4–2 victory. Greeting Ruth at home are teammate Lou Gehrig and batboy John McBride.

Babe Ruth tries to keep warm on the Yankee bench during a May 1933 game at Comiskey Park. Ruth struck out twice and left the game, but the Yankees didn't need him as they rolled to a 10–2 victory.

Lefty O'Doul had a less-than-stellar career as a pitcher. His most notorious moment may have come on July 7, 1923, when Red Sox manager Frank Chance, angry that O'Doul had been breaking curfew, refused to remove him from a game in which he was getting pounded. When it was over, O'Doul had surrendered 13 runs. The next season, however, he was traded to the Giants and turned into an outfielder, where he prospered, hitting .319. He hit .398 for the Phillies in 1929, and finished his career in 1934 with a .349 life-time batting average.

Manager Bill Terry keeps tabs on the action from the New York Giants dugout in 1937. Terry was a brilliant hitter and first baseman who took on the additional duties of manager in 1932. He led the Giants to pennants in 1933, '36, and '37, but never became a fan favorite because of his differences with the press.

Leo Durocher was a weak-hitting, good-fielding shortstop who came to the St. Louis Cardinals in 1934. Cocky, abrasive, and always ready to fight, he captained "The Gashouse Gang" the next season.

Lou Gehrig and fiancee Eleanor
Twitchell of Chicago take
advantage of a Yankee day off
to relax in the park. They met
at a party in 1929, and four
years later were married in
New Rochelle, N.Y.

The Washington Senators' Heine Manush waits his turn in the on-deck circle
at Comiskey Park in 1934. A left-handed line-drive hitter, he twice batted
.378 and hit .330 over a 17-year major-league career.

Gabby Hartnett was one of the cornerstones for the Cubs in the 1920s and '30s. A career .297 hitter—his best effort was .354 in 1937—and a solid defensive catcher, Hartnett was also a favorite of teammates and fans. Upon his death, Cubs owner Philip K. Wrigley said, "He was one of those ballplayers who played for the sheer joy of it."

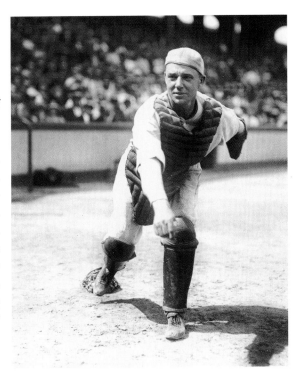

Ernie Lombardi, seen here in a 1933 photo, could hit. He won the National League batting title in 1938 with a .342 average and was named league MVP that season. But he was also known for being slow afoot, and the wisecracks— "Lombardi was once out stretching a double into a single"—became a sore point with him. "All anybody wants to remember about me was that I couldn't run," he once said after he had retired. "They still make jokes. Let them make jokes."

Lou Gehrig had the disadvantage of following Babe Ruth in the Yankee batting order for 11 years. "When I get to bat," he once said, "people are still talking about what Ruth has done. If I stood on my head and held the bat in my teeth, none of the fans would pay the slightest attention. But I'm not kicking."

Babe Ruth, as a member of the Boston Braves, sits in the dugout with manager Bill McKechnie on May 20, 1935. Less than two weeks later, at McKechnie's insistence, the Braves gave Ruth his unconditional release. It was the end of his 22-year career.

Eleanor and Lou Gehrig pose for photographers at Comiskey Park.

Detroit Tigers outfielder Goose Goslin rips a single against the White Sox in 1935. Goslin had more than 2,700 hits and one batting title (.379 in 1928) in an 18-year career. In the 1935 World Series, his RBI single in Game 6 beat the Cubs and made the Tigers world champions.

Out of uniform, White
Sox pitcher Ted Lyons
cuts a dashing figure.

The wife and parents of Lon Warneke watch him work six shutout innings
against the Detroit Tigers in Game 5 of the 1935 World Series. Warneke won
two games in the Series, the only two the Cubs would win, as the Tigers
beat them in six.

Two of the greatest New York Giants ever, Mel Ott (left) and Carl Hubbell, wait for batting practice at Wrigley Field in 1936. That year, Ott hit .328 with 30 homers and Hubbell went 26–6 with a 2.31 ERA as the Giants won the National League pennant.

Woody English was a good hitter on some very solid Cubs ball clubs in the early '30s. He hit .335 in 1930 and .319 the following season.

Pitchers Dizzy Dean of the St. Louis Cardinals and Lon Warneke of the Cubs
meet before a game in April 1935.

Larry French waits to take the mound against the Pittsburgh Pirates in a 1936 game at Wrigley Field. He gave up only eight hits and got the victory, one of 18 he picked up in 1936, his best year in the majors.

Phil Cavarretta visits with his parents before the Cubs' game on July 19, 1935, his nineteenth birthday. Cavaretta came to the Cubs at age 18, right out of high school, late in the 1934 season. He spent 20 years with the Cubs and two more with the White Sox, retiring with a career .293 average.

White Sox manager Jimmy Dykes (left) and coach Muddy Ruel talk things over before a 2–1 loss to the Philadelphia Athletics in June of 1936.

Red Ruffing pitches batting practice to his Yankee teammates in May 1937 at Comiskey Park. Ruffing came to the Yankees from the Red Sox in 1930 having been one of the losingest pitchers in the league over the previous five years. With help from manager Bob Shawkey—and having hitters like Babe Ruth and Lou Gehrig to support him—Ruffing turned his career around. He won 231 games for the Yankees between 1930 and '46, including four consecutive 20-win seasons from 1936 to '39.

Billy Myers was a light-hitting short-stop whose greatest strength was defense. He spent six seasons with the Reds before coming to the Cubs in 1940.

White Sox manager Jimmy Dykes and some of his players take a quick tour of Comiskey Park before an April 1936 exhibition against the Cubs. Looking things over are (from left) Italo Chelini, Ira Hutchinson, George Stumpi, Red Evans, Dykes, Marshall Mauldin, Mike Kreevich, and Joe Morrissey.

Playing in Philadelphia's cozy Baker Bowl, with its 280-foot right-field fence, Chuck Klein was a hitting machine. From 1928 to 1933, he averaged 201 hits, 32 homers, and a .359 batting average. He came to the Cubs before the 1934 season, and although he had two decent years (.301 and .293), his production fell short of his Philadelphia numbers. He was traded back to the Phillies during the 1936 season.

Billy Herman works out around second base during the 1936 season. Herman was a right-handed hitter with outstanding bat control—he was the league's best hit-and-run man—and an excellent second baseman. A 10-time All-Star, he had a career .304 batting average over 15 seasons, 10 of them with the Cubs. "I gave a thousand percent every day in my playing career," he once said. "Baseball was serious as hell to me. Baseball was my life."

Cubs mascot Paul Dominick and pitcher Charlie Root sport mustaches as part of festivities marking the 60th anniversary of the founding of the National League in August 1936. Players dressed in 1876-era uniforms and played a short exhibition game before the regular contest, which the Cubs lost to the Reds 6–4.

Early in the 1934 season, the only four American League pitchers who had no-hitters to their credit crossed paths at Comiskey Park: Boston's Wes Ferrell and the White Sox's Ted Lyons, Bill Dietrich, and Vern Kennedy.

Seventeen-year-old Bob Feller sits on the Indians bench before a 1936 game against the White Sox. He had made his major-league debut about six weeks earlier, striking out 15 St. Louis Browns. Feller spent 18 seasons with the Indians, posting six 20-win seasons and leading the league in strikeouts seven times. He had a 266–162 lifetime record.

Rogers Hornsby's managerial career—here he's with St. Louis in 1936—would have been much longer had he not been so brutally honest. When a player made a mistake, Hornsby told him, in no uncertain terms. His lack of tact and inability to get along with his bosses proved to be his undoing in Chicago and elsewhere.

When Joe DiMaggio came to the Yankees as a rookie in 1936, two of the
players who took him under their wing were Tony Lazzeri and Frank Crosetti.
Here the three wait their turn in the batting cage at Comiskey Park.

Wally Stephenson slips into the tools of ignorance before a 1936 game at Wrigley Field. It was a rare opportunity for Stephenson, who appeared in only six games for the Cubs that season.

Four of the reasons the Yankees swept the Cubs in the 1938 World Series—Red Rolfe, Bill Dickey, Joe DiMaggio, and Lou Gehrig—await the start of Game 1 at Wrigley Field. It was the third consecutive world championship for the Yankees, who would also win it in 1939.

Dizzy Dean's days as an overpowering pitcher were behind him when he came to the Cubs in 1938, the year this photo was taken, but he still went 7–1 with a 1.81 ERA to help them win the National League pennant.

White Sox
catcher Luke
Sewell gets some
sun and catches
up on the news
before a game at
Comiskey in
1937.

Augie Galan came up to the Cubs
in 1934 as an infielder, but was
moved to the outfield the following season. There he led the
league in runs scored and stolen
bases and hit .314 to help the Cubs
to the pennant. His career was
hampered by injuries; in fact, the
Cubs traded him to the Brooklyn
Dodgers in 1941 figuring his best
days were behind him. But Galan
had eight more seasons in him,
including four in which he hit
better than .300.

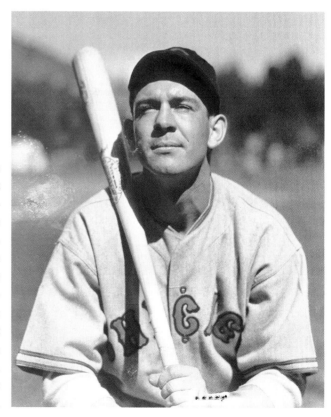

Manager Pie Traynor shouts encouragement to his Pittsburgh Pirates during a 1938 game at Wrigley Field. The teams went to the final days of the season neck-and-neck, with the Cubs edging the Pirates for first place by two games.

Red Sox Lefty Grove delivers a curve to a White Sox hitter in a June 1938 game at Comiskey. The 38-year-old Grove went 12 innings in beating the Sox 4–3, running his record to 11–1. He finished with a 14–4 mark that season.

Yankee rookie Charlie Keller waits on deck at Comiskey Park in 1939. He was another of those talented young players the Yankees brought up like clockwork in the late '30s. He hit .334 in his first season and was a steady contributor until suffering a back injury in 1947. He required surgery, and was never again the slugger he once was.

Cubs catcher-manager Gabby Hartnett waves to the crowds during a parade celebrating the Cubs pennant on October 3, 1938. Just five days earlier, Hartnett had hit his "homer in the gloamin'," a ninth-inning blast that beat the Pirates and put the Cubs in first place and sent them on their way to the pennant. Riding with Hartnett is Chicago Alderman Jacob Arvey.

Ted Williams, the Red Sox's 20-year-old rookie, talks to manager Joe Cronin at Comiskey Park in 1939. Williams hit .327 that season, the first of his 18 seasons at .300 or better.

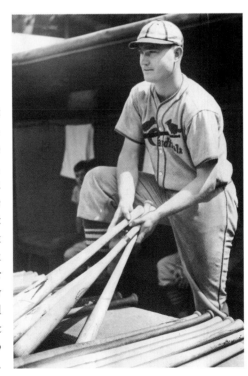

Johnny Mize was one of the most skilled hitters of the 1930s and '40s. He hit with power, blasting 359 home runs in his 15-year career, but unlike most sluggers seldom struck out. He debuted with the St. Louis Cardinals in 1936 and hit .336 for them over the next six seasons. Traded to the New York Giants, he continued producing for five seasons, then went to the New York Yankees, where he finished out his career as a backup first baseman and one of the game's top pinch-hitters.

190

Boston Red Sox pitcher
Wes Ferrell grounds out
during a 1937 contest
against the White Sox.
Not only was Ferrell a
good pitcher—he won
193 games over 15 sea-
sons—he was one of the
better hitting pitchers.
He had a lifetime .280
average and hit .347 in
1935. The Sox catcher is
Luke Sewell.

Pepper Martin played the game with
abandon, hence his nickname "The
Wild Hoss of the Osage." He hustled
in the field, and he ran the bases like a
madman. Martin had a career .298
average and batted .418 in three World
Series. He was a perfect fit on the St.
Louis Cardinals' "Gashouse Gang."

In his later years, Joe DiMaggio was intensely private and reserved. But early in his career he was much more out-going. Arriving in Chicago for a series with the White Sox in 1939, he posed with teammate Babe Dahlgren and hammed it up for press photographers.

Pirates great Honus Wagner watches from the Pittsburgh dugout in 1935.
Wagner was brought back as a coach in 1933 and spent the next two decades
helping young players—he was a big influence on shortstop Arky Vaughan—
and serving as a goodwill ambassador for baseball.

Joe DiMaggio made hitting look easy, almost as if he could do it with his eyes closed. Seen here ripping a single against the Sox in 1940, he had a career .325 batting average.

Luke Appling pops one up in batting practice. A natural hitter, he homered in the first Cracker Jack Old-Times Game in 1980 at the age of 73.

The Boston Red Sox's Bobby Doerr takes his cuts in batting practice at Comiskey Park in the late '40s. One of the best fielding second basemen of his day, Doerr was also a decent hitter, accumulating more than 2,000 hits and a .288 average over 14 seasons.

1940–1950

By the 1940s, baseball's fortunes were climbing. The game, and the nation, were escaping the grip of the depression. Major-league attendance would reach 9.8 million in 1940, the highest since that incomparable season of 1930. And young players such as Joe DiMaggio, Ted Williams, and Bob Feller had established themselves as solid stars.

THE WAR YEARS AND REBIRTH

Any fans who were giving baseball only a passing glance surely couldn't ignore Opening Day of the 1940 season. In front of a Comiskey Park crowd that included his parents and sister, as well as comedians Joe E. Brown and Eddie "Rochester" Anderson, the 21-year-old Feller threw a no-hitter as the Cleveland Indians beat the White Sox 1–0.

It was the beginning of a remarkable year for Feller and the Indians. By mid-June manager Oscar Vitt had aggravated enough players to precipitate a team-wide mutiny—11 veteran players, including Feller, went to owner Alva Bradley and asked that the stern Vitt be fired. Bradley refused, and the players backed down. With that behind them, the Indians positioned themselves at or near the top of the American League standings for the rest of the season. Leading the way were Feller and second-year shortstop Lou Boudreau. The Indians' fate was decided in late August and early September when they lost six of nine games to their main rival, the Detroit Tigers. The two teams had one last showdown, September 27 at Municipal Stadium in Cleveland. The second-place Indians sent Feller to the mound. The first-place Tigers went with Floyd Giebell, just recalled from the minors, where he had been 12–15. Feller allowed just three hits, but one was a home run and Detroit won 2–0 to clinch the American League pennant.

The Tigers, led by Charlie Gehringer, Dick Bartell, Rudy York, Hank Greenberg, Schoolboy Rowe, and Bobo Newsom, were matched against the Cincinnati Reds, easy winners in the National League.

The Reds had a memorable year as well, only one tinged with tragedy. They had something to prove, having been swept by the New York Yankees in the 1939 World Series. They started strong and were a half-dozen games ahead of second-place Brooklyn when they were shaken in early August. Catcher Willard Hershberger, apparently blaming himself over some recent close losses, killed himself in a Boston hotel room. Despite the emotional upheaval, the Reds stayed the course and wound up winning 100 games, a franchise record.

In the World Series that year, pitchers Bucky Walters and Paul Derringer each won two games, and Mike McCormick and Billy Werber provided the offense, as the Reds outlasted the Tigers in seven games for their first world championship since 1919.

The following season, the Tigers, Reds, and all other teams in baseball would wind up as supporting players as two of the game's greatest hitters—Ted Williams and Joe DiMaggio—gave performances that still evoke awe 60 years later.

Williams had broken in with the Boston Red Sox in 1939. He made a big splash, driving in 145 runs to lead the majors and set a rookie record. He was equally impressive in 1940, hitting .344 with 113 RBIs and 23 homers. In 1941, he became the dominant hitter in the game, batting .406 with 37 homers and 120 runs batted in. His average was well above .400 most of the summer, but he faded in September and was at .3995 going into the final day of the season, a doubleheader in Philadelphia. By all rights, he could have taken the day off and his average legitimately would have been rounded to .400. But Williams refused to take the charity, even if it was only .0005 of a percentage point. He played both games of the double-header, getting six hits in eight at-bats to finish at a robust .406.

But Williams's batting title was not the biggest story of 1941—DiMaggio saw to that. Over a two-month period, the Yankee Clipper got hits in 56 consecutive games and captured the nation's attention along the way.

DiMaggio was an old hand at hitting streaks. In the minors, he had one of 61 games, and in his first three seasons with the Yankees he had streaks of 22,

23, and 18 games. Then in the spring of 1941 he hit safely in the Yankees' last 19 exhibition games and their first eight regular-season games for a string of 27. And that was just a preview of what was to come.

His most well-known streak began on May 15 in New York with a single off White Sox pitcher Ed Smith. As the streak grew, so did the spotlight. By early June, papers across the country were keeping tabs. The modern National League record of 33 games fell on June 21; the American League mark of 41 on June 29, and the all-time record of 44, set in 1898 by Wee Willie Keller, was broken on July 2. Two weeks later, DiMaggio's first-inning single off Cleveland's Al Milnar upped the streak to 56, and that's where it would end.

"I can't say I'm glad that it's over," he told reporters. "Of course I wanted to go on as long as I could." DiMaggio, incidentally, picked up the next day where he left off when he got a hit to start a 16-game streak.

When DiMaggio's streak began, the Yankees were 15–15 and in fourth place. When it ended, they were in first place by seven games. They pulled away down the stretch and wound up beating their nearest competitors, the Red Sox, by 17 games. Despite being outhit by the Red Sox's Williams in just about every offensive category, the more popular DiMaggio was voted the American League's most valuable player.

The Yankees' opponent in the World Series was the Dodgers, who slipped past St. Louis thanks to the hitting of National League MVP Dolph Camilli and the pitching of Whit Wyatt and Kirby Higbe.

New York had a two-games-to-one lead, but Brooklyn was on the verge of tying the Series in Game 4, leading 4–3 with two out in the ninth. Then came another one of those legendary baseball moments. Batter Tommy Henrich swung and missed at strike three for what should have been the game-ending out. But the ball got past Dodgers catcher Mickey Owen and Henrich reached first. The Yankees then rallied to win 7–4 for a three-games-to-one Series lead, and polished the Dodgers off the following day.

Williams, DiMaggio, and the exciting World Series were just part of what made 1941 one of the most memorable seasons in baseball history. Other news included the death of Lou Gehrig, Lefty Grove's three hundredth career victory, the retirement of veteran umpire Bill Klem, and the debut of Stan Musial for the St. Louis Cardinals.

After the attack on Pearl Harbor and the United States' entry into World War II, baseball became a different game. At one point there was even some question as to whether the entire sport should be put on hold, but with prodding from

President Roosevelt, owners decided to play on. They did it, however, without some of their biggest stars. Bob Feller, Ted Williams, Hank Greenberg, Stan Musial, Warren Spahn, and Joe DiMaggio—and thousands of others—all gave up prime baseball years to serve in the armed forces. The effects of the war on the game were evident in other ways, such as 15-year-old rookies (Cincinnati's Joe Nuxhall), one-armed outfielders (St. Louis' Pete Gray), and batting champions most people have never heard of (New York's Snuffy Stirnweiss, 1945).

The war also changed history in Chicago. The Cubs had planned to install lights at Wrigley Field, and owner Philip K. Wrigley ordered the steel and cable for the job during the 1941 season. The materials were stored under the stands, and the cutting of the steel was to begin on December 8. The morning before, of course, Pearl Harbor was attacked. That same day, Wrigley placed a call to the War Department offering the steel to the government. The offer was graciously accepted. The Cubs tried again to light their field during 1944 season, but the war production board turned down their application. After the rejection, Cubs general manager Jim Gallagher told reporters, "The Cubs will confine their baseball to the daylight in Chicago this season, at least. . . . However, the Cubs have not been and are not now sold on night baseball. But this situation may change after the war." It took them only 43 years to change their minds.

The 1942, '43, and '44 National League seasons were dominated by the St. Louis Cardinals, who won the pennant all three years and the World Series in '42 and '44. Key players on some of those ball clubs were Musial, Enos Slaughter, Marty Marion, and brothers Walker and Mort Cooper. The Yankees won in '43 and were surprised—along with the rest of baseball—when the St. Louis Browns won the American League pennant in '44.

That season was wartime baseball at its best. Or worst, depending on how you look at things. The Browns, with an all-4F infield, the majority of their players over 30, and a number of athletes salvaged from baseball's scrap heap, jumped out to a 9–0 start. With most other teams severely depleted by the war, the Browns were able to sneak home with the first pennant in their 43-year history, finishing one game ahead of Detroit. The Browns' magical season ended in the World Series, however, where they lost to the Cardinals in six games.

By 1945, baseball was starting to recover from the war-induced talent shortage as Feller, Greenberg, and Charlie Keller were among those who returned from the service. But the recovery wasn't complete. The American League batting title was won by Yankees second baseman Stirnweiss (.309), who also led the league in hits, runs, triples, slugging percentage, and stolen bases. Players who hadn't appeared in the majors in years—like Babe Herman, who had retired in 1937—found roster spots. And 42-year-old batting practice pitcher Paul Schreiber was activated by the Yankees. Hours later, he worked 3⅓ hitless innings in his first major league appearance in 22 years.

One team still feeling the effects of the war was the St. Louis Cardinals. They lost first baseman Stan Musial for the entire season and catcher Walker Cooper for all but four games. And, tired of his contract squabbles, they traded three-time 20-game winner Mort Cooper to the Boston Braves. These troubles, while devastating for the Cardinals, worked in favor of the Cubs.

The 1940s had not been kind to the Cubs, who had a fourth, two fifths, and two sixth-place finishes in their previous five seasons. In '45, under Charlie Grimm, who began his second tour of duty as manager in '44, the Cubs bested the second-place Cardinals by three games. Key players were first baseman Phil Cavarretta, who hit .355 and was the National League's most valuable player; pitcher Hank Wyse, their only 20-game winner; and, most important, pitcher Hank Borowy.

Borowy had been a solid pitcher for the Yankees for 3½ seasons. On July 27, 1945, New York sold him to the Cubs for nearly $100,000 in a transaction that the next morning's *Tribune* called "the most spectacular player deal of the year." Writer Ed Burns went on: "If Borowy is available all season the deal should guarantee the National League pennant for the Chicago club." Burns was on the money. Borowy went 11–2 the rest of the season for the Cubs, who, at one point, won 26 of 30 games to take control of the pennant race.

In the American League, the addition of a familiar face boosted the Detroit Tigers to the pennant. Greenberg, who had gone into the service in May of 1941, returned to the lineup on July 1 and celebrated with a home run. He hit 12 more in his abbreviated season, none more important than a ninth-inning grand slam on September 30 that beat St. Louis and clinched the pennant in the Tigers' season finale.

Borowy and Greenberg played key roles in that World Series. Borowy shut out the Tigers in Game 1, took the loss in Game 5, and pitched four scoreless innings to get the win in Game 6. Greenberg had a three-run homer in Game 2 and three doubles in Game 5 to spark a pair of Detroit victories. The Series came down to a decisive Game 7. Grimm elected to start Borowy after only one day's rest, and he just didn't have it in him. The Tigers opened the game with three consecutive singles, knocking Borowy out, and scored five runs in the first inning on their way to a 9–3 victory and world championship. "The Detroit Tigers may be one of the weakest clubs that ever has won a world series," wrote *Tribune* sports editor Arch Ward, "but they convinced 41,590 spectators in Wrigley Field yesterday they are the best team in 1945 baseball. They had the batting punch and pitching strength to whip a team with far greater speed and steadier defense."

It would be the last World Series appearance for the Cubs, who fell to third in 1946 and drifted through the second division for the next 20 years.

The World Series had barely faded from the front pages when the baseball world was shaken by the October 23 announcement that the Brooklyn Dodgers had signed a black ballplayer to a contract. Jackie Robinson, the 26-year-old shortstop of the Negro Leagues' Kansas City Monarchs, was signed for the Dodgers' International League team in Montreal. "I can't begin to tell you how happy I am that I am the first member of my race in organized ball," Robinson told reporters. "I realize how much it means to me, to my race, and to baseball. I can only say I'll do my very best to come through in every manner."

It would be more than a year before Robinson would get his chance in the majors. In the meantime, with the war over, life was returning to normal in the American and National Leagues. The 1946 season saw the return of the rest of the players who had gone off to war. None made a bigger impact upon his return than Ted Williams. He batted .342, hit 38 homers, and drove in 123 runs as Boston turned the American League pennant race into a runaway. Williams's year was notable on another front. During a game against the Red Sox in July, Cleveland Indians manager Lou Boudreau instituted what became known as the Ted Williams shift, positioning all of his fielders to the right of second base except for his left-fielder, who played a deep shortstop. Williams, a dead pull hitter, was stymied as other managers copied the defense over the rest of the season (and his career). Williams did manage the last laugh when he hit an opposite-field, inside-the-park home run against the Indians on September 13 to clinch the pennant.

The pennant race was considerably closer in the National League, where St. Louis, bolstered by the return of Musial, came from 7½ games back in July to tie Brooklyn for the pennant. The Cardinals won a best-of-three playoff series in two games to advance to the World Series. Boston and St. Louis battled to a seventh game, where the Cardinals scored the deciding run in the bottom of the eighth in another of those memorable baseball moments. Enos Slaughter scored from first on a double by Harry Walker when Boston shortstop Johnny Pesky held the ball and hesitated making the throw home.

The next spring, baseball entered a new age when Brooklyn purchased Robinson's contract from Montreal. Few welcomed Robinson, and even his teammates were initially cold to him. A protest petition signed by some of the players in spring training angered general manager Branch Rickey and manager Leo Durocher, who threatened to trade anyone who didn't want Robinson as a teammate. Opponents—most famously the Philadelphia Phillies—taunted Robinson on the field, and fans on the road often targeted him. He stood up to the critics, the racists, and the doubters to hit .297 and lead the league in stolen bases. His performance earned him Rookie of the Year honors.

Often lost in the frenzy of Robinson's arrival in the majors is Larry Doby. Three months after Robinson broke in with the Dodgers, Doby became the first black player in the American League when he was signed by Cleveland Indians owner Bill Veeck. Doby's road was equally difficult. As former National League president Bill White told the *Tribune*, "When he played his first big-league game (July 5, 1947 against the White Sox at Comiskey Park), he had to go into the opposing team's clubhouse to get a first baseman's mitt. None of his Cleveland teammates offered him a glove." Reluctant teammates and belligerent fans were a way of life for Doby too, but, in Robinson's shadow, he was usually forgotten. "That doesn't bother me—Jackie Robinson was No. 1 and he deserves that," Doby said in 1997, "but when people ask me, 'Did he make it easier for you?'—that's a stupid question. It was 11 weeks between the time Jackie Robinson and I came into the majors. Eleven weeks. Come on. Whatever happened to him happened to me."

Doby was further hurt by the fact that Robinson and the Dodgers enjoyed the national spotlight that went with both playing in New York and going to the World Series in 1947. Waiting for them were the New York Yankees, who breezed to the American League pennant. Leading the way was DiMaggio, who would later win American League MVP honors despite Ted Williams's Triple Crown season. For the third year in a row, the Series went seven games, with the Yankees prevailing behind the hitting of Tommy Henrich and the pitching of Spec Shea and Joe Page.

Over the next two seasons, Robinson became the heart of the Dodgers. They slumped to third place in 1948, but won the pennant in 1949 when he led the league in hitting and stolen bases.

A sidelight to the Robinson story was the fact that, in more enlightened times, he could have been leading the White Sox instead of the Dodgers. Robinson had had tryouts with other major-league clubs, including one in 1941 with the White Sox. In mid-March, Robinson and pitcher Nate Moreland appeared at Brookside Park in Pasadena, California, where the Sox were training. They asked for a tryout, and manager Jimmy Dykes and his staff put them through a workout. Afterward, Dykes reportedly told Robinson that he was faster than anyone he had on the Sox, but Dykes and the players all knew the tryout wouldn't lead anywhere because of baseball's color line.

And it certainly wasn't like the Sox couldn't have used Robinson. Their highest finish in the '40s came in 1941, when they went 77–77 and placed third, and in only two seasons did they finish above .500. Their biggest stars were two old standbys, Ted Lyons and Luke Appling. But things were looking up by the end of the decade. In 1948, Frank Lane became general manager, and he began rebuilding the franchise through his legendary trades.

Sox fans should have taken heart in 1948, when the story of the season was the success of two perennial also-rans. The Boston Braves, who hadn't won a pennant since 1914, won the National League, and the Cleveland Indians, non-winners since 1920, captured the American League. Boston had the hitters—Tommy Holmes, Al Dark, Eddie Stanky, Jeff Heath, and Mike McCormick were all over .300—and a pitching staff that consisted of Johnny Sain and Warren Spahn and not much else ("Spahn and Sain and pray for rain"). The Indians were led by player-manager Boudreau, who hit .355, and a pitching staff anchored by Bob Lemon, Bob Feller, and Gene Beardon. But something else Cleveland had going for it was owner Bill Veeck.

The son of the former Cubs president, he had gotten his start in baseball with the Cubs, mailing out tickets when he was only 11. He and his partners had purchased control of the team in 1946. Perhaps the most important move he made in 1948 was part baseball, part showmanship. In July he signed veteran Negro Leagues pitcher Satchel Paige. Much of the baseball world scoffed, but Paige became a key component for the Indians' pennant drive. He went 6–1 in 21 games, one of his victories a 5–0 decision over the White Sox in August in front of more than 51,000 fans at Comiskey Park. A week later he shut out the Sox on three hits, winning 1–0, in front of more than 78,000 fans in Cleveland.

The Indians needed every one of Paige's victories, as they and the Red Sox finished in a tie for the American League pennant. The champion was decided in a one-game playoff, which the Indians won thanks to two home runs by

Boudreau. Cleveland's pitching was too much for the Braves in the World Series, and the Indians won in six games.

As close as the pennant races were in 1948, they were even tighter the following season. Both the Yankees, under new manager Casey Stengel, and the Dodgers won pennants by one game. In the Series, New York again made short work of Brooklyn, winning in five games. The '49 season was equally notable for some outstanding individual performances. Philadelphia Athletics right-hander Bobby Shantz pitched nine no-hit innings in relief against the Tigers in May; Pittsburgh's Ralph Kiner hit 54 home runs for his fourth straight National League homer crown and had 127 RBIs; and Mel Parnell won 25 games for the Boston Red Sox.

A couple of new names popped up in 1949. The Dodgers brought up pitcher Don Newcomb, while Monte Irvin debuted for the New York Giants. In Cleveland, rookie pitcher Mike Garcia led the American League in earned run average, and the New York Yankees signed an Oklahoma high school phenom named Mickey Mantle.

Club presidents Warren Giles of Cincinnati and Branch Rickey of Brooklyn talk business at league meetings in Chicago in 1946.

Long ago banished from baseball for his part in the Black Sox
scandal, former Sox third baseman Buck Weaver held a variety of
jobs, including installing tile. Here he works on an elevator in the
early '50s.

Cleveland Indians manager Lou Boudreau talks with Larry Doby on July 5,
1947, the day Doby became the first black player in the American League.
Doby, 22, had been hitting over .400 for Newark of the Negro National
League when his contract was purchased by the Indians. He appeared as a
pinch-hitter in his first game, striking out in the seventh inning against the
White Sox.

When Lefty Grove came to the New York Yankees he relied almost entirely
on a devastating fastball. Later in his career, when his fastball had lost its zip,
he became a control pitcher with an effective curve and knuckleball. Either
way, he was a winner. Gomez had 189 victories in 13 years with the Yankees,
including four 20-win seasons, and twice led the league in ERA.

Ruth Steinhagen is taken away in a police patrol wagon after shooting Phillies first baseman Eddie Waitkus in 1949. Steinhagen, 19, had developed an obsession for Waitkus. She checked into the Edgewater Beach Hotel in Chicago and had a note sent to Waitkus's room saying she had to see him. When he arrived at her twelfth-floor room, she shot him in the chest, just below the heart. He eventually recovered and played for six more seasons. Steinhagen was declared insane and committed to Kankakee State Hospital. In 1952 she was judged sane and freed.

Umpire Beans Reardon gets a different view of a 1940 game at Wrigley Field—from the seats. The fun-loving and hard-drinking Reardon was one of the most colorful umpires of his era. He umped from 1926 to 1949.

A view of Wrigley Field from the visitors' dugout in 1942.

Cubs pitcher Lon Warneke towels off after giving up five runs to the New York Giants in a 1942 game at Wrigley Field.

Brooklyn Dodgers manager Burt Shotten sees some things he likes—and some he doesn't—during a 1948 game at Wrigley Field. In his three full seasons as the Dodgers manager, Brooklyn finished first twice and second once.

Joe DiMaggio and an unidentified partner enjoy an evening out at the
Blackhawk Restaurant.

Johnny Vander Meer warms up on the sidelines before taking the mound for the Cincinnati Reds against the Cubs. Vander Meer had a 13-year career, 11 of them with the Reds. He won 119 games, including back-to-back no-hitters in June 1938.

Cleveland Indians pitcher
Satchel Paige talks to boxers
Gene Burton (left) and Joe
Louis before making his first
appearance at Comiskey Park as
a major-leaguer in August 1948.
A crowd of 51,013 filled the
ballpark—several thousand
more were turned away and
jammed the streets outside—
and saw Paige shut out the
White Sox on five hits.

Pittsburgh Pirates slugger Hank Greenberg talks hitting with a young
admirer at Wrigley Field in 1947.

Brooklyn Dodgers catcher Mickey Owen allowed the most famous passed ball in baseball history. In Game 4 of the 1941 World Series, the Yankees' Tommy Henrich struck out to seemingly end the game, but the ball got past Owen and Henrich reached first base. The Yankees rallied to win the game, and the Dodgers, who were on the verge of tying the Series at two games apiece, never recovered. New York went on to win Game 5 to wrap up the Series.

Outfielder Moose Solters takes batting practice in 1940, his first—and best— year with the White Sox. Solters hit .308 with 12 homers in 116 games.

The first night game at Comiskey Park, on August 14, 1939, was a novelty not only for managers Jimmy Dykes of the White Sox and Fred Haney of the St. Louis Browns, but for the fans as well. More than 35,000 of them attended, and after Charles Comiskey II threw the switch, they saw the Sox win 5–2.

The 1943 Cubs were the last stop in catcher Al Todd's 11-year major-league career. A lifetime .276 hitter, he also played for the Phillies, Pirates, and Dodgers.

Herb Adams inspects his bat before batting practice in 1949. Adams hit .293 in 56 games for the Sox that season.

INDEX

222

Greenberg, Hank, 114, 198, 200, 201, 214

Grimes, Burleigh, 83, 151

Grimes, Oscar, 86

Grimes, Ray, 86

Grimm, Charlie, 79, 104, 105, 112, 126, 138, 150, 201

Grimm, Lillian, 138

Grimm, Mae Gene, 138

Groh, Heine, 97

Grove, Lefty, 57, 97, 110, 187, 199, 207

Grube, Frank, 116

Haas, Mule, 111

Hack, Stan, 132

Hadley, Bump, 121, 161

Hafey, Chick, 111

Haney, Fred, 216

Harris, Bucky, 55

Hartnett, Gabby, 114, 142, 150, 151, 167, 188

Hayes, Jackie, 111

Heath, Jeff, 204

Hemsley, Rollie, 150

Hendrix, Claude, 24, 26, 44

Henrich, Tommy, 199, 203, 215

Herman, Babe, 109, 201

Herman, Billy, 80, 150, 179

Hershberger, Willard, 198

Herzog, Buck, 27, 43, 45

Higbie, Kirby, 199

Highlanders (New York), 7

Hildebrand, George, 34

Holmes, Tommy, 204

Hooper, Harry, 22, 54, 58

Hornsby, Rogers, 56, 57–58, 76, 104, 105, 106, 110, 112, 113, 118, 122, 148, 182

Hoyt, Waite, 51, 56, 158

Hubbell, Carl, 114, 135, 172

Huggins, Miller, 41, 48, 149

Hurst, Don, 129

Hutchinson, Ira, 178

Indians (Cleveland), 66, 67, 203, 204

Irvin, Monte, 205

Isbell, Frank, 7

Jackson, Joe, 25, 26, 27, 48

Jennings, Hughie, 34, 146

Johnson, Ban, 5, 6, 13, 23

Johnson, Walter, 16, 54, 55, 79

Jolley, Smead, 125

Jones, Davey, 4

Jones, Fielder, 7, 12, 24

Jones, Sam, 120, 121

Judge, Joe, 55, 66

Jurges, Billy, 104, 112

Kamm, Willie, 58, 82

Kauff, Benny, 53

Keller, Charlie, 188, 200

Keller, Wee Willie, 199

Kelly, George, 54

Kennedy, Vern, 111, 123, 181

Kerr, Dickie, 58–59

Killian, Ed, 4

Killifer, Bill, 28

Killifer, Red, 29

Kiner, Ralph, 205

228

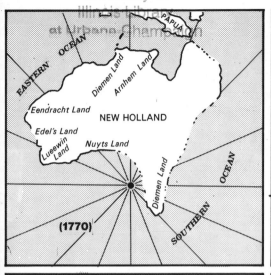

(1770)

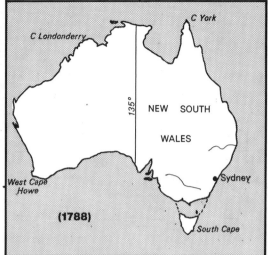

(1788)

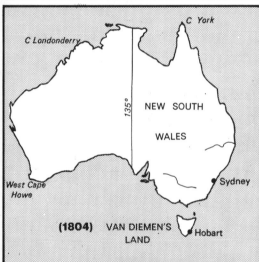

(1804)

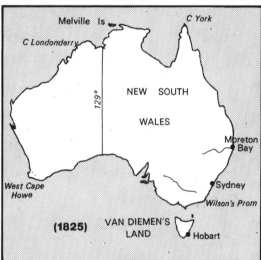

(1825)

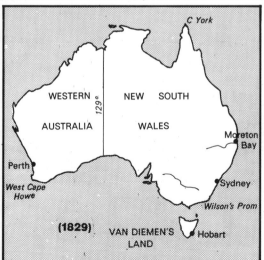

(1829)

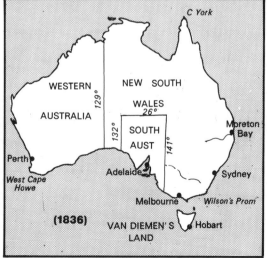

(1836)

The
Origins of Australia's Capital Cities

Australia
1788-1988

This publication has received financial assistance from the
Western Australian Government
to celebrate Australia's Bicentenary in 1988

Studies in Australian History

Series Editors
Alan Gilbert and Peter Spearritt

The
Origins of Australia's
Capital Cities

Edited by

Pamela Statham

Department of Economic History
University of Western Australia

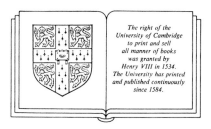

Cambridge University Press

Cambridge

New York   New Rochelle   Melbourne   Sydney

Published by the Press Syndicate of the University of Cambridge
The Pitt Building, Trumpington Street, Cambridge CB2 1RP, UK
32 East 57th Street, New York, NY 10022, USA
10 Stamford Road, Oakleigh, Melbourne 3166, Australia

First published in 1989

Printed by Macarthur Press, Sydney.

National Library of Australia cataloguing-in-publication data

The Origins of Australia's capital cities.

Includes bibliographies and index.

1. Cities and towns—Australia—History. 2. Australia
—History. 3. Australia—Capital and capitol. I.
Statham, Pamela, 1944-   . (Series : Studies in
Australian history (Cambridge, England))

994

British Library cataloguing in publication data

The Origins of Australia's capital cities.
1. Australia. Capital cities ; history.
I. Statham, Pamela
994′.00973′2

ISBN 0 521 36242 3

CONTENTS

MAPS

Inside back and front covers . . . The Evolution of Modern Australia

TABLES

CONTRIBUTORS

Geoffrey C Bolton   Professor of History, Murdoch University. Educated at the University of Western Australia (where he was later Professor of Modern History) and at Oxford, he is a prominent author and commentator on current affairs. He has recently completed editing the new *Oxford History of Australia* to which he also contributed the final volume. His writings on Western Australian history are numerous, the two best known being *Alexander Forrest* (1958) and *A Fine Country to Starve In* (1972).

James Cameron   Dean of the Faculty of Education, Darwin Institute of Technology. Dr Cameron was educated at the University of Western Australia, and is a geographer with a particular interest in Australia in the first half of the nineteenth century. In addition to many articles he is the author of *Ambition's Fire: The Agricultural Colonization of Pre-Convict Western Australia* (1981) and *The Atlas of Northern Australia* (1986).

Mel Davies   A Welshman and cyclist of some note, is Lecturer in Economic History, University of Western Australia. He was educated at Coleg Harlech, the University of Kent at Canterbury, and Adelaide University. While at Adelaide his two main interests were Aboriginal affairs and the early copper mining industry. Publications include 'Apartheid— Australian Style' in *Origin* (1971), 'Copper and Credit: Commission agents and the SA Mining Association', AEHR 1983, 'Corsets and Conception' in *Comparative Studies in Society and History* (1982) and, with R.T. Appleyard, a chapter in *Australian Financiers: Biographical Essays* (1988).

Tony Denholm   Reader in History, University of Adelaide. Graduating from the University of Wales, he has taught at the Manchester Polytechnic; the University of Hong Kong and, since 1968, at the University of Adelaide. His publications include *France in Revolution: 1848* (1972).Tony Denholm is currently working on aspects of South Australian and British urban history.

Brian H Fletcher   Bicentennial Professor of Australian History, University of Sydney; he is Vice-President of the Royal Australian Historical Society and co-editor of its Journal. He has published numerous articles on the early history of New South Wales, including an edited, annotated edition of David Collin's *Account of the English Colony in New South Wales*; *Landed Enterprise and Penal Society* (1976); *Colonial Australia before 1850* (1976); *Ralph Darling A Governor Maligned* (1984), and *The Grand Parade, A History of the Royal Agricultural Society of New South Wales* (1988).

Ross Johnston Associate Professor of History, University of Queensland. His publications include a volume on British imperial history, *Great Britain Great Empire* (1981), and several Queensland histories: *The Call of the Land* (1982); *A Documentary History of Queensland* (1988); and *A Guide to the History of Queensland* (1985).

Helen Gregory Research Assistant, History, University of Queensland. She is an independent writer specialising in early Brisbane, and worked with Ross Johnston on both Queensland chapters.

Ged Martin Director of Canadian Studies, University of Edinburgh. Previously research fellow in history, Magdalene College, Cambridge and at the Australian National University, Ged Martin also spent some time teaching at the University of Cork before moving to Edinburgh. Apart from editing his well-known book on *The Foundations of Australia* (1978, 2nd edition 1981) he is author of *The Durham Report and British Policy* (1972) and, with Ronald Hyam, *Reappraisals in British Imperial History* (1975).

Roger Pegrum Director of Architecture, Federal Dept. of Administrative Services and Associate Professor of Architecture, University of Sydney. He has degrees in Arts, Architecture and Town Planning. His previous publications include *Australian Architects* and *Details in Australian Architecture*, as well as *The Bush Capital*, upon which his chapter is based.

Susan Priestley Freelance Historian. After taking a degree in Arts at the University of Queensland she became Assistant Archivist at the University of Melbourne. Publications include several local histories eg *Echuca* (1965) and *Warracknabeal* (1967), and most recently Volume 3 of the sesqui-centenary series *The Victorians* entitled *Making their Mark* (1984).

Robert Reece Professor of Australian History, University College Dublin and Senior Lecturer, Murdoch University, WA. He worked as a journalist in Malaysia and Singapore. His main published works are *Aborigines and Colonists: Aborigines and Colonial Society in NSW in the 1830s and 1840s* (1974); *The Name of Brooke . . .* (1982); and '*A Place of Consequence*': *A Pictorial History of Fremantle* (1983). Also, he has recently contributed entries for the *Northern Territory Dictionary of Biography*.

Gordon Rimmer Emeritus Professor of Economic History, University of New South Wales. Educated at Cambridge and Harvard, he has held chairs in History at the University of the West Indies and University of Tasmania as well as that of Economic History at the University of New South Wales. His main publications are *Flaxspinners, 1788–1886* (1960); *Portrait of a Hospital: the Royal Hobart* (1981); and *In Time for War* (forthcoming).

Lloyd Robson Senior Lecturer in History, University of Melbourne. He was educated at the University of Tasmania, the University of London and the Australian National University and he is the author of numerous books and articles in the field of Australian history. His best-known works are *The Convict Settlers of Australia* (1965); *The First AIF* (1970); and *A History of Tasmania*, Vol. I (1983).

Alan Shaw   Emeritus Professor of History, Monash University. Educated at Melbourne, Oxford and Newcastle. His publications are manifold and have made a significant contribution to Australian history, the best known being *Economic Development of Australia* (1946); *Story of Australia* (1955); *Modern History* (1959); *Convicts and the Colonies* (1966); and *Sir George Arthur, 1784–1854* (1980).

Pamela Statham   Senior Lecturer in Economic History, University of Western Australia and Research Fellow, Economic History, Australian National University 1987–8. Educated at Monash University and the University of Western Australia, her main interest lies in early nineteenth century Australian economic development. Publications include *The Dictionary of Western Australians*, Vol. 1, 1829–1850 (1979); *The Tanner Letters: A Pioneer Saga of Swan River and Tasmania 1831–45* (1981); and *'Swan River Colony 1829–1859'* in C.T. Stannage (ed), *A New History of Western Australia* (1981).

ACKNOWLEDGMENTS

This book has had a long gestation period and a difficult and protracted birth, which is why my thanks are particularly wholehearted. The Department of Economics, University of Western Australia gave me the travel grants and office support to initiate the project and assisted in its early preparation. My contributors have patiently endured my suggestions for redrafting, often three and four times, and have helped by believing in the worth of the project and giving encouragement when the usual trials of editorship nearly put an end to it. My sincere gratitude also goes to the Economic History Department, Research School of Social Sciences, Australian National University which, during a year's secondment, gave me the breathing space and practical support necessary to finish the book. To the Research School's Cartography unit, and especially Manlio Pancino, I am also indebted, for the wonderful job done on redrafting the maps throughout the book. For editorial assistance I would like to thank Alan Shaw, John McCarty and Gordon Sheldon; for typing assistance Mary Dobbie, Margaret Grigg, Barbara Gramza and Winnie Pradela.

For the handsome grant they gave to get the book into print I shall be eternally grateful to the Western Australian Bicentenary Authority, while to Robin Derricourt and Cambridge University Press go my thanks for undertaking the publishing of the project and for their professional job in its production.

My thanks also go to staff at the Battye Library, Western Australia; Mitchell Library, New South Wales; and the National Library for assistance with sources and illustrations. And finally, I must thank all my family, John Jackson and Noel Butlin without whose moral support and encouragement this book might never have seen the light of day.

Pamela Statham

ABBREVIATIONS USED IN THE NOTES

A.A.A.G   Annals of the Association of American Geographers
A. & R.   Angus & Robertson
A.D.B.   *Australian Dictionary of Biography*
A.E.H.R.   *Australian Economic History Review*
A.G.S.   *Australian Geographical Studies*
A.H.R.U.   Architectural History Research Unit
A.N.U.   Australian National University
A.O.N.S.W.   Archives Office of New South Wales
A.P.I.J.   *Australian Planning Institute Journal*
B.A.H.   *Business Archives and History* (Journal)
B.P.P.   British Parliamentary Papers
C.O.   Colonial Office Entry Books
C.P.P.   Commonwealth Parliamentary Papers
C.S.   Colonial Secretary's office correspondence
C.U.P.   Cambridge University Press
E.H.R.   *English Historical Review*
F. of A.   *The Founding of Australia: The Argument about Australia's Origins* (ed Martin, G.) (Hale & Iremonger 1978 and reprint 1981)
H.R.A.   Historical Records of Australia
H.R.N.S.W.   Historical Records of New South Wales
H.R.V.   Historical Records of Victoria
J.A.S.   *Journal of Australian Studies*
J.E.H.   *Journal of Economic History*
J.H.C.   *Journals of the House of Commons*
J.O.L.   John Oxley Library (Queensland)
J.R.A.H.S.   *Journal of the Royal Australian Historical Society*
J.R.G.S.   *Journal of the Royal Geographical Society*
J.R.H.S.Q.   *Journal of the Royal Historical Society of Queensland*
J.R.W.A.H.S.   *Journal of the Royal Western Australian Historical Society*
L.A.   Legislative Assembly
M.L.   Mitchell Library, Sydney
M.U.P.   Melbourne University Press
N.S.W.G.G.   New South Wales Government Gazette
P.R.O.   Public Records Office (London)
O.U.P.   Oxford University Press
R.G.S.A.   Royal Geographical Society Archives
R.G.S.A.   Royal Geographical Society of Australia
R.S.N.S.W.   Royal Society of New South Wales
S.A.P.P.   South Australian Parliamentary Papers
S.R.P.   Swan River Papers
S.U.P.   Sydney University Press
S.W.A.H.   *Studies in Western Australian History* (Journal)

T.H.R.A.	Tasmanian Historical Research Association
U.A.	University of Adelaide
U.M.	University of Melbourne
U.N.S.W.	University of New South Wales
U.Q.	University of Queensland
U.Q.P.	University of Queensland Press
U.T.	University of Tasmania
U.W.A.	University of Western Australia
U.W.A.P.	University of Western Australia Press
V. & P.	Votes and Proceedings
V.G.G.	*Victorian Government Gazette*
V.H.M.	*Victorian Historical Magazine*
W.A.A.	Western Australian Archives, Alexander Library, Perth
W.P.E.H.	*Working Papers in Economic History*, ANU Series

Table 1: Dates and Important People

City	Date made capital	Date founded	Founder	Colonial Secretary (London)	Prime Minister (London)	Monarch
Sydney	1788	1788	Arthur Phillip	Lord Sydney	Pitt	George III
Hobart	1825	1804	David Collins	Lord Hobart	Pitt	George III
Perth	1829	1829	James Stirling	Murray	Wellington	George IV
Adelaide	1836	1836	William Light	Glenelg	Melbourne	William IV
Melbourne	1850	1835	Capt. Lancey (Batman and Fawkner)	Glenelg	Melbourne	William IV
Brisbane	1859	1825	Lt. Miller and John Oxley	Bathurst	Liverpool	George IV
Darwin	1911	1869	George Goyder	Lord Granville	Palmerston	Victoria
Canberra	1927	1913	Henry Parkes		Bruce (Australia)	George V

Table 2: Conversion Table

(Imperial measures have been used throughout the book)

1d	= 0.83 cent
1s	= 10 cents
£1	= $2
1 guinea	= $2.10
1 acre	= 0.405 hectare
1 inch	= 25.4 millimetres
1 foot	= 30.5 centimetres
1 yard	= 0.914 metre
1 mile	= 1.61 kilometres
1 ounce (oz)	= 28.3 grams
1 pound (lb)	= 454 grams
1 ton	= 1.02 tonnes
1 bushel	= 0.036 cubic metre

Introduction

DARWIN

?

BRISBANE

PERTH

ADELAIDE

CANBERRA   SYDNEY

MELBOURNE

HOBART

Chapter I

Patterns and Perspectives

Pamela Statham

Despite the size of the Australian continent and its empty spaces, most of its population live in just eight capital cities. Moreover, despite separation by distances that amaze foreign visitors, these capital cities share a surprising degree of similarity. That this came about is all the more remarkable when it is considered that the eight capital cities were founded in three different centuries and in very different ways. Sydney, the eighteenth-century capital, was founded as the centre of a penal settlement while Perth, the first city founded as a capital in the nineteenth century, was established as the heart of a private enterprise experiment, closely followed by Adelaide, the model capital of a systematically colonised territory. Hobart, Brisbane and Melbourne began life as the centres of outposts of New South Wales and became capitals only when their territories gained the status of separate colonies. Darwin, or Palmerston as it was first called, was the last of the present capitals to have been founded in the nineteenth century and it too was for years the centre of a territory governed from elsewhere. Finally, there is Canberra, a twentieth-century city which was planned from the outset as a federal capital. Why these capital cities are located in the particular corners of Australia that they are, why and how they were founded, how their similarities and differences evolved, and whether there was anything uniquely Australian in their early moulding that explains their primacy today, are the fundamental questions that prompted this book.

Previous studies have drawn attention to the paradox that, though Australians like to present their country to the world in terms of rural images and the bush, it is actually one of the most highly urbanised nations in the world—and has been so almost since its European foundation.[1] This was pointed out for the first time in 1899 in a classic comparative study of international urban growth by Adna Weber who noted that Australia was founded so late that it inevitably shared in 'the tendency towards concentration and agglomeration' that was affecting the entire western world.[2] What Weber *did* find surprising was that Australia's urban population 'was massed in so few cities'.[3] Unlike Europe and even America, Australia has few large urban centres between the metropolitan capital of each colony/state and the small town[4]—a condition known as city primacy[5] that is as true today as it was in the 1890s. The permanence and primacy of Australian capital cities therefore makes the choice of their initial location particularly interesting. Did the founders have infallible insight? All the current state capitals are still located on the original sites chosen—and almost all the sites were determined before the surrounding country-side had been fully explored. As has been pointed out elsewhere:

> hitting on the best spot for the heart of a modern city before alternative sites in the same area had been exhaustively assessed might be accounted a lucky chance in one or two cases. When it can be shown to have happened in six separate city foundations, however, some other general explanation seems necessary.[6]

A capital city is by definition the seat of government of a territory. It is the takeover, acquisition or movement into new *territory* that gives rise to the need for an administrative centre, or principal town, while the status of *capital* is attained only when the territory administered from that town is separately delineated and its administrators given a degree of independent government. In Australia this was at first achieved by the granting of separate colonial status and the appointment of a governor. The origins of capital cities thus cannot be divorced from the origins of settlement in the territories of which they are the capitals. This duality has meant that in investigating the origins of Australia's eight capital cities two separate issues have had to be tackled: first, the reason for initial settlement of the territory concerned, that is, *why* it was decided to plant a new settlement in a particular quarter and second, the way in which the particular capital city evolved, that is, *how* its location was determined, how it took shape and how it resisted possible challenges for primacy from alternative urban centres. It is admitted that the distinction between the issues of *why* and *how* is a trifle arbitrary but it does provide a focus for presenting the material necessary to answer the questions initially posed.

Although there is a large and growing international literature on the growth of cities, subscribed to by a diverse group of geographers, sociologists, historians, architects and now urban researchers, the question of city origins, and particularly capital city origins, has been relatively neglected. Guttkind's monumental six-volume work on the rise of cities in various regions of the world[7] and Mumford's *The City in History*[8] are exceptions, but even so their emphases are more on city growth than city beginnings. Of course they were dealing primarily with cities that evolved over time, from tiny hamlets to market towns, industrial towns and finally metropolises, a pattern which differed totally from the experience of cities in regions of more recent settlement where cities were 'planted', starting life as relatively modern commercial and administrative centres. John McCarty made this point in his 1970 article on 'Australian Capital Cities in the Nineteenth Century',[9] as did Sean Glynn in a monograph published in the same year[10] but both again were concerned more with the growth of cities, the urbanisation process, than with origins. City origins have of course been treated in numerous individual city histories, and in the Australian literature Graeme Davison's *The Rise and Fall of Marvellous Melbourne* is a notable example.[11] But again such studies rarely question whether the cities' locations are the best that could be found or what the similarities and differences are between the establishment of the city under study and that of other cities. One reason for the lack of such comparative studies in Australia has been the dearth of source material. In the light of the millions of words that have been written on the foundation and early development of Sydney this would seem an absurd statement, but for anyone wishing to study or compare the origins of *all* Australia's capital cities, relevant material has been difficult to obtain. General histories tend to detail the beginnings of first established cities but rarely cover those established at a later date. The various publications brought out in state centenary and sesquicentenary celebrations have been specific to their own regions, while the few comparative city volumes that are available are either illustrated coffee-table works or studies of modern problems.[12]

The purpose of this book is therefore to fill this gap. The essays that follow draw together material on the origins of all eight Australian capital cities, so providing the essential first step for comparison and analysis. A start to the latter will be attempted in this introduction but it is to be hoped that it will be continued by others in years to come. Authors were selected on the basis of their previous work on the city concerned, so their backgrounds differ widely, reflecting the range of interests involved in international urban studies. With historians, economic historians, an architect and a geographer contributing chapters, style and emphasis naturally vary as do methods of treatment. A large degree of independence for authors has been considered essential, however, both to provide evidence of the range of specialist interests in the field and to deal with the different periods and vastly different circumstances involved. Given the nature of the twin questions initially posed, each capital city in the book except Canberra has two separate chapters. The first of the two chapters is concerned primarily with initial settlement—the so-called *why* issues—while the other deals basically with the capital city itself, the *how* issues.

To provide a loose framework for individual treatments of each city certain key themes were identified in prior discussion with contributors. In the 'why settled' chapters these keys themes involved the motives behind settlement (ie for defence, trade etc); the accuracy of pre-settlement reports about the territory; the nature of any abortive attempt at settlement and the reasons for its failure; the method of settlement, including what was offered by whom and who came; the extent of pre-foundation planning; and finally the identity of individuals who took any major part in the decision-making process. In the 'how settled' chapters key themes included reasons for the choice of city location, the nature of early town plans and origin of street names; the nature and function of early buildings; any challenge to the city's location; the growth of suburbs and the direction of city growth; the nature and extent of specialisation within the city; and finally the economic basis of the city's growth. The rules were by no means hard and fast, however, and in cases such as Hobart and Adelaide the choice of city location fell more naturally into the first rather than the second chapters.

A major problem for authors of the second chapters was where to stop. The attainment of capital city status was clearly no help as some cities were capitals from the start, while others became capitals when already mature. The date of conferment of responsible government provided no easy benchmark either as it would have meant that the Perth chapter became a book, for Western Australia did not receive responsible government until 1890. The size of the city in terms of numbers of residents again was no help as Sydney in its second year had a far larger population than Perth in its twenty-first. The only benchmark that seemed to make sense as a finishing point for an analysis of the beginnings of a capital city was when the nucleus of the modern city had been established: in other words, when major buildings had been erected, principal roads constructed and specialisation within the city was sufficiently well established to make a change of location of the administrative heart of the territory extremely unlikely. As no precise date could be given for this achievement contributors could use their own discretion on a finishing point, but given the need to limit the size of this book it has been necessary to conclude at the earliest possible date. The many urban histories now emerging should enable interested readers to follow up the various city beginnings presented here.

Because each chapter concentrates on only one city or region and one period, certain background material has had to be taken for granted within each chapter and comparisons kept to a minimum or ignored. Yet the questions which prompted the drawing together of these individual studies demand comparison and contrast. For this reason an attempt will now be made to draw together information from the essays that follow to provide a starting point for future discussion and, it is hoped, to revive interest in the question of origins, which for far too long has been considered to be somewhat 'blah' by academics and left to the valiant efforts of local historians and novelists. After a short introduction, setting Australian cities in a world context, this overview will examine and assess the reasons for the foundation of each of the Australian capital cities; the choice of their locations; the nature of early city planning; the forces responsible for early city growth; the nature and direction of city specialisation and spread; and, finally, the reasons for the continued primacy or dominance of the capital cities.

Australian cities in a world setting

As already mentioned, Australian cities differ considerably from those in the old world for they did not evolve slowly over time. They do have much in common, however, with cities in other regions of recent settlement such as the United States, Canada and New Zealand. As McCarty pointed out:

> their economic and social structures tended to vary as their rural hinterlands varied but as commercial cities, linking the hinterlands to world markets, each was fully exposed to the levelling effects of the expanding world capitalist economy.[13]

All, moreover, shared a common British heritage and all were essentially 'planted' before the resources and possibilities of their hinterlands had been fully assessed. Instead of growth through natural increase and rural-urban drift, the cities of the new regions grew primarily through immigration and, what is more to the point, involved migrants from predominantly urban backgrounds.[14] By developing in advance of rural settlement and industrialisation the new-world cities reversed traditional experience and imposed on the new region, in a moment of time, the values, institutions and socioeconomic characteristics that had evolved gradually in a totally different environment. All the newly settled regions had abundant land resources, for example, but were settled by people from land-scarce areas whose whole institutional and functional heritage was geared to close settlement. All therefore faced the task of adaptation.

Despite these and many other commonalities the new world cities do differ considerably. Dissimilar physical environments, resource endowments and historical influences have made them develop along divergent lines. The primacy of Australian capital cities compared to the more even distribution of city sizes in Canada and the United States is one such marked difference, and one that will be explored a little later. Another way in which Australian capital cities differ is through their basic similarity. Each city, for example, was settled by immigrants from the United Kingdom who brought with them the same basic laws, customs, institutions, education and language. This differentiates Australia from Canada and South Africa, where the French and the Dutch respectively had a profound influence, and even from the USA where continental European immigrants had a significant influence during the foundation years. Australia's relatively homogeneous ethnic background meant not only that the early inhabitants of each city would make similar everyday decisions, but also that city planners and builders would share a common heritage that would tend to minimise extreme differences in approach. This was reinforced, moreover, by the short time in which the majority of the present capital cities were founded. Sydney, Hobart, Perth, Adelaide, Melbourne and Brisbane were all founded before 1838, only fifty years after Phillip's landing at Sydney Cove. The effect that time can have in changing values, building styles, technology and taste was therefore minimised. As a trivial example of this, all these cities have prominent George and/or William Streets, reflecting the fact that all were founded within the reigns of George III, George IV and William IV. In contrast, the majority of the American colonial state capitals were founded over a far wider span of time and significant differences in their original architecture and layout quite vividly illustrate this even today. Australia's homogeneous beginning was further accentuated by the fact that every settlement bar Canberra was orchestrated by a single planning office in London—the Colonial Office—and, because of the clustering of settlements in time, by just a few influential people connected with that office. Was there, then, as James Cameron suggests in Chapter XIV, a 'grand design' in the minds of those British officials involved in the settlement of Australia? To answer this question the reasons for the settlement of each of the Australian colonies should be compared.

Why were the territories settled?

A review of the 'why settled' chapters that follow reveals four major reasons for the settlement of the various Australian colonies. It also reveals in certain cases the disagreement between writers on which of the four motives was of paramount importance in the decision to plant each new settlement on Australian shores; most settlements involved more than one major motive and often several minor ones. Religious freedom, which was such a major factor in the initial settlement of the British colonies in America, was only a minor influence in Australia, even in South Australia, the so called 'Paradise of Dissent'. The four major motives specified in the accompanying essays as pertinent to the Australian case, either singly or in various combinations, were defence, trade, penal expediency and private investment or speculation.

A dispute has raged for many years over the reasons that lay behind Phillip's landing at Sydney Cove. The traditional belief that this event was inspired simply by Britain's desire to dump her unwanted convicts still has its modern adherents, but there have been challengers aplenty. Evidence and ingenuity have been drawn on to advance quite convincing cases for a defence imperative and, again, for trade reasons to underline Australia's foundation. Ged Martin, in Chapter II, admits to a penchant for the China tea-trade argument, which he outlines, but believes that in fact the decision to found New South Wales was the result of an amalgam of factors, and was reached by a process not unlike the decision to buy a new house. If such a combination of trade, defence and penal considerations was responsible for the foundation of Sydney in 1788 then it would seem reasonable to suppose that similar factors were responsible for Hobart's beginnings in 1804. But Lloyd Robson, in Chapter IV argues that in this case defence reasons were predominant. 'Governor King,' he states, 'made the decision to settle Van Diemen's Land as an outstation of New South Wales, and he did it as a direct reaction to French presence in the region!'[15] King chose the Derwent, rather than the Tamar, as the settlement site mainly on the advice of Bass and Flinders who in 1798 had examined the area discovered by D'Entrecasteaux and had reported French interest in it, as others did a little later.

In the past a similar defence motivation has been given for the foundation of the first settlement on the opposite side of the continent. Fear of the French as a motive for initial settlement has been denied, however, by Pamela Statham, in Chapter VI. Instead, it is maintained that the military outpost established at King George Sound in December 1826 was intended to be a penitentiary for re-convicted convicts, but was not needed when pressure for the relocation of the Moreton Bay convict depot eased with the opening up of new pasture lands to the south. In consequence the King George Sound outpost stagnated. At that stage the British government was most unwilling, mainly on the score of expense, to establish further colonies in Australia (Van Diemen's Land having been given separate colonial status in 1825) and it was left to the ambition and drive of Captain James Stirling to force its hand by convincing a large enough group of private individuals of wealth and influence that the new territory was a worthwhile investment. It is therefore argued that Swan River Colony, and Perth its capital, was founded purely as a private enterprise initiative—though Stirling did use trade and defence arguments, including the French threat, in his efforts to persuade the British government to give colonial status to his proposed settlement.

Even before Western Australia was settled, outposts had been established in what is now Queensland and in the Northern Territory, both in 1824. Governor Brisbane gave the orders that led to the establishment of the Moreton Bay depot and he did so, as he told Colonial Secretary Bathurst, because encroaching pastoral interests were threatening the security of the Port Macquarie penitentiary for re-convicted convicts. As Ross Johnston and Helen Gregory note in Chapter XII 'the settlement that was eventually made at Moreton Bay was essentially a response to the problem of how to control convicts in New South Wales and Van Diemen's Land—and indirectly in Britain. Economic considerations were not paramount . . . [and] strategic concerns also took a secondary place', although, they admit, 'Moreton Bay can be seen as part of a wider imperial strategy—to ensure the exclusion of a foreign power from the unclaimed parts of the continent.'[16]

James Cameron, however, believes that commercial and strategic concerns at this stage were of far more than secondary importance. In Chapter XIV he argues that they were 'two dimensions of Britain's imperial impulse in the period after the Napoleonic Wars'. Cameron gives a good deal of credit to John Barrow, second secretary of the Admiralty and a leading geographer of his day, for settlement decisions in this period including the 1824 settlement of Fort Dundas on Melville Island. In Barrow's own words this settlement was to 'become another Singapore', protecting British ships involved in the Eastern Trade through the largely Dutch archipelago from the other side. It was also part of what would later be called 'an ambitious plan to encircle the Australian continent with strategic outposts', providing a ring fence to deter all foreign interests.[17] Unfortunately the Melville Island site lacked fresh water and was not easily accessible to shipping, so a new outpost was formed on the mainland at Raffles Bay.

If the ring fence idea has any credence, it would seem to have been very short-lived. By the end of 1828 the order had been given for the abandonment of both of the northern settlements and in 1831 the small depot at King George Sound was dismantled and handed over to the administration of Swan River Colony. Only the Moreton Bay depot continued, driven primarily by increasing numbers of convicts. Even this settlement, however, was 'earmarked for abolition after 1832', but managed to survive, partly through

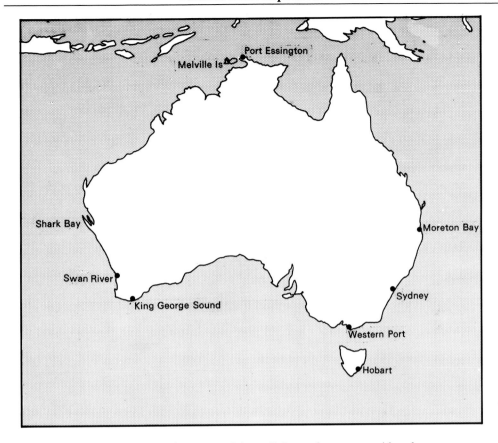

Figure 1: 'A ring fence round Australia'—settlements considered up to 1830

inertia and partly because Governor Bourke 'wanted to avoid the problem of an uncontrolled grab for land . . . that [had] happened when the Port Phillip district was thrown open to free settlement'.[18] Private enterprise, in the form of the expanding pastoral frontier, thus ensured Brisbane's continued life.

Melbourne and Adelaide were both outright products of private enterprise. It is true, as Alan Shaw shows in Chapter X, that defence considerations (including that of splitting the convict body to prevent riots) led to the abortive initial settlement attempt by Collins in 1803, but had little or no influence on eventual settlement in 1835. The impetus then was simply 'the great difficulty of now obtaining any extent of tolerably good land' for grazing in Van Diemen's Land.[19] Faced with a *fait accompli,* the Colonial Office bowed to the inevitable in 1836 and countenanced another Crown-administered settlement with the justification that settlers 'in reality [may have] given birth to undertakings, which deliberate reflection would have recommended rather than discouraged'.[20]

By that stage moves were well under way in Britain for the establishment of another new Australian crown colony. Mel Davies thinks the area selected for the colony of South Australia was quite appropriately situated in the region specified by Swift for his 'Lilliput Land'. In Chapter VIII he likens the disagreement among Swift's Lilliputians to the dissent accompanying Adelaide's beginnings. Born of an ideal of systematic colonisation, the foundation of this colony owed all to private enterprise and initiative—grander imperial motives played no part at all. The British government acted as a somewhat unwilling partner in what was basically to be a company-run settlement under the auspices of the South Australia Association, a chartered company vested in trustees. The government retained political power for framing laws and appointing officers, while the commissioners appointed by the Association's London board did the rest. It was, as Davies comments, 'a compromise between the Colonial Office and the promoters but unlike the Great Lustrog's pronouncements many of [its features] were to prove abrasive rather than salving during the early days of the Colony'.

It is perhaps ironic that the Northern Territory, for which South Australia took responsibility in 1863, experienced the same sort of tensions between promoters and government officials in the run up to settlement. Darwin, as Robert Reece shows in Chapter XV, was hurriedly founded under the name of Palmerston to quieten the demands for compensation then facing the South Australian government from angry land-order holders in Britain and elsewhere in Australia. Darwin therefore also falls into the private-enterprise/speculative category as far as motives for settlement were concerned, though it was also soon needed as a maintenance and service station as the first Australian base of the London-Australia telegraph cable.

If the major reasons for founding settlements in the various territories are now compared and X's given to explicitly recognised motives and queries attached to motives that were possibly involved, a table can be drawn up as follows:

Table 3: Motives for Settlement

Territory	Penal	Trade	Defence	Investment or speculation
NSW	x	x	x	na
VDL	x	?	x	na
WA	x	?	?	x
SA	na	?	na	x
QLD	x	na	na	x
VIC	na	?	?	x
NT	na	x	?	x

na = not applicable

A 'grand design' in Australian settlement presumably would have required trade and/or defence motives to have been dominant reasons for settlement but, quite clearly from the table, decisions by individual British private investors were paramount in the overall founding of the Australian territories, while penal motives—especially the relocation of second offenders—played a more pervasive role than hitherto believed. That each territory became a British colony, with the full panoply of civil and military establishment services paid for by the British Treasury, can basically be attributed to that government's unwillingness to allow private individuals to control and benefit from the disposal of what were seen to be Crown land resources.

As the major incentive for early (pre-gold) private investment in Australia was the acquisition and use of land and as even the penal colonies were expected to be self-sufficient in food, it is perhaps surprising that capital cities, the focuses of settlement, were all perched on the seaboard perimeter. To some extent this can be explained by reliance on imports brought from Britain and access to information which all came initially by sea. It can also be explained by the previously mentioned fact that almost all the cities were established before their surrounding areas had been fully explored. It does not, however, satisfactorily explain why the capitals were not moved further inland, following the tide of settlement, when the exigencies of establishment were overcome. Did the initial sites possess advantages that outweighed those of centrality to settled and productive areas? Such a question raises three issues: why were the cities located where they were, how and why did they grow to dominate their territories, and why was their supremacy not challenged by other sites? The last issue brings back the question raised earlier, that is, were the founders infallible in their choice of sites? What criteria did they use—and did they have any common background?

Why were the capital cities located where they are?

In general the person who chose the city site for the Australian capitals did not design its layout. Location was usually determined by the governor of the territory or his representative and shape or form by the chief surveyor. Having said that, the experience of Adelaide and Darwin immediately arises to contradict, for in these cases the surveyor general both chose the site and determined its layout. Nevertheless, as separate issues were involved in each instance, choice of site and layout will be treated independently.

Phillip's rejection of Botany Bay and his selection of Sydney Cove on the Tank Stream as the site for his settlement is well known. 'I fixed on the one [site] that had the best spring of water and in which ships can anchor so close to the shore that at a very small expense quays can be made at which the largest ships can unload,' he stated.[21] Brian Fletcher, in Chapter III, stresses fresh drinking water as the major reason for the move,[22] but Ged Martin, in the companion chapter, asks an interesting question: if the initial party had been smaller, would the facilities at Botany Bay have sufficed? He thinks that 'Phillip found its low ground did not provide enough drinking water for the numbers under his command',[23] and so was forced to move. Others have drawn attention, however, to Phillip's insistence that the site be elevated and 'free of swamps and undrained areas' and assume that he ruled out Botany Bay for health reasons.[24] The most important reason Phillip himself cited for leaving Botany Bay was because it was 'so very open' that it did not afford proper shelter. A deep and safe anchorage close to shore was imperative and Botany Bay was 'so shoal' that ships had to anchor near the entrance exposed to heavy seas. Phillip was after all a naval captain and a safe accessible anchorage would have been his prime consideration.

Lieutenant Governor David Collins, who chose the site of Hobart, was also a naval man, an officer of the marines,[25] and it is not surprising therefore to find that anchorage and access considerations were important reasons for his decision to move the site of the capital from Risdon Cove, where a base had been set up by a party from New South Wales some months earlier, to Sullivan Cove on the opposite side of the Derwent River. As Robson shows in Chapter IV, Collins settled without hesitation as soon as he found a good flow of water at a spot where his settlement could command the approaches.[26]

Collins was also critical of the difficulty of access at Risdon through silted approaches and a steep ascent on landing, and argued that the main settlement site should be a gradual run up near a deep water unloading point.[27] So, a deep anchorage reasonably close to shore, fresh water and suitable terrain (ie with a moderate elevation) were the major considerations in the choice of the site of Hobart.

Governor James Stirling, another naval man, gave weight to anchorage facilities in his initial proposal to examine the Swan River area as a potential site for settlement, but did not then place his capital at the port. This decision not only broke with tradition, but also had unfortunate consequences when early ships' captains, who did not venture upriver to see the improvements at Perth, carried back to England tales of a colony on the brink of collapse. Their reports reflected the makeshift situation at Fremantle where incoming settlers waited for land grants to be allocated further up river. As it was in some ways an odd decision it is interesting to note that Stirling had been instructed to:

> weigh maturely the advantages which may arise from placing it in so secure a foundation as may be afforded on various points of the Swan River, against those which may follow from establishing it on so fine a port . . . as Cockburn Sound.[28]

As Geoffrey Bolton relates in Chapter VII Stirling later explained that it had been immediately apparent on arrival that the topographical features of the colony required the main agricultural settlement to be situated on the fertile upper reaches of the river, an area separated by a broad swathe of sandhills and swampy limestone country from the mouth of the Swan, which was the obvious choice of site for a port. For ease of administration therefore the new governor thought the capital should be midway between the two.[29] As a naval man he also wanted his settlement out of range of naval bombardment,[30] near fresh water and suitable building materials and in a picturesque setting. He eventually chose Frazer Point as the site for Perth, a peninsula in the river below Mount Eliza and some seven miles from the sea. So for Perth's location, fresh water, administrative convenience (ie midway between port and agricultural land) beauty and building material availability were prime considerations.

That Perth and Adelaide are both situated inland from their ports to some extent reflects the improvement in firing power of naval cannon during the Napoleonic Wars. In David Collins' time, cannon shot could never have penetrated five or more miles inland, but by the late 1820s artillery improvements had made such distances quite feasible.

Colonel Light, the surveyor general appointed by the South Australian Association, was given entire responsibility for selecting the site of Adelaide, a fact bitterly resented by Governor Hindmarsh who subsequently criticised every move he made. Light's initial instructions were to examine Port Lincoln on Spencer's Gulf and the south-eastern shores of the Gulf of St Vincent near the mouth of the Murray River. Light, however, rejected the Murray mouth site as too exposed; Port Lincoln, the site favoured by the governor, as lacking good land for settlement purposes; and Nepean Bay on Kangaroo Island, which afforded an excellent harbour and had been chosen as the initial site for disembarkation, as lacking both sufficient agricultural land and enough fresh drinking water for a permanent settlement. As Davies shows in Chapter VIII, he preferred an extensive level area above the Torrens River near the fertile western foothills of the Mount Lofty Ranges and some six miles distant from a reasonable harbour.[31] Governor Hindmarsh, a naval man, did not like the army-trained Light's selection of a site for a capital so far from a port, and made several moves to override him. Light was adamant, however, that the port sites

Hindmarsh favoured lacked fresh drinking water and would be too low and subject to flooding. So, Light's criteria for selection of the site of Adelaide were fresh water, convenient location between port and agricultural land, an elevated area free from swamps and flood risk, and an accessible harbour.

A naval background was most probably responsible for Collins' abandonment of the attempt to settle Port Phillip Bay in 1803. As Alan Shaw comments in Chapter X 'though easily defensible, . . . it [ie Port Phillip] was no good as a naval post in Bass Strait if it was to be difficult for ships to leave the Bay in pursuit of any enemy' (which it was) 'and there was little fresh water near the Heads, where, for fishing and defence purposes, the settlement ought to be'.[32] By the early 1830s, when interest in the area rekindled, the emphasis of economic activity had swung away from fishing to grazing, and shipping and defence capabilities had improved. The issues were then different. Choice of the eventual site of Melbourne has been attributed variously to John Batman and to John Fawkner, both leaders of groups of Van Diemen's Land squatters seeking new grazing land. Shaw, however, gives the honour to a hitherto unknown master mariner, John Lancey, who, though of Fawkner's party, preceded him because Fawkner had been detained by business in Launceston.[33] Lancey, captain of the *Enterprize,* chose a situation on the River Yarra (the only fresh water river they came across in their exploration of the eastern side of Port Phillip), just below the falls—a low basalt reef which separated fresh water from the tidal estuary. At this point there was a reasonable anchorage for small boats, and easy access to the bay where larger vessels could anchor in shelter, and nearby was a hill (later Batman's Hill) which afforded a view of approaches. Although Batman sketched a broad area in this same vicinity for the site of his township, Shaw maintains it was too large and vague an area, and Batman's diary entry too ambiguous, to indicate that he had actually determined a precise spot for settlement. Anyway, it would have been surprising if he had, Shaw believes, for that 'was not the prime object of his journey'.[34]

Melbourne thus differs from all the other cities in that its site was chosen by two private individuals and their parties, as a headquarters for exploiting the surrounding land and not primarily as an administrative centre. That it so became was a product of chain migration (following Batman's and Fawkner's lead) and Governor Bourke's sense of order, in that he could not countenance illegal occupation of what he considered to be Crown land under his jurisdiction. He could not evict them, especially given the potential legal conflict over Batman's so-called 'purchase' of land from the Aboriginals, so he advised legalising the settlement. The Colonial Office's reaction has already been cited. In all, fresh water, a moderate elevation near a hill, a satisfactory anchorage and the good land that had attracted the graziers were the major considerations in the choice of the site of Melbourne.

Brisbane shares with Melbourne a situation on a river some distance from the harbour. The instructions given to John Oxley, New South Wales Surveyor General, regarding the selection of a site for the new penal settlement were perhaps appropriate but not promising as far as future development was concerned.[35] Of three possible locations, Port Curtis (now Gladstone), Port Bowen (now Port Clinton) and Moreton Bay, he was to choose the site with 'fewest recommendations of soil' and 'least accessible to ships'. Oxley, however, was given the right to choose. He was a strong-minded man with a naval career behind him when he travelled north on this mission in 1823. He was also a great believer in the existence of an inland sea and river system, and Ross Johnston and Helen Gregory, in Chapter XII, feel that this influenced his choice of site. On discovering the Brisbane River, Oxley deduced that this strongly flowing north-easterly stream carried inland waters into Moreton Bay, so giving that location an incalculable advantage. As a result, other suggested sites were only cursorily examined and then dismissed—Port Curtis as incapable of holding a large permanent population, and Port Bowen as climatically unsuitable. Having chosen Moreton Bay, Oxley's problem was then to select a specific site, but his difficulty was that 'the Brisbane River presents so many superior situations'.[36] He therefore recommended initial settlement at Redcliffe point on Moreton Bay, which could function later as a port or military post, while further exploration sought a better permanent settlement site on the river. This, however, had to wait until the following year when Oxley returned with Lieutenant Miller, the first commandant, and his party of convicts and men. Oxley extolled two particular sites on the river, the first, which he had noted on his previous journey, at Enoggera or Breakfast Creek which ran into the Brisbane River at the end of the sea reach, and the second some seventeen miles from the sea and the actual site of Brisbane. Johnston and Gregory give Miller the distinction of having selected the latter site, though Oxley's journals reveal that he had thought it 'by no means an ineligible situation for a first settlement up river'.[37] Governor Brisbane and Chief Justice Forbes actually recommended the Breakfast Creek site on their visit in November 1824 but, in 1825 when the move was finally made, Miller settled further upstream. Johnston and Gregory believe he could have made a mistake, for his instructions to move seventeen miles did not specify from where, and while the distance from Redcliffe would have taken him near to Breakfast Creek, seventeen miles from the river mouth landed him at the present site of Brisbane.[38] Alternatively, he could have thought Breakfast Creek too floodprone, the river at that point too shallow, the area too open for easy defence and the Aboriginals too numerous and threatening.[39] It is certain that Oxley was concerned about a sufficiently deep anchorage near the shore at Breakfast Creek and that he made a special point of the abundance of fresh water at the seventeen mile spot. Fresh water, good soil and timber, a reasonably deep water anchorage close to shore and moderate elevation were the criteria specified in Oxley's field books and, as Brisbane was one of the two sites he selected, can be taken as the major reasons for its location.

The site of Darwin, as already noted, was finally chosen by George Goyder, South Australian surveyor general, in 1869. Goyder was the first 'founder' with a purely civilian background, having served as an engineer/draftsman before his appointment. He had chosen the rough whereabouts of the northern capital before leaving Adelaide, on the basis of all the reports submitted to that time, but within the Port Darwin area he selected a site on a point that had fresh water, was moderately elevated so being 'healthy and free from swamp', had a reasonable harbour and, he believed, a hinterland suitable for all kinds of agriculture.[40]

The selection of the twentieth century federal capital, Canberra, was very much a political affair. In Chapter XVI Roger Pegrum gives a fascinating account of the arguments in favour of and against the various sites suggested. But, as no single person was responsible for the site of Canberra and it is, as it were, 'in another place at another time', it will be omitted from the following comparative remarks.

The first striking feature of the various city site decisions is the narrowness of criteria used. There were basically only six determinants, of which the most important was fresh water. As the following table shows, most founders also chose sites which had a reasonably deep anchorage nearby and moderate elevation to avoid floods and swamps. These three criteria were common to all seven city sites and can be regarded as the necessary preconditions of site choice. Thereafter, differing emphases were placed by each founder on defensibility, soil fertility, availability of building materials and administrative convenience—the latter being used as an umbrella term to cover the decision by Stirling and Light to place the capital between the port and the best agricultural land.

Table 4: Capital City Choice

Capital	Date founded (made capital)	Fresh water	Deep anchor-age nearby	Good soil	Moderate elevation, defend-able	Build-ing mater-ials	On river between port—agriculture	Chosen by	Back-ground
				Criteria used					
Sydney	1788 (**1788**)	x	x		x	x		Gov Phillip	Navy
Hobart	1804 (**1825**)	x	x		x			Lt Gov Collins	Navy
Perth	1829 (**1829**)	x			x	x	x	Gov Stirling	Navy
Adelaide	1836 (**1836**)	x	x	x	x		x	Col Light	Army
Melbourne	1835 (**1850**)	x	x	x	x			Capt Lancey	Mariner
Brisbane	1825 (**1859**)	x	x	x	x			Lt Oxley	Navy (surveyor)
Darwin	1869 (**1911**)	x	x	x	x			Goyder	Civil (surveyor)

The particular emphasis given in choice of location seems to have depended on the time period in which the site was determined, for priorities changed over time, for example, from defence to good grazing land. It also depended on the background and experience of the founder. In examining their own written rationales for their choice of site it is interesting to note, as James Bird did in a similar comparative exercise in 1965, that the founders gave 'more reasons . . . for the choice of site than for choosing its land situation', that is, its position relative to the area it was to serve.[41] Partly, as Bird points out, this was because the hinterlands had not been fully explored before the town was founded, but it must also be attributed partly to the predominance of naval backgrounds among the decision makers. Land transport considerations would not have been uppermost in their minds. River/harbour navigability and good anchorages close to shore would have been far more important, together with the defensibility of the site, including command of approaches.

As each of the sites chosen remains the city centre today it is pertinent to question the wisdom of the choices made—given the benefit of hindsight. If Phillip had had more time and fewer people under his command he himself admitted he might have chosen differently. 'Had I seen the country near the head of the harbour I might have been

13

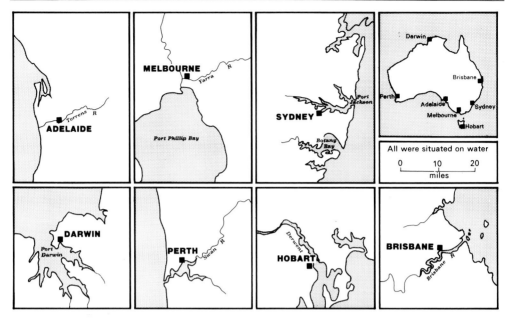

Figure 2: All nineteenth century capitals (or administrative centres) were on rivers or near the coast

induced to have made the settlement there',[42] near Rose Hill (now Parramatta)—and so have avoided the congestion and building problems that have since beset Sydney. Yet, when the Rose Hill area was discovered only three months after landing, no move was made to change the site of the capital. Launceston would in many ways have made a more suitable capital than Hobart, and indeed it even challenged Hobart's supremacy in the early years. Governor Arthur also wanted to move the capital to New Norfolk, further inland, but his proposal was vetoed in London mainly because of the expense of new government buildings.[43] As Gordon Rimmer points out in Chapter V, the establishment of a bureaucratic hierarchy concomitant upon being made the administrative centre or capital of a territory gave that centre an 'unusually elongated social scale for a recently established town' and thus a momentum all of its own.[44] Bird agrees, maintaining that the early Australian cities were not only commodity markets and financial centres but also seats of political influence and power—features which he sees as derived from the very act of proclamation:

> To have a regular market of whatever kind presupposes the publishing or proclamation of a set of rules and regulations. The proclamation which establishes the legal basis of the market . . . is the great impulse converting the primitive site of a pioneer settlement into the recognised site for a regional centre.[45]

He thus concludes that the founders did not display infallible foresight in their choices of sites, but that they were infallible in obtaining official recognition for their choices. Such an argument falters, however, when Moreton Bay is compared with King George Sound and the early northern settlements at Melville Island and Raffles Bay. All were established as outposts, and proclamations were read in each instance establishing not only a claim over territory but also rules and regulations for settlement. Yet only Brisbane at Moreton Bay became a long-lasting major administrative centre.

14

A more pertinent issue would seem to be the extent of initial investment in the site chosen. Hindmarsh, for example, could not persuade the British government or the South Australian settlers to move from Adelaide, though he tried several times, and that was mainly because of the costs of removal.[46] Further discussion of the reasons for the continued permanence and primacy of the capital cities will follow later, but it is worth noting now that some of the features that the founders thought advantageous became liabilities over time. The island Collins extolled in Sullivan Cove as a secure base for stores had to be obliterated if Hobart's port area was to be developed;[47] the curve of the Brisbane River that attracted Oxley for its command of approaches has disadvantaged that city's layout and made it susceptible to flooding ever since;[48] and similarly Perth, on its picturesque peninsula, was jammed between river and swamps and required extensive reclamation work to allow growth.[49] It has also been argued that South Australia 'is not so rich in its resources of really productive land that it could afford to build a large city on the Adelaide plains . . . it is a garden made sterile'.[50] Once established, however, in each case a momentum appears to have set in which precluded locational change.

In this context it is interesting to ask whether settlement *as a capital* differed to any marked extent from settlement as a major but outlying centre governed from elsewhere, as was the case with Hobart, Brisbane, Melbourne and Darwin. From the viewpoint of site choice, there would appear from the foregoing to have been very little if any difference, though Stirling's and Light's consideration of administrative convenience in siting their capitals midway between the port and agricultural interests might be so termed. The situations of Melbourne and Brisbane are so similar to those of Perth and Adelaide, however, that it can be concluded that the function of the future city had minimal bearing on site choice. There seems little doubt, nevertheless, that all the founders (except perhaps Brisbane's) realised that they were choosing sites for a future city and not just a village centre. This, together with the short time span in which the majority of the Australian capitals were founded, possibly accounts for the narrowness of criteria and similarity of situations chosen (ie all are on rivers or near the sea.) One obvious explanation for this similarity that has not yet been broached is the question of instructions. Were all the founders following a set of similar instructions from the same Colonial Office in London? From the evidence it would appear not, for correspondence cited in the various chapters reveals that each founder was given complete discretion in site choice. This does not deny that verbal instructions could have emphasised the need for ready access by ship, but this would have been commonsense anyway for settlements that would be dependent on imported supplies and communications for at least several years.

If the function of the future city had no major influence on choice of site, did it affect the city's layout or design?

How were the Australian capital cities laid out or designed?

As can be seen by comparing the town plans on pages 62, 98, 147, 182, 225, 260, 308 and 335, all but one are based on a simple grid structure. Canberra is the exception and belongs to an entirely different school of urban design. The nineteenth century city layouts, however, belong to a tradition of colonial planning that long antedates the earliest cities in the United States of America. When the Romans colonised Britain they used the grid as the basis for city planning and even then it was by no means an innovation. As Mumford comments in *The City in History*:

the geometric plan was not an easy one to apply to sites with an irregular topography, but it had one advantage that gave it currency in the 6th Century BC and made it universal once more in the 3rd Century BC . . . it provided a single and equitable method of dividing the land in a new city formed by colonization.[51]

He goes on to say that:

the standard gridiron plan in fact was an essential part of the kit of tools a colonist brought with him for immediate use. The colonist had little time to get the lay of the land or explore the resources of a site: by simplifying his spatial order he provided for a swift and roughly equal distribution of building lots (and public spaces).[52]

This would tend to explain why there are no detailed instructions regarding city layout in Colonial Office correspondence—though planners were advised to place blocks at right angles to water-frontage to maximise access to river transport.[53] Bigge recommended the adoption of rectangular land surveys in Australia in the 1820s, following the American model, but he made no specific reference to city planning.[54]

If the grid was the basis for Australian town plans, it was clearly not a sacrosanct guide since most capitals exhibit irregularities in the grid which arose for topographical, historical or accidental reasons. Jeans has noted that New South Wales town grids are 'outstanding for their irregularity'[55] and that a major cause of this was inaccurate compass use and fraudulent use of the chain-measure (in which links could be added or subtracted to favour one particular party).[56] In some instances roads went around buildings so as not to inconvenience their owners. This occurred in Hobart and is said to have happened in Perth around the house of Surveyor General Roe, although this charge has been denied by Bolton in Chapter VII.[57]

In general, the character of early Australian capital cities can be likened to some of the medieval European planned towns in that the layout of the latter also:

was dictated by practical considerations, . . . It was a planning from above, moulded by military expediency and the desire to produce convenient results with a minimum of effort, imagination and cost, in a minimum of time.[58]

Tony Denholm takes up this theme in Chapter IX when he asks whether Adelaide can be considered a Victorian version of a medieval bastide or fortress-town. The origins of most existing medieval planned towns were military in nature but colonial authorities too could impose their will and plan from above when setting up 'cities in the wilderness'.[59] They too were motivated by the need for speed and administrative expediency and so, just as in the medieval planned towns, 'streets were laid out first and houses relegated to the left over space between them,'[60] in total contrast to the traditional town where houses (and people) were supreme and streets wandered haphazardly in between.

Loss of social intimacy is the feature that most critics of the grid system emphasise. Neat geometric order does not provide a civic nucleus. Shops for example were in straight lines along a single road, public buildings were often dispersed and parks and open spaces kept to a regimented minimum. Gridiron critics also refer to the 'additional tax on the time and energy of inhabitants'[61] imposed by the grid's lack of attention to contours and topography. Even the orientation of streets so that buildings could maximise (or minimise) sunlight, 'a principle known to the Greeks and the Chinese', was completely overlooked in applying the grid, as was 'any functional differentiation between the residential, industrial, commercial and civic quarters'.[62] Only on strictly commercial principles did the gridiron plan answer, believes Mumford, as it provided 'as no other plans did for the shifting

16

values, the accelerated expansion, (and) the multiplying population, required by the capitalist regime'.[63]

How do the Australian capitals measure up against such criticisms? It has already been noted that McCarty would agree with Mumford's 'commercial' classification for Australian cities, but how relevant are the other comments, especially those of lack of regard for topography and functional differentiation in the use of the grid system?

These questions are difficult to answer as the cities generally went through several stages of planning and were often influenced by more than one individual. It emerges from the following essays, moreover, that several Australian cities were influenced by the same people. Oxley, the surveyor, for example, made comments on Hobart as well as being very influential in the choice of site and layout of Brisbane.[64] Again, Oxley's assistant in planning Queensland's first settlement was Robert Hoddle, who later was responsible for the layout of Melbourne.[65] Governor Macquarie not only supervised the redesign of Sydney town but also made it his business to frame a regular plan for Hobart.[66]

Earliest plans of both Sydney and Hobart show a cluster of tents on high ground near freshwater streams, with the governor's residence set a little apart from the rest and separated by military or marine quarters from the convicts. Even given the temporary nature of first settlement, however, extant sketches show a rudimentary order with tents and early buildings in roughly straight lines and usually parallel with or at right angles to the waterfront. Topography was vital at this stage for delineating function. As Fletcher points out in Chapter III, the ridge overlooking the cove was made the site for Government House and the civil and criminal courts in the Phillip-Dawes plan of July 1788.[67] Phillip envisaged major streets converging on Government House, which therefore faced the principal street with parade grounds for the marine guard on the right.[68] The marine, or afterwards military, barracks and convict huts were situated below, facing each other across the Tank Stream. Phillip was very conscious of the need for planning and so situated the principal streets at angles 'to admit free circulation of air'. He was also concerned to 'preserve uniformity in the buildings, [and] prevent narrow streets and the many inconveniences which the increase of inhabitants would otherwise occasion hereafter'.[69] By the time he left, however, 'Sydney was not quite as the governor had planned, possibly because closer acquaintance with the landform had shown the original concept to be impractical'.[70] Another possible reason was his quarrel with the gifted engineer-astronomer-surveyor Lieutenant William Dawes who had initially planned a layout for the town but had been estranged when he refused Phillip's order to take part in a punitive expedition against the natives.[71] Early development around the cove was therefore largely unplanned, but as the town grew to the south it took on a more regular grid pattern as may be seen in Meehan's sketch plan of Sydney Town in 1809, on the eve of Macquarie's arrival.

Though Fletcher maintains that much had been done to quite high standards before Macquarie's arrival, he also admits the significance of Macquarie's contribution. 'He combined a wide vision with a passion for order and symmetry and possessed the strength of character to ensure that his wishes were heeded.'[72] In so doing, Macquarie left both Sydney and Hobart a legacy of straight streets and fine public buildings. Existing streets were renamed and realigned—except in the immediate vicinity of the port where the old throughfares remained—and new streets were added.

In Hobart, where he arrived in November 1811, Macquarie found no recognisable plan to the collection of buildings near the port and immediately issued orders 'respecting the dividing of Hobart Town into one principal square and seven streets' (three long and four cross streets), and in so doing set the spatial pattern of future development.[73] The grid was not completely regular, however, as some streets had to be angled 'so as not to interfere with many houses which are now erected'. Macquarie was very conscious of topography and gave most of his public buildings, for example the hospital, barracks, court house and gaol, commanding positions on ridges surrounding the towns. Government House, situated in both Sydney and Hobart on a rise near the main port, was given the best possible view of incoming shipping.

Vista was also important to Captain John Septimus Roe, the first surveyor general of Swan River Colony, who laid out the town of Perth. Unlike Sydney and Hobart, Perth and later Adelaide did not go through a tent stage, as early arrivals camped near the main anchorage while the city was being surveyed further inland. Roe, and later Light, therefore had a free hand and in both cases the whole city was laid out at once in a regular fashion. Perth, however, was not as extensively planned as Adelaide for Roe was under enormous pressure from increasing arrivals to survey not only Perth but also land for agricultural grants, the town of Fremantle for merchants and wayfarers, and the water approaches to Fremantle following several bad shipping accidents. Nevertheless, he marked out a regular grid on the level ground under Mt Eliza facing the river with angled streets running up the hill. Later development broke the neat grid as surveyors encountered swamps on the opposite side of town to the curving river.[74] This problem also occurred in Brisbane when Wade's regularly planned grid was superimposed in 1842 on the more flexible original plan established by Hoddle and Oxley. After the second survey poor Thomas Lenehan 'applied for permission to exchange an allotment in consequence of its being under water', but was refused, the governor and surveyor general agreeing that it 'would be setting a bad precedent to do so'.[75]

Light's plan for Adelaide was by far the most comprehensive of Australian city plans and was used by Goyder and his assistant J Brooks as a model for setting out what is now Darwin, though in that case a smaller, more elongated city was called for as it directly faced the water. Melbourne's layout was simplified by the large open area allocated for it, but its format is unique mainly for the 'little' streets that were placed between the city's cross avenues to allow ease of rear access and so remove the unsightly spectacle of loading and unloading from the eyes of passers-by. Apparently Hoddle based the layout of Melbourne on his predecessor 'Robert Russell's memory of a township plan lying around in the government offices in Sydney . . . The grid was superimposed on the land with no consideration for the natural features of the site 'with unfortunate consequences' as the river flooded low-lying parts of the town and traffic congested the more level streets while avoiding those which toiled up the sides of the steepish Batman's and Eastern Hills.[76]

Overall then, topography was made far less important a feature of early Australian cities than it was, for example, in Canberra and Washington. Some functional planning was typical, in that sites for Government House, military barracks, churches and a hospital were generally included even in early plans, but it was very limited. Residential and commercial areas were rarely separated, though of course in Perth and Adelaide many commercial enterprises tended to cluster in the port, and in other cities on or near the wharves. Only Roe and Light gave any real thought to suburban development in their initial town plans when they included residential 'villa' blocks on the opposite side of the river in Perth and Adelaide respectively. In the chapters that follow care has generally been taken to outline and analyse the nature and direction of city spread. This topic will be referred to again but it is interesting to note here that city spread was intimately related to a particular feature of the gridiron plan and that was the effect it had on land values.[77] By setting out the whole town at once, creating in a sense an artificial scarcity, and by parcelling out urban lots in standard, rectangular blocks that could easily be surveyed, described and transferred on standard legal documents, the grid favoured speculation and rising urban land prices. As Denholm points out, it was this which largely accounts for the early move out from Adelaide into the suburbs, a feature noted in almost all the city chapters. Before taking this point further in connection with city growth, one other facet of early city layout should be mentioned and that is the matter of city street names.

With the exception of Adelaide, all main streets of nineteenth-century cities are named either after British personalities at the time of founding or local personalities and landmarks. The British set includes the King or Queen (George, William, Adelaide); other members of the royal family, for example dukes and princes (York, Clarence, Albert etc); the prime minister (Pitt, Wellington, Peel); the secretary of state for colonies (Bathurst, Murray and Liverpool); the permanent undersecretaries (Stephen, Hay and Twiss); and sometimes that of a key member of parliament. Local personalities include governors or commandants and their wives (King, Hunter, La Trobe, Bourke, Collins, Elizabeth after Mrs Macquarie); explorers (Flinders, Sturt and Mitchell) and then doctors, military men and lawyers. The remainder are named after local features such as Mill Street, Pier Street, Bazaar Terrace, Bridge Street etc. Brisbane stands out for having the largest percentage of female names; indeed it is the only capital whose main long streets bear the names of kings (Albert, Edward etc) and cross streets those of queens (Margaret, Mary, Charlotte etc). In Adelaide the twelve-man committee set up to name the city streets preferred the names of local identities, including explorers and members of the association that inaugurated the colony. Again Adelaide differs in that streets converge on a central square and there change names—except for the one avenue—King William Street, which runs north-south midway through the town. Limits to the city are also set by North, South and West Terraces, East Terrace following a series of steps that would allow expansion.

Expansion of the capital cities, however, was linked inextricably to the prosperity of the settlement as a whole and this raises a new question, what were the forces that resulted in city growth?

Why did the capital cities grow in the pre-rail era?

Once railways were introduced in fan patterns with branch lines that converged on the capital cities from a large hinterland, the expansion of the city hub is understandable, even though many have argued that railways increased the opportunities for population dispersal. Railways did have a striking impact, but except for Darwin and Canberra the capitals were all well established by the time the railways were introduced to Australia, so they cannot be held responsible for creating the momentum that set the capital cities on the path to primacy. What then, were the forces that led to capital city growth in the pre-rail era, and how rapid was that growth?

In analysing the forces responsible for city growth in the United States in the pre-rail era, most historians have laid primary emphasis on the 'physical size, population and fertility of their hinterlands'.[78] City growth was fed by the needs of the export sector. This view has also been held of Australian cities. In 1970, JW McCarty tested his belief that the size and early rate of growth of the Australian capital cities depended on the wealth and rate of growth of their rural hinterlands and found it to be substantially correct.[79] Indeed, for many years it was held that Australia's rapid urbanisation was due to the growth and nature of her major exports, especially wool, as this industry required few rural labourers (and fewer families compared to other types of farming) yet needed a large number of urban-based services, such as transport, warehousing, insurance, banking and shipping. Believers in the export staple theory of colonial growth could thus be quite comfortable with figures which showed that 'increments in non-metropolitan population and income appear to have been accompanied by proportionally greater increments in metropolitan population and income'.[80] However, the work of several eminent economic historians has cast substantial doubt on the whole premise of export led growth in Australia[81] and for present purposes it is of little help. Wool (indeed any major export) post-dated the early growth of most Australian capital cities. The wool export trade in New South Wales, for example, was insignificant before the mid 1820s yet, as Fletcher shows in his chapter, by 1821 Sydney was a thriving well-established city. It is true that the pastoral push from Van Diemen's Land led to the founding of Melbourne but, as Susan Priestley notes in Chapter XI, it was commerce and the processing of primary produce for the local market that provided the real stimulus for expansion and helped recovery from the depression of the early 1840s.

By 1850, when Victoria was recognised as a separate colony with Melbourne its capital, the city:

> was already generating some of its own growth energy through primitive manufacturing in vehicles, building materials and food processing, although its role in channelling goods to and from its hinterland remained crucial.[82]

To this time, moreover, Melbourne had had none of the advantages of a large, British-paid bureaucracy, as major administration and authority rested in Sydney. The advantages of the latter, as already mentioned with regard to Hobart, was that a top echelon with high and independent incomes (being paid from Britain) and high conspicuous consumption traditions (for status should be seen) created a demand for goods and particularly services (groomsmen, gardeners, maids, butlers etc) that led to a trickle-down of wealth. Such officials, and the officers of the military regiments in each colony who were also paid from the British Treasury, were not blind to the investment opportunities open to them in the colonies and quickly became involved in multifarious concerns from trading, shipowning and whaling, to land and pastoral deals. To protect their reputations (as trade was a socially inferior occupation for a gentleman), and because they were full-time government employees, civil officials and military officers were forced to employ others to run such concerns. As NG Butlin has noted:

> Military pride apart, an officer could neither direct his farm in detail nor manage the details of purchasing or resale of goods . . . To purchase and transport grain or meat from ex-convict farmers, to dispose of liquor stocks or other goods at retail required a chain of transactions and a chain of subordinate humans . . . Convicts or ex-convicts were in a position of scarcity to demand and secure a transfer of part of the benefit that officers transferred to themselves . . . The terms of bargaining shifted real income above subsistence standard towards, if not necessarily approaching, the level of that of the officials.[83]

So, 'even though wealth was not directly shared, the opportunity developed for wealth accumulation at lower income levels'. Butlin was particularly concerned here with early Sydney and consequently emphasised the trickle-down to convicts and ex-convicts, but the principle he outlined operated in exactly the same way in the non-convict colonies. In Perth, for instance (which remained convict-free till 1850), civil and military officials were also paid from Britain and also became involved in various business enterprises that required employees. In this case, however, ex-indentured servants brought out by other masters filled the bill—and shared in the trickle-down of incomes received as salaries from outside the colony.[84]

Where all this was crucial for the early growth of Australian capital cities lies in the twin facts (a) that most of the local demands imposed by those on British salaries were for urban *services* and (b) that the majority of Australia's early immigrants, convict and free, were from urban, and not rural, backgrounds and consequently were able to fulfil the diverse service demands imposed.[85] For with the growing urban population and the unequal distribution of wealth went a rising demand for people to perform a myriad of personal services: to build, furnish and clean their homes, to wait on them, stitch, wash and cook for them, sell them necessities and luxuries, transport them and run messages for them, get them into or out of gaol, entertain them, educate them, heal them and bury them. Given the multiplier process, this employment created a considerable urban market for consumable primary produce—and hence supported hinterland growth. This in turn meant that wool prices, for instance, could vary considerably as long as the local market for meat, hides and tallow provided the pastoralist with a reliable basic income.

The importance of urban services and commerce in the early growth of Australian cities runs through each of the city chapters that follow. Rimmer in his chapter on Hobart is quite precise:

> Over half the workforce [in the late 1830s] was engaged primarily in service industries. In addition to the town's commercial community, most of the island's professional men practised in Hobart. The twelve principal departments of civil government and almost as many auxiliary departments employed two to three hundred people, a fifth of whom had professional training. In 1836 the town had twelve clerics, eleven military officers in charge of 324 other ranks. Altogether some three hundred people in Hobart were involved in administration and the provision of professional services for the islanders while another three hundred were on garrison duty. And the middle classes employed close on a thousand full and part-time domestic servants along with a swarm of clerks, messengers, boatmen and porters. Combining the functions of both a colonial capital and a port, Hobart had an unusually large tertiary sector.[86]

Emphasis here, then, is again on the government and port functions, and not on convicts. One can argue that convicts necessitated a large government sector and in doing so provided indirectly the impetus to growth but, although the relative size issue is admitted, Perth, as already shown, as well as Melbourne and Adelaide, give the lie to the necessity for convicts in order to provide a government-led impetus (and British-financed) to urban growth based on services. Once begun, 'the self perpetuating mechanism of initial advantage . . . compounded every year'[87] as continued inflows of immigrants with urban backgrounds chose not to move into the alien hinterland. Why other urban centres did not develop to challenge the initial site is a separate question tackled a little later, but imports played a crucial role. Australia, like other regions of recent settlement, remained dependent on the old world for heavy industrial and manufactured goods for well over a century. As the unloading, storage, transport and retailing of such imports was very labour-intensive it tended to concentrate population near the point of entry—the ports attached to the capital cities. The volume and value of imports, moreover, remained throughout most of the nineteenth century far higher than that of exports, as salaries from abroad and overseas investment in Australia allowed higher incomes than those generated just by exports, and hence supported a deficit balance of trade. This in turn tended to generate faster urban than rural growth.

How were the cities affected by the increase in urban incomes? Was suburban spread and increased specialisation within the city a response to increased incomes? Or did they occur simultaneously?

What was the nature of city growth and spread?

In Chapter IX Denholm cites the traditional view 'that there is a necessary relationship between the overpopulation of the city and the growth of suburbs',[88] but he then argues that Adelaide did not conform. Indeed the Australian experience as a whole contradicts such a view for, in almost all cases, suburban growth, that is, the growth of urban areas, usually residential, near to but separated from the business or administrative centre, occurred simultaneously with the city's growth. Just how they grew is the subject of several theories advanced by urban geographers but in simplest terms it can be said that suburbs arise in two major ways. They can begin as satellite villages at points that could more readily service the needs of particular economic activities, for example near ports or rich agricultural land. The roads or waterways that linked these villages to the cities then become ribbons of development which, over time, expand to end the early separation. This form of suburban growth in Australia was typified in early Sydney, Brisbane and, to an extent, in Perth. The other major type of suburban development involves the emergence of a distinct city fringe of mainly residential areas, and in Australia seems truest of Adelaide, Melbourne and Darwin. Hobart exhibited a little of both of these major trends but its early suburban growth was really too limited to classify.

Before the end of 1788 Sydney had a rival town in Parramatta situated near the head of the habour and with far better soil for agriculture than that around Sydney. Indeed, by 1792 'Sydney remained the headquarters of the colony but its population was less than that of Parramatta' and remained so until after 1800.[89] These, of course, were the starvation years and agriculture was the life blood of the settlement, but Parramatta was just the first of a series of villages set up to serve rapidly expanding agricultural areas. Windsor, for example, was established in 1794 when the Nepean and the Hawkesbury areas were opened up. Newcastle, or Coal River as it was first aptly named, situated at the mouth of the Hunter, was settled a decade later. Under Macquarie the townships of Liverpool, Campbelltown, Wilberforce, Pitt Town, Richmond and Castlereagh were opened up reasonably near Sydney but 'this proliferation of townships did not affect Sydney to the extent that had been the case earlier [with Parramatta]'.[90] They became channels passing goods and services to and from the hinterland as it moved outwards, and were connected to Sydney by increasingly busy thoroughfares.

Sydney Town itself also developed up to Macquarie's period although, as Fletcher points out, 'urban was so blended with the rural as to make a distinction between the two extremely difficult'.[91] Before Macquarie arrived, there was some functional specialisation in the town with the brickfields area clearly marked out, windmills on the ridges and warehouses and traders near the harbour. Under Macquarie this specialisation was extended. He moved the market place to the edge of the residential area near a new wharf, and encouraged small manufacturers to move to Cockle Bay. Although the town was not at that stage 'sufficiently developed for it to be divided into separate work and residential areas'[92], a certain amount of class distinction had emerged spatially reflecting the convict basis of the colony. The 'St James' portion of Sydney, home of civil and military officials and wealthy free immigrants, was located on 'the eastern side of George St, along the waterfront of Sydney Cove and on the higher land stretching up towards Macquarie St'.[93] Near the harbour, the land was more valuable and houses were located closer together, while further away they were situated on larger grants which permitted substantial gardens. This created a sprawl which surprised visitors such as Cunningham, who commented 'Sydney, from the scattered state of its buildings, necessarily occupies a great extent of ground'.[94] Mechanics, shopkeepers and artificers lived and worked in houses on the western side of the town [the 'St Giles area'] while the worst housed and behaved were in the Rocks area above the harbour. By 1821 therefore the stage was set for Sydney to expand out towards the already established villages, which had in essence begun the suburban trend.

Hobart also reflected its convict origins in that a separate residential area for the free was established from the very beginning at New Town, two miles north of the centre at Sullivan Cove.[95] By 1826 one-third of all those who owned their own houses lived at New Town, making it a very exclusive suburb. Proprietors of shops and lodging houses or taverns dwelt close to the centre and the rest rented accommodation on the western and northern sides of the town[96] in a nascent suburban fringe. Functional specialisation really began with Macquarie's masterly planning when government buildings, churches and schools were located in the town centre, and cowsheds, abattoirs, tanneries, flour and timber mills, soap boilers and shipyards relegated to the outskirts. Mt Wellington, towering behind the town, tended to push development along the river either side of the town [but mainly to the north], while 'very high rents'[97] in the city proper tended to encourage an earlier separation of workplace and residence. The area around Sullivan Cove itself was zoned commercial in 1826 and even by this time a considerable amount of reclamation and excavation had been done to enlarge the port. Further suburban growth, however, slowed after 1840 as the sources of Hobart's early rapid progress 'shrivelled up'.[98] So, apart from the early New Town development, Hobart's suburban growth was of the fringe type, but very slow[99] and mainly in a north-west direction [towards New Town] for the most part of the pre-1850 era.

In Perth, suburban villa lots were included in the original town plan fronting the river upstream to Claisebrook and also on the opposite side of the Swan River.[100] Development of the latter blocks was slow as it was not until 1843 that a bridge or causeway was constructed to link the two areas. Development of suburbs around Perth was limited too by Stirling's initial decision to found three townships, Fremantle at the port, Guildford at the navigable head of the Swan, and the capital, Perth, midway between. By 1837 all three townships had grown. Perth, with 620 inhabitants was the largest but most of the population lived on their rural grants in the surrounding territory. With the rapid immigration of 1840-43, however, suburban development took off and in 1841 speculators were announcing a new 'City of Albert' to rise at Claisebrook to the east of Perth where cheaper land was encouraging residential settlement.[101] As immigration ceased with the 1840s depression this particular project never came to fruition but when suburban development did resume, it fanned out on both sides of Perth, towards Fremantle and Guildford which were really villages on the opposite side of the river. Functional specialisation was slow to develop in Perth, mainly because her sister towns were specialised by design. Port, trading, merchanting and warehousing ventures and their servicing requirements were centred at Fremantle; agricultural markets, teamsters and farm service requirements were mainly at Guildford; while Perth was the centre for all government activity, the military, professionals, schools, banks, newspapers and retail stores.[102] Small processing establishments, such as flour mills, tanneries etc, were to be found on the outskirts of all three towns but, as import replacement was very limited, no specific industrial area emerged until quite late in the century.

Although Adelaide, much like Perth, developed as the hub of villages, there were more villages at an earlier stage clustering just beyond the parklands in Light's town of Adelaide, so suburban development in this instance was more of a fringe type. This occurred, moreover, 'long before the city as laid out by Light was full either of buildings or of people'.[103] It was again the 'high cost of city blocks' that forced artisans, mechanics and labourers 'into nascent suburbs beyond the parkland fringe'.What was different, however, was that these suburbs right from the start 'frequently took on a unique, specialised, occupational or functional character'.[104] Some grew to house those engaged in the carrying trades, another became a suburb of brickworks and tanneries, while others were simply residential quarters for the well-to-do. The last was true of North Adelaide, the suburb planned by Light, but it in fact grew more slowly than the elite suburbs of Kensington and Norwood to the east of the town; as North Adelaide was separated by the river it was not till 1843 that a connecting bridge was built.

Despite its lack of convicts, South Australia began life with the largest initial population of any Australian colony to that time. This population, moreover, was not only large—it was occupationally diverse, which encouraged specialisation and differentiation in the city and suburbs right from the beginning. Within four years of its foundation Adelaide exhibited a degree of specialisation that emerged only slowly in other capitals. Hindley Street, and later its extension, Rundle Street, was the main retail area, lawyers congregated in Grenfell and Currie Streets, while North Terrace and King William Streets hosted the banks and most early public buildings. Nevertheless, because urban speculation kept town lot prices high, even by 1860 at least 'a quarter of the city acre sections were undeveloped, whilst areas just beyond the parkland, where land prices dropped dramatically, were burgeoning.'[105] The ready availability of such suburban land and its low cost encouraged a very high expectation of home ownership among 'even the lowest section of the community' at a very early stage. The working men's suburbs tended to grow to the north and west of Adelaide, forming a corridor to the port. They grew moreover with the city centre, rather than as a response to the city's growth. This makes it all the more strange that 'unlike many of its American counterparts Adelaide rapidly acquired a civic pride and corporate identity'.[106]

Priestley also deals with the emergence of corporate identity and municipal government in her chapter on Melbourne, but that is one of the many strands in the following chapters that have had to be left out of this overview. Suburban development in Melbourne, she shows, again occurred simultaneously with the city's growth. Before 1839 suburban land averaged one twentieth of the town price and most of this land was 'at one remove from the central grid.' By 1841 there were suburban clusters along the bay at Williamstown, Port Melbourne, St Kilda and Brighton. Others were on the eastern hill at Newtown [later Fitzroy] and at Jolimont, and more stretched along the Yarra at Richmond, Abbotsford, South Yarra and Hawthorn. On the south side of the river immediately opposite Swanston Street [with access by punt] there was a canvas town to accommodate new immigrants.[107] Like Adelaide, Melbourne grew very quickly, and even before the gold rushes had devel-

24

oped functional specialisation. Medical and other professional men by 1850 had clustered premises 'along the eastern hill at the top of Collins Street', while Elizabeth and Lonsdale Streets housed hotels, shops, churches and a school and were considered 'no longer appropriate for a gentleman's villa.'[108] Half way up Bourke Street a hay and general market area attracted a number of smaller home-run businesses and hotels, while Batmans Hill, which was later levelled for Spencer Street railway station, was the original site for race meetings.

As in other capitals, businessmen and traders often lived in rooms in the hub of the town close to or partitioned off from their workplace, but rising urban land prices forced those who wished for a more genteel and spacious lifestyle to move to the suburbs. These rising prices, however, had little to do with productive efficiency and rising per capita incomes, for even as early as the 1840s urban land prices were far more a reflection of absentee speculative investment and colonial land policy, including the specification of city boundaries.

Beginning life as a penal outpost, Brisbane's early growth was slow. As Johnston and Gregory comment:

> uncertainty as to its future led to stagnation and decline. By 1839 Brisbane was taking on a deserted air, and this situation was compounded by the government's failure to make a definite plan for the area's future.[109]

When the western districts were finally thrown open in 1842 'rival urban groups soon developed to challenge Brisbane Town.' Problems with the city site, such as difficulty of access for store vessels due to the bar at the river mouth and several shoals, impure water supply and the restricted amount of flat land for settlement,[110] encouraged the growth of villages outside the town and construction of a store base on Stradbroke Island. Three main communities grew quickly around Brisbane Town, South Brisbane, Kangaroo Point and Fortitude Valley. South Brisbane had a more favourable position for commerce than the original city on the northern bank, and despite similar urban land prices, outpaced Brisbane Town till 1850. Further inland Ipswich, originally called Limestone from its position on the limestone hills above the Bremer River west of Brisbane, also took off in the early 1840s, as it was 'an obvious supply base for the growing number of stations in the [Darling Downs] hinterland'.[111]

Functional specialisation within Brisbane was reduced by the early development of these suburban villages and so the city retained its convict legacy for many years. But in terms of function, commercial development was at first centred in South Brisbane, as already mentioned, while Kangaroo Point became mainly industrial and residential and Fortitude Valley the reception area for new immigrants.[112] With the rising tide of immigration and the spread of settlement came early calls for the administrative centre to be moved north, or for the division of what is now Queensland into two or three separate colonies.[113] Indeed, it was not until the 1850s that it became clear that Brisbane would be the capital city of the new colony of Queensland, which gained its separate identity in 1859. Brisbane had survived as the focal point of a growing number of outstations and so, like Sydney, suburban development could follow the lines of communication between the centre and villages until the latter were engulfed in the city itself. Brisbane's location so far south within its territory, however, has led to the growth of a larger number of sizable towns than in other states, a point that will be taken up again later.

Darwin, or Palmerston as it was first called, was modelled by Surveyor Goyder on

25

Light's plan for Adelaide and so it is not surprising to find that suburban development along the arms of the bay was included in plans right from the beginning.[114] Its development was thus of the fringe type and, as it was regarded in the early period as basically just a supply and administrative depot, it was slow to develop any real functional specialisation.

Overall then, it appears that in Australia, suburbanisation took place simultaneously with the capital cities' development, rather than as a response to crowding or rising incomes. Continued suburban growth around the capital cities, not examined here, possibly helped those cities to retain primacy in their respective territories, but many other factors were also involved.

Why have the original capital cities retained their primacy?

In an article on urbanisation in the United States in the pre-rail era GR Taylor noted that 'no single American city dominated the American scene at the close of the colonial period [1770s] as did London in Great Britain or Paris in France.'[115] Instead, there were over twenty large cities in the thirteen colonies, a trend that continued so that even today there is no large gap in the size ranking of cities and towns in the same state region.[116] Indeed, state capitals in America are often smaller than other cities within the same state, for example, Sacramento, the capital of California, is considerably smaller than Los Angeles and San Francisco. In Australia the pattern has been entirely different. In 1850, on the eve of the gold rushes, Sydney was clearly the dominant Australian city, though Melbourne at that time had a faster rate of growth. In each colony, moreover, there was a clear gap between the population of the capital and that of the next largest town in the same region. McCarty has calculated that in 1900, fifty years later:

> Brisbane had 7 times the population of Rockhampton, its nearest rival, and Sydney 9 times the population of Newcastle; Perth and Melbourne had ratios of 10 and 11 and Adelaide a ratio of 23 to 1. Hobart had only one-third more population than Launceston[117]

. . . and so Hobart is the only capital whose primacy was not abundantly evident. Why had this pattern developed? After all, the first American cities were also seaports yet they were superseded or at least challenged by fast-growing inland towns as development ensued.[118] The whole answer to this question cannot really be drawn from the essays that follow for they deal, by design, with establishment and very early challenges. Nevertheless it is a pertinent question, for the origins of Australia's capital cities are fascinating partly because these cities have remained capitals since inception and partly because they are so dominant in their respective territories.

The whole question of primacy attracted a lot of attention in the mid 1960s and early '70s, mostly from urban geographers.[119] Arguments were two-pronged, reasons for initial city growth being separated from the issue of later primacy. With regard to the first, perhaps the most accepted view was that metropolitan growth was attributable to the demands for goods and services created by a large, productive, and export-oriented hinterland. Thus one can attribute 'the rapid growth of Melbourne and Sydney to their large productive hinterlands . . . and Hobart's slow growth . . . to its small and relatively stagnant hinterland, which it has to share with Launceston.'[120] Other theories, however, stressed internal growth-generating forces within the city and the important part played by the immigration of labour and inflows of capital.[121] Once firmly established, it was then argued, the cities' primacy was assured by resultant economies of scale and location, immigrant preference and perhaps by the failure of businessmen to perceive non-metropolitan investment opportunities.[122]

These theories are useful in providing a general background for discussion of urban primacy but they do not adequately take into account the specifics of the Australian situation. In particular it is necessary first to explain why Australian society became urbanised at such an early stage, and second why that urbanisation was concentrated into so few capital cities. The second question is beyond the scope of the essays which follow, but they combine to provide evidence for a more closely focused answer to the first. It can be argued that Australia's early urban concentration resulted directly from five factors: (1) the low population potential of most areas of the continent, (2) the relatively low labour intensity of most rural activities undertaken, (3) the high standard of wealth generated initially by British subsidy, investment and markets, (4) the high urban orientation of most immigrant skills; and (5) the high costs of early overland transport.

In Australia the vital natural resources that support a large population, that is, freshwater and reliable rainfall, fertile soil, good timber and a temperate climate, are all concentrated in the east, south-east, and south-west of the continent. This contrasts with their more even distribution in Canada and the United States where the land could support a constantly western-moving frontier of new immigrants, and support them, furthermore, when they reproduced the labour-intensive uses of land that they were used to in the old world. Australia's average land quality was poorer, and in most parts of the country soils and climate precluded intensive farming (especially with nineteenth century techniques). From the beginning, moreover, Australian agriculture was mainly commercial.' It produced for sale, and often for export, rather than for consumption on the farm or in the local region,'[123] and through this specialisation it moved away from the labour-intensive, self-supportive farming of the kind then common in Europe and eastern North America. Australian land was suited, however, to extensive forms of land use such as pastoralism which required low labour densities and did not encourage family participation, as for example, did dairy farming or grain production. Thus, geographic and economic factors combined to prevent an even distribution of settlement in Australia. Likewise they induced (primarily because of the high costs of good quality livestock) an unequal distribution of wealth. This trend was reinforced by the colonial heritage, whereby Britain annually injected thousands of pounds for defence and administration, thus producing a standard of wealth unachievable by other means. As previously outlined, the existence of a wealthy elite gave rise to a demand for the many and diverse services available in the old world, and so provided employment for the predominantly urban-based skills of both the willing and unwilling immigrant labour force. The range of specialist skills available in the cities, from immigrants who had neither the desire nor the ability to take up rural land, together ensured that the rural-based wealthy (permanently and temporarily so) would go to the cities to satisfy their varied needs, including entertainment.

In the early period, costly overland transport ensured that many small towns emerged, about one day's bullock-team drive from each other to satisfy the overnight needs of travellers, but generally such towns did not develop far because of the high cost of introducing and housing a large variety of goods and service personnel. In early America such costs were offset by the large markets provided not only by the surrounding area but also by the constant passage of new immigrants going out to the frontier. The lack of a fertile hinterland large enough to support dense populations and perhaps, too, the lack of significant numbers of rurally bred immigrants (who were attracted to America instead) prohibited this sort of market development in Australia. Major markets remained in the cities where employment opportunities were widest and where consumers could bear transport costs.

This then explains why Australia urbanised at such an early stage, but does it explain why such urbanisation was concentrated in a single centre in each colony? With one further qualification it does. It follows from the argument above that the site chosen as the administrative centre of a colony, or territory governed from elsewhere, will tend strongly to become the focal point for the injection of funds needed to defend and administer it adequately. This instantly creates the hub of a market for goods and particularly services which in turn will have multiplier effects. Employment opportunities thus created will have a strong attraction for new immigrants, especially those from urban backgrounds as experienced in Australia. When to this is added the relatively low labour requirements of rural activities, the high costs of pre-rail overland transport and the dependence on imports for so many everyday needs, the tendency for agglomeration on the initial site is understandable. As the city grew, moreover, economies of location and scale became available which reinforced the trend and increased the costs of establishing elsewhere. 'Once cities are established and pass a certain size, vested interests of business (and government) lead to a process of cumulative causation.'[124]

The one qualification to be added to this argument is the impact of railways. The walking city had defined physical limits which, even with dense settlement patterns, placed a limit on the attainable size of any one viable city. Such restraints were removed by the advent of railways which, through commuting, enabled suburbs to spread and the city to service far larger hinterlands than previously thought possible. Moreover, because railways were constructed in Australia *after* the planting of the city, they were generally focused on that city and consequently channelled all hinterland activity towards it. In these circumstances the city hub developed economic, social, political and information-gathering advantages that effectively precluded any challenge from urban centres anywhere else in the region, thus ensuring city primacy.

Queensland was something of an exception to this fan pattern of railways in that several of the northern coastal towns, as well as Brisbane, became railheads for their hinterlands and so shared some of these advantages. They failed, however, to challenge Brisbane's established lead as Queensland's major market centre, particularly for all kinds of services, and have remained simply collecting and distributing centres. So, early concentration into a few principal cities was continued, partly because economies of scale and location made it natural to develop further the partially developed, and partly because railways were introduced at a crucial stage in Australia's history, allowing the city to spread out from its walking limits and to develop a fan and hub pattern that concentrated hinterland activity on the capital.

The above explanation of the early primacy of Australian cities derives essentially from the high incomes earned initially by those in receipt of British funds (public and private). Colonial status resulted in an injection of funds from the mother country into a single administrative centre, where concentrated high non-rural incomes created, through a trickle-down process and the urban oriented skills of willing and unwilling immigrants, higher per capita wealth than that obtainable purely on the basis of export earnings. The United States of America was deprived of this influence by the War of Independence and, in being thrown back on her hinterland resources, developed instead a broad swathe of large cities and an interlocking, rather than a fan-based, pattern of railways. Canada simi-

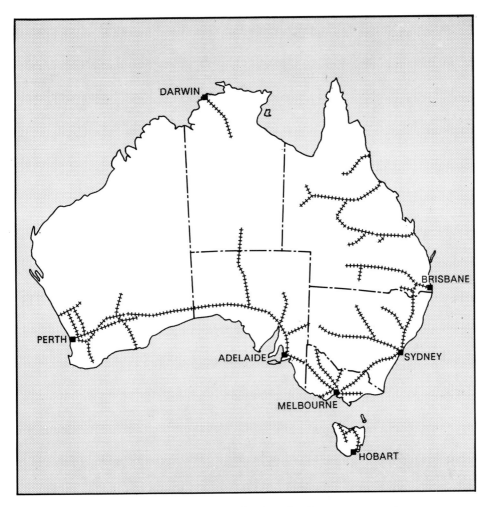

Figure 3: A fan-shaped pattern of railway development converging on the major cities

larly was deprived of major British subsidy by earlier responsible government, a different administrative system and, of course, no convicts. It also had a far richer hinterland which encouraged closer settlement and this, in the absence of a large, single, service nexus accompanying the administration of a big subsidy, led to the development of a larger number of sizable towns. This in turn made it possible for the capital of Ontario, for example, to be shifted several times to different cities within the province during the nineteenth century—a total contrast to the Australian experience.

Conclusion

In the first section of this overview, under the heading 'Why were the territories settled?', it was argued that the settlement of Australia *as a whole* owed less to British government imperial design than to private investment decisions and penal expediency. The British government's unwillingness to allow private individuals to control the disposal of lands annexed for the Crown basically led to its administrative intervention in each colony, and to the consequent expense of maintaining both civil and military establishments. The answer to the next question, 'why were the capital cities located where they are?' is less straightforward. Three essential preconditions have been isolated, namely a good supply of fresh water, sufficient elevation to be free of swamps and flooding, and proximity to a deep water safe anchorage near shore to facilitate the loading and unloading of visiting vessels. The last condition, however, could be met by a port site removed from but accessible to the capital, as in the case of Perth and Adelaide. Thereafter, given the span of time covered from 1788 to 1869, the reasons for choice of site varied according to when foundation took place as well as with the background and circumstances of the founder. It was also clear that although each founder knew that he was choosing the site for a city, whether that city was to be a capital or simply a regional centre had minimal influence.

The layouts of all capital cities other than Canberra were loosely based on the gridiron plan that had been used in colonial situations since the Roman period. Irregularities occurred in each city, however, for topographical, historical or accidental reasons—though topography in general was not featured as it was for example in Canberra. Because most city centres were planned and thrown open as a whole from the start, vacant town lots remained for quite some time after foundation, a situation that could be expected to have deterred any early move into the suburbs. In fact quite the opposite occurred. In almost every Australian capital, suburban growth took place simultaneously with the growth of the city centre. One explanation for this was that speculators and investors bought up and held centre city lots, so causing high prices and the search for cheaper suburban blocks. This did not occur in the earliest established cities, for then town lots were granted rather than sold. In these instances the move had more to do with the desire by the wealthy for estates large enough to support a lifestyle on the grand scale, or conversely the aspirations of labourers to achieve partial self-sufficiency on a few acres by keeping goats, pigs or poultry and an extensive garden. Other explanations for the early move into suburbs surrounding the city centre involve early class distinction by residential area, gradual functional specialisation in particular areas, and service demands along key transport routes.

The answer to the next question, 'why did the capital cities grow in the pre-rail era?' is complex. It has been argued that exports had little to do with early city growth, for in most instances successful export trades well and truly postdated the establishment and early development of the capital cities. Rather, the early growth of Australian cities has been attributed to the demand for goods and particularly services from well-paid civil government and military personnel taken together with the urban-oriented skills of most immigrants. The trickle-down of externally derived wealth enabled the cities to maintain a far higher rate of importation than was possible on the basis of exports, and hence created further employment and fostered diversification. The fact that Australian agriculture, except in the very early stages, was largely commercial and non-labour-intensive reinforced the dominance of the cities as also did high overland transport costs in the pre-rail era, for they made substantial industry and market development in inland towns uneconomic.

The continued primacy of Australia's capital cities has been attributed in turn to location economies and scale economies that developed as the market, initially created by the injection and trickle-down of government funds (mainly British), expanded because of Australian local activity and demands. It has also been linked to the pattern and timing of railway development in Australia in that railways were appended to existing cities just as (or before) they reached their pedestrian and horse-drawn limits. The resulting fan pattern of rails, linking small inland towns to the centre, consolidated the latter's port and central administrative functions. The consequent advantages (economic, social, political and information gathering) then held by the city hub effectively precluded any challenge and ensured primacy.

This interpretation of the origin and growth of Australian capital cities has highlighted the importance of government expenditures and centralised decision making in a period long before the twentieth century welfare state. The prominence of government expenditures, subsidised by Britain, at such an early stage in Australian development had a profound effect on the structure, function and growth of each of the colonies/states and on their respective capital cities, an effect that is only now beginning to be explored. For example, there has been little or no research into the financial, demographic, entrepreneurial and skill contributions of the British regiments stationed in the Australian colonies until 1871. Yet their influence in each of these fields was by no means insignificant and their role in Australian history far exceeds that of showy manoeuvres against rebellious convicts, bushrangers and insubordinate Aboriginals.

As indicated by the lack of mention under any of the previous headings, Aboriginal influence on the pattern of urban settlement in Australia was minimal, unlike America where Indian warfare necessitated fortress towns in some areas. This was not because the Aboriginals passively accepted the European takeover; far from it. Almost every city chapter that follows details early conflict with the Aboriginals and the intrepid resistance of some of their leaders. The problem rather was that the effectiveness of Aboriginal resistance was undermined by a severe reduction in numbers through introduced disease. It is believed that smallpox epidemics in 1789 and 1829-31 spread widely and wiped out half to two-thirds of the Aboriginal population in south-eastern Australia, while those in direct contact with whites also suffered from venereal disease and the debilitating effects of alcohol.[125] On the other side of the continent tuberculosis, influenza, measles and alcohol similarly undermined potential resistance.[126] Whenever direct competition for scarce food resources arose, conflict was sharp and violent. That such incidents were not more frequent than they were has been attributed to the fact that fewer Aboriginals reduced their resource needs and thus delayed confrontation until 'whites began to absorb the proportion of resources exceeding the proportion of black population already lost'.[127] By the time this occurred the whites were well entrenched and, in terms of numbers and firepower, non-evictable. Most skirmishes thus occurred only on the perimeters of settlement and in seasons of acute food shortage and did little to influence the process or nature of Australian urbanisation.

It is hoped, in conclusion, that this collection of essays will give scholars new insights into the reasons for the settlement of each of the Australian colonies and the growth of each capital city; that it will cater for all those who cherish an interest in Australian beginnings but lack the time and access to specialised material to pursue that interest themselves, and finally that it will encourage new research, and particularly comparative research, into Australia's capital city origins.

Notes

[1] Glynn, Sean. *Urbanization in Australian History*, (Thomas Nelson, Aust. 1970), pp.2-3.

[2] Weber, A.F. *The Growth of Cities in the Nineteenth Century. A Study in Statistics.* (New York, 1899, reprinted Ithaca, 1965), p.1.

[3] *Ibid.*, p.138.

[4] McCarty, J.W. 'Australian Capital Cities in the Nineteenth Century', in McCarty, J.W., and Shedvin, C.B., (eds) *Australian Capital Cities: Historical Essays,* (Sydney University Press, 1978), Ch. 2, p.15.; and Robinson, K.W. 'Processes and Patterns of Urbanization in Australia and New Zealand', *New Zealand Geographer*, Vol. 18, 1962, p.33.

[5] Glynn, *op.cit.*, p.2.

[6] Bird, James. 'The Foundation of Australian Seaport Capitals', *Economic Geography*, Vol. 41, No. 4, October, 1965, pp.283-4.

[7] Guttkind, E.A. *International History of City Development*, Vols. 1-6, (Collier Macmillan, London, 1971).

[8] Mumford, Lewis. *The City in History*, (Penguin Books, 1961).

[9] McCarty, J.W. 'Australian Capital Cities in the Nineteenth Century', *A.E.H.R.*, Vol. 10, No. 2, September, 1970, pp.107-111.

[10] Glynn, *op.cit.*

[11] Davison, Graeme. *The Rise and Fall of Marvellous Melbourne*, (M.U.P., 1978).

[12] Eg. Bremer, Stuart. *Living in the City: A Pictorial Record of Australian Cities*, (S. & L. Brodie, South Australia. 1983).

[13] McCarty (*A.E.H.R.*), *op.cit.*, p.109.

[14] Neutze, M. 'City, Country, Town: Australian Peculiarities', *Australian Cultural History*, No. 4, 1985. p.14.

[15] Robson, Chapter IV, p.80.

[16] Johnston and Gregory, Chapter XII, p.236.

[17] Cameron, J., Chapter XIV, p.277.

[18] Johnston and Gregory, Chapter XII, p.243.

[19] Shaw, Chapter X, p.208.

[20] *Ibid.*, p.211.

[21] Bird, *op.cit.*, p.284.

[22] Fletcher, Chapter III, p.52.

[23] Martin, Chapter II, p.48.

[24] Bird, *op.cit.*, p.284.

[25] *A.D.B.*, Vol. 1, Entry for D. Collins, p.236.

[26] Bird, *op.cit.*, p.285.

[27] Robson, Chapter IV, p.86.

[28] *H.R.A.*, III, vi, p.600.

[29] Bolton, Chapter VII, p.143.

[30] Stannage, C.T. *The People of Perth: A Social History of Western Australia's Capital City*, (Perth City Council, 1979), p.1.

[31] Davies, Chapter VIII, p.170.

[32] Shaw, Chapter X, p.205.

[33] *Ibid.*, p.210.

[34] *Ibid.*, p.209.

[35] Johnston and Gregory, Chapter XII, p.236.

[36] Bird, *op.cit.*, p.287.

[37] *Ibid.*

[38] Johnston and Gregory, Chapter XII, p.242.

[39] Bird, *op.cit.*, pp.287-288.

[40] Reece, Chapter XV, p.309.

[41] Bird, *op.cit.*, p.295.

[42] *H.R.N.S.W.*, Vol. 1, Part 2, pp.348-349.

[43] *H.R.A.*, III, v, pp.180-6, and Vol. vi, pp.246, 386.

[44] Rimmer, Chapter V, p.114.

[45] Bird, *op.cit.*, p.297.

[46] Davies, Chapter VIII, p.170.

[47] Solomon, R.J. *Urbanization: The Evolution of an Australian Capital*, (A. & R., 1976), pp.75-77.

[48] Wheeler, J. 'Notes on the Moreton Bay Settlement', *A.P.I.J.*, Vol. 4, No. 3, July, 1966, p.76.

[49] Bolton, Chapter VII, p.154.

[50] Roper, Gil. 'Afterthoughts on Colonel Light', *A.P.I.J.*, Vol. 2, No. 7, 1963, p.212.

[51] Mumford, *op.cit.*, p.224.

[52] *Ibid.*

[53] Jeans, D.N. 'The Breakdown of Australia's First Rectangular Grid Survey', *A.G.S.*, Vol. 4, No. 2, October, 1966, p.123.

[54] Pitt Morison, M. 'The Shaping of Early Perth 1829-1845' in *Western Geographer*, Vol. 6, No. 1, January, 1982, p.50.

[55] *Ibid.*, p.119.

[56] *Ibid.*, p.127.

[57] Bolton, Chapter VII, p.146.

[58] Guttkind, E.A. *International History of City Development: Urban Development in Western Europe: The Netherlands and Great Britain.* Vol. 6, (Collier Macmillan, London, 1971), p.212.

[59] Bridenbaugh, C. *Cities in the Wilderness: The First Century of Urban Life in America. 1625-1742*, (A. Knopf, N.Y. 1955).

[60] Guttkind, *op.cit.*, p.211.

[61] Mumford, *op.cit.*, p.482.

[62] Mumford, *op.cit.*, p.483.

[63] *Ibid.*, p.484.

[64] Solomon *op.cit.*, p.28 and Wheeler *op.cit.*, p.69.

[65] Wheeler, *op.cit.*, p.69.

[66] Solomon, *op.cit.*, p.29.

[67] Fletcher, Chapter III, p.53.

[68] Auchmuty, J. (ed), *The Voyage of Governor Phillip to Botany Bay*, (A. & R., 1970), pp.69-71.

[69] *H.R.A.*, I, i, p.48.

[70] Fletcher, Chapter III, p.55.

[71] Fitzharding, L.F. *Sydney's First Four Years: Tench's Narrative and Complete Account*, (A. & R., 1961), p.80.

[72] *Ibid.*, p.16.

[73] Solomon, *op.cit.*, p.29.

[74] Bolton, Chapter VII, p.144.

[75] Wheeler, *op.cit.*, p.72.

[76] Turner, I.A.H. 'The Growth of Melbourne: An Historical Account', in Troy, P.N. *Urban Redevelopment in Australia*, (A.N.U., 1967), pp.31-32.

[77] Mumford, *op.cit.*, pp.480-486.

[78] Rubin, Julius. 'Growth and Expansion of Urban Centres', in Wakstein, H.M. *The Urbanization of America: An Historical Anthology* (Houghton-Mifflin, Boston, 1970), p.89 and Taylor, G.R. 'American Growth Preceding the Railway Age', *J.E.H.*, Vol. 27, No. 2, 1967, (hereafter cited as 'Pre-rail').

[79] McCarty (*A.E.H.R.*), *op.cit.*, pp.121-122.

[80] Glynn, *op.cit.*, p.12.

[81] Notably Butlin, N.G. in *Investment in Australian Economic Development 1861-1900*, (C.U.P., 1964).

[82] Priestley, Susan, Chapter XI, p.218.

[83] Butlin, N.G. 'Free Lunches Antipodean Style: N.S.W. Economy 1788-1810', *W.P.E.H.*, *A.N.U.*, No. 57, October, 1985, p.50.

[84] Statham, Pamela. 'The Role of the Commissariat in Early West Australian Economic Development', *A.E.H.R.*, Vol. 24, No. 1, March, 1984, pp.31-2.

[85] See Statham, Pamela. 'Swan River Colony 1829-1850' in Stannage, C.T. *A New History of Western Australia*, (U.W.A. Press, 1981) p.185. and Butlin, N.G. 'White Human Capital in Australia 1788-1850', *W.P.E.H.*, A.N.U., No. 32, April, 1985, pp.30-32.

[86] Rimmer, Chapter V, p.107.

[87] Williams, M. 'The Making of Adelaide', in McCarty and Schedvin, *op.cit.*, p.116.

[88] Denholm, Chapter IX, p.183.

[89] Fletcher, Chapter III, p.55.

[90] *Ibid.*, p.66.

[91] *Ibid.*, p.69.

[92] *Ibid.*, p.70.

[93] *Ibid.*

[94] *Ibid.*

[95] Rimmer, Chapter V, p.97.

[96] *Ibid.*, p.109.

[97] *Ibid.*, p.108.

[98] *Ibid.*, p.115.

[99] Solomon, *op.cit.*, p.51.

[100] Bolton, Chapter VII, p.151.

[101] Statham, P. 'Swan River Colony', *op.cit.*, pp.199-202.

[102] Bolton, Chapter VII, p.151.

[103] Denholm, Chapter IX, p.183.

[104] Chapter IX, p.183.

[105] *Ibid.*

[106] *Ibid.*, p.190.

[107] Priestley, Chapter XI, p.220.

[108] *Ibid.*, p.224.

[109] Johnston and Gregory, Chapter XII, p.244.

[110] *Ibid.*, p.245.

[111] *Ibid.*, p.246.

[112] *Ibid.*

[113] *Ibid.*, p.247-248.

[114] Reece Chapter XV, p.309.

[115] Taylor (Pre-rail), *op.cit.*, p.316.

[116] *Ibid.*

[117] McCarty (*A.E.H.R.*), *op.cit.*, p.113.

[118] Bridenbaugh, C. 'The Foundations of American Urban Society', in Wakstein, *op.cit.*, p.76.

[119] See review in Linsky, A.S. 'Some Generalizations Concerning Primate Cities', *A.A.A.G.*, Vol. 55, 1965, p.506 and fns. For Australian references see Glynn, S., *op.cit.*

[120] Stillwell, F.J.B. 'Economic Factors and the Growth of Cities', in Burnley, I.H. *Urbanization in Australia: the Post-War Experience*, (C.U.P., 1974), p.34.

[121] *Ibid.*, p.36.

[122] *Ibid.*, p.37.

[123] Neutze, M., *op.cit.*, p.9.

[124] *Ibid.*, p.18.

[125] Butlin, N.G. *Our Original Aggression: Aboriginal Populations of South Eastern Australia 1788-1850*, (Allen & Unwin, 1983), pp.81-85, (hereafter 'Aggression').

[126] Green, N. 'Aborigines and White Settlers', in Stannage *op.cit.*, pp.78, 88 & 90.

[127] Butlin ('Aggression'), *op.cit.*, p.103.

Sydney

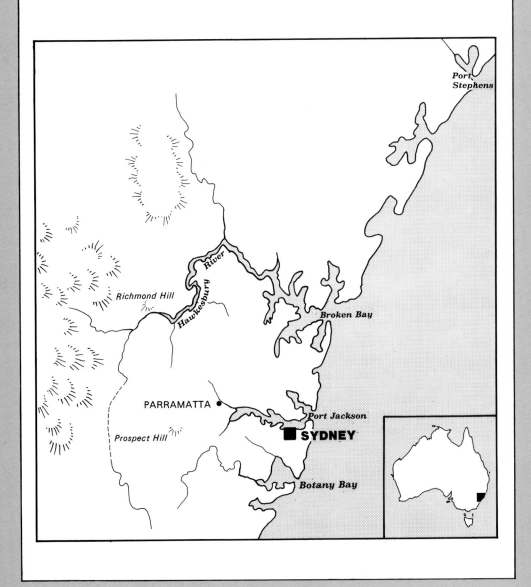

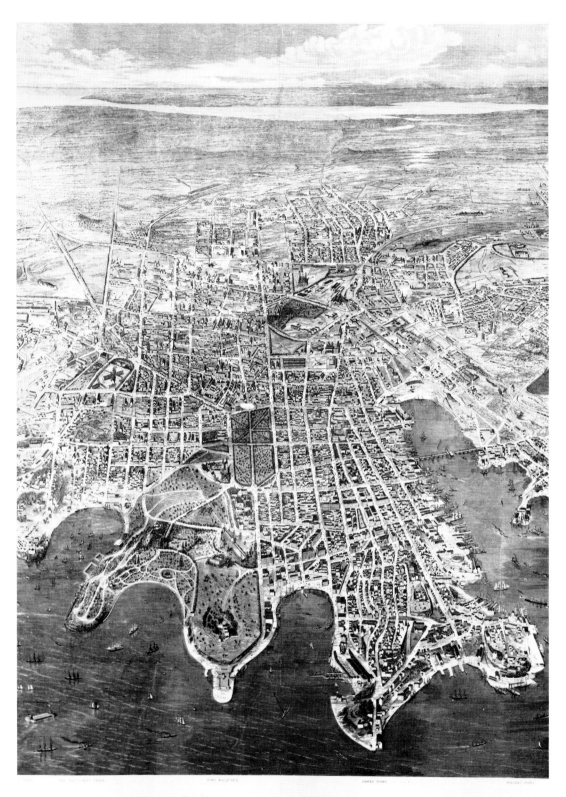

SYDNEY

Chapter II

The Founding of New South Wales

Ged Martin

In January 1788 an expedition containing over one thousand people, two-thirds of them convicts, arrived from England to settle at a place on the thinly inhabited east coast of Australia which had only once before been visited by Europeans. Thus was founded the colony of New South Wales and, more haphazardly, the city of Sydney. What motives lay behind the decision to send this expedition? What is the significance of the fact that so many people arrived at such a time and in such a way? How has this event been interpreted? At the outset of a book seeking to explain the origins of Australia's states and cities it is important to look not merely at explanations given, but also at the way in which historians have constructed those explanations. The best starting point for that line of enquiry is to survey the three main theories put forward for the establishment of New South Wales.[1]

For the first century of Australian historical writing, one simple account held the field. The British, it was argued, dumped their unwanted convicts in Australia, partly because the empty continent was far away, and partly because no other suitable outlet could be found once the American colonies asserted their independence and made it clear, after 1783, that they would not accept transported felons. Although a few individuals could not shake off the hope that some nobler motive might have entered British calculations, most Australians were probably happy enough with that explanation: the British normally slighted Australia's interests, and there was some pride in concluding that Australia had triumphed despite a sordid start. The 'convict dumping' theory has never been wholly abandoned among historians and, despite attack in the 1960s and 1970s, Manning Clark and A G L Shaw have stood firm in arguing that the evidence did not permit any other interpretation, a line defended by Alan Atkinson and GJ Abbott and more recently by M Gillen and D Mackay.[2]

In 1952 a fresh explanation was posited by KM Dallas, who argued that the settlement was founded as a trading post to spearhead British penetration of the Pacific and to service an alternative sea route to China. For this Dallas should be given full credit for he was asking questions and launching large theories at a time when most scholars kept to conservative lines of enquiry.[3] However, some of Dallas's ideas stretched the known evidence a little too far, such as his argument that Botany Bay was settled to encourage fur trading in North America or whaling in the South Pacific. Recently even these ideas have gained some credence through the work of Margaret Steven, who has unearthed new evidence to support a theory of deliberate commercial policy behind Prime Minister Pitt's actions in the late eighteenth century.[4] Critics of Dallas in the 1950s, however, made the mistake of assuming that because they could fault some parts of his hypothesis, all of it could be rejected—thus overlooking the potentially significant link between the colony and the China tea trade. In his 'Historical Studies' article in 1960 and the first volume of his mighty *History of Australia* in 1962 Manning Clark virtually eliminated the Dallas theory from the corpus of Australian historiography in an authoritative condemnation of those who stressed 'the mundane benefits from an expansion of commerce'.[5] Yet by the end of the decade, H T Fry had fleshed out the 'China route' part of the Dallas theory, with a careful demonstration of the concern felt in British official circles, right down to the very week in August 1786 when the decision to establish the colony was made, for the security of trade routes to China.[6]

Geoffrey Blainey was also unconvinced by the Dallas theory but he did share the intuitive Dallas assumption that some more positive motives for the founding of the colony must have existed. In 1966 he proclaimed a third approach, contending that the British government had aimed to secure new supplies of mast timber—by using Norfolk Island pine for its warships—and of flax, the plant from which ropes and sailcloth were manufactured, and which in strategic terms was as important as uranium is today.[7] Some sharp, immensely enjoyable but not always entirely helpful discussions ensured, with Blainey taking this stand on the references to flax and mast timber in the documentation of the mid 1780s, and his critics both casting doubt on the status of the sources and asking why so little had been done to develop these supposedly vital supplies after 1788. Like Dallas, Blainey was probably too sweeping and global in launching his theory, for whatever the documents said or did not say, it was hard to understand why the British government should have invested so heavily in unknown timber resources in the Antipodes when it had ample reserves of pine in the forests of Canada. This objection was largely removed during the 1970s by an impressive series of publications from Alan Frost, who fine-honed the Blainey thesis to argue that the British sought supplies for their fleets in eastern waters, which needed to refit without sailing home if they were to defend the British hold in India against the machinations of the French.[8] Although this modification might have seemed to have opened up the possibility of rapprochement with Fry and the China route, Frost remained convinced that no specific commercial motive, and certainly none relating to China, lay behind the decision to settle New South Wales.

Consideration of the reasons for the founding of New South Wales must, in large part, involve consideration of the way in which historians have debated the question, and it must be stressed that their writings throw as much light on the mental processes of modern academics as upon those of bygone politicians. Historians are not 'experts' who *know*, but rather craftsmen who reconstruct, and the quality of their reconstructions depends both upon their skill and sensitivity, and upon the shards of surviving evidence available to them. Historians work from documents and of documents there are broadly two kinds—the 'thinking' and the 'doing'. The first explain why something is to be done or should be done, the second explain or order how it is to be done. Since the second kind are normally directed at underlings, and underlings take orders, there is not much need to include any explanation for the motives behind the instructions—and unfortunately, much of the surviving documentation for the establishment of the New South Wales colony is of this kind. But thinking documents also fall into sub-categories, for explanations given on paper may not reflect the actual reasons behind a decision. The thinking documents we have for the founding of New South Wales illustrate this problem. Frequently they are very persuasive, but so they should be: they were invariably written by people who wanted to convince those in power that the government should settle New South Wales, or—in the case of newspaper reports after the decision was taken—convince others that their bold folly was really a master stroke.[9]

Historians can generally allow for the motives behind thinking documents, but they are less happy when they have to deal with the context in which they are written. If something is not put down on paper, does this mean that it was not considered, or even known about—or does it mean that it was taken for granted? Historians set out to make tidy patterns of explanation, arranging verifiable pieces of evidence in set order, and they distrust arguments which assume that other, unverifiable, factors played a part. There is good reason to do this, for if a firm line is not drawn conclusions would quickly drop to the level of 'must have': New South Wales 'must have' been founded for commercial or economic motives, because 'obviously' no other explanation will do. Yet innocent men have been hanged because juries were persuaded that they 'must have' committed the crime. Preventing enthusiasms from colouring the evidence, however, does not entirely solve the problem of context. For instance, Alan Frost disagrees with those who argue that the ministers chose Botany Bay for their penal settlement knowing that convicts could be sent out in empty tea ships en route to China. Frost shows, quite convincingly, that it was not until a month later, when the government advertised for transport, that an enterprising shipowner, William Richards, put forward the idea that the export of criminals might be married to the import of tea and, in seeking the approval of the powerful East India Company, the government did behave as if this was a new idea.[10] At face value, the documents support Alan Frost, but his argument assumes that those who had taken the decision had not and could not have thought of the idea for themselves. The decision was probably taken largely by two men: the imperially minded Prime Minister, William Pitt, and Evan Nepean, the Undersecretary for Home Affairs. Now there is evidence that Nepean had known of the possibility of combining the two traffics, for in 1784 James Matra had sent him a calculation, made by Sir George Young of the Admiralty, of the costs of sending convicts to New South Wales in merchant vessels, and had asked him to pass on the information to the Home Secretary, Lord Sydney, who was also closely concerned in the decision to settle New South Wales.[11] But even without this written evidence, Frost's argument asks us to accept that Pitt—with his grandiose plans for British world trade, including in 1784 a slashing of the duties on tea to foster the eastern trade—had not seen the link for himself. There is no concrete evidence—nothing, that is, in writing—for this, but, by the same token, there is no written evidence that Pitt knew that the world was round: it is something that has to be deduced from the facts that Pitt was an intelligent and educated man and intelligent and educated men of his time believed in a circular planet.

At this point, lest the argument becomes too convincing, all cards should be placed on the table. Of all the historians involved in the debate, this writer has placed most emphasis on the postulated interconnection between tea ships going out empty and convict ships coming home empty. Faced with Alan Frost's evidence it would be easy to retreat to a 'must have' riposte by triumphantly citing Matra's letter to Nepean, which establishes that *someone* had seen the connection two years earlier, but that does not prove that it was in the minds of decision makers in August 1786. Nepean was a very busy man and Matra, a displaced American loyalist, was not very important. Nepean might have discounted and forgotten what was a mere postscript to a letter. There is certainly no evidence that

Nepean passed on the information to Sydney, as Matra requested, and none at all that Sydney explained the idea to the Cabinet, as Matra optimistically hoped. For what it is worth, this writer still believes that Pitt, Nepean and Sydney selected Botany Bay in the knowledge that convicts could be sent out cheaply in tea ships. It is true that the shipping agent, Richards, thought he originated the idea at a later date, and was very pleased with himself for saving the government so much money, but then, as he was still lobbying for the contract, he can be forgiven for exaggerating his own contribution.[12]

This problem—that historians arrange facts into convenient boxes to the exclusion of inconvenient assumptions—can also be illustrated by the twin paths which can be taken to the moment in August 1786 when the British government decided to establish a colony at Botany Bay. One path leads firmly to New South Wales, moving vigorously from one proposal for an Australian colony to another. The other ranges across the face of the globe, pursuing possible outlets for British convicts, uncertain whether there were, or were not, other places to which they might be sent. Only occasionally do these two odysseys intertwine. Europe first learned of the east coast of Australia in 1771, on Cook's return from the South Seas. The next few years were dominated by the crisis of American independence, which made new colonial ventures unlikely, although it was the closing of the old outlet for transported felons in Virginia and Maryland which led Joseph Banks to suggest Botany Bay as a prison site in 1779.[13] Proposals for colonies in New South Wales and Norfolk Island were made by James Matra and Sir George Young in 1783-5, and rejected by the government and the East India Company, despite various commercial and economic incentives pressed by the promoters. As Mollie Gillen and others have argued, the government did not look favourably on New South Wales until driven to do so by its convict crisis of 1786—although that is not to say that they had forgotten the seductive arguments of Matra and Young.[14]

The colony route to Botany Bay, then, is fairly short and on the whole unconvincing. The convict route is both more circuitous and more controversial. Much ink and ingenuity has been spent on tracking down other places to which convicts were sent or might have been sent after 1776. These include the United States once again—for a few shiploads were dumped there, including one from Ireland as late as 1788, after the sailing of the First Fleet; British North America (variously Newfoundland, Hudson's Bay, Quebec, Nova Scotia—the last two of which were reported to have been promised to the city of London as destinations late in 1788),[15] the West Indies and the coast of Honduras, the latter seeming for a time in 1784-5 to be the answer, and the coast of Africa. West Africa had many supporters; but it disposed of criminals as fast as the gallows and at greater cost. Southern Africa was a more likely possibility in 1785-6, and it is possible that Arthur Phillip's designation as commander of the First Fleet originated in outline planning for a penal settlement in either Namibia or the eastern Cape, since he had previously served with the Portuguese navy on convict ships in the south Atlantic. A ship was sent out to Das Voltas Bay, West Africa and returned at the end of July 1786 with discouraging reports of the aridity of the land, an impossible climate and insect infestation. Ministers considered these reports with what seems to have been painstaking desperation, before deciding on the Australian site three weeks later.[16]

Reaching Botany Bay by the convict route does not, unfortunately, mean reaching agreement on the motives for its selection. New South Wales 'was simply the last choice left in a succession of attempts to find a destination to which British convicts could be sent after the American destination had been closed to them'.[17] In this picture, every other

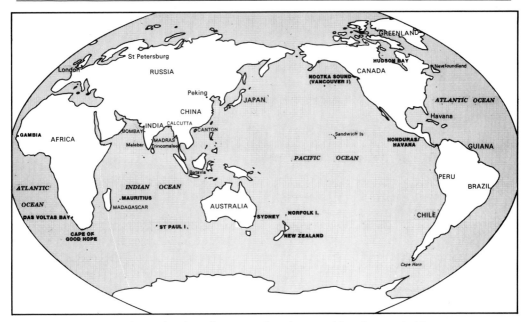

Figure 4: Alternative dumping grounds—sites considered are in bold type

door had clanged shut, and only the one marked 'Australia' was still ajar. This is not necessarily the case. Other doors could still have been forced open had there seemed more to be gained than lost in so doing. British authority might have been imposed on the anarchic Honduras settlements at less cost than was involved in sending several hundred marines to the shores of the Pacific. That it was not thought worth doing would seem to imply that there was no likely gain, no improvement in the Honduras timber trade, to be expected in return. If the aim was to send convicts to some place whence return would be difficult, why not face the likely opposition of the Hudson's Bay Company and ship them to the Arctic? If the overriding need was to be rid of them, why not West Africa, with its attendant and punitive horrors? The objection to West Africa had been not so much its nastiness, although that was a comforting theme for humanitarians, as its sheer inefficiency. Thus in retreating to New South Wales, it seems reasonable to expect that ministers comforted themselves with hopes of some positive advantages in their choice, for New South Wales was not without problems of its own, chiefly of distance and lack of detailed information. Or is that a 'must have' argument? Even Gillen is not free of 'must have's. Despite long-established evidence that Pitt's government was actively concerned with the promotion of British trade, she asserts as a general principle of past and present affairs, that governments 'are not renowned for foresight'. This causes her some difficulty when she reveals—and a most interesting fact it is—that as early as January 1786 ministers were seeking estimates of the cost of sending felons to New South Wales. Despite the lack of ministerial foresight this move was 'clearly a precautionary reserve plan in case Das Voltas failed'.[18] But 'clearly' is a great 'must have' word!

In any case, even if it was accepted that the American and African doors were shut, it does not necessarily mean that the government's choice had narrowed to the east coast of New South Wales. At most, the argument implies that the government's choice was limited to the south-west Pacific. The question, therefore, should not be simply why were convicts

41

sent to Australia, but rather why they were not sent to New Zealand.[19] Despite the reported ferocity of the Maoris, Cook had favoured colonising the North Island. Moreover, the uncooperativeness of the local population had not inhibited the campaign for a West African site: indeed, it had added to the deterrent horrors of transportation. Why, then, Botany Bay rather than the Thames River area of New Zealand's North Island? One reason was probably the support given to the former by Banks, the country's leading man of science, for Banks was still available to argue for his choice. The selection of an Australian, rather than a New Zealand location seems to argue conclusively against a desire to exploit New Zealand flax or trees as a major motive behind the decision. Moreover Botany Bay made sense as a port of call on a route to China; New Zealand did not.

Three objections arise to this argument. The first is the intuition which detects a 'must have' assertion. It can be combated. Banks had favoured Botany Bay as a place of fertility: the colony would thus quickly become self-sufficient (and so save money, unlike convicts held on hulks at home). If it grew food, it would provide what long-distance sailing ships most needed—fresh meat and vegetables. The second objection, argued by Shaw and still echoed by Frost, is that Phillip's instructions positively forbade the colonists to trade.[20] No one wanted to help criminals escape, and no one planned an Australian settlement as a step towards fostering *Australian* trade. That, however, is very different from seeing the settlement as a useful adjunct to *British* trade, which in that part of the world meant trade carried on by and licensed by the East India Company. The prohibitions in Phillip's instructions were designed to defend the company's monopoly, including its monopoly right to make use of the new colony. Phillip's instructions were drawn up after the arrangements to tender licensed tea ships—clear evidence that the ban on colonial trading was not directed at the East India Company. The third objection to the argument that Botany Bay was chosen as a way station for the China trade is unspoken, but it should not remain so. All too often Australia's place in the world is seen only in terms of Mercator's projection which normally locates Australia in the bottom right-hand corner and implausibly remote from China. This is simply the result of the solution devised by a sixteenth century map maker to the problem of depicting a spherical planet on rectangular pages; but in terms of great circle routes Sydney is not so inconvenient as a port of call between the Cape and Canton. Add the prevailing winds which dictated all routes in the days of sail, and an Australian route to China becomes entirely feasible.

So the argument continues, and will continue, about the motives for the British decision to found the first Australian colony. Perhaps it is necessary to stand back a little and concentrate less on the reasons for choosing Australia and more on a prior assumption—that there is in human affairs something called 'a decision', made at a finite moment by an identifiable person. There must indeed have been a moment at which the decision to send convicts to New South Wales was taken. It may well have been in an office in Whitehall, perhaps with the windows closed to fend off the summer stench from the nearby Thames. It was probably not a particularly solemn moment and, insofar as those who took the decision had anything dominating their minds, it was no doubt the problem of getting rid of the surplus prison population. But to understand how, where and why, the decision must be seen as a wider and more subtle process, one which cannot simply be distilled from existing documentary evidence.

To start, it is reasonable to suppose that the selection of the Australian site was ultimately the decision of the Prime Minister, William Pitt—partly because the documents indicate his involvement, and partly because as head of government it was his ultimate responsibility. The pressures and influences which led to that decision, however, can be examined, through the relationship of four other men who took some part in the process. First there was James Matra, the American who sailed with Cook and thus had some first-hand knowledge of Botany Bay. It was Matra who in August 1783 had adduced the cultivation of flax as a reason for settling New South Wales. It was Matra who—after conversation with Lord Sydney—outlined how convicts might be sent out to start the new colony.[21] Matra lobbied for his ideas between 1783 and 1785 without winning much conviction and then appears to have lost heart: Matra *qua* Matra, then, cannot be pointed to as the man behind the decision in August 1786. Nonetheless, Matra's contribution raises questions for the historian, since he was not only one of the first to link convict transportation to the idea of an Australian settlement (although in this he appealed, fairly enough, to the testimony of Sir Joseph Banks) but also was apparently the pioneer in associating the prospect of a flax supply with the new colony. What, then, was Matra's motive in putting forward these arguments? The answer is fairly straightforward, and eminently creditable to the man himself. He was an American who had refused to join his countrymen in opting for independence. Many of his friends and associates had been driven from their colonial homes, especially in 1783 when the British finally withdrew from New York, Matra's own home province. Their expulsion from the United States was one of the greatest refugee crises in the history of the English-speaking world. Having visited New South Wales, Matra saw the southern hemisphere as a suitable place of refuge for his countrymen, and naturally enough slanted his arguments to meet the concerns of the men he hoped to persuade: his motives, then, must be sought in American, not Australian, history.

It is easy enough to see how Matra could take on board convict transportation in his pleas for an Australian colony. 'When I conversed with Lord Sydney on this subject it was observed that New South Wales would be a very proper region for the reception of criminals condemned to transportation.'[22] It does not much matter which of the two steered the discussion round to the convict problem: Matra concluded that he could gain a sympathetic hearing from Sydney by combining his crusade for his refugee friends with Sydney's pressing concern to empty the prisons. After all, a convict workforce despatched to Australia would be both a convenience to the loyalists and to the government, combining an act of justice with one of political expediency.

What of Matra's reference to the flax plant? 'I must not omit the mention of a very important article', he wrote in introducing his argument that a New South Wales colony could cultivate the New Zealand flax plant.[23] The formulation suggests an afterthought, a special plea designed to bolster a case made on other grounds. At whom might it have been directed? The answer perhaps lies in Evan Nepean and the Bridport connection. The former has been vividly brought to life by Alan Frost;[24] the latter may be one of the missing pieces in the founding of Australia. Nepean was indeed a remarkable man. The son of a shipwright, he rose to influential office despite his lack of aristocratic connection. Slow, taciturn, immensely hard working, he was one of Pitt's most trusted administrative colleagues. As Undersecretary of State for the Home Office, he was in effect a senior public servant and certainly in far more day-to-day control of business than the mildly ineffectual minister, Lord Sydney. In the eighteenth century no definite distinction existed between top public servants and junior ministers, and Nepean also sat in parliament. He was MP for Bridport, the small coastal town two miles from his country home at Loders in Dorset. Just as Sheffield was synonymous with knives, so Bridport was a byword for rope-making:

the hangman's noose was nicknamed 'the Bridport dagger'. The broad streets of the small town were designed to twist and wind cordage, and the surrounding villages were also engaged in the trade. It would make sense for Matra to have inserted his reference to the strength of ropes made from New Zealand flax to gain Nepean's interest in the settlement of New South Wales. Of course, a man of that time did not have to be MP for Bridport to understand the strategic importance of flax, but the Bridport connection probably explains why Matra felt that Nepean would be interested in his proposal. There can be little doubt that the flax argument would appeal widely, but when Matra first introduced it, it may well have been aimed at just one man.

Now to the role played by two other men, Lord Sydney and George III: in different ways, the decision to go to New South Wales required their acquiescence. Sydney was the Home Secretary. He was not a particularly effective minister, nor one held high in Pitt's esteem, but he did concern himself over several years with the problem of the convicts, and it was his signature which was appended to the letter of 18 August announcing the New South Wales project. That Pitt above and Nepean below had the real charge of the business should not disguise the fact that Sydney was a consenting party in the decision. Nor should the King be forgotten. George III was not the cypher that subsequent monarchs proved to be. With Pitt as Prime Minister, he did not attempt to be in overall charge of business, but he was capable of bursts of activity and of busying himself with particular problems. In opening parliament in January 1787, George referred baldly to the First Fleet project:

> A plan has been formed, by my direction, for transporting a number of convicts; in order to remove the inconvenience which arose from the crowded state of the gaols in different parts of the kingdom . . .[25]

What should be made of those three words, 'by my direction'? All government actions in a monarchy are done by royal direction—why was this one singled out with a redundant phrase? Was it a signal that the King himself was vitally involved in the plan to settle New South Wales? The evidence, as it happens, so far as the destination is concerned, is discouraging. The speech made no mention of the advantages of an Australian colony, but simply alluded to the crowded prisons. A search in the Royal Archives has established that no submission to the King outlining the proposal for a new settlement survives from that period. Nor is there any indication of discussion with ministers in the days before the decision was made: published court circulars show that the King was out of London on a holiday tour except for a brief visit, indeed on the 18th, but mainly for the purpose of a formal diplomatic reception.[26]

Nonetheless, a project of such breathtaking magnitude could hardly have been launched without the King's general acquiescence, and there is ample evidence to indicate that in August 1786 George III was very concerned about convicts and penal policy, and concerned for a very direct and personal reason. On the morning of 2 August, as the King descended from his carriage at St James's, a mad woman rushed at him with a knife, although she failed to strike home. The modern world has become sadly inured to political assassination and it is not easy to recall the traumatic horror which this incident aroused. Assassination seemed a foreign weapon, associated in the folk memory with the murder of William the Silent in Holland and the dastardly plot by Guy Fawkes to blow up James I, which was still marked by bonfires every November. The poor relationship between the King and his heir, the Prince of Wales, added to the possible political significance of the attack, although the woman herself was quickly found to be deranged, crossed in love and convinced that she was the rightful queen of England. Sydney himself took the lead in questioning her—an unusual task for a senior minister—and she was eventually subjected to a five-hour grilling by the entire Cabinet, reinforced by no less a personage than the Archbishop of Canterbury, and finally sent to an asylum.[27]

Among the founders of Australia, a small niche should be found for mad Margaret Nicholson, for there is nothing like an attack on royalty to convince those in authority that extreme steps are necessary to curb the rising tide of crime. The King withdrew to Lord Harcourt's country house in Oxfordshire, where he was evidently much concerned about the state of the prisons. He had his host carry out enquiries at the local gaol, partly because he wanted to mark his providential escape by issuing a royal pardon to suitably reformed felons, and partly because he was interested in an experiment by the local magistrates to subject criminals to close confinement with hard labour, rather than leave them to rot as was the normal practice. The King was certainly in the mood to accept a ministerial plan which would empty the prisons and combine hard labour with the hope of reformation. But would that acceptance extend to a plan for a new convict settlement so far away?

Another set of concerns, both for Sydney and the King, intersected here. In the week in which the decision to go to Australia was taken, Sydney had an interview with the chargé d'affaires of the newly independent United States—perhaps sounding him out on the possibility that the Americans would change their mind about taking convicts[28] Throughout that week he studied the gloomy reports about Das Voltas Bay. On the Wednesday, he received a British officer just back from Mauritius where an agreement had been patched up to defuse a developing Anglo-French tussle in India. At 3.15 pm Sydney sent an urgent report to the King, who was at Windsor, and within three hours George III was sending an express reply, welcoming the news but indicating concern at the ease with which the French could convert commercial vessels in the east into warships.[29] Both Sydney and the King were thus in a frame of mind to accept a penal settlement in New South Wales as a reinforcement of British strategic interests in eastern waters.

To assess the decision to settle New South Wales, it is also necessary to understand not only the arguments put forward but the nature of a decision itself. Most people will have observed this in the exercise of buying a house. First, there is the resolve to tackle a perhaps long-contemplated move. Then lists are made of ideal features and locations. But invariably the final selection satisfies few, maybe none, of these desiderata. The process of making a decision tends to take over, and the pressure to finish the business one way or another becomes paramount over finding an ideal choice. As with dream-homes, so—we may fairly conclude—with colonies. By August 1786, British ministers had reached the first stage: they were publicly committed and under political pressure to take some step to transport convicts. A number of promising alternatives in 1785-6 had collapsed, leaving them obliged to be seen to act decisively. Various promoters had urged colonisation in Australia, usually coupling their own arguments with other incentives they hoped would appeal to the government.

Eventually all these elements came together, and half-remembered gambits were seized upon as rationalisations, arguments for founding a colony which a decade later would be discredited and forgotten. All notions of rational explanation need not be abandoned but it should be recognised that once particular pressures required a decision, layers of incentive combined in different ways and in different minds to shape the decision to go to New South Wales. A survey of comments on New South Wales made by a London newspaper, the *Daily Universal Register,* just before the sailing of the First Fleet in May 1787 would indicate that an alternative sea route to China was seen as the major motive behind the new settlement,[30] although what appeared in the press was not necessarily a guide to government motives. However, in late 1786 there was concern about Britain's relations with the Dutch, who had the power to block the existing sea route to China through the East Indies.[31] A year later, in October 1787, when there seemed danger of a rupture with Russia instead, which would break off the main supply of Baltic flax to Britain, the same newspaper announced that there was nothing to fear, since the new colony would soon supply Britain with an altogether superior article.[32]

The truth seems to be that all these arguments were present in the minds of the men who selected the Australian site. The government would not have selected New South Wales if it had not felt obliged to dispose of a sizeable part of the prison population. It would not have selected New South Wales, rather than elsewhere, had the decision not been capable of presentation in some advantageous form. It would probably not have selected New South Wales if the timetable for decision had not forced the matter to a head in mid August 1786.

*   *   *

In January 1788 an expedition containing over one thousand people, two-thirds of them convicts, arrived to settle at a place on the thinly inhabited east coast of Australia. What was the real significance of this event? Historical facts do not have significance in isolation; significance must be measured, surely, by noting that Australia was settled at that time and in that way, rather than in some other manner or not at all. One may start with the point that the eastern Australian coast had been visited only once before by Europeans. This unavoidably meant that little was known about the coast, with the exception of the few points where Cook had called, and also that considerable reliance had to be placed upon the testimony of Sir Joseph Banks. In the event, his view of the fertility of Botany Bay proved either wrong, or was unperceived by Phillip, who shifted his headquarters, at a few days' notice, to drier ground on Port Jackson. Because there was only one, highly incomplete, report available in London on Australia's east coast, Phillip was limited to a small area for his landing, and forced to make a quick decision. He could not foresee that the camp he established on the Tank Stream would grow into a city with twice the population of the London he knew, but it is hard to avoid the conclusion that Sydney was in many respects an unfortunate choice, and certainly one which helped shape the subsequent growth of eastern Australia. Of course Port Jackson was a good harbour, 'in which a thousand sail of the line may ride in the most perfect security', but other east coast harbours would have been just as convenient for the small ships of the time, one thousand of which were hardly likely to arrive at once. The major disadvantage of Sydney was that it was hemmed in to the west by mountains, a circumstance which has created a wholly unnecessary aura of the heroic about their crossing in 1813: routes to the south-west, for instance, were much less dramatically barred.

Suppose the settlement had not been made in 1788, but at some later stage. More would have become known about the east coast: La Pérouse, after all, was hard on Phillip's heels in 1788. The wars might have encouraged more detailed naval exploration, and at least some whaling, even if illegal, would have started in Australian waters. An occasional ship would have been shipwrecked, and information about the interior obtained from survivors. Coastal exploration and some inland travel would probably have established that the Hunter River was the best way into a pastoral interior (although, remarkably, it did go undiscovered for seven years after the settlement of Port Jackson) and the chief city of eastern Australia might well have taken root further north, perhaps on the equally magnificent Port Stephens. Such a city would have found it correspondingly harder to have rivalled Melbourne in controlling the trade of the Riverina, but would have been better placed to have withstood or limited geographically the northern separatist movement which established Queensland. Thus the whole process of settlement in eastern Australia might have run along different lines, the political boundaries could have been different, and maybe federation harder to achieve as a greater Victoria faced a more tropical New South Wales.

What of the significance of the fact that most of the original settlers were English? It certainly did not mean that Australia was endowed, in the 1780s, with democratic institutions—any more than Britain was—but it did mean that the colony was heir to a set of legal and constitutional traditions which—even in its unpromising pioneer form as a prison—could be developed along democratic lines. Of course, the Englishness of the colony was quickly modified by the arrival of Irish convicts, with the corresponding cleavage of religion and national identity. However, the convicts did share a common language, for the most disturbed parts of Ireland in the 1798 rising were English-speaking counties, like Wexford and Antrim. This affinity of language with each other was coupled with a continuing affinity of language with the home country: a colony founded after the invention of printing was much more likely to maintain a standard form of its home language— unlike medieval colonists like the Anglo-Saxons in England or the Norsemen in Iceland, who evolved distinct languages of their own. (The emergence of Afrikaans in South Africa is a special case, involving the deliberate fostering of distinct forms. It has not happened to the French in Canada).

This in turn again raises the significance of the date, 1788. Does it matter that any part of Australia has an eighteenth century origin? To most of the southern and western sections of the continent, it may seem to matter very little. In any case there was a time-lag in the transmission of fashions and ideas to the colonies which in effect extends the eighteenth century in Australia almost to 1840: some of the country's finest 'Georgian' architecture dates from the Regency and afterwards. Since New South Wales was not visited until 1770, after which Britain was engulfed by a decade of colonial problems in America, it is hardly likely that any settlement could have been made earlier—certainly not by Britain. Yet the possibility that some foothold might have been established by another European power, probably the French or Dutch, ought not to be ruled out. Australia is so often thought of as 'a nation for a continent and a continent for a nation' that the very remarkable fact that it fell, entire, to one distant power tends to be overlooked. In all probability, any such settlement would have remained a tiny enclave, like the five French towns in India, since only Britain had the naval supremacy, emigrant population and capital surplus to sustain large-scale colonisation. Nowadays the foreign foothold would probably be a pleasantly exotic place to go for a holiday, like New Caledonia, or the little part-French town of Akoroa in New Zealand. Then again, East Timor may remind us that colonial enclaves can mean political difficulty, and even New Caledonia, hundreds of miles out to sea, was a disturbing neighbour for much of the last century. In the 1980s Australia again became uneasily aware of this colonial problem on its doorstep. Of course, a single British settlement at Port Jackson did not in itself engross the whole continent: it was forty years before sovereignty was claimed over the western half, and probably to forestall the French. If anything, the First Fleet, followed by La Pérouse, might have stimulated a rival settlement. In that case, the significance of the date is not so much that it was 1788, as that it was one year before 1789, when the outbreak of the French Revolution fully occupied that nation's attention.

The year 1788 was part of a significant transitional period, when British opinion was turning against non-white slavery, but had not yet become disgusted by convictism. Phillip was determined not to introduce slaves from the Pacific Islands, nor did he need to. By contrast, post-1815 colonies had as little to do with convictism as possible, although transportation continued, more or less by inertia, to the older penal settlements until the mid nineteenth century. Thus the question, 'what is significant about 1788?' widens into a much more intangible riddle, 'does it matter that Australia was founded by convicts?' Some might point to elements of authoritarianism in modern Australian bureaucratic government as the legacy of days when officials had power to flog the public, but the same qualities can be traced in New Zealand, British Columbia and South Africa, and must owe more to frontier life than to the status of the population. In one respect, however, the predominantly convict origins of New South Wales can be seen as significant, and that is in the establishment and preservation of a 'white Australia' throughout the nineteenth century. Less than one-fifth of the first settlers were women, and there remained a massive imbalance between the sexes throughout the early decades of New South Wales. The male settlers were almost all subject either to prison or military discipline, without which their sexual behaviour could not have been controlled. Hundreds of free men would surely have imported women from the islands, establishing a mixed-blood community. This might have led to greater racial tensions with the more sexually balanced influx of free British migrants in the second half of the nineteenth century (as with the coloureds of South Africa), or perhaps alternatively to some modification of the rhetoric of 'Britishness' which underlay the emerging sense of Australian identity by the early twentieth century.

The size of the First Fleet is also of more significance than the cheerfully innumerate historical profession has recognised. Not all of the estimated 1350 arrivals stayed, but the population of the colony in its first year (1024) was upwards of ten times the 102 Pilgrim Fathers whom the *Mayflower* had carried to America in 1620. It was also as large if not larger than any other initial settlement in Australia or New Zealand (and the fact that it was planned for 750 convicts from the outset does add considerable weight to the 'convict dumping' theory).

What, then, is the significance of this large number of arrivals? It helps to explain why Phillip abandoned Botany Bay for Port Jackson: Banks probably thought of a much smaller settlement when he urged the bay, but Phillip found that its low ground did not provide enough drinking water for the numbers under his command. The size of the colony also helps to account for its early problems: one hundred people can improvise with a failure in basic supplies better than a thousand. They can also more effectively ensure that their latrines and their drinking water are kept apart, and epidemics reduced to a minimum, a consideration when the sickly Second and Third Fleeters turned the infant camps into an instant town. The disorganisation and shortages which ensued not only underlined the already omnipotent role of government, but placed its resources disproportionately in the hands of the officer corps, thus beginning the Australian tradition by which powerful private interests demand government support but denounce government control. The size of the population also tends to explain the inertia of its settlement pattern. A smaller, more tentative expedition, could have been shifted to a more suitable location, like the first Port Phillip convict settlement, or removed altogether—like the later 'limpet port' on Melville Island (described in later chapters). New South Wales remained, and Sydney grew, partly because its initial size conferred upon both a form of instant permanence.

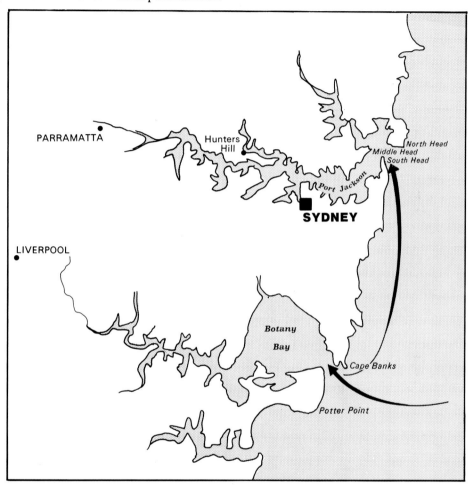

Figure 5: 'Not Botany Bay'—the initial choice—but Port Jackson

The last issue which calls for comment is the thinly inhabited coastline. The size and timing of the First Fleet must surely have been traumatic to the Aboriginal peoples who lived around Port Jackson. There had been only one fleeting contact eighteen years before, and suddenly without warning 1350 white people—not to mention La Pérouse and his men—arrived out of nowhere, disciplined in their organisation, armed with superior weapons and with ominously firm intentions to stay. The effect would have been similar to that of a Martian invasion on the world today. The tribes lost a large area of their hunting grounds on the south side of Port Jackson (while the settlers, ironically, were too numerous to subsist on the available game) and it may well be that they also suffered from

49

over-fishing by the newcomers. The failure of the First Fleeters to develop an effective fishery is a subject which cries out for study, but it does seem that the bumper hauls caught in Botany Bay and Port Jackson in January and February 1788 reduced the supplies available to native fishermen, a connection noted by Phillip as early as July of that year.[33] Within a few months the local Aboriginal population had declined, in European eyes, from the proud nobility which Phillip had saluted in the naming of Manly Cove to wretched remnants of sick and hungry savages. With regard to the age-old Australian continent, we rightly think of the first white colony as a kitten's paw of a touch, barely noticed by the abiding earth. In terms of the impact upon the age-old local population, it was a clenched fist which delivered a shattering blow.[34]

This point may be underlined by asking how Aboriginals might have adjusted to a slower and slighter process of contact with Europeans—the occasional exploring expedition, some shipwrecks, perhaps some timber-cutting settlements and a few refugees from whalers, involving smaller numbers of white men in non-military organisations. The balance of force between the sides would have been more equal, especially as Aboriginals proved in other parts of the continent that they could play off knowledge of terrain against superior weaponry. The ravages of European bacteria might have been less pronounced if contact had been made with fewer people over a wider area and a longer period. Food supplies would have been less threatened. It is even possible that in some areas, Aboriginal technology and society would have had time to make its own compromises with the new ways. Maoris in the northern part of New Zealand quickly adopted gun warfare (with devastating results) and similar though more complex pressures probably underlay the military revolutions in Africa which culminated in the rise of the Zulu empire. Instead of being a figure of sad fun, Bennelong today might hold a place alongside South Africa's Shaka or New Zealand's Hongi as an innovative warrior leader. Whether this could have happened is, of course, a might-have-been. What seems certain is that the size, organisation and timing of the First Fleet ensured that it did not.

*   *   *

New South Wales was founded for a mixture of motives and in a welter of rationalisations which can probably never be fully analysed. The need to empty the prisons compelled a decision for transportation, but the circumstances of August 1786 could in themselves do no more than incline ministers towards selecting New South Wales, since neither its availability nor the non-availability of alternative sites can be regarded as immutable qualities. Some balance of perceived problems in alternative sites and comforting optimism about the possible advantages of New South Wales led to the selection of the Australian outlet, but the nature of that balance may not have been entirely clear to those who found themselves taking the decision, let alone capable of clarification by historians two hundred years later. The timing of the new settlement may be of significance to modern Australia in endowing the country with a mixed legacy of the brutalities and decencies of late eighteenth-century Europe. It is probably largely responsible for the continent's single language and its political structure. Its size and suddenness help to explain the location of the country's largest city, and to account both for its early struggle to survive and for its virtual destruction of local Aboriginal society. Thus, a decision taken two hundred years ago for reasons which still remain obscure can be regarded as having exercised a considerable and continuing influence on the shaping of modern Australia.

Notes

[1] The articles referred to below are collected (except where noted) in Martin, Ged, (ed.) *The Founding of Australia: the Argument about Australia's Origins*, (hereafter cited as 'F. of A.'), (Sydney, 1978 and 1981). The 1981 revised edition has been used in all references).

[2] Gillen, Mollie. 'The Botany Bay Decision, 1786: Convicts, not Empire', *E.H.R.*, ccclxxxii, 1982, pp.740-66. Mackay, David. *A Place of Exile: The European Settlement of New South Wales*, (Oxford, 1985). Abbott, G.J. 'The Botany Bay Decision', *J.A.S.*, May, 1985.

[3] Dallas, K.M. *Trading Post or Penal Colony*, (Richmond & Sons, Tasmania, 1969).

[4] Steven, Margaret. *Trade Tactics & Territory: Britain in the Pacific 1783-1823*, (Melbourne, 1983).

[5] Clark, C.M.H. *A History of Australia: I, From the Earliest Times to the Age of Macquarie*, (Melbourne, 1962), pp.26-9.

[6] Fry, H.T. 'Cathay and the Way Thither', 'F. of A.', pp.136-49.

[7] Blainey, G. *The Tyranny of Distance*, (Melbourne, first ed., 1966); 'F. of A.', pp.79-90, (1980), pp.16-33, (1971).

[8] Frost, Alan. *Convicts and Empire: A Naval Question 1776-1871*, (Melbourne, 1980).

[9] Documents are printed in *H.R.N.S.W.*, Vol. I, Part II, pp.1-22; and in Clark, C.M.H. (ed.), *Select Documents in Australian History*, Sydney, 1950, pp.15-41.

[10] Frost, *op. cit.*, pp.130, 190-1.

[11] 'F. of A.', pp.16-17.

[12] Gillen, *op. cit.*, pp.757-8.

[13] *J.H.C.*, xxxvi, 1-4-1779, pp.310-11.

[14] Gillen, *op.cit.*, esp. p.742, and Mackay.

[15] 'F. of A.', p.160.

[16] Mackay, D.L. 'Direction and Purpose in British Imperial Policy, 1783-1801', *Historical Journal*, xvii, 1974, pp.489-90.

[17] Gillen, *op.cit.*, p.741.

[18] *Ibid.*, pp.741-54.

[19] 'F. of A.', p.245. Shaw had earlier made the same point, *Ibid.*, p.126.

[20] Frost, *op.cit.*, p.190.

[21] 'F. of A.', pp.9-18.

[22] *Ibid.*, p.14, probably written soon after 23-8-1783.

[23] *Ibid.*, p.9, Bolton. G.C. 'The Hollow Conqueror: Flax and the Foundation of Australia', *A.E.H.R.*, Vol. IX, No. 2, 1969.

[24] Frost, *op.cit.*, pp.129-30.

[25] *J.H.C.*, xlii, 23-1-1787, p.4.

[26] I am grateful to Miss Jane Langton of the Royal Archives at Windsor Castle for enabling me to search the correspondence of George III for this period. The surviving correspondence for August 1786, however, is distinctly thin and might suggest the record is incomplete. Court news was published in the *Daily Universal Register*.

[27] Aspinall, A. *The later correspondence of George III*, Vol. 1, (C.U.P., 1962), pp.240-41.

[28] *Daily Universal Register*, 15-8-1786.

[29] Aspinall, *op.cit.*, p.244.

[30] Reprinted in 'F. of A.', pp.169-84.

[31] *Ibid.*, pp.138-84.

[32] *Daily Universal Register*, 18-10-1787.

[33] *H.R.N.S.W.*, i(ii), pp.177-8.

[34] Butlin, N.G. *Our Initial Aggression*, (Allen & Unwin, 1983).

Chapter III

Sydney: A Southern Emporium

Brian Fletcher

Between 1788 and 1821, Sydney was the capital of a colony that served a unique purpose as the dumping ground for British convicts. Whatever the reasons underlying the decision to despatch the first fleet, the fact is that its human cargo was composed exclusively of convicts and their gaolers. Thereafter, a steady trickle of felons, increasing to a rapid stream after 1815, flowed into Port Jackson. Their presence affected every facet of life both in New South Wales as a whole and in its principal town. Yet, it would be misleading to imagine that no other influences were at work during this period. The new settlement was by no means static and although in origin a prison it had by 1821 developed beyond this state. Some of the attributes of a free society were present from the outset in the decision of the British government to make provision for ex-convicts and migrants to own grants of land. The subsequent emergence of a private enterprise economy in New South Wales had significant consequences for Sydney. The township grew steadily and, while retaining some of its original characteristics, acquired additional dimensions that made it more than the mere headquarters of a gaol.[1]

Pitt's government was responsible for selecting New South Wales as the site for a penal colony, but it was Governor Phillip who fixed the location of the capital. His practical mind was quick to perceive the inadequacies of Botany Bay where he had been instructed to land the first fleeters. On 21 January 1788 he took a small party to examine Port Jackson and there found 'a noble and capacious harbour, equal if not superior to any yet known to the world'.[2] One of the coves possessed what Botany Bay lacked, namely a stream of water for drinking purposes, and here colonisation began. On 26 January the convicts were landed after a ceremony on the preceding evening when the Union Jack had been unfurled, shots fired by the marines in salute and a toast to the Crown, the Royal Family and the success of the new colony, drunk by the officers.[3] For some months there was confusion about whether the locality had an official name. According to Surgeon White, the governor had intended to provide one on 4 June 1788 when he nominated 'the district which he had taken possession of, Cumberland County'. Unexpected difficulties 'in clearing the ground and from a want of artificers', however, prevented him from laying 'the first stone' for the township on this occasion. White believed that Albion was the preferred name and in July, Daniel Southwell advanced the same opinion. 'Whether the name is yet determined on I cannot tell', he informed his wife, 'but have heard Albion mentioned'.[4] In fact, Phillip had from the outset decided that the cove should be called after the Secretary of State for Home and Colonial Affairs. He made this clear in his first despatch of 15 May 1788 which was headed 'Sydney Cove, New South Wales'. Quite abruptly and for no stated reason he abbreviated this to 'Sydney' in a despatch of 14 June 1790 and thereafter the shortened version was used. No public occasion marked any of these developments, which was typical of the aloof, reserved governor. Presumably, word gradually filtered through to the inhabitants. From July, private letters used the heading Sydney Cove instead of Port Jackson, or 'Camp'. That Phillip should have selected this name was understandable given the eighteenth century patronage system, but the lethargic Lord Sydney was scarcely the appropriate person to be commemorated in what was to become a dynamic and bustling metropolis.

Sydney began its existence on the shores of the harbour at what is now the Circular Quay area. Originally, as a sketch by the naval officer William Bradley revealed, it was a mere collection of canvas huts[5] but a map by the convict Francis Fowkes in April 1788 showed some advances.[6] On level ground between Sydney Cove and the adjacent Farm Cove nine acres of land had been cleared and put under cultivation. Between the farm and the water a building, misleadingly described as a 'mansion' was said to be under construction for Phillip's use until a proper government house could be built. Like other officers the governor still occupied temporary accommodation. His hut, together with that of the judge advocate, his aide and the Reverend Richard Johnson, was located on the western shore of Sydney Cove, where there were also a smithy, the governor's garden, a marine guard house and, towards the head of the cove, separate camps for male and female convicts. On the opposite side were strung out the quarters and parade ground for the marines and two more convict encampments. From there, moving towards Maskelyne (later Dawes) Point, were the Bake House, the General Hospital, Lieutenant Ball's house and garden and the observatory that had been built to locate a comet which was supposed to appear in 1789. These buildings were of simple design and construction. The marine guard house was made from the soft timber of the cabbage tree palm and the convict huts were 'still more slight, being composed only of upright posts wattled with slight twigs and plaistered up with clay'.[7] While adequate in warm weather they were scarcely suitable for the wet and colder seasons. Nor could they cater for more than the existing number of colonists and there was every reason to expect the arrival of additional convicts.

Phillip was well aware of this. By July 1788, with the help of Surveyor Alt and Lieutenant Dawes, he had prepared a plan for future development.[8] To the line of buildings along the western side of Sydney Cove he added the site for a church. On an incline, overlooking the cove, he set aside land for the main guard room, the civil and criminal courts and Government House. This last building faced the principal street, to the right of which was the parade grounds. Behind Government House an area was reserved for future development. Careful thought had gone into these arrangements. Phillip situated the principal streets so as 'to admit free circulation of air' and stipulated that each was to be 200 feet wide. He urged his superiors to ensure that when permission was given for town blocks to be issued as grants each should have a frontage of sixty feet and a depth of 150 feet. This would 'preserve uniformity in the buildings, [and] prevent narrow streets and the many inconveniences which the increase of inhabitants would otherwise occasion hereafter'.[9] Already, clay suitable for making bricks and a tree, pine-like in appearance with timber resembling that of the English oak, had been found thus making more durable structures feasible.

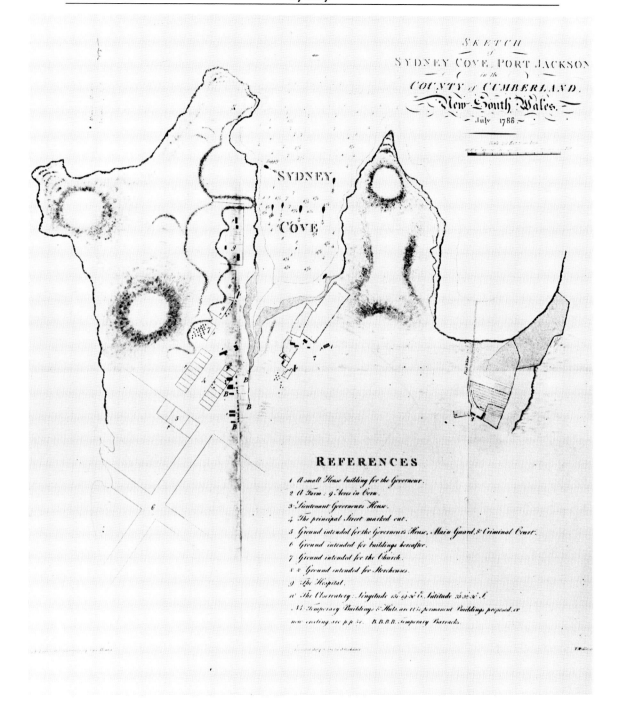

Figure 6: First settlement at Sydney Cove, 1788. Drawn from an engraving in the National Library

Phillip's intentions were only partly fulfilled during his term as governor. A map of December 1792 throws interesting light on what had been achieved by the time of his departure.[10] The buildings near the mouth of the cove included a prison, a barracks and a new storehouse. At the head of the cove, marine barracks and convict huts faced each other on either side of the Tank Stream over which two bridges had been constructed. Between the convict huts and the cove lay the workshops and beyond those, at the point where present-day Phillip and Bridge Streets join, Government House had been constructed and the government domain had been marked out by means of a ditch. Bricks were now being produced in substantial numbers at Brickfield Hill and stone was also being quarried. As a result many of the buildings had taken on a more permanent appearance, although the lack of limestone necessitated the use of clay as a bonding agent and this could not support walls higher than twelve feet. Many of the old buildings remained and some of the more recent ones were of wood, whitewashed with pipe clay. Phillip, however, was convinced that they would last. His own house, located on a different site to that originally chosen, contained twice the rooms he had intended and was sufficiently well built to stand 'for a great number of years'.[11] The changes in this building were paralleled by those made in others. The line of the main street now ran directly from the head of Sydney Cove to the brickfields and a number of sites had been moved to fresh positions. Sydney was not quite as the governor had planned, possibly because closer acquaintance with the landform had shown the original concept to be impractical. Development was also less than Phillip had anticipated.

The limited early progress of Sydney was largely a consequence of the slow development of the colony. By December 1792 the total population was still only a little over three thousand. The convicts had proved unwilling workers and in the early years were forced by acute food shortages to exist on inadequate rations that reduced their ability to engage in manual labour. Since practically all tasks had to be carried out by hand, the construction of roads and buildings was necessarily impeded. Moreover, the development of Sydney was influenced by the fact that it was the economic centre of the colony only during the early months of its existence. The soil near Farm Cove proved unsuited to agriculture and, following the discovery of better soil further inland, Phillip established a settlement at Rose Hill in November 1788. Nearby, he laid out the township of Parramatta around a main street, 205 feet wide and a mile long, 'commencing near the landing place, and running in a direction west, to the foot of the rising ground named Rose Hill', where a house was built for the governor.[12]

On either side of the street huts and public buildings were constructed for the convicts and marine detachment. By the end of 1792 a small but flourishing township had emerged to provide accommodation for the military garrison and the men employed on the government farm, and services for the small number of private settlers who occupied land grants in the vicinity. Sydney remained the headquarters of the colony but its population was less than that of Parramatta and it was not to regain a leading position until after the turn of the century.

During the eight years after 1792, when the colony was ruled first by the military and then by Governor Hunter, Parramatta continued to expand as the surrounding area attracted increasing numbers of farmers. In 1794, Lieutenant Governor Grose opened a new region on the banks of the river Hawkesbury some twenty miles to the north west. Pioneered by a small group of settlers led by the emancipist and former Parramatta farmer, James Ruse, this area, with its rich alluvial soil quickly attracted emancipists and

Figure 7: Plan of Parramatta. Inset is a map of the County of Cumberland. From *Baker's Australian Atlas* (Courtesy of the Mitchell Library, State Library of New South Wales)

Figure 8: Hunter's map of the Sydney settlement, 1796 (*Historical records of New South Wales* vol. II)

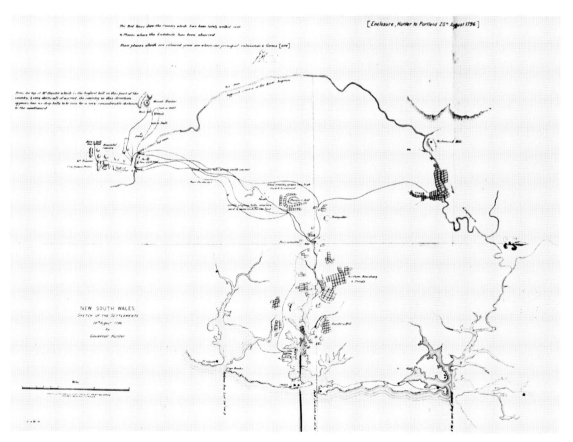

other smallholders.[13] So productive was the land that the district supplanted Parramatta as the colony's main food producing area. A township, known originally as Green Hills and later as Windsor, was established near the junction of South Creek and the Hawkesbury river. Located along the banks of the river on the only ridge that was above flood level, it acted as a service area for the surrounding district and contained quarters for the convicts and military, a storehouse and other necessary buildings.[14]

The spread of settlement and the emergence of Parramatta and Windsor necessarily affected the growth of Sydney. Both were located within twenty miles of the capital and although their potential was more restricted than that of Sydney they did in the short run retard the latter's development. By 1800 three towns existed to serve the needs of a population that amounted to only 4936.[15] The majority of colonists lived outside the Sydney region and had little immediate contact with the capital. Nevertheless Sydney did not stagnate. Some of the newly arrived convicts remained there and the nearby Cooks River and Georges River area attracted private settlers for whom Sydney was their main centre. It was from here that they obtained supplies and also sent their produce for sale at the market. Moreover, each year saw additional convicts in all parts of the colony complete their sentences and a proportion of these chose to live in the capital. New houses were constructed and the centre of population began to move away from the Cove and towards Brickfield Hill. This process was furthered by Lieutenant Governor Grose who erected huts along the main street for his soldiers. By December 1793, one hundred and sixty had been completed. They were mainly made of timber with shingled roofs, but 'upwards of fourteen hundred bricks' were allowed for a chimney and floor. In addition, five barracks had been constructed, two of which were for the officers. This reflected Grose's concern for the well-being of his troops who had hitherto been poorly accommodated. The lieutenant governor also improved the Parramatta road and, to make travel safer, encouraged settlement along its route. He was less forthcoming when the Reverend Richard Johnson sought assistance in building a church. As yet none existed, much to the amazement of a visiting Roman Catholic priest at whose instance Johnson was said to have approached Grose. When refused, Johnson seized the initiative and on 10 June set convicts to work on a thatched building of 'strong posts, wattle and plaster' near the corner of present-day Hunter and Bligh Streets. It was completed within six weeks and the first service was held on 25 July 1793.[16]

Despite Phillip's hopes, most of the buildings were still made of material that was unlikely to last. Governor Hunter, who arrived in September 1795, endeavoured to improve matters. Among his more important contributions to the development of Sydney was the construction of better buildings. He replaced the surgeons' 'wretched huts' with 'a perfect suite of barracks, built of brick' and erected new barracks for military officers. When Johnson's church was burnt down on 1 October 1798, he laid the foundation for a stone structure which was named after the first governor. It was built on a site opposite the present church and completed in 1810. He also devoted considerable attention to buildings of public utility. There had long been a need for a power-driven mill to replace the hand-driven machine that had been constructed in 1793 by a former convict, John Baughan. Not until September 1795 did the parts of a windmill arrive and in June 1796 an Irish convict, 'rough and uncouth in his manners' but with the necessary expertise, began a tower on a hill overlooking the western side of Sydney Cove.[17] This, and a second stone mill, were put into operation under Hunter. Located on the skyline they were later supplemented by the other windmills which formed a distinctive feature of Sydney. The appearance of the town was also enhanced by the construction of a square brick tower on the brow of Church Hill. This housed the clock that had been brought to the colony in June 1797, and also served as an observatory. Utilitarian ends influenced the other buildings for which Hunter was responsible, namely, 'a strong double-logged gaol' that was replaced with a stone structure after being burnt down, a brick granary, a military hospital and dispensary and a variety of other lesser structures including some for naval purposes. As a governor, Hunter had serious shortcomings but these were not evident in the services he performed for Sydney.[18]

To outsiders, however, the town left much to be desired. The botanist, George Caley, noted on arrival in 1800 that it 'had more the appearance of a camp than a town, mixed with stumps and dead trees'.[19] Captain James Colnett of the *Glatton* found in September 1803 that 'Every object on shore declared the poverty of the soil'. He described how, 'The buildings called Sydney town was a little relief to the eye. I could compare them to no other than a miserable Portuguese settlement'. Assistant Surgeon Thomson, writing midway through the following year, found nothing worthy of praise.[20] By that stage, Governor King had been in office for over three years. He added to the number of windmills, enlarged Government House, built a tannery, a manufactory for canvas, two bridges over the Tank Stream, a printing office and a guardhouse.[21] Yet, in the history of Sydney, he deserves to be remembered less for his building program than for formulating policies that promoted economic development. A man of vigour and ambition, he sought to diversify the economy and widen the range of activities. He permitted colonists to trade in sandalwood with nearby Pacific Islands, promoted the cedarwood industry on the south coast, took steps to encourage the production of flax, and exported coal to the Cape of Good Hope from the new penal establishment at Newcastle. A friend of Samuel Enderby, head of the British whaling firm, he promoted this industry and helped persuade the East India Company to relax its charter so that whaling vessels could bring goods for sale to the colonists. All this, and the establishment of a government store, designed to help the lesser settlers obtain supplies at moderate rates, gave a boost to the development of commerce. Since 1792 merchant vessels had been arriving from as far afield as Boston and the British settlements in India. In 1798 the Calcutta firm of Campbell, Clarke and Company established a permanent base and its representative, Robert Campbell, became Sydney's first free merchant.[22] His activities and those of others were to expand under King.

As the colony's only port, Sydney was well placed to benefit from these developments. The free settler, George Suttor, predicted in 1800 that:

> Sydney will become the Emporium of the Southern Hemisphere when it has a sufficient population to make it available to commerce, no city in the world has a safer or more extensive harbour, a finer climate, or greater natural resources.[23]

Under King, Bligh and the ensuing rebel administration, Sydney began to develop more rapidly. By this stage the colony as a whole was on a secure footing. Population rose to just over 10,000 by 1810 and although convicts under sentence formed the largest single group, nearly half of the residents catered for themselves. The majority who fell into this category were former convicts who found employment as tradesmen or labourers. But increasing numbers of emancipists had settled on the free grants of land that were made available by the British authorities. They were joined by a sprinkling of migrants and by the officers of the New South Wales Corps who, in 1793, had received permission to farm land on their own behalf. The free and freed population provided a ready market for goods of all kinds and in response to this commercial life and even manufacturing developed in Sydney.[24]

Evidence of this can be seen in the advertising columns of the colony's first newspaper, the *Sydney Gazette*, which was founded in 1803. The name of Robert Campbell, whose wharves and warehouse were located just around from Dawes Point, regularly appeared. So too did those of other free resident merchants such as Garnham Blaxcell who arrived as acting purser on the *Buffalo* in October 1802 and soon established himself as a leading entrepreneur; William Tough, agent for Chace, Chinnery and Company of Madras and James Birnie, agent for Alexander Birnie and Company of London.[25] In addition to these were the more enterprising emancipists such as Simeon Lord, James Underwood, Isaac Nichols and Mary Reibey, all of whom made a mark on the colony. They often owed their start to the officers of the New South Wales Corps who, contrary to government orders, engaged in trade. Partly to avoid exposure, partly because it would have been unseemly for them openly to have acted as traders, they used assigned servants as their agents. The more energetic of these convicts set up businesses of their own after completing their sentences. After 1800 they competed with the officers and in a number of cases established warehouses in Sydney.[26] Not all retailers, however, had been given a start by their employers. Some convicts brought goods with them to the colony and built up capital while under sentence. Others of frugal instinct saved money gained by working outside hours and invested this after completing their sentences. Once they had a house in Sydney there was nothing to stop them trading from it and a number took advantage of this. One such person was J Colles of 34 Back Row East who advertised 'at reduced prices' articles ranging from cotton goods to groceries and toiletries. Others, like Joseph Davis of Pitt's Row, were more specialised. A watch and clock maker, he offered 'fashionable gold and silver watches' and 'a handsome assortment of jewellery, at very moderate prices'. These two advertisements[27] show that there was a trade not only in articles of necessity but also in luxury items for which there was a demand among the better off settlers. Indeed, the range of goods that could be purchased in Sydney was quite remarkable.

By 1810, therefore, Sydney was already becoming a centre for commerce and trade. Private entrepreneurs, besides controlling the retailing industry also engaged in manufacturing. The scope for this form of activity was limited by the lack of raw materials, the primitive state of the economy and the restricted size of the market. Nevertheless, specialised industries that could draw on available skills did emerge. A number of privately owned flour mills were constructed on the Macquarie Street ridge of the town, opposite those owned by the government which were 'on the western ridge near the government granary'.[28] Governor King's attempts to encourage the brewing of beer as a means of promoting grain production and reducing the importation of spirits, resulted in the establishment of several small breweries in Sydney between 1804 and 1809.[29] Boatbuilding was carried on around the harbour and there were a number of tanneries as well as a salt manufactory on the northern shore of Sydney Cove.

The presence of private residents and entrepreneurs in primarily penal Sydney-town created administrative problems for governors. Shortly before leaving the colony, Phillip had issued a plan defining the area to be occupied by the town. Acting on his instructions, the surveyor had traced a line running from the 'Head of the Cove which is to the Westward of Sydney Cove to the Head of Garden Cove'. Within this boundary no land was to be granted or leased, and any houses were 'to remain the property of the Crown'.[30] In issuing this injunction Phillip clearly envisaged this area of Sydney as a place of temporary

residence for convicts, troops and government officials. Their quarters and other necessary structures, such as hospitals, storehouses and workshops were to comprise the only
buildings. As Phillip left before the first free and freed persons demanded the right to
make a livelihood in Sydney, he did not have to deal with the consequences of his policy,
but his successors did and accordingly adopted the practice of issuing temporary leases.
At first this was done on an ad hoc basis, but in June 1801 Governor King promulgated a
General Order allowing five-year leases and laying down conditions of occupancy.[31]
Subsequently he sanctioned a number of fourteen-year leases but insufficient care was
taken to ensure that land thus rented was not required for governmental purposes. His
successor, Governor Bligh, warned occupants that if they constructed buildings it was at
their own risk and announced his intention to recall leases whose location was open to
objection. Several of the leading inhabitants, including John Macarthur, were affected
and Bligh's refusal to offer compensation added fuel to the fire of his growing number of
enemies.[32]

Bligh's actions were depicted as those of an unjust tyrant but, although he could have
handled the matter more diplomatically, justice was on his side and the individuals
involved formed only a small proportion of leaseholders. In any event, he was removed
from office before he could carry out his threat. His rebel successors renewed the leases
of thirty-four tenants and issued 141 leases to new residents.[33] It is unlikely that this was
merely an attempt to win favour among the townsfolk for the bulk of leases were issued
not by Colonel Johnston, who was most in need of support, but by Colonel Paterson who
had no reason to fear anything from the British authorities. More open to question was
the action of Colonel Foveaux, the second of the military administrators. In converting to
grants the leases of several wealthy emancipists, and allowing John Macarthur to exchange
a grant at Parramatta for one at Sydney, Foveaux had alienated land that should have been
kept in the hands of the government.[34]

One of the principal objections to the existing leases was that they discouraged residents from effecting improvements for fear of losing their land when the tenancy expired.
Macquarie, who was concerned at the situation, was advised on arrival that 'in most cases
the private buildings are of a mean and perishable character'. He himself was appalled at
the state of many of the public buildings which:

> Were in a most ruinous state of decay, and the greater number of them in such a state of dilapi-
> dation as to render them incapable of bearing repairs.[35]

The general hospital, warehouses, civil officials' barracks and most of the military barracks, in his opinion, fell into this category. Earlier, Colonel Foveaux had painted a similar
picture, describing how:

> The public buildings of every description [were] in a state of shameful delapidation [sic] or of
> rapid decay. The streets of Sydney were almost impassable, and the principal roads and bridges
> were, if possible, in a still more dangerous and neglected state.[36]

That there was substance in this view can scarcely be disputed. A shortage of labour and
a preoccupation with other issues had prevented King from repairing buildings and Bligh
who drew attention to this fact, held office for too short a period to achieve anything
worthwhile. Some of the older buildings had fallen down and even the stone bridges which
King had built over the Tank Stream and opened on 1 April 1804 were in a bad state.[37]

Even so, it would be misleading to depict Sydney on the eve of Macquarie's long
governorship as a mere collection of decaying structures and ill-kept streets. Foveaux had

placed the 'extension, ornament and improvement of the towns, especially Sydney' among his foremost objectives. He claimed to have effected repairs, constructed a 'new range of brick barracks', and laid the foundation for a new granary and provision store sufficiently close to the water for easier discharge of cargoes from large vessels.[38] Macquarie was impressed and arranged for the granary building to be completed. He also praised Robert Campbell and Simeon Lord for having constructed 'very spacious and elegant houses and warehouses . . . at a very great expense.[39] Meehan's 1809 plan illustrates this progress.

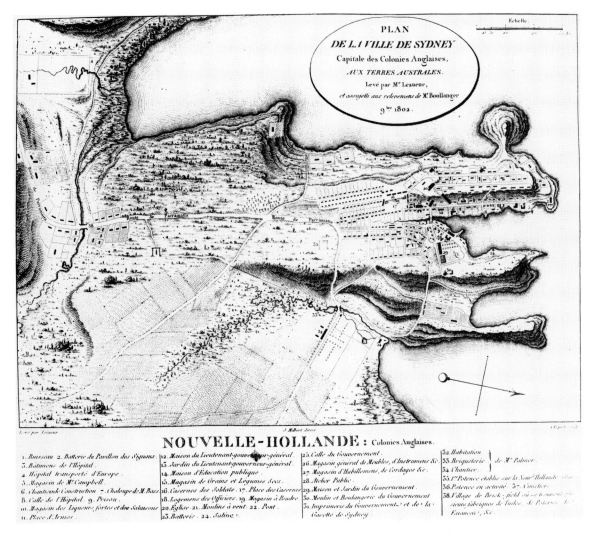

Figure 9: Sydney in 1802, from Mathew Flinders' *Voyage to Terra Australis* (London, 1814) (Courtesy of the Reid Library University of Western Australia)

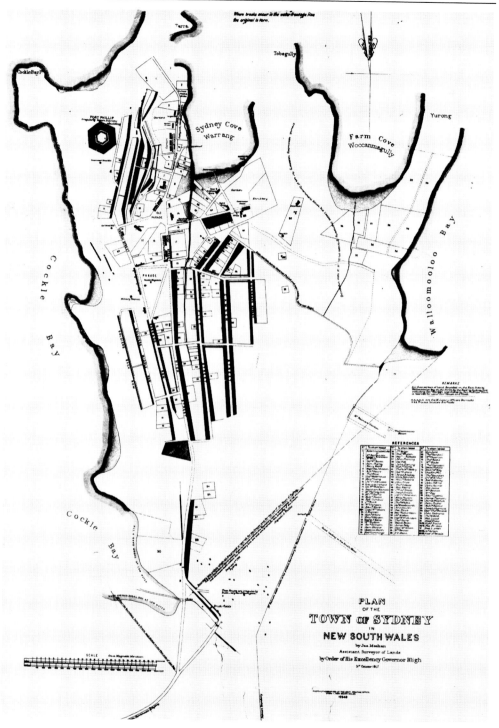

Figure 10: Meehan's map of Sydney, 1809 (Courtesy of the Mitchell Library, State Library of New South Wales)

The most detailed description of Sydney on the eve of Macquarie's accession, that by the emancipist D D Mann, confirmed and enlarged upon this view. He described Lord's stone dwelling as 'by far the most magnificent in the colony' and instanced others such as the imposing brick residence and warehouse of James Underwood, the long brick house belonging to Garnham Blaxcell, and the stone buildings occupied by Isaac Nichols. In the Rocks area he also found 'very comfortable habitations'.[40] Neither the verbal picture which Mann presented, nor the attractive coloured illustrations which illuminated his book, gave any hint of the problems referred to by Foveaux and Macquarie. The paintings, taken from two different angles, reveal an attractive collection of one and two-storeyed buildings, some white, others yellow, with roofs that were either red or grey. The whole group of structures was located on rising land around a busy harbour in which native canoes intermingled with river boats and an overseas vessel. This peaceful setting with its rolling parkland, shrubs and trees was doubtless over-romanticised and unduly Anglicised. Yet Mann, a former government clerk, had lived in Sydney since 1799 and knew much about its development. His *Present Picture* thus provides a caution against assuming that Sydney possessed no redeeming features before it entered the Macquarie era.

To say this is not to underestimate the significance of Macquarie's contribution to the development of Sydney. Earlier governors had taken a largely utilitarian view which was reinforced by limited resources and lack of personnel with architectural or planning skills. Macquarie believed that Sydney was destined to become as 'fine and opulent a town as any one in His Majesty's other foreign Dominions'. He combined a wide vision with a passion for order and symmetry and possessed the strength of character to ensure that his wishes were heeded. After 1816 he enjoyed the services of the emancipist architect, Francis Greenway, who after being transported for forgery in 1814 was allowed to practise as an architect. Macquarie used his services, at first in an advisory capacity and then in March 1816 as the official civil architect and civil engineer. An arrogant, difficult man, Greenway made many enemies and eventually antagonised the governor. Yet he possessed outstanding talents to which a wide variety of edifices bear testimony. Among those in Sydney are the lighthouse overlooking Watson's Bay, the Government House stable, the Hyde Park barracks and St James's Church. Their construction on so ambitious a scale bore testimony to Macquarie's desire to make Sydney a place in which he would long be remembered.[41]

Macquarie's building program was by no means motivated solely by personal considerations. He recognised that improvements were needed and from 1815 was also faced with an unprecedented increase in population. While the Napoleonic Wars continued, convicts arrived in a slow, steady and predictable stream—1908 between 1810 and 1813 and 2265 in the next two years. The situation, however, changed dramatically thereafter and in the first six years of peace the total reached 13,046, an annual average of 2174 as compared to 695 during the preceding six years.[42] Before 1815 most convicts found employment on privately owned properties but so many arrived after that date that Macquarie was forced to keep increasing numbers in government hands, because private settlers could not absorb them. Against his better judgment he expanded public farming and opened a new agricultural settlement at Emu Plains. Yet there were limits to how many could thus be absorbed and large numbers had to be kept in Sydney. Later Macquarie was criticised by Commissioner Bigge for not having dispersed more into the country, but the reality was that, given the employment situation, he had no choice. It was the need to accommodate and provide jobs for new arrivals that explains why so many public works projects were commenced during the second half of his administration. The program was a result more of necessity than of choice.[43]

Even before 1815, however, Macquarie had achieved much. During the first half of his administration he completed the four-storeyed granary that had been started by Foveaux and built a 'new range of excellent barracks capable of containing 250 soldiers' to replace the existing ones which were 'in a most ruinous decayed state'. Additional soldiers were now stationed in the colony and to meet their needs he constructed further barracks as well as a new regimental hospital. Around these buildings he erected a high wall to prevent 'the constant intercourse which at present subsists' between soldiers and populace. 'A good respectable and commodious dwelling house with offices' was built for Judge Advocate Bent whose previous residence had been 'scarcely habitable'. Quarters were also constructed for the chaplain, the commissary, the governor's secretary and the provost marshal, who would otherwise have been given rented accommodation. More noteworthy was the new 'Rum Hospital', built at no cost to the government by Wentworth, Blaxcell and Riley in return for a temporary monopoly over the sale of spirits.[44] This replaced an earlier hospital which was too small and tumbling down.

Although most of these buildings were less architecturally outstanding than those designed by Greenway, they did not lack merit. All were built of brick or stone and were properly roofed with tiles that, like the bricks, were manufactured locally. Particularly impressive was the hospital which, 'being on an airy and elevated situation . . . is rendered a conspicuous and handsome object'. Wentworth included it, along with the public stores and the convict barracks, in his list of buildings 'which would not disgrace the best parts' of London.[45] The hospital was financed privately, but to help meet the expenses of the other buildings Macquarie established a police fund which drew on the proceeds from the duty of three shillings a gallon imposed on imported spirits. This fund was initially used also to finance the improved roads which Macquarie constructed to improve the links between Sydney and other leading centres. Tolls were introduced for this purpose and the proceeds of the police fund were employed in connection not only with Sydney but also other towns.[46]

Macquarie's interest in Sydney extended beyond providing better public buildings. His earliest measures included restoring bridges across the Tank Stream, repairing existing streets and opening new ones. In August 1810 he gave W H Alcock charge of these projects and allocated convict gangs to work under him. Stumps were removed from the main streets which were also widened and given names of more historical significance than those then in use. First to be changed was the name of the street running from Sydney Cove to Brickfields Hill. Over most of its length it had been called High Street, but in the Rocks area it became Sergeant Major's Row. Macquarie called it George Street 'in honour of our revered and gracious Sovereign'. Pitt's Row became Pitt Street after the Prime Minister, and Chapel Row, Castlereagh Street after that leading statesman. Back Row became Elizabeth Street and a new street commemorating the governor was also opened. The royal Dukes of York, Clarence and Kent were remembered in three thoroughfares and there was also a Prince Street. Nor were Macquarie's predecessors forgotten. Phillip, Hunter, King and Bligh were all honoured.[47]

Besides improving and renaming streets, Macquarie made other changes to the town. He moved the market place to a piece of open ground, formerly used in part by the Blaxlands as a stockyard and located at the edge of the residential area. Bounded by

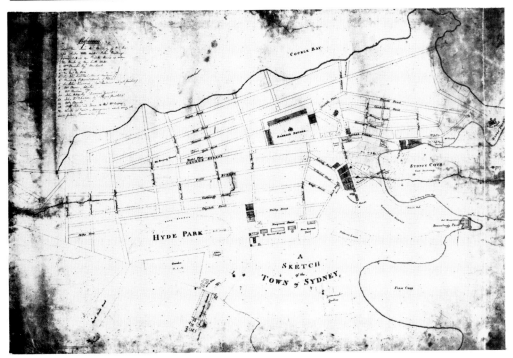

Figure 11: Macquarie's Sydney (Courtesy of the Mitchell Library,
State Library of New South Wales)

George, York and Market Streets, it was linked to a new wharf and had better access than
the old site. Covered buildings were erected, pens installed for animals and a clerk
appointed to maintain supervision and ensure that Macquarie's regulations for the management of the market were heeded. In the interests of public health he employed public
gangs to clear out the stream which provided the water supply and issued orders designed
to reduce the risk of pollution. Animals were not to drink from the stream and no clothes
were to be washed in it.[48] Nor were dogs to roam unattended. Attention was also paid to
the recreational interests of the residents. An area was cleared in front of St Philip's
Church and named Charlotte Square. A second square, this time called after the
governor, was set aside near the domain and a number of derelict buildings were removed
from it. At the southern end of the town the whole of the unoccupied area known variously as 'The Common', 'Exercising Ground', 'Cricket Ground', and 'Race Course'; was
reserved 'for the recreation and amusement of the inhabitants of the town, and as a field
of exercise for the Troops'. Designated Hyde Park it was closed off from the nearby
Brickfields and brickmakers were banned from using any part of it for their trade.[49]

Macquarie was also anxious to encourage improvements in private buildings. He
believed that 'a considerable number of opulent merchants and others' were willing to
construct 'handsome and permanent houses', provided they were given more security of
land tenure. On his own initiative, he permitted Robert Campbell and Simeon Lord, both
of whom already owned impressive residences, to convert their leases into grants. In
informing his superiors of this step, he recommended that a similar concession be
extended 'to all such other persons as are able and willing to erect substantial and hand-

some buildings within the town'.[50] The Secretary of State concurred, provided that land required for public use was not affected. The concession, however, applied only to the wealthy who could carry out adequate improvements and so most residents continued to lack a permanent title to their land. It was not until after Governor Darling arrived that the situation was regularised.[51] Nevertheless, there were indications of greater attention being paid to appearances and there were many homes even on rented land that were well cared for.

Under Macquarie, therefore, Sydney became a more attractive, better regulated and more varied town. This was due not simply to the presence of an enlightened governor but also to the fact that the period was one of substantial economic growth. Admittedly there were seasonal setbacks, resulting from alternate drought and floods, and there was a commercial depression between 1812 and 1814 which adversely affected mercantile interests.[52] Yet in general the decade saw greater advances than ever before and the rate of expansion accelerated after the end of the Napoleonic Wars. In addition to an influx of convicts, peace brought an increase in the number of free immigrants, most of whom possessed capital to invest in the pastoral industry. Each year also saw more convicts complete their sentences, adding to the free population. These developments gave a great boost to farming and grazing, expansion of which pushed settlement into the furthermost parts of the Cumberland Plain and even beyond. This in turn benefited the existing townships and created new ones. Liverpool, which already existed as a service centre for the western regions when Macquarie arrived, was laid out afresh, as was Windsor. Four additional centres, Wilberforce, Pitt Town, Richmond and Castlereagh were founded on the Hawkesbury-Nepean river system.[53] This proliferation of townships did not affect Sydney to the extent that had been the case earlier. The capital was by 1810 sufficiently well established to withstand competition and it attracted a substantial share of new arrivals over the next decade. Additional free people and former convicts became traders and opened businesses in Sydney. Moreover, the importance of the township as a market for produce increased and it was also able to benefit from the greater wealth of the interior. Important too was the development of an export trade, initially in whale oil and seal skins, but later in fine merino wool, the potential of which had been revealed by men like John Macarthur and the Reverend Samuel Marsden. The first exports of wool in 1811 attracted favourable prices even though the quality was indifferent and this, far more than the example set by Macarthur in 1805, encouraged others to begin production for the British market.[54] Each year saw additional quantities despatched and in 1821 the total reached 175,433 lbs. Even more significant, so far as the growth of Sydney was concerned, was the fact that imports also expanded to meet the demands of a colonial population that grew from 10,452 in 1810 to 29,963 in 1821.

It was commerce that gave Sydney its first major boost in the years after 1810 and it was this again which enabled it to forge ahead during the following decade. The commercial depression did drive some merchants out of business, but those who remained put their affairs on a sounder basis. Names such as those of the free men, Richard Brooks, Robert Campbell senior and junior, and Thomas McVitie appeared regularly in the advertising columns of the *Sydney Gazette*. So too did those of the older emancipist firms who were joined by Solomon Levey, Robert and Daniel Cooper and Samuel Terry, the 'Rothschild of Botany Bay'. By 1821 there were more wholesalers, retailers and auction houses than ever before and there was also a variety of butchers, bakers, ropemakers and other specialised shops.[55]

Manufacturing also expanded as existing firms increased their business and new ones were founded. A 'Wood-Screw Manufactory' opened in 1815, while a year later a small factory which made agricultural implements appeared on the scene. In 1811 Simeon Lord, the emancipist, started a hat manufactory in partnership with Francis Williams and Reuben Uther. Subsequently Lord and Williams, who had a long association, began glassmaking and also sought apprentices for weaving, spinning, pottery and dyeing. The firm broke up in 1813 but a year later Lord built a factory at the mouth of the Lachlan Swamps on Botany Bay and was soon employing sixty convicts. He produced shoes, hats, stockings, leather goods and woollen cloth for the government. Milling also expanded and by 1821 the town of Sydney contained eight windmills, two watermills and a steam flour mill. The last was powered by the colony's first steam engine which had been bought by the Scottish-born John Dickson in October 1813. An engineer and millwright, Dickson was given a town grant at Cockle Bay where he established his mill and began operations in 1815.[56]

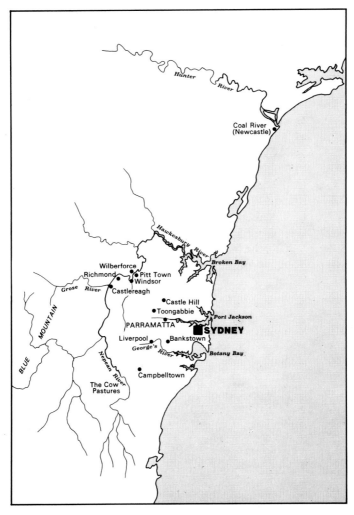

Figure 12: Sydney and its villages, circa 1820

67

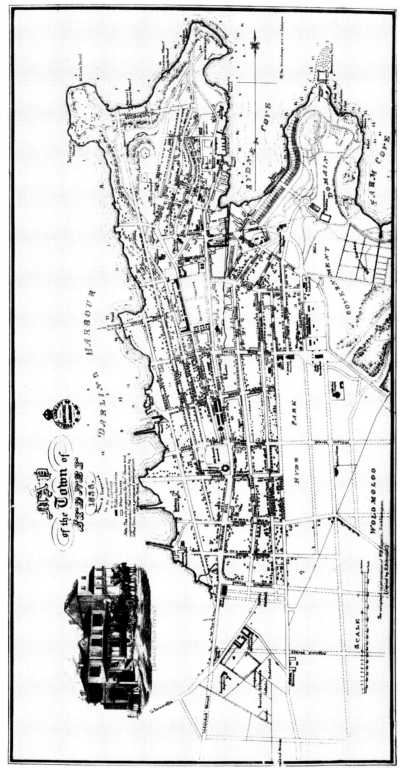

Figure 13: Sydney Town a decade after Macquarie (Courtesy of the Mitchell Library, State Library of New South Wales)

The history of Sydney between 1788 and 1821, therefore, is that of an expanding township whose economic basis continued to diversify. Apart from being the centre of government, it also contained most of the colony's wholesalers, retailers and manufacturers. Moreover, in April 1817 the Bank of New South Wales, which had been founded under Macquarie's auspices, opened its doors for business. Located in Macquarie Place, it marked the beginning of Sydney's history as a financial centre.[57]

But what of social life and conditions in the capital? What developments occurred in this field before 1821? It is difficult to provide accurate details of the number of residents because the estimates provided by contemporaries were often vague and contradictory. One writer stated in September 1798 that the total was 4000, but six years later Surgeon Thompson gave it as 'about 3000'. William Charles Wentworth claimed in 1819 that the 'town does not contain above seven thousand souls', but this was no more than a guess.[58] Another estimate, which at first glance appears to provide an accurate picture, gives a base total in 1790 of 1455 rising to 2397 in 1796 and 2537 by the turn of the century. Numbers then rose gradually to 3163 in 1805 but nearly doubled over the next five years. Under Macquarie the total declined from 6158 in 1810 to 5475 in 1815 and then rose to a peak of 12,079 in 1820. Coghlan is cited as the main source of these figures but there is no indication where he obtained them.[59] Admittedly the governors' returns normally included an entry for 'Sydney', but the term clearly referred both to the town and surrounding districts, which stretched as far as Botany Bay. Residents were obliged to come to Sydney for the periodical muster and no attempt was made to distinguish between them and the town dwellers in the official returns. To the extent that Coghlan drew on these muster records he overstated his case. Making allowance for all this it is probably reasonable to conclude that by 1821 Sydney had a population which was approximately five times larger than when settlement began. This meant that even as late as 1821 the total was little greater than that of a reasonably sized modern country town. Indeed for the whole of its early history Sydney must have possessed much of the atmosphere of such a town. It existed in a colony that drew most of its wealth from the land and had close associations with its surrounds. Farms and farmers impinged on everyday life and the urban was so blended with the rural as to make a clear distinction between the two extremely difficult. At a time when land was a badge of respectability, as well as a source of wealth, many of the leading town dwellers owned country properties. Moreover, there was a regular flow of settlers coming into Sydney bringing goods for sale on the open market or to the commissariat. Some travelled by land but most used the small vessels that plied along the Parramatta River or which came from the Hawkesbury via Broken Bay.

Sydney also attracted numerous overseas visitors. As a port it formed the gateway to the outside world. Convict transports, merchantmen and whalers came regularly as did vessels in need of supplies. There were also from time to time visits from scientific and other expeditions. The Sicilian nobleman, Alessandro Malaspina arrived on a voyage for the Spanish government in 1794 and there were visits by French explorers beginning with François Peron and Nicholas Baudin in 1802 and ending with Louis de Freycinet in 1820.[60] The presence of such visitors gave Sydney, even at this early stage, something of a cosmopolitan atmosphere. Ships' officers were entertained by leading colonists, thus helping to enliven society and break down isolation. On the other hand, crew members brought to Sydney other features associated with the world's ports. Their presence contributed to the existence of unsavoury areas around the waterfront and complicated the task of preserving law and order.

Although Sydney had a large floating population most of its residents were permanent. At the apex was the governor whose presence ensured a supremacy for Sydney as the centre of government and society. Wealth helped to determine who came next on the scale, but important too was the question of whether the individual concerned had arrived as convict or free. The leading military officers, civil officials, merchants and landholders saw themselves as a group apart. They were willing to engage in business dealings with the well-off emancipist traders and manufacturers, but they regarded this element as socially inferior. Nevertheless, wealthy 'superior citizens', whether free or emancipist, lived intermingled on the eastern side of George Street, along the waterfront of Sydney Cove and on the higher land stretching up towards Macquarie Street. This, later observed the visiting surgeon, Peter Cunningham, was considered to be the St James's portion of Sydney. Near the harbour the land was valuable and the houses were located closer together. Further away they were situated on larger blocks and were usually:

> Built in the detached cottage style,—of white freestone, or of brick plastered and whitewashed, one or two stories [sic] high, with verandahs in front, and enclosed by a neat wooden paling, lined occasionally with trim-pruned geranium hedges.[61]

Most had substantial gardens 'decked out with flowers and teeming with culinary delicacies'. The size of the building blocks, besides making such gardens feasible also created a sprawl noted by contemporaries who were used to the more compact English towns. Wentworth estimated that the area occupied by 7000 people in Sydney would have catered to 20,000 in England. Cunningham likewise noted that 'Sydney, from the scattered state of its buildings, necessarily occupies a great extent of ground'.[62]

The western side of Sydney, known as the St Giles' area, mostly contained lesser elements—'fishermen, mechanics, shopkeepers, butchers' and the like. Worst housed and behaved were those to be found in the Rocks area, so named because of the 'bare mass of white sandstone' which rose in successive layers above Sydney Cove. The locale, as Cunningham pointed out, did 'boast of many handsome houses with highly respectable inmates', but for many years its ruggedness, difficulty of access and 'the total absence of order in its houses' made it 'more like the abode of a horde of savages than the residence of a civilised community'. This was by no means typical of the lesser sections of the community as a whole. Contemporaries spoke highly of the appearance of houses in other parts. 'Sydney in general', noted John Slater, 'commands the attention of a stranger for its neatness even in the poorer orders of society, every house having a garden attached, and most gardens being stocked with the peach tree..'. These houses, particularly when the occupant was a tradesman or shopkeeper, were also a place of work. This was true of others such as the merchant, Robert Campbell, whose residence adjoined his warehouse and wharf. Traders in general selected sites that were close to the harbour. As yet, the town was not sufficiently developed for it to be divided into separate work and residential areas. Houses, shops, warehouses, government offices and military barracks were all intermingled.[63]

Although dominated by free and freed people, Sydney still bore the imprint of its penal beginnings. By 1821 the convict huts which were a feature of the early days had long since been removed. Convicts employed in tending the government horses, bullocks and carts were housed in the Carters Barracks located on the road leading from Hyde Park through the Brickfields to Parramatta. Most convict employees, however, were kept in the three-storeyed, handsome brick barracks that had been constructed near Hyde Park. A number spent their days in the barracks but most worked in the township performing tasks for the government. They could be seen daily:

> Marching backwards and forwards from their work in single military file, and the solitary ones straggling here and there with their white woollen Parramatta frocks and trowsers, or grey or yellow jackets with duck overalls (the different styles of dress denoting the oldness or newness of their arrival), all daubed over with broad arrows P.B.'s, C.B.'s, and various numerals in black, white and red . . .[64]

Some were employed at the colonial dockyard maintaining government vessels, while those with trades worked in the lumber yard which consisted of a 'range of workshops forming a square to the left of George Street'. In addition to the convicts from the barracks there were the gangs from the gaols where those who had committed offences after arrival were kept. They were generally used on unskilled tasks, such as unloading government ships and their 'jingling leg-chains', noted Cunningham, 'told a tale too plain to be misunderstood'.[65] Less conspicuous were the better behaved convicts who were allowed to dress as they pleased and find private quarters in the town. Most had tickets-of-leave and were allowed to work for themselves provided they behaved and reported regularly to the authorities.

The presence of convicts and emancipists gave Sydney an unusual flavour and threatened to undermine law and order. Shortly after his arrival Macquarie claimed that the:

> Streets frequently exhibited the most disgraceful scenes of rioting, drunkenness, and excesses of every kind, and each morning brought to light the history of thefts, burglaries, and depredations which had been committed the night before.[66]

That vice was endemic can scarcely be disputed, given the evidence of contemporary observers and the records of the Criminal Court. Efforts had been made to cope with these problems from the outset. Phillip had appointed constables and watchmen chiefly from among the better convicts. Hunter followed the practice of many English parishes and arranged for the election of constables on a twelve-month basis. No monetary payment was offered but the governor did provide a range of other inducements, including a pint of rum (later reduced to half a pint) on a Saturday night. Macquarie found the 'Police of the town of Sydney very defective and totally inadequate' and established the first real police force in New South Wales. He divided Sydney into five districts, giving each a watch-house, a District Constable and six 'constables in ordinary'. Their responsibilities were laid down with great care and the force was brought under the acting principal surgeon, D'Arcy Wentworth. Many of the alterations which Macquarie made to the streets and layout of the town were designed to improve the prospects of securing 'peace and tranquility'.[67]

Although matters may have improved, Macquarie certainly did not eradicate crime, for the opportunities of avoiding detection were considerable and there were many prepared to run the risk of committing offences. Yet although crime persisted it was on a smaller scale and of a kind different from what might have been expected given the background of convicts and emancipists. Murders and crimes of violence were comparatively rare and thefts although not uncommon were not unduly numerous. It is unlikely that the residents of Sydney were any more exposed to attack or robbery than were their counterparts in major English towns. The contemporary DD Mann reached such a conclusion, claiming that:

the morals of the colony are by no means so debauched as the tongue of prejudice has too frequently asserted . . . The instances of drunkenness, dishonesty and their concomitant offences, are not more common than in the mother country.[68]

Whether Mann was correct in his reference to drunkenness is more open to question. Heavy and prolonged drinking was characteristic of the group from which the convicts were drawn and there is ample evidence to prove that their habits persisted after they reached New South Wales. Liquor was first brought to the colony by overseas merchants in 1792 and thereafter a steady stream was landed, some, during the years before 1810, at the instance of the officers of the New South Wales Corps. These men used their agents to sell it and were possibly behind some of the public houses that opened in Sydney and elsewhere. Efforts were made by all governors to curb imports of liquor and ensure that retailing was confined to licensed dealers of sound character who operated under prescribed conditions. Hunter was the first to introduce a licensing system and in 1796 granted permission for ten public houses in Sydney. By 1809 the number had increased to sixty-two or approximately one per one hundred residents. Not surprisingly, Macquarie reduced the number of licensed houses. Far from producing the desired effect, however, this merely brought about a growth in the number of illicit grog shops, forcing Macquarie to issue additional licenses. Neither he, nor his predecessors found it possible to bring the liquor trade under control but his reforms did have limited success, especially his attempts to improve public houses. Often these in the past had been little more than a room set aside in a private residence and furnished according to the whim of the owner. Several were run by women and all followed the English practice of advertising their existence by means of a board bearing colourful, and sometimes provocative names.[69] Macquarie brought them under his town planning regulations and partly in response to this, partly due to the emergence of a more demanding clientele, amenities were improved and standards did rise. Nevertheless primitive, unlicensed premises could still be found in the less salubrious parts of town. As Cunningham later observed:

Sobriety . . . by no means ranks among the conspicuous virtues of our general population;—many, very many of our dear citizens, keeping up devoutly the religious festival of St Patrick from year's end to year's end.[70]

Drinking was not the only leisure activity for the lower orders. Gambling was also a favourite pastime according to Mann, and 'next to drinking' constituted 'the chief pleasure and amusement of the lowest classes of prisoners'. He found the practice was carried to such excesses that 'in some cases, the most abandoned of the prisoners have actually staked the clothes which they wore, and when those were lost, stood amongst their companions in a state of nudity . . .'[71] Blood sports were also popular. Bull baiting attracted large crowds and so too did cockfighting. Boxing did the same, so long as matches could be held without the knowledge of the authorities. No such problems attached to foot racing, which occasionally attracted attention.[72]

For a time there also existed another form of entertainment which drew audiences from the lower as well as the better-off elements of society. In June 1789 a group of convicts engaged in the first theatrical performance in Australia when they took part in Farquhar's comedy *The Recruiting Officer* to celebrate the King's birthday.[73] Six and a half years later, on 16 January 1796 a playhouse was opened at Sydney in what is now Bligh Street. Owned by Robert Sidaway, the colony's first baker, it was managed by a convict, John Sparrow, and the company included five convicts. Five plays, all of a popular variety were performed over the next six months, but the playhouse was closed by Governor Hunter after finding that the houses of members of the audience were robbed while they were watching the plays. Moreover, admission fees were sometimes paid in provisions and convicts who used this currency were 'unable to pursue their labour with proper energy and activity'.[74] The building itself 'was levelled to the ground' and although a new company was formed in 1800 it too was dissolved after two performances. Nothing further was attempted until after 1821.[75] In the interim, according to Mann:

> The sources of amusement have been confined to cricket, cards, water-parties, shooting, fishing, hunting the kangaroo, or any other pleasures which can be derived from society where no public place is open for recreations of any description.[76]

Most of these activities seem to have cut across social groups and interested most inhabitants. Cricket was played from an early stage in Sydney on the open area later included in Hyde Park. 'The late intense weather', noted the *Sydney Gazette* on 8 January 1804, 'has been very favourable to the amateurs of cricket, who have scarcely lost a day for the last month'. It is not clear which sections of the community were interested in cricket, but horseracing was mainly confined to the wealthier free residents. Already well established by 1810, it was popular among the military and the large landed settlers, some of whom had residences in Sydney. These men were responsible for importing bloodstock first from the Cape of Good Hope, then from India and England. Under Macquarie it developed further and several meetings a year were held, generally as part of celebrations such as the King's birthday, on the new track at Hyde Park. Macquarie took steps to ensure that they remained respectable and during race week banned 'all species of Gaming, Drunkenness, Swearing, Quarelling, Fighting, or Boxing' from the vicinity of the ground.[77] Meetings were invariably followed by private dinner parties which together with the occasional ball were popular among the upper echelons of society.

There was one further element of society for whom special provision was made, namely, young people. A number of children arrived with their parents and others were born in the colony. Anxious lest the convicts contaminate children the British authorities had from the outset urged governors to 'interfere on behalf of the rising generation and . . . educate them in religious as well as industrious habits.' Phillip and Hunter could not spare the time for such matters, but King established a female orphan school in September, purchased a house for its use and appointed a committee to manage it. Plans were laid for a male orphan institution, but no building had been completed by the time a master arrived in 1810. Macquarie opened a public charity school for children of both sexes soon after arriving and in January 1819, after transferring the female orphans to Parramatta, gave their building to the males. In addition to these government institutions Sydney also contained a number of privately run, fee-paying schools generally conducted in the house of the teacher. Although there was no system of education in Sydney as yet, opportunities to acquire instruction did exist.[78]

A varied and interesting life was therefore possible in Sydney before 1821. Admittedly, outsiders used to the sophistication of English cities were critical of what they found and lamented the absence of libraries, musical entertainments, learned societies and a flourishing theatre. Cunningham later complained that 'agreeable amusements' were much wanted. He found that because 'people knew too much of each other's private affairs' idle gossip became a substitute for intelligent discussion.[79] This, however, was only to be expected in what was the capital of a small, recently settled community. Sydney like the colony as a whole had, by 1821, made significant progress and had already risen above its exclusively convict beginnings. Its foundations had been securely laid and it had emerged as a township in its own right. Already some of the buildings that were to remain landmarks had been erected, and streets had been given their permanent location and their modern names. Thus far Sydney had served a small colony that after thirty-three years was still concentrated mainly within the narrow coastal plain bounded by the Blue Mountains. With settlement about to spread and the wealth of the interior soon to be tapped new possibilities were opening that in the coming decades were to transform the capital.

Notes

[1] See Fry, E.C. 'The Growth of Sydney' in McCarty, J.W. and Schedvin, C.B. (eds.) *Australian Capital Cities*, (S.U.P., 1977), p.29; also Birch, A. and Macmillan, D.S. (eds.) *The Sydney Scene 1788-1960*, (M.U.P., 1962).

[2] Auchmuty, J.J. (ed.), *The Voyage of Governor Phillip to Botany Bay*, (Sydney, 1970), pp.23-4.

[3] White, J. *Journal of a Voyage to New South Wales*, (hereafter cited as 'White, Journal'), (ed.) A.H. Chisholm (Sydney, 1962) p.112 and D. Collins, *An Account of the English Colony in New South Wales*, (hereafter cited as 'Collins, Account'), (ed.) B.H. Fletcher, (Sydney 1975), Vol. 1, p.405.

[4] 'White, Journal', *op.cit.*, p.140, *H.R.N.S.W.*, Vol. II, p.692 12-7-1788. 'Collins, Account', *op.cit.*, February, 1788 entry, and Tench, W. *Sydney's First Four Years*, (ed.) Fitzhardinge, (Sydney 1961), p.60. (NB - presumably it was the County and not the Cove that was officially named in this 4-6-1788 reference).

[5] Bradley, W. *A Voyage to New South Wales, the Journal of Lieutenant William Bradley R.N. of H.M.S. 'Sirius', 1786-1792*, (Sydney, 1969).

[6] The map is reproduced in Kelly, M. and Crocker, R. *Sydney Takes Shape*, (Sydney, 1977), p.2.

[7] 'White, Journal', *op.cit.*, p.118-9; 'Collins, Account', *op.cit.*, Vol. 1, pp.15-6.

[8] Auchmuty, *op.cit.*, p.70; *H.R.A.*, I, pp.47-8, (9-7-1788); Johnson, P.A. 'The Original Sydney, A Geometrical and Numerical Analysis of Phillip's Plan', *A.H.R.U.*, Paper (U.N.S.W., 1982).

[9] *H.R.A.*, I, i, p.48.

[10] Kelly and Crocker, *op.cit.*, p.7.

[11] On Government House see, Irving, R. *The First Australian Architecture*, (M. Arch. Thesis, U.N.S.W., 1975), and Gillespie, R. *Viceregal Quarters, An Account of the Various Residences of the Governor of New South Wales from 1788 until the Present Day*, (Sydney, 1975).

[12] See, 'Collins, Account', *op.cit.*, Vol. 1, p.103; Jervis, J. *Parramatta, Cradle City of Australia*, (Parramatta, 1963), Proudfoot, H. *Old Government House: the Building and its Landscape*, (Sydney, 1971), pp.9, 11; Johnson, P.A. 'The Original Parramatta, A Geometrical and Numerical Analysis of the Earliest Plan', *A.H.R.U.* Paper, (U.N.S.W., 1982). For the spread of settlement see also Perry, T.M. *Australia's First Frontier, The Spread of Settlement in New South Wales, 1788-1829*, (Melbourne, 1963), and Fletcher, B.A. *Landed Enterprise & Penal Society: A History of Farming & Grazing in New South Wales before 1821*, (hereafter cited as 'Landed Enterprise'), (S.U.P., 1976).

[13] Fletcher, B.H. 'Grose, Paterson and the Settlement of the Hawkesbury', *J.R.A.H.S.*, Vol. 51, 1965, pt.3.

[14] Bowd, D.G. *Macquarie Country, A History of the Hawkesbury*, (Melbourne, 1969), pp.1-6.

[15] *H.R.A.*, I, ii, pp.679-80, (30-9-1800).

[16] See 'Collins, Account', *op.cit.*, Vol. 1, pp.251, 258 and general 263 and 175.

[17] 'Return of Public Buildings erected . . .', *H.R.N.S.W.*, Vol. 4, pp.151-6; for mills see 'Collins, Account', *op.cit.*, Vol. 1, pp.359, 395, 399.

[18] *A.D.B.*, Vol. 1, entry for Hunter; Wood, G.A. 'Governor Hunter', in *J.R.A.H.S.*, Vol. 14, 1928, pt. 6.

[19] Quoted in Kelly and Crocker, *op.cit.*, p.9.

[20] *H.R.N.S.W.*, Vol. 5, p.209, (14-9-1803); p.390, (28-6-1804).

[21] *Ibid.*, pp.196-7, 7-8-1803. See also *A.D.B.*, Vol. 2, entry for King; and Roe, M. 'Phillip Gidley King', in *Australian Quarterly*, Vol. 30, No. 3, September, 1958.

[22] Steven, M. *Merchant Campbell 1769-1846, A Study in Colonial Trade*, (Oxford, 1965).

[23] Suttor, G. *Memoirs*, (London, 1800), p.61; for background see Hainsworth, D.R. *Builders and Adventurers: the Traders and the Emergence of the Colony 1788-1821*, (M.U.P., 1968).

[24] See Abbott, G.J. and Nairn, N.B. (eds.), *The Economic Growth of Australia 1788-1821*, (M.U.P., 1969), chapters by Shaw, A.G.L., Stevens, M. and Walsh, G.P.

[25] *Ibid.*, chapter by Hainsworth, D.R. p.267 ff. also index to the *Sydney Gazette*, Vols. 1-7, Council of the Library of New South Wales (Sydney, 1964-70).

[26] Articles on leading emancipists will be found in *A.D.B.*, Vols. 1 and 2; see also Hainsworth, D.R. *The Sydney Traders, Simeon Lord and his Contemporaries, 1788-1821*, (hereafter cited as 'Sydney Traders'), (S.U.P., 1972) and Fletcher, 'Landed Enterprise', *op.cit.*, pp.67-8.

[27] *Sydney Gazette*, 4-8-1810 and 14-7-1810.

[28] Chapter by Walsh, in Abbott and Nairn, *op.cit.*, p.247-9.

[29] *H.R.N.S.W.*, Vol. 4, p.824, (29-8-1802).

[30] Kelly and Crocker, *op.cit.*, p.8.

[31] See Grimes *Plan of Sydney*, 1800, *H.R.N.S.W.*, Vol. 5, p.838; and Government and General Order, 11-6-1801, *H.R.N.S.W.*, Vol. 4, p.402-3.

[32] *H.R.N.S.W.*, Vol. 6, p.359-60, (31-10-1807); *Kings Papers*, Vol. 8, p.245, (25-10-1807). (M.L.).

[33] *H.R.A.*, I, vii, p.4, (20-2-1809) and p.304 ff., (30-4-1810); p.654, (7-11-1812).

[34] *Ibid.*, p.4, (20-2-1809) and Note 3, p.793.

[35] *H.R.A.*, I, vii, p.209, (4-5-1809), p.528, (9-11-1812).

[36] *H.R.N.S.W.*, Vol. 7, p.298, (27-2-1810).

[37] *H.R.A.*, I, vi, p.98 ff., (25-1-1807), p.169, (31-10-1807); *Sydney Gazette*, 1-4-1804.

[38] *H.R.N.S.W.*, Vol. 7, p.298, (20-2-1809, 27-2-1810); *H.R.A.*, I, vii, pp.4, 116, (10-6-1809).

[39] *H.R.A.*, I, vii, p.254, (30-4-1810), p.269.

[40] Mann, D.D. *The Present Picture of New South Wales 1811*, (hereafter cited as 'Present Picture'), (facsimile Sydney, 1979), p.56, ff.

[41] *H.R.A.*, I, viii, p.554, (24-6-1815), and see Ellis, M.H. *Francis Greenway*, (Sydney, 1949).

[42] Shaw, A.G.L. Chapter in 'Abbott and Nairn', *op.cit.*, p.113.

[43] Fletcher, 'Landed Enterprise', *op.cit.*, pp.160-4.

[44] *H.R.A.*, I, vii, pp.384-5, 401-5, (18-10-1811) and pp.529-30, (9-11-1812).

[45] Ellis, M.H. *Lachlan Macquarie*, (Sydney, 1947), p.192; Wentworth, W.C. *Statistical, Historical and Political Description of the Colony of New South Wales*, (hereafter cited as 'Statistical . . . Description), (London, 1819), p.8.

[46] *H.R.A.*, I, vii, p.387, (18-10-1811); Government Order, *Sydney Gazette*, 31-3-1810.

[47] *H.R.A.*, I, vii, pp.342-3, (27-10-1810); Government Order, *Sydney Gazette*, 6-10-1810.

[48] Government Order, *Sydney Gazette*, 15-9-1810 and 20-10-1810, and 18-11-1820.

[49] Government Order, *Sydney Gazette*, 6-10-1810.

[50] *H.R.A.*, I, vii, p.269, (30-4-1810); p.366, (26-7-1811).

[51] Fletcher, B.H. *Ralph Darling, A Governor Maligned*, (Oxford, 1984), p.175.

[52] Steven, M. 'The Changing Pattern of Commerce in New South Wales 1810-1821', *B.A.H.*, Vol. 3, No. 2, August 1963.

[53] Bowd, *op.cit.*, pp.41-4; Lachlan Macquarie, *Journal of His Tours in New South Wales*, (Sydney, 1956), p.23 ff.

[54] Ker, J. 'The Wool Industry in New South Wales 1803-1830', *B.A.H.*, Vol. 1, No. 9, May, 1956.

[55] Ritchie, J. *The Evidence to the Bigge Reports*, (hereafter cited as 'Evidence'), (Heinemann, 1971), Vol. 1, pp.105-18. Dow, G.M. *Samual Terry, The Botany Bay Rothschild*, (Sydney, 1974).

[56] For manufacturing details see Hainsworth, *Sydney Traders, op.cit.*, *S.G.*, 4-12-1819 and the memorial by Dickson, 1-7-1812, *C.O.*, 201/63, f.173 and *Sydney Gazette*, 3-6-1815 and 25-8-1821.

[57] Holder, R.F. *The Bank of New South Wales, A History*, Vol. I, (Sydney, 1970).

[58] In order, figures from 'A Letter from Sydney' *H.R.N.S.W.*, Vol. 3, p.486, (14-9-1898); *H.R.N.S.W.*, Vol. 5, p.390, (28-6-1804); Wentworth, W.C. 'Statistical... Description', *op.cit.*, p.8.

[59] See Fletcher, Landed Enterprise, *op.cit.*, pp.57, 199.

[60] 'Collins, Account', *op.cit.*, Vol. I, pp.230-1; Dunmore, J. *French Explorers in the Pacific*, Vol. I, (Oxford, 1965); Peron, F. *A Voyage of Discovery to the Southern Hemisphere*, (London, 1809).

[61] Cunningham, P. *Two Years in New South Wales*, (hereafter cited as 'Two Years'), (London, 1827), Vol. I, p.40.

[62] Wentworth, 'Statistical... Description', *op.cit.*, pp.7-8, Cunningham, 'Two Years', *op.cit.*, Vol. I, p.47.

[63] Cunningham, *op.cit.*, p.40; and Slater, J. *A Description of Sydney, Parramatta, Newcastle, etc.*, (London, 1819), p.5.

[64] Bigge, J.T. *Report of the Commissioner on the State of the Colony of New South Wales*, 1822, pp.448, 22-3; Cunningham, 'Two Years', *op.cit.*, Vol. I, p.46.

[65] Cunningham, 'Two Years', *op.cit.*, Vol. I, pp.51 and 52.

[66] *H.R.A.*, I, vii, p.385, (18-10-1811).

[67] *Ibid.*, p.385, the evidence of D'Arcy Wentworth in Ritchie, 'Evidence', *op.cit.*, Vol. I, pp.40-62 and Vol. 2, p.32 ff; King, H. *Problems of Police Administration in New South Wales 1825-1851*, *J.R.A.H.S.*, Vol. 42, 1956, pt. 5; and the Government Order, *Sydney Gazette*, 6-11-1810.

[68] Mann, 'Present Picture', *op.cit.*, p.53; and Cunningham, 'Two Years', *op.cit.*, Vol. I, p.62.

[69] Freeland, J.M. *The Australian Pub*, (Melbourne, 1977), pp.6-19.

[70] Cunningham, 'Two Years', *op.cit.*, Vol. I, p.58.

[71] Mann, 'Present Picture', *op.cit.*, p.53.

[72] For sports see *Sydney Gazette*, 4-6-1810, 16-6-1810, 4-8-1810, 20-10-1810; also Cumes, J.W.C. *Their Chastity Was Not Too Rigid* (Melbourne, 1979), pp.1-59.

[73] 'Collins, Account', *op.cit.*, Vol. I, pp.57-8; Kardoss, J. *A Brief History of the Australian Theatre*, (Sydney, 1955).

[74] 'Collins, Account', *op.cit.*, Vol. I, p.375; Mann, 'Present Picture', *op.cit.*, p.54.

[75] Cumes, *op.cit.*, p.54.

[76] Mann, 'Present Picture', *op.cit.*, p.54.

[77] Government Order, *Sydney Gazette*, 6-10-1810; and race report *Sydney Gazette*, 5-6-1819.

[78] See Cleverley, J. *The First Generation: School and Society in early Australia*, (Sydney, 1971), also *H.R.A.*, I, iii, pp.43, 425; Mann, 'Present Picture', *op.cit.*, p.34; *H.R.A.*, I, x, p.94, (24-3-1819), p.679, (27-7-1822); and advertisements in *Sydney Gazette*, 7-1-1810, 4-8-1810, 22-9-1810, 14-11-1820.

[79] Cunningham, 'Two Years', *op.cit.*, p.52.

Hobart

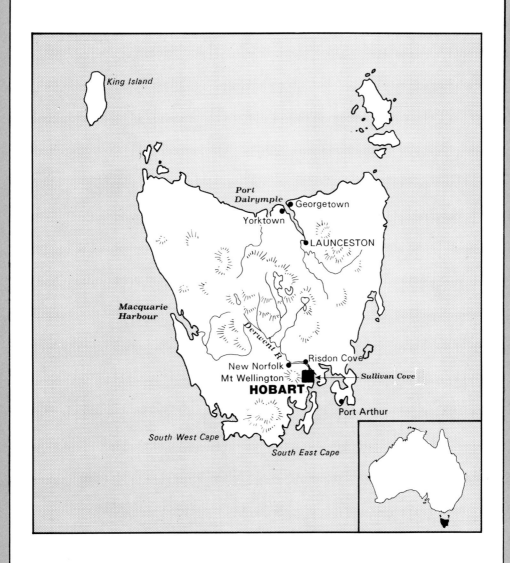

King Island

Port Dalrymple

Georgetown

Yorktown

LAUNCESTON

Macquarie Harbour

Derwent R.

Risdon Cove

New Norfolk

Mt Wellington

Sullivan Cove

HOBART

Port Arthur

South West Cape

South East Cape

HOBART TOWN.

Chapter IV

Settling Van Diemen's Land

Lloyd Robson

The island of which Hobart Town became capital was discovered in 1642 by Abel Janszoon Tasman, an employee of the Dutch East India Company. Finding no evidence of ready treasure or useful natural products, the Dutch made no settlement at that time and concentrated their trade and business energies elsewhere. Tasman nevertheless named the island Van Diemen's Land, after his employer, a name which was used until changed to Tasmania in 1855.

During the eighteenth century, commercial and scientific motives of exploration came to be associated with a curiosity concerning people of the exotic Pacific region. For these reasons numerous French and British expeditions visited Van Diemen's Land before 1800, the French better equipped for scientific study as a result of government encouragement and subsidy. Though leaving a considerable cartographic legacy no suggestion of permanent settlement emerged from these voyages.

The existence of Van Diemen's Land was well known, then, when Arthur Phillip came with the first fleet to Botany Bay in 1788, although it was still assumed that Van Diemen's Land was part of Australia proper. It was not known for certain to be an island until the voyage of circumnavigation made by Bass and Flinders in the summer of 1798-9. Some fifteen years of European settlement of New South Wales elapsed before it was considered necessary to extend the area of British occupation beyond the bridgehead of Sydney and the remote outpost of Norfolk Island. Van Diemen's Land was then made an administrative dependency of New South Wales, until separation in 1825, and had only a nominal capital city till that date.

Whoever seeks for the origins of the settlement of Van Diemen's Land and the establishment of its capital should look not to London or Sydney but to Paris. By the end of the eighteenth century, three major French expeditions to the Pacific had been conducted: those of Bougainville (1766-69), La Pérouse (1785-88) and D'Entrecasteaux (1791-3).[1] Then, in 1800, a fourth exploratory voyage was organised by the French. With the address and date of Paris, 7 Vendemiaire, year 9 of the French Republic [29 September 1800], Pierre Forfait, Minister of Marine and Colonies, transmitted to Citizen Nicholas Baudin, Post Captain, commander-in-chief of the corvettes *Géographe* and *Naturaliste*, instructions to examine in detail the south-west, west, north-west and north coasts of New Holland. By combining the results of this survey with the work done by English navigators on the east coast of New South Wales and of D'Entrecasteaux on Van Diemen's Land, the French government would come to know the entire coastline of the area, stated Forfait. Citizen Baudin was enjoined to employ assiduously the scientists, engineers, artists and means placed at his disposal, to determine precisely the geographical position of the principal points along the coast and to study the inhabitants, animals and natural products.[2]

The aim of the expedition, it was stressed, was to increase the scientific field and illuminate for foreigners the liberal designs of the First Consul for the pacification of Europe. The instructions given by the revolutionary republic were silent on the ultimate purpose to which such new knowledge might be put.

Baudin's ships sailed from Le Havre on 19 October 1800, the *Géographe* under his command and the *Naturaliste* in the charge of Emmanuel Hamelin. After charting the Western Australian coast the expedition arrived off the coast of Van Diemen's Land on 13 January 1802. From the channel named after D'Entrecasteaux, Baudin's ships proceeded along the east coast until they lost touch with each other on the night of 7 March. They did not come together until they reached Sydney. In the meantime, one of them surveyed the east and north-east coasts of Van Diemen's Land between Schouten Island, named by Tasman after a member of the Dutch East India Company, and the river later to be named Tamar.

Before leaving again in November 1802, the French ships remained some five months at Port Jackson, where the then governor, Philip Gidley King, entertained grave doubts about the purity of their scientific exploratory motives. On 9 November 1802 he wrote to London of the loss of a French schooner, the *Surprise*, which had arrived from Ile de France to catch seals and the like in Bass Strait. The governor rejoiced that such a fate might deter any more adventurers from that quarter.[3] On the twenty-second of the same month, King again evinced anxiety about French intentions and issued orders to Acting Lieutenant Charles Robbins to proceed on the colonial schooner *Cumberland* to Storm Bay in southern Van Diemen's Land, a large body of water named by Tasman, and there to establish a settlement. If the winds prevailed strongly in the west or south, however, Robbins was directed to sail to King Island and Port Phillip, taking care to hoist His Majesty's colours every day on shore during his examination of these places.[4] Port Phillip had been discovered independently by Flinders and Lieutenant John Murray earlier in 1802. Murray had politically named it Port King, but the governor graciously declined the honour and renamed it after the first governor of New South Wales.[5] After all, King Island had been given his name the previous year by a British ship's captain.

King later stated that his instructions to Robbins were actually a bluff, deliberately designed to mislead Baudin, though whether they would have achieved their object is very doubtful if the French had made up their minds to put men ashore. Robbins actually encountered Baudin at King Island and the French navigator, rather amused at the fuss he was creating, informed the Englishman that France did not contemplate settlement. But whatever the case, it was certainly Governor King who made the decision to settle Van Diemen's Land as an out-station of New South Wales, and he did it as a direct reaction to French presence in the region.

The settlement decision was facilitated by the arrival at Sydney of the *Glatton* on 11 March 1803. This ship contained convicts but also carried on board Junior Lieutenant John Bowen, a naval officer, and Mr Jacob Mountgarrett, a naval surgeon. Both were to have been sent to Norfolk Island but, when approached by King, readily agreed to form part of an expedition to southern Van Diemen's Land. By instructions dated 28 March 1803, King appointed the twenty-three-year-old Bowen commandant and superintendent

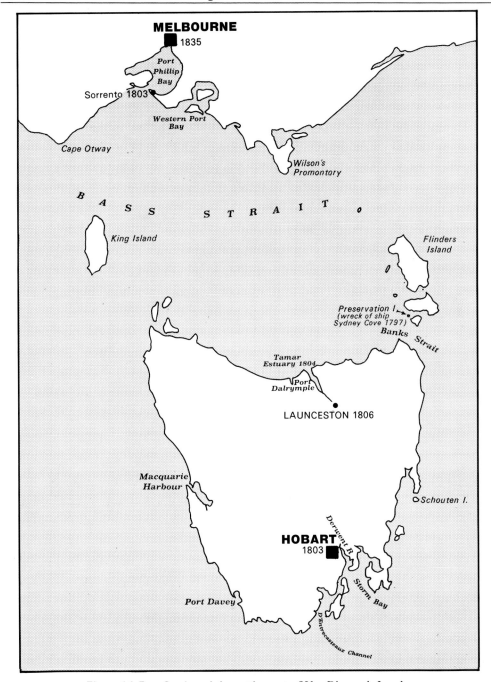

Figure 14: Bass Strait and the settlement of Van Diemen's Land

of a settlement to be formed at the River Derwent. This very large river had been named the Riviére du Nord by D'Entrecasteaux in 1793 but then, two months later, named the Derwent by the English Lieutenant John Hayes who was quite unaware that D'Entrecasteaux' expedition had preceded him.[6]

81

Over and above his obsession with forestalling any French settlements, King's decision to plant the flag in Van Diemen's Land was supported by several other factors: Bass and Flinders had reported favourably on the site; it would divide the convicts; it would secure another place for procuring timber and any other natural products that might be discovered and found useful; it would have the advantage of raising grain for the parent settlement; and would enable the promotion of a seal fishery. Bowen was later to confirm that his agreement with the governor's wishes to establish a settlement was on account of the valuable fisheries and because the French and the Americans had been surveying the coast.[7] King's motivations were probably best summed up by James Colnett, Captain of the *Glatton*, who maintained that the governor sought, by promotion of British interests and securing the advantages that might be derived from the fisheries and related enterprises, to thwart any projects or plans which might be shaped by France.[8]

Before his departure from Sydney, Bowen was authorised to wear the uniform of a commander, though without the accompanying pay, so that greater respect and attention might be paid to him, particularly by foreign nations. He was also presented with a written memorandum from King explaining how he was to provide for his little detachment of officials, settlers and convicts, prepare the ground for crops and generally be on the alert to prevent misconduct by the prisoners, to the extent of searching them for weapons such as knives, and examining their irons. Cattle and sheep were to be secured and the prisoners employed at public labour in rendering snug the provisions and stores, and building huts. Free settlers were to have land granted to a maximum of a hundred acres apiece and to be victualled from the government stores (commissariat) for twelve months, allowed the labour of two convicts each for the same period, and supplied with stock, equipment and clothing.[9]

On 12 September 1803, Bowen in the *Lady Nelson* arrived at Risdon Cove on the Derwent, the *Albion* having preceded them by five days. This site was chosen because of the availability of fresh water and there the vessels unloaded. Bowen soon occupied the hill above the creek and thereby commanded a perfect view of the river. The young commandant judged the land excellent and concluded that settlers should also occupy the countryside above Herdsman's Cove where the salt water gave way to fresh. Bowen reported that the Aboriginals were a shy people who retreated when the Europeans arrived. There were forty-nine newcomers, including Bowen and Mountgarrett, a storekeeper named Thomas Wilson; one lance sergeant and seven private soldiers from the NSW Corps with three women and a child; three free settlers—William (or Aaron) Birt, William (or Richard) Clark(e), and an overseer named Smith from Grose Farm at Sydney—with three women and a child; and twenty-one male and three female convicts. In addition, there were two women and one man whose names are unknown.

Bowen sent his first report back to King on Monday 20 September, three days after his arrival.[10] The following Monday he reported that the settlers had not been despatched up the river after all, but sensibly kept in a body near the main site. He further noted that work was proceeding and that soldiers and prisoners occupied very comfortable huts.[11]

King applauded young Bowen's efforts and sent him more hands in the person of Lieutenant William Moore of the New South Wales Corps and fourteen non-commissioned officers and private soldiers. In addition, King supplied his subordinate with copies of orders followed on Norfolk Island in February 1788 (presumably Phillip's instructions to King) thinking that the circumstances of settlement were very similar. They were, except that the Derwent was a safe and easy anchorage whereas Norfolk Island was the opposite. Another similarity was the governor's concern with flax. Hearing that there was a great abundance of grass further up the river which produced a type of flax, King asked for samples to try how far it would answer for bags, rope and other purposes so important for a maritime nation.[12] In this emulation of Phillip in 1788 there was another parallel between the settlement of Port Jackson and Van Diemen's Land.

Early in the New Year of 1804, Bowen left the settlement for Sydney in the whaler *Ferret*. He said that he wanted to report on and bring about the conviction of prisoners including a member of the New South Wales Corps who had been detected in a dangerous plan to rob the stores, but Bowen really wanted to rejoin the navy; war with France had broken out again, he had heard. Moore remained in charge, but in February Bowen was sent back from Sydney, and after a difficult passage reached the Derwent to find that a superior officer had arrived on the scene. This was Lieutenant Governor David Collins who had in fact been sent from England to establish a settlement at Port Phillip, not at Van Diemen's Land at all.

Towards the end of November or very early in December 1802 an unsigned, undated and unaddressed memorandum had been written at the British Colonial Office drawing attention to the two French vessels surveying and exploring the western and southern coasts of Australia. These were named as the *Géographe* and *Naturaliste*. Attention was also drawn to 'recently received' communications from Governor King wherein that official had recorded his belief that the French had failed to discover either Port Phillip or King Island. This was a reference to despatches dated 9 and 21 May 1802, written at Sydney by King during the period when Baudin's party was refreshing itself at Port Jackson, and after Lieutenant John Murray and then Flinders had identified and explored Port Phillip and reported favourably upon it.[13]

There is no obvious evidence that the British were acting on information received from sources other than King, ten thousand miles away out in New South Wales, but it is reasonable to suppose that they kept themselves informed on French policy as it was shaped in Paris. Information was sufficient, however, for the government to decide to send another expedition across the world instead of directing King to establish an out-station at Port Phillip, as he had done at the Derwent. It should be noted that King's action in despatching Bowen to Van Diemen's Land was taken before he had received information from Lord Hobart (Secretary of State for War and the Colonies 1801-4) that a similar settlement was to be established at Port Phillip. Hobart's despatch was dated 14 February 1803 and acknowledged by King on 1 March 1804, the governor having decided at the end of March 1803 to send Bowen and party to the Risdon site. Hobart's information about a settlement at Port Phillip direct from Britain was then still in transit to King. This formal despatch informed the governor of New South Wales that the government of His Majesty had determined upon the establishment of a penal settlement at Port Phillip, it being evident that the attention of other European powers had been drawn to the Australian region.[14] Not only were American whalers and sealers and inquisitive French scientists in the area of New South Wales at that time: on 27 June 1803, Hobart had written to inform King that the Russians intended to send the *Neva* and *Nadegada* on a voyage of circumnavigation and discovery and that he was to show them every mark of hospitality and friendship should they arrive.[15]

It was observed that the establishment of any foreign power on the southern coast of New South Wales might, in the event of hostilities, greatly interrupt communications with Port Jackson and materially endanger the tranquility and security of British possessions in that area. The Colonial Office also noted that Sydney was growing and should be spared the introduction of any more prison labour for a while. Stress was laid too on the importance of the seal fisheries in Bass Strait for the proposed new settlement. In the same manner as Norfolk Island had been so swiftly and urgently occupied from Port Jackson in 1788, now instructions were sent out that King Island, stated to be a valuable seal fishery, was similarly to be occupied from Port Phillip as soon as the British expedition arrived.[16]

David Collins, the commander of the Port Phillip expedition,was judge advocate with the first fleet to Botany Bay. Returning to England in 1797, he was reduced to half pay, and in collaboration with his wife Maria, employed his talents in the production of a most elegant *Account of the English Colony in New South Wales*. His knowledge of that part of the world induced the British government to select him to command the enterprise to Port Phillip. In January 1803 he was commissioned Lieutenant Governor of the proposed new dependency under the governor of New South Wales. Evidently having no alternative attractive employment, Collins accepted a salary of £450 a year and was obliged to stand the cost of outfitting himself, thereby running up a considerable debt. It was to be his final parting from Maria.[17]

The *Calcutta* was commissioned on 27 October 1802 and, with the storeship *Ocean*, comprised the fleet; the former vessel embarked 308 male convicts and the wives of some thirty of their number. Free settlers and guards were also on board, together with a civil establishment of officers, livestock, seeds and equipment. Collins' instructions in fact enabled him to settle at any part of the southern coast of New South Wales or islands in Bass Strait, provided always that he communicated with the governor on this point. The Colonial Office was concerned with establishing a British presence on the southern coast of New South Wales to the north of Bass Strait, rather than at any special spot. In fact, a strict reading of Collins's commission actually precluded a settlement in Van Diemen's Land.[18]

The *Ocean* arrived at Port Phillip two days before the *Calcutta*, and the commanders of both ships were at once alarmed at the difficulty of entry into the port. Collins was supplied with descriptions of it, however, and spent several fruitless days seeking a spot which had the necessary advantages of a good supply of fresh water, timber for building and soil for agricultural purposes.[19] He finally and uneasily settled on a spot near the heads, to the west of Arthur's Seat at what later became known as Sorrento. Did Collins feel obliged by the French threat to restrict his options to areas near the entrance of Port Phillip? In November 1803 news had reached New South Wales of the existence of a state of war with France[20] and this intelligence may have weighed with Collins. But there is strong evidence that Collins and his officers quickly realised that the huge port they had entered was in reality guarded by nature from hostile occupation by the French or anyone else. Lieutenant J K Tuckey, in his report to Collins of a survey of Port Phillip, observed that scarcity of water and poorness of soil at Collins's site for the camp near Arthur's Seat outweighed the convenience of that situation, but from the extent of the huge body of water in which they found themselves (the extremes being sunk in the horizon) it was naturally supposed that more convenient spots might be found.[21] None was. Without adequate water, any settlement was doomed and it is clear from Tuckey's observations that, though suspecting the presence of a river, he had missed the Yarra Yarra and Werribee rivers completely.[22]

It is perhaps important that Collins, when he reached the Derwent, settled without hesitation as soon as he found a good flow of water at a spot where his settlement could command the approaches. Transport in this era of colonial development in Australia was all by sea, and it was vital that there be maritime access to places of refreshment and replenishment of supplies. Fertile soil was clearly a great advantage but, as was to be exemplified in the case of the settlement at Hobart Town, the relative scarcity of extensive good soil as observed by the invaders did not prevent settlement when the harbour was good—indeed, quite superb—and ample fresh water was to hand. To this extent, Collins was quite correct to abandon Port Phillip and, safe at the Hobart Town site on the Derwent, he congratulated himself on being removed from the burning land winds which had so annoyed at Port Phillip.[23] When Collins concluded that Port Phillip would never do for speculative men, he knew exactly what he was talking about; speculation for him and his generation was speculation in trade by sea and especially the seal and whale fisheries. For these purposes, Port Phillip was quite unsuitable in 1803. The difficulty of egress from the port was also of profound importance. Tuckey observed it to be a most formidable obstacle, and he correctly noted that the prevailing southerly winds blew to such an extent and with such force that whalers would never make the port a place of rendezvous.[24]

Finding no eligible place at Port Phillip, then, Collins was confronted with two other possible sites. One was Port Dalrymple (named by Governor Hunter after Alexander Dalrymple, hydrographer to the Admiralty) situated at the mouth of an estuary on the north coast of Van Diemen's Land. The estuary belonged to the River Tamar, named by William Paterson in 1804 after the English river separating Devon and Cornwall, on which stood Launceston, the birthplace of Governor King. The other site was at the Derwent, with Bowen. A strict adherence to his commission would have left Collins no choice but Port Dalrymple and Governor King also tended to favour that site. However, reports from both the schooner *Governor King* and a reconnaissance expedition sent across Bass Strait by Collins, regarding difficulties in navigating the river there and hostile Aboriginals, influenced him in the opposite direction. In addition, Collins was having trouble with the military guard at Port Phillip for they had become restless and turbulent at drill. Such discontent was known to be dangerous in a penal settlement and had to be quelled—the lieutenant governor was faced with the alarming situation where if any officer became ill he would not have enough to form a court martial. This difficulty would be overcome at the Derwent by the presence of Lieutenant Moore. Thus Collins explained his removal from Port Phillip, adding that the situation at the Derwent was more adapted for commercial purposes than Port Dalrymple anyway.[25]

After leaving Port Phillip on 30 January 1804, Collins had a long and unpleasant passage to the Derwent and the *Ocean* was forced to anchor for three days in Frederic Henry Bay, east of the Derwent estuary, so tempestuous was the weather. By the fifteenth the weather had moderated and the vessel was able to get under way and make sail for the Risdon settlement, which it reached that day. Some twenty-four hours later, on Thursday, 16 February 1804, Lieutenant Governor Collins left the ship and it saluted him with eleven guns as he went ashore for the first time in Van Diemen's land.[26]

Nothing about the Risdon encampment pleased Collins that February Thursday: the 'town' was situated on several high hills, and on landing at the creek the visitor was compelled to ascend a very steep climb which, though leading to a fine lookout was most inconvenient. Further, Collins found that the settlers were obliged to fetch water a considerable distance from the creek in summer—there had been no rain for four months—and that the settlement was much exposed to the cold south winds which appeared to descend from the Table Mountain across the river.[27]

In his official despatch to King dated 19 February 1804, Collins detailed other reasons for his dissatisfaction with Risdon: he found the landing place in the creek accessible only at a certain time of the tide; to make the channel at all practicable for loaded boats it would be necessary to remove 140 yards of mud which, from its being mixed with sand, would be always liable to break down and fill up the channel again; the storehouse was built so low that he dreaded the consequence of heavy rain and therefore would have to build another one on higher ground, a most difficult and laborious undertaking; the land about the settlement did not appear as excellent as he had expected, and he hoped to find as good or better lower down the harbour.

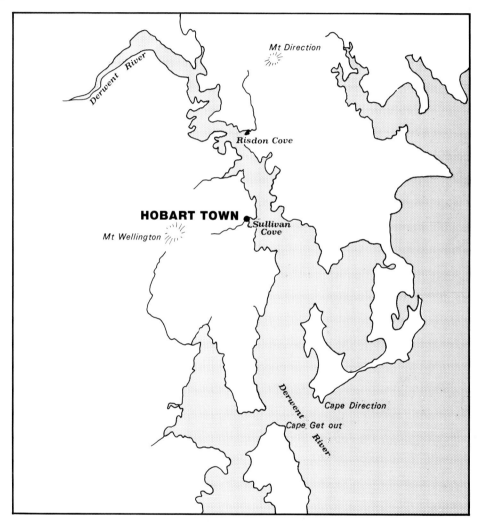

Figure 15: Risdon and Sullivan Coves—sites of first settlement

Collins pitched tents at the cove, however, in case the search for a new site should fail and on the morning of Friday the seventeenth sent Surveyor George Prideaux Harris, in search of a more advantageous place. That officer soon discovered a fine run of water on the opposite side of the river closer to its mouth and to that extent more suitable as a site than Risdon. There was good land, a most convenient cove and, for stores, an island safe from the depredations of the convicts because it connected with the shore by a spit at low tide and could readily be guarded.

Despite very strong gales, on Sunday 19 February the *Ocean* got down to Sullivan Cove, (named in honour of John Sullivan, Undersecretary to the Department of War and the Colonies), and about two miles from shore dropped anchor, the heavy wind blowing from the north-west preventing the vessel getting further in. The next day the weather was better and under the direction of Lieutenant Lord a party of the convicts and stores was landed and organised on Hunter's Island, where a temporary wharf was swiftly constructed and store tents pitched.

On Wednesday the twenty-second the Reverend Robert Knopwood, chaplain to the expedition, and AWH Humphrey, a mineralogist, accompanied Collins on shore and took possession of their marquees. Two days later more of the party landed and trees were cut for a bridge over the stream. On the Sunday the military paraded at ten in the morning and half an hour later, the convicts and settlers also being assembled, Collins and all officials of the new colony heard Divine Service.[28]

The term 'Hobart' had already come into existence as a place name: the settlement near Arthur's Seat at Port Phillip had been termed 'Hobert' (sic) by the Reverend Knopwood and the name was used by Bowen in dating his second despatch from Risdon Cove. Indeed, he later distinctly took the credit, stating that 'I named my settlement Hobart'. In the second commission granted to Bowen on 13 October 1803, Governor King referred to the settlement of 'Hobart' in the county of Buckinghamshire and it appears likely that it was King who so decided to honour the Secretary of State for War and the Colonies. Collins first used the name 'Hobart Town' in an entry in his order-book for 5 May 1804. The first despatch to use the term 'Hobart Town' was dated 24 April 1804, earlier communications bearing the address 'Headquarters Camp, Sullivan Cove'.[29]

Finding that the Risdon settlement had been placed on two-thirds rations, Collins immediately advised Lieutenant Moore to restore full rations as there were two months of provisions in hand and supplies were expected from Sydney. He also thought it his duty to inform King that not a single acre was in preparation at Risdon for grain upon government account. In these circumstances Collins announced that he was going to supply the settlers Clark and Birt as well as Moore with grain for planting and would succour the starving pigs with Indian corn brought for his own stock, not yet arrived.[30]

Following the successful landing of the stores on Hunter's Island (actually part of the 'estuary' of the stream which became known as the Hobart Town Rivulet) various parties explored the region in the direction of Herdsman's Cove. They came across a river where they found specimens of coal and so named it the Coal River, they climbed Table Mountain (so named by Bligh, called Le Plateau by the French and finally, at an uncertain date, Mt Wellington) and journeyed about eighty miles up the Derwent. Humphrey and the eminent botanist Robert Brown journeyed also to the Huon River (named after Captain Huon de Kermadec of the *Esperance* in D'Entrecasteaux' expedition) by way of Table Mountain, returning along the shores of Storm Bay.[31]

On Saturday 10 March Bowen returned from Sydney in the American schooner *Pilgrim*, and the *Ocean* went back to Port Phillip for the rest of the party and provisions left there. They found, however, that there had been an extensive loss of livestock and that wheat and rye were rendered useless by overheating and weevils. The *Ocean* finally returned to the Derwent on 25 June.[32]

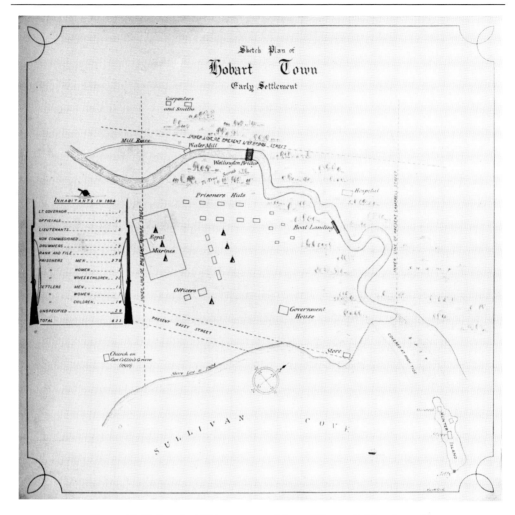

Figure 16: Hobart in 1804—note position of Hunter's Island, used
as a store base until subsumed in later wharf development (In
private hands)

The history of the first seven years or so of the settlement at Hobart Town is one of
muted conflict with the Aborigines against a background of constant anxiety about food
supplies and provisions in general. There was never enough food produced on the spot
to feed the population of free and freed settlers, convicts and military, numbering about
800 by 1809. The whole administration was rendered more difficult for Collins by the
absence of legal powers other than those exercised by the magistrates, and by the practice
of re-transporting prisoners from Sydney to the Derwent, thus presenting Collins with
hardened and abandoned wretches who were a great trouble. The fact was that no criminal court proceedings were possible in Van Diemen's Land because Deputy Judge Advocate Samuel Bate did not arrive until 14 May 1806, and turned out to be incompetent as
well as two years late. Then, for twelve years the British government failed to forward the

necessary documents to create a criminal court, so that serious cases had to be sent to Sydney. This was usually not done, because it led to much inconvenience and loss of labour and time and money. As an example to evildoers, one prisoner was sent to Sydney for trial and, adjudged guilty, returned to the shores of Van Diemen's Land and hanged at Hobart Town, but Collins feared that even this salutary example would not hold in check the proclivities of the vicious. Thus was the law brought into disrepute and contempt during the establishment of Hobart Town.[33]

Collins despaired and spoke of the strange neglect of the British government. On the face of it this was indeed extraordinary, even for the Colonial Office, because Collins received no response during six years to despatches sent straight to London. It may be that Collins was considered directly responsible to the governor of New South Wales and so was writing through the wrong channels—but if so, he was never officially informed. This was typical of the British neglect of the settlement at Hobart Town.[34]

Conflict with the Aboriginal people began at Risdon in May 1804, when the Reverend Knopwood, in the Hobart Town camp, was startled to hear the sound of a cannon from across the river. It had been fired on the orders of Lieutenant Moore when a group of Aboriginals appeared in or near the Risdon site. Casualties apparently were inflicted when the Europeans either panicked or decided to demonstrate their firepower. There is evidence that the Aboriginals did not constitute a war party, if indeed such existed in their culture, for they were accompanied by women and children. There were certainly isolated clashes during the following seven years but there is no reason to suppose, from the fragmentary evidence, that there ever existed a state of war. There were not many Europeans. In 1807 the Reverend Knopwood mingled easily with an estimated 250 to 300 Aboriginals at Brown's River, south of Hobart Town (possibly named after the botanist Robert Brown) but there were cases of hostilities and bloodshed.

Early in 1805 the Aboriginals set fire to a sealers' hut and robbed the men of their provisions and destroyed about 2000 skins—or so the sealers claimed. The next year the Reverend Knopwood reported a case where the Aboriginals wounded a kangaroo hunter with a spear, killed or wounded three of his dogs and took three kangaroos from the men. The Aboriginals evidently did the same thing in November and then in early 1807 there occurred what may well have been a ritual killing. This concerned Robert Waring, transported for fourteen years on the *Calcutta*. When hunting kangaroo for the deputy commissary, he was forced from a hut by the Aboriginals, who came in great numbers. He was taken some distance and one of the Aboriginals threw a spear at him which entered his side. Waring pulled it out and on the Aboriginals going to pick up the spear to throw it again, Waring shot and killed one of their number. Struggling down river towards the settlement and safety, he died of wounds.

There is some evidence that the conflict between European and Aboriginal was exacerbated or possibly largely caused by competition for kangaroo meat and kangaroo products during the period that the colony was desperate for fresh food, but the relations between the two peoples in these early days are very shadowy. Evidence from Aboriginals is almost non-existent although some later told GA Robinson, who sought to rescue the demoralised remnants of their people in the 1830s and place them in what were virtually concentration camps, of incidents of European attacks. One of the very few European reactions is that of Surveyor Harris who considered that the Aboriginals would be quiet if left unmolested, but that escaped convicts wantonly murdered the poor wretches and kidnapped their women. This led to acts of revenge.[35]

Hobart Town was the hub of what was first, last and always a penal settlement; the dispersal, treatment and labour of the convicts was Collins' main concern and no one was ever permitted to forget it. The daily account of robberies committed during the night by the ever-present convicts was one of the few enlivenments for officers who regarded themselves as surrounded by the most infamous of convicts, their lives and careers characterised by stealing and flogging. Some combined order and gratification by taking convict women as mistresses, so that there was no respectable society at Hobart Town. Indeed the atmosphere of a raw penal colony on the edge of civilisation and the borders of starvation was not calculated to induce fine feelings. Even Collins took up with the wife of the convict Matthew Power and then with Eliza Eddington; Edward Lord who became lieutenant governor during Collins's absence, associated with Maria Risley, evidently transported in 1804 for stealing in a dwelling house.

When Edward Lord succeeded to the command of the Marines and acted as lieutenant governor during the temporary absence of Collins, he placed a convict named Mary Granger in the stocks for an hour on suspicion of stealing a tumbler. Some of Mary's friends among the convict women then interceded with Mrs Maria Lord and reminded that lady of her previous civil condition. But Maria evidently took no action to help Mary Granger, at which one Martha Hudson, a friend of Granger's then abused Mrs Lord. Infuriated, Lieutenant Lord then and there tied Martha Hudson to the cart's tail and flogged her to the sound of drum and fife down the Parade, without any surgeon attending. This greatly annoyed Magistrate G P Harris, who heard the uproar and whose wife was then in the last stages of pregnancy. When he demanded whether the punishment was a military or civilian one, Lord responded, 'Do you know who I am? I am now Governor and Commanding Officer and will do as I like without you interfering.' The upshot of Harris's strenuous objections was that he was placed under house arrest by armed soldiers, and then proceeded to embark on a very lengthy correspondence with Collins to demand the entire transaction be aired at a court martial. This was rendered unnecessary, however, when Harris died in October 1810.[36]

Organisation of convict labour was related to the urgency of work. Within a few months of the settlement at Hobart Town, Collins had recognised that economic necessity militated against penal theory when he perceived that more labour was to be obtained from prisoners by piecework (taskwork) than by day work, but he was compelled to prefer the latter on the grounds that the convicts thereby had less time for concerting mischief. Despite this, he allowed a farm gang to be tasked, in order to get in a crop of wheat.[37] From earliest times a chronic shortage of effective labour militated against the severity of penal discipline.

Labour prices had to be fixed by Collins in 1804 when he learned that several mechanics, artificers and labourers took advantage of their skills to sell to the highest bidder and charge an unjust and enormous price for work performed by them in their extra time. He laid down that no men, especially the highly valuable sawyers, who had not performed the government work assigned for the week, were to be permitted to work for private individuals in their free time.[38]

The health of the all-important labour force was a constant problem. Scurvy broke out to an alarming degree in the late autumn of 1804, and Collins was obliged to buy kangaroo meat at sixpence a pound, the sourness of the ground impeding the growth of vegetables which might have checked the scourge. As an anti-scorbutic, the meat was boiled into soup with rice and vegetables from the government garden. Deaths from scurvy of such as sawyers and carpenters were particularly lamented by Collins, reducing even further his slim labour force, but the need for timber workers diminished somewhat when he discovered that very durable bricks could be made from the local clay. That was in early summer 1804, and thereafter Collins's men produced no fewer than 30,000 bricks, a great acquisition when so many chimneys were required. Collins also noted that tiles turned out well, and were a safer and more expeditious covering for buildings than thatch, which had hitherto been brought a long distance by water.[39]

In response to Collins's plea for food supplies, King instead persisted in forwarding consumers: thirty female convicts were sent on the *Sophia* in January 1805.[40] By mid 1806, some 465 persons were victualled at Hobart Town, of whom only 165 could be used for public labour and several of these were perfectly useless. As the entire labour force for twelve months had been scantily clad and badly fed, it could not be expected that much labour could be obtained.[41] Yet the population continued to increase. The main source of increased numbers was not from Sydney but from Norfolk Island. This convict settlement had been established in 1788 but, largely because of difficulties in landing stores, it was ordered to be wound up in 1804 and its population gradually transferred to Van Diemen's Land. By this time, however, the great majority of Norfolk Island convicts had served out their sentences and hence came free to the southern settlement. By September 1808, arrivals totalled 333, all demanding that they be assisted after the inconvenience of being uprooted from their erstwhile home in the Pacific; the next month 242 more came.[42]

The arrival of the Norfolk Islanders emphasised the administration's constant preoccupation with problems of stores, provisions and food. These supplies were especially closely guarded and numerous injunctions issued. For example, no boat was permitted to come into the creek or land on Hunter's Island after the taptoo (that is, a tattoo, or signal for curfew) had been beaten.[43] Not only were food supplies limited but stores such as tools and equipment were no good: axes were so soft that the commonest woods of Van Diemen's Land turned their edges, gimlets were worn out after one use, the iron being rolled instead of wrought; sewing thread for mending the convicts' clothes was nearly all rotten; shoes were of bad quality, all the one size and completely worn out in a fortnight, so that kangaroo skins had to be tanned. Although making very good upper leathers, kangaroo skins were too soft for sole leather, and as there were few substitutes shoes remained scarce. The ordnance also was incomplete; medical instruments were second-hand and in many cases of old-fashioned design; there was neither borax, glue, resin nor a bar of steel to be had. Yet some of the meat was excellent, added Collins fairly, finding some joy in a catalogue of woe.[44] As may be seen, the establishment of Van Diemen's Land presents a splendid example of how the establishment of colonies offered the opportunity for exploitation and sale of defective or non-existent goods.

The instruction to close down the Risdon settlement (its establishment embarked on the *Ocean* on 29 July 1804) meant that Collins was enabled to augment his precious stock by the addition of one bull, nine cows and seven calves, twenty-nine sheep and sixteen lambs.[45] The *Lady Barlow* had also arrived, but the promised provisions of pork and flour on board turned out to have gone bad. However, a valuable cargo of 230 cows, one bull, sixty oxen, fifty-nine sows, two boars, one stallion and three mares were landed from this vessel.[46]

Twelve months later the settlement at the Derwent still existed, precariously balanced between hard and desperate times. The lieutenant governor remained short of supplies and begged King for an immediate supply of grain and, if possible, salted meat, because otherwise Hobart Town would soon be without either. If nothing were sent, stressed Collins, then the current weekly ration of four lbs of flour would be halved.[47] In late September 1805, Collins began to betray signs of emotion and a desperate urgency quite at odds with his usual laconic communications. If nothing came before 1 October, he would be able to serve only two lbs of flour a week to each person, at which rate he could continue for six weeks. But what was that, he asked rhetorically? No one could last long in such conditions, and had it not been for the kangaroos and emus which afforded the people of Van Diemen's Land as providential a source of supply as the Mt Pitt birds once did the wretched inhabitants of Norfolk Island, there would have been no meat at all. Provisions continued to be augmented by kangaroos, hunted by those who owned dogs, affording relief to the extent of the commissariat purchasing at a shilling a lb and distributing more than 17,000 lbs in the period August to October 1805.[48] This perennial shortage of provisions led Collins early in 1806 to issue new imports of inferior salted pork which, if subjected to serious inspection, would surely have been condemned. The scoundrels who had casked it at Norfolk Island had imposed on the government by putting a few pieces of good meat at each end of the casks and filling the remainder with meat that should have been thrown away.

There was no consolation in drink either: the spirits supplied by the victualling office were deficient, and when Collins appropriated this most necessary item from the *Myrtle* for issue to the military, part of his supply was at once stolen. Altogether the year 1806 contained little joy. The *Venus*, one of the supply ships from Sydney, was piratically seized by her crew at Port Dalrymple and so Hobart Town settlement lost a considerable quantity of private comforts sent on board for the enjoyment of the officers, and about 17,000 lbs of salt pork, flour and meal. By midwinter a desperate Collins feared that he would be compelled to evacuate the settlement, and wrote to the chief of HM forces at the Cape of Good Hope requesting food supplies, having been reduced to committing his reserves by issuing grain intended for seed. Once again, kangaroo meat was the only shield against starvation and this item was issued after being hunted mainly in May and July.[49]

Upon his arrival at Sydney, Governor Bligh sent a much-needed shipment of supplies to Hobart Town. He was in the nick of time—the local kangaroo hunters had declared themselves on strike unless they were supplied with bread, for without it they maintained they could not hunt. In September 1807 Harris noted that Hobart Town people had been without bread for upwards of two months and were subsisting on coffee made with bran without sugar, and kangaroo fried in rancid pork in lieu of bread.[50]

During this period of early subsistence, officers began and continued their economic activities. For instance, AWH Humphrey bought five dogs for £25, to kill about 1000 lbs of kangaroo meat a week, for which he received sixpence a lb from the commissariat. He also exchanged 400 lbs of this meat for flour from the captain of the *Ocean*. And any quantity of rum could be bought, said Humphrey, the commissariat to be repaid in a given time. The established price was a guinea a gallon, 'but we can make four times that of it', he wrote gleefully. Friends and allies were important in trading enterprises, he continued, congratulating himself on being befriended by such as Lieutenant Lord, a first cousin to Sir Hugh Owen of Wales, no less, and a brother of a counsellor in Lincoln's Inn. 'It was necessary for me to join with someone, who would look after the stock in my absence in the country, and Lieutenant Lord is prudent and steady', observed Humphrey piously. Lieutenant Lord was more than that. By 1820 he was said to be the richest man in Van Diemen's Land.[51]

Harris too was involved in trading, though he leavened his account of commercial dealing with descriptive passages in his letters home. In surroundings he described as idyllic, Harris rejoiced that the immense, beautiful country romantically abounded with kangaroos, emus, duck, teal and black swans. It was a great thing, he thought, to have such a supply of fresh meat. Especially was this so, given the local style of barter and trade, as sellers would accept payment for goods in wheat, flour, salt pork, beef or kangaroo meat. He himself had managed to come into possession of some hundredweight of valuable flour from a ship by the simple exchange of fresh kangaroo meat.

It was next to impossible to gain a competency other than by trading or farming, explained Harris, but the former was forbidden to officers in the colony on pain of losing commission, and the latter would only answer in respect to a stock farm.[52] Anyway, all the means of making money out of the colony were monopolised by one or two individuals, he complained. If this was so, it is very probable that Edward Lord was one of their number. What else were colonies for, and especially penal colonies, but to exploit individually and collectively? Coming into possession of a valuable proportion of the breeding stock at the Derwent, Lord and Humphrey had been favoured with grants of land. With an excellently developed sense of survival, Lord had managed by 1809 to possess himself of a large and valuable herd of cattle, and had secured Collins's sanction to appropriate 500 acres for grazing and agricultural purposes.[53]

It was particularly irritating to Collins that incompetence at the Colonial Office actually militated against the potential success of the colony centred upon Hobart Town: the land was sufficient for extensive agricultural purposes, the water supply was reliable and the climate appeared to be subject to none of the sudden and distressing changes of cold and heat that characterised Port Jackson and Port Phillip. Furthermore, the harbour was extraordinarily easy of access, sounding at fourteen to twenty fathoms right up to the settlement's edge.

As if he had not enough problems, Collins suffered further handicaps such as the inadequate supply of specie, which obliged him to direct the commissariat to issue small promissory notes, not less than £1 in value, which proved a great accommodation as they passed into circulation. Again, in September 1804 King transmitted to Collins a General Order discouraging or preventing foreign vessels clearing from the Australian settlements on whaling voyages, which in effect compelled him to turn away much-needed supplies. Commercial dealings with the American ship *Criterion* for example, appeared to contradict the order because this would involve communication with the possessions of the East India Company as well as the China Coast.[54]

Whaling enterprises were largely conducted by ships from Britain and the United States, but some local whaling was prosecuted and Collins enthused dutifully that the utility of colonies could never be better evinced than by their natural products becoming articles of commercial importance to the mother country. The Derwent estuary was resorted to by whalers every season, many filling their ships with black and sperm whale oil procured there, in the adjacent bays and off the south-east coast, and then taken to England. Even as the first settlers came to the Derwent, British whaling ships sailed into the mouth of the Derwent, unaware that settlement had occurred in Van Diemen's Land. Knopwood heard whales sounding opposite his cottage and sometimes found it dangerous to travel across the river, his boat being liable to be overturned by the surfacing leviathans.[55]

Sealing was one of the interests which the British were interested to extend when they

93

came into the region, and to this purpose government occupation of King Island was ordered from London. The sealers complained that this would frighten away their quarry, but their own rapacity in ruthlessly exploiting this resource, asserted Collins, would more effectually extirpate the seals than any system of settlement as suggested by the Colonial Office.[56] But Collins had no means of occupying King Island and it remained uninhabited for years.

The desirability of utilising the natural resources of the settlement was never overlooked. Nature's bounty was there for the British colonisers to grasp and exploit. Hearing that the 'cedar' tree was to be found at Adventure Bay (named after Captain Furneaux' ship in 1773) Collins despatched Harris and Knopwood to examine the Huon area. Knopwood brought back some Huon pine, which was destined to become an extremely valuable commodity for such purposes as shipbuilding because of its amazing resistance to insects and worms.[57]

The accession to power of the insurgents at Sydney in 1808 and the ousting of Governor Bligh was greeted with great caution by Collins, but Johnston and his cronies appeared very anxious to keep on good terms with the Hobart Town base, and forwarded extensive food supplies. This may not have been unrelated to the fact that the northern settlement of Van Diemen's Land, also made in 1804 as a result of King's anxieties, was under the control of William Paterson who, as it happened, was second in command of the New South Wales Corps, and therefore next in line to the usurper Johnston. Paterson, indeed, was finally and most reluctantly obliged to leave Port Dalrymple and return to take over at Sydney.

Despite the assistance of the rebels at Port Jackson, by winter 1808 Collins was yet again forced by the arrival of the Norfolk Island settlers to have recourse to the bush for food. He caused the commissariat to purchase increasingly scarce kangaroo meat at a shilling a lb, and issue it in the ratio of seven lbs to each four lbs of pork. But by now at least Collins had managed to put a twelve-month supply of grain in the stores.[58] Bligh's stay at the Derwent, where he awaited news of rescue and support from England, was a nuisance to the Hobart Town settlement but of no historical significance. Collins's problems continued to be those of foodstuffs and manpower right to the end of his regime and little was done in the way of increased provisions or labour until, in 1812, there arrived the convict ship *Indefatigable*. It brought 200 male prison labourers, embarked in England as a result of a plea from Governor Macquarie for more men to work the southern colony.[59]

But by then Lieutenant Governor Collins lay dead and the turbulent colony of Van Diemen's Land was about to enjoy the boon of having its ports freed and its superb pastoral lands flooded by a great increase of free settlers direct from the United Kingdom. With the arrival of these men the nature of Hobart Town was to change from an embattled encampment to a thriving maritime and pastoral centre, ready to play its role in the further invasion, colonisation and exploitation of Australia.

Notes

[1] Plomley, N.J.B. *The Baudin Expedition and the Tasmanian Aborigines 1802*, (Hobart, 1983), p.6.

[2] Baudin, N. (trans. C. Cornell), *Journal of Post Captain Nicolas Baudin, Commander-in-Chief of the Corvettes Géographe and Naturaliste, assigned by order of the government to a voyage of discovery*, (Adelaide, 1974), pp.1-9.

[3] *H.R.A.*, IV, p.145, (9-5-1803).

[4] *Ibid.*, p.259, (9-5-1803).

[5] Giblin, R.W. *The Early History of Tasmania: The Geographical Era 1642-1804*, (London, 1928), pp.206, 233.

[6] *H.R.A.*, I, iv, p.144, (9-5-1803). Giblin, *op.cit.*, p.140.

[7] C.O. 201/38, ff.245-51, 22-7-1805.

[8] Baudin, *op.cit.*, p.xii; *H.R.A.*, III, i, pp.190-1, (29-3-1803).

[9] *Ibid.*, p.191, pp.193-4, (10-6-1803).

[10] *Ibid.*, p.197, (20-9-1803).

[11] *Ibid.*, p.199, (27-9-1803).

[12] *Ibid.*, p.99, and pp.202-5.

[13] November-December 1802, Memorandum of a Proposed Settlement in Bass's Straits, *H.R.A.*, III, i, p.1; *Memoir of a Chart of Port Phillip*, surveyed in October, 1803, by Lieutenant James Tuckey of His Majesty's Ship *Calcutta*, *H.R.A.*, III, i, pp.110-1, notes 76 and 77.

[14] *H.R.A.*, I, iv, p.9, note 2, (14-2-1803).

[15] *Ibid.*, p.306, (27-6-1803).

[16] *Ibid.*, note 2, (14-2-1803).

[17] *A.D.B.*, Vol. 1, entry for David Collins.

[18] Collins Commission *H.R.A.*, III, i, p.4, 14-1-1803; *H.R.A.*, I, iv, p.10.

[19] *H.R.A.*, III, i, p.22, (15-7-1803); p.25, (22-8-1803) and pp.26-7 and note 19, (5-11-1803).

[20] A Journal of the Proceedings on Board His Majesty's Ship *Calcutta*, *H.R.A.*, III, i, p.105, note 74, (13-12-1803) and I, iv, p.605, (1-4-1804).

[21] Memoir of a Chart of Port Phillip, *H.R.A.*, III, i, pp.110-11 and 116.

[22] *H.R.A.*, III, i, p.110, note 77.

[23] *Ibid.*, p.287, (10-11-1804).

[24] Memoir of a Chart of Port Phillip, *op.cit.*, p.110.

[25] *Ibid.*, *H.R.A.*, III, i, p.218, (28-2-1804).

[26] *Ibid.*, pp.147-8.

[27] *The Diary of the Reverend Robert Knopwood, 1803-1838, first Chaplain of Van Diemen's Land*, (ed. Mary Nicholls), (Hobart, 1977), (hereafter cited as 'Knopwood Diary'), entry 27-2-1804. *Hamilton and Greville Papers*, British Library, 42071, letter of 1-8-1804.

[28] *H.R.A.*, III, i, pp.222-4, (29-2-1804) and pp.148-9, (17 to 21-2-1804); 'Knopwood Diary', entry (26-2-1804).

[29] *C.O.*, 201/38, ff.245-51, 22-7-1805; 'Knopwood Diary', *op.cit.*, undated entry preceding 17-10-1803; *H.R.A.*, III, i, pp.791, 810, notes 38, 142.

[30] *H.R.A.*, III, i, pp.224-5, (29-2-1804).

[31] Hamilton and Greville Papers, *op.cit.*, letter from Humphrey 1-8-1804; *H.R.A.*, III, i, p.241, (15-5-1804).

[32] *H.R.A.*, III, i, p.150, (10-3-1804); pp.248-9, (31-7-1804); p.242, (15-5-1804) and p.169, (25-6-1804).

[33] *Ibid.*, i, p.409, (23-10-1808); p.764; p.226, (29-2-1804); p.817, note 186; p.811 note 146; and pp.356-7, (20-4-1806).

[34] *Ibid.*, p.811, note 146.

[35] Robson. L.L. *History of Tasmania*, (Melbourne, 1983), Vol. 1, pp.45-51, 220-53; Marie Fels, 'Culture Contact in the County of Buckinghamshire, Van Diemen's Land 1803-11', *T.H.R.A.*, Papers and Proceedings, Vol. 29 No. 2, June, 1982, pp.47-9.

[36] *A.D.B.*, Vol. 1, entries for David Collins and G.P. Harris; *Harris Papers*, British Library, 45, 156, ff.23-5, 29-31, letters from G.P. Harris, 7-8-1804, 12-10-1805; 45, 57; Robson, *History of Tasmania*, p.131.

[37] *H.R.A.*, III, i, p.241, (15-5-1804).

[38] *Ibid.*, pp.265-71.

[39] *Ibid.*, pp.286-7, (10-11-1804).

[40] *H.R.A.*, III, i, p.305, (8-1-1805); p.313, (22-2-1805); p.315, (26-2-1805).

[41] *Ibid.*, p.363, (17-6-1806).

[42] *Ibid.*, p.245, (23-7-1804); p.339, (17-12-1805); p.347, (24-12-1805); pp.403-4, (1-9-1808); pp.407 and 409, (23-10-1808).

[43] *H.R.A.*, III, i, p.271, (24-6-1804).

[44] *Ibid.*, pp.232-3, (4-3-1804); p.320, (1-3-1805) and p.343, (18-12-1805).

[45] *Ibid.*, p.249, (31-7-1804).

[46] *Ibid.*, p.279, (18-8-1804); p.307, (20-2-1805).

[47] *H.R.A.*, III, i, pp.326-7, (28-9-1805).

[48] *Ibid.*, pp.330-2, (15-10-1805).

[49] *Ibid.*, p.369, (2-8-1806); and pp.376-8, (31-8-1806).

[50] *Ibid.*, p.380, (18-10-1806); Harris Papers, *op.cit.*, letters 1-2-1805 (1806?) and 3-9-1807.

[51] Hamilton and Greville Papers, *op.cit.*, letter from Humphrey, 1, 5-8-1804; *A.D.B.*, Vol. 2, entry for Edward Lord.

[52] Harris Papers, *op.cit.*, letters 14-2-1804, 7-8-1804, 12-10-1805 and 10-4-1806.

[53] *H.R.A.*, III, i, pp.346-7, (24-12-1805); p.415, (25-3-1809).

[54] *Ibid.*, p.231, (4-3-1804); p.262, (3-8-1804); p.282, (30-9-1804); p.377, (31-8-1806).

[55] *Ibid.*, p.316, (26-2-1805); pp.404-5, (1-10-1808); Harris Papers, *op.cit.*, letter 14-2-1804; 'Knopwood Diary', *op.cit.*, entries for 28-6-1804, 1-7-1806.

[56] *H.R.A.*, III, i, p.227, (29-2-1804).

[57] *Ibid.*, pp.291-2, (8-12-1804); 'Knopwood Diary', *op.cit.*, entry 28-11-1804.

[58] *H.R.A.*, III, i, p.402, (11-6-1808); p.403, (1-9-1808).

[59] *H.R.A.*, I, vii, pp.382-3, (18-10-1811) and p.488, (19-5-1812).

Chapter V

Hobart: A Moment of Glory

Gordon Rimmer

Located in a predominantly rural world, western Europe's towns had grown slowly over the centuries with the result that four-fifths of them had less than 20,000 inhabitants at the beginning of the nineteenth century.[1] Hobart, planted in 1804, had 13,000 inhabitants within thirty years. At the time of its foundation little was known about Tasmania apart from the fact that it was an island and, despite sanguine reports from the first commandants about the Derwent valley's agricultural and commercial potential, the newcomers were confronted by a strange, forbidding landscape. The British government, engulfed in hostilities with France, simply wanted an out-station there for strategic reasons. What would become of it in the future was not clear.

When Governor Lachlan Macquarie toured the island in November 1811, some 600 people lived in Hobart and another 400 further up the Derwent at New Norfolk. Hobart still had the appearance of a temporary encampment. A few dozen huts, constructed of logs, turf, split palings and wickerwork covered with clay, were 'indiscriminately scattered on both sides of a very fine stream of water' which curved round to the south-west.[2] Many were occupied by convicts. Others served as taverns, lodging houses and shops. On a low hill, a few hundred yards south of the stream, the marines' tents stood in regular lines. A government store, built of brick for security, dominated the jetty at the mouth of the stream. The free settlers who had arrived seven years earlier had chosen land two miles further north at Newtown. Their 'white cottages' were surrounded by 'tolerable good gardens', but frequent cropping had already exhausted the soil.[3] Hobart was little more than a village, but no ordinary village. Three-quarters of its inhabitants were not free, and the remainder consisted mainly of soldiers and civilian officials. For the fifty years that Tasmania remained a penal colony, a military garrison and the convict department's headquarters were located there.

By the mid 1830s, Hobart, including Newtown, had 13,394 inhabitants, thirty per cent of the island's population. The town, spread over a thousand acres, had twenty streets intersecting at right angles in a grid-shaped pattern. Almost half the streets had been levelled and macadamised, and five, with more than a hundred dwellings each, contained half the town's 1300 houses. Government House, the Court House, Treasury and Commissariat Office clustered around St George's Square in the centre. Nearby stood the gaol, Anglican church, offices, banks, and lawyers' chambers in Devil's Row. The store, hospital

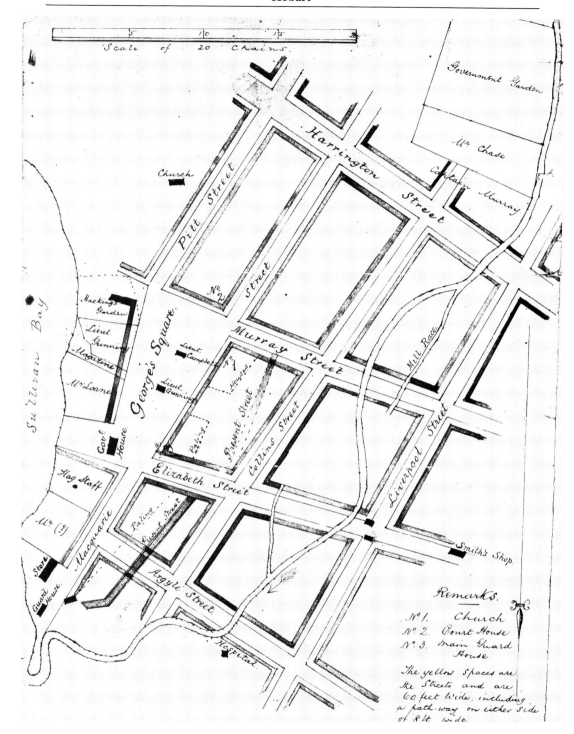

Figure 17: First street plan of Hobart, 1811 (Courtesy of the
Hobart Lands Department)

and prisoners barracks were situated a few blocks away, and the old and new wharves were surrounded by lofty warehouses for the growing volume of merchandise carried by close on 200 sailing ships a year. Within the built-up area there were half a dozen places of worship, and as many schools, and taverns, common lodging houses, dwellings and workshops. On a nearby hill stood the town's biggest group of buildings, the military barracks. Around the outskirts were cowsheds, abattoirs, tanneries, flour and timber mills, breweries, soap boilers and shipyards. Four out of ten buildings were constructed of stone or brick, and the trend towards more specialised land use was reflected in differential property valuations.[4]

Hobart had become more than just the administrative centre of a penal colony. It was the island's main port, a manufacturing centre and the cultural and religious capital of Tasmania. With the arrival of Anglican and Catholic bishops in 1843, it attained the status of a city and, as the 'Athens of the Southern Ocean', enjoyed a brief moment of glory, rising to second place in pre-eminence amongst Australia's towns.[5]

*   *   *

How was this small penal outpost transformed within a generation into a 'populous metropolis'? Before the twentieth century, growing towns were invariably more than political and social capitals. Urban growth depended mainly on trade and industry, and Hobart's early development was determined by the diversification of its economic structure in a predominantly market economy. As in other colonies of settlement, economic growth depended initially on imported capital, labour and commodities. Some 17,000 convicts and 14,000 free settlers had come to Tasmania by the mid 1830s. The free settlers brought capital worth over half a million pounds sterling while the British government allocated some £2 million for commissariat expenditure on local purchases. At the same time commodity imports jumped from £20,000 a year at the end of the Napoleonic Wars to more than £300,000 a year in the mid 1830s.

The distribution of capital and labour throughout the island was the outcome of countless decisions by officials and merchants in Hobart. Some resources were retained in the town but most, after 1815, went into the development of the hinterland. Pressure for an agricultural surplus came from urban initiatives and institutions. Hobart merchants found markets abroad for wheat and wool, expedited the direct capital formation that was essential for commercial agriculture, provided credit for farmers, and financed the shipment of exports. Urban retailers and craftsmen likewise provided the services and goods that farmers could not produce for themselves, and urban professionals attended to rural legal and medical requirements. So rural development was underpinned by urban organisations, and urban growth depended in turn upon rural expansion. The relationship was reciprocal. The progressive exploitation of the hinterland by British immigrants was a co-requisite for urban growth based on primary product exports. Exports from Hobart increased from less than £20,000 a year around 1820, to well over £100,000 by the mid 1830s.

In the final analysis, of course, Hobart's rapid economic growth depended on import substitution. At first everything the settlers required was imported. Import replacement began with the local production of basic foodstuffs and spread to semi-manufactured and manufactured goods. In the absence of exports the cost of imports was initially met by grants from the mother country. As primary produce became available for export, the income received provided an additional source of foreign exchange for the purchase of imports. Because the foreign exchange available for imports was derived both from Britain *and* from exports, the colonists were able *at a very early stage* to import a broad range of goods, and this accelerated the process of substitution by greatly extending the spectrum of opportunities for import replacement. So urban development was the product of a circular process: as local products replaced imports, the foreign exchange thus saved could be used to buy different kinds of imports, and the advent of these imports provided Hobart businessmen with fresh opportunities for import replacement. Before the 1820s this process of import substitution and structural diversification made little headway owing to labour scarcity. But from the later 1820s there was a decade of rapid replacement. By the 1840s two-thirds of Hobart's exports went to Britain and one-third to other British colonies. As the outcome of market forces a simple trading pattern had evolved, involving the exchange of raw materials from an agrarian economy for manufactured products from a metropolitan economy. Even though the quantities traded multiplied over time, the pattern itself remained constant because Hobart's manufacturers soon reached the limits of what was then technologically feasible. Industrial diversification beyond the level already attained could not occur without a corresponding increase in import substitution. But local craftsmen lacked the expertise to make high-quality goods and the island's market was too small to sustain a factory system. Close at hand, the mainland colonies had no more industry than Tasmania and their purchases from the island consisted of meat, grain, fish, timber and bark rather than craft goods. So further diversification through import substitution was circumscribed and Hobart's industrial structure remained frozen for more than a generation.[6]

The scope for processing rural products in Hobart for subsequent export was likewise limited. Considerable value could be added in the town to some products sold there by slaughtering livestock, tanning hides, making casks, salting meat, boiling oil and grinding flour. But less than a fifth of Hobart's exports fell into these categories. Wheat and wool, which accounted for more than half of the town's exports, required little processing. Indeed Hobart's main contribution to trade took the form of providing banking, insurance and storage services. Consequently, the value of imports consumed *in the town* was probably not fully matched by the value added there through servicing and processing commodity exports. In this sense, Hobart's rapid growth and rising living standards in the generation after 1815 depended less upon economic activities undertaken within the town, than upon the development of the hinterland and escalating grants from the British government for the maintenance of the convict establishment.

Two points require mention before the growth of Hobart is considered as the product of agricultural, industrial and commercial interaction. First, although it is useful to distinguish between primary, secondary and tertiary sectors of economic activity, the inhabitants of undeveloped economies are invariably occupied in more than one sector. Second, unlike other Australian colonies, the exploitation of Tasmania's interior was undertaken, not from one town which eclipsed all others, but from two: Hobart in the south and Launceston in the north. Before the mid 1820s, while the inflow of capital, labour and merchandise was still spasmodic and sluggish, Hobart was virtually the only port of entry. When the flows became stronger after 1826, the island's external trade was increasingly shared between Hobart and Launceston.[7] However, by that time Hobart's predominance was ensured. Its merchant houses already controlled most of the island's trade. And the seat of government remained in Hobart after the island was proclaimed a separate colony in 1825 despite an attempt by Lieutenant Governor Arthur to relocate it elsewhere.[8] If the administration had been moved inland as happened in many British North American colonies during the eighteenth century, Hobart would not have grown so rapidly. But the island was a penal colony and few settlers could influence political decision making: consequently, despite northern representations, there was never any real likelihood that the Secretary of State for the Colonies would agree to shift the administration elsewhere.[9] As long as Hobart's commercial community determined the course of rural development, their economic hegemony was assured.

*   *   *

Agricultural development was the first and most important cause of Hobart's growth. The production of primary produce accounted for 45 per cent of Tasmania's small Gross Domestic Product (GDP) of £108,800 produced each year by white settlers between 1815 and 1819, and 52 percent of the much larger GDP of £1,442,500 produced annually between 1835 and 1839.[10] In two decades, the island's GDP increased thirteen-fold in current prices, and the value of its primary produce fifteen-fold. By 1835-9 arable farming and fisheries contributed £470,300 to GDP, and animal husbandry £275,000.[11] Figures in this form inevitably imply a greater degree of rural specialisation than was actually the case. Mixed farming was the predominant type of agriculture in Tasmania at the time.[12] It not only provided subsistence but enabled those on the land to adjust to variable market conditions. Despite statistical categorisation, therefore, no sharp distinction really existed between arable and animal husbandry.

With 1325 acres under plough in 1813 wheat production in the vicinity of the Derwent met local requirements. When the first convict ship to reach Hobart in almost a decade arrived in that year, half the prisoners were added to the agricultural workforce. In the following season surplus grain was shipped to Port Jackson which was stricken by drought.[13] By 1816, 3204 acres had been cleared in southern Tasmania, and half the wheat crop of 48,006 bushels was sent to the parent settlement. By the early 1820s, twice as much wheat again was being produced and exported. This expansion of arable husbandry depended upon favourable market conditions, additional labour, Tasmanian productivity and transport costs. Since tillage required a heavy input of labour, the extension of grain production was constrained before 1818 by the dearth of immigrants. When the workforce subsequently increased, market conditions became less buoyant. Local demand expanded with population growth, though the proportion of the population victualled by the government fell and a fixed price system was replaced by tendering. As farmers with supplies in excess of subsistence and store requirements competed to dispose of growing surpluses at public auctions and after 1820 at Hobart's weekly wheat market, grain prices tumbled. The main export market at Port Jackson concurrently became sluggish because Hawkesbury farmers could normally produce 'the vast bulk' of that settlement's requirements and, in the absence of crop failures, the marginal demand there depended upon transport costs, cheaper land clearance and higher productivity in Tasmania, and the superior quality of the island's wheat which 'was alone held to be sufficient to meet transport costs'.[14]

Wheat prices dropped in the early 1820s to between five and six shillings a bushel. Owing to soil exhaustion farm production costs rose and transport costs played an increasingly decisive role in determining the limits of wheat growing. Farmers situated further away from Hobart found themselves at a disadvantage. To eliminate toll and ferry charges and to protect farmers on the frontier against bushrangers and Aboriginals, Governor Arthur tried in 1825 to move the seat of government to Brighton or New Norfolk in the upper Derwent.[15] But he was unsuccessful, with the result that, although two-thirds of the acreage under wheat in the island was located in the south where three-quarters of the population lived, the arable frontier there extended inland no further than thirty miles. Farming also flourished independently in the north, where conditions for grain growers were more favourable and yields higher. With less than a quarter of the island's inhabitants, the north had a third of the wheat acreage and accounted for almost half the island's grain exports in 1821. During the next twenty-seven years Tasmania's wheat acreage increased eight-fold to the point where nearly half the wheat acreage of Australia and 57 per cent of the island's enlarged acreage was located in the north, which became known as 'the granary of Van Diemen's Land'.[16] In the 1840s, 42 per cent of Tasmania's wheat crop was exported, four-fifths of it through Launceston, to new settlements at Port Phillip and Adelaide. By that time wheat was sown on two-fifths to half of the island's acreage, the other cash crops being barley, oats, potatoes and turnips. The area under these crops had increased to 60,000 acres in two decades and, with the exception of potatoes, much of this produce was exported through Launceston.

Animal husbandry required more land than arable farming. Ninety-four per cent of the land that had been alienated by 1815 was used for livestock. In that year 42,000 sheep and 5000 cattle grazed 30,000 acres. Initially this industry too was developed mainly in the south. In 1821, 71 per cent of the island's pastures and three-quarters of its livestock were located in the southern half of the island. Production costs were low. Land was virtually free and little labour was required. As meat supplies increased, prices fell along with the capital value of the prolific herds. With prices down to sixpence per lb, large producers responded by salting and shipping carcases in casks to Port Jackson, and something like a fifth of the island's meat was exported. But with freight at £3 a ton, producers netted no more than fourpence a lb which 'barely leaves a profit'.[17] As the days of high meat prices drew to a close, livestock producers, like arable farmers, sought other opportunities. They sold hides and skins and produced dairy products once the manufacture of butter proved profitable in the early 1820s; and, since livestock specialists operated further away from the market, there was always the prospect of land speculation.[18] Livestock production thus remained 'a profitable method of investing money'.[19] However, whereas the number of cattle increased by 78,000 by 1841, the number of sheep rose by more than a million following the rapid occupation of the Midland Plains, an area of some 4000 square miles which became available as the Aboriginal population was wiped out. The use of this resource to promote a new export industry provided an additional stimulus to urban growth after the mid 1820s.

The opportunity to export large quantities of wool to Britain arose through an unexpected stroke of good fortune. The expansion of wool production could not have been predicted at the time because it required a coincidence of favourable market conditions in both Britain and Tasmania. The genesis of the island's pastoral industry involved several independent variables: postwar fluctuations in the level of activity in Britain's woollen industry and a shift towards the manufacture of worsted cloth; the imposition in 1819 of a protective tariff against foreign wool which gave colonial producers an advantage until 1825; the relative decline of coarse wool prices; and the reconstruction of the island's pastoral industry so that fine wool could be produced for export.[20] Tasmanian capitalists had little more than a decade in which to respond to these changes in order to meet the Yorkshire woollen industry's raw material requirements. If the opportunity had arisen before 1820 or after 1840, the burst of growth that occurred in the later 1820s and 1830s would have been less explosive, though the island's economic structure would doubtless have evolved along much the same lines.

The acceleration of pastoral farming coincided with grants by Governor George Arthur totalling one million acres of crown land in the six years before 1832. By that date more wool was exported to England from Tasmania than from New South Wales. Fifteen years later when all the colony's best grazing land had been alienated, its sheep population reached a peak of 1.7 million. But whereas three-quarters of the island's sheep had been in the south in 1820, the majority were in the north by that time and Launceston was exporting as much wool as Hobart. All told, wool accounted for three-quarters of the island's export earnings and it integrated Tasmania's economy with a flourishing British factory industry.

The aggressive exploitation for commercial gain of more than two million acres by a few thousand people in the fifteen years before 1840 was a remarkable achievement. Resourceful pastoralists obtained free land grants before 1832 which, supplemented by lease and purchase, enabled them to operate on a relatively large scale. Between fifty and a hundred had more than 18,000 acres each, and several hundred around 10,000 acres. Although animal husbandry contributed less to the island's GDP than arable farming, average earnings were high because fewer people were involved commercially on a large scale. Many 'wool barons' earned £1000 to £4000 a year, and they used their lightly taxed private wealth to acquire public status by constructing imposing town and country houses and by seeking public office which conferred a legitimacy on those who fancied themselves as gentry.[21]

Whaling and sealing provided another source of income from primary production and the fisheries had more impact on Hobart than on any other port in the island. Coastal sealing lasted for a generation until the industry was ruined in the 1830s by reckless destruction. Once the British government reduced the duty on imported whale oil in the late 1820s colonial entrepreneurs also participated in bay whaling. This industry reached its peak in 1836-8 when nine of the island's ten whaling stations exported their products through Hobart and the town became 'one of the great whaling ports of the world'.[22] As such it derived economic benefit from victualling and repairing whalers and from the expenditure of crews. But this industry too was soon destroyed by indiscriminate slaughter and Hobart vessels subsequently took little part in deep-sea whaling.

In sum, primary production flourished in the 1820s and 1830s. The beneficiaries were the small landowners who earned their livelihood by mixed farming, and the larger landowners who exported wool, hides and meat. The economic cost was shouldered mainly by the Aboriginals and by convicts assigned to the interior. By the end of the 1830s, Tasmania's most accessible land had been alienated, its fisheries exhausted and settlers were migrating across Bass Strait in search of fresh opportunities. The first phase of fast economic growth had come to an end and primary product expansion no longer provided a stimulus for further urban development.

*　　　*　　　*

The second cause of urban growth and prosperity was external trade. Even after the rise of Launceston in the 1820s, Hobart remained the main port of entry for most imports. Four-fifths of the colony's trade passed through the town in 1828, and from 1840 to 1847, 48 per cent of the island's exports and 63 per cent of its imports. The average annual number of shipping arrivals increased from under 30 before 1820 to 185 in the late 1830s.[23]

Initially all shipping berthed at the Old Wharf on Hunter's Island at the northern end of the cove. As the number of arrivals increased, congestion became a problem because it took at least a fortnight to discharge and load cargo and provision a ship for the long voyage to England. So a second wharf was constructed at the southern end of the cove. This undertaking began in 1818 with the resumption of land and the excavation of an embankment to provide level ground for the erection of warehouses in what became Salamanca Place. Work on the quay proper started in 1830 and from that date ships could berth alongside. But it was not until 1836 that fresh water could be piped directly into vessels. From start to finish the project took eighteen years to complete and at times involved a work force of a hundred convicts. In 1828, well before its completion, the engineer's office was planning a new scheme involving extensive reclamation work along the shoreline between the Old and New Wharves for the accommodation of twenty-two warehouses, a Customs House and a careening basin with workshops. Work on the western foreshore began in 1839. By 1847, half the town's sixty-two warehouses were located near the wharves, and port facilities along the waterfront which in 1820 had covered thirty-five acres occupied twice as much space two decades later.[24]

About 20 per cent of Hobart's adult males were involved in trade and commerce in 1820, and a further ten per cent may have been employed on a casual basis. Twenty years later 982 inhabitants, 31 per cent of the workforce, were engaged in 'commerce'. By 1824 the town had twelve merchants, all either free settlers or ex-officers (serving personnel were barred from trade in Tasmania). The high risks initially involved in such enterprise were covered by big mark-ups and by diversification. Merchants invested in rural properties, acquired urban real estate for rental, owned ships, ventured into whaling, supplied timber, and formed partnerships to provide banking and insurance facilities. Generating income out of all proportion to their numbers, these men played a key role in the town's development by forcing the pace of agricultural expansion and, owing to their familiarity with local conditions, by undertaking worthwhile investments that were beyond the reach of outsiders.[25]

*   *   *

The third source of Hobart's growth was industrial development. The process of import substitution involved both crafting local materials for domestic needs and applying finishing touches to merchandise imported in an unfinished state. Unfortunately the trading aggregates for this period are so fragmentary that Hobart's industrial genesis cannot be properly analysed along these lines and the full effects of import replacement remain obscure.

Processing local raw materials such as grain, hides, skins and timber obviously provided scope for import replacement. Four watermills on the Hobart rivulet were grinding corn in 1822. By 1847 there were nineteen, five powered by steam engines. In 1824, two years after the distillation of spirits had been legalised, Hobart had four distilleries. When the

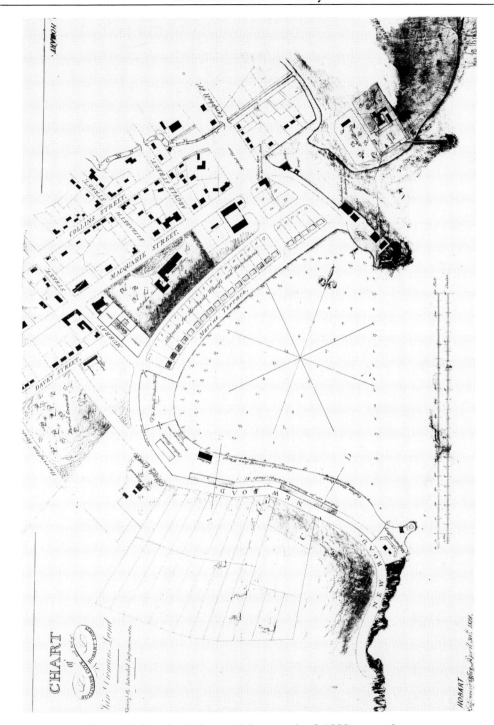

Figure 18: Plan for Hobart and the new wharf, 1828—note the absorbtion of Hunter's Island (Courtesy of the Hobart Lands Department)

government raised its excise duties two of them closed. The other two consumed 12,500 bushels of grain in 1838 just before their licences were revoked. By 1824 Hobart also had four breweries. Twenty years later eleven breweries produced enough beer to meet local demand and provide a surplus for sale in Port Jackson. Although most of the island's hides and skins were exported, tanning and currying was carried out in a small way near slaughterhouses. By 1847 some 60,000 animals a year were butchered in four abattoirs on the outskirts of the town and a dozen tanneries supplied leather which was fashioned into boots, saddles and straps.[26]

The best-known industry in the town was shipbuilding. It required large amounts of capital and mainly used local materials. Four yards at Battery Point built vessels up to 600 tons weight at an average cost of between £7 and £8 a ton. In the 1840s 'Hobart turned out more shipping than the other Australian colonies together'.[27] This in turn stimulated associated trades such as cooperage, mast and blockmaking, ropemaking, sailmaking and sawmilling. More important in terms of employment and capital formation was building. Apart from public buildings, taverns, shops and warehouses, an average of a hundred houses a year were built in Hobart between 1820 and 1841. All this construction provided work for free, emancipist and convict labour as carpenters, joiners, bricklayers, glaziers, plasterers, plumbers, painters, tilers, brickmakers, sawyers and smiths. By the 1830s window frames, doors, nails, hinges and glass which initially had to be imported were produced locally.[28]

By that time a considerable amount of metalworking was also undertaken in the town. From shoeing horses and repairing coaches, craftsmen went on to make ironmongery for buildings and boats, and produce castings and engines. Seven agricultural-machine makers supplied threshers and ploughs besides repairing broken ones. Other enterprises drawing on local skills and materials sprang up in these boom years. In the 1820s craftsmen produced earthenware pots, pans, soap, candles, hats, salt and glue. By the 1830s there were manufacturers of snuff, pipes, carts, parchment and a small sugar refinery. There was also an increasing number of craftsmen-retailers—printers, pharmacists and tobacconists—who imported semi-finished materials which they processed for sale.[29]

In 1841, forty-two per cent of the town's work force—1350 people—were engaged in 'manufacturing'; and a Return of Manufacturers in 1842 shows that they worked in eighty-six enterprises in twenty-two 'industries'.[30] To be sure, these operations were undertaken on a small scale; but even in Britain's factory towns only a small proportion of the labour force worked in large establishments. For instance, between 1801 and 1841 four out of every five additional workers in Leeds, the leading industrial town in the West Riding woollen district, were employed in household and craft workshops, not in textile mills and engineering plants. In 1840 the average number of workers in that town's establishments was ten.[31] In Hobart the average was higher. For a new settlement which had been in existence for barely a generation, a remarkable amount of industrialisation had taken place. The market in Tasmania—after discounting a high degree of rural self-sufficiency and the effects of convict production in the public sector—was of the order of 20,000 people in the 1840s, about the same size as the markets of Europe's smaller urban centres, but just big enough to foster the development of craft industry. By 1830, local materials including coal were readily available; wage rates were falling; the risk of the market suddenly being swamped by a glut of imported craft goods had diminished; and, although traders obtained more profit from swapping the island's primary produce for British manufactures, settlers who did not have the capital to become merchants and landowners could set up as craftsmen and participate as independent proprietors in the mainstream of the island's development.[32] What seems surprising in view of the limited market, the preference of pastoralists for imported goods, and the scarcity of local capital for manufacturing enterprise, is not so much the lack of industry in Hobart as the progress that had been achieved by 1840.[33] In the 1840s, of course, the process of diversification faltered. Import substitution beyond the level already attained involved the production of goods which were beyond the capacity both of local manufacturers and the island's market. At that time rather than earlier, technological backwardness and market size became a drag on further urban development, ending Hobart's early phase of relatively rapid growth.

Over half the work force was engaged primarily in service industries. In addition to the town's commercial community, most of the island's professional men practised in Hobart. The twelve principal departments of civil government and almost as many ancillary departments employed 200-300 people, a fifth of whom had professional training. In 1836 the town had twelve clerics, eleven qualified medical practitioners, twenty-nine lawyers, and eleven military officers in charge of 324 other ranks. Altogether some 300 people in Hobart were involved in administration and the provision of professional services for the islanders while another 300 were on garrison duty. And the middle classes employed close on a thousand full and part-time domestic servants along with a swarm of clerks, messengers, boatmen and porters. Combining the functions of both a colonial capital and a port, Hobart had an unusually large tertiary sector.[34]

*   *   *

How did the economic factors which determined the *level* of urbanisation in Hobart affect the town's demographic, physical and social development? Hobart's population (including soldiers and convicts) rose from 600 in 1810 to 3500 in 1820, 6000 in 1830, and 15,000 in 1841.[35] Induced by job opportunities, this growth was primarily the result of increasing immigration and a fairly low mortality rate. Between 1818 and 1841, 35,000 convicts and 16,000 settlers arrived in Tasmania. Over a third of the free settlers, and perhaps the same proportion of emancipists, ended up in Hobart. In addition there were usually 2000 convicts in the town during the 1820s and twice as many in the next decade. The vast majority of the townsfolk then were immigrants: free settlers seeking a more rewarding life; emancipists, whose numbers increased rapidly in the 1830s; and convicts who were 'better off . . . than the poor in England, only more confined'.[36] Tasmania's birth rate, less than twenty per thousand, was low by contemporary standards, not because of infertility, since most women had large families, but because 70 per cent of the inhabitants before 1840 were male. And once the initial hardships of settlement had been overcome, immigrants and native-born alike enjoyed an unusually long life span because the colony had a low death rate—fifteen per thousand in 1830. This was the effect not merely of a salutary climate, but also the result of an abnormal age distribution. Until the 1840s the population contained few young children and old people.[37]

Demographic changes in Hobart, unlike those elsewhere in Tasmania, made for normal family life by the later 1830s. In the previous decade, with the occupation of the interior, rural population had increased faster than urban population, and the proportion of convicts stationed in Hobart had decreased. Two-thirds of the 11,000 convicts who arrived in the 1820s were assigned to a few thousand settlers in the hinterland. So, even though the total number of convicts in Hobart continued to increase, the proportion of prisoners in the town's population declined from three-fifths to two-fifths. By 1837 three-quarters of Hobart's inhabitants were free and the town had a more balanced sex ratio; 1.3 males (excluding convicts) for every female. With most people able to lead an ordinary family life, natural increase became more important as a source of population growth, and concern for the welfare of a new generation of native-born Tasmanians began to affect attitudes and institutional arrangements.[38]

*   *   *

Under the impulse of economic and population growth, Hobart's physical appearance was transformed. In 1811, Governor Lachlan Macquarie had drawn up a town plan, named the streets, and reserved sites for future public buildings. He called the centre of the projected town St George's Square—a market place flanked by a church, town hall and guardhouse. Running westwards, there were to be four 'long' streets intersected by four 'cross streets' in a north-south direction. These streets were to be sixty feet wide, with a further twenty feet before the building line on each side 'as an area or inclosure in front of the Houses'.[39] Macquarie's street layout remains unchanged together with seven of the nine names he chose: St George's Square eventually became Franklin Square and Pitt Street became Davey Street.

Work on the construction of the town did not begin in earnest until 1814. Twenty-one houses and huts were demolished and their owners belatedly compensated. The gaol and military barracks were erected in 1816; two years later, the military hospital, followed by Government House and St David's Church, and in 1819-20 the Colonial Hospital.[40] 'The Town is improving fast and the settlement is likely to be of consequence', wrote Maria Lord in 1820, shortly before Macquarie's second visit.[41] It was now 'near one mile in length from north to south, and about half a mile in breadth, containing 300 houses, occupied by a population of from 1100 to 1200 persons'.[42] Although most private houses were still single-storey timber buildings, widely spaced and enclosed by gardens, there were fifteen to twenty brick dwellings, several of which were two storeys high. 'On entering Hobart Town, every one must be surprised to see so substantial and well constructed a place in a colony of such recent foundation,'[43] commented one visitor. 'New buildings are rising up every day', Curr wrote, a development he attributed to agricultural sluggishness in the early 1820s when labour was diverted from the countryside.[44] From one vantage point 'it looked like the *beginning* of a town . . . all interspersed with the poles and scaffolding of houses being built, and it looked as if a lot of people had come only the night before and had begun to set up a city to dwell in.'[45] Three hundred huts disappeared as the original cabins were replaced by brick buildings. The number of private houses doubled to 600 by 1823 when the population reached 4000 and Hobart became 'an expensive place to live in'. Rents were 'very high', a large house in the centre commanding between £200 and £300 a year and small houses on the outskirts, which had cost £250 to build, fetched £60 to £80 a year.[46] Such prices indicate just how fast the town was growing. Another sign was the rising value of urban land which the Land Commissioners priced at between £3 and £60 an acre in 1826 compared with half-a-crown to seven shillings for rural property.[47] By the time Tasmania was proclaimed a separate colony in December 1825, Hobart 'had begun both to look [like] and function as a town'.[48]

In 1826 Governor Arthur's Land Commissioners produced a new plan for the town's future development.[49] It doubled the number of streets in each direction; zoned the area around Sullivan's Cove for commerce; relocated Government House on the Domain; provided for a twenty-foot nature strip on both banks of the rivulet and a bridge; removed a slaughterhouse from the edge of the Domain; and reserved sites for two more churches, a school, another marketplace, a ten-acre burial ground, a gaol and customs house. Although the hilly terrain made some of the commissioner's proposals impractical, the recommendations on additional streets and public buildings were for the most part put into effect.

In the later 1830s when the construction boom petered out, Hobart had 2000 private houses.[50] Six hundred families were sufficiently affluent to own their own homes and almost a third of them lived in the 'suburb' of Newtown. Others occupied spacious two-storey villas in Davey Street, Fitzroy Gardens and Battery Point on the south-western fringes while many proprietors of shops and lodging houses still dwelt close to the centre. The remaining four-fifths of the population, unable to afford property, rented three- and four-room cottages on the western and northern sides of the town. The town's largest developer, the government, owned twenty-two buildings and other premises. Public offices, constructed in freestone—far too expensive for private use—were located near St George's Square. In the same vicinity twenty to thirty buildings more modest in appearance provided offices for professional men and bankers. Down by the cove, forty-five warehouses clustered around the wharves. West of the square as far as Bathurst Street most of the town's 400 retail outlets were to be found, with 'the best shops' in Elizabeth Street, and many of the hundred pubs, the lodging houses and workshops were located in this district. Further afield, on the outskirts of the town, were the new cemetery, tanneries, shipyards and breweries. The product of public decree and free enterprise 'the shape of the city was [now] firmly fixed' between the towering mass of Mount Wellington and the fast-flowing Derwent.[51]

As the town increased in size, the usual urban problems emerged and had to be solved if growth was to continue. Congestion at the wharves has already been referred to. In 1835, after a decade of petitions, a public meeting was called to discuss the water supply in view of the 'lamentable sickness' caused by its impurities.[52] At that time the town's water came from the rivulet which also served as a sewer and dried up in summer. No action was taken and at the end of 1839 Hobart experienced its first serious epidemic. In seven weeks 914 people were stricken by typhoid fever and eighty-two died. Although the victims were mostly convicts, public opinion was shaken. The administration responded by extending the Colonial Hospital and devising a scheme to improve the water supply. But its implementation was delayed more than a decade owing to the capital cost and opposition from property owners. Pressure was also applied to remedy long-standing nuisances such as garbage disposal, street cleaning, paving and lighting. Poverty, too, became more acute and widespread: the number of destitute emancipists in Hobart increased; men who went to the mainland did not always provide for the dependents they left behind; and to make matters worse, Hobart was severely affected by economic depression in the early 1840s— unemployment rose, houses were left vacant, and vagrancy increased as country people drifted into the town seeking work. Private charities could no longer cope. To control public squalor, provide for those in need and preserve the town's social fabric, the relationship between the community's taxable capacity and public welfare had to be reassessed, and the implications for income redistribution was one of the factors that aggravated the struggle for constitutional change.[53]

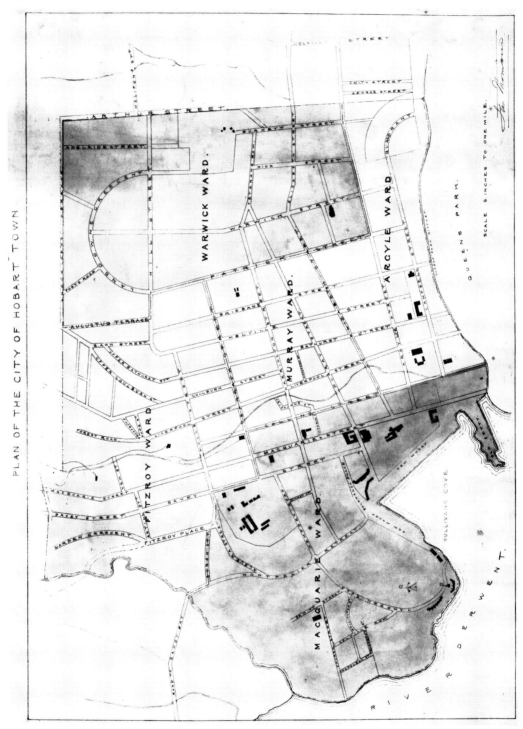

Figure 19: Hobart in 1850—note crescent development (Courtesy of the Mitchell Library, State Library of New South Wales)

*   *   *

Ralph Dahrendorf's concept of 'life chances' provides one way of evaluating social change in Hobart before 1840.[54] Did the inhabitants of the town in the later 1830s have fewer or more opportunities for advancement and for social commitment than their predecessors in 1810-15?

At the outset the range of available opportunities and the network of social bonds were strictly limited. Although the Reverend Robert Knopwood referred to Hobart as a 'town' for the first time in 1814, the Reverend John West more accurately described the settlement as a 'mere camp'.[55] It contained no permanent buildings, no roads that led anywhere and the nearest town was 600 miles away by sea. Its 600-odd inhabitants came from the same country and spoke the same language but beyond this they had little in common. The male population, nine-tenths of the inhabitants, was segregated into two unequal groups: one-fifth armed, four-fifths unarmed. For the military, the Derwent was a temporary residence; the convicts under their control would remain there for the rest of their days. Life in the camp rotated around the dull routine of a peacetime garrison: for the soldiers, parades, sentry duty, patrols, chasing escapees, courts martial and corporal punishment for fraternising with convicts; for the prisoners, manual work, subordination, and punishment in the pillory or triangle.[56]

As convicts, 70 per cent of the town's inhabitants had no choice but to carry out orders from above. Their 'private' activities were limited to providing shelter for themselves on the quarter-acre lots which they were allocated and to labouring on their own account after working hours. Except as outlaws they were unable to use their initiative to exploit the island's resources. In marked contrast the civil and military officers at the other end of the social scale were well placed to make the most of any opportunities that came their way. Salaries paid in London provided them with money. They could obtain gifts of land and acquire livestock. Their official positions enabled them to bend rules to secure more convict labour than they were strictly entitled to and obtain preferential treatment at the store. So these men exploited their positions whenever possible. Yet none of them succeeded in making substantial gains. Lieutenant Edward Lord, who reputedly became 'the richest man in the Island' by 1821, had not made much progress in that direction before he resigned his commission in 1812.[57] Opportunities for gain were circumscribed. Officers were not permitted to engage in trade and ships from Britain or India could not anchor in the port before 1815. Moreover, as long as there was an acute shortage of labour, economic activity was restricted to fishing, hunting and animal husbandry. And most officers did not remain in the island long enough to reap any long-term benefit from land ownership. That they had so little to show for their endeavours was due to the dearth of available opportunities for making money.[58]

Owing to their station in life, however, these officers had a strong sense of superiority. Through education and training, family ties, property and patronage they were conscious of their origins, regimental traditions and responsibilities. If, as is sometimes suggested, they led dissolute lives once they set foot on Sullivan's Cove, the implication is that the effectiveness of such bonds diminished in Tasmania. Some no doubt behaved differently away from home. But it does not follow that everyone did. Officers had to carry out their duties and to gain advancement, they had to conduct themselves in an acceptable manner. Their superiors in Port Jackson watched them like hawks. Of course, David Collins and his staff may not have been men of high intelligence, integrity or courage. Indeed it would have been surprising if outstanding officers had been sent to this outpost in time of war. The administration of a convict settlement did not involve much of a challenge and the Derwent provided little scope for the display of initiative or heroism. Their duties were routine and what these officers needed most during their stay was companionship, domesticity and recreation, requirements difficult to come by in such a male-dominated convict community. Some officers took convict women as mistresses. Some drank too much. Just as whites were supposed to disintegrate morally in the tropics, the character of British officials in Tasmania allegedly degenerated because the conventional decencies of life were forgotten in this socially barren environment.[59] Moral values and judgments, however, tend to be culturally determined and the factual basis for this view is dubious. Liquor consumption in the colony's early years was no higher than in England, and some officers were accompanied by their wives while others made respectable marriages in the settlement. 'Moral laxity' was probably not exceptionally widespread, but merely very conspicuous in such a small community.[60]

Enough has perhaps been said to suggest that between 1810 and 1814 Hobart's inhabitants had limited opportunities to improve their lot. The place was little more than a prison camp and those who dwelt there were bored and lonely.

During the next thirty years Hobart was transformed. It became the capital of a colony with 50,000 inhabitants; a busy port with processing industries; its built-up area expanded into the surrounding hills; roads radiated into the countryside; and the silhouettes of tall buildings, spires and masts on the skyline became a familiar image in the colony. In short, Hobart had the appearance of a town and functioned as a town. No longer quite so isolated from the rest of the world, the inhabitants had put down roots and felt they belonged there, identifying their goals in life with the fortunes of the local community.[61]

Moreover, for the majority of inhabitants, human existence was no longer a cycle of endless toil after a brief childhood. Most people received some education after which they alternated work with leisure for the rest of their days. Almost everyone's lifestyle had improved over time, and those who wanted to achieve something had greater opportunities for doing so as well as more scope than the first generation of newcomers for climbing social pyramids in voluntary organisations.

The 'possibilities of choice' had increased in several ways.[62] With twenty-three times as many people, three-quarters of them now free, there was a gain in personal liberty and individual mobility. Most of those who remained permanently in the town presumably did so from choice. Economic development provided fresh opportunities for investment and employment. Real incomes per head in Tasmania more than doubled in the fifteen years before 1840 and the proliferation of shops and places of entertainment provided Hobart's consumers with greater variety than before.[63]

These opportunities were not available, of course, to everyone on an equal basis. Inequality was probably greater than it had been a generation earlier. A classification based on occupations and property ownership shows that the town had three groups of free adult males each with differing prospects: 5 per cent were relatively well-off—office-holders, skilled professionals and businessmen who owned their own houses; 37 per cent earned up to £200 a year and a third of them owned houses; the remaining 58 per cent—a third of whom were emancipists—were labourers largely dependent on casual work.[64]

Those in the first category with access to information and resources, with rare skills and positions of authority, were better placed than others to take advantage of the colony's unfolding cornucopia. Indeed, the businessmen and officials of this time have been criticised for their obsession with money.[65] After 1840, however, when the era of continuous growth drew to a close, personal advancement became more difficult. Land was no longer given away and the best land was in private hands. Settlers no longer received cheap labour in the form of assigned convicts. Some industries declined, industrial diversification faltered, and the spectre of higher taxation raised its head. Business and professional men looking for easy gain went to the mainland.

Opportunities for skilled and unskilled workers continued to increase as long as the pace of economic development was maintained and labour remained scarce. Job vacancies mounted, money wages rose, and tradesmen had the chance to set up in business. But as more emancipists entered the workforce, the free settlers' position deteriorated; wage rates declined, and in the early 1840s unemployment became widespread. Some skilled workers reacted by forming trade societies which practised discrimination, and emancipists soon found themselves barred from the public service and professions and from holding hotel licences.[66] Denied opportunities open to others, ex-convicts were too unorganised to respond. Unfortunately, apart from the remarkable careers of a few emancipists, little is known about their fate. Although many left the island, several thousand probably still lived in Hobart in the early 1840s.

The chance to multiply relationships, strengthen social bonds, develop a sense of direction and create a basis for community action, went hand-in-hand with enhanced opportunities for personal advancement. The number of people committed to living in Hobart had increased significantly by 1840. Over half the inhabitants were native-born. With women comprising 46 per cent of the population, the majority of citizens led normal family lives, displayed an attachment to house and garden, and began to question the continued use of the island as 'a dumping ground for home rubbish'.

Peter Bolger has painted a vivid portrait of middle-class fraternity in this 'paragon of a place' during Franklin's administration.[67] The elite in spacious houses, staffed by servants and surrounded by beautiful gardens, could entertain relatives and friends, provide for the future by investing in the education of their offspring, and realise their social aspirations by forming exclusive associations. In the early 1840s Hobart had some forty voluntary institutions, many of them run by professionally trained clergy and doctors. That they served an important purpose in middle-class life is shown by the fact that three private schools, seven places of worship, five voluntary relief agencies, a library, museum, theatre, choral and musical societies, the Tasmanian Society and a host of sporting clubs existed largely through the support of just a few hundred families. Middle-class boys were groomed to be gentlemen through a grounding in scripture, classics and sport. Their parents, through cultural societies and charitable work, familiarised themselves with the main traditions of the West. Even if these efforts at character building and acculturation were not always successful, and even if a double standard sometimes prevailed, the middle classes at least tried to improve themselves. A generation earlier such institutions did not exist. Except for race and regatta meetings, social life in Knopwood's day had been confined to the small circle of officers who regularly met at Government House. By 1840 a vice-regal invitation had become a sign of public recognition and several hundred citizens were received by the Franklins in a courtly setting. Indeed the baronial government house planned for the Domain was 'acknowledged to be the best belonging to any British colony' in the Empire shortly after its completion.[68]

The social realm of the lower orders was less organised, and by comparison very restricted. Even so it was more tolerable than that experienced by the few dozen free settlers thirty years earlier. Men and women had more opportunities as workers and more scope for family life. They had time too for sport, the pub, Sunday chapel, the Mechanics Institute. In time of need private bodies now provided a preferable alternative to convict department institutions. Through self-improvement every settler could aspire to the ideal of working-class respectability. Those who missed out were the misfits trapped in the human swamp of the poorest streets where casually formed relationships could easily be severed by the insecurities of working class life.[69]

The one aspect of life in which there had not been much improvement in the thirty years before 1840 was political involvement. Settlers were still excluded from sharing in the exercise of political power. Administrators were appointed in London and although the lieutenant governor picked eight non-official members to speak on behalf of sectional interests in the Old Council, the colony had no representative institutions. In Hobart where even garbage was disposed of by a government department, 'everything was administered.'[70] Under the law the inhabitants had certain liberties—personal inviolability, free speech and property rights—though the government rode roughshod over individuals whenever the interests of the convict department were at stake. But as the settlers' sense of community matured and their emotional attachment to the island strengthened, the lieutenant governor's authority began to be questioned. In the 1840s, Tasmanians were presented with a blueprint for change. And the prospect of a self-governing society without convicts and based on limited political participation, led in due course to constitutional change. But that belonged to the future.

Before 1840 the most common source of conflict in Hobart was more narrowly institutional. Every major institution in the island had its headquarters in the capital. Twenty government departments were headed by bureaucrats, more senior, more powerful and better paid than their predecessors a generation earlier. All these career administrators constantly jostled one another for resources and advancement. The lieutenant governor's authority to control the military commandant, the deputy inspector of hospitals and Anglican clergy was sometimes called into question. Junior officers in the Convict Medical Department clashed with their seniors, and the department's surgeons vied with immigrant physicians over the right to treat fee-paying patients. In both the Anglican and Catholic churches existing incumbents opposed newcomers and interdenominational strife flared up with the advent of nonconformist ministers on the scene. The most protracted struggle of all involved Bishop Francis Nixon's attempts to ensure for the Church of England the same exclusive position that it had occupied in Britain.[71]

Much of this infighting originated in the burgeoning bureaucratic hierarchies of Hobart and was amplified by the editors of the town's 'neurotic press'.[72] But the mere presence of so many important dignitaries also meant that Hobart had an unusually elongated social scale for a recently established town, and this in turn had the effect of excluding humbler citizens from playing a more prominent role in public affairs. Whereas in Hobart authority unmistakably flowed down from above, in Launceston, a town with a narrower social scale, businessmen and shopkeepers participated to a much greater extent in community life. Indeed, the more democratic character of society in this northern town which was rarely plagued by the sort of administrative skirmishing that occurred in Hobart, helps to account for the spirit of north-south rivalry that developed as the island's economic centre of gravity shifted northwards.[73]

If Hobart's population and economy had continued to expand, the city's conspicuous vice-regal establishment, its civil and ecclesiastical courts, and its parliament and public offices would not have featured so prominently in the long run in its functional profile. But the 1840s was a turning point in the development of the Derwent settlement, just like the end of 'starvation time' a generation earlier. Although the inhabitants of Hobart, accustomed to 'progress', may not have realised exactly what was at stake, fundamental adjustments were taking place that sealed the city's fate and deflated its citizens' expectations for the rest of the century. Though it retained its multi-functional role as capital, port, commercial and manufacturing centre, once the sources of its growth had shrivelled up, Hobart was transformed again, this time into 'a pleasant, neat, old-fashioned English country town, perhaps twice as large and straggling as Dorchester, Ipswich or Bury but ten times more stagnant, dull and lifeless'.[74]

Notes

[1] Schmal, H. (ed.), *Patterns of European Urbanisation since 1500*, (London, 1981), pp.86, 95. (NB - only 30 per cent of the 363 cities listed experienced an annual growth as high as 0.5% between 1500 and 1800).

[2] Lieutenant Oxley, R.N. quoted in Solomon, R.J. *Urbanisation: The Evolution of an Australian Capital*, (Sydney, 1976), p.28; Robson, L.L. *A History of Tasmania*, Vol. 1, (Melbourne, 1983), pp.118-9.

[3] Solomon, *op.cit.*, p.28.

[4] *Ibid.*, p.71, and pp.61-5.

[5] Bolger, Peter, *Hobart Town*, (Canberra, 1973), p.27.

[6] Solomon, *op.cit.*, pp.99-104; Curr, *An Account of the Colony of Van Diemen's Land*, (Hobart, 1824); (facsimile edition, 1967), pp.144-5, 123; Hartwell, R.M. *The Economic Development of Van Diemen's Land 1820-50*, (Melbourne, 1954), p.102; Wentworth, W.C. 'Statistical . . . Description', (London, 1819), pp.155-6.

[7] See Reynolds, J. *Launceston, History of an Australian City*, (Melbourne, 1969), Chs. 2 and 3; Morris-Nunn, M. and Tassell, C.B. *Launceston's Industrial Heritage: a Survey*, (Launceston, 1962), pp.11-14; Dyster, Barrie. 'The Port of Launceston Before 1851', *The Great Circle*, Vol. 3, No. 2, (1981), pp.103-124; Curr, C. *op.cit.*, pp.42-6; Solomon, *op.cit.*, p.88; Robson, *op.cit.*, p.209.

[8] *H.R.A.*, III, 5, pp.179, 180, 186-7, 305-12, 386.

[9] Reynolds, *op.cit.*, p.55; Robson, *op.cit.*, pp.318, 519.

[10] Butlin, N.G. and Sinclair, W.A. *Australian Gross Domestic Product 1788-1860: Estimates, Sources and Methods*, (ANU Source Paper No. 2), p.6; and Butlin, N.G. *Contours of the Australian Economy 1788-1860*, (W.P.E.H., A.N.U., No. 21, 1984), p.32.

[11] Butlin and Sinclair, *op.cit.*, p.6.; Butlin, *op.cit.*, p.32.

[12] See, for example *Geils Papers*, (Crowther Collection, State Library, Hobart); McKay, Anne (ed.), *Journals of the Land Commissioners for VDL 1826-8*, (Hobart, 1962), pp.8, 92; and Rimmer, W.G. *Two Early Views of Van Diemen's Land*, (Hobart, 1965), pp.4-6.

[13] Fletcher, B.H. *Landed Enterprise and Penal Society: A History of Farming and Grazing in New South Wales before 1821*, (Sydney, 1976), pp.146, 150-1.

[14] Fletcher, *op.cit.*, p.226; Scott, Peter, 'Farming' in Davies, J.L. (ed.) *Atlas of Tasmania*, (Hobart, 1965), p.58; see also chapter by Rimmer in Abbot, G.J. and Nairn, N.B. (eds.) *Economic Growth of Australia 1781-1821*, (Melbourne, 1969), esp. p.345, pp.343-4; Robson, *op.cit.*, p.91. For low-level productivity, see Curr, *op.cit.*, pp.14, 112, 114; Henderson, John. *Observations on the Colonies of New South Wales and Van Diemen's Land*, (Calcutta, 1832), pp.46, 93, 96.

[15] See McKay (ed.), *op.cit.*, pp.31, 109-17; Jacob, W. 'Practicality of Establishing Permanent Communications . . .', in the *Tasmanian Directory 1832*, (M.L.); also *Maria and James Lord Letterbook*, (M.L.), entry for 15-4-1820; Robson, *op.cit.*, pp.5, 112-4; McKay, (ed.), *op.cit.*, pp.63-4, 52, 92, 111, 115-6.

[16] Curr, *op.cit.*, p.45 and pp.26, 33-4; see also Hartwell, *op.cit.*, pp.134-6; *Tasmanian Year Book* No. 4, (Hobart, 1970) pp.227-8; Scott in Davies, (ed.), *op.cit.*, p.58; Linge, *Industrial Awakening*, (Canberra, 1979), p.129.

[17] *H.R.A.*, III, 3, p.222. See also Robson, *op.cit.*, pp.72, 111, 116-7.

[18] Curr, *op.cit.*, pp.65-7, 84-5; Hartwell, *op.cit.*, pp.124-5.

[19] Curr, *op.cit.*, pp.87, 126; Morris-Nunn and Tassell, *op.cit.*, p.346; *Tasmanian Year Book* No. 4, (Hobart, 1970), p.228.

[20] Chapter by Abbott, in Abbott and Nairn, *op.cit.*, pp.229-32; Robson, *op.cit.*, p.112; Hartwell, *op.cit.*, pp.107-23; Curr, *op.cit.*, pp.68-84; Smart, W. *Economic Annals of the Nineteenth Century 1801-20*, (London, 1910), p.685; Jenkins, D.T. and Ponting K.G. *The British Wool Textile Industry 1770-1914*, (London, 1982), pp.43-8; Geraint Jenkins, J. (ed.), *The Wool Textile Industry in Great Britain*, (London, 1972), Chs. 4 and 5.

[21] Robson, *op.cit.*, pp.196, 264-5; McKay, (ed.), *op.cit.*, pp.7, 18, 53, 64, 73.

[22] Robson , *op.cit.*, p.261; Hartwell, *op.cit.*, pp.139-43; Olsen, A.M. 'Fisheries' in Davies, (ed.), *op.cit.*, p.74.

[23] Solomon, *op.cit.*, pp.75 and 79. For imports and exports see pp.89, 90, 100 and 103. Also Linge, *op.cit.*, pp.122-3.

[24] See Solomon, *op.cit.*, pp.75, 81, 166, and Robson, *op.cit.*, pp.75, 257-9. For bridges see McKay, (ed.), *op.cit.*, pp.109-17; Robson, *op.cit.*, p.267.

[25] Solomon, *op.cit.*, pp.166-7, 74; Hartwell, *op.cit.*, pp.164, 169, 170-3, 179; Robson, *op.cit.*, p.74; McKay, (ed.), *op.cit.*, p.93; Lord Letterbook, *op.cit.* N.B. Arthur informed Bathurst in 1824 that Hobart's merchants 'drained the Agricultural Interest to the last degree . . .'; *H.R.A.*, III, 5, p.181.

[26] Hartwell, *op.cit.*, pp.145, 147-50; Linge, *op.cit.*, pp.124, 127-34; Robson, *op.cit.*, pp.73, 256-66; Solomon, *op.cit.*, pp.167, 169; Curr, *op.cit.*, p.145; Rimmer, in Abbott and Nairn, *op.cit.*, pp.345-6; Morris-Nunn and Tassell, *op.cit.*, p.5.

[27] Hartwell, *op.cit.*, p.156, see also pp.156-60; Robson, *op.cit.*, p.266; Solomon, *op.cit.*, p.169; Linge, *op.cit.*, p.127.

[28] See Solomon, *op.cit.*, p.65.

[29] Robson, *op.cit.*, p.266; Hartwell, *op.cit.*, pp.150-2; *The Van Diemen's Land Almanac 1831-6*, (M.L.), Morris-Nunn and Tassell, *op.cit.*, p.373; Curr, *op.cit.*, pp.94-5.

[30] Solomon, *op.cit.*, pp.166-7.

[31] Rimmer, W.C. 'The Industrial Profile of Leeds, *Publications of the Thoresby Society*, Vol. L, Part 2, (1967), pp.147-8.

[32] See Hartwell, *op.cit.*, p.85; Linge, *op.cit.*, p.132.

[33] See Bolger, *op.cit.*, p.12; also Linge, *op.cit.*, p.118, 122-4; Hartwell, *op.cit.*, p.144.

[34] Based on The Van Diemen's Land Almanac, *op.cit.*; Solomon, *op.cit.*, p.71; Robson, *op.cit.*, pp.434, 476; Rimmer, W.G. *Portrait of a Hospital: The Royal Hobart*, (hereafter cited as 'Portrait') (Hobart, 1981), pp.56-60.

[35] Solomon, *op.cit.*, pp.56-61, 110.

[36] Robson, *op.cit.*, p.173 and pp.102, 106, 171; see also Solomon, *op.cit.*, p.63; Hartwell, *op.cit.*, pp.67-9; Shaw, A.G.L. *Convicts and the Colonies*, (London, 1966), pp.364-8; Robson, *op.cit.*, p.70; Bolger, *op.cit.*, p.20.

[37] Solomon, *op.cit.*, p.65 and pp.63-5; Robson, *op.cit.*, pp.116, 164, 167; *Tasmanian Year Book* No. 11, (Hobart, 1977), pp.180-2, 193. (The crude death rate was about 11/1000 in 1830 and 9/1000 in 1840); Henderson, John, *op.cit.*, pp.19-22, 101; *Geils Papers*, *op.cit.*, entry for 3-5-1817; Rimmer, 'Portrait', *op.cit.*, pp.29-32.

[38] Rimmer, 'Portrait', *op.cit.*, p.6; Solomon, *op.cit.*, pp.32, 41-5, 53, 57, 61; Hartwell, *op.cit.*, p.71; Robson, *op.cit.*, pp.74, 116, 168.

[39] Cited in Solomon, *op.cit.*, p.29, also pp.30-1; Macquarie, L. *Journal of his Tours in New South Wales and Van Diemen's Land 1810-22*, (Sydney, 1956), pp.61-2. Previous quotation from West, John, *History of Tasmania*, (Launceston, 1852), Vol. 1, p.50. See also *Reminiscences of James Backhouse Walker*, (Archives, U.T.), pp.46-9.

[40] See Shaw, *op.cit.*, p.365; Robson, *op.cit.*, pp.66, 68; Fletcher, *op.cit.*, p.136; Solomon, *op.cit.*, p.31; Nicholls, Mary, (ed.), *The Diary of the Reverend Robert Knopwood 1803-1838*, (Hobart, T.H.R.A., 1977), p.185.

[41] *Lord Letterbook*, *op.cit.*, entry for 14-1-1820.

[42] Lieutenant Colonel Jeffreys, *Van Diemen's Land, Geographical and Descriptive Delineations of the Island of VDL*, (London, 1820), cited in Solomon, *op.cit.*, p.41.

[43] Curr, *op.cit.*, p.5. See also Rowcroft, Charles, *Tales of the Colonies*, (London, 1843), Vol. 1, p.16, cited in Solomon, *op.cit.*, p.41.

[44] Curr, *op.cit.*, p.5.

[45] Rowcroft, in Solomon, *op.cit.*, p.41.

[46] Curr, *op.cit.*, p.9; Robson, *op.cit.*, p.111; Solomon, *op.cit.*, p.153. See also Bolger, *op.cit.*, p.16.

[47] Solomon, *op.cit.*, pp.39-41.

[48] *Ibid*, p.56.

[49] McKay, *op.cit.*, p.101 and Appendix A, pp.101-8.

[50] See Solomon, *op.cit.*, pp.45-8, 63-5, 113-4, 145-73. (Figures are derived from the Assessment Lists of 1847,

the first comprehensive survey of property values in Hobart. They suggest that the depression of 1841-5 did not have as great an impact on construction in the private sector as might be expected). See also Butlin and Sinclair, *op.cit.*, p.6, and West, *op.cit.*, Vol. 1, pp.223-4.

51 Bolger, *op.cit.*, pp.65, 16; Solomon, *op.cit.*, p.43.

52 Solomon, *op.cit.*, pp.49, 50-1.

53 Rimmer, 'Portrait', *op.cit.*, pp.45-6, 49; Bolger, *op.cit.*, pp.65-6; Backhouse Walker, *op.cit.*, pp.48-50, 52-4, 56; Brown, Joan C. *'Poverty is not a Crime': The Development of Social Services in Tasmania, 1803-1900*, (Hobart, 1972), Ch. 2; West, *op.cit.*, p.255; Roe, Michael, 'The establishment of local self-government in Hobart and Launceston 1845-58', *T.H.R.A. Papers and Proceedings*, Vol. 14, (1966), pp.21-45.

54 Dahrendorf, Ralf. *Life Chances: Approaches to Social and Political Theory*, (London, 1979), pp.29-39, 40-53, 74-84.

55 Nicholas, (ed.), *op.cit.*, p.157; West, *op.cit.*, Vol. 1, p.53.

56 Nicholas, (ed.), *op.cit.*, pp.63, 100, 115, 122, 179.

57 Letter of 12-6-1821, cited by Rimmer, in Abbott and Nairn, *op.cit.*, p.327. See also Butlin, S.J. *Foundations of the Australian Monetary System 1788-1851* (Sydney, 1953), pp.51-74; Nicholas (ed.) *op.cit.*, 132; Curr, *op.cit.*, pp.5-8.

58 Nicholas, (ed.), *op.cit.*, p.189, and Geils Papers, *op.cit.*

59 Robson, *op.cit.*, pp.79, 82, 83; Bolger, *op.cit.*, pp.13, 18, 21; West, *op.cit.*, Vol. 1, p.38; Curr, *op.cit.*, pp.10-11, 150; Henderson, *op.cit.*, p.45.

60 West, *op.cit.*, Vol. 1, p.28; Butlin, N.G. 'Yo, Ho, Ho and How Many Bottles of Rum', *A.E.H.R.*, xxiii, 1983, pp.1-27; (NB - George Harris, Edward Lord, William Collins married in Hobart between 1805 and 1808).

61 Bolger, *op.cit.*, pp.30, 34, 37, 39; Robson, *op.cit.*, pp.177-8, uses the diaries of G.T.W.B. Boyes, to make the point that the rising generation of native-born inhabitants had a 'passionate love' for 'the country of their birth'.

62 Dahrendorf, *op.cit.*, p.130.

63 Butlin and Sinclair, *op.cit.*, p.6; Solomon, *op.cit.*, p.110.

64 Solomon, *op.cit.*, pp.63-5, 145-73; Hartwell, *op.cit.*, pp.31-58; Robson, *op.cit.*, pp.350, 386, 395; Rimmer 'Portrait', *op.cit.*, p.55; Townsley, W.A. *The Struggle for Self-Government in Tasmania 1842-1856*, (Hobart, 1951), pp.40 to 51 lists the salaries paid to public officials in 1860. Davey received £750 a year as Lieutenant Governor, Franklin got £2500 and Eardley-Wilmot £4000. Whereas the first Anglican clergyman was paid £182, the Archdeacon received £2000 a year in the 1830s. The Colonial Surgeon from 1821-37 could make £2000 a year from private practice, ten times as much as his salary.

65 Robson, *op.cit.*, p.175.

66 Roe, Michael. *Quest for Authority in Eastern Australia 1835-1851*, (Melbourne, 1965), p.99; Bolger, *op.cit.*, pp.18, 26, 34, 35; Solomon, *op.cit.*, p.111; Robson, *op.cit.*, p.420.

67 Bolger, *op.cit.*, p.25; see also pp.24-32, 34, 41; and Walker, *op.cit.*, pp.27, 33; Robson, *op.cit.*, pp.175-181, 184; Curr, *op.cit.*, p.150.

68 Trollope, Anthony. *Australia and New Zealand*, (Melbourne, 1874), p.368, cited in Bolger, *op.cit.*, p.81, see also pp.31, 41-2; Robson, *op.cit.*, pp.325, 337; Nicholls, *op.cit.*, pp.175, 178.

69 Robson, *op.cit.*, pp.177, 281-360; Bolger, *op.cit.*, pp.32, 36-40; Roe, *op.cit.*, pp.101, 194-5.

70 Walker, *op.cit.*, pp.45, 46; Robson, *op.cit.*, pp.310-3, 334; Townsley, *op.cit.*, pp.60-96.

71 Robson, *op.cit.*, pp.271-2, 286-8, 336-8, 350-3, 400-10; Roe, *op.cit.*, pp.19-20, 120; Rimmer 'Portrait', *op.cit.*, pp.39-43, 46-53; West, *op.cit.*, Vol. 1, pp.195-6, 205-14.

72 Robson, *op.cit.*, p.328.

73 Robson, *op.cit.*, pp.176, 318, 322, 358, 519; Petrow, Stefan. *Sanatorium of the South? Public Health and Politics in Hobart and Launceston, 1875-1914*, (M.A. Thesis, U.T., 1984), pp.40-83; Green, F.C. *A Century of Responsible Government 1856-1956*, (Hobart, 1956), pp.67-70; Blainey, Geoffrey. *The Rush that Never Ended*, (Melbourne, 1963), p.40. In Tasmania, north-south rivalry replaced the more characteristic rural-urban rivalry of the mainland colonies: See Reynolds, *op.cit.*, pp.55, 109-10, 185-6; Rimmer, 'Portrait', *op.cit.*, p.176.

74 Martineau, John, *Letters from Australia*, (London, 1869), p.61; Rimmer, 'Portrait', *op.cit.*, p.109.

Perth

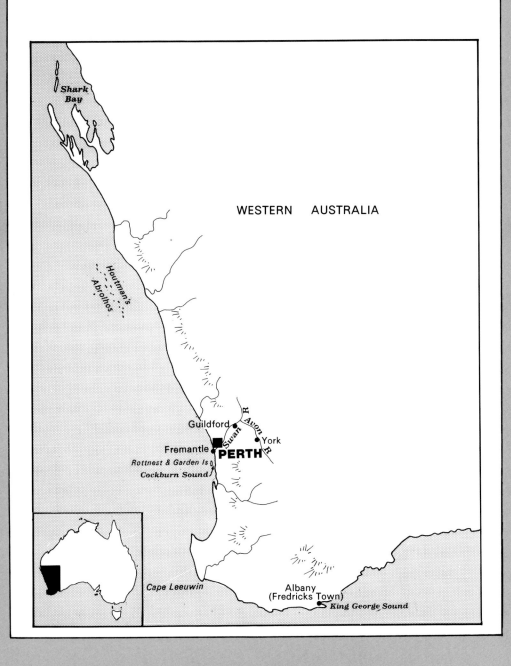

Shark Bay

WESTERN AUSTRALIA

Houtman's Abrolhos

Swan R.
Avon R.
Guildford
York
Fremantle
PERTH
Rottnest & Garden Is.
Cockburn Sound

Cape Leeuwin

Albany
(Fredricks Town)
King George Sound

Chapter VI

Western Australia becomes British

Pamela Statham

The establishment of the Swan River colony in 1829 was surprisingly late given that the western coast of Terra Australis had been known to Europeans since Hartog's discoveries in 1616.[1] True, the west coast had acquired a very unsavoury reputation. Early Dutch and British explorers had reported dangerous coastlines, barren shores, unappealing natives, heat and flies. But William de Vlaming had noted and named Swan River in 1696, and in 1718 Jean Pieter Purry had even suggested that the Dutch East India Company form a settlement on the south-west coast between Cape Leeuwin and Fowlers Bay.[2] Purry claimed, just as Captain James Stirling did later, that such a settlement would be of immense strategic value and provide a victualling station for the East Indies.[3]

That these early Dutch observations and suggestions went unheeded can be attributed more or less directly to Western Australia's apparent lack of commercially exploitable resources, such as the precious metals, ores, spices, sandalwood, silks and cotton that were the *raison d'être* of the Dutch East India Company. Little did they know at that time that inland and over the hills lay sandalwood, gold and other minerals aplenty. Further exploration, however, was precluded by the Dutch East India Company's deteriorating financial situation and its need for quick returns. Thus, 'after more than a century of contact, the Dutch forsook the opportunity to claim the western side'.[4]

The first English reports of the west coast came from William Dampier who visited the Shark Bay region in 1688. His accounts confirmed the general impression that the west coast was barren. The search for a southern paradise then swung east to the Pacific, culminating in Cook's discoveries and the foundation of Botany Bay in 1788. Thereafter, the British had no immediate incentive to look west, the Dutch were finished and the French, who had shown some interest in the west coast in 1772,[5] were busy fighting the Napoleonic wars from 1793 to 1815.

The story of Western Australia's emergence as a British colony—and of Perth as its capital—really began in 1825 when Ralph Darling, the seventh governor of New South Wales, was handed his commission. In that document the British extended their sovereignty from the 135° to the 129° longitude.[6] This brought the Melville Island Settlement, established in 1824, into what was then still New South Wales,[7] and also defined the present eastern border of Western Australia.

Explanations of the events of 1826 that led Governor Darling to send a party from New

South Wales to found an outpost at King George Sound (so named by Vancouver in 1791 after King George III) have stressed the fear of French territorial acquisition.[8] It is true that French vessels visited southern and western Australian waters in the mid to late 1820s but Governor Brisbane, who preceded Darling, had expressed no alarm in any of his despatches to the Colonial Office, and neither did Darling in his first year. Brisbane had been far more concerned with another problem which at first sight seems to have little connection with Western Australia. This was the problem of what to do with re-convicted convicts. Gaols in Sydney were required for convicts arriving from England, and maximum security detention centres at Norfolk Island and Port Macquarie were overcrowded. When Brisbane sent convicts to a new penal settlement at Moreton Bay in 1824, he had informed the Colonial Office that this location was also not suited as a long-term high-security detention site because of its fitness for general colonisation.[9] The Colonial Office would not wish to have to build and then dismantle successive security prisons as the tide of settlement moved out. What was clearly needed was a really isolated site for worst offenders.

These circumstances throw new light on two key despatches written in March 1826 which ordered the survey and occupation of the Western Port region (in what is now Victoria) and a survey of the Shark Bay area on the west coast.[10] The ostensible reason for such instructions was that:

> the sailing of two French ships on a voyage of discovery have led to the consideration of how far our distant possessions in the Australian seas may be prejudiced by any designs which the French may entertain of establishing themselves in that quarter, and more especially on that part of the coast of New South Wales which has not yet received any colonists from this country.[11]

This sentence has frequently been cited as evidence that fear of French interest led to the establishment of an outpost in Western Australia, despite the fact that it specifically points out that uninhabited regions of New South Wales were more at risk. Lord Bathurst actually gave a far more direct reason for exploring the Shark Bay region on the western coast. He said that information was to be procured about this site:

> In order that should it be deemed advisable to establish a penal settlement at some distant point . . . Moreton Bay, the settlement which is already employed as a second place of punishment on the East coast might then become that to which prisoners convicted for the first time of offences in the colony and convicts occasionally from here may be consigned, and Port Macquarie which is now devoted to that purpose may be thrown open to colonization as suggested by Sir Thomas Brisbane . . . [12]

Ten days later, Lord Bathurst instructed Darling to ignore the previous order regarding Shark Bay, as it was reportedly barren, and to examine King George Sound instead, which had the 'added advantage of lying on the direct route of vessels sailing from England to Port Jackson thus facilitating future supply and communications.'[13]

Darling readied the two expeditions as ordered but warned Bathurst that:

> King George's Sound will be found totally unfit for the purpose *even of a penal settlement* . . . communication must I understand be at all times tedious and difficult and during a part of the year will be hardly practicable . . . I am informed that the country around both Shark Bay and King George's Sound is perfectly barren and destitute of vegetation. The French would therefore find it difficult to maintain themselves at either of these places . . . [14]

In secret instructions given to Major Lockyer, who was to lead the party of twenty military men and twenty convicts to King George Sound, Darling stated that:

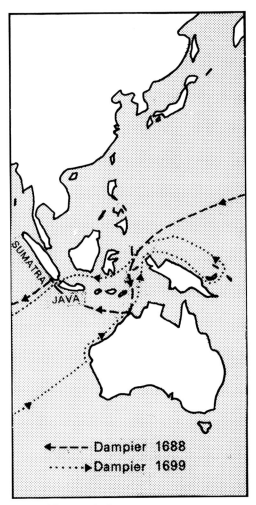

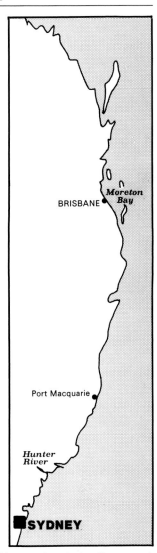

Figure 20: Dampier's voyages

Figure 21: Pushing penitentiaries (for second offenders) further and further up to coast—first Sydney, then Port Macquarie and finally Morton Bay

> You will . . . land the troops . . . and signify that it is considered the whole of New Holland is subject to His Majesty's Government and that orders have been given for the establishment of King George's Sound as a settlement for the reception of criminals.[15]

Lockyer and his party duly arrived at King George Sound on Christmas Day 1826 and proceeded to carry out instructions. His claim to the whole of Western Australia, however, was later totally ignored by the British government. Two and a half years were to pass before the tiny outpost was joined by the settlement at Swan River, and a further two years before the convicts were withdrawn and the outpost transferred from the New South Wales government to the administration of the new colony.[16]

Figure 22: The settlement at King George Sound, founded Christmas Day, 1826

A major motive for this first European settlement in Western Australia was thus clearly penal. That King George Sound was never actually used as a detention centre for second offenders may be attributed in part to the difficulties of supply and communication that Darling had foreseen, but more cogently to a lessening of the pressure to release the Port Macquarie and Moreton Bay sites as the settlement movement in New South Wales swung south in the late 1820s. That the depot was not withdrawn earlier, however, would have to be explained in strategic terms as Darling's perception of the 'French Threat' increased from late 1826 and became a dominant issue in despatches of 1827. It was this concern that paved the way for the second settlement in Western Australia at Swan River.

The train of events that led to the first detailed appraisal of the Swan River region began when the Colonial Office learned in 1825 that all was not well with the tiny outpost on Melville Island in Northern Australia.[17] As Cameron relates in Chapter XIV this depot proved to be off the route of Malay traders; surrounded by navigational hazards; lacking fresh water and, at this time, dangerously low on supplies. The British East India Company, which had instigated the establishment of the depot to provide protection and relief for its ships in the area, requested a better site. The Colonial Office agreed, and arranged with the Admiralty to detail a commander and ship-of-war and sent Governor Darling instructions to 'afford the necessary co-operation to the Naval Officer who may be employed on this service'.[18]

The officer appointed to carry out the relief of the depot and the search for an alternative site was the then thirty-five-year-old Captain James Stirling who had been on half-pay since 1818. He was one of the many young men who had served with distinction in the French Wars only to be retired when Napoleon's final defeat made so many like him redundant. Stirling probably owed his Australian commission to his father-in-law, James Mangles of Woodbridge, Surrey, a shipping magnate and a director of the East India Company. Stirling had married Mangles' sixteen-year-old third daughter, Ellen, in 1823 and had settled with his wife's people at Woodbridge.[19] It is more than probable therefore that Stirling discussed his assignment with his father-in-law before departure and thus knew the major reasons behind the East India Company's desire to see a British outpost maintained in northern Australia. In essence these were to control the trade of and through the Southern Archipelago; to secure company shipping from pirates; and to provide a safe re-victualling and convalescent station.[20]

In January 1826 Stirling was given command of the *Success* and in April left for Sydney. This was his big chance. The long voyage to New South Wales would have given him plenty of time to search the known charts for alternative sites that would meet the East India Company's objectives. The Swan River region on the west coast, which lay in the same temperate latitude as Sydney, would have attracted attention as it had never been explored, surveyed or charted by a British officer yet strategically was very well placed. Stirling clearly gave considerable thought to the advantages of a settlement in that region, for he presented Darling with a detailed proposal only a week after arriving in Sydney in early December 1826.

Finding that the Melville Island depot was no longer in urgent need of relief, Stirling asked Darling for permission to explore the Swan River region[21] giving four reasons for his request. First, the navigational and strategic value of the Swan River site as it lay at the pivot of 'two strong opposing wind forces' that would give ships stationed there control over the whole Indian Ocean. Second, its trade potential, as the temperate climate would allow production of commodities that could be traded with tropical neighbours. Third, its re-victualling and convalescent potential for the Indian establishments. And, fourth, its cost-advantage to Britain, both in support of the East India Company and because supplies for Swan River would provide an outward cargo for ships engaged in the China trade. Stirling also urged that action 'should immediately be taken to prevent Britain being anticipated in the occupation of a position of such value.'[22]

It was a persuasive proposal, but nonetheless a risky venture and it is not clear why Darling, essentially a cautious man, agreed to it without official sanction; for the *Success* was under Admiralty orders. Fear of the French may have been one reason, but Lockyer had already been sent to King George Sound to establish Britain's claim and could have been instructed to obtain information about the Swan River site, obviating any necessity for Stirling's trip. Another possible reason is that Darling may have hoped to distract official attention from the turbulent domestic affairs of New South Wales at that time. In November 1826 two military men had been excessively punished for a minor crime, on the governors' orders, as an exemplary deterrent. The punishment caused the death of Sudds, one of the unfortunate men. This event, known as the 'Sudds affair' provided ammunition for William Charles Wentworth who in articles and public meetings called for the governor to be brought to trial.[23] As complaints of settlers in the past had led to the recall in disgrace of some of his predecessors, Darling would undoubtedly have been disturbed by the general hue and cry and could perhaps have seen Stirling's arrival in the midst of the fracas as fortuitous. A despatch enclosing Stirling's proposal and enlarging on the French threat would reach England about the same time as reports of the Sudds incident and could thus provide a valuable counter-irritant.

The *Success* eventually sailed out of Sydney Harbour on 17 January 1827 and anchored on 5 March off Rottnest Island just opposite the mouth of the Swan River.[24] During the next sixteen days Stirling and Charles Frazer, the NSW government botanist, explored the Swan River to its furthest navigable point, while a smaller party examined the Canning River which leads off a broad expanse of the Swan called Melville Water some twelve miles from the sea. Stirling then spent a further nine days examining the coast between Rottnest and Geographe Bay before the *Success* departed for Sydney by way of King George Sound. This survey, although more thorough than any other that had preceded the formation of an Australian colony,[25] was still very incomplete. By taking the river as the route inland, Stirling and Frazer gained an exaggerated impression of the fertility of the area and failed to appreciate the extent of the sand-dunes and swamps that predominated beyond the river. Moreover, the climate during their stay was exceptionally mild and taken together the balmy weather, sparkling river and inland water, the evergreen trees and bush scrub turned the whole venture into something of a 'picnic episode'.[26]

Stirling wrote a detailed and persuasive report, as did Charles Frazer, which they submitted to Darling early in April 1827. Their summary pronounced the land seen on the banks of Swan River as superior to any in New South Wales 'not only in its local character but in the many existing advantages which it holds out to settlers'.[27] Both men were obviously impressed by the area: the ratio of favourable to unfavourable adjectives in each of the reports of land quality, for example, was more than ten to one. Leaving aside the use of adjectives such as 'delicious', 'stupendous' and 'majestic', how accurate was the factual content of the report? This is difficult to assess, for many inaccuracies can be shown to have stemmed from the adoption of English-based criteria of land evaluation and from pure chance. For example, it was simply chance that dictated the benign weather conditions which effectively obscured deficiencies in Cockburn Sound and nearby anchorages, and good fortune that enabled the *Success* to pass through one of the few narrow channels into Cockburn Sound without mishap, so discouraging thorough survey of the area and reinforcing Stirling's impression of a fine, safe harbour. It was largely chance again that determined, through river depths at that time, the farthest point of the Upper Swan River that boats could navigate. Thus, the fact that the only exhaustive soil tests took place at this furthest navigational point, which happened to be the most fertile region in the whole Swan River area, can also be attributed to chance. On the other hand, the English criteria that Frazer, the botanist, and to a lesser extent Stirling, used to assess the quality of soils were basically unsuitable for evaluating Australian lands.[28] In England tall trees and green vegetation were a positive indication of soil fertility, and similar soils produced very similar types of vegetation. Therefore when the fertile soils of the Upper Swan region were observed to produce tall green vegetation and undergrowth similar to that covering land at some distance, it was concluded that the soils of the latter must share the same basic fertility. This proved to be incorrect as the permanently grey-green Australian bush covered markedly different soils.

It is significant, in view of later calumny by certain settlers, that Frazer, the botanist, rather than Stirling, the future governor, was responsible for proclaiming the land to be generally fertile. Stirling's observations on the land, its quality and capabilities were extravagant but basically accurate. Assessment and evaluation of soil quality he left entirely to Frazer, the acknowledged expert in such matters, no doubt realising that Frazer's expertise would count with government authorities. In fact, Frazer's four-point summary was accepted unquestioningly, even though each of the points he made could have been challenged simply through comments made elsewhere in the same report. For example, Frazer's summary drew attention to the 'advantage of water-carriage to [the settler's] door and the non-existence of impediments to land carriage' despite the fact that details had been given earlier in the report of difficulties encountered in ascending the Swan River owing to sandbanks and very shallow areas. Heavy coastal sand-dunes that would inevitably impede land carriage had also been described in the body of the report but 'forgotten' in the summary.

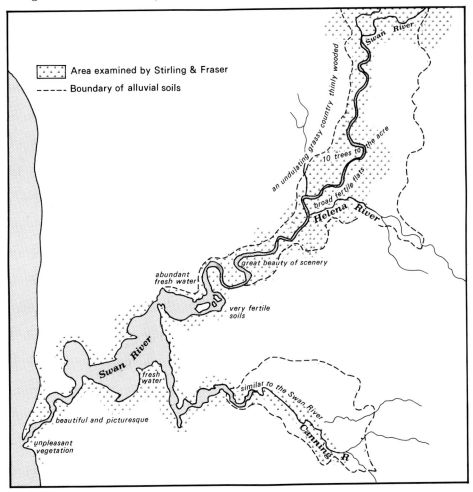

Figure 23: Stirling and Frazer's examination of the Swan River area, March, 1827 (Courtesy of Dr James Cameron)

As the proportion of the final report spent in description of the terrain far outweighed that given to facilities for shipping, it would appear that on arrival Stirling's initial conception of the area as a strategic outpost of Empire, based on a port town, was expanded to encompass a larger agricultural colony, a valuable opportunity for British private investors who would want the fullest possible information on the land and its resources. With this objective in mind, limited time at his disposal and no perceived need for detailed appraisal of shipping approaches and anchorages because of their lucky entry into Cockburn Sound, Stirling's failure personally to check observations made by his ship's master was perhaps forgivable. Nevertheless, it was extremely unfortunate because his expertise in this area gave credence to judgments in the report that were based on hasty and inadequate surveying.

In contrast to Stirling and Frazer's rhapsodical report the despatch sent to Darling by Major Edmund Lockyer, who had returned on the *Success* with Stirling, was a brief and prosaic account of experiences during the first months of settlement at King George Sound.[29] Submitted at the same time as Stirling's, Lockyer's report challenged by implication several of the Stirling/Frazer claims. For example, Lockyer's descriptions of the terrain actually cultivated and found to be poor at the sound were very similar to Frazer's description of the coastal soils at Swan River, which the latter had claimed to be extremely fertile!

Although Lockyer's comments on the advantages and safety of the large King George Sound harbour and the variety of marine life to be found there were factual and held promise, the most important part of his report, in view of later events, conveyed information about Swan River which he had obtained from two boat crews of British sealers who had been left by their mother-ship to seal along the south-west coast.[30] One crew, led by James Everett, had entered the Swan River and journeyed about twenty miles upstream, encountering a number of natives brandishing spears and shouting. They also reported 'a Bar entrance [to the river]; no vessel could get in; that the anchorage outside was bad' and that 'the open roads off Rottnest Island [were] too dangerous to load and unload cargoes or refit'.[31] Stirling had reported the existence of the bar but had made light of it claiming that it could be 'removed without difficult or great expense':[32] a far cry from the truth for the bar impeded shipping for many decades to come.

When in receipt of both reports, however, Governor Darling unreservedly accepted Stirling and Frazer's views and did not even mention points raised by Lockyer when writing to the Colonial Office. His despatch of 21 April 1827 concluded with the comment:

> As Captain Stirling's visit to Swan River may attract attention, and the report find its way into the French papers, it appears desirable, should His Majesties Government entertain any intention of forming a settlement at that place, that no time should be lost in taking the necessary steps.[33]

So certain were Stirling and Darling of the British government's favourable reaction, that Stirling, with Darling's support, wrote to Bathurst on 19 May just before leaving for Melville Island, applying for the honour of the new establishment's 'Superintendence and Governance'.[34] By the time Stirling received the answer—a flat 'no'—he had removed the Melville Island depot to Raffles Bay, and had joined his base station in East India. His only compensation was two large land grants in NSW awarded by Governor Darling.[35]

The first hint Darling received of the British government's attitude came in December

1827 when he received a despatch, written the previous July, ordering the abandonment of the western port outpost (in Victoria).[36] No mention was made of the depot that had been founded simultaneously at King George Sound. This Darling found odd, for, as he stated in an immediate reply, King George Sound was 'still more inconveniently situated' and should be abandoned as well, unless its retention was 'a matter of policy'.[37]

On 28 January 1828 the Colonial Secretary finally answered the Darling and Stirling despatches regarding Swan River. A new settlement in that region was totally 'out of the question, unnecessary on either of the grounds that had precipitated the settlement of the Eastern Colonies' (ie penal and possibly trade considerations) and 'inexpedient on grounds of expense'.[38] Behind this rejection lay not only severe government expenditure constraints but also the attitude of John Barrow, Secretary to the Admiralty, a major advocate of imperial expansion and an acknowledged authority on all matters pertaining to the Southern Hemisphere.[39] As the government expert, Barrow received all material relating to Australia as a matter of course. His initial reaction to the Stirling report, however, was anything but favourable. Not only did he receive second-hand a report on an exploratory voyage of which he, as Secretary to the Admiralty, should have been first informed, but Stirling's rash action appeared likely to 'jeopardize his carefully unfolding pattern of territorial expansion in Australia.[40]

> I cannot but regret very much that General Darling should have so easily come into the quixotic expedition proposed by Captain Stirling, in direct contradiction to his orders, and in utter ignorance of what he has proposed . . . If Captain Stirling had read the accounts of the French Surveys . . . or those more recent ones of Captain King he must have known that, excepting in Shark Bay, to the Northward, there is not a safe anchorage on the whole western coast, that a reef of rocks runs across the entrance of Swan River, and that within it there is not more than 5 or 6 feet of water; that the whole of the neighbouring coast is represented as a continued succession of 'sandy dunes', barren and utterly unfit for any kind of cultivation, and that there is no fresh water.[41]

His comment on the actual report was terse: 'while it [is] abundantly clear . . . that all the physical elements required for a settlement exist . . . here I think its advantages end'.[42] The whole coast was far too dangerous for Swan River to became a vital trade centre or a regular convalescent station. Further, given the difficulties of supply and administration from New South Wales, a separate colony would have to be founded with 'all the expense of a direct Government'. That Barrow's comments convinced Hay is evident from the similarity between his points and the reasons for refusal given in the Official Despatch of 28 January 1828. Even fears of French occupation had by that time well and truly cooled. In March 1827 Hay had informed Darling that his 'fears of French interest were groundless',[43] while in June Barrow stated that the western coastline was so barren and dangerous that there could be no objection to 'the French trying what they could make of it.'[44]

Given the circumstances in Britain at that time, it is understandable that the government was not in favour of financing a colony that to all intents and purposes appeared unnecessary. Throughout the 1820s, the English economy had been considerably affected by financial constraints resulting from government management of the large war debt[45] and stringent Treasury budgeting internally and externally was held to be imperative. In fact, even the withdrawal of the King George Sound depot was under discussion in January 1828.[46]

It was about this time that Stirling received news of the government's negative decision about Swan River.[47] He refused to accept it and within just six months the Colonial Office had changed its mind. This dramatic reversal has been ascribed by historians to a combination of linked influences: Stirling's persistence and force of argument on his return from India: the declared willingness of wealthy capitalists to invest in Swan River; renewed fear of French interest in the region excited by reports of French vessels off King George Sound and by despatches from France; and finally the changes that took place within the ruling Tory party during the period 1827-29.[48]

The resignation of Lord Liverpool in February 1827 brought to an end forty years of strong Tory leadership that had kept widening party differences under tight control. Thereafter, the ultra-conservative and reformist factions of the party openly divided, which led to three rapid changes in prime ministership before the party lost the General Election of November 1830. The third of these changes, in January 1828, conferred leadership on the hero-figure of Waterloo, the Duke of Wellington,[49] who was in sympathy with the more reformist faction of the party,[50] and made Robert Peel, a known progressive, his Home Secretary. It was therefore not surprising that the views of contemporary political economists, regarding the value of colonies as outlets for Britain's surplus population, began to exert a stronger influence over the policies of a government that had been known in the past for its anti-imperialist stance.[51]

The January 1828 change in Tory administration thus created a political atmosphere in which the foundation of a third Australian colony was less unlikely. Moreover, as Wellington appointed his old quartermaster-general and chief-of-staff, Sir George Murray, as Secretary for War and the Colonies, good fortune played into Stirling's hands.[52] Murray was the member for Perth in Scotland (hence Stirling's later choice of name for the capital of the new colony) and was an old friend of the Lanarkshire-based Stirling family. He was therefore predisposed to grant Stirling a sympathetic hearing, but he was also a rather weak civil head.[53] In this situation, his two undersecretaries exercised considerable influence. Robert Hay, who had been undersecretary since 1825 was a very decisive man and a close friend of Barrow's (even employing the latter's son as his own private secretary).[54] The second undersecretary was Horace Twiss, a younger and more recent appointee who had apparently been a school friend of Stirling's and provided another invaluable channel for negotiations.[55] Altogether the changes of late January 1828 created a far more auspicious climate for an official reconsideration of the Swan River proposal. But, despite more favourable circumstances, any positive Colonial Office action was hamstrung by the expenditure constraints imposed by Treasury. Of these constraints, however, Stirling was well aware.

Arriving back in England on grounds of ill health,[56] Stirling lost no time in advocating his Swan River scheme. On 30 July 1828 he began his campaign by outlining all his previous arguments, concluding with the comment that without prompt action by the British government, 'some Foreign Power may see the advantage of taking possession'.[57] Immediately following this he made two separate suggestions for low-cost settlement. The first, that Swan River be made 'a place for the reception of convicts',[58] was no doubt made in the belief that the Colonial Office was still concerned with the issue of an isolated penal settlement in Australia. His second suggestion was to include free settlers with convicts and to keep expenses down by employing a 'Vessel of War' there, and 'placing every individual settler for a certain time under the control of Naval discipline', thereby obviating 'many of the inconveniences attending the early stage of all settlements'.[59]

Hay was evidently impressed by these arguments as he arranged an immediate meeting with Stirling and Barrow to enable the latter to reconsider the Stirling Report. Barrow was finally convinced and recommended that the King George Sound depot be moved to Swan River.[60] On 4 August 1828 a jubilant Stirling informed his brother that negotiations were well in hand and he expected to be soon on his way to govern the new colony.[61] Two weeks later, however, he 'found them trembling at the thought of increased expenditure' and unwilling to take action of any kind.[62]

Frustrated with official indecision, Stirling now began to advocate private settlement to his acquaintances in the London clubs, to family connections and naval friends. This change in attitude was reflected in a letter to Hay, written in conjunction with Major Thomas Moody, a former member of the Colonial Office and an expert on the West Indies and the slave trade.[63] Dated 21 August it read:

> As the expense of maintaining settlements . . . may be thought a reason sufficient to prevent their formation by the Government, we venture to ask whether in such case any objection would be made to the unsupported employment of private capital and enterprise in the occupation and improvement of that territory; and whether we may be permitted to form an association with a view to obtaining a Proprietary Charter upon principles similar to those formerly adopted in the settlement of Pennsylvania and Georgia.[64]

The response from the Colonial Office was discouraging. Sir George Murray felt it was 'desirable to exercise a more immediate control over the settlement by government than by such an arrangement it would possess'.[65] This rebuff disheartened Moody who dropped out but Stirling remained undeterred. If the government would not allow private settlement, private interest could still be used to force the government's hand. Private companies such as The Australian Agricultural Company (1824), The Van Diemen's Land Company (1825), The Cressy Company of Van Diemen's Land (1823) and The Australian Company of Edinburgh (1822) were already operating successfully on a charter basis, and included members of parliament as well as prominent capitalists among their shareholders.[66] As his promotional activities during August and early September had assured Stirling that there was sufficient private interest in Swan River for such a company to be formed, he left England for a brief sojourn on the Continent to restore his health. He returned early in October to find everyone 'absent in the country'.[67]

It was mid October before Stirling could arrange another meeting with Barrow and Colonial Office staff. He was then advised that his case for settlement by private charter company would be far stronger if he could demonstrate considerable support and provide names of potential investors. As the number of individuals he could contact personally was limited, Stirling persuaded the *Hampshire Telegraph* to print a long description of Swan River, highlights of which were reprinted in *The Times, The Sun* and other London papers.[68] Almost immediately the Colonial Office began to receive enquiries, most from individuals already considering New South Wales,[69] but none would commit themselves to Stirling's scheme without firm assurance that the government intended to form a colony.[70] Private settlement that met all military, judicial and government expenses would clearly be unprofitable. But the government also wanted to avoid additional expense. Thus, despite all Stirling's efforts, the Swan River question appeared to have reached a stalemate by late October 1828. Nevertheless, Stirling continued to press the Colonial Office to at least send a ship-of-war to prevent Western New Holland's acquisition by a foreign power.[71] As he was well aware of Lockyer's formal claim this was game-playing at its best.

Suddenly it seemed to pay off. On 5 November, Sir George Murray ordered the Admiralty Commissioners to despatch a ship-of-war from the Cape of Good Hope 'to proceed to the Western Coast of New Holland and take possession of the whole territory in His Majesty's Name'.[72]

Stirling's renewed agitation about possible French interest, and the refusal of the Colonial Office to act on any of the settlement schemes he had advanced have led historians to interpret the order of 5 November as a preventative measure only. J S Battye, for example, wrote that: 'Although this action set at rest the question of actual possession, there does not appear to have been at that time a definite decision to establish a colony forthwith'.[73] Evidence for this view, however, is slim.

Various factors indicate that the Colonial Office had far more than prevention in mind when it gave the annexation order. Western New Holland had been claimed for the British Crown by Lockyer, in 1826, yet rumours of foreign interest had grown during 1827[74] and occupation, not proclamation, was the international rule for determining territorial rights.[75] Also, if the main aim was to prevent Swan River falling into foreign hands the simple and least costly solution would have been to shift the King George Sound settlement to Swan River, as suggested by Barrow. Alternatively, the Raffles Bay depot which Murray had ordered to be closed (with personnel transferred to King George Sound) in November, just before the Admiralty order,[76] could have been moved to the Swan. Instead the Colonial Office chose to send a warship which was to 'remain stationed at Swan River until further instructed'[77] a move that was far more in keeping with a precursor to settlement. Of course this alone did not signify an intention to settle, but it is revealing when coupled with the fact that, on 12 November, Twiss had asked the Admiralty for another ship to convey a small detachment of military to the Swan River,[78] orders already having been sent to the army for the selection of men, particularly those with varied basic skills.[79] As the *Challenger*, the ship eventually assigned under the command of Captain Fremantle to undertake the annexation,[80] carried a company of 189 men including fifty fighting marines,[81] purely protective motives would have made the stationing of an additional military guard at the Swan an unwarranted expense. On the other hand, a military guard was an essential provision for a new Crown colony, especially during the period of foundation and first settlement.

The conclusion that can be drawn from this, namely, that the Colonial Office had already decided on 5 November to establish a Crown colony at Swan River, is significant because, as previously indicated, it means that the Colonial Office had already decided on a method of settling the region at minimum Crown expense. Such a conclusion appears, however, to conflict with another widely accepted view: that the major influence on the method of settlement employed at Swan River was a proposal put forward by the syndicate led by Thomas Peel, cousin to the then Home Secretary. For Peel's proposal was not submitted until 14 November.[82]

The Peel Association, which also included the well-known and wealthy capitalists, Captain Vincent, Colonel Potter McQueen and Mr Edward Schenley,[83] had been formed to enable a pooling of funds to invest in the territory glowingly described by Captain Stirling. Their plan was to finance the large-scale transportation of labouring men and their families, goods, livestock and equipment to the Swan and to establish a settlement there at little or no expense to His Majesty's government but at the same time fully responsible to the Crown. In return they requested that the government grant them land in strict proportion to the total value of their investment, that proportion being one acre for each 1s 6d invested. They estimated that 10,000 people would be transported over four years at a cost of £30 per head, their total outlay thus entitling them to a grant of four million acres.

Returns on this planned investment were expected to accrue from the sale of marketable crops such as tobacco, sugar, cotton and flax, and from raising livestock to both mount and provision His Majesty's forces stationed in the Indian Ocean area.[84]

This plan bore a marked resemblance to earlier proposals for Australian settlement, such as Purry's 1718 submission to the Dutch East India Company and Matra's 1783 submission to the British government for the settlement of Botany Bay, which was mentioned in Chapter II.[85] The central proposal of the Peel plan, that land be granted in proportion to capital invested, was also not new but based on the then current policy of land grants in New South Wales. This system, moreover, was well known to at least one member of the Peel group, Colonel Potter McQueen, who held a 10,000-acre grant in New South Wales, managed by an overseer, awarded in 1823 on the basis of the value of labour and assets he had introduced.[86]

A land-grant system had been implemented in New South Wales as early as 1789, although at that time grants were purely at the governor's discretion and involved no conditional investment outlay by the grantee.[87] The latter was introduced in 1817 and modified to include penalty clauses in 1826. At that stage the proportion between the value of assets and the amount of land granted was set at £500 for one square mile (or three shillings per acre).[88] The new laws were not popular with colonists, and problems of evasion and duplicity in grant applications plagued Darling through the remainder of the decade. Thus, problems in the past application of the grant system, as well as its limited success in attracting free British settlers,[89] would have led Colonial Office authorities to discount the possibility that a land-grant system could provide a feasible basis for establishing a new colony.

In this context the Peel Association's willingness to invest in virgin territory purely in return for Crown grants of newly annexed land provided convincing evidence that a land-grant system could constitute a viable and low-cost method of colonisation. As such, their proposal could well have tipped the scales towards the annexation order, except for the fact that the Peel proposal was forwarded nine days *after* the order to the Admiralty.

Although this date inconsistency supports the traditional assumption that the Peel proposal had no direct effect on the annexation order, there are reasons for challenging this view. Common prudence would dictate that formal commitment should be delayed until satisfactory evidence of Crown intent towards annexation, administration and protection of the territory had been provided. The fact that the group submitted their proposal to the Colonial Office indicates *ipso facto* that they in no way planned to form an independent or purely private settlement at Swan River. Again, given the personal connections that existed between members of the Peel Association and government officials, including Colonial Office staff, it is extremely doubtful that the association would have submitted its proposal without prior consultation.[90] Indeed, correspondence cited by Peel's biographer, Alexandra Hasluck, includes a letter from Peel to Twiss, the Colonial Undersecretary, dated 6 November, which refers to an even *earlier* meeting between Twiss and the association.[91]

There is thus little doubt that *before* the annexation order of 5 November the idea of using a low-cost land-grant colonisation scheme had overcome the government's financial objections to a new Crown settlement at Swan River.

Further assurance for the government was provided by continued queries from potential investors in late November, including another substantial settlement proposal by Colonel Peter Augustus Lautour,[92] co-founder of The Cressy Company of Van Diemen's

Land, who had heard of the scheme from Colonel Potter McQueen. Such queries, however, shifted the government's attitude towards the Peel proposal. Concern was expressed, particularly by Stirling, that the size of the grant requested by the association (some four million acres) would 'stem the flow of interest from individuals with more limited finances . . . [while] an organisation of such a size in the infant settlement would impede efficient unbiased administration'.[93]

On 6 December 1828, almost a month after their initial submission, the Peel Association received a reply.[94] The government agreed, in principle, to the scheme but limited the amount of land to be granted to one million acres—half to be made available on arrival and the remainder when all assets and labour had been landed. All land would be granted in fee simple (ie titled) if it was cultivated or improved at the end of 21 years, but the association was not to have priority of choice or exclusive settlement rights. In fact, a broadsheet was enclosed with the reply entitled 'Regulations for the Guidance of those who may prepare to embark as settlers for the new settlement on the West Coast of New Holland'. While setting out the guidelines for land grants, these regulations also specified that colonists emigrated at their own risk. Stirling was announced as civil superintendent of the new settlement which was not to have the full status of a colony but be attached to New South Wales in the same way that had applied initially to Van Diemen's Land.

These terms broke the Peel Association. Members felt they undermined the scheme's potential profitability and that they would be 'little better than lunatics were we to attempt further to proceed'.[95] But Peel, with financial support from the emancipist, Solomon Levey, did proceed and his story is told elsewhere.[96]

The general regulations broadsheet included in the reply to the Peel Association represented, in effect, the government's formal commitment to a new settlement at Swan River. It included acceptance of the financial burden of providing a minimal government machinery and the clear intimation that the settlement would be open to *any* interested investor who would actually emigrate. Two factors appear to have influenced these decisions: first, the government's antipathy, based on past experience with the powerful East India Company, towards granting exclusive rights to a few individuals, and second, the receipt of news from a British envoy late in November that the French government was again taking a serious interest in Western New Holland, making *rapid* occupation of the Swan River region desirable and best achieved by encouraging any interested investor.

The catalytic effect of the news from France was mentioned in a letter from Hay of the Colonial Office to the Treasury, dated 31 December 1828. This despatch also set out in some detail the nature of the government's commitment to the new settlement:

Being fully aware of the necessity of adhering to the strictest economy in carrying into effect the proposed undertaking, Sir George Murray has provided that the Expedition which is preparing should be on the least expensive scale compatible with the nature and effectual accomplishment of the project in view. For the full security of those who may be inclined to embark their capital in this scheme and for the protection of those who may be employed by His Majesty's Government in administering the affairs of the Colony and in superintending the public works which it may be expedient to erect, it has been thought proper to send out a detachment of 60 men with a proportionate number of officers, and females of the Regiment. The number of the Civil establishment to be employed (excluding the Governor) has been fixed at seven, and it has been considered feasible to place their salaries at a lower rate. In (the three) cases where no salary is stated, it is not intended that any should be given at least until the duties should appear to be such as to require compensation. They will be entitled, however, to a free passage, which is also given to all those who go out on the Public Account . . .

. . . The Secretary of State feels his inability to prepare any estimate of the expenditure which may be required but he does not doubt that before the expiration of the year he will have it in his power to submit calculations to the Lords Commissioners which may answer their Lordships' purpose in making the necessary application to Parliament.[97]

This communication clearly reveals one of the major constraints on the future development of the new colony, namely: the minimal number of civil staff appointed to administer the new settlement and the meagre funds set aside to meet establishment costs. Nevertheless, provision *was* made for an independent and separate government which Stirling had forcefully requested in a memorandum of 28 December. However, while the government did agree to a separate colony, it only allowed Stirling the title of Lieutenant Governor, placing him on the same footing as Arthur in Van Diemen's Land, but below Darling in the senior colony of New South Wales.[98]

The collapse of the Peel Association began about the same time as these negotiations took place but appears to have caused little concern. As Cameron has argued elsewhere, 'for the Colonial Office, the collapse of the Association was an unfortunate but minor annoyance. It was now fully extended in meeting requests for information about Swan River from prospective colonists . . . Twenty-four requests were handled in November and seventy-six in December. By the end of January a further eighty-five had been dealt with . . . (many being quite substantial proposals) . . . Support for the colony was so overwhelming that its success seemed assured without the involvement of Peel's Association and the terms offered to the Association were re-examined and broadened to take account of this'.[99]

The new regulations were issued first on 13 January 1829 and later, with minor modifications, on 3 February.[100] In essence they encompassed three principles. First, that apart from provision of a minimal civil and military establishment the government would incur no expense in carrying settlers to or from the new private enterprise colony or in supplying it with necessities after foundation.[101] Second, to attract maximum numbers of private investors and settlers, 40 acres would be granted for each £3 invested in assets suitable for farming (ie one acre = one shilling and sixpence which was cheap compared with the going rate of three to five shillings an acre in other colonies). Money was not to be admitted as a basis for land-grant applications but former government servants (civil and defence) were permitted to exchange their present and future pension entitlements for a grant of land. As no convicts were to be introduced and costs of passage (£15 a head steerage) would deter the emigration of labourers, settlers were to be granted two hundred acres for every adult introduced at their own expense, and smaller acreages for children according to age. Third, to ensure that assets and labour admitted for land entitlement were actually applied in productive land use, settlers were initially to be given only occupation rights to their grants. Title, and hence ownership and transfer rights, was to be withheld until grantees had 'improved' every acre to the value of at least one shilling and sixpence by cultivation, drainage, fencing etc. Fines were to be imposed on settlers who failed to improve at least a quarter of their grant within three years of occupation, and grants not wholly improved within ten years (reduced from the original twenty-one) were to be resumed by the Crown.

The Times pointed out:

It is obvious that none but men of some capital are wished for by the King's Government as undertakers of the projected enterprise. The State is to be at no expense whatever. The Colonist is to support himself and family throughout the voyage and after the disembarkation, and

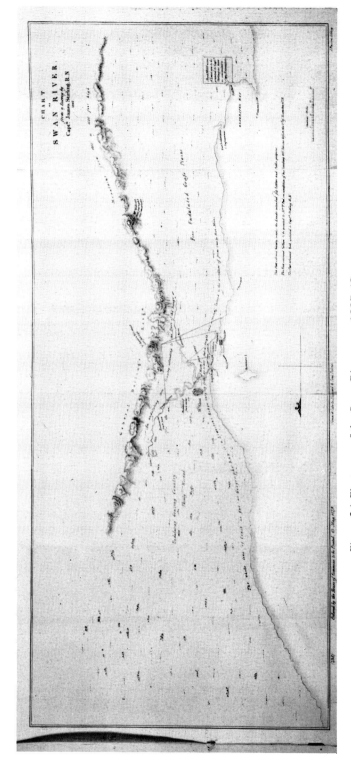

Figure 24: First map of the Swan River area, 1827 (Courtesy of the Battye Library, Perth WA)

to protect from want, at his own proper charge, any labourer or servant he may take out from England.[102]

As the only detailed information on which colonists could make decisions was contained in the Stirling/Frazer report and this was a confidential government document and not leaked to the press until April 1829,[103] Stirling was a key figure in all early preparations, but he left on board the *Parmelia* with his small civil staff and their families on 8 February. Thereafter, lack of detailed information, combined with inaccuracies in the report itself, led to speculation and rumour in the London press which reached mania proportions by mid year. Misinformation in turn severely distorted the decisions that young potential settlers made regarding their needs in the new colony, and consequently slowed its early development far more than need have been the case.[104]

The *Parmelia* did not, as is often thought, carry the first free independent settlers. It was chartered by the government to convey the civil officials and their families, servants and government labourers to the Swan. At first all had been expected to travel on the *Sulphur*, the naval vessel commissioned to take the military troops to the Swan.[105] But Stirling objected so strongly to such overcrowding that he eventually persuaded the government to charter the 443-ton *Parmelia* to transport the civil establishment and public stores to the colony at £4 · 10 · 0 per ton register.[106] The civil staff consisted of the surveyor, Lieutenant JS Roe, who accompanied Phillip Parker King in his 1817 survey of the Western Australia coast and assistant HC Sutherland, Colonial Secretary Peter Brown (later Broun), storekeeper J Morgan, surgeon Charles Simmons, harbour master MJ Currie, naturalist J Drummond, and a clerk, seventeen-year-old William Shenton, who was a cousin of Stirling's.[107] No public works officer, treasurer, or judge was initially appointed. Somehow Colonial Office authorities expected this small group to administer effectively a territory known to be larger than England. Moreover, Stirling was granted an initial cash reserve of only £1000 (in sterling and Spanish dollars) to meet contingency needs over the first two years.[108]

Apart from granting the right to draw bills on Treasury when required, the British government provided no definite terms of reference regarding the nature of the governor's financial responsibilities or the extent of its own total financial commitment before the departure of the *Parmelia*, an omission that was to cause considerable problems in the first few years of settlement when demands upon government finance were naturally high.

Once the decision to settle Swan River had been made, the speed with which it was put into effect was striking. Within less than two months General Regulations were drawn up, appointments made, stores ordered, ships and finance arranged and troops readied for departure. Such haste clearly denied any chance of careful planning or assessment of the problems that might stem either from the 'conditions' imposed on private settlers or from the minimal government resources allocated to cover the inception of the most isolated colony in the world. However, despite the rapid and largely unplanned nature of official decision making, the departure of the *Parmelia* and her escort the *Sulphur* on 4 February, marked the beginning of an 'experiment in colonisation by free settlement'.[109] Their arrival at Swan River on 1 June 1829, followed by the first private settlers on the *Calista* in August, can be said to have marked also the realisation of one man's dream. Without James Stirling's persistence and ambitious endeavours there is some doubt that Western Australia would have become British at all.

Notes

[1] For detailed discussion see Appleyard, R.T. and Manford, T. *The Beginning*, (U.W.A.P., 1979); Schilder, Gunter. *Australia Unveiled*, (Theatrum Orbis Terrarum Ltd., Amersterdam, 1976); and Wood, G.A. *The Discovery of Australia*, (Macmillan, 1969).

[2] Appleyard and Manford, *op.cit.*, p.16 and Wood, *op.cit.*, pp.237-8.

[3] Cameron, J.M.R. *Ambition's Fire: The Agricultural Colonization of Pre-convict Western Australia*, (hereafter cited as 'Ambition's'), (U.W.A.P., 1981), pp.9-11.

[4] Appleyard and Manford, *op.cit.*, p.19.

[5] Marchant, Leslie. *France Australe*, (Artlook Books W.A., 1982), Ch. 3.

[6] See Darling's Commission 1825, *H.R.A.*, I, xii, p.77.

[7] See Cameron, Ch. XIV, pp.277-79 and also Eddy, J.J. *Britain and the Australian Colonies: The Technique of Government*, (Oxford, 1969), p.23, and *H.R.A.*, I, xii, pp.226-7.

[8] See Battye, J.S. *Western Australia: A History from its discovery to the Inauguration of the Commonwealth*, (hereafter cited as 'History'), (Oxford, 1924), Ch. III.

[9] *H.R.A.*, I, xii, p.321.

[10] *Ibid.*, pp.193-5.

[11] *Ibid.*, p.195.

[12] *Ibid.*, p.194.

[13] *H.R.A.*, I, xii, p.218.

[14] *Ibid.*, pp.640-1.

[15] *Ibid.*, p.700.

[16] *Proclamation*, 7-3-1831.

[17] *H.R.A.*, I, xii, pp.226-7.

[18] *Ibid.*, pp.224-5.

[19] *A.D.B.*, Vol. 2, entry on Stirling, pp.484-5 and Cameron, J. 'Sir James Stirling The Founder', in Hunt, L. (ed.) *Westralian Portraits* (U.W.A.P., 1979), pp.5-9.

[20] Eddy, *op.cit.*, p.23; Spillett, P. *Forsaken Settlement*, (Melbourne, 1972), p.13.

[21] *H.R.A.*, I, xii, pp.729, 775-6 and 777-780.

[22] *Ibid.*, p.780.

[23] See *The Monitor*, 28-11-1826, *The Australian*, 6-12-1826, 13-12-1826, 27-12-1826; Clark, C.M.H. *A History of Australia*, (M.U.P., 1968), Vol. 2, pp.71-5.

[24] *H.R.A.*, III, vi, pp.501-6.

[25] Cameron, J.M.R. 'Prelude to Colonization: James Stirling's examination of Swan River, March 1827: (hereafter cited as 'Prelude'), in the *The Australian Geographer*, XII, 4 (1973), p.318.

[26] Bassett, Marnie. *The Henty's: An Australian Colonial Tapestry*, (hereafter cited as 'Henty's') (O.U.P., London, 1954), p.85.

[27] *H.R.A.*, III, vi, pp.583-4.

[28] Cameron, 'Prelude', *op.cit.*, pp.319-323.

[29] *H.R.A.*, III, vi, pp.491-506.

[30] *Ibid.*, pp.489-9.

[31] *H.R.A.*, III, vi, pp.604-6 and p.504.

[32] *Ibid.*, p.575.

[33] *H.R.A.*, I, xiii, p.265.

[34] *Ibid.*, p.307.

[35] Cameron, 'Ambition's', *op.cit.*, p.34.

[36] *H.R.A.*, I, xiii, p.450.

[37] *Ibid.*, p.667.

[38] *Ibid.*, pp.739-40.

[39] See Eddy, *op.cit.*, p.235 and *H.R.A.*, III, vi, pp.751-3.

[40] Cameron, J.M.R. 'The Foundations of Western Australia Reconsidered', (hereafter cited as 'Foundations'), in *S.W.A.H.*, Vol. III (November, 1978), pp.5-6.

[41] *C.O.*, 323, Vol. 149, p.135.

[42] *C.O.*, 201. Vol. 185, pp.23-6.

[43] *C.O.*, 207, Vol. 17, p.44.

[44] *C.O.*, 323, Vol. 149, p.135.

[45] Deane, P. and Cole, W.A. *British Economic Growth 1688-1959*, (C.U.P., 1962), pp.164-172.

[46] *H.R.A.*, I, xii, p.714 ff.

[47] *H.R.A.*, II, vi, p.584.

[48] See Battye, J.S. 'Causes which led to the colonization of Western Australia', *J.R.W.A.H.S.*, Vol. V, September 1918 and Battye, 'History', *op.cit.*, p.57. Portus, G.V. *Australia Since 1606*, (Melbourne, 1932), pp.98-9; Hasluck, Alexandra. *Portrait with Background*, (Melbourne, 1955), pp.15-16 and also *Thomas Peel of Swan*

River, (hereafter cited as 'Peel'), (Melbourne, 1965), pp.20-36; Crowley, F.K. *A Short History of Western Australia*, (Melbourne, 1959), pp.9-12 and also *Australia's Western Third*, (London, 1960), p.6; Uren, M.J. *Land Looking West, The Story of Governor James Stirling in Western Australia*, (London, 1948), pp.27-58; Bassett, Marnie. 'The Henty's', *op.cit.*, pp.74-5; Henn, P.U. 'French Exploration on the Western Coast', *J.R.W.A.H.S.*, Vol. 11, Part XV, 1934; Cameron, 'Foundations', *op.cit.*, and Statham, P. 'Swan River Colony 1829-50', in Stannage, C.T. (ed.), *A New History of Western Australia*, (U.W.A.P., 1980).

[49] See Webb, R.K. *Modern England*, (Allen & Unwin, 4th ed., 1975), Ch. 4, p.183; Beales, Derek. *From Castlereagh to Gladstone 1815-1885*, (Nelson Sphere Books, London, 1969), Appendix C, pp.281-2; and Young, D.M. *The Colonial Office in the early 19th Century*, (London, 1961), pp.16-19 and 111-113.

[50] See Webb, *op.cit.*, Ch. 4; Thompson, D. *England in the Nineteenth Century (1815-1914)*, (Penguin, London, 1964), Ch. 3, pp.52-62.

[51] See Coates, A.W. (ed.) *The Classical Economists and Economic Policy*, (Methuen, 1971), p.24; Finlayson, G.B.A.M. *England in the Eighteen Thirties: Decade of Reform*, (Edward Arnold, London, 1964), Ch. 1, p.6; Chapters by Winch and Ghosh in Shaw, A.G.L. (ed.) *Great Britain and the Colonies 1915-65* (Methuen, 1970), Chs. 4 and 5.

[52] Eddy, *op.cit.*, p.19 and Uren, *op.cit.*, p.49.

[53] Eddy, *op.cit.*, p.19.

[54] Young, *op.cit.*, p.86.

[55] Hasluck, 'Peel', *op.cit.*, p.26.

[56] *Ibid.*, p.18.

[57] *H.R.A.*, III, vi, p.585.

[58] *Ibid.*, p.586.

[59] *Ibid.*

[60] *C.O.*, 18 Vol. 1, pp.96-8.

[61] *Stirling Letters*, A.S. 139/1 M.L. (letter 4-8-1828). See also Cameron, 'Foundations', *op.cit.*, p.8.

[62] Stirling Letters, *op.cit.*, letter 4-8-1828.

[63] Young, *op.cit.*, pp.71-74.

[64] *H.R.A.*, III, vi, p.586 and note 122, p.864.

[65] Cited in Battye, 'History', *op.cit.*, p.70.

[66] For details of these private companies see Roberts, S.S. *A History of Australian Land Settlement*, (hereafter cited as 'Land Settlement'), (Macmillan Australia, 1968), Ch. 6, pp.56-67; list of shareholders in Campbell, J.F. 'The First Decade of the A.A. Co.' *J.R.A.H.S.*, 1923, Vol. 9, p.118; Mudie, *The Affairs of the Australian Agriculture Co.*, (London, 1833); Bischoff, *Sketch of the History of Van Diemen's Land*, (London, 1832).

[67] Stirling Letters, *op.cit.*, letter of 11-10-1828 (NB - by 1827, the Australian Company had 'nearly 2000 tons of shipping in the trade with no intention of immediate increase'. See note 129 *H.R.A.*, I, xiii, pp.553-4.

[68] *Hampshire Telegraph*, 18-10-1828; *The Times*, 20-10-1828, etc., cited in Cameron, 'Foundations', *op.cit.*, p.9.

[69] *C.O.*, 202, Vol. 23, p.74; *C.O.*, 18, Vol. 1, p.266; *C.O.*, 18, Vol. 2, p.86.

[70] This was admitted by Stirling, see *C.O.*, 18, Vol. 1, pp.67-9.

[71] *Ibid.*

[72] The original is missing, but referred to in another letter, see *H.R.A.*, III, vi, p.587.

[73] Battye, 'History', *op.cit.*, p.71.

[74] Cited in Battye, 'History', *op.cit.*, p.62.

[75] See *H.R.A.*, I, xii, p.700.

[76] *H.R.A.*, I, xiv, pp.410-11.

[77] *H.R.A.*, III, vi, p.587.

[78] *Ibid.*, p.589.

[79] See Whitely, E.S. and C.G.S. *The Military Establishment in Western Australia 1829-63*, (Unpublished MS, W.A.A., April, 1970), Q 355-009, Ch. 1.

[80] H.M.S. *Tweed*, was first given this commission, but soon afterwards Captain Fremantle, commander of H.M.S. *Challenger*, was ordered to relieve *Tweed* at the Cape and carry out the Admiralty's instructions. For details see Parry, Ann. *The Admirals' Fremantle*, (Chatto and Windus, London, 1971), p.142.

[81] See list of the ship's company in *S.R.P.*, Vol. 2.

[82] See *H.R.A.*, III, vi, p.588.

[83] Details of the background of these men and the Association are given in Hasluck, 'Peel', *op.cit.*, Ch. 3.

[84] The proposal is stated in full in *H.R.A.*, III, vi, pp.588-90.

[85] See Clark, C.M.H. 'The Choice of Botany Bay', *F. of A.* Ch. 11, p.66.

[86] Details in *H.R.A.*, I, xi, pp.142-3 and xii, p.795.

[87] See Clark, C.M.H. *Select Documents in Australian History 1788-1850*, (A. & R., 1975), Section 5, pp.218-9 and *H.R.A.*, I, i, pp.124-6; Auchmuty in Ch. 2 Crowley, F. (ed.) *op.cit.*, pp.46-7; Robinson, K.W. in Ch. 5 of Abbott and Nairne, (eds.) *Economic Growth of Australia 1788-1821*, (M.U.P., 1969), pp.91-4; Mills, R.C. *The Colonization of Australia 1829-42*, (1915, Reprinted 1968), Ch. VII, pp.157-161; Roberts, 'Land Settlement', *op.cit.*, Ch. 4, pp.36-40.

[88] *H.R.A.*, I, xii, pp.377-8.

[89] For evidence of slow free immigration before 1830 see Madgwick, R.B. *Immigration into Eastern Australia 1788-1851*, (S.U.P., 1969, 2nd impression), Ch. 3, pp.53-58.

[90] See Young, *op.cit.*, p.20; Hasluck, 'Peel', *op.cit.*, Ch. 2.

[91] Hasluck, *Ibid.*, p.211.

[92] See *C.O.*, 18 Vol. 1, p.242 (17-11-1828) and 270 (12-12-1828).

[93] Cameron, 'Foundations', *op.cit.*, p.11.

[94] *H.R.A.*, III, vi, pp.593-4.

[95] Cameron, 'Foundations', *op.cit.*, p.12; Hasluck, 'Peel', *op.cit.*, pp.31-2. (NB - McQueen withdrew first and was followed by Vincent and Schenley in January 1829).

[96] Hasluck, 'Peel', *op.cit.*, Bergman, G.F.J. 'Solomon Levey — From Convict to Merchant Prince', *J.R.A.H.S.*, Vol. 54, 1968, pp.22-4; for Peel's acceptance of conditions see *H.R.A.*, III, vi, pp.610-11.

[97] *C.O.*, 18, Vol. 1, pp.142-5. (In this draft copy the date 12th December has been crossed out and replaced by the 31st, indicating consideration over several weeks.)

[98] *H.R.A.*, III, vi, p.598-9 and pp.600-2.

[99] Cameron, 'Foundations', *op.cit.*, pp.12-13.

[100] For details see *H.R.A.*, III, vi, p.606 and ff.

[101] See *B.P.P.*, (Shannon Ireland, 1970), Colonies General, Vol. 2, pp.80-1.

[102] *The Times*, 17-1-1829.

[103] See the *Quarterly Review*, April 1829, and following publicity in other journals.

[104] Statham, 'Swan River Colony', *op.cit.*, pp.184-6.

[105] See *The Collie Letters*, W.A.A. 332, Letter of 22-11-1828.

[106] *C.O.*, 18, Vol. 3, pp.247-251.

[107] *H.R.A.*, III, vi, pp.600-2.

[108] This amount and its breakdown is listed as the initial colonial cash credit in the 1829-30 accounts presented to the London Colonial Office (see CS Vol. 1/54-60). It is also referred to in Butlin, S.J. *Foundations of the Australian Monetary System, 1788-1851*, (M.U.P., 1953), pp.379-80.

[109] Mills, R.C. *op.cit.*, p.73.

Chapter VII

Perth: A Foundling City

Geoffrey Bolton

Responsibility for the site of the city of Perth can be placed directly on two men, Captain Sir James Stirling, the first governor of Western Australia, and John Septimus Roe, the first surveyor general. Stirling was an ambitious visionary, the first of a long line of leaders and entrepreneurs who have sketched grand schemes for the development of Western Australia without scrupulously counting the human and financial costs which would result from encouraging others to embark on these schemes before they were adequately researched and planned. Roe, although by no means lacking an eye to his own advantage, was a much more methodical character, hard-working, efficient and loyal. He was the first great Western Australian public servant, and the forerunner of engineer-administrators such as CY O'Connor and Sir Russell Dumas. This combination of the charismatic politician and the sober bureaucrat has been present at many of the great leaps forward in Western Australian development.[1]

Characteristically it is Stirling who is more lavishly commemorated. The main road between Perth and its port of Fremantle is Stirling Highway. The broadest thoroughfare leading north from the city centre is Stirling Street. His statue stands in the central city area in the forecourt of the headquarters of the only Western Australian bank. Even in his own time a critic complained that 'The name 'Stirling' appears in so many places on the Maps . . . that people . . . begin to suspect they have been duped by a Company of mere speculators.'[2] Roe on the other hand had the misfortune to give his name to a street which from the turn of the century until 1958 was noted for housing Perth's brothels. It is only in recent years that he has been commemorated by a freeway, still largely incomplete, which in time will constitute a ring road for the Perth metropolitan area. Nevertheless Roe claims equally with Stirling the status of godfather to Western Australia's capital city.

As shown in Chapter VI, none of Stirling's forerunners had given the Swan River such enthusiastic praise as Stirling did on the basis of a fortnight in March 1827, fortified by the opinion of the botanist, Charles Frazer. Vlaming in 1696-7 and Heirisson in 1801 had charted the river with its two great lake-like reaches behind a deceptively narrow mouth blocked by a sandbar, but neither expedition led to European annexation.[3] Stirling and Frazer, arriving at the end of what was apparently an uncommonly cool, moist summer, were misled by the tallness of the northern jarrah forest and the quality of the alluvial soils close to the river into believing that the coastal plain would offer fertile farming and grazing. It was, Stirling wrote, equal to the plains of Lombardy; and he persuaded himself that the cool easterly land breeze of these early autumn nights must originate from a range of snowy mountains. On even slimmer evidence he predicted that coal would be found.[4] Having formed these optimistic misconceptions he returned to Sydney convinced that a colony must be planted at the Swan River.

Two years later his dream had become reality. On returning to Britain in 1828 he had cajoled the Colonial Office into authorising the foundation of a colony in Western Australia with himself as governor. While the British government intended to keep its expenditure on the settlement to a minimum it stimulated private investment by publicising an even more exaggerated version of Stirling and Frazer's optimistic claims for the Swan River region. Settlers were attracted by the prospect of securing land grants in this Arcadia at the rate of forty acres for every £3 of invested capital. During 1829, 669 settlers and 100 military, seamen, and officials were to make the journey to the Swan River, followed by another 1050 in 1830. Few were experienced farmers. None had Australian experience.[5] No preparations whatever had been made for their arrival. It was to be Stirling's triumph that from such unpromising beginnings the colony would eventually survive and grow.

Having landed the first settlers in June 1829 on the wind-swept dunes of Garden Island, Stirling considered the question of founding a town site. His instructions from the Secretary of State for Colonies, Sir George Murray, informed him that among his earliest duties would be the determination of the future seat of government. When this town site had been selected its streets should be laid out on a regular plan, sufficient land should be reserved for public purposes, and a central zone of 1920 acres should be available only for leasehold for up to twenty-one years so that it might be disposable for future resumption as the town expanded. The Colonial Office also suggested that the town should be situated at the confluence of two waterways, and that Stirling's first efforts should be concentrated on the south side of the Swan. In the upshot most of Murray's advice was disregarded, although it was in recognition of him that Stirling decided at an early stage that the new capital would be christened 'Perth' after Murray's constituency in the House of Commons. Sydney and Hobart had both been named for the Colonial Secretary of their day, and it is curious that Stirling did not choose the name 'Murray' instead of disguising the compliment. Perhaps he thought that Murray, a baffled old warhorse who owed his place in the Duke of Wellington's Cabinet largely to army loyalties, was not distinguished enough. Perth in Scotland on the other hand was a pleasant place, although it was to be the Georgian 'New Town' of Edinburgh which eventually provided a model for the later layout of the Western Australian capital.

But first a site had to be found, for the settlers soon wearied of camping by the seashore in a rainy winter. Roe was taken from his task of surveying a harbour and sent in quest of a town site. Cockburn Sound looked like a fine location for a seaport, but the initial problems of inland communication through unmapped bush required the use of the Swan River as a waterway. It was easy enough to fix on a landing place at the river mouth which would become the nucleus of Fremantle, but Stirling's hopes of establishing an upstream port at Rocky Bay or Freshwater Bay were doomed as soon as he realised that the bar across the mouth could not easily be removed (it survived until the creation of the artificial Fremantle Harbour in 1897-9). Some thought seems to have been given to cutting a canal from Rocky Bay to the coast north of Fremantle, but this was clearly impracticable in the short term. Fremantle itself was ruled out because it could not be defended against a foreign foe as readily as an upstream site. To our eyes this may seem far-fetched, as in 200 years of European settlement foreign navies have only once attacked an Australian city even minimally, but it was a significant factor in contemporary thinking; in 1867 Fremantle was to be thrown into panic for fear that American privateers would bombard the port and release the convicts.[7] Defence considerations probably ruled against two possible sites a few miles north of Fremantle, Buckland Hill, and the head of Freshwater Bay (now the site of Claremont). Both places were reserved from alienation, but neither was developed.

Another factor told against Fremantle or its close environs as an administrative centre. Stirling and Roe soon realised that the bulk of the country within 20 miles of the coast was sandy plain, unsuited to the arable farming contemplated by many of the settlers. The most fertile land lay on the upper Swan, above its confluence with the Helena, and here Stirling, Roe and other leading officials and their friends thoughtfully allocated themselves land grants when the first subdivisions were made. To serve these holdings a separate capital had to be established upstream. Thus Stirling departed from established practice in the British colonies, so creating a precedent for Colonel William Light when in 1836 he separated port and capital in South Australia.

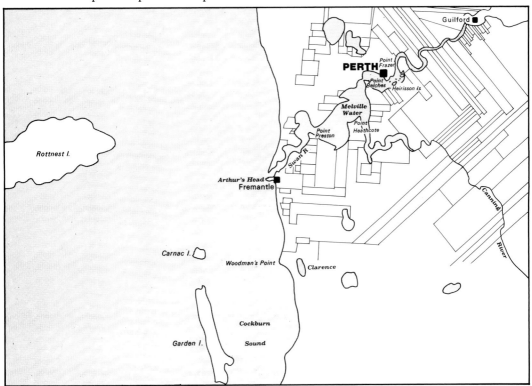

Figure 25: Perth, midway between the navigable head of the river at Guildford and the port of Fremantle

Seddon and Ravine have analysed the motives which led Stirling to select the present site of Perth rather than the alternative at Point Heathcote in what is now the suburb of Applecross.[8] Point Heathcote was in many ways a superior site. It met the criterion of fronting two important waterways, the Swan and its major tributary the Canning, with access to potential farmlands in both hinterlands. Compared to the site eventually chosen, Point Heathcote was much less cramped for future growth, had easier access to Fremantle and the inland, possessed a better anchorage, was better ventilated by the summer sea breezes, was well watered and accessible to building materials—although, defending his decision after the event, Stirling claimed that Point Heathcote was inferior to Perth in the two last respects. He was wrong. The only advantage which Seddon and Ravine discern in his ultimate siting of Perth is its picturesqueness—for although Point Heathcote commands admirable river views it lacks a backdrop as fine as Mount Eliza, and its eastern sky-line offers a less distinct view of the Darling Scarp. Stirling also claimed that a site above the Narrows would be easier to defend than Point Heathcote. But although Seddon and Ravine do not say so, it is hard to resist the thought that a great attraction of the site chosen for Perth was its accessibility to the lands chosen on the upper Swan by Stirling, Roe and others of the colonial elite.

On 12 August 1829 Mrs Helen Dance, the most senior officer's wife who was not incapacitated by pregnancy, founded the city of Perth by striking a blow with an axe on a casuarina tree.[9] During the ensuing weeks Roe laid down the outlines of Perth's first street pattern, almost certainly following specific instructions from Stirling. In defining a site of three square miles he was constrained by Mount Eliza to the west, the Swan to the south and east, and to the north by a chain of swamps which drained into Claise Brook. Within these boundaries a rectangular town site could be laid out. This led the street plan into following the model of 'New Town' of Edinburgh, where the original terrain imposed comparable constraints, although in the early nineteenth century many new colonial town sites were planned on similar principles of layout.

Roe tilted the oblong plan of the town site so that its lateral streets ran parallel to the river. As 'Front Street' he marked out a spacious terrace designed to front an open space of river bank. This might have been named King George's Terrace, but the dilapidated George IV was not an impressive figure to many of his subjects, and the patriotic compromise of St George's Terrace was chosen instead. Going inland three further streets were marked paralleling St George's Terrace, the most northerly of them edging the swamplands. Having drawn these lines on the map; Roe then must have named them in hierarchical order. The top line, furthest from the river, was named after the Prime Minister, the Duke of Wellington; the next for his subordinate, Murray, the Colonial Secretary; the third for Murray's Undersecretary, R W Hay. Paradoxically it was Hay Street which became the most important thoroughfare, since it ran along the east-west ridge one block back from St George's Terrace, and was not subject to flooding like parts of Wellington and Murray Streets.

Roe's intention was to divide the town site into two portions. West of Barrack Street would be the focus for trade and commerce. The central block of the site between Barrack and Pier Streets would form an open space reserved for public purposes and including the military cantonment. To the east would lie the administrative quarter grouped around a square on a small hill, now Victoria Square. At some point soon after the end of 1830 news arrived of a change of government in London, and Stirling or Roe must have considered it diplomatic to commemorate the new Whig ministers. Accordingly Murray Street east of the cantonment became Goderich Street after the new Colonial Secretary, and Hay Street was matched by Howick Street for the new undersecretary; but for some reason Wellington Street retained the same name throughout, and the eastern extension of St

George's Terrace along the riverfront became Adelaide Terrace, after the wife of the new monarch William IV. The King himself was allocated one of the cross-streets in the western part of the town.

Stirling and Roe had made a promising start. Despite all the pressures they had planned spaciously, allowing for large central allotments well aligned to take advantage of the local environment. Even the constraining influence of the swamplands to the north might have been overcome. As W E Bold, the influential and innovative town clerk of Perth was to argue a hundred years later, 'It is a pity that no avail was taken of the opportunities which presented themselves at that day of laying out an ideal garden city, by taking advantage, for ornamental purposes of the chain of lakes from the eastern end of the City to Monger's Lake in the north-west.'[10] But such planning would have required financial and engineering resources far beyond the reach of an impoverished colony struggling for survival. Economic stringency, inept directions on land policy from London and a shortage of skilled workers soon dimmed the brightness of the original vision.

There was also the problem of the Aboriginals, perhaps 400 in number, who inhabited the Swan coastal plain.[11] Unlike Batman in Melbourne a few years later Stirling made no attempt to enter into treaty with the Aboriginals for the occupancy of their grounds. If he gave the matter a thought at all, he probably assumed that people without agriculture and a formal political system had no title to the land, following the precedent of the annexation of New South Wales.[12] After about a year of peaceful coexistence conflict broke out between settlers and Aboriginals, culminating in the execution of Midgigooroo in May 1833, the murder of Yagan two months later, the Aboriginal raid on Shenton's mill in April 1834 and the decisive battle of Pinjarra six months later after Stirling's return from a visit to England.[13] These hostilities must have discouraged the spread of settlement beyond central Perth and account for the prominence of the site chosen for the military barracks in Perth's central square.

Somehow the colony survived. During 1830 Western Australia experienced serious shortages of foodstuffs and of liquid funds. The result was virtual stagnation. Between 1831 and 1837 the non-Aboriginal population increased only from 1875 to 2032. The main stimulus to the economy came from the commissariat servicing the military required for guard duties and Aboriginal hostilities. The opening of the Avon valley after 1830 met the demand for good farming country and brought into existence the town sites of York, Northam, and Newcastle (Toodyay). Nearer to Perth, Guildford was established on the upper Swan and Kelmscott on the Canning as gateways to the inland. But almost the only export was a little wool. Perth's growth was still slow and largely improvised. The Crown land regulations of 1831 setting an upset price of five shillings an acre for land sales ended the system of free grants which was almost Western Australia's sole attraction to investors; but it also put an end to the practice of reserving townlands on twenty-one-year leases, so that before long the central area of Perth had been alienated as freehold and the government was without suitable land for its own purposes. This was to impede long-term planning for the future. The central reserve behind the military cantonment was cut up and abandoned and, during Stirling's absence in 1834, the land between St George's Terrace and the river was also subdivided for sale, with Roe's active consent, thus blocking what would have become a magnificent public site. Stirling on his return repurchased land east of Barrack Street to form the site of Government House and the adjacent gardens, paying from his own pocket, but his original concept was irreparably lost.[14]

The pressure for land on St George's Terrace was due partly to its prestige as the main street, partly to its access to the westerly sea breezes which cooled hot summer afternoons, and partly to the official policy which required buildings erected on the Terrace to be of a value of at least £200. Within a few years it was clear that St George's Terrace would become the 'best' street in Perth. Its west end, and its continuation up Mount Eliza which became Mount Street, would house some of Western Australia's elite families until well into the twentieth century. So would its eastern continuation, Adelaide Terrace, for many years distinguished from St George's Terrace by a dog-leg which local myth attributed to Roe's wish to preserve his front garden, but which Seddon and Ravine show convincingly to have been a deliberate device to define the eastern end of the town centre.[15]

Hay Street, only one block back, would become the precinct for retail commerce. This meant that the more northern portions of the townsite, more prone to flooding and less exposed to the benefit of sea breezes, would be taken up by the less affluent members of the community. Consequently the square at the eastern end of the city centre, designed as a focus for the administrative quarter, never fulfilled its early expectations. The Anglican Church declined the site, preferring to conduct its worship in the fashionable quarter of St George's Terrace, and it eventually fell to the Catholic community and became the site of St Mary's Cathedral. But it was 1843 before the first Catholic clergy arrived, and by this time the square was renamed Victoria Square in honour of a new sovereign.

Unfashionable the northern end of town may have been, but it offered the most convenient room for expansion. As early as 1833 the first map of Perth town site, engraved by Arrowsmith of London, shows a number of thoroughfares laid out among the swamplands north of Wellington Street, though there was little if any occupancy, and Seddon and Ravine shrewdly conjecture that they were largely dummy streets marked out to give the British authorities an exaggerated view of Perth's progress. The most impressive of them, Stirling Street, ran north from the central cantonment reserve and was probably designed as the major northern outlet from the city, but with the alienation of the central reserve shortly afterwards it was destined to survive only as an anomalously wide street in inner suburbia.

Behind the plans of the map makers lay a modest little town of few pretensions.[16] It could boast a number of public buildings by the end of its first decade. One of the oldest, the Anglican church, was simply built of rushes over a timber frame; but several erected between 1834 and 1839 used brick, at first imported, later of local manufacture. Plain but not inelegant examples of late Georgian idiom, nearly all of them have been destroyed, some surprisingly recently. Several were designed by the engineer, HW Reveley, once the friend of the poet Shelley in whose company he gained some acquaintance with Mediterranean architecture. The most prominent among them was the two-storeyed Government House (1834-64) with a Doric portico and single-storey wings. The commissariat, a two-storeyed building with shingled roof, was erected in 1837 at the river end of the central reserve; it was later used for a time as the Supreme Court and was demolished in 1902 to make way for its successor. Adjacent to the commissariat was the first courthouse, completed in 1839, which now survives as the Law Society museum and is usually claimed as Perth's oldest building. A little to the west in St George's Terrace was Hedges' Hotel, also built in 1839, which as the United Services Hotel survived with a gold-rush facade until

Opposite: Figure 26: Earliest map of Perth Township, 1832. Redrawn from
deteriorating originals by Margaret Pitt Morrison (Courtesy of the
Department of Architecture, University of Western Australia)

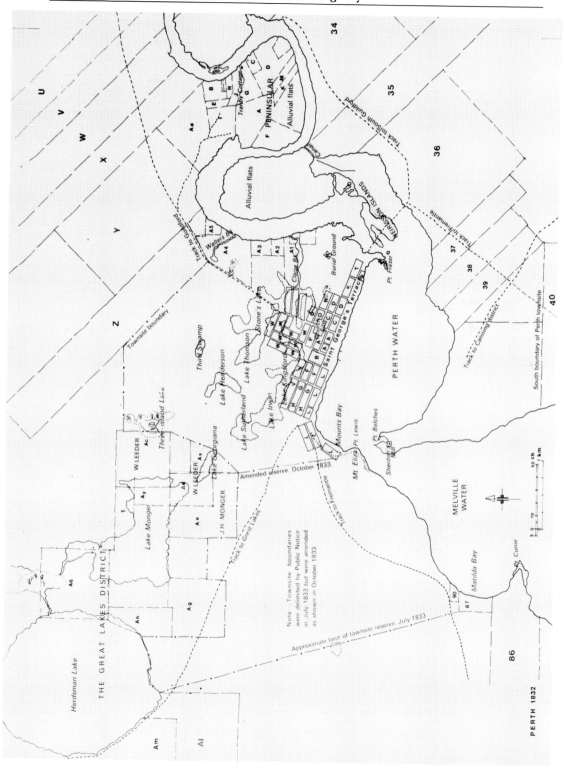

PERTH 1832

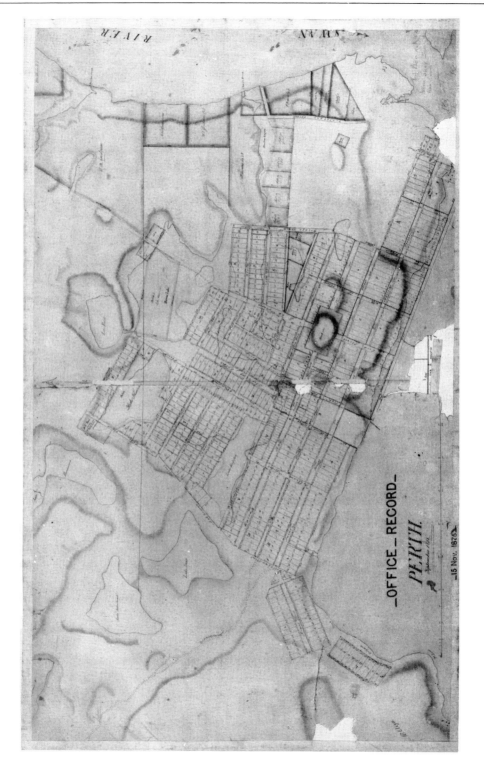

demolished to make way for a multistorey office block in 1968. Besides these major buildings a number of substantial houses were put up in the late 1830s and early 1840s. Some were an index of growing business confidence. Between 1839 and 1842 Lionel Samson, probably the colony's leading merchant, built a house, store and auction room reputed to cost £3000, a sum then equivalent to Western Australia's entire wool exports. But this house and all its contemporaries were wiped out in the gold-rush boom. Perth has no equivalent of John Cadman's cottage in Sydney.

This building activity reflected a somewhat healthier tone in the economy. Woolgrowing was the main staple; the value of exports built up from £1500 in 1836 to £3000 in 1841. In 1837 local entrepreneurs went in for whaling, though the shore-based catch never matched the activities of the American and French ships present in Western Australian waters from the 1820s. In 1837 also a group of local investors founded the first bank, and when that was taken over by outside interests established another in 1841 which lasted until a takeover in 1926. Partly because of this renewed activity, British investors were once more tempted to look to Western Australia. Between 1839 and 1842 a project went forward for a new settlement about 100 miles south of Perth on Leschenault estuary. As its name Australind suggested, the newcomer was intended as an entrepôt for trade with India and south-east Asia. The enterprise failed because of indecision and lack of confidence at the London end.[17] However it resulted in the arrival of 300 more migrants and the beginnings of the port of Bunbury.

This was the last time that Perth was seriously troubled by the prospect that another town might develop elsewhere to become the infant metropolis of Western Australia. Albany, although two and a half years older, was never serious competition. With the withdrawal of the convict garrison in 1831 it became subsidiary to Perth and remained in that state because its hinterland was too poor for successful farming. Over a hundred years later it would be discovered that certain trace elements were lacking, but at the time it meant that Albany survived mainly as a port and as a base for a handful of graziers. The other landing places in the south-west, Augusta and the Vasse (Busselton), remained insignificant. Fremantle, as port and whaling centre, presented something more of a challenge. By 1836 it was surveyed almost as extensively as Perth, and the local limestone presented an attractive building material; but it was a notoriously sandy spot.[18] Stirling and his successor as governor, John Hutt (1839-46), never deviated from the support of Perth as the major administrative centre.

This determined the location of other amenities. A public hospital, after two abortive starts in the 1830s, was eventually established in 1840.[19] Between 1841 and 1845 the Anglicans replaced the old 'rush' church with a more substantial edifice across the road from Government House. Known inevitably as St George's, it was topped by a short tower and cupola in the elegant and uncluttered late Georgian idiom which resulted from limited means and isolation from contemporary trends. In 1846 a Congregational church was completed in St George's Terrace. In the same year the Catholic Sisters of Mercy established a convent on the south-east side of Victoria Square adjoining the cathedral site abandoned by the Anglicans.[20] Both buildings still survive, albeit as portions of larger complexes.

Optimistic portents of suburban spread began to emerge. In 1837 Roe's deputy, Alfred Hillman, marked out the first planned suburban development, a row of allotments along

Opposite: Figure 27: Hillman map of Perth, 1838 (Reproduced courtesy of
the Department of Lands Administration, Perth, Western Australia)

149

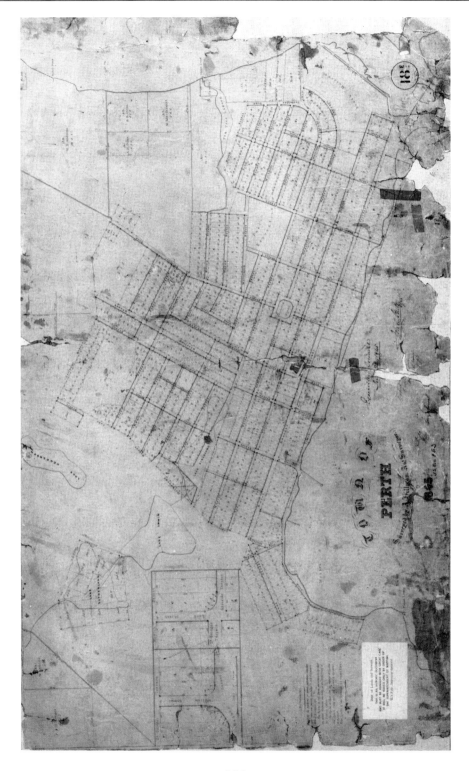

the riverfront on the south side of the Swan. A map prepared by Hillman a year later also shows considerable subdivision in East Perth, where a new prospect of streets was laid out at a diagonal to the existing road system. But this new development was not persisted with. Instead, by 1845 East Perth was largely replanned as an extension of the central grid, but with two graceful crescents at the eastern-most high ground overlooking the river and commanding fine views of the Darling Scarp. It may have been expected that Waterloo Crescent would grow into a fashionable residential district. Three years before, in 1842, a hopeful promoter had advertised real estate for sale in a subdivision named Albert in honour of Queen Victoria's new husband; it fronted the river and Claise Brook.[21] Buyers failed to come, and East Perth never found favour, possibly because of its proximity to the cemetery. In any case it was premature in the 1840s to expect that Perth would experience rapid suburban growth.

Premature maybe but not, in the long run, unrealistic. Perth was the centre for administrative services, the home of the colony's two newspapers, the site of the first gentlemen's club and Mechanics' Institute.[22] Already the colony's transport system was beginning to show the first signs of that centralisation on the metropolis characteristic of most Australian colonies. The process began with the blazing of a trail between Albany and Perth in 1836 after seven years of communication by sea; Stirling on his return from visiting Britain in 1834 had been delayed at Albany for several weeks by contrary winds. For many years afterwards Albany and Perth remained separated by a sense of psychological, if not physical distance; in 1881, when Queen Victoria's two grandsons spent three weeks in Albany it was not thought practicable to send them to Perth.[23] The Avon valley settlers were linked to Perth by what was known for many years as King Dick's Road, after the Aboriginal guide who accompanied the survey party. From 1842 Perth was joined to Australind and Bunbury by what was known as the Old Coast Road. Meanwhile Perth's claims as entrepôt were boosted by the bridging of the Heirisson Islands by a causeway in 1840, the opening of a town jetty in 1842 and the completion of a bridge across the mouth of the Canning in 1843. As the first landing place below the barrier of the Heirisson Islands, Perth became a staging point for produce and passengers ferried upriver from Fremantle.

Development was still desperately slow. If an energetic policy of public works was to be pursued, the colony would require a cheaper and more numerous work force than it had yet been able to attract. Landowners in the Avon valley and the south-west spoke of their need for shepherds and labourers. The Swan River colony could not hope to attract large-scale migration while reports of its early difficulties lingered in Britain, inflated by the self-serving propaganda of publicists such as E G Wakefield. Nor could it hope to compete with the thriving eastern colonies, New South Wales, Van Diemen's Land, or even the newer settlements of Port Phillip and South Australia, particularly now that convict transportation was gradually drawing to a close and the proportion of free migrants was on the increase. Grudgingly, uneasily, Western Australia's influential men edged towards an unwelcome conclusion. New South Wales and Van Diemen's Land had arrived at their point of economic take-off largely because of the start given by the input of labour and government capital introduced by convict transportation. Western Australia in its turn should become a convict colony.[24]

Opposite: Figure 28: Perth, 1845—note crescent development (Reproduced
        courtesy of the Department of Lands Administration, Perth,
        Western Australia)

151

Between 1850 and 1868, 9721 male convicts arrived in Western Australia.[25] In addition 1191 pensioner guards arrived with almost twice as many dependants. Some young Irishwomen were also brought out under official auspices as a somewhat calculated corrective to the imbalance of sexes. The total white population of Western Australia quadrupled from under 6000 in 1850 to over 24,000 in 1868. Over the same period the number of sheep pastured in the colony grew even faster: from 128,000 to 649,000. The wool industry expanded into the Champion Bay district behind Geraldton, 310 miles to the north of Perth, and from thence leapt in 1861 to the north-west based on Nicol Bay and Roebourne. Pastoralists also moved out east of Perth until by 1870 the frontier had moved as far as Esperance.[26] Exports began to diversify. Sandalwood cutting, after a tentative start in the 1840s, became from 1857 a not unimportant item among the colony's exports. 'Swan River mahogany', the term more or less indiscriminately applied to Western Australian hardwoods, also contributed modestly, although it would be the mid 1870s before the industry came to the fore as a major export. Lead and copper were sent from the Geraldine mines, north of Geraldton, after 1853. None of these commodities challenged the dominance of wool, nor was industrial growth of any significance but, in all, the Western Australian economy was throwing off some of its sluggishness.

Farmers found themselves a home market in the convict establishment. The roads between Perth, Fremantle, York, Bunbury and Albany were all upgraded, increasing the capacity of settlers to market their produce, although it would take the coming of the railways in the 1880s to overcome the problems of inland freight. The economic growth generated by convict transportation during the 1850s and 1860s undoubtedly helped Western Australia to withstand the massive counter attractions of the gold discoveries in New South Wales and Victoria, which during those years drew off a considerable number of free colonists. This achievement had its social costs, as Stannage has reminded us.[27] It also had a lasting effect on the built environment of Perth and its surroundings.

The first priority, unsurprisingly, was the construction of prisons. Fremantle was chosen for the major penitentiary, 'the great grey gaol by the sea'[28] of Randolph Stow's phrase, still a landmark of the central port area. Between 1854 and 1856 Perth also acquired a substantial gaol on the unfashionable north side of the town. The Colonial Hospital, built between 1853 and 1855, was similarly placed on the northern side of town, its aspect facing the Swan River and excluding sunlight as far as possible.[29] A growing need for working-class housing also encouraged the gradual northward spread of the built-up area. The swamplands, which had been taken up for market gardening in the 1840s and early 1850s, were partly drained in 1854. This proved insufficient to avoid major flooding during the unusually wet winters of 1862 and 1872, and the draining of the lakes into Claise Brook was necessary in order to facilitate future suburban expansion. This low-lying land, at a distance from river views and sea breezes, was destined in future decades to support cheap housing for the working class, to be followed during the twentieth century by successive inflows of migrants—Italians, Greeks and Vietnamese—and eventually to include that inner-suburban gentrification which has emerged in all Australian cities during the last twenty years. Its development marked one of the first steps in Perth towards geographical social stratification. Unlike Australia's larger cities, however, the working-class areas were not identified with a manufacturing district because until the last decade of the century Perth's industrial growth remained rudimentary.

Major public buildings continued to be concentrated on St George's Terrace and Hay Street. St George's Terrace, planted on both sides with deciduous Cape lilac trees, was levelled in the early 1850s, and in 1862 became the first major thoroughfare to be macadamised. This was an early achievement of the Perth City Council, formed in 1856 by the upgrading of the former Town Trust.[30] By the early 1860s the first priorities for government convict labour—roadmaking and the construction of gaols and hospitals—had largely been met, and in the modest prosperity of these years it was possible to think of new projects. A new Government House, five years in the building, was completed in 1864, its progress faithfully recorded by one of Perth's first photographers, Alfred Stone. At the other end of St George's Terrace the western vista was closed off by the erection between 1863 and 1867 of a barracks for the pensioner guards.

Thus for a century St George's Terrace was dominated by a relic of the authority of a convict colony. Behind the barracks there would arise during the twentieth century the state Parliament House, and in the 1960s the Brand government would decide that the barracks should be razed, to be replaced in the public eye by the building which should have symbolised constitutional democracy. Unfortunately most of Perth's citizens were more interested in aesthetics than in symbolism, and they liked the look of the slightly sham-Tudor red brick of the barracks better than the modernism of Parliament House. After long debate the two wings of the barracks were pulled down in 1965 but the central arch was allowed to remain, no longer a symbol of penal authority but a reminder of the supremacy of public opinion over even the most well-meaning of parliaments. There was also some symbolism apparent in the design of the Flemish-style Perth Town Hall erected between 1867-70. Its clock face was flanked by openings in the shape of broad arrows and arched by ornamentation not unlike a hangman's rope, and although this appears to have been entirely unintentional, civic legend persists in attributing these flourishes to the mordant humour of convict builders.[31]

As a corrective to convictism there came an upsurge in church building. Between 1859 and 1865 the Anglicans put up a house for the bishop at the salubrious west end of St George's Terrace, another for the dean only a few steps from St George's Church, and two small suburban churches, St John's for the respectable working class at the intersection of Wellington Street and Melbourne Road, and St Bartholomew's in East Perth as a cemetery chapel. The first Catholic cathedral, dedicated to the Immaculate Conception, was finished in 1863. A new Congregational church arose in St George's Terrace in 1865, and Wesley Church, with its distinctive spire, was completed at the corner of Hay and William Streets in 1867. The Anglican bishop, Matthew Hale, established a large boys' school operating between 1858 and 1872 in a building known as the Cloisters. As with the Town Hall and Wesley Church, local brick was used to produce a fifteenth-century Flemish effect which coexisted harmoniously enough with the surviving late Georgian public buildings. This was the trademark of Richard Roach Jewell, clerk of works from 1853 to 1884 and architect of many of Perth's public buildings from that era.

The more substantial private housing was also in brick, with shingled roofing. Corrugated iron came late to Western Australia, and was described as a novelty in 1879 although it was first manufactured in Britain forty years earlier. On the whole technological lag had a beneficial effect on the appearance of early colonial Western Australia. Perth, still no more than a large village of five or six thousand inhabitants in the 1860s, appealed to visitors as having a certain sleepy charm. Although this was mainly due to the Mediterranean colours of its riverside situation something was also owed to the unpretentious building of honest colonial craftsmen a little behind the times.

Viewing Perth through the hindsight of the photographic record it is easy to forget some of the less agreeable characteristics of that charming small town. In summer it stank. Many of the poorer residents kept pigs. For most, sanitation consisted of cesspits, and these were thought to contaminate the wells from which they drew their domestic water supply. Mosquitoes infested the summer nights, although this nuisance became a little milder after the draining of the northern swamps in 1873-5. The town was not well provided with parklands until Governor Weld (1869-75) authorised the gazetting of the large reserve on Mount Eliza as a public park in 1871. This was the forerunner of Kings Park, often described as natural bush, although in fact by the time Weld reserved it the original jarrah cover had nearly all been removed by timber-cutters and replaced by secondary growth; remains of the sawpits may still be found.[32] About the same time the first provision was made for a park reserve in the northern part of the town, its name, Weld Square, still commemorating its origins. A few years later Weld Square was considered as a site for the town's central railway station, but a route closer to the city centre was preferred. So it was that the railway built between 1879 and 1881 had the effect of creating a barrier between the town centre and the northern suburbs, and in future decades was to constrict the flow of traffic quite as effectively as the swamps of an earlier era. Perth in short not only lagged far behind cities such as Melbourne, Sydney and Adelaide, but even newcomers such as Ballarat and Bendigo. It remained, however, the beneficiary of the hopeful planning of Stirling and Roe.

Stirling died in 1865, an admiral and a knight. He never revisited Western Australia. Roe on the other hand lived out all his remaining years in Perth, dying an octogenarian patriarch in 1878. Surviving into the years of mild recession which followed the ending of convict transportation, he yet lived to witness the coming of the intercolonial telegraph which ended Western Australia's isolation, the planning of the first railways and the expansion of the colony's timber, pearling and mining industries, forerunners of the unimaginable growth and development which would follow the finding of gold in 1885-94. These were the portents of transformation for Perth, as were the first suburban subdivisions which took place in Claremont, Subiaco and South Perth within five years of Roe's death. A century later this transformed Perth would boast more than a million inhabitants, but it was still the creature of Stirling and Roe's original plan. St George's Terrace would remain Perth's major boulevard, though the Cape lilac trees were long gone, and shade was cast rather by multistorey office blocks, the facades of which dominated the parklands of the Swan's reclaimed northern shore, and pierced the skyline of many suburban landscapes. The constricting influence of the railway, following as it did the line of the earlier swamps, would continue to squeeze the pattern of urban development until the planning of a cultural centre precinct and the proclamation of Northbridge as Perth's attempt at a Latin Quarter. Even so, the northern suburbs on the whole would prove less attractive to the affluent than those favoured areas commanding views of open water. One hundred and sixty years after Stirling made his reconnoitre and formed his resolve, the city of Perth *still* looked to the Swan river as its pride and focus. By then the 'foundling city' of the early nineteenth century had been transformed, and emerged as a prosperous and self-confident metropolis.

Notes

[1] For Stirling's biography see Uren, M. *Land Looking West*, (London, 1948); Appleyard, R.T. and Manford. T. *The Beginning*, (U.W.A.P., 1979). For Roe, see Mercer, F.R. *Amazing Career*, (Perth, 1962) and Burton Jackson, J.L.; *Not an Idle Man: A Biography of John Septimus Roe, W.A.'s first Surveyor General*, (Fremantle Arts Centre Press, 1982); and respective entries in the *A.D.B.*

[2] Cameron, J.M.R. 'Sir James Stirling, the Founder' in Hunt, L. (ed.), *Westralian Portraits*, (U.W.A.P., 1979), p.11.

[3] Marchant, L.R. *France Australe*, (Perth, 1982), esp. Chs. 5-6.

[4] *H.R.A.*, III, vi, p.567 and p.576.

[5] Population figures from Statham, P. 'Swan River Colony 1829-1850', in Stannage, C.T. (ed.), *A New History of Western Australia*, (hereafter cited as 'New History'), (U.W.A.P., 1981), pp.181-210; analysis on p.185.

[6] *H.R.A.*, III, vi, pp.600-02.

[7] Bolton, G.C. 'The Fenians are coming, the Fenians are coming', *S.W.A.H. IV: Convictism in Western Australia*, (Nedlands, 1981), pp.62-7.

[8] Seddon, G. and Ravine, D. *A City and its Setting: Images of Perth, Western Australia*, (Fremantle, 1986), pp.68-73.

[9] Seddon, G. and Ravine, *op.cit.*, pp.76-7. See also the comments by Stannage, C.T. *The People of Perth*, (hereafter cited as 'People'), (Perth City Council, 1979), p.11.

[10] Cited in Seddon and Ravine, *op.cit.*, p.86.

[11] Green, N. 'Aborigines and White Settlers in the 19th Century', in Stannage, 'New History', *op.cit.*, pp.79-89, Stannage, 'People', *op.cit.*, pp.40-44.

[12] Frost, A. 'New South Wales as *terra nullius*: the British Denial of Aboriginal Land Rights', *Historical Studies*, Vol. 19, 1981, pp.513-23.

[13] Green, *op.cit.*, pp.84-5.

[14] Seddon and Ravine, *op.cit.*, pp.98-9.

[15] *Ibid.*, pp.270-71.

[16] *Ibid.*, Ch. 6; also Pitt Morison, M. and White, J. Both 'Builders and Buildings', in Stannage, 'New History', *op.cit.*, pp.515-25 and *Western Towns and Buildings* (U.W.A.P., 1979), pp.9-24, 74-89.

[17] Statham, *op.cit.*, p.198; Battye, J.S. *A History of Western Australia*, (Oxford, 1924), pp.154-60.

[18] Reece, R. and Pascoe, R. *A Place of Consequence*, (Fremantle, 1983).

[19] Bolton, G.C. and Joske, P. *History of Royal Perth Hospital*, (Nedlands, 1982), Ch. 1.

[20] Byrne, G. *Valiant Women*, (Melbourne, 1981).

[21] Statham, *op.cit.*, p.202.

[22] Stannage, 'People', *op.cit.*, Ch. 2.

[23] Garden, D.S. *Albany*, (West Melbourne, 1977), pp.181-2.

[24] Statham, P. 'Why convicts I: an economic analysis of colonial attitudes to the introduction of convicts', 'Why convicts II: the decision to introduce convicts to the Swan River', *S.W.A.H. Vol. IV*, (Nedlands, 1981), pp.1-18.

[25] Taylor, S. 'Who were the convicts?', *ibid.*, pp.19-45; Hasluck, A. *Unwilling Emigrants: a Study of the Convict Period in Western Australia*, (Melbourne, 1959).

[26] For the wool industry, see Fyfe, C. *The Bale Fillers: Western Australian Wool 1826-1916*, (U.W.A.P., 1983).

[27] Stannage, 'People', *op.cit.*, pp.88-101.

[28] Stow, R. *Midnite: The Story of a Wild Colonial Boy*, (Melbourne, 1967).

[29] Bolton and Joske, *op.cit.*, Ch. 2.

[30] Stannage, 'People', *op.cit.*, pp.152-60.

[31] Oldham, R. and J. *Western Heritage: a Study of the Colonial Architecture of Perth*, (Perth, 1961).

[32] Hughes, V. *The History of Kings Park*, (B.A. Hons. thesis, Murdoch University, 1978).

Adelaide

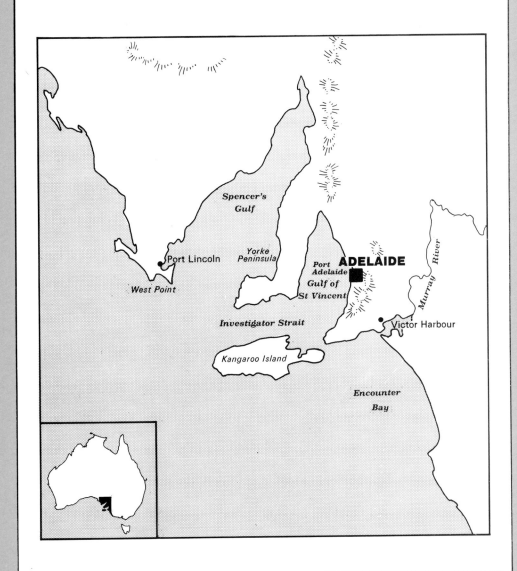

ADELAIDE

Chapter VIII

Establishing South Australia

Mel Davies

The amazing story of one Lemuel Gulliver who bade farewell to Bristol from the decks of the *Antelope* on 4 May 1699 will no doubt be familiar to readers. On reaching the Antipodes fate determined that a tempest north-west of Van Diemen's Land on latitude 30 degrees 2 minutes south should wreck the vessel and cast Gulliver, unconscious, upon the sands of a strange shore. Captive to a host of dimunitive beings, Gulliver's wonder soon turned to bemusement as he noted societal animosities and discord among those who populated Lilliput and surrounding lands. Foremost in dissent were the Trameckson and Slameckson, the adherents of fashion, favouring respectively high-heeled or low-heeled shoes, who found unbearable the audacity and bad taste of the other. Even more serious, for it resulted in military hostilities, was the dispute between Lilliputians representing the 'small-enders' and their opponents the Blefusian 'big-enders' each convinced eggs should be eaten from those respective ends, despite the teachings of the great prophet Lustrog who had sensibly decreed in compromise that 'all true Believers shall break their Eggs at the Convenient End'.

Had Jonathan Swift, Gulliver's creator, been a soothsayer his work would now be heralded as prophetic. Similar tempestuous events, ridiculous argument and disharmony surrounded the foundation of South Australia—the very coast on which according to Swift's latitudinal reference Gulliver had been so unceremoniously dumped at the turn of the eighteenth century.

Both Douglas Pike's cryptically named *Paradise of Dissent* [1] and AG Price's *Foundations and Settlement of South Australia* [2] provide detailed accounts of the acrimonious relationships among the colonisers, though even between these two major contributors to South Australian historiography there is some apparent difference of opinion. The former stresses (perhaps too forcefully) the importance of nonconformist settlers and planners striving for a brave new world of religious and political toleration while Price gives greater (and perhaps more realistic) emphasis to the economic and social ambitions of South Australia's capitalistic settlers. Like the Great Lustrog, the historian's egg is open-ended and its interpretation can be viewed from both ends!

The plan to settle South Australia followed close on the heels of the foundation in 1829 of its western neighbour, the Swan River Colony. What is surprising is that the British government should have countenanced the idea of another 'self-supporting' colony so soon

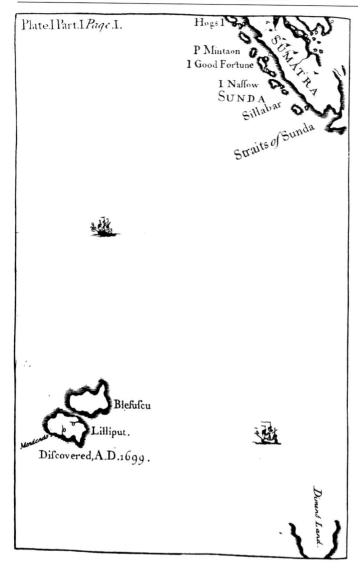

Figure 29: Swift's positioning of Lilliput land—from Swift J. *Gulliver's Travels* vol. I, London, 1727

after the fiasco of the private-enterprise endeavours at Swan River. Perhaps the answer to this riddle lies in the persuasive pen and personality of Edward Gibbon Wakefield whose self-seeking strategies, it has recently been claimed, included deceit, bribery, fraud and 'motiveless malignity' to achieve his own ends[3], though subtle persuasion was perhaps his major weapon. This is not to deny the important part played in the political thrust and manoeuvres by such dedicated individuals as Robert Gouger and Colonel Robert Torrens who along with Wakefield presented a coherent plan that was guaranteed to appeal to the new breed of political economists and to negate most opposition. By highlighting (and often distorting) the mistakes of the neighbouring western colony in his voluminous works, Wakefield was also able to distance his plan for settlement of South Australia from the earlier experiment at Swan River.

The settlement of South Australia occurred within a period of upheaval and turmoil, at a time when the British middle and working classes were emerging as distinct entities, each fighting for new rights and changes to the old order of society. It was a time of rapid oscillation in economic activity and a period when social, political, religious and educational institutions and policies were under attack from the liberal minded. While the panacea for the many problems of the 1830s was seen by the various new radicals to be either in free trade, religious toleration, parliamentary reform, attacks on nepotism, promotion of socialism or other attractive reforms, a determined minority was beguiled with the idea of 'escapism', a fresh start and a divorce from old-world restrictions and conservatism. Even the reformed parliament of 1832 was a disappointment for many middle-class hopefuls who found that the claw of restriction by the House of Lords, and often by conservative Commoners, cramped their full aspirations. Thus, many supporters of the idea that healthy societies required fewer restrictions and more competition saw fulfilment of their utilitarian ideas not in frustratingly slow reform but in complete separation and emigration to uninhabited lands where there existed new opportunities for those prepared to take the plunge. In the case of South Australia this migrant philosophy appears to have been more pronounced than in any other colony, though the overriding emphasis appears to have been more upon individual gain *per se* rather than upon the more widespread benefits to society as a whole, as extolled by Bentham's democratic individualism and laissez faire. As Pike states, many of the so-called reformers motivated by frustration sought 'little more than a redistribution of the spoils'.[4] Few of the actual planners ever became emigrants but many were involved as absentee landowners and speculators, evincing more interest in material gain than the achievement of any wider and more philosophical goals. Nevertheless, in the wave of economic and social legislation following the Parliamentary Reform Act of 1832 many of the major proponents, such as Grote, Molesworth, Hume and Roebuck, were also active in the organisation to colonise South Australia.[5] Within the plans to colonise South Australia we therefore see the first seeds of dissent between those who were interested for reasons of pure self-interest and speculation, and those who had far higher philosophical aims.

Many historians concerned with the origins of the National Colonisation Society of 1830 (the springboard for South Australia's foundation) have noted with irony that its emphasis upon the ideal of a taintless society had been conceived in the fertile minds of Newgate gaolbirds Wakefield and Gouger. The latter became enamoured with the idea of settling South Australia while incarcerated in Newgate prison with a roving sea captain, Henry Dixon, who extolled the virtues of Kangaroo Island and nearby lands.[6] Gouger's resolve was strengthened in late 1830 when glowing reports of land in the vicinity of Gulf St Vincent arrived in England from explorer Captain Charles Sturt.[7] However, the first official approach to government was not made until February 1831 when Major Anthony Bacon (another intimate of Gouger's from Newgate Prison) approached Lord Goderich of the Colonial Office with a plan to settle South Australia with himself as governor. When his request was bluntly rejected he joined the Wakefieldians who later that year formed the South Australian Land Company. This involvement, according to one writer, was like a kiss of death, for Bacon was a direct descendant of the impeached Chancellor of the Exchequer, Harley, whose links with the disastrous and fraudulent South Sea venture affair in the early eighteenth century was enough to make London businessmen lock their coffers and turn away.[8]

Wakefield's active pen was soon at work and his circular, setting out the aims and plans for colonisation of the new South Australian Land Company,[9] were only slightly modified before being presented to Goderich in July 1832.[10] The submission stressed that the demands of the company were 'limited to *mere sanction* of Government' (original emphasis).[11] There was to be no call on government aid nor participation. For doing absolutely nothing, it was stressed, the Crown would gain great benefit: first, through emigration, which would reduce the country's oversupply of labour and thus help reduce poor relief; second, by providing a new source of primary materials for British consumers and manufacturers; and, third, by creating an additional market for Britain's finished goods. As for the company, its capital of £500,000 was to be used for the rapid development of the colony and the benefit of shareholders. Labour was to be brought out in strict relation to land sales, therefore ensuring the healthy equilibrium between land, labour and capital that had been the main thrust of Wakefield's theory. In the first instance the company was to be given unalienable rights to purchase the best lands at five shillings an acre, the then ruling minimum price in the other Australian colonies. This price was claimed to be 'artificially low' but was accepted as a bonus as its superior true value would be realised by subsequent incremental price rises until market demand could establish a 'true' equilibrium price. As the company would occupy lands fit not only for agriculture but also for the seat of government and commerce then the speculative return to shareholders through sales and rents would be assured.[12] Until the population reached 50,000 (originally 10,000 was specified) the colony was to be administered by a governor chosen by the company and the cost of government in this period later recouped from the Crown (with interest). The governor would make and amend laws and members of the judiciary would be elected locally. While there would be no Crown taxes, a land tax of sixpence per acre would offset the expenses and administrative responsibilities of the company. The company would also be accorded the power to raise loans. The proposal stressed the need for industrious labour of both sexes who would be chosen by the company—no convicts were to taint the proposed colony. No customs rates were to be imposed nor any other restrictions on imports or exports, while such things as freedom of the press and religious toleration would be written into the company's charter. In true Benthamite fashion, education, as a tool to dispel ignorance and raise the moral tone and the dedication of the settlers to hard work, was another plank in the platform.

Not surprisingly RW Hay on behalf of Lord Goderich responded on 14 July 1832 by calling the plan a 'subversive' measure. It was rejected in no uncertain terms on the grounds that it was undesirable to provide such a vast territory to a private company that had the power to administer the law, raise the militia (another right claimed by the company), exclude the Crown from imposing duties and ignore the Navigation Acts in promoting free trade, which together would amount to handing over power to a republican state within the realm of the British monarchy.[13]

While appreciating the personal and philosophical goals of the promoters, it may well be asked whether the authors of this initial submission were really serious in their approach to government? Surely they must have been aware that most of their points would prove anathema to the Crown authorities even in that year of political reform. Was Wakefield naive or was his strategy to aim ridiculously high and then to submit an amended but more reasonable proposal which would answer most of the objections and thus provide the company with all it really desired? Within two days of the government's rejection of their plan, the promoters, men of principle, graciously offered to 'abandon every proposal in the charter, except the land sale and emigration fund proposals and the eventual privilege of a legislative assembly', an offer caustically rejected by Goderich on the grounds that he had 'serious misgiving as to the maturity of the knowledge and counsels of the promoters'.[14]

Following this debacle, interest revived in 1833 with the publication of Wakefield's influential *England and America* which clearly enunciated his theories and boosted the image of South Australia. The book's launching coincided too with a visit to London by Captain Charles Sturt who publicised the favourable discoveries made by himself in 1829-30 and by Captain Colet Barker in 1831 of lands in the vicinity of Gulf St Vincent and along the Murray Valley. In December 1833, buoyed by this tide of publicity and the positive interest of a number of influential parliamentarians the South Australian Association was launched.[15] Promoted at first as a chartered company vested in trustees, the organisation was soon persuaded by Colonial Office opposition to abandon any political control. In their wisdom the promoters agreed that South Australia should become a Crown colony in which the Wakefieldian system of land sales and emigration would be controlled by government-appointed officials. Before parliament agreed to sanction the Act political opposition had to be nullified including that of the reputedly obstinate and powerful 'Iron Duke' of Wellington. Soothed by the cultivated friendship of Gouger and the silver-tongued Wakefield, Wellington was converted into a forceful ally after being persuaded that colonisation should not be seen as a party affair. Still, this was a strange marriage, linking as it did the radical promoters of the Bill and an arch conservative, though it is claimed that the duke, like lesser mortals, had his weaknesses; one being flattery, a point which Wakefield was adroit to observe and exploit.[16] Thus the promise that Wellington's name would be recorded for all time by bestowal on the capital of the colony (a promise which Wakefield later honoured when settling New Zealand) was one lever to change his point of view. Another was the scare tactic. The French bogey was always guaranteed to raise the Iron Duke's blood pressure and when it was gently pointed out that in the aftermath of the Baudin expedition of 1802-3 Spencer's Gulf had been named Golfe Bonaparte and the Gulf of St Vincent, Golfe Joséphine, it was enough to bring on apoplexy and instant conversion to the need to plant the Union Jack.[17]

Political opposition finally overcome, the Act for the Establishment of the Colony of South Australia was passed on 15 August 1834. In effect, the Act was a number of compromises between the Colonial Office and the promoters but unlike the Great Lustrog's pronouncements, many of the compromises were to prove abrasive rather than salving during the early days of the colony. In the political sphere the usual colonial problems associated with distance of local administration from seat of government in England were exacerbated by a split of power into *four-way* control. In London a board of commissioners, appointed by the Colonial Secretary, was to manage land sales and emigration and to provide for costs of government while the Crown retained direct responsibility for framing laws and appointing officers. Essentially the governor had the power to govern—subject to the British government authorities and especially the Colonial Office, while the commissioners held the purse strings, being responsible in turn to their London board. This division of powers resulted in a tug-of-war over areas of hazy responsibility and within the new colony the situation was exacerbated by personality clashes between the governor and the board's representative domiciled in South Australia. But divisions occurred even within bodies. According to Wakefield the London board, with one or two exceptions, was represented by a pack of bumbling amateurs.[18] Included in this category was the board's chairman, Colonel Robert Torrens MP who, despite a persuasive pen, was generally viewed as a quick-tempered, insensitive schemer whose verbosity was used as a means to bludgeon opponents and to enforce his often misleading points of view.[19] When incompetence on the board was accompanied by political divisions between Whigs and Tories the result proved deleterious to the interests of the new colony.

The inadequacies of the board may be linked directly to the personality problems and incompetence of a substantial proportion of the officers it selected for actual service in South Australia. Some were chosen by the size of their bank balances rather than by their skills, reflecting the board's anxiety to attract capitalists and ensure land sales. Some were chosen because of their faithfulness to the cause of colonisation over the years, and others by nepotism. It could also be argued that competence was limited by the narrow area of choice, for not many men of proven talent cared to participate in setting up new colonies. While the Colonial Office delegated the responsibility of choosing officers to the board, its own only direct appointment, that of Chief Justice, Sir John Jeffcott, would hardly give credence to the idea that better quality officers would have been chosen had the board been ignored. Jeffcott, who unfortunately drowned within twelve months of arrival, had the doubtful distinction of having killed a man in a duel and of having had to creep like a thief in the night aboard ship for embarkation to South Australia in order to escape his creditors. Fortunately, a few intelligent, conscientious, dedicated and competent officers *were* appointed, such as Robert Gouger the first Colonial Secretary,[20] but much of their hard work was thwarted by the large number of self-seeking individuals who placed private speculation before public duty.

Under the final agreement, the affairs of the colonists were to be largely regulated by the Board of Commissioners until the population reached 50,000 at which juncture a representative assembly was to be constituted. However, settlement itself was not to proceed until certain conditions were met. Lands to the value of £35,000 had to be sold and an additional £20,000 raised and invested in bonds before the Act could come into operation. Loans to a ceiling of £200,000 secured against future anticipated revenues in the colony were also to be raised by the commissioners, a difficult though vital responsibility due to the fact that they had talked themselves into a corner by stressing the 'self-supporting' principle of financing.

It was the pre-sale of lands, however, that was the main problem for the commissioners. With land sales slower than hoped or anticipated, several attractive carrots were dangled before prospective parties. The first (which was to raise the eyebrows of those who had long opposed the settlement scheme owing to fears of speculation and 'jobbery') was the granting of one acre of city land for every eighty acres of rural land purchased. The second (even more suspect for it fostered speculation) was the reduction of the original selling price of rural land from twenty to twelve shillings per acre in order to stimulate land sales, with the proviso that lands would, within a short period, be increased again to their original price. 'Jobbery' certainly appears to have been at work in this sphere, for the opportunity was taken by George Fife Angas, a member of the Board of Commissioners, to circumvent the previous objections by the Colonial Office to settlement being based on a profit making joint-stock venture, when he floated a new South Australian Company. The objectives of the company were to acquire rural lands and town lots for the benefit of shareholders. Angas, who had been involved in the overtures of 1832, was cognisant of the speculative returns as enunciated in the Land Company Proposal[21] whereby it was realised that the town development generated its own impetus to growth, and that such growth spelt increased town property values and enhanced the value of adjacent rural lands.[22] As the Act for the Establishment of the Colony of South Australia stipulated that first purchasers would have first selection, there was the double advantage of holding town lots and greatly undervalued rural lots. While the myth has grown that Angas was the 'saviour' of South Australia in that he boosted land sales when the picture looked black, it is virtually certain that such sales would have taken place expediently *without* the formation of the company, due to the attraction of the publicised speculation to private individuals.[23]

It seems doubtful that Angas, and others of similar ilk saw any dilemma in the conflict between speculation, exploitation and the loftier moral goals associated with their religious and philosophical beliefs. Angas the philanthropist saw, for example, great merit in rescuing numbers of German immigrants from religious persecution, but behind that was the hard practical belief that such an inflow would keep down the rate of wages.[24] Such thought was more akin to his belief in the hallowed laws of demand and supply than his Christian morality. Neither he nor his representatives showed any qualms of conscience in selling these migrants lands he had acquired at £1 an acre for £7 to £10 an acre plus interest,[25] sums which would take many up to 30 years to pay off!

Wakefield too appears to have been unconcerned at such speculative activity. Despite showing no initial objection to land sales at £1 an acre he dissociated himself from the South Australian project in 1836 on the grounds that such a price was *too low* and would thus enable labourers to acquire land too quickly and so upset the equilibrium between the factors of production.[26] While Wakefield lost his battle for a higher 'sufficient price', he did triumph over those who had recommended auctions and differential land prices when his plan for fixed-price land sales won the day. But that was to be his last influence on the new colony; his attentions then moved elsewhere and out of this South Australian saga.

One of the major problems that faced the early settlers was that of slow and tardy surveying. This problem, which had proved disastrous in the settlement of Swan River Colony, was anticipated by the planners of South Australia but their desire for surveys to be undertaken before the arrival of immigrants was thwarted by the Act for the Establishment of the Colony of South Australia, which stated that no action should be undertaken by the board until the stipulated sums had been raised from the sale of lands.[27] Nevertheless, when the indecent haste in which settlers were transported to the new colony, following realisation of the requisite conditions, is considered, this would appear to be a poor excuse.

Between July and December 1836, before Surveyor General Colonel William Light had found time to lay out his first survey chain, fifteen immigrant vessels had arrived in South Australia from England. The deputy surveyor, the pompous, quarrelsome and incompetent George Strickland Kingston, who was on board the *Cygnet* with a large part of Light's surveying team, did not arrive for some seven weeks after Light's vessel the *Rapid*, despite having left some five weeks before it. Kingston, who had bullied the captain of the *Cygnet* into wasting a number of valuable weeks at Rio so that he and the team might wine and dine, wasted even more precious time on arrival in South Australia by dallying at Nepean Bay, Kangaroo Island, for a month before Light was made aware of his presence. Light had therefore been forced to work almost single-handed between his arrival on 20 August 1836 until mid October upon the mammoth and unrealistic task set him by the Board of Commissioners.[28]

Although Sturt and Barker's reports had led to a recommendation that the Holdfast

Bay of St Vincent's Gulf would be the most suitable site for settlement, there was some uncertainty about this because it conflicted with reports by Flinders and Baudin, who had visited the region some thirty years earlier. Moreover, the views of later visitors, such as Captain Sutherland and Captain Jones, and the doctored publications of the planners who, in an effort to paint a glowing picture of the proposed colony, had omitted any deleterious evidence from the reports they cited, further confused the issue and proved a painful burden for the gentlemanly, forbearing Light.

Flinders and Baudin had each examined the Port Lincoln region on Spencer's Gulf and formed very disparate views. While Flinders noted the unsuitable nature of Port Lincoln, with its dangerous seaway approach and barren soil, Baudin's naturalist compatriot, Peron, had waxed idyllic in its praise:

> Shall I now revert to what I have before stated as to the fertility of the soil? Shall I speak of the beautiful valleys, which appeared to indicate the existence of springs or streams of fresh water? Ought I to dwell on the numerous fires we perceived along the shores, which led us to conclude that this spot was far more thickly peopled than any other part of the southern coast? . . . Equal if not superior to Port Jackson, Port Lincoln is in every respect one of the best and most beautiful harbours in the world: and of all those we discovered or visited on the coasts of Australia, it appears to be . . . the most inviting, the most advantageous for the establishment of an European colony.[29]

Flinders' doubts were overridden by the promoters on the grounds that his report was written in despondency, his Port Lincoln visit having occurred immediately after the tragic loss of a number of his crew off Cape Catastrophe. To reassure readers the promoters tapped the rather hazy but rosy memories of surviving members of his crew. In particular they extracted reports on the size of trees in the vicinity—seen by the questioners as an evident sign of fertility—a serious misunderstanding of the local ecology and a repetition of the mistake made by botanist Charles Frazer who had investigated land along the Swan River with Captain Stirling in 1827.

In contrast to his views on Port Lincoln, Flinders had waxed ecstatic on the fertility of Kangaroo Island, a sentiment later endorsed by a Captain Sutherland, a visitor to the island in 1819, and by George Goold who had visited in 1827-8 aboard the *Jackson* on a sealing venture. An adverse report by Peron regarding the island was however omitted from the evidence presented by the 1831 Land Company and by the South Australian Association in 1834. On the strength of the positive viewpoint presented the South Australian Company chose to set up its first station of 320 acres at Nepean Bay, Kangaroo Island, in July 1836 but was soon to abandon the settlement because of its unsuitability.

All these varied reports created a dilemma—where should the major settlement be sited? There were supporters aplenty for Port Lincoln including the first governor, Captain John Hindmarsh, the naval hero who had fought with distinction at the Battle of Trafalgar and Battle of the Nile with Nelson but who proved in South Australia to be rather a bumbling landlubber. Trained on the quarterdeck Hindmarsh had a headstrong and often tactless approach to civilians which became even more intractable when he discovered his muted powers over the colonial officers and administration of the colony. Under the misapprehension that he was omnipotent, Hindmarsh had instructed Light before the latter sailed for South Australia to place the site of the capital at Port Lincoln,

Opposite: Figure 30: Adelaide coastline, from the 1839 Arrowsmith map
(Courtesy of the South Australian Library Board)

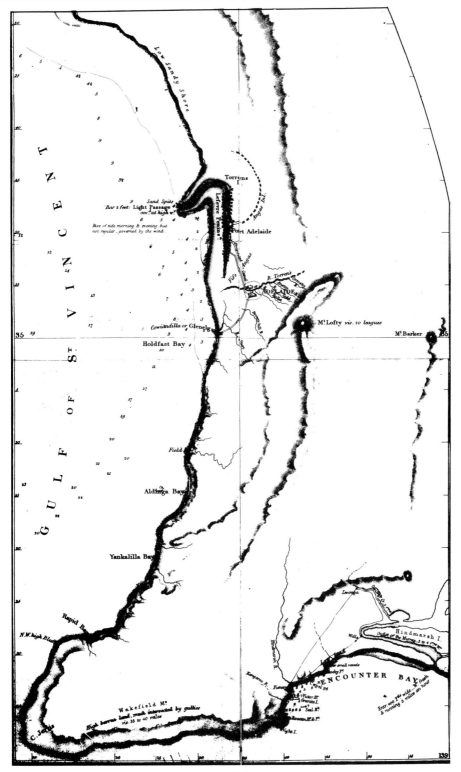

167

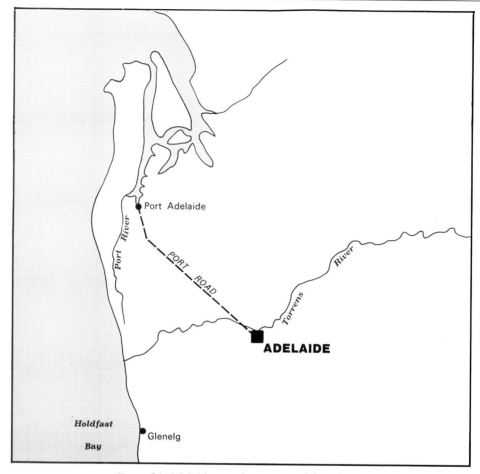

Figure 31: Adelaide was also separated from its port

a decision based simply on the belief that the port presented an easily defended naval facility, rather than on its suitablility as the centre of an agricultural settlement.[30]

Light, in fact, was set an imposing if not impossible task. Not only was he undermanned and under-equipped but within a couple of months the commissioners expected him to survey all likely harbour facilities from the mouth of the Murray to Port Lincoln, thus covering a coastal span of some 1500 miles. He was also expected to determine the site and survey the capital, to survey sites of secondary towns and to begin the survey of rural lands including the 'special surveys' which might be located anywhere in the colony. In the absence of deputy surveyor Kingston and most of the surveying team Light was, in effect, sent on a hectic wild goose chase along the coastal belt, probing and testing and often being led astray by inaccurate reports. Valuable time was lost, for instance, when he searched for the site of a supposedly 'magnificent' harbour on Gulf St Vincent which had been inaccurately plotted on a map by a Captain Jones in 1833. The harbour in question turned out to be the mouth of the 'Sixteen Mile Creek', subsequently the inlet to Port Adelaide, but this came to light only after weeks of inconvenience and time wasting for the harassed surveyor general. Following his investigations around the mouth of the Murray

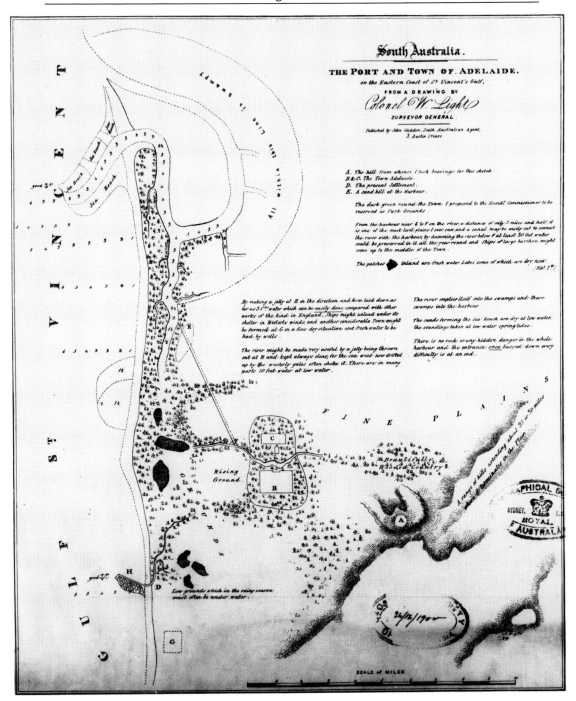

Figure 32: Light's 1837 survey of the Adelaide region (Courtesy of the Mitchell Library, State Library of New South Wales)

and at Port Lincoln, Light was convinced that his first impressions were correct, and from early November 1836 new arrivals were instructed to camp temporarily at Holdfast Bay on the Adelaide Plain, despite opposition from bickering officials.

Having officially proclaimed the colony at Glenelg, off Holdfast Bay, on 28 December 1836, the governor was invited two days later by Light to inspect the site for the capital which he had chosen on a rise above the Torrens River. Hindmarsh, with his fixation on harbour facilities, declared that the site should be shifted to the port, but Light politely demurred because it lacked a suitable supply of drinking water. The obdurate governor thereupon insisted the site should at least be positioned a couple of miles closer to the port and Light was prepared at first to compromise with this position, until he found evidence that the new site was subject to flooding. Finally Light announced that the site of Adelaide should be situated on the rise above the Torrens that he had originally suggested.[31] This minor battle illustrates the irritating position for both Light and Hindmarsh—the surveyor having been given the final power to select the city site, with the governor having to be consulted for his opinion—a situation with which Hindmarsh, with his desire to command, was not easily reconciled.

Perhaps piqued by his lack of real power, Hindmarsh did not let the matter lie. In February 1837, a full month after the city survey began, he backed a public move to have the city site removed to Port Adelaide but it was defeated by the vote of selectors by 218 to 127. The meeting did however recommend that those who so desired could establish their town acres at the port and subsequently twenty-nine acres were surveyed there.[32]

This was still not the end of the matter. There were those, including such sensible individuals as Gouger, who still had doubts whether the best site had been chosen. It was possible that more suitable sites for the centre of administration had still to be discovered. Port Lincoln remained a possibility in the minds of many colonists while others, remembering the reports of Sturt and Barker, opted for a site closer to the Murray mouth. Despite reports by Flinders and later explorers that the dangerous open coast in the vicinity was not going to provide the hoped-for haven, with access to the interior via the Murray River, hope still lived on.

Light completed the 1042-acre survey of Adelaide in an amazingly short time, just two months between 11 January to 10 March 1837. This can be favourably compared to the five months it took surveyors to lay out the 240-acre town of Melbourne.[33] But Hindmarsh was still not satisfied. In December 1837 he wrote to the Secretary of State in London announcing his intention of shifting the site of the capital on account of a magnificent harbour discovered near the Murray mouth. The report had emanated from a Kangaroo Island sealer by the name of Walker who with a friend had discovered:

> twenty-five miles to the south-eastward of the river discovered by Sturt, a fine harbour, into which a river leading directly from Lake Alexandrina, empties itself. Ships of any size may enter the harbour, and vessels might lie close upon the banks of the river in four fathoms of water and discharge their cargoes. The land in every direction was beautiful, and the place fitting for a capital.[34]

The bemused Light, knowing Walker to be a hopeless alcoholic, recognised the claim as a farce. Not so Hindmarsh, who immediately despatched expeditions to investigate the area and prematurely lodged claims for allotments at 'Walker's Harbour'. It was on one of these investigative expeditions that tragedy struck, for Judge Jeffcott, Captain Blenkinsop and two sailors were drowned when breakers upset their boat at the mouth of the Murray.[35] Despite this accident, one of Hindmarsh's supporters was adamant that a site close to the Murray could be obtained with the construction of a breakwater at Granite Island, Encounter Bay (now Victor Harbour). Carried away by this suggestion, Hindmarsh wrote again to Lord Glenelg on 18 December 1837, seeking authority to remove the capital to Encounter Bay. He suggested that the harbour could hold up to fifty vessels and access could be made to the Murray via a canal connected to Goolwa.[36] All this flew in the face of previous information from Sturt who had reported the harbour was capable of taking at the most five to seven vessels, though even these could be affected by certain adverse conditions. His judgment was vindicated shortly after Hindmarsh's letter to Glenelg when five South Australian Company vessels were sunk at the site.

The fight over the city site was one of the many burdens imposed upon Light. Ill-trained and inexperienced officers, shortages of stores and equipment, low wages and overwork led to labour disputes and further inefficiency. Light's position was also undermined by the conniving Kingston who returned to England in order to plead for a better deal for the surveying party. While there he managed to cast doubt on Light's competence while elevating his own, despite the fact that he hardly knew a surveyor's chain from a dog lead.[37] Meanwhile, the now sick and ailing Light attempted to continue with rural surveys. His already scant resources were further stretched by the commissioners' directive that the first choice of country surveys were to be carried out for landowners belonging to the preliminary purchaser group of 437, who were originally to choose their locations within an area limited to 150 square miles around the metropolis. This directive, however, was overridden by Resident Commissioner Fisher who extended the choice to some 1000 square miles in districts to the south.[38] So, rather than concentrating his effort, Light was forced to cater for the varied claims and whims of the influential preliminary purchasers. This proved detrimental to other settlers who wished to go about their business on the land, and further weakened efficient use of his already inadequate resources. Economic activity also suffered because a large proportion of the preliminary land orders was held by absentees who had purchased land for speculation rather than for development.[39] Despite these trials, Light trigonometrically surveyed 150,000 acres, mapped large areas, and staked 150 sections over a period of fifteen months.[40]

Dissatisfied with this progress, the London-based commissioners, wishing no doubt to cast blame for their own inadequacies and goaded by adverse reports from Hindmarsh and Kingston, sought the 'temporary' suspension of Light from his position of authority while elevating Kingston to supervise the surveys. Their ultimatum was received per the *Rapid* on 21 June 1838. The following day Light resigned in disgust, a move followed a few days later by the resignation of the whole of the surveying team bar three assistants. Within a month, the source of much of Light's irritation, Governor Hindmarsh, was also relieved of his position[41] and replaced by the more sympathetic and energetic Captain George Gawler. Arriving on 17 October 1838, Gawler also took the position of resident commissioner, thus replacing Fisher whom it was claimed had been slipshod in his duties, being more inclined to concentrate on personal mercantile activities rather than upon the interests of the commissioners.[42]

Despite Light's valiant efforts, the majority of *bona fide* settlers were still sitting on their assets in downtown Adelaide when he handed over to Kingston in mid 1838. Neither did the problem go away with the arrival of Gawler, despite his dismissal of Kingston and the appointment of the more competent Boyle Travers Finniss as surveyor general. In 1839 the London commissioners complicated matters when they decided that priority should be given to 'special surveys' for purchasers of 15,000 acres or more chosen anywhere in the colony.[43] Not only did this create public resentment and resource problems for the general survey department, but it was a move which appeared diametrically opposed to one of the main tenets of the Wakefieldian plan—that of *concentration*. By allowing settlement only in contiguous blocks, he claimed, infrastructure costs would be lowered; factors of production would flow freely and the benefits of *civilisation* be extended to all settlers.[44]

Despite this stress on geographical propinquity, Wakefield also held that 'the only restriction on liberty of choice [in his ideal colony] would be the sufficient price; but that would apply to quantity alone, not at all to locality.'[45] In 1838 Gouger, while lauding a system of land allocation which 'avoided dispersion caused by huge land grants', added the rider that a policy of 'concentration' did not prevent capitalists purchasing land where they liked—free selection was allowed as 'commonsense . . . would dispose capitalists to purchase land where labour was concentrated.'[46] Like Wakefield, Gouger could hardly have imposed strictly planned contiguous development when this would have contradicted the fundamental laissez faire belief in freedom of choice and self-interest.[47]

Problems of surveying thus proved a disconcerting start for South Australia both in terms of economic development and in terms of harmony. But lack of harmony was seen in almost every level of decision making among the upper echelons of the local society. In 1837, for example, Governor Hindmarsh took it as his prerogative to name the streets of Adelaide, but was opposed by the hairsplitting Resident Commissioner Fisher who believed this was the responsibility of the Board of Commissioners. In compromise it was finally agreed that the streets should be named by a committee of twelve prominent settlers who even then failed to reach a unanimous decision as members' sympathies were split between the Hindmarsh and the Fisher factions.[48] Another acrimonious incident involved Gouger and Colonial Treasurer Osmond Gilles, a cantankerous character whose only redeeming feature appears to have been his business acumen and willingness occasionally to use his ample personal funds to prop up the colonial coffers.[49] Gilles was a 'Governor's' man, which explains why the more temperate and serene Gouger, a 'commissioner's functionary,' was relieved of his post as Colonial Secretary following a public fracas in which he and Gilles attacked each other with fists and umbrellas in the centre of Adelaide. Gilles, however, later fell foul of Governor Gawler, who looked askance at the time he devoted to his chandlery business. Gawler refused to brook his slipshod and, as it turned out, deficient methods, which were timidly described by the commissioners (who tended to be afraid of alienating this wealthy pariah) as 'moral irregularity'.[50]

For the *bona fide* settler, with no aspirations other than to get on to the land, the situation must have been exceedingly frustrating. They were the victims of inefficiency, caused in large part by petty-minded officials more interested in feathering their own nests[51] than in working wholeheartedly for the betterment of all colonists, and in part by the failure of the London-based commissioners and Colonial Office to ensure adequate pre-settlement preparation. In the face of such adversity most colonists were helpless.

That the colony finally prospered there is no doubt, though it was far more the result of accident than careful planning. Despite an early period characterised by blunders reminiscent of those made in the establishment of the Swan River Colony, there were some positive facets which help to explain why South Australian growth and development proved more rapid and successful than its neighbour in the west. In the first place the land on the Adelaide Plains and over the adjacent hills proved exceedingly fertile, lightly wooded and easily cleared and admirably suited to agrarian and pastoral pursuits.[52] Secondly, Wakefield's belief that he could transplant English agricultural and societal conditions had encouraged him to opt for eighty-acre lots,[53] a fortuitous decision given the fertile nature of the soil, which allowed successful farming by small landowners and lease-holders using family labour, and without the necessity to apply large amounts of capital to the land. In other colonies, 640 acres was the minimum land holding, though more often than not such acreages were on the small side where land was only suited for 'exten-sive' pastoral activity. The third feature, despite criticism made previously regarding its early speculative activities, was the activity of the South Australia Company as it endowed the colony with substantial capital and, supposedly, carefully selected labour inputs. Other benefits endowed by the South Australia Company included the early introduction of banking which succeeded to some degree in oiling the wheels of commerce, and the provision of roads, bridges and harbour facilities.[54] Such company-financed facilities, when combined with the vigorous programme of public works engendered by Gawler, did much to lay down a solid foundation of social overhead capital on which rapid develop-ment could take place.

Wakefield's principle of financing labour migration by land sales, while exhibiting some negative traits such as denying revenue to other areas of need including surveying, also had its positive aspect. Coupled with a successful publicity campaign and the benefits held out to speculators, land sales were high over the first three years of settlement and this ensured rapid population growth. Despite leakages from the economy through the high import levels that accompanied both a large population and limited production in the early years, South Australia's economic progress was relatively rapid. Population tended to generate activity and, while Swan River in its twenty-second year, 1851, had a popu-lation of only 5886,[55] South Australia could boast 63,700 inhabitants in the same year, just fifteen years after foundation. In fact, by 1850 South Australia had truly answered the prayers of its planners—it was the recognised granary of Australia and, as a bonus, it was also the greatest mineral producer. The rich Kapunda copper discovery of 1842, followed by the exposure of the fabulous deposits at Burra Burra in 1845, spelt not only prosperity for the copper magnates but also employment for well over 1000 miners. By 1848 Burra Burra alone had a population in excess of 5000, making it by far the largest inland town in Australia. The wealth it created, the linkages it extended to local farmers and the multivarious suppliers of services, as well as the export earnings generated, turned envi-ous eyes from other colonies on the good fortune which nature had bestowed upon this colony. Whether Wakefield could pat himself on the back for the part his plan played in this success is a moot point. The principles of the plan worked in South Australia's case primarily because of the fertility of the soil, but the way the plan was administered nearly spelt ruin for the colony. Indeed, success appears to have been achieved *despite* the activi-ties of the commissioners and the host of quibbling officials sent out to establish South Australia. It may also be claimed that development only really took off when George Grey, who succeeded Gawler as governor, managed in 1842 to take complete control of the col-ony in the name of the Crown, no longer having to brook interference from the com-missioners. South Australia's administration was thus placed on the same footing as all of Britain's other Crown colonies. Lustrog's sought-after harmony was restored.

*　　*　　*

South Australia had been founded during a period in which the Colonial Office was subjected to an evangelical-humanitarian thrust[56] which was echoed in a determination by the House of Commons to secure the observance of justice and protection of rights for all Aboriginal peoples. Indeed, in 1836 parliament appointed a select committee to examine the 'Treatment of Native Inhabitants of Countries where British Settlements are made . . .' and its comprehensive report was published just as Adelaide received its first European settlers in 1837.[57] As scathingly noted by this committee, the South Australian Foundation Act of 1834 had in its deliberations completely ignored the existence of the Aboriginals, describing the province as one of 'unoccupied lands'.[58] In consequence, settlement plans were delayed while amending clauses were drafted and passed— amendments which declared that the Aboriginals were not to be disturbed in enjoyment of the lands over which they held proprietary rights and which they refused to voluntarily transfer.[59] But this, along with an agreement to forbid the hunting of game and to purchase the like from Aboriginals,[60] was simply empty rhetoric by a Board of Commissioners who, save for Angas,[61] showed no interest even in the evangelical goal of saving savage souls. However, with the gilded belief in the power of administrative direction and the appointment of a government-funded 'Protector',[62] the philanthropic humanitarians sat back in Whitehall satisfied that the nascent colony would prove a triumph for their theories and dreams. This was especially so because South Australia was to be peopled by a 'superior' type of settler.

The basic principles of the humanitarians were simple—Aboriginals were to be protected and granted equality before the law and also exposed to the benefits of Christianity as a vital step on the path to 'civilisation' and 'amalgamation'. Amalgamation (assimilation) was primarily to be achieved through the great leveller 'education', for, stated the humanitarians, the native mind if properly nurtured was as receptive and intelligent as that of the white man.[63] The key to the whole process of Aboriginal amalgamation was seen to be religion, as the canon of Christianity would overcome 'the indolence and the spirit of independence natural to their race' thus making them passive and pliable in the hands of their saviours.[64] Rather than saving souls, however, the underlying emphasis was on cultivation of the work ethic and support of a master-servant relationship. The work ethic particularly was emphasised in South Australia. Despite the planned balance between factors of production under Wakefieldian immigration theory, the 1840s saw acute labour shortage and high wages.[65] The insistence upon a 'taintless' society divorced the settlers from a convict remedy and so Aboriginal labour was seen as a means to drive down the price of labour.

The first step in the process of civilisation was to bring the local natives into proximity with whites, a move expected to excite in them a desire for all things European. Thus in 1838 it was triumphantly announced that some tribes in the vicinity of Adelaide had 'abandoned their former erratic life' and settled in a village environment consisting of twelve huts and a school where many natives, especially children, were learning English.[66] But complaints in later years that the shelter provided was used only in rainy weather and 'usually only as a repository for spears, shields, etc,'[67] along with continued reference to the natives leaving for the bush, proved that these early reports were too optimistic.

Frustration was continually expressed at the lack of diligence of the Aboriginals, much of the blame for their 'mendacity and idleness' being placed on the availability of handouts in Adelaide which they preferred to a life of systematic employment.[68] In 1840 Protector Moorehouse wrote despairingly that indolence 'is the characteristic of the whole. During the last half-year we have averaged 106 Natives in Adelaide . . . and they altogether have not done as much work as an European would do in one month.'[69] Yet it was the Aboriginals who were largely responsible for filling the gaps in the labour force in pastoral and agricultural pursuits during the exodus of the 1850s gold rush to Victoria.[70]

In a bid to induce Aboriginals to marry and settle, several eighty-acre reserves were selected in the vicinity of Adelaide during 1840 under the auspices of Governor Gawler.[71] This raised the ire of some of the resident preliminary land-order owners, including Angas, who argued that as the Foundation Act of 1834 had not recognised the existence of Aboriginals, no compulsory provision for them could thereafter be demanded by the Commissioners. Although illegal, the reserves were subsequently recognised by the Colonial Office in the guise of 'Public Lands' under Clause 3 of the Waste Land Act of 1842.[72] The same Act allowed *up to* 15 per cent of gross proceeds of land sales to be used for Aboriginal welfare—though such sums were seldom if ever put to that use. In addition, 10 per cent of proceeds of the sales of all *Waste Lands* were to be similarly used—though this practice was abandoned in 1845.[73]

The idea of the eighty-acre reserves was to encourage the Aboriginals to settle, but as they were not attracted to such small plots it was decided to wait until they were ready 'to take to the plough'. Until such time, it was agreed to tender or auction the reserves on seven-year leases to European settlers, rents being paid into the Treasury and funds being appropriated for use of the Aboriginals.[74] Subsequently, such revenue became recognised as a substantial source of funds to offset expenditure by the Aboriginal Department.[75] By 1849 rents raised were £112 out of the total expenditure of £1445, which climbed to £995 out of £2398 by 1859—though these total sums were minuscule compared to total colonial expenditure and illustrate the tight funding allowed for Aboriginal affairs.

The Protector of Aborigines, Dr Matthew Moorehouse, had predicted in 1840 that the decision to set aside reserves would be seen as 'a propitious event—an event which the Aborigines of this province will, at a future period, fully appreciate, and one which all real philanthropists will rejoice to hear.'[76] But his prognostications proved as empty a shell as all other areas associated with original aspirations for the welfare and well-being of the Aboriginals of South Australia. The Aboriginals themselves soon realised that the professed desire of the wider community to accept them as equals was a fallacy. Even those professing Christianity found that they did not improve their position, and that the doctrine of the 'brotherhood of man' was not universally acceptable.[77]

In hindsight it is easy to realise from the experience of other European colonising ventures that the outcome of settlement would be a clash of interests and cultures. Also inevitable was the tragic and rapid increase in Aboriginal mortality which accompanied the process, a situation which would appear to have been flippantly dismissed in a conscience-salving statement by the Bishop of Adelaide when he exclaimed 'I would rather they died as Christians than drag out a miserable existence as heathens . . .'[78]

*   *   *

In summary, both the physical settlement of South Australia and the treatment of its native population evidence a confusion between theory and its practical application. In both spheres the theory had been developed on the basis of experience in other British colonies, but the interpretation of this experience and the remedies proposed proved inadequate to resolve the problems actually faced by administrators and settlers. For example very little heed appears to have been taken by planners of the early trials and tribulations of the adjacent Swan River Colony, probably because Wakefield held the myopic view that all of its problems were due solely to the generosity of the Crown in allocating overlarge and scattered grants. The matter of tardy surveying is but one example of a situation unnecessarily repeated.

That the Colony of South Australia proved, within a relatively short span of time, to be agriculturally bountiful and well endowed with mineral wealth enabled it to recover from the blunders of the planners. Without this fortuitous combination of natural endowments, South Australia, despite its 'Plan', would in all probability have suffered the same slow development as Swan River. It can therefore be surmised that it was not 'planned settlement' that triumphed over Swan River's 'free enterprise' but rather the natural endowments of the land which paved the way for smoother development.

Notes

[1] Pike, Douglas. *Paradise of Dissent: South Australia 1829-1857*, (hereafter cited as 'Paradise'), (M.U.P., 2nd ed., 1967).

[2] Grenfell Price, A. *The Foundation and Settlement of South Australia 1829-1845. A Study of the Colonisation Movement, Based on the Records of the South Australian Government and other Authoritative Documents*, (hereafter cited as 'Settlement'), (Adelaide, 1924).

[3] Manning, H.T. 'E.G. Wakefield and the Beauharnois Canal', *The Canadian Historical Review*, XLVIII, 1967, pp.1-25; see also Manning, H.T. 'The Present State of Wakefield Studies', *Historical Studies*, Vol. 16, No. 63, October, 1974, pp.277-84; and Pike, *op.cit.*, pp.75, 77.

[4] Pike, *op.cit.*, p.12.

[5] Fitzpatrick, Brian. *The British Empire in Australia. An Economic History 1834-1939*, (M.U.P., 2nd ed., 1949), pp.6-7.

[6] Pike, Douglas. 'South Australia: A Historical Sketch', in Best, Rupert J. (ed.), *Introducing South Australia*, (Adelaide, 1958), pp.3-20.

[7] Price, 'Paradise', *op.cit.*, p.55.

[8] Sutherland, George. *The South Australian Company, A Study in Colonisation*, (London, 1898), p.43; Fitzpatrick, *op.cit.*, p.22; Pike, 'Paradise', *op.cit.*, p.56; Grenfell Price, A. *Founders and Pioneers of South Australia*, (hereafter cited as 'Founders'), (Adelaide, 1929), p.10.

[9] *Proposal to His Majesty's Government for Founding a Colony on the Southern Coast of Australia*, (1831, S.A. facsimile ed., No. 10, Public Library of S.A., 1962), (hereafter cited as 'Proposal . . . for a colony'); Lloyd-Pritchard, M.F. *The Collected Works of Edward Gibbon Wakefield*, (Collins, 1968), p.31, fn. 8.

[10] B.P.P., Papers Relating to Australia 1840-41, Colonies—Australia, Vol. 6, pp.363-375.

[11] 'Proposal . . . for a Colony', *op.cit.*, p.3.

[12] *Ibid.*, pp.9-11.

[13] B.P.P., Colonies—Australia, Vol. 6, p.376.

[14] Pike, 'Paradise', *op.cit.*, p.62.

[15] *Ibid.*, p.64.

[16] Harrop, A.J. *The Amazing Career of Edward Gibbon Wakefield with Extracts from 'A letter from Sydney'*, (Allen & Unwin, London, 1928), pp.71-2.

[17] Sutherland, *op.cit.*, pp.28-9; see also Cooper, H.M. *The Unknown Coast Being the Explorations of Captain Matthew Flinders, R.N., Along the Shores of South Australia 1802*, (Adelaide, 1953), pp.121-3; and Howell, P.A. 'The South Australia Act, 1834', in Dean Jaensch (ed.), *The Flinders History of South Australia—Political History*, (Wakefield Press, Adelaide, Vol. II, 1986), p.43.

[18] Price, 'Founders', *op.cit.*, p.60.

[19] *Ibid.*, p.62; Pike, 'Paradise', *op.cit.*, pp.92-3.

[20] Pike, 'Paradise', *op.cit.*, p.53; Dutton, Geoffrey. *Founder of a City. The Life of Colonel William Light, First Surveyor-General of the Colony of South Australia: Founder of Adelaide, 1786-1839.* (Melbourne, 1960), p.154.

[21] See *above*, p.4.

[22] Of the 437 Preliminary Land-Orders, 322 were held by absentees or for speculation. See *B.P.P.*, Colonies—Australia, Vol. 7, 1842-44, p.215, and Vol. 6, pp.517-8.

[23] Price, 'Settlement', *op.cit.*, p.35.

[24] Price, 'Founders', *op.cit.*, p.200; Pike; 'Paradise', *op.cit.*, p.209.

[25] Pike, 'Paradise', *op.cit.*, p.209; Price, 'Settlement', *op.cit.*, p.156.

[26] See Letter LII, *The Art of Colonisation*, in Lloyd-Pritchard, *op.cit.*, p.949, and, Letter XLVII, p.935.

[27] Light very soon recognised the problem. See Light, William. *A Brief Journal of the Proceedings of South Australia with a few remarks on some of the Objections that have been made to them*, (Adelaide, 1839), p.20.

[28] Dutton, *op.cit.*, pp.180-2.

[29] 'Proposal . . ..for a Colony' (1831), *op.cit.*, p.26, quoting M. Peron, *Voyage de decouvertes aux terres Australes*, Vol. III, p.162. (NB—the 1834 edition of *Plan of a Colony* contains a slightly different translation.)

[30] Dutton, *op.cit.*, p.164.

[31] Light, *op.cit.*, p.39.

[32] *Ibid.*, p.61.

[33] Dutton, *op.cit.*, p.219, quoting Light; Price, 'Settlement', *op.cit.*, pp.106-7.

[34] Dutton, *op.cit.*, p.235, quoting the *Register*, 11-11-1837.

[35] *Ibid.*, pp.236-7.

[36] *Ibid.*, pp.238-9.

[37] Price, 'Settlement', *op.cit.*, pp.70-94 passim; Dutton, *op.cit.*, pp.225, 250-66.

[38] Pike, 'Paradise', *op.cit.*, pp.174-5.

[39] See *B.P.P.*, Colonies—Australia, Vol. 7, 1842-44.

[40] Price, 'Settlement', *op.cit.*, pp.90-1; Dutton, *op.cit.*, p.246.

[41] *B.P.P.*, Colonies—Australia, Vol. 6, 1840-41, letter 21-2-1838 and enclosure dated 22-9-1837, p.404.

[42] Pike, 'Paradise', *op.cit.*, pp.28, 30; see *B.P.P.*, Colonies—Australia, Vol. 6, 1840-41, p.249.

[43] For further details see *B.P.P.*, Colonies—Australia, Vol. 6, 1840-41, pp.517-8.

[44] Wakefield, *England and America*, in Lloyd-Pritchard. *op.cit.*, p.541.

[45] Wakefield, *The Art of Colonisation*, in Lloyd-Pritchard. *op.cit.*, pp.981-6.

[46] Gouger, Robert. *South Australia in 1837 in a Series of Letters with a Postscript as to 1838*, (London, 1838), pp.3-4; see also Torrens, R. *Colonisation of South Australia*, (London, 1835), pp.137-9.

[47] See Pike, 'Paradise', *op.cit.*, p.94; and Roberts, Sir Stephen. *History of Australian Settlement 1788-1920*, (Macmillan, Melbourne, 1968), pp.91-3.

[48] Pike, 'Paradise', *op.cit.*, pp.104-5; Price, 'Founders', *op.cit.*, pp.104-5.

[49] Dutton, *op.cit.*, p.154; Pike, 'Paradise', *op.cit.*, pp.107-8.

[50] Pike, 'Paradise', *op.cit.*, pp.107-8, 234-5.

[51] See *B.P.P.*, Colonies—Australia, Vol. 6, 1840-41, 'Returns Relating to Land in South Australia', p.130.

[52] Pascoe, J.J. (ed.), *History of Adelaide and Vicinity with a General Sketch of the Province of South Australia and Biographies of Representative Men*, (Adelaide, 1901), p.64, (NB—yields were reported to be as high as 30 or 40 bushels per acre on some lands in 1840).

[53] Lloyd-Pritchard, *op.cit.*, pp.17-18.

[54] Thornton, Robert. 'The South Australian Company, 1835-1849, A Research Note', *South Australia*, Vol. 21, 1982, pp.114-9; Pascoe, *op.cit.*, p.23; Sutherland, *op.cit.*, pp.53-4, 133-5 and Gouger, *op.cit.*, p.80.

[55] Battye, J.S. *Western Australia: A History from its Discovery to the Inauguration of the Commonwealth*, (Oxford, 1924); Pascoe, *op.cit.*, Appx. D, p.619.

[56] Gibbs, *op.cit.*, p.62.

[57] *B.P.P.*, 'Report from the Select Committee on Aborigines in British Settlements, 1836', 1837 Session.

[58] *Ibid.*, pp.4, 12.

[59] See *B.P.P.*, Colonies—Australia, Vol 5, Appx. 5, p.192; *B.P.P.*, Colonies—Australia, Vol. 4, 'First Report of Commissioners on Colony of South Australia, 1836', p.480; *Ibid.*, No. 43, 'Letters Patent Erecting and Establishing the Province of South Australia', 19-2-1836.

[60] Dutton, *op.cit.*, pp.162-3; Pascoe, *op.cit.*, p.30; Gibbs, *op.cit.*, p.64.

[61] Angas was forced to resign from the Board in 1835.

[62] Merivale, *op.cit.*, p.494.

[63] *Ibid.*, pp.534-5.

[64] *Ibid.*, pp.524-5, 534.

[65] See Davies, Mel. 'Blainey Revisited: Mineral Discovery and the Business Cycle in South Australia', *A.E.H.R.*, XV:2, 1985, pp.114-5.

[66] *B.P.P.*, Colonies—Australia, Vol. 5, 'Third Annual Report of the Colonisation Commission of South Australia', pp.313-4.

[67] *B.P.P.*, Report of Protection of Aborigines, 14-6-1840, p.353.

[68] For example, *B.P.P.*, Colonies—Australia, Vol. 7, 'Report from the Protector of Aborigines', 14-1-1840, p.350; *Ibid.*, Vol. 8, 'Report from Protector of Aborigines' 4-1-1844, p.351.

[69] *Ibid.*, Vol. 7, 27-7-1840, p.354.

[70] Hassell, *op.cit.*, p.134; Rowley, *op.cit.*, p.83.

[71] *South Australian Parliamentary Papers*, (hereafter cited as S.A.P.P.), 'Report Upon the Select Committee . . . upon the Aborigines, 1860', Vol. 3, No. 165, items 2499 and 2500; evidence Matthew Moorhouse, item 2512.

[72] See despatch No. 7, 28-4-1841 in *B.P.P.*, Colonies—Australia, Vol. 8; No. 5, 26-5-1843; No. 6, 6-8-1843; and 14-11-1843, p.339; Gibbs, *op.cit.*, p.70; Hassell, *op.cit.*, pp.48-9.

[73] S.A.P.P., 'Report on . . . Aborigines, 1860', p.5 (NB—*S.A.P.P.* pages are misnumbered, p.5 should be p.3); *Ibid.*, evidence Matthew Moorhouse, items 2512, 2518.

[74] *B.P.P.*, Colonies—Australia, Vol. 8, No. 5, p.337.

[75] See *S.A.P.P.*, 'Report on . . . Aborigines, 1860', *op.cit.*, items 1024-86, 2387-92, 2410-11, 2512 and 1518.

[76] *B.P.P.*, Colonies—Australia, Vol. 7, 'Report of Protector of Aborigines', 27-7-1840, p.354.

[77] Berndt, R. and C. *From Black to White in South Australia*, (Cheshire, Melbourne, 1951), pp.92-3.

[78] S.A.P.P., 'Report on . . . Aborigines, 1860', *op.cit.*, evidence Bishop of Adelaide, item 98.

Chapter IX

Adelaide: A Victorian Bastide?

Tony Denholm

At first sight there is little in common between a medieval bastide of thirteenth century Europe and a colonial city founded by Britain in the nineteenth century. Bastides were created by feudal lords to prevent depopulation of their lands and to serve chiefly as agrarian colonies and military strongholds in remote, often disputed territories. But even in this general way the parallels with the settlement of South Australia are not so tenuous as might at first appear. The settlement of South Australia, as shown in the previous chapter, was based at least in theory, on Wakefield's principles of scientific colonisation—where land was to be sold at a 'sufficient price', its release controlled to prevent speculation and keep settlement 'concentrated', and proceeds from land sales to be used to finance new migrants. Essentially this was a system designed to open up new agricultural land, to accommodate 'surplus' British farmers and agricultural labourers dispossessed by enclosure and to provide food for the teeming industrial cities of the mother country. Not least, there were hidden strategic considerations, as British settlement in the remote South Seas would counter French influence and ambitions in the Pacific region. Some of these features are evident in the instructions Colonel Light received for deciding the site of the colony's capital city. It was to have a year round safe harbour; a 'considerable tract of fertile land immediately adjoining'; fresh water; 'extensive sheepwalks'; as well as good communications with its hinterland and other ports. Secondary considerations included a supply of building materials, and the presence of coal.[1] While the latter suggests a keen eye on the industrial needs of Britain, clearly the prime function of the new colony was emphatically agricultural.

A closer parallel with earlier bastides becomes more apparent when one considers the expectations of the new citizens. For thirteenth century bastides it was:

> above all, the improvement in social status and the promise of liberty that seemed to advance migration to the new communities.[2]

The nineteenth century Englishmen who responded to the blandishments of the South Australia Company's propaganda in the late 1830s expected no less. They sought freedom from the hidebound class divisions of early Victorian Britain, the opportunity to advance their economic and social status, and for some the freedom to worship untrammelled by the tenets and tithes of the established church in a 'paradise of dissent'. Unlike their thirteenth century counterparts they had to buy their building plots but their expectations

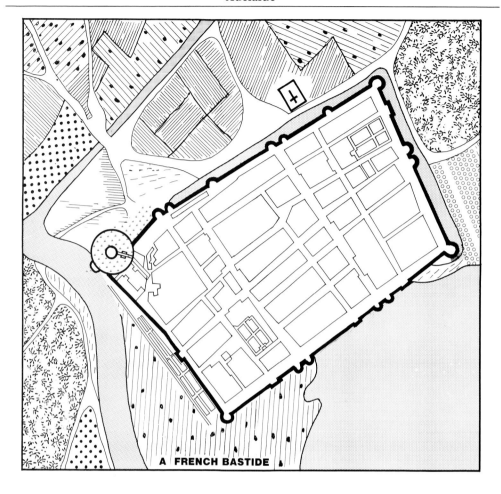

A FRENCH BASTIDE

were much the same. The medieval peasant looked to the status of free citizen and exemption from the personal services and taxes of the feudatory. His nineteenth century cousin looked to obtain property, respectability and a chance for self-improvement. Both settled on virgin land to be worked and made fruitful, both undertook the task of building their city from a bare site and to develop the hinterland from the city base.

So too, as the bastides were the 'all essential elements of the urbanisation of France' reflecting the 'consolidation of commerce and industry, and the growing power of the middle class',[3] Adelaide needed British capital, worldwide connections and the protection of the Empire. Britain, in turn, needed land for its citizens and food for its population, and sought to consolidate its imperial role in far-flung regions. It has been argued that the city itself formed the 'linchpin' in colonialist movements, and that urban forms which:

> evolved earlier in Europe were transplanted from the outset as part of an initial development phase. Thus descendants of the bastide appear as part of the occupation process in these new lands.[4]

Although this was postulated with specific reference to American urban settlement, it is no less true for Australia in general and for Adelaide in particular. Even the grid pattern of Adelaide's streets and the division of North from South Adelaide, separated by the River Torrens, is a classic bastide example of the variation of the grid pattern being determined by the site itself.[5]

Like medieval bastides, Adelaide was laid out on a more or less regular ground plan with a public square in the centre and a geometrical street pattern which made it easy to divide into plots of equal dimension, so providing 'a symptomatic expression of the social equality of all inhabitants'.[6] The open plain, between the Mount Lofty ranges and the sea, slightly elevated some six miles from the coast, was an excellent choice of site for a 'bastide' city, free from irregular contours and other topographical hazards. In rejecting other proposed sites—Kangaroo Island, Encounter Bay, the River Murray mouth—and in choosing a site in the middle of a reasonably flat plain, it would have been surprising if Light had *not* chosen a basic grid pattern. Blocks, squares and streets could be laid out unhindered by natural features like hills, estuaries or fast-flowing rivers. In fact only East Terrace on the very perimeter of the city follows the contours, zigzagging 'like to a series of steps'.[7] Unlike most medieval 'bastides' Adelaide had no military function or town wall, though one could argue that the belt of parklands, first authorised by Governor Gawler in September 1838, in many ways served some of the same purposes as a wall by effectively separating the outlying suburbs from the city centre. Gawler's purchase of the parklands has been aptly described as 'an inspired decision which has left North and South Adelaide cocooned in a belt of parklands that is the envy of other cities and a constant source of pride to Adelaideans themselves'.[8] In fact, generations of Adelaideans have now successfully upheld surveyor Light's vision or 'conscious theoretical purpose'[9] in defending and using their parkland space, laying out and preserving the squares, beautifying the boulevards and embellishing the noble terraces with fine buildings.

There is, however, a need to place the settlement of Adelaide in the broader context of nineteenth century urbanisation. Much attention has been spent on its uniqueness and its 'sense of difference', and there is some truth in both assertions, but the settlement of Adelaide, as of most Australian cities, is but part of a global process of urbanisation in the nineteenth century, and many features and factors are shared in common with other countries. Three major and recurring features have been identified in the diffusion of urbanisation to the non-European world: the defensive strong point to secure the new territory; the church, whether to convert the indigenous peoples or to reconcile the settlers to a hard life; and the market, 'by which the territory was exploited through an established and controlling central place which became the focus of community and of organisation'.[10] In the case of Adelaide it can be argued that the Royal Navy rendered the first unnecessary and that the nonconformist ethic, especially the work of some founding fathers like George Fife Angas, provided the second. On the third there can be no argument, for by 1861 Adelaide had successfully established itself as the prime city in the province, in spite of many attempts to move the capital city—to either Port Adelaide, the Murray mouth, or Victor Harbour. Light's choice of site proved durable, chiefly because 'investment was already so great, the impetus of initial advantage so forceful, and alternative sites so unsuitable that nothing was done'.[11]

One cannot draw the 'bastide' parallel too closely, however, for unlike its medieval counterpart, and indeed many contemporary European cities, Adelaide quickly and in some respects surprisingly, experienced the phenomenon of suburbanisation. Bastides concentrated settlement *within* the defined urban area and many European, though not British, nineteenth century cities opted similarly for high density, vertical growth, rather

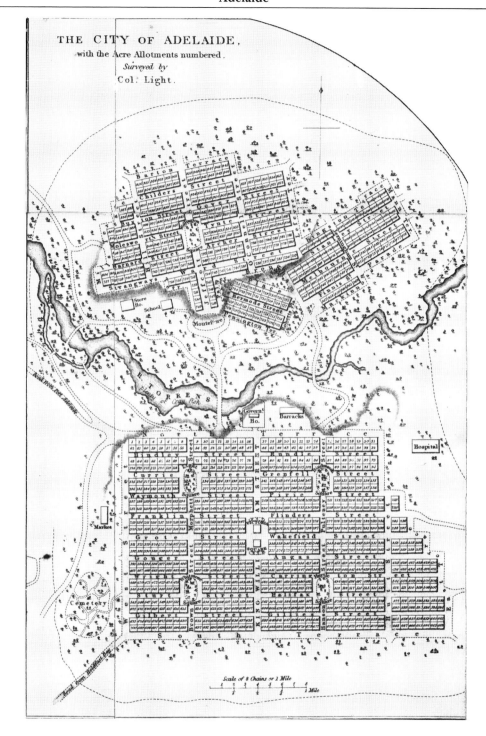

Figure 34: Light's plan for the city of Adelaide (Courtesy of the
Mitchell Library, State Library of New South Wales)

than horizontal suburban development. Traditionally it has been thought that there is a necessary relationship between the overpopulation of a city and the growth of suburbs.[12] But the Adelaide experience challenges this, because Adelaide had a history of suburbanisation long before the city, as laid out by Light, was full, either of buildings or of people. Once the surrounding plains were thrown open to settlement, after 1840, some thirty villages appeared, the result of speculators buying up notionally rural sections of land, and then subdividing them into half-acre blocks to sell to labourers, artisans and mechanics.[13] The high cost of city blocks forced this section of the community into nascent suburbs, beyond the parkland fringe, where they frequently took on a unique, specialised occupational or functional character. Some like Hindmarsh, Bowden, and Prospect, straddling the chief routes out of the city, grew to house those engaged in the carrying trades. Thebarton became an industrial suburb of brickworks and tanneries. Others like Walkerville, Kensington and Norwood developed as residential quarters largely for the well-to-do. Klemzig, settled initially by German migrants, retained a rural function and foreign flavour for a while. Salisbury, and the other northern villages of Adelaide, had a population of 100-200 people by 1848 and had become suburban nucleii.[14] Their layout was 'uncompromisingly rectilinear', and they developed quickly because the flat terrain made it easy to set them out and provide communication with the city itself. Though these northern villages, like Enfield and Salisbury, were not as attractive as areas to the south and in the hills, they had good water and soil and allowed quick speculative profit. District councils after 1853 gave a measure of self-government to these communities but they never really developed into towns in their own right. Only Gawler achieved this status. The villages had grown around a church, a school, a hotel, a carpenter's shop and a smithy and differed essentially from their English counterparts only in the absence of a squirearchy. But they also lacked any distinct character of their own, and were thus easily digested into suburbs as the city enveloped them.

The villages or suburban 'nodes', exercised a permanent influence on the morphology of the city for the mostly straight tracks which ran over the dusty plain, linking them to the city, became in the course of time the main suburban trunk routes, around which 'ribbon' development clustered. Almost from the beginning newly arrived migrants were attracted into the suburbs because of the cheapness of the blocks, and thus suburban development became an integral part of the whole process of urbanisation. The suburbs grew with the city, not after it. This continued into the 1850s and 1860s because the price of city land remained high. Even as late as 1860 over a quarter of the city acre sections were still undeveloped, while areas just beyond the parkland, where land prices 'dropped drastically',[15] were burgeoning. By 1860 only about half the total population within the urban area of Adelaide lived within the actual city as set out by Light. The districts to the south of Flinders and Franklin streets, which covered more than half the central city, were very sparsely populated. This pattern of dispersal within an area that could accommodate the population of a large European city has been regarded as both 'remarkable' and a 'new concept of an urban area'.[16]

Suburbs, characterised by social, spatial and functional differentiation, were present then in Adelaide almost from the beginning of settlement, unlike most nineteenth century British and European cities where the process of suburbanisation was much slower, and due as much to population pressure as to the high cost of city land. In Adelaide rich and poor suburbs also emerged early. By 1861 the better class suburbs, like Kensington and Norwood, Walkerville and Glenelg, contained houses built mainly of brick or stone, while

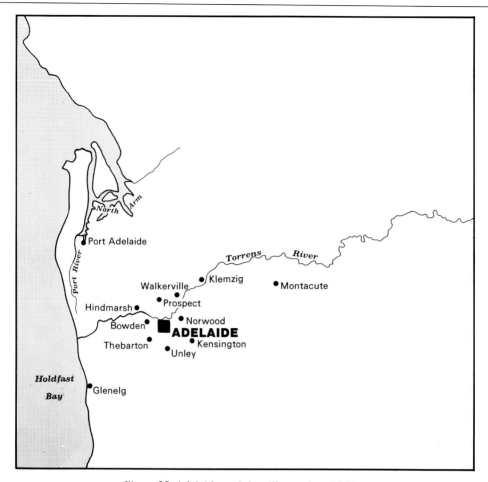

Figure 35: Adelaide and the villages circa 1840s

in the poorer western districts there were still large numbers of wooden and even mud dwellings. Within the city itself in 1861, 98.4 per cent of the houses were built of durable materials, for quarries both on the plain and in the hills provided an abundance of stone suitable for building.[17] Indeed, the high proportion of stone and brick buildings became a distinctive mark of South Australia compared with all other colonies.

The unique form of suburban development around Adelaide was yet another nail in the coffin of the Wakefieldian dreamtime, for even the lowest section of the community looked to the early ownership of land upon which to build a home. It set up high expectations of home ownership for the humblest new arrivals who could settle in town rather than move on into the country. It thus deprived the countryside of the large, mobile, labouring class that the Wakefield system required. Furthermore, this high expectation of home ownership set the Adelaide working man well apart from his contemporary British or European cousins, who lived most of their lives in rented, poor quality (often slum) accommodation.

The overall pattern of the townscape as laid out by Light has remained largely intact, though from the beginning there were encroachments on the parklands for amenities ranging from the hospital and the gaol (1840), to the cemetery on West Terrace and the ten acres Light set aside as a site for Government House (1839). Of the fifty-one main streets of North and South Adelaide (with six squares) surveyed by Light, none was less than sixty-six feet wide, many were in fact wider and the surrounding terraces were no less than a hundred feet in width. Within this overall framework of streets however there were additions of lanes and alleyways until by the 1880s the number of streets in the city had increased to over 360 due, according to Thomas Worsnop, Adelaide's Town Clerk in 1880, to 'private speculations and the exigencies of traffic and population'.[18]

A comparison between Arrowsmith's official 1839 map of Light's plan, and a sketch map of 1853 by CH Barton reveals some interesting features. The cluster of suburbs built right up to the parklands is evident from the Barton map. Bowden, Thebarton, Unley (laid out in grid pattern), Kensington, Norwood, Walkerville and Little Adelaide (Prospect) cling to the outer ring of parklands like the suburbs around a medieval walled city. To the east, south and north-west this perimeter took the form of roads leading to the main exit routes—west to Port Adelaide, south to Noarlunga and Willunga, and north to Gawler, Kapunda and Burra. Barton's map shows that North Adelaide had not developed as fully as the South, chiefly because it was more residential and less commercial. Barton's shaded area gives the impression that South Adelaide was largely built upon, though we know that even seven years later there were 221 vacant acre sections out of the 700 in the city.[19] One must remember too that it is only a rough sketch map, and in fact Barton left out two of the main east-west streets. Clearly though, settlement is concentrated in the northern part of South Adelaide along the Hindley Street/Rundle Street axis and particularly around the intersection with King William Street. The black dots indicating inns or taverns confirm this as the busiest part of town. Over forty inns and taverns marked on Barton's map would suggest that Adelaide was a city of pubs long before it became a city of churches. The site of Barton's own house should remind us too that North Terrace, now given over to a happy blend of cultural, educational, commercial and medical functions, was at this time chiefly residential in nature.

Barton's Adelaide was still a primitive frontier town, on the point of recovering from, and capitalising upon, the rush to the Victorian goldfields two years earlier. Still, it had come a long way since 1839 when the city was described as 'a seedy collection of shacks, tents, and stores, its streets muddy scratches through the grass, its squares a tangle of gum trees and wombat holes'.[20]

A committee had been set up in 1837 to name these 'muddy scratches' of streets, and many of Adelaide's early elite looking to posterity liberally distributed their name tags to the highways and byways of their city. James Hurtle Fisher gave his middle name to a square, Jeffcott, McLaren and Gouger had streets named after them along with the more prestigious Wakefield. The Iron Duke, Wellington and the hapless first governor Hindmarsh each warranted a six acre square. At the centre of the grid pattern, like a forum in a Roman 'civitas', was an eight-acre square which had the honour of becoming the first of many streets and squares throughout the Empire to be named after the new Queen, Victoria.

Governor Gawler, the second governor of South Australia, set about the task of constructing solidly built official buildings between 1838-41 as part of his effort to reverse the province's economic plight. A gaol, a barracks, the hospital, houses for officials, as well as a new mansion for himself, were all part of his public works program. At the site of the landing of the first settlers in 1836 in Holdfast Bay a new town, Glenelg, was established

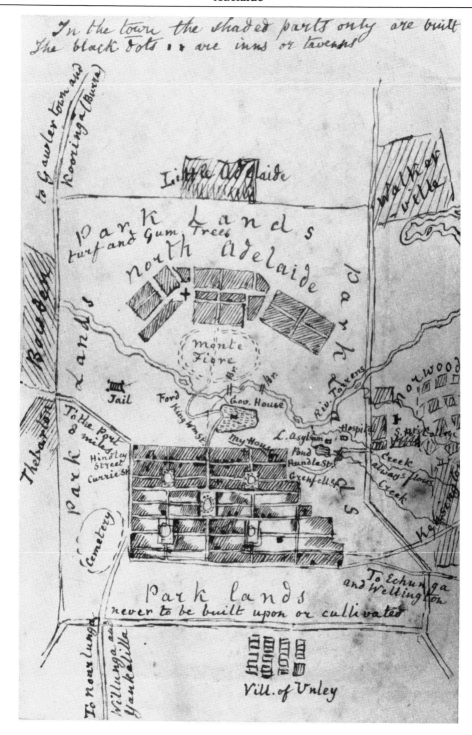

Figure 36: Barton's 1853 map of Adelaide (Courtesy of the
Corporation of the City of Adelaide Archives)

in 1839 and a wharf constructed there in the same year. This town, along with Port Adelaide a few miles to the north, served as points of seaborne entry to the city. By 1841 Gawler's work and confidence were beginning to have an effect on the townscape. Apart from public buildings, there were now flour mills, a bank, stone-built shops and offices as well as 1960 houses, stores and workshops.[21] By the mid 1840s Trinity church on North Terrace, built of stone, had replaced a prefabricated wooden church brought from England but never properly erected. The nonconformists followed, building solid chapels in Hindley Street, Gawler Place, Grenfell and Gouger Streets,[22] thus adding to the growing concentration of city life around the Hindley/Rundle and King William Street cross. A Literary and Mechanics Institute sited just to the east of Government House on North Terrace was opened in 1838 and began the long association of that gracious boulevard with the cultural and intellectual life of the city, for later years saw the arrival of a museum, an art gallery and the university along the northern side of the terrace.

During Gawler's administration a bridge had been constructed over the Torrens linking North and South Adelaide but it soon fell into disrepair. The first ill-fated city corporation was financially unable to act and it was left to private citizens to raise the money for repairs by subscription, though the governor allowed stone and timber to be taken from the parklands. The bridge, named the City Bridge, was reopened by the mayor with a great flourish of congratulations on the virtues of self-help in June 1843.

As already shown, the early economic life of the city was exceedingly precarious and it was not until the early 1840s that 'the success of the venture seemed assured'.[23] The elected city corporation, set up on the basis of English legislation,[24] at first consisted of 'almost all the prominent unofficial men in the colony'[25] but it fell foul of successive governors, was unable to raise sufficient rates for public works and was £600 in debt by January 1842. Worsnop described the critical situation at that time as follows:

> Everything was at the lowest ebb possible, and at one time it was thought that it would be fatal to the existence of the young colony. It has been stated that the lateness of the period at which the surveys became available, had prevented the settlers from obtaining their land at the time when they were prepared to cultivate it, and that this circumstance had been followed by a condition of idleness and want of enterprise on their part.

This, however, was only part of the problem and perhaps only a minor irritant to economic well-being. The greatest handicap lay in the evils of land speculation which were identified as:

> a system of land jobbing, and of mortgaging the land and hypothecating the produce, until the people were reduced to such a condition that neither merchants nor bankers could help them. A class of monopolists had arisen whose influence upon trade deprived the mercantile portion of the community of their legitimate profits—so that the greater part of the whole body of the colonists suffered severely.[26]

Governor Grey who took over in 1841 was soon at odds with the city corporation over new taxes, drainage schemes, and slaughter houses and, of course, over his desire to amend legislation to give him greater powers over the corporation.

Economic improvement and renewed confidence only came after the home government baled the colony out at the end of 1842. This was followed by the first export shipment of 260 bags of flour to Western Australia, and a cargo of wheat to Mauritius. The financial injection given by the home government in 1842-3 by writing off debts incurred by both Gawler and Grey, and the conversion of a loan into a free gift, were the strongest indication since settlement of British commitment to the colony. Adelaide was a 'planted' city, set down in the midst of undeveloped land and like other cities settled in virgin territory it needed the substantial support of the dominant authority to establish itself. Only then could the city get on with the task of fully exploiting its hinterland. Unlike 'organic' cities which grow as a result of the expansion of the surrounding district, planted ones need tender cultivation before they can generate their own growth and that of their uncolonised hinterlands. By 1843 this phase was complete—a city had been successfully established and 'now it was over . . . farmers fanned out over the plains'.[27]

The two decades following the 1842 crisis witnessed the take-off of the South Australian economy, based chiefly on agricultural produce and mineral wealth. In spite of the foundation of a number of country towns and new ports, Adelaide retained its tight grip on the colony's economy. It established a pre-eminence over all other urban settlements partly of course because it was the proclaimed capital and the seat of government and administrative initiative. But there were other factors. Adelaide always retained a high percentage of the total population of the province, and though this dropped from around 35 per cent in 1843 to 27 per cent in 1861,[28] Adelaide remained the only major urban centre—its merchants and financiers brooked no rivals. The hinterland was settled from the city as newly arrived migrants stayed first in Adelaide before moving out to the countryside, although as previously shown many of the early migrants settled initially in the suburbs. It has been claimed too that the 'self-perpetuating mechanism of initial advantage of the existing site . . . compounded every year'[29] was an important factor in ensuring Adelaide's supremacy. Certainly improved communications, notably the railways to Gawler, Kapunda and Burra, and to the agricultural hinterland, were centred on Adelaide. Materials, supplies, services, finance and labour emanated from the city and its port. Mining and country towns as well as the countryside itself were dependent on the virtual monopoly of specialist functions held by the bankers, lawyers, merchants, agents and carriers in the dominant city. One of the most characteristic features of South Australian towns both close to, and far from Adelaide, was their failure to challenge the dominance of Light's foundation. At first the hinterland was too close to entertain rivals and by the time settlement had reached a great distance from the metropolis, Adelaide had already established a complex network of manufacturing, distributive and financial functions. The arrival of the railway system only reinforced this *fait accompli*.

Yet in spite of this nineteenth century pre-eminence, Adelaide remained in many ways a pre-industrial city. The basic economic functions of Adelaide in the 1840s and 1850s were not unlike those of many European cities before industrialisation. It is true of course that Adelaide had merchants engaged in long-distance trade but a significant proportion of its population, like those in early modern European towns, were 'artisans working for the local and regional market, exchanging their products for the raw materials and foodstuffs provided for them by the agricultural population'.[30] The changing occupational patterns in Adelaide from 1845 to 1865 have recently been analysed and clearly show how the number of farmers, gardeners and other primary producers dropped over these twenty years as the 'urban character of the settlement was more firmly stamped on the ground'.[31] Also over these years there was a four-fold increase in the number of people engaged in manufacturing industries of the craft type, especially in metal, woodworking and clothing trades. By the 1860s whatever the household needed and the shops wished to store was now manufactured in Adelaide rather than imported.[32] Yet there were few factories as such, industrial activity was essentially of the artisan kind. This pre-industrial view of Adelaide up to 1861 is further reinforced if one accepts the argument that South Australian agriculture was virtually at subsistence level until 1855.[33] Only after this did the farmers and graziers look more towards overseas markets and themselves become increasingly dependent on higher technology imports. Until then Adelaide manufacturers served their needs.

A sure sign of confidence in the economy were proposals for a railway linking Adelaide to the port. First mooted in 1846 by private interests, construction was finally begun in 1852 by the government. However, the relative prosperity of the city in the late 1840s was abruptly arrested by the discovery of gold in Victoria in 1851. There was a sudden and dramatic exodus of male citizens from Adelaide as well as from the Burra mines and the countryside. Altogether about 16,000 South Australians left the colony. Trade came to a standstill, coin was scarce as the diggers took funds with them, properties deteriorated, and rate assessment became difficult if not impossible. Women and children were left without support and the Destitute Board, set up in 1849, provided outdoor relief to those families with somewhere to live while the Destitute Asylum took in the homeless and incapable. Women turned to prostitution and crimes of assault, robbery and drunkenness increased markedly. The high moral tone of the colony, which figures so prominently in the propaganda of the colonising commissioners and which was supposed to distinguish South Australia from the convict colonies, was now under threat. Public officials were sacked and the police force reduced thus exacerbating the problems of unemployment and crime.[34] As Worsnop commented:

> All the labours and anxieties of the preceding fifteen years seemed to have been suffered in vain. Ruin compounded every one and every interest in the place.[35]

The crisis however was short-lived. Many emigrants found gold and after the establishment of a protective escort of mounted police much of it was sent back to Adelaide. The government made it legal tender and an assay office was established. As men returned with their wealth Adelaide took on an extravagant and flamboyant flavour. The economy of the city quickly recovered as the newly rich went on a spending spree. Those with greater foresight, however, invested their gold in land and it is perhaps no accident that the extensive agricultural development of the hinterland dates from the mid 1850s. A diarist recorded the return to normality in March 1855:

> The town has subsided into its ordinary state. We do not now see any mad diggers galloping through the streets, still less do we see or expect to see gorgeous weddings celebrated between drunkards and whores.[36]

From very early days the nucleus of a central business district appeared along the Hindley Street/Rundle Street axis at the intersection with King William Street. It is not surprising that land in this part of town should have fetched very high prices. The area was close to the exit road to the port, from whence came supplies and materials, it was close to the river for water, and adjacent to the political power generated from Government House. The first council meetings too were held in premises in Hindley Street. Only businessmen opening shops, warehouses, banks and offices could afford the high land prices in this part of town. The early speculation in town land is also responsible for this. Town blocks which had originally sold from between £2-£14 when first auctioned in 1837 were selling for £300-£2000 two years later, due mainly to the 'constant arrival of new settlers with supplies of cash and negotiable assets.'[37]

In the 1850s this nucleus of the central business district expanded into neighbouring

Currie and Grenfell Streets, and changed shape a little as Rundle Street replaced Hindley Street as the major retailing area. This eastward shift is attributed by some to the purchasing power of the prosperous eastern suburbs of Kensington and Norwood whose population sought shops closer to their places of residence. Nevertheless, the intersection of both these streets with King William Street remained the focal point of the Central Business District. Nearby Grenfell and Currie Streets became occupied by warehouses and offices for mercantile firms and lawyers. Most of the banks were built in King William Street, though some early ones were situated in North Terrace. Eventually the Town Hall, Treasury buildings, the Post Office, the law courts as well as warehouses, offices and shops found their home on King William Street. In the 1860s and 1870s many palatial buildings, architectural variations of the Italian Renaissance style, lined what Worsnop claimed was 'one of the handsomest streets in the southern hemisphere.'[38] Close by, the North Terrace railway station was built linking the centre of the city to Port Adelaide and Gawler. When the colony received self-government in 1857 Parliament House was also situated on North Terrace, adjacent to the railway station. Along with Government House and the government printing office, political authority joined commercial and financial interests in a concentrated nexus of power. Not surprisingly the Adelaide Club, the resort of the merchant and squatter-elite built its clubhouse nearby on North Terrace in 1863. Newspaper offices, the South Australian Club, the Exchange and the Chamber of Manufacturers also established themselves in close proximity.

Adelaide's economy was in many ways typical of frontier cities. It fluctuated in direct relationship to the exploitation of the minerals and land of its hinterland. Like early American cities before independence the city's primary orientation was towards the sea, and both in form and function it was clearly related to the home country by which its security was assured.[39] This aspect of Australian urbanisation is often neglected. Adelaide needed no elaborate fortifications or even a substantial garrison. British naval power was the silent but effective sentinel, behind whose protective shield both city and province could grow without fear.

Other comparisons are noteworthy. Adelaide shared some of the Utopian and boom characteristics of some contemporary American towns as the urban frontier moved towards the Rockies. Like these, Adelaide's economy was influenced by gold discoveries and its expansion, if not its survival, owes a great deal to the railway. Like them and indeed most other Australian cities, Adelaide was 'the product of the second quarter of the nineteenth century when technological, social and political changes and advances enabled major towns to consolidate their hold on their tributary areas in a way they had never been able to before.'[40] It has been claimed that a town 'has to dominate an empire, however tiny, in order to exist'.[41] Adelaide was fortunate, first, in having the mechanism of colonisation to acquire a huge 'empire' to dominate, and then the wherewithal in terms of labour, capital and technical expertise which allowed her to control it so thoroughly.

Unlike many of its American counterparts, Adelaide rapidly acquired a civic pride and corporate identity, partly attributable to a sense of difference, and partly to the self-conscious adoption of the civic traditions and values of the mother country. Adelaide was to be the model city of a model colony. Utilitarian theory, 'the greatest happiness of the greatest number'; freedom both to worship as one wished and to pursue one's economic advantage were part of the colonising theory. Only sober, industrious persons of good character were to be allowed to immigrate. Unlike other Australian colonies it was to be free of convicts, and preferably of alcohol too. However, convicts crept in and took to the hills, and drunk and disorderly behaviour could not be wished away. In 1854, 58 per cent of all arrests were for drunkenness, 17 per cent of which were women.[42] Dreams of a non-conformist new moral order faded quickly in the face of greedy land jobbers, ambitious would-be politicians, hard times and human frailty. Lip-service continued to be paid to these ideals, and indeed, by the efforts of some like George Fife Angas, attempts were made to sustain them. But perhaps the most tangible survival of the ideals of the colonial theorists, lay in the early attempts by the citizens of Adelaide to set up their own municipal government.[44]

The 1830s had witnessed the origins of modern town government in England with the passing of the Municipal Corporations Act in 1835, and the colonisation commissioners successfully sought to extend the principles of this legislation to the new colonial capital once its population had reached 2000. In 1840 Gawler passed the first Municipal Councils Act permitting the election of nineteen councillors, a mayor and three aldermen by males who owned city property to the value of £20 per year and who had been resident for six months in the province. Criminals and recipients of public relief were excluded. No person could be elected unless he owned or occupied a city dwelling to the value of £50 or possessed personal property of £500. As in England, property was regarded as the rightful index to power in both municipal and national representative institutions. Almost all the prominent non-official men in the colony were members of the first council and 'very great expectations were formed as to the results of their joint exertions'.[45] But these high hopes were soon dashed. The salaries of the mayor, the treasurer and other officials, amounted to 80 per cent of the calculated rate revenue, and from the outset the council was beset with financial problems. It met in one room in Hindley Street and began to tackle the problems of street improvement and the regulation and control of the market and slaughterhouse, but it never had enough money. Increased rates met with resentment and evasion by the citizenry; the council quarrelled with Governor Grey when he raised money by imposing harbour dues, but it still lost the respect of the people in spite of organising protest meetings against the Governor. In October 1842 when new elections were due only 135 citizens bothered to enrol, and in the next year Grey obtained Colonial Office approval to wind up the bankrupt council. Given the imperial legislation of 1842 which abolished the colonisation commissioners, governors were now free to rule South Australia and its capital city without the restraints of divided authority or municipal decree. The brave experiment in self-government was temporarily abandoned and the governor was given a nominated Legislative Council to assist him to rule in traditional Colonial Office style.

In 1849 Governor Young, who had succeeded Grey, set up his own City Commission to raise rates and handle the problems of the municipality. This five-man operation worked for over two years and had to cope with the initial deleterious effects of the gold rush exodus from the city. Although considerable improvements in the collection and dispersal of rates were made, the critical factor in the success of this commission was the additional financial support of the government. Even Thomas Worsnop, town clerk and historian, later admitted that:

> Whatever objections the citizens might have had to the principle of taxation without representation, embodied in the constitution of the Commission, there is no doubt that the City progressed immensely under its management.[46]

The fact is of course that for the first fifteen years Adelaide was not large or prosperous enough to support on rate revenue alone the many varied civic projects—street paving, bridge building and repairs, slaughterhouse and market regulation among them, that were so necessary. The government was obliged to take over these responsibilities and had to bear the financial burden. However, with the return to prosperity in 1852, after the gold rush, a new and more permanent instalment in municipal government was introduced by Governor Young.

The new corporation comprised four aldermen, representing new wards; and twelve councillors one of whom, J H Fisher, became mayor. All male householders who had property in the city and who lived there, or within seven miles, were entitled to vote. The corporation met in the Blenheim Hotel, though the governor allowed it to take possession of a town acre which had been set aside for a town hall. New assessments of city property were made and committees established to deal with finance, streets, bridges and markets. In 1854 new powers were given to the corporation in connection with the making of private streets and building regulations though control of markets and the power to license public conveyances were still left under the authority of the police commissioner. This situation, which was not rectified until 1861, meant that the corporation was deprived of considerable revenue, which went instead to the government, and led to a division of authority that caused considerable inconvenience.[47]

In 1857 after the passing of the Australian Colonies Government Act, the Legislative Council was increased in size to twenty-four members, sixteen of whom were elected by males owning property to the value of at least £100, or who paid £10 a year in rent. Along with the more representative nature of the city corporation it could now be claimed that, twenty years after the foundation of the province, a property-owning democracy was established in South Australia.

The corporation and the government set about the task of making the city healthier and more beautiful. The squares were properly laid out and £1000 was spent on Victoria Square alone. The first eight acres of the Botanic Gardens at the eastern end of North Terrace had been planted in 1855 and the public admitted in 1856. By 1880 they had been extended to forty-six acres and were a great source of pride and joy to citizen and visitor alike. A new road to North Adelaide was cut through part of the government domain in line with King William Street, and a new bridge over the Torrens was opened in 1856, though its costs were borne entirely by the government not the corporation. The city surveyor was instructed to design improvements along the line of the Torrens, to construct a weir and improve the flow. The banks of the river were to be grassed and the city parklands were to be provided with trees, shrubs and roads for the better enjoyment of the citizens. Shortage of funds, however, delayed many of these admirable projects. Public baths were opened in 1861, the water being supplied free of charge by the government from the new waterworks.

One of the initial advantages of the site for the city had been the availability of water from the Torrens and other streams coming off the ranges into the plain. Private wells and two water-carrying companies were sufficient to meet needs until the 1850s when piped water from a newly constructed reservoir, east of the city at Thornden Park enabled the people of Adelaide to consume more and more water, enhancing personal hygiene and encouraging gardens of all kinds. Port Adelaide was brought on-line in 1866 and a new reservoir at Hope Valley to serve the suburbs was in operation by 1871. Provision of water on this scale, for needs other than drinking and washing, enabled Adelaide to become the garden city so admired by visitors in the later nineteenth century:

> The city is environed by suburban municipalities, almost hidden in luxuriant and well culti-
> vated gardens, where fruit trees of great variety and richness, when clothed with their
> blossoming garments . . . afford as many evidences of prosperity as the city.[48]

Provision for the disposal of sewage, however, was tardier. Cesspits, the Torrens and the
parklands were used and proper piped drained sewerage and treatment works had to wait
until the 1880s. Even so, Adelaide was earlier than other Australian cities in gaining both
piped water and sewerage disposal. In large part this can be attributed to Adelaide's
topographical and political circumstances—the 'gently sloping plains' aided the natural
flow of water, and the establishment of a central authority initially under a Commissioner
of Public Works in 1876 placed both facilities under semi-government control. This
'avoided the fragmentation and dispute between councils that happened . . . in
Melbourne'.[49]

In the broad context of settlement the history of Adelaide is but part of the European
colonisation of the world whereby the whole of the 'earth's surface became characterised
by cities as the basic settlement feature'.[50] In this process of urban diffusion 'native
peoples were all but eliminated so that exploitative colonisation became effective settlement and occupation'.[51] This was indeed the fate of the Aboriginals who had lived in and
around the site of Light's vision. Early friendly relationships between the Kaurna tribe
and white settlers and the good intentions on the part of the new arrivals, described in the
previous chapter, gave way to:

> a confrontation between two totally different worlds. The weaker went to the wall, and for the
> Kaurna there remained only an increasingly debased twilight existence on the fringe of the fine
> new city dedicated to progress and profit . . . they lingered for a time on the parklands and
> beaches, then they faded away.[52]

After twenty-five years of European settlement the society of the city was not quite what
the theorists, utilitarian or nonconformist, had envisaged though in many ways they had
cause to congratulate themselves. Like their medieval counterparts the settlers had created a city out of the bare soil. Hundreds of square miles of land had been brought under
cultivation and a venue for 'profit and progress' firmly established. The initial impulses
for greater economic and religious freedom had in a large degree been satisfied. It is true
that the self-supporting principles had floundered from time to time and the home government had had to come to the financial rescue on more than one occasion, but by 1861
all this was in the past. Internal self-government for the province and municipal self-
government for Adelaide brought greater responsibility. The leaders of the new civic community had fought for and made society free from the established church—it was a
'paradise' for dissenters and they stamped their mark on the townscape with a motley collection of churches in a wide range of styles. But no new Jerusalem appeared.

It is perhaps a little unfair to dismiss the early inhabitants simply as a 'colony of socially
elite but misplaced English gentry and dissatisfied middle and working-class families' as
has been done in the past. One can agree that the early inhabitants of Adelaide considered
themselves different from settlers in the other Australian colonies for they harboured the
illusion that they would create a society free from crime and poverty because they were
themselves superior immigrants. Adelaideans above all considered themselves
'respectable'. They shared none of the rebellious traditions of the convict settlers, and the
near balance of the sexes made for a contented society based on complete nuclear
families.[53] The early police force, though lacking in funds, was accepted by the public and

considered necessary chiefly to track down escaped convicts who it was generally agreed were the cause of most crime.[54] But, as already noted, drunkenness was from the outset a great problem, exacerbated by high wages and the low cost of alcohol,[55] and actually accounted for most arrests made by the police. More serious strains appeared in the social fabric with economic depression and the initial effects of the exodus to the goldfields. The resources of the Destitute Board were overstretched and petty theft and prostitution flourished. Police Commissioner Dashwood was nevertheless fairly sanguine about the latter, reporting in 1851 that though the number of brothels was on the increase they were 'fairly quiet and orderly and confined to certain notorious areas of town'.[56] In fact depression and the gold rushes had a significant and unexpected effect on the ideal of a pure society as it led to the realisation that it was 'necessity which caused people to resort to crime and destitute relief'.[57]

By the early 1860s then Adelaide had not fulfilled all the expectations of pious founders like Angas, even though the city 'already preened herself as the moral, civic and constitutional model of a new community'.[58] Neither had it become the 'idyllic community of country squires, respectful yeomen, and even more respectful peasants'[59] that the Wakefield theorists had contemplated. Instead, most of its citizens had reacted as most planted settlers had done since the time of the bastide foundations. Their time and efforts were spent making their livelihoods in a new and strange environment, establishing homes of increasing durability on their own land and tending their vegetable plots. They seized opportunities as they came, whether these were on the goldfields of Victoria or in servicing the needs of those who created the agricultural and mineral wealth of the hinterland. They took their pleasures cheaply, in drink and family life according to their persuasion. The theatre and horseracing figured prominently in early leisure activities. Above all they had fully vindicated an old German saying 'town air sets a man free'. After a quarter of a century's endeavour, despite setbacks and disappointments, the 35,000 citizens of Adelaide and its suburbs had reason to be satisfied with their creation. They were poised for further successful civic enterprise, fleshing out Light's skeleton of streets with fine, sometimes elegant, stone and brick buildings. Commercially, its merchants had shrugged off any challenges from other towns; industrially, it was at the point of further expansion; politically and administratively, it was unquestionably the capital city of a province whose agricultural and mineral wealth had been hacked out of empty land. Situated as it was at the frontier of a great empire, it was indeed a most successful 'bastide'.

Notes

[1] Whitelock, D. *Adelaide 1836-1876. A History of Difference*, (St Lucia, Q.U.P., 1977), p.7.

[2] Guttkind, E.A. *Urban Development in Western Europe: France and Belgium*, Vol. 5, (New York, 1970), p.9.

[3] *Ibid.*, p.54.

[4] Carter, H. *An Introduction to Urban Historical Geography*, (London, 1983), p.50.

[5] *Ibid.*, p.44.

[6] Guttkind, *op.cit.*, p.52.

[7] Worsnop, T. *Adelaide and its Environs*, (hereafter cited as 'A. and E.'), (Adelaide, 1880), p.2.

[8] *Ibid.*, p.12.

[9] Stretton, H. *Ideas for Australian Cities*, (Adelaide, 1970), p.143.

[10] Carter, *op.cit.*, p.61.

[11] Williams, M. 'The Making of Adelaide' in McCarty, J.W. and Schedvin, A.B. (eds.) *Australian Capital Cities*, (Sydney, 1978), p.113.

[12] Thompson, F.M.L. *The Rise of Suburbia*, (Leicester, 1982), p.5.

[13] Williams, *op.cit.*, p.114.

[14] Lewis, J. *Salisbury, South Australia, a History of Town and District*, (Adelaide, 1980).

[15] Williams, *op.cit.*, p.119.

[16] *Ibid.*, p.119.

[17] *Ibid.*, p.121.

[18] Worsnop, 'A. and E.', *op.cit.*, p.2.

[19] Williams, *op.cit.*, p.119.

[20] Whitelock, *op.cit.*, p.36.

[21] *Ibid.*, p.60.

[22] Pike, D. *Paradise of Dissent*, (London, 1967), pp.265-66.

[23] Williams, *op.cit.*, p.116.

[24] Worsnop, T. *History of the City of Adelaide*, (hereafter cited as 'History'), (Adelaide, 1868), p.18.

[25] *Ibid.*, p.19.

[26] *Ibid.*, p.44.

[27] Williams, *op.cit.*, p.116.

[28] Calculated from the population table in Williams, *Ibid.*, p.116.

[29] *Ibid.*, p.116.

[30] Van Werveke, H. in Postan, M.M., Rich, E.E., and Miller, E. (eds.), *The Cambridge Economic History of Europe*, (C.U.P.), Vol 3, p.22.

[31] Williams, *op.cit.*, p.118.

[32] *Ibid.*, p.118.

[33] *Ibid.*, p.125.

[34] Much of this information comes from an unpublished paper by Pearson, S. *The effect of Victoria's gold discovery on South Australia's family life and social attitudes towards crime and poverty 1850-1855*, (History Department, U.A., 1981).

[35] Worsnop, 'History', *op.cit.*, p.97.

[36] Quoted by Pearson from the diary of James Allen, in 'The effect of Victoria's gold discovery . . .', *op.cit.*, p.13.

[37] Williams *op.cit.*, p.114.

[38] Worsnop 'A. and E.', *op.cit.*, p.31.

[39] Carter, *op.cit.*, p.56.

[40] Williams, *op.cit.*, p.125.

[41] Braudel, F. 'Pre-Modern Towns' in Peter Clark (ed.), *The Early Modern Town*, (London, 1975), p.54.

[42] Mayo, J.A. *The South Australian Police Force 1838-1857*. (Unpublished M.A. thesis. History Department U.A.), p.43.

[43] Carter, *op.cit.*, p.62.

[44] Worsnop, 'A. and E.'. *op.cit.*, p.2.

[45] Worsnop, 'History', *op.cit.*, p.19.

[46] *Ibid.*, p.94.

[47] *Ibid.*, p.115.

[48] Worsnop, 'A. and E.', *op.cit.*, p.4.

[49] Williams, *op.cit.*, p.134.

[50] Carter, *op.cit.*, p.50.

[51] *Ibid.*, p.50.

[52] Whitelock, *op.cit.*, p.16.

[53] Pearson, 'The effect of Victoria's gold discovery . .', *op.cit.*, p.4.

[54] *Ibid.*, p.5.

[55] *Ibid.*, p.5.

[56] *Ibid.*, p.26.

[57] *Ibid.*, p.28.

[58] Whitelock, *op.cit.*, p.77.

[59] *Ibid.*, p.77.

Melbourne

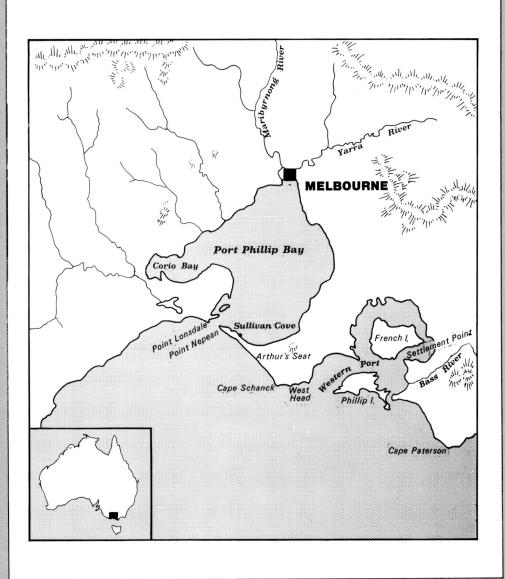

Maribyrnong River

Yarra River

MELBOURNE

Port Phillip Bay

Corio Bay

Sullivan Cove

French I.

Settlement Point

Point Lonsdale
Point Nepean

Arthur's Seat

Bass River

Western Port

Cape Schanck

West Head

Phillip I.

Cape Paterson

MELBOURNE 1880

NATIONAL LIBRARY OF AUSTRALIA · CANBERRA

Printed at The Griffin Press, Adelaide, for

NATIONAL LIBRARY OF AUSTRALIA

Chapter X

The Founding of Melbourne

Alan Shaw

The site of Melbourne was chosen as a place of settlement only after two other abortive attempts had been made to locate an establishment somewhere on the northern shores of Bass's Strait. After the naval surgeon George Bass had discovered Wilson's Promontory and Western Port in January 1798, he and the young Lieutenant Matthew Flinders had confirmed in November-December that the long-suspected strait really existed and that Van Diemen's Land was an island, by sailing through the one and around the other. The Colonial Office in London did not receive news of this discovery for fifteen months, but when it did, in March 1800, the Secretary of State, the Duke of Portland, reacted quite quickly. The previous month he had sent out Lieutenant James Grant, in the 60-ton brig *Lady Nelson*, to survey 'the unknown parts of the coast of New Holland', especially on the south. He told Grant to note any considerable rivers, the fertility of the soil, and so forth, and 'in all places which appear to him of any importance to Great Britain, either on account of the shelter for shipping or the probable utility of the produce of the soil, . . . to take possession in His Majesty's name'.[1] Then, when he learned of the discovery of the strait, he sent a message to him at the Cape of Good Hope, telling him to sail through it, surveying it 'minutely'.[2]

Unfortunately, Grant's investigations were less thorough than they might have been. As he sailed from Cape Otway to Wilson's Promontory,* at the end of his voyage, late in 1800, he did not see the entrance to what was later to be known as Port Phillip Bay, lying at the head of the bight between these two headlands. Nor did he do so when the Governor of New South Wales, Philip Gidley King, sent him back in March 1801 to examine the strait in more detail. 'His discoveries,' complained King on his return, 'have extended no further than making a minute survey' of Western Port, which Bass had named 'from its relative position to the hitherto known parts of the coast'. As it lies between Cape Schanck and Wilson's Promontory, and therefore east of Port Phillip, this name is somewhat misleading, and so was part of Grant's report. True, as he had told King, it was 'a safe and spacious harbour for any number of ships', but it was unfortunately not true that the soil

---

* The promontory was named after Thomas Wilson, a London friend of Matthew Flinders. Cape Otway and Cape Schanck were named after commissioners of the Transport Board, which later became part of the Admiralty.

thereabout was 'equal in goodness to that of Norfolk Island'. But this was not yet known, and for the moment King concluded that:

> the important situation of that port, and its relative connexion with this settlement, points it out as a proper and necessary place to have a settlement at, not only from its convenient situation in the center [sic] of the straits for ships to stop at . . . but also from its advantageous situation for a seal fishery.[3]

So in October that year the governor sent the *Lady Nelson* back to the straits, now under the command of her mate, 'a very active and deserving young man', Acting-Lieutenant John Murray. He did sight Port Phillip Bay, and after he had sent his mate in a small boat to find a passage through the heads, he entered the harbour on 15 February 1802.[4] Bowen, the mate, who with his small crew was the first British seaman to enter the bay, had reported it as 'a most noble sheet of Water, larger even than Western Port, with many fine Coves and entrances in it, and the appearance and probability of Rivers'. Murray was equally impressed, noting:

> thick Brush . . . Stout Trees . . . and in some places [it] falls nothing short in Beauty and Appearance from Greenwich Park . . . The Ground was hard and pleasant to walk on, the Trees are at good distances from each other and no Brush intercepts you; the soil is good as far as we may be judges.[5]

He found 'plenty of fresh water', but on the other hand after initial friendliness, suffered what he called a 'Treacherous and Unprovoked Attack' from Aboriginals, in which one native was killed and another wounded. He did not visit the northern end of the bay, but before leaving, on 9 March 1802, took possession of what he called Port King in the name of George III. King welcomed the annexation but changed its name to Port Phillip 'after my worthy and dear friend the Admiral, who until now has not had his name bestowed on either stick or stone in the colony'.[6]

Murray was followed after only six weeks by Matthew Flinders, who was returning to the colony, sent like Grant in 1800, to investigate and survey the coasts of New Holland. Sailing along the south coast, he entered Port Phillip on 23 April, climbed the mountain which Murray had christened Arthur's Seat, from its likeness to that near Edinburgh, and from its summit, 1026 feet high, saw a 'port so extensive that even at this elevation its boundary to the northward could not be distinguished'.[7] Being short of provisions, he could not examine it all thoroughly, but he climbed a peak 1154 feet high in the You Yang hills (after the Aboriginal name Yowang), and from the summit saw the full extent of the bay and some of its hinterland, as far as Mount Macedon, 33 miles distant. He described the country as being 'low, grassy and very slightly covered with wood, presenting great facility to a traveller desirous of penetrating inland', and thought the bay 'capable of receiving and later sheltering a larger fleet of ships than ever yet went to sea'; however, he noted that its entrance was narrow, with rocks and shoals making 'breakers in which small vessels should be careful of engaging themselves', and inside, more shoals were 'a great obstacle to a free passage up the port'. Flinders found no fresh water, but thought the country 'had a pleasing, and in many parts a fertile appearance', was fit for agriculture and even more suited for sheep. The southern peninsula, ending at the point which Murray had named after Evan Nepean, the Secretary to the Admiralty, was sandy and a

Opposite: Figure 37: Portion of Matthew Flinders' chart of the south coast of Australia, from Cape Otway to Cape Liptrap near Wilson's Promontory; from the charts accompanying his *Voyage to Terra Australis* (London 1814)

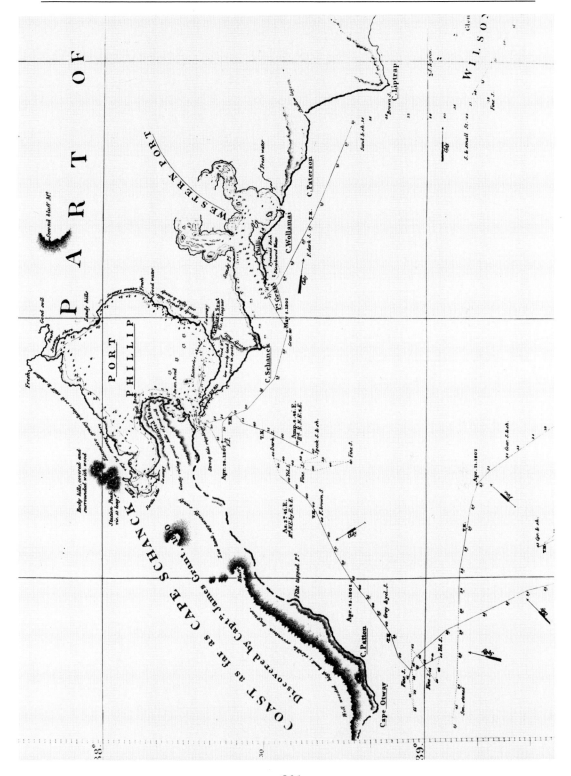

great deal of the eastern shores were swampy, but on the western side, the Bellarine (from the Aboriginal 'balla') Peninsula looked 'particularly agreeable'.[8]

These reports so encouraged King that, as he told Sir Joseph Banks in June, 'I have in a very earnest manner recommended the making a settlement at Port Phillip'. It would enable him to reduce the convict numbers at Sydney—which he expected to increase since at that moment it seemed that the French war was over—and it was also desirable 'from the French having it in contemplation to make a settlement' in the Straits. 'The soil is excellent and the timber thin', he wrote. There was 'a great abundance of sea elephants . . . and other seals' on the coast, 'the security and expansiveness of the harbour seems to point it out as absolutely necessary that a settlement should be made there', and it would be 'a better wheat country' than Sydney and its environs.[9] However, he knew it would be some time before the Colonial Office could act, and he was worried by the intentions of the French, so in November, on his own initiative, he sent Lieutenant Charles Robbins to make further surveys in Bass Strait. Robbins reached Port Phillip on 19 January 1803, and accompanied by Charles Grimes, the colony's surveyor-general, carried out that 'most minute investigation of that spacious harbour' which King had instructed him to make.[10]

To do this, Grimes and his party, which included the gardener, James Flemming who kept a journal, walked around the bay. They thought the eastern side disappointing, but at its head they found the mouth of a river. They first went up its Salt Water Branch (the Maribyrnong River) as far as Solomon's Ford, Braybrook, and then the freshwater stream (the Yarra), reaching the future site of Melbourne on 4 February, and proceeding as far as Dight's Falls, in what is now Kew. They had a friendly meeting with a party of Aboriginals, and returned around Corio Bay (Aboriginal 'Corayo'—the land around the bay) to the heads. They concluded that 'the most eligible place for a settlement . . . is on the Fresh water river', where there was 'fine black soil', and though it was very hot and dry when they were there, they thought 'that there is not often so great a scarcity of water as at present from the appearance of the herbage. The country in general is excellent pasture and thin in timber'.[11] But on Grimes' chart are frequent notes that the soil near the shore of the Bay was 'sandy', 'swampy', 'very shallow and light', 'barren', 'very bad', 'stony' etc, and King now told Lord Hobart, the new Secretary of State, that Grimes and Robbins had 'no very promising hopes' of Port Phillip being 'an eligible place for a large agricultural settlement', making similar comments in letters to Banks and Sir Evan Nepean at the Admiralty. But that was not the end of the matter, for he also assured Banks that the bay was well situated and likely to be useful for the fishery of the sea-elephant, and he told Hobart that it was for him to decide whether a settlement should be made at Port Phillip 'from its being situated at the western extremity of the entrance of the straits'.[12] However, his immediate worries had been lessened by his decision in March, after the return of Robbins and Grimes, to send Lieutenant Bowen to establish a settlement on the Derwent; though not accomplished until Bowen settled at Risdon in September, this fulfilled his desires to divide the convicts, obtain more timber and grain, promote the fisheries and anticipate any possible French occupation.[13]

Meanwhile in London, Hobart had been considering King's accounts of the visits of Murray and Flinders. As a result he had decided, before the less favorable report on Grimes' investigation reached England, that a new settlement should be established at Port Phillip. Writing in February 1803, he declared that this was desirable since 'the attention of other European powers had been drawn to that part of the world' and a foreign establishment there might greatly 'interrupt the communication with Port Jackson, and

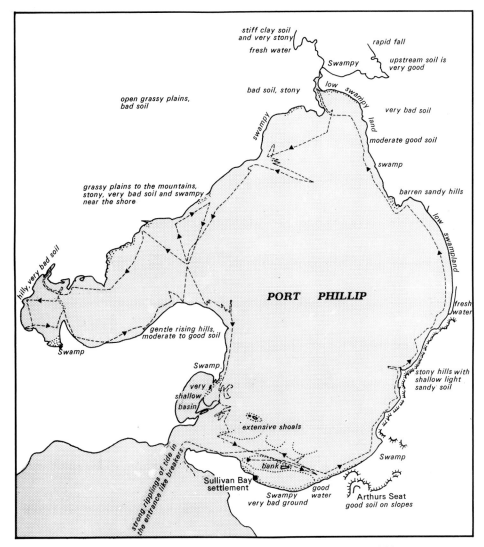

stiff clay soil
and very stony

rapid fall

fresh water

Swampy

upstream soil is
very good

bad soil, stony

low swampy land

open grassy plains,
bad soil

very bad soil

swampy

moderate good soil

swamp

grassy plains to the mountains,
stony, very bad soil and swampy
near the shore

barren sandy hills

low swampland

hilly, very bad soil

PORT PHILLIP

fresh water

gentle rising hills,
moderate to good soil

Swamp

stony hills with
shallow light
sandy soil

Swamp

very shallow basin

extensive shoals

Swamp

strong ripplings of tide in
the entrance like breakers

bank

Sullivan Bay
settlement

good water

Arthurs Seat
good soil on slopes

Swampy
very bad ground

Figure 38: Port Phillip Bay, drawn from Grimes' chart, 1803
(*Historical Records of New South Wales*)

materially endanger the tranquillity and security of our possessions there'; moreover, it would encourage the fisheries, and in any case, another convict settlement was desirable, as King had already pointed out. 'Sydney, I think is now completely saturated', Hobart had told Banks. 'We must let it rest and purify for a few years, and it be again in a position to receive'.[14]

Consequently on 27 April 1803, two ships, the *Calcutta* and the transport *Ocean*, with 307 convicts (of whom eight died en route), forty-eight marines and various others sailed for Port Phillip under the command of Captain David Collins, the former Judge-Advocate of New South Wales.[15] They arrived in October, when Collins chose a site for the settlement west of Arthur's Seat at Sullivan Bay, near modern Sorrento. It was not far from the heads, and he had found fresh water there by sinking casks near the shore, but it was also

203

near the place where Flinders had anchored, and he had clearly reported 'unfavorably' on this 'southern peninsula'. Collins received his first 'unfavorable impression' of the bay itself from the master of the *Ocean,* which had arrived two days ahead of him. This view, he told King, he was 'truly concerned to observe a more minute Survey . . . has only tended to strengthen'.[16]

Why, with Flinders' report before him, he should have selected this site is not easy to understand, though certainly he wanted to disembark without delay, and a quick examination found nothing better nearer the heads. But he had not seen Grimes' report, and he now sent Lieutenant James Tuckey from the *Calcutta,* with GP Harris, his deputy surveyor, to survey the harbour. They were not inspired by it. 'The Land in general . . . carries a deceitful appearance of a Rich Country', reported Harris, but the soil was 'for the most part Sandy'; it was not likely 'to repay the cares of the Husbandman', and on the western side, there was not enough water' for the smallest cultivation'.[17] Tuckey was also critical. Although at first he thought the country 'most beautifully picturesque'—a place whose appearance 'flattered us into the most delusive dreams of fruitfulness and plenty'—upon examination he too found the soil sandy, the timber small, many places swampy but fresh water scarce; except possibly on the north-west, there was no spot within five miles of the shore that would 'answer for raising wheat or any other grain which requires moisture'. Certainly he noticed that at the head of the bay there was 'a break in the land which had the appearance of a river mouth', as indeed Grimes had noted earlier in the year: but he did not have Grimes' report at this stage, and 'the badness of the weather at the time, being a dead lee shore with a heavy surf beating on it prevented a more minute examination'—which Collins did not see fit to carry out even after he had been told of the existence of the River Yarra.[18]

There were other objections too, which Tuckey elaborated both then and later. The weather was disconcerting. He had had trouble with Aboriginals on the northern shores of Corio Bay. Fish were too scarce to be relied on for food in an emergency. Most important of all, the navigation was 'exceedingly difficult', and since the settlement was to guard Bass Strait, and to provide a rendezvous for sealers, it was of 'first consequence' that there should be 'easy access for shipping'.[19] But, explained Tuckey, this was not the case. With a wind from the south—and he found it steady in this direction 'for many days together and often blowing very hard'—a ship leaving Port Phillip could not clear Point Schanck or Cape Otway; the difficulty of getting out meant that whalers would not willingly come in, all the more bearing in mind that the:

> heavy swell that constantly tumbles on the coast between Port Phillip and Wilson's Promonotory will render it impossible . . . to keep off the shore, which here represents a continued barrier of rock that denies the smallest hopes of escape to those dashed upon it.[20]

All these considerations influenced Collins' decision to leave. On 5 November, after only twenty-seven days in the Bay, he told King that he wanted to move:

> I cannot but suppose that all the disadvantages are as well known to Your Excellency as they are to myself at this moment. If they are, you will have anticipated this Report; but it may not have entered into your contemplation that there are at this moment three or four hundred People sitting down chearfully [sic], with no other or more certain supply of Water than what is filtered daily through the perforated sides of Six or Eight Casks which are sunk in the Sand.
> I do not see . . . that by staying here I can at all answer the intentions of Government in sending hither a Colonial Establishment. The Bay itself, when viewed in a Commercial light, is wholly unfit for any such purpose, being situated in a deep and dangerous Bight . . . to enter which

[ie the Bay] must ever require a well-manned and well-found Ship, a leading Wind, and a certain Time of Tide, for the Ebb runs out at the rapid Rate of from five to seven Knots an hour [sic] . . . With a gale of wind upon the coast . . . a Ship would be in imminent risk and danger.

Moreover, if he were to move to the north of the bay, he would run into hostile natives—and would need 'four times the force I have now' as a protection.[21] To Lord Hobart, in London, he reiterated the difficulties of navigation:

The Boat that I sent to Port Jackson was three days lying at the Mouth of the Harbour before she could get out, owing to a swell occasioned by the Wind meeting the strong Tide . . . When all the disadvantages attending this bay are publicly known, it cannot be supposed that Commercial People will be very desirous of visiting Port Phillip.[22]

King agreed with these misgivings. He told Collins that his observations had 'been fully anticipated', and it seemed clear that Port Phillip was 'totally unfit in every point of view to remain at'. He now sent Grimes' and Robbins' reports to Collins, which, of course, the latter had not seen in London, and though he drew attention to their comments on the 'Upper part of the Bay at the head of the Rivers', he noted that they had been unfavorably impressed and concluded that unless 'you should have made any further Observations to encourage your Remaining' he would 'presume it will appear to you that removing from thence will be the most Advisable for the Interest of His Majesty's Service'.[23] But by the time Collins received this letter he had already made his decision to leave. He made no further investigation of the Yarra, and he was soon to add to his reasons for departure his dislike of the weather and an 'improper spirit' among his military; the latter meant he would need reinforcements from Port Jackson, unless he joined with the detachment of the New South Wales Corps which had by then been sent to guard the new settlement at Risdon on the Derwent.[24]

Thus the first plans to settle in Port Phillip were abandoned, and despite Grimes' report no attempt was made to establish a settlement at the present site of Melbourne on the Yarra. For this, Victorian patriots and historians later in the century were very critical, alleging that Collins had been too easily put off and that even before leaving London he hoped to move to Tasmania (though for this I have found no evidence). But this decision was not surprising. The reports of the land at Port Phillip from Murray and Flinders, which he had been given in London, were more optimistic than the later more careful survey by Grimes and Robbins appeared to justify. The government's objectives were not to be easily achieved. The difficulties of entering and leaving the bay made it an unsuitable base for fisheries; though easily defensible, as Flinders said, it was not good as a naval post in Bass Strait if it was to be difficult for ships to leave the bay in pursuit of any suspected enemy, and there was little fresh water near the heads where, for fishing and defence purposes, the settlement ought to be. The timber, about which the government was immediately concerned, was poor.[25] There was, as yet, little interest in the pasture lands that Flinders had seen, but there was a great interest in growing food, and about this, reports were uniformly unfavourable. If a new penal settlement were needed to split up the convicts, it would be better established elsewhere, and that was what Collins proceeded to do.

King, however, did not entirely give up the idea of an establishment at Port Phillip. He told Collins to leave a small party behind 'as well for the purpose of advising any Ships that may hereafter arrive, as for other Advantages that will attend that measure'. Collins did not do this, so when in 1804 King sent Colonel Paterson to form a settlement at Port Dalrymple, on the north of Tasmania, he asked him to send someone to examine:

how far you consider Port Phillip or Western Port the most [sic] eligible for forming a Post at—not so much with a view to it being considered a present Agricultural Settlement as a Post of Occupancy.[26]

So, towards the end of 1804, Lieutenant Robbins made another exploration of Bass Strait. But he found nothing. There was no other harbour than Port Phillip and Western Port, and the latter possessed 'no great advantages to render it an eligible place for a Settlement'. It was bady watered and swampy, and in comparison with Port Phillip, which he had visited with Grimes in 1803, there was no part of it 'so eligible as the freshwater river at the head of Port Phillip'. Another naval surveyor, Lieutenant Oxley, reiterated this judgement. Western Port was, he said, sandy, muddy, stony, swampy, with little timber and little fresh water. 'If Port Phillip was found Bad, this Port is certainly much worse, and can never in any Point of View be found a fit place for a Settlement'.[27]

Nevertheless, it was here that the next settlement was made. This followed the reports of the explorers, Hamilton Hume, a New South Wales settler, and William Hovell, a retired sea-captain, who were sent to 'ascertain the character of the country' between Lake George (near Canberra) and Bass Strait, in accordance with the suggestion made in 1823 by J T Bigge, the commissioner inquiring into the affairs of New South Wales. He wanted this area to be investigated because he thought that:

> the extent of its surface, and the natural pasturage for sheep and cattle that there is reason to expect it will afford, the superior attractions of its climate and the facility of intercourse with the northern settlements of Van Diemen's Land and the islands in Bass's Straits, all constitute reasons for attempting the colonisation of this tract; first by a careful survey of the country itself, and afterwards by the gradual introduction of free settlers.[28]

Travelling overland, Hume and Hovell reached the southern coast, discovering en route 'one of the finest parts or tracts of country yet known in Australia. It is chiefly immense Downs and Forests, partially wooded; the whole of which is easy of access and well watered'. From the coast inland was country eighty to one hundred miles square 'fit for any purpose of agriculture or grazing'; it would be:

> a real and invaluable acquisition to this and the mother country, inasmuch as its advantages for Shipping, Agriculture or the depasturing of Stock etc. are much superior to any discoveries yet known in New South Wales.[29]

Unfortunately they mistook Corio Bay, which was where they had gone, for Western Port, so when another settlement was made in what was later Victoria, it was again put in the wrong place, not on the shores of Corio Bay, which they praised so highly, but at Western Port, which had been strongly condemned more than twenty years before. For at this moment, London was thinking again of a settlement on the south coast in order to anticipate French designs, and Hume's reports encouraged the Colonial Office, forgetful of the earlier investigations, to instruct Governor Darling to establish a settlement at a place which seemed to it so favorable for colonisation. Darling was more sceptical. He thought it had little prospect of becoming a place of importance, but he obeyed his orders, thinking that the possible French threat overrode economic considerations, and ordered the establishment of a penal settlement at Western Port.[30]

The expedition sailed in the sloop *Fly*, commanded by Captain F Wetherall RN. It settled on the eastern shore of the port at what is now Corinella, but it was not a success. Wetherall thought the harbour had its difficulties—like Port Phillip. The Commandant, Captain Wright, reported:

the very small quantity of good land, in the neighbourhood of the Settlement that I have been able to discover, and the sterile, swampy and impenetrable nature of the country, surrounding Western Port to a great extent, lead me to believe that it does not possess sufficient capabilities for Colonisation on a large scale.[31]

However, though Wetherall concluded that it was 'very evident' that it was not the country which Hume and Hovell had described, declaring flatly that 'they could never have been there', he also thought that despite the criticisms he had made, the place should 'not be deemed either unproductive or unpromising'. There must be 'abundance of good land to the Eastwood'. There were 'many places' suitable for sheep pasture. The port would be a place of refuge for ships in bad weather, and it might be convenient as a fishing station. But these reservations did not convince Darling, who remained certain that 'Western Port does not possess the necessary requisites for a Settlement'. It could be useful only:

when the Settlement of the colony is so far extended to the Southward . . . as to render it desirable to have a post for the introduction for the Settlers in that neighbourhood, and the Exportation of the Produce . . .

Since this would not be the case 'for a very considerable period of time', he sought and obtained permission to withdraw the outpost, and this was done without delay.[32]

The Colonial Office and the Admiralty were soon to have second thoughts. The Secretary of State told Darling that the settlement would be a useful connecting link with Van Diemen's Land, and as it seemed that the country was better than had been first reported, it would be valuable for 'the prosecution of grazing and agricultural operations'.[33] Others thought so too, and Darling was wrong in saying that there was no 'disposition on the part of the Inhabitants to settle' near Western Port. This may have been true in Sydney, but at the Colonial Office Undersecretary Hay noted that naturally no one would want to go if they thought the settlement was about to be abandoned, and 'in other circumstances' it might be 'a popular place of resort'; in fact two men in London and two partners in Hobart had applied for land near the new establishment.[34] They may have been misled by the first reports of the Hume and Hovell expedition, but there was without doubt an interest in the unoccupied land which the explorers had praised so highly, and the time of settlement would not be so far in the future as Darling thought.

At that moment neither the government in Sydney nor the Colonial Office was anxious to extend the limits of settlement, and even when in 1834 Darling's successor, Sir Richard Bourke, suggested a change in policy, and supported a proposal to establish a settlement at Twofold Bay, on the far south-east coast of New South Wales, the Secretary of State vetoed it; but as grazing was becoming more profitable and extensive, there was an increasing number who wanted access to more land—all the more so as good and well-situated pastures were beginning to become scarce—especially in Van Diemen's Land. There, the sealing and whaling parties, which frequently visited the mainland, constantly spoke of the excellent grazing country across the strait.[35] The change of government policy in 1831, which replaced granting Crown land by selling it for cash, was a further incentive to look for 'fresh fields and pastures new' where land might once again be obtained (and it was hoped be kept) without payment, or on credit. In Van Diemen's Land, John Aitken, later to be one of the first settlers at Port Phillip, had suggested to George Russell in '1833 or 1834' that he and others should join in sending sheep across Bass Strait to form 'a squatting establishment'. Following a letter from a group of Launceston capitalists to the Secretary of State in London in August 1834, seeking permission to buy land on credit on the mainland because 'of the great difficulty of now obtaining any extent of tolerably good land' in the colony, JH Wedge, then a government surveyor in Van Diemen's Land and soon to be a major participator in the Port Phillip Association, told Governor Arthur in Hobart that there was:

> very little doubt . . . that the Southern parts of New Holland afford every advantage and a boundless field for the enterprising Colonist, and that it will at no distant period become a Colony of considerable importance.

More dramatically, after an earlier reconnoitre, in November 1834, Edward Henty followed a similar request by directly squatting at Portland Bay, on the western coast of the future colony of Victoria; more important still was John Batman's expedition to Port Phillip the following May.[36]

Spurred on by Hume's stories of his exploration, Batman had sought land at Western Port in 1827, in conjunction with the lawyer and landowner, Joseph Gellibrand, in order to pasture sheep and other livestock. Now, seeking no permission from any authority, he sailed to Port Phillip as the emissary of the fifteen members of a syndicate called the Port Phillip Association. This body of capitalists and landowners, including Batman, Wedge, Gellibrand, and Charles Swanston, the banker, had been formed in Van Diemen's Land to investigate the possibilities of grazing enterprise on the northern coast of Bass Strait, and if they seemed promising, to take up land there. Batman sailed from Launceston in the *Rebecca* and landed on 29 May 1835 at Indented Head on the Bellarine Peninsula (where Flinders had been thirty-three years before) armed with Flinders' map. He formed a base there and then walked and sailed round Corio Bay, finding to the south-west, west and north 'nothing but grassy plains, of good soil, with plenty of grass, well adapted either for sheep or agricultural purposes . . . with scarcely any timber', or as he noted three days later, the 'most beautiful sheep pasturage I ever saw in my life'. On 6 June he 'bought' from the Dutigalla tribe, for an annual tribute of supplies worth about £200 about 600,000 acres of land at the head of the Bay and extending to Geelong; he then returned to the mouth of the Yarra, where he picked up the *Rebecca* to return to Launceston, leaving a small party with three months' supplies at the camp on Indented Head.[37]

Batman had told them to build a hut there, plant potatoes and 'put off any person who might trespass on the land I have purchased from the natives', but at this stage he did nothing about the site of the future Melbourne. Whether he had even visited it depends on the interpretation of a somewhat ambiguous phrase in his journal. He had gone up and come down the Maribyrnong, but on his return, when expecting to reach the *Rebecca*, at its mouth, 'to our great surprise', his party struck the Yarra flowing into it. Camping there at the river junction, he sent for the ship, which came up to it, but when next day, 8 June, he wanted to sail for Van Diemen's Land he found that the wind was 'foul this morning for Indented Head. We tried but could not get out of the river'. So, he went on:

> The boat went up the large river I have spoken of which comes from the east [i.e. the Yarra], and I am glad to state, about six miles up found the river all good water and very deep. This will be the place for a village.

But did 'this' mean 'six miles up' or refer to the place where Batman was writing his journal? and was Batman in the boat upstream or at the junction waiting to sail out? Strictly, one would expect that the last two sentences in the journal entry were linked, but at the same time the phrasing suggests that Batman did *not* go upstream in the boat but

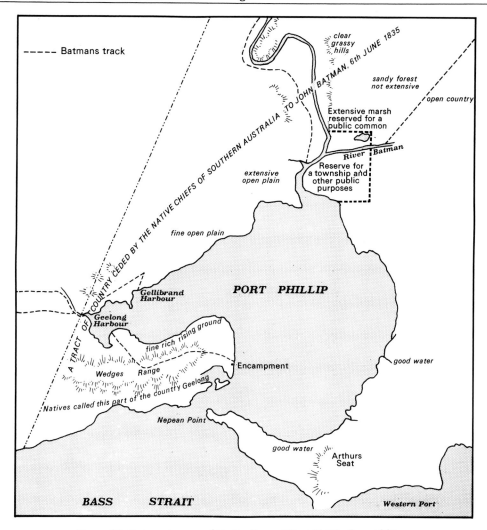

Figure 39: Batman's map of Dutigalla and Port Phillip Bay, 1835.
Drawn from the Report of the Select Committee on the Disposal of
Lands in the British Colonies (Parliamentary Papers UK, 1836)

stayed at the junction; one would certainly expect fuller comments if he had actually seen the site. On his map, Batman marked around this area a section on the south side of the river to be 'reserved for a township and other public purposes', and on the north, 'an extensive marsh to be reserved for a Public Common'—referring to the West Melbourne marsh now largely occupied by Victoria Dock. But it is all rather vaguely sketched, and though it suggests that he was thinking of the south bank rather than the north, probably he had no very precise spot in view at all, since picking one was not the prime object of his journey.[38]

Back in Van Diemen's Land, he tried to persuade Governor Arthur to recognise officially the 'purchase' of land from the Dutigalla tribe, meanwhile dividing it up between the other members of the Port Phillip Association. Arthur correctly forecast that the Colonial Office would refuse Batman's claims, despite the latter's attempt to show how much he would help the Aboriginals. But before either could receive any reply from London, naturally enough the confirmation of the reports of good land encouraged competitors. Two who were immediately active were John Pascoe Fawkner and John Aitken, whose ships left Launceston on 27 July. As a boy, when his father had been a convict, Fawkner had been with Collins' party. Now he was a tradesman, farmer, publican, bookseller and journalist, anxious to make money, if he could, from a colonising expedition to the mainland. Unfortunately for him, he had to disembark at George Town, at the mouth of the River Tamar, in order to settle his debts, but his party, backed by five other settlers and led temporarily by John Lancey, a master mariner, went on in the schooner *Enterprize*, laden with livestock and provisions. The men first looked at the country round Western Port, which they not surprisingly found unsatisfactory, and then examined the eastern side of Port Phillip. This too seemed unpromising until, on 20 August, they reached the mouth of the river at the head of the bay. Three days later they found fresh water up its eastern branch, (ie the Yarra—soon to be named, in a sense mistakenly, from the Aboriginal Yarrow Yarrow, meaning falling water) above low falls which checked the incoming tide. They returned to the ship, got her over the bar at the river mouth with some difficulty and warped her up to the river junction, where they got a breeze to sail up to the falls. Here they could land their stock and provisions near the site they had chosen to settle at, so on 29 August, Lancey was able to moor their vessel at the foot of what he called Pleasant Hill (later Batman's Hill) and begin to unload her, 'much to the satisfaction' of the horses, he noted. The land was measured into 'parcels in order to accommodate each party with a fresh water frontage', and Lancey chose for Fawkner a plot 'with beautiful grass, a pleasant prospect, a fine fresh water river and the vessel laying alongside the bank discharging at a musket shot's distance from a pleasant hill, where I intend to put your house'.[39] Thus began settlement on the site of the future city.

They were not to remain alone for long. On 2 September, after the *Enterprize* had been unloaded and while a store was being built, J H Wedge arrived. He had resigned his position as a government surveyor in Van Diemen's Land to investigate for himself the prospects of the Port Phillip Association of which he was a member. On 7 August he had arrived from Launceston at the Indented Head camp with Henry Batman, John's brother, and their servants; and he walked up to Lancey's establishment to assert the rights which Batman and the association claimed on the strength of their 'purchase' from the Dutigalla Aborigines. Lancey and Wedge agreed to refer their claims to those at Launceston and Lancey departed next day, but in the meantime, Sir Richard Bourke, Governor of New South Wales, having heard of Batman's activities, had issued a proclamation on 26 August declaring the 'treaty' or 'sale' to be void, and that all persons at Port Phillip were 'trespassers and liable to be dealt with in like manner as other intruders upon the vacant lands of the Crown'.[40]

Settlement proceeded none the less. John Aitken had gone back to Launceston, to return with sheep the following March, but the other members of Lancey's party at once began to plough five acres, even though they were within the area Batman claimed to have purchased. On 16 September, Henry Batman also came up from Indented Head and landed at the Yarra settlement. Exactly a month later Fawkner followed. He read Divine Service on Sunday, 18 October, and soon rivalled Henry Batman's sod hut by building a house, which he and his wife moved into on 7 November. Two days later John Batman arrived too, and as Fawkner put it, 'pulled up to the Settlement with us'.[41] Fawkner shows in his journal that the two were then on quite good terms, and later that month he agreed that Batman should buy his farm on the north of the Yarra, and he would move to the other side. During the summer of 1835-6, other settlers arrived with their stock, and other huts were built on the river bank, while Bourke in Sydney was waiting for London to reply to the despatch he had sent on 10 October 1835 recommending that the government recognise the settlement.[42]

At first the Colonial Office had doubts about doing so. When the news of Batman's treaty reached London from Van Diemen's Land's Governor Arthur, Undersecretary Hay wrote a critical minute, on the lines of the answer given to Bourke about a proposed settlement at Twofold Bay in New South Wales the previous year. 'All schemes of this kind have been of late years discountenanced as leading eventually to the establishment of fresh settlements and fresh expense', he noted:

> if everyone were allowed to follow his own inclination by selecting a fit place of residence on the coast of New Holland, all hope of restricting the Circuits of our settlements in that quarter must be at once abandoned.

Moreover a settlement at Port Phillip would almost certainly provide 'an asylum for runaway convicts'.[43] But though this was the tenor of the reply to Arthur, such language was rather like that of Canute's courtiers, and the reply about Port Phillip to Bourke three months later was more favourable. New South Wales was 'marked out by Nature for a Pastoral Country', decided Lord Glenelg, the new Secretary of State. Settlement would inevitably be scattered, and it would be:

> wholly vain to expect that any positive Laws . . . will be energetic enough to repress the spirit of adventure and speculation in which the unauthorised settlements . . . have originated . . . It may indeed admit of serious doubt whether the Settlers . . . have not in reality given birth to undertakings, which deliberate reflection would have recommended rather than discouraged.

Port Phillip would probably form 'the nucleus of a new and flourishing settlement' and be 'reinforced by a large number of Emigrants, and a considerable introduction of Capital'. So when Bourke received this answer he was able to issue a notice on 9 September 1836 officially recognising the existence of the settlement which was then more than a year old.[44] It remained, of course, part of New South Wales, but he appointed Captain William Lonsdale of the 4th Regiment to be police magistrate in general charge of the district. The following March, 1837, he visited the new township himself, and found between sixty and seventy families there; he thought the population of the district was about five hundred, with more than 100,000 sheep, so, as he told Glenelg, there was 'little doubt that this Settlement will increase rapidly in numbers and wealth'. He fully agreed with those who had been there before him, including Grimes, Batman's first party, Lancey, Wedge, Fawkner, Lonsdale and others that the best site for a township was indeed that which had already been chosen, near the falls in the River Yarra, and he named it Melbourne, after the British Prime Minister, calling the port, at the mouth of the river, William's Town, after King William IV. He arranged for the town to be surveyed and the first land sale to be held on 1 June; this would mean that those so far trespassing on Crown Land would then become the legal owners of their township lots, and while they were laying the foundations of a future metropolis, a rapidly expanding squatting occupation was proceeding to transform the countryside.[45]

Why was the foundation this time successful when previous attempts to establish a settlement at Port Phillip, or anywhere else in Bass Strait, had failed? The important difference was that of motive. Early in the century the considerations that were important were of defence, fisheries, timber and a second penal settlement with its necessarily associated farming operations. For none of these was Port Phillip particularly suitable. Its timber was poor. Its harbour was so dangerous and difficult that it would never be an easy recourse for shipping and it was an unsuitable base for any naval operations. At all times, passage through the heads demanded favorable wind and tide, and though the latter was regular the former was not. A penal settlement needed to be self-sufficient and the prospects of growing food did not seem promising. Above all, water was scarce—except, according to Grimes, at the head of the bay, on the Yarra. That this site might have been further explored earlier is true; but those who deplore the failure to do this forget that the Yarra site was not a good one for other reasons. It was too far from the heads. It had poor timber, and the navigation of the bay, though not so difficult as that of the heads and the rip, was not easy either.

Thirty years later, objectives were different. What was sought was good grazing country. Reports from Hume and Hovell were encouraging, but their mistaken notion of their destination led to a further setback. However, the increasing shortage of readily available land in Van Diemen's Land made the search for new pastures urgent, and although as Bourke noted, the shores of the bay were 'not for the most part well watered', this agreement with the judgment of the early visitors was less important than his other conclusion that 'generally the pasture may be described as superior in quality to the average of the districts of New South Wales, which have been earlier settled.[46]

It was of even greater benefit to Van Diemen's Land where Arthur thought that because of the short trip across Bass Strait, it 'might very rapidly be covered with flocks and herds from this Colony'—and others had thought this too, before Batman set out on his pioneering visit. So the prospects encouraged 'trespassing', or unauthorised settlement, by men ready to follow the examples of the squatters in the interior of New South Wales, where, explained Bourke:

> the proprietors of thousands of acres already find it necessary, equally with the poorer settlers, to send large flocks beyond the present boundary of location, to preserve them in health throughout the year. The colonists must otherwise restrain the increase or endeavour to raise artificial food for the stock—

two courses both of which seemed 'a perverse rejection of the bounty of Providence'.[47] Moreover, small colonial vessels, whether coming from Sydney or northern Van Diemen's Land, could pass through the heads, tricky though the navigation was, much more easily than the big square-rigged ships which Collins and the other naval men had been thinking of a generation before. In these schooners and barques, sloops and cutters, settlers with their livestock and provisions could go up the bay, where they would find plenty of fresh water in a place well suited to be the centre of an expanding pastoral movement. To be able to go by sea so far into the interior, as it were, was an advantage not a drawback. Certainly the Yarra itself was not at first easily navigated either and only small craft, drawing up to about ten feet, could go up the river. Many goods had to be taken by barge to and from ships at Williamstown or in Hobson's Bay, and this was the subject of criticism for years. But the need for and the value of the land now opening up in the Port Phillip district overbalanced such difficulties, and the necessity of fresh water determined the site of the city.

Geelong (Jillong: a place of cliffs) might have proved a rival, but its approach also was obstructed by a bar; its water supply, from the Barwon River, was less accessible than that of the Yarra, and though well situated for graziers in the Western District, it was not so well suited for those moving to the north and north-east—areas which became increasingly important as the overland movement of squatters from New South Wales increased in volume, after the reports of Major Mitchell's explorations in Australia Felix in 1836 became widely known. Apart from that, of course, once Bourke had decided to make Melbourne an administrative centre, government business played a part in the growth of the city. It was proclaimed as a legal port, and soon came to be not only an important commodity market but also a disembarkation place for immigrants.

Was Melbourne founded by Batman or Fawkner? This question has been hotly debated for years, but the true answer should probably be 'neither', though this largely depends on what is meant by 'founder'. Is he, as P L Brown has argued, the 'man who showed the way there and first imagined it'? If so, the man is Batman, for his expedition and example led to the opening up of the district; his 'purchase' or 'treaty' with the Dutigalla tribe and his camp on Indented Head were the first steps towards permanent settlement on the shores of Port Phillip Bay.[48] But the site of the settlement on the Yarra was effactually chosen by Captain Lancey and his party when they arrived in the *Enterprize* at the end of August 1835, and though Fawkner had sent out the schooner, he was not there to found a city—or even to establish a settlement. So perhaps Lancey was the founder, for certainly during the next couple of months, neither Wedge from Indented Head, nor Henry Batman, nor Fawkner, nor John Batman wanted to shift the settlement from the site Lancey had selected. Still, if one thinks the prize belongs to the man who was the first to build a *permanent* residence, with the intention of remaining in it, that man is Fawkner, though the place for it was chosen before he even saw the Yarra. But what became a bitter personal vendetta between the two pioneers and their supporters, who all chose to ignore the strong claims of Lancey, is perhaps not a matter of great historical consequence. Both Batman and Fawkner played an important part in the establishment of the new city, in which incidentally they are singularly little commemorated officially, neither having much more than a park named after him; both were men of enterprise, but neither was a discoverer, and after the lapse of years a remarkably unfruitful controversy may well be left to rest.

Notes

1. Reporting Bass Strait: *H.R.A.*, I, ii, pp.381, (15-8-1799), pp.498-500, (26-2-1800).
2. *Ibid.*, p.498, (22-4-1800); and p.501, (8-4-1800).
3. Flinders, Mathew. *A Voyage to Terra Australis*, (hereafter cited as 'Voyage'), (London, 1814, facs., Adelaide, 1966), Vol. 1, p.cxiii; and *H.R.A.*, I, iii, p.116, (8-7-1801).
4. *H.R.N.S.W.*, Vol. iv, p.602; *H.R.A.*, I, iii, p.267, 274; p.482 and note 191, p.795, (29-3-1802). (NB—Bowen, Murray's mate, should not be confused with Lieut. John Bowen who established the settlement at Risdon on the River Derwent).
5. Murray's log, quoted in Labilliere, F.P. *Early History of the Colony of Victoria*, (1878), Vol. i, pp.86-7.
6. *Ibid.*, pp.91-2 and 97; and *H.R.N.S.W.*, Vol. iv, p.783, (5-6-1802).
7. Flinders, 'Voyage', *op.cit.*, Vol. i, pp.211-3.
8. *Ibid.*, pp.216-9; Blake, L.J. *Place Names of Victoria*, (1977), p.37.
9. *H.R.N.S.W.*, Vol. iv, p.875, (5-6-1802); *H.R.A.*, I, iii, p.490 and 528.
10. *H.R.A.*, I, iii, pp.737-9, (23-11-1802).
11. Journal of Explorations of Charles Grimes, kept by James Flemming, in Shillinglaw, J.J. (ed.), *Historical Records of Port Phillip . . .*, (ed. C.E. Sayers, Melbourne, 1972), p.34; Boys, R.D. *First Years at Port Phillip 1834-1842*, (Melbourne, 1959), p.17.
12. Grimes' Chart, in *Journal of the Exploration of Charles Grimes, Acting Surveyor of N.S.W.*, (1879); *H.R.A.*, I, iv, pp.144-5 and 249, (9-5-1803); *H.R.N.S.W.*, Vol. v, p.137, (9-5-1803).
13. *H.R.A.*, I, iv, pp.144-5, (9-5-1803); 152-3; 248-9 and 415.
14. *H.R.A.*, I, iv, pp.8-9, (14-2-1803); *H.R.N.S.W.*, Vol. v, p.835, Memorandum on proposed settlement, *H.R.A.*, III, i, pp.1-2 and note 1, p.781.
15. *H.R.A.*, I, iv, pp.8-9, 18, and note 8, p.783, and note 16, pp.786-7.
16. *H.R.A.*, III, i, p.26. (NB—The *Ocean*, had arrived on 7 October, and the *Calcutta*, with Collins, on 9 October 1803).
17. *Ibid.*, p.27; and Harris' report, *Ibid.*, p.31.
18. Lieutenant James Tuckey, 'Memoir of a Chart of Port Phillip' (hereafter cited as 'Memoir'), 1803, *H.R.A.*, III, i, pp.114ff., esp. 116-7; cf. Tuckey, J.H. *An Account of a Voyage to Establish a Colony at Port Philp [sic] in Bass Strait . . .*, (hereafter cited as 'Account'), (London, 1805), pp.157-9, and Pateshall, N. *A Short Account of a Voyage Round the Globe in HMS 'Calcutta', 1803-1804*, (Melbourne, 1980), p.61.
19. Tuckey, 'Account', *op.cit.*, pp.164 and 166; and *H.R.A.*, III, i, p.287, (10-11-1804), and Pateshall, *op.cit.*, p.61.
20. Tuckey, 'Account', *op.cit.*, pp.5-6 and 157, and 'Memoir', *H.R.A.*, III, i, p.110.
21. *H.R.A.*, III, i, pp.28-9, (5-11-1803).
22. *Ibid.*, pp.35ff.
23. *Ibid.*, pp.39ff. See also Grimes' Journal *op.cit.*
24. *H.R.A.*, III, i, pp.217-8, (28-2-1804); cf. Garrison Orders, *Ibid.*, pp.88-9
25. Tuckey, *op.cit.*, p.153; on timber, see *H.R.A.*, I, iv, p.146, (9-5-1803).
26. *H.R.A.*, III, i, p.152, (30-12-1802); and p.589, (1-6-1804).
27. See *H.R.A.*, I, v, p.223, (20-12-1804); p.283, (16-1-1805); *C.O.*, 201/36, ff. 164-5; and Oxley's remarks, *H.R.A.*, III, i, pp.776-7.
28. *Reports of the Commissioner of Inquiry on the State of Agriculture and Trade in the Colony of New South Wales*, *B.P.P.*, 1823, No. 136, pp.18-19; *H.R.A.*, I, xi, p.98, (31-7-1823); and p.555, (24-3-1825).
29. *H.R.A.*, I, xi, p.555, *H.R.A.*, I, xii, p.643, (24-1-1825), p.656, (20-4-1826).
30. *H.R.A.*, I, xii, pp.192-3 and 194-5, 1-3-1826; *Ibid.*, p.699; p.701 and *H.R.A.*, III, v, pp.827ff.
31. *H.R.A.*, I, xiii, p.74, (4-2-1827); *H.R.A.*, III, v, pp.842-6, (24-1-1827); *Ibid.*, p.854.
32. *H.R.A.*, III, v, pp.835 and 848-9; *H.R.A.*, I, xiii, pp.240 and 667; and p.450.
33. *H.R.A.*, I, xiii, p.734, (20-1-1828); *H.R.A.*, III, v, pp.854ff, (27-3-1827); *C.O.*, 201/182, ff.19-20, (6-4-1827); and 201/185 ff.23-5.
34. *H.R.A.*, I, xiii, p.240; *C.O.*, 201/182, ff.19-20; *C.O.*, 201/190, ff.341, 4-1-1827, f.376; Gellibrand and Batman to the Governor of N.S.W., cited, Labilliere, *op.cit.*, ii, pp.34-5.
35. *H.R.A.*, I, xvii, p.468, (4-7-1834); and p.615, (25-12-1834); Hartwell, R.M. *The Economic Development of Van Diemen's Land*, (Melbourne, 1954), p.39; Perry, T.M. *Australia's First Frontier*, (Melbourne, 1963), Ch. 4; Bassett, Marnie, *The Hentys*, (Melbourne, 1954), Part v, Ch. 7; *A.D.B.*, entries for William Dutten, Vol. 1, p. 340, John and Charles Mills, Vol. II, p.231, and John Hart, Vol. III, p.355; *Argus*, (31-3-1854).
36. Brown, P.L. (ed.), *The Narrative of George Russell of Golf Hill*, (1935), p.92; Bell, G.P. and others to the Secretary of State, cited Labilliere, *op.cit.*, ii, p.36; Bassett, *op.cit.*, pp.291-2; and p.283ff, (18-4-1834); Boys, *op.cit.*, pp.34-8.
37. Billot, C.P. *John Batman and the Founding of Melbourne*, (Melbourne, 1979), Ch. 9, citing Batman's Journal; Boys, *op.cit.*, p.40.

[38] Billott, (Batman's Journal), *op.cit.*, p.101; *C.O.*, 201/58, 4-7-1835, No. 53, *B.P.P.*, 1836, No. 512, *Report from Select Committee on the Disposal of Lands in the Colonies*, p.224; Billot (Batman's Journal), *op.cit.*, p.309, note 24; Long, C.R. 'Who founded Melbourne', *J.R.A.H.S.*, Vol. XIX (1934), pp.67-71.

[39] Billot, C.P. (ed.), *Melbourne's Missing Chronicle: Fawkner's Journal at Port Phillip, 1835-6*, (Melbourne, 1982), pp.1-6; Boys, *op.cit.*, pp.43-4; Greig, A.W. (ed.), 'Some new documentary evidence concerning the foundation of Melbourne—Lancey's diary', *V.H.M.*, Vol. xii, (1927-8), pp.109-14.

[40] Anderson, Hugh. 'The Place for a Township', *V.H.M*, Vol. xii, (1970), pp.350-9; Proclamation 26-8-1835, *V.G.G.*, (2-9-1835).

[41] Billot, (Fawkner's Journal), pp.10-12; *op.cit.*, p.45.

[42] *Ibid.*, pp.12-16; Boys, *op.cit.*, pp.43-4, *H.R.A.*, I, xviii, pp.153-8, (10-10-1835).

[43] *H.R.A.*, I, xvii, pp.615-6, (25-12-1834); *C.O.*, 280/58, f.179, 4-7-1835.

[44] *H.R.A.*, I, xvii, pp.379-81, (13-4-1836); p.540 and Government Notice, p.833.

[45] *H.R.V.*, Vol. 1, (1981), Chs. 3 and 7.

[46] *H.R.A.*, I, xviii, p.781, (14-6-1837).

[47] Arthur to Spring Rice, cited in Labilliere, *op.cit.*, ii, p.48, (4-7-1835); *H.R.A.*, I, xviii, p.781, (10-10-1835).

[48] Brown, P.L. 'The Batman Stone', *V.R.M.*, Vol. xxxiv, (1963), p.11.

Chapter XI

Melbourne: A Kangaroo Advance

Susan Priestley

After the landing of the Batman and Fawkner parties in the winter of 1835, just over a year elapsed before the governor in Sydney, Sir Richard Bourke, received the despatch from Lord Glenelg, Secretary of State for the Colonies, which bestowed official status on the Port Phillip settlement. The despatch was dated 13 April 1836[1] and reached New South Wales more than four months later. William Lonsdale, appointed by Bourke as the first police magistrate, brought the news to Port Phillip when he arrived on 27 September after a voyage around the coast of only six days. With 'contrary winds' ships could take up to three weeks.[2] The alternative of travelling overland from Sydney in 1836 was really out of the question because of the 'very mountainous and impracticable country which intervenes'.[3]

The ensuing fourteen years saw the transition of the settlement on the Yarra, sometimes called Bearbrass or Bearpurt by the Vandemonian vanguard,[4] into the city of Melbourne, the chief urban centre of a newly independent colony. This was a remarkably swift metamorphosis, especially since economic conditions in the burgeoning southern district of New South Wales were so volatile. An initial feverish speculative boom based on wool and land sales, which reached its height in 1839, overlapped with enthusiastic waves of imported goods and immigrant people. In May 1836 less than a hundred persons were in the camps and huts strung out at no great distance from the landing spot on the northern river bank. By September 1838 more than a thousand people were included in William Lonsdale's rough population count for the 'town of Melbourne'.[5] The town plan, as marked out by surveying pegs, then extended for a mile along the Yarra and three-quarters of a mile to the north-west.

The newcomers were motivated by strong commercial instincts. The market demand for land was so intense that, by December 1839, central Melbourne land purchased at five separate sales of 117 acres had raised an average of £209 per acre for government revenue. Suburban land, that is within five miles of the central grid, averaged one twentieth of the town price. Most of this land immediately adjoined the central area to the east, the north and across the river to the south. To the west was swampy land leading to the Saltwater or Maribyrnong River, and south-west beyond that was the port of Williamstown where twenty-seven small parcels of town land had also been sold. About 130 country lots, usually square mile blocks, averaged sixteen shillings an acre, but even this value was enhanced by its Melbourne connection. It was all in the county of Bourke which extended not more than thirty or forty miles into the interior. Mt Macedon was the northern limit.[6]

Merchants, bankers, builders, stock and land agents flooded in to buy land and gain a foothold in the new trading centre. In 1838 four banks including a local enterprise opened for business, but the Port Phillip Bank did not survive beyond 1843 and the depths of the business collapse. However, a Port Phillip Savings Bank which opened in January 1842, was the foundation for the present State Bank of Victoria. After 1840, when Melbourne was declared a free port, shipping warehousing and wharfage businesses multiplied, bolstering the western end of town on the rise above the river as the natural hub. Wooden wharves at last began to edge the river basin and stretch downstream. There were bond storage sheds and a specialist dock to off-load building lime and stone which was carried down on lighters from west of the Maribyrnong. Warehouses for storing the wool and hides produced in the hinterland were among the first buildings to use bluestone, the blue-grey basalt which was to become a prized characteristic of the city.

At the census of March 1841, there were nearly 4500 Melbourne residents, which was more than one third of the whole population of the southern district of New South Wales.[7] However, with pastoral and trading enterprises so interdependent there was as yet little distinction between town and out-of-town attitudes. Pastoralists and traders signed the original petitions seeking Port Phillip immigration schemes and independence from New South Wales. Urban and rural outlooks merged even closer during the general gloominess of the depressed years 1841-4, although townsmen were worse affected by debts incurred in buying land and speculating in merchandise. Those with purely pastoral interests had to buy stock and basic supplies but paid only an annual licence fee for their land and so were less likely to be forced to the depths of bankruptcy. Some town-dwellers went bush where living was certainly cheaper. While they were living in Melbourne, lawyer Andrew McCrae's wife, Georgiana, rarely bought fish because it was expensive, but paid the baker's wife five to seven shillings for beef and pigeon pies. In 1843 she moved reluctantly to a pastoral lease down the bay near Arthur's Seat where her husband and other workers, or Aboriginals who befriended them, spent time catching fish and small game which were salt-dried or turned into pies by their house servant.[8]

In rural districts Aboriginal skills in gathering food supplies, in locating water and in the easy handling of European stock animals where they were so disposed, won them a small degree of acceptance from Europeans, but in Melbourne the Aboriginals were almost entirely displaced in the first few years of settlement. After William Thomas began his field work as 'Assistant Protector of Aborigines' in the central districts in April 1839, he was taken to task severely if any Aboriginals gathered in the town area. The river flats and lagoons which had been their rich larder grew foetid with town drainage and the trees which sheltered opossums and yielded building bark, manna and sweet gum were felled at an alarming rate for European fuel and timber.

Recovery from economic depression in the late 1840s hastened Aboriginal dispossession and intensified town development. The recovery of town fortunes, based as they were on commercial agencies and processing pastoral products like meat and hides, took a season or two longer than the pastoral upturn. This had been sparked by selling tallow recovered through the boiling-down process, and consolidated by a gradual rise in wool prices on the English market.[9] The census of March 1851 showed that the whole Port Phillip population had increased sevenfold since 1841, and that almost 23,000 people lived within the five-mile radial boundaries of Melbourne. This meant that the city (for it had achieved this status with the appointment of an Anglican bishop, Charles Perry, in June 1847) had nearly six times as many people as in 1841. However, people living in an arc of satellite villages outside the five-mile limit but totally bound to the city's fortunes may have been counted in the total. Brighton to the south, Heidelberg to the east and Pentridge (now Coburg) to the north all supplied food and fuel to the city proper. Outside Melbourne, Geelong was the only other town of any size in 1851 and although it had grown twentyfold during the decade it still claimed only 8291 residents.[10]

By mid century, Melbourne was firmly established and dominant in the southern district of New South Wales. It was already generating some of its own growth energy through primitive manufacturing in vehicles, building materials and food processing, although its role in channelling goods to and from its hinterland remained crucial. Officially and practically, that hinterland comprised the whole colony of Victoria when proclaimed by a British Act of August 1850. The northern boundary was the Murray river, extended by a line from the river's source to Cape Howe on the east coast. The western boundary was longtitude 141 degrees E from the Murray river to the southern coast. Extended economic links across the Murray were forged when trafficable river crossings along its middle and upper reaches were formed by settlers who found it easier to get to Melbourne than to Sydney.

Essential to Melbourne's progress were lines of communication with the economic wealth of the hinterland, as well as with Sydney, the nearest focus of authority, and with Britain, the ultimate authority and the pastoralists' marketplace. In February 1839 the first mail sent direct to London and not by way of Sydney went on a ship that took away some of the wool clip, but not until June 1841 did the imperial authorities allow mail from Britain to be unloaded anywhere but Sydney. Mail for Melbourne was then charged again for its passage southwards, a matter which heightened the popular grievance against New South Wales authority. The deepest source of grievance however lay with Governor George Gipps' refusal to allow money collected from the Port Phillip land sales to be used entirely for bringing immigrants to Port Phillip. Gipps insisted on using a great deal of it on immigrants to Sydney. Similarly the Melbournians wanted increased expenditure on public works on the grounds that they were a new settlement and Gipps' efforts to economise in this area, on orders from London, were not popular.

Attempts were made from the earliest days to create passable lines of road feeding into Melbourne. The Sydney road, taking a roughly diagonal line across the district, guided inland settlers to the bay port and in 1838 a horseback mail was introduced. By 1843 the overland mail time had been reduced from sixteen to seven days, the service was twice weekly and the volume of mail demanded that a light-wheeled vehicle be used. It was 1848, however, before a covered conveyance, which gave weather protection to the mails and the occasional passenger, was put on the run. Private overland travel was still regarded as somewhat heroic. It took the newly appointed Roman Catholic Bishop, James Alipius Goold, nineteen days including four rest days to travel from Sydney in 1848. Despite high fares and mail rates during most of the 1840s the sea route to Sydney was preferred because of its greater speed and comfort—if the weather was not too unfavourable! Once steamers were introduced, in 1840, they were less likely to be blown off course and could make the journey in four days, but vessels rugged enough to provide a regular service to Sydney and across Bass Strait to Launceston could not be put on the routes until 1843. By then smaller steamers made regular daily trips between the Yarra wharves, Williamstown and Geelong. Westwards along the coast, steamer services to Port Fairy, Portland and Adelaide were arranged only 'as opportunity afforded'.[11] The most practical routes into Gippsland fanned out from the sea-landing at Port Albert. By 1850 year-round overland travel, at least along the main mail routes, was possible in western Victoria where basalt plains provided a firm base and the rivers were not broad. By contrast heavy traffic churned up long stretches of the Sydney road making impassable bogs in wet weather or when rivers spread out in flood.[12]

Commerce was the lifeblood of Melbourne's growth and communications its arteries, but the complexities of urbanism can be better understood from a whole range of interconnecting viewpoints. A classic model used by sociologists suggests as major viewpoints the physical structure of an urban centre, its social organisation and the set of attitudes and ideas which shape and control characteristically urban behaviour.[13] Aspects of each of these factors influenced the attainment of Melbourne's position in 1850.

*   *   *

In March 1847, Robert Russell, one of Melbourne's early surveyors and designers, who was largely forgotten in his old age, acknowledged in his diary after some time away that 'Port Phillip has advanced wonderfully'. But he added somewhat wryly 'its advance has been that of a kangaroo, a long jump and a long rest after it'.[14] Even so, there were signs of a gathering of the limbs in 1847 ready for the next bound which reached a high point in 1849-50.

Melbourne was named by Governor Bourke on his visit of inspection in March 1837. It was then a motley collection of tents, mud, timber or wattle and daub huts with a few small houses roofed with shingle and thatch. Fourteen months later, a new immigrant, William Waterfield, noted that building activities on the grassy town site were like extensive preparations for a rural fair, 'many of the buildings being wood and more like Booths than houses'.[15] Energy for this first long leap in physical growth came from the six sales of town and suburban land between June 1837 and June 1840. In March 1841 the *Port Phillip Herald* noticed the 'great alteration' in Melbourne's appearance during the previous year:

> [B]uildings are erecting, gardens laid out, old houses pulled down, and their places supplied by neat and elegant structures of brick and timber.[16]

Presbyterian parson James Clow certainly intended an impression of elegance when in 1838 he built a thirteen-roomed prefabricated house on several isolated acres facing Lonsdale Street near the Swanston Street corner. It boasted an impressively large ballroom, and a verandah, while ornamental and kitchen garden, horse paddock and stables completed the setting. Most houses were much simpler—two or four rooms sometimes joined as a terrace row with a narrow front garden strip and a long backyard for the outhouses. Businessmen and traders often lived in rooms in the hub of town, close to or partitioned off from their workplace.

In 1841 public buildings had begun to assume an air of permanence. The churches of St James and St Francis and chapels in Collins Street belonging to the Wesleyans and the Independents were either newly completed or under construction in brick or stone. Government offices remained unimposing. The police office was still being described as a wooden dog kennel in 1846.[17] Only the Customs House facing the river wharves was of stone, although its construction had suffered long delays due to changing contractors and lack of funds. The gaol and courthouse remained in inadequate temporary quarters until stone buildings were begun on a rise to the north-east, well away from the commercial hub which was bounded by William, Bourke, Swanston and Flinders Streets.

True suburban development accelerated from 1839 at one remove from the central grid. By 1841 there were suburban clusters along the bay at Williamstown, Port Melbourne, St Kilda and Brighton. Others were on the eastern hill at Newtown (later Fitzroy) and at Jolimont, and more stretched along the Yarra at Richmond, Abbotsford, South Yarra and Hawthorn. On the south side of the river immediately opposite Swanston Street, with access provided by a punt and later a wooden bridge, there was a canvas town to accommodate new immigrants. It was begun about 1838 and was refurbished to accommodate the gold immigrants of the 1850s.

During the depressed years 1841-4 town construction slackened noticeably. Even public works funding was limited, most effort being put into the gaol and into raising the level of the dam across the Yarra at the falls. This work was to prevent rising salt tides and drainage wastes from polluting the residents' drinking water. The latter was drawn up by pumps set on the river bank upstream from Swanston Street. Private water carriers paid a weekly charge to fill large barrels mounted on drays, and then hawked the water to householders, filling the house casks set just inside front or rear fences.[18] Apart from the rather muddied quality of the river water itself, keeping the house supply fresh for a week was a problem, especially in summer when the casks leaked through shrinkage, and heat encouraged 'animacules' to multiply in the remaining moistness.

Complaints about the water supply, however, were never as vociferous as complaints about the condition of the streets, chiefly the volume of dust or mud. Flooding was common. There was so little drainage that lakes or 'veritable ravines' formed readily in wet weather, especially in Flinders and Elizabeth Streets. There were periodic outcries against piles of refuse, builders' rubbish, putrefying animal carcasses ranging from horses to cats, and general filth.[19] Cesspits were less common than the practice of emptying slops on vacant land or into the vestigial drains. It was hardly surprising that in November 1842 'dysentery and infant cholera [were] decimating' young children, as Georgina McCrae noted sadly in her diary.[20]

Rotting carcases were however less immediately alarming than the hazards presented by live animals. Bolting horses, ferocious dogs, steers, goats and pigs roaming the streets almost daily threatened town dwellers or at least their dignity. Garryowen (Edmund Finn) claimed that at the inaugural procession of town councillors in December 1842, the constable Joseph Hooson, who was leading the way with a square of red calico attached to a baton, was charged by a bullock in William Street and only escaped by immersing himself in a slushy ditch near Flinders Lane.[21]

After the town council began business meetings in earnest early in 1843, attempts were made to improve street orderliness. Droving cattle, sheep and pigs through the main streets was restricted, at least in business hours, once butchers' killing yards and the cattle market were confined to the outskirts. The cattle market was held on open land north of Victoria Street just beyond the cemetery. However, the dog problem remained. GW Miller who grew up in Melbourne during the 1840s, recalled that every household had loose claim to one or more dogs, mostly the large breeds like Newfoundlands, mastiffs and 'kangaroo dogs'. In September 1849, 1200 wandering dogs were reported as

Opposite: Figure 40: Russell's plan of the Town of Melbourne, 1837
(Courtesy of the Mitchell Library, State Library of New South Wales)

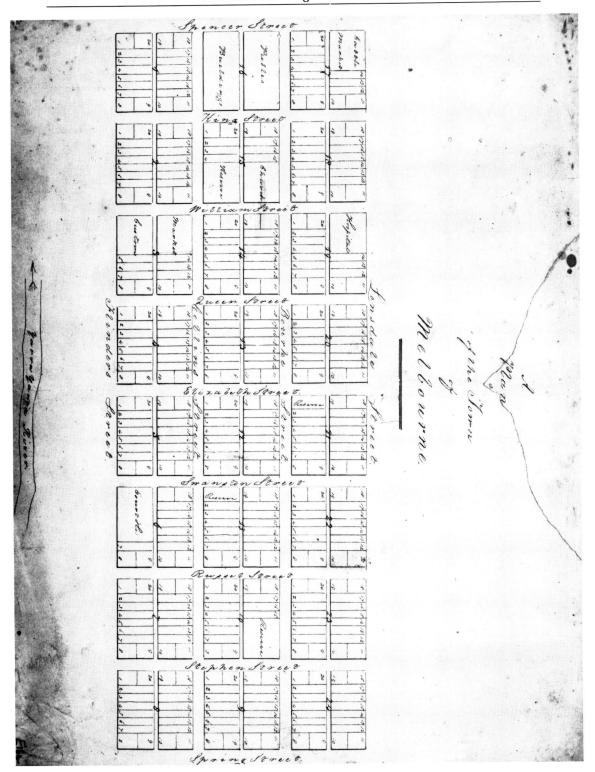

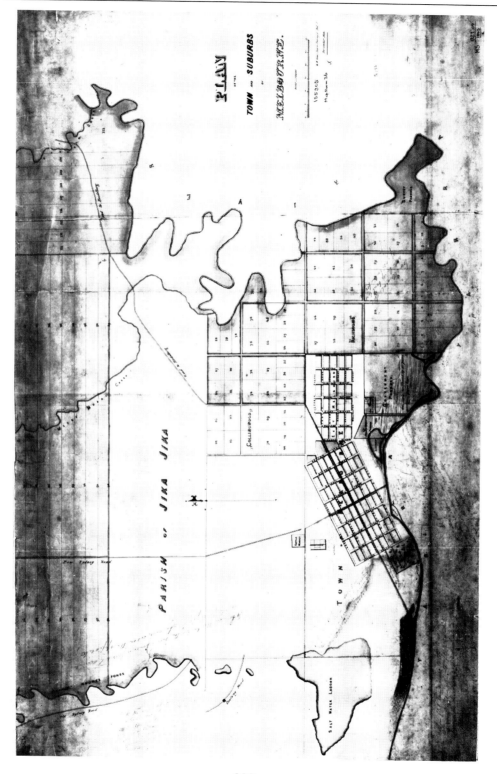

destroyed by police in an attempt to rid the streets of this 'intolerable pest'.[22] Several hundred more were added to the toll up to June 1850, but the *Argus* still complained that harassment by roaming street dogs had not appreciably diminished.[23]

There was little improvement in the condition of the streets either. From March 1843 the council took on about 150 of Melbourne's unemployed men to do road work but funds only lasted six months.[24] Some road metal was laid in the central area, but as late as 1850 newcomers ranging from the working class Chandler family to the aristocratic Hugh Childers and his wife, were jolted into comment by hazardous encounters with logs and stumps still lying around in Collins and Bourke Streets.[25]

Even the wood-lined drains built to take water away from main intersections had their dangers. In December 1850 a team of bullocks slipping on the rain-soaked surface of Elizabeth Street went into the drain under the impetus of a loaded dray, which almost capsized as a wheel caught the wooden edge.[26] Such an upset could have started a panic among other street traffic, or crushed pedestrians on the footpath. But at least central footpaths were provided by 1850, with gravelling to reduce the walking discomfort of mud or dust. Moreover pedestrians with a coin or two to spare could take up the offer of 'Keb sir keb?' from drivers of brougham-type cabs known as 'growlers', which since 1847 had been allotted cab stands in major thoroughfares like Collins Street.[27]

The increasing solidity of Melbourne between 1846 and 1850 was marked by construction works such as the stone police office and cells near the Collins-Swanston Street intersection, a corner of which was also set aside for the future town hall. There was also excitement over the single-arched stone Princes Bridge slowly taking shape to replace a wooden toll bridge, while new city churches and a synagogue were matters of public as well as denominational pride.

In September 1850, James Graham, a Melbourne merchant and managing agent wrote to one of his clients, the widow of J D L Campbell who had died from heart disease six years previously. After advising her of the pleasing rise in rents which he could now obtain for her city properties, Graham commented:

> You would not know Melbourne again—not only from the vast increase in size but also from the improvement in the style of the buildings . . . within ten months upwards of one thousand houses [have] been built in Melbourne. This is not a mere guess, but ascertained from the Official returns of the valuation lately laid before the City Council.[1]

Graham's observation would suggest that most of the 1739 houses built in Melbourne between the censuses of 1846 and 1851 went up in 1850. The 'improvement in style' which pleased his eye was partly the outcome of using brick and stone for walling. Only sixty of the 1739 were built in timber, for city council regulations had discouraged timber buildings as a fire safety measure. By 1851 the proportion of brick to timber in Melbourne's 4000 houses was three to one, an indication that the building trades together with brickmaking and quarry work provided many of the jobs available to new immigrants.[29] The improved quality of six new hotels, first licensed in the year to June 1850, was also welcomed by the *Argus* newspaper, then one of the newest voices in Melbourne's journalistic cacophony. It declared the 'Bull and Mouth' in central Bourke Street to be unsurpassed in 'these Colonies . . . for beauty of design and execution'. Seven of the old shanty-style pubs had been de-licensed.[30]

Three months later, the *Argus* was pleased to report that the 'unsightly and useless'

Opposite: Figure 41: Melbourne and suburbs 1843 (Courtesy of the Mitchell Library, State Library of New South Wales)

Lonsdale Street frontage to the horse bazaar was to be totally rebuilt. Moreover wealthy pastoralist and investor Hugh Glass was financing the building of an adjoining eight 'elegant shops'. He had already built substantial commercial premises in Elizabeth Street.[31] Such construction as far north as Lonsdale Street indicates the city's expansion. By 1850 James Clow's house at the Lonsdale-Swanston Street corner was overlooked from the north-west by the new red-brick Melbourne Hospital. Westwards along Lonsdale Street there were shops, a hotel, the horsemarket and St Francis church and school all clustered near the Elizabeth Street intersection. The area was no longer appropriate for a gentleman's villa. When sold, Clow's substantial house became the Caledonian Hotel, which advertised the ballroom as an attraction for hire.

The city was also expanding along the eastern hill at the top of Collins and Bourke Streets. In Collins Street, medical and other professional men built residences which incorporated consulting rooms, and a tiny village style St Peter's church was built on a corner of what was to become the Parliament House reserve. Halfway up the Bourke Street hill a hay and general market area attracted a fringe of smaller businesses and the inevitable hotels, but there was still open space on which tents and primitive theatres could be erected for circuses and other popular entertainments. Cricket matches and race meetings were also held on open spaces around the town perimeter. Batman's Hill, long since levelled for Spencer Street railway station, was originally the main venue, but by 1850 races were being held at Flemington and the Melbourne cricket ground was established across the river at South Melbourne. The transfer to its present site was necessary when Melbourne's original rail line to Port Melbourne was built in 1854.

The social organisation and attitudes which characterised Melbourne in 1850 had grown as an amalgam of the cultural baggage brought in by immigrants to Port Phillip and shaped by the local issues which affected them most closely. Of the latter, the nature of immigration and the desire for separation from New South Wales were the most persistent. Both served to unite Melburnians into a reasonably coherent community.

In the beginning the local need was simply for an ordered official structure, since those who had launched pastoralism in the south as a risk enterprise could not prosper without it. Until 1837 such people came largely from Van Diemen's Land and New South Wales, where convictism and colonialism had honed and moulded their inbred Britishness. In June 1836 thirty-one of these newcomers signed a petition to Governor Bourke asking that a resident magistrate be appointed.[32] They met at the house of John Batman and sent their petition to Sydney with George Stewart, a visiting magistrate whom Bourke had sent to investigate reports of attacks on Aboriginals by white men. The meeting also appointed a local 'arbitrator', James Simpson, with power to fine, who would act in all disputes except those relating to land. He would monitor and investigate any 'aggression committed upon or by the Aborigines', while the residents pledged themselves to protect the natives and keep firearms out of their ken. Furthermore, seeing the destruction of 'wild dogs' as crucial to their economic survival, the residents agreed to collect subscriptions for a fund to provide a five shillings reward for each dog destroyed. This would have been enticing bait for the servants of stockholders whose contract wage was generally less than £1 (twenty shillings) a week.[33]

The thirty-one signatories to the petition can be seen as a cross-section of the infant community. Sixteen were men who had brought over stock, mostly sheep, to settle along the Barwon, the Moorabool and the fresh upper reaches of the Maribyrnong River. Some were overseers or the managing member of pastoral partnerships. Already a little apart,

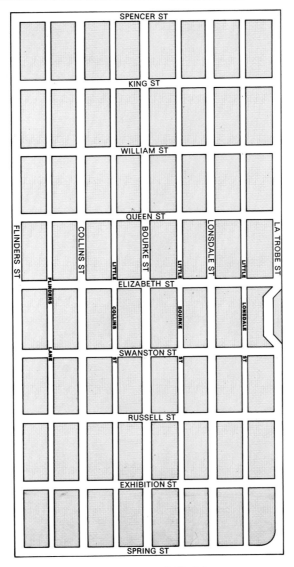

Figure 42: Melbourne's 'little' streets

John and Henry Batman and JP Fawkner largely confined their interests to the Yarra settlement. So did George Hollins who became John Batman's overseer, while publican Michael Carr, boat-builder William Winberry, carpenter William Diprose, Michael Leonard and John Hyland seem to have had an urban outlook from the beginning. Carr and Hyland were among the buyers at the first Melbourne land sales. William Buckley, lately returned to European contact after three decades with the Aboriginals, signed a mark, and so did three of the remaining four petitioners. These four remain shadowy in the later historical record but they or their namesakes were town or pastoral labourers, contract sawyers, petty thieves and occasional drunkards.

The petitioners' request for a resident magistrate was answered when William Lonsdale

225

arrived with his wife and infant daughter at the end of September 1836 in the *Rattlesnake*. Another party in the *Stirlingshire* followed a week later. The new arrivals included a military detachment of thirty-three soldiers; three surveyors; three constables; two customs officers and personal servants as well as their wives and families.

From the outset Port Phillip was regarded as a haven for the free and enterprising of all classes. Stockholders like Batman, Thompson and Wedge who had faced 'lawless and intimidatory behaviour' from many of the 'lower order of people who had come over on adventure'[34] especially welcomed the protection of the magistracy. Even so subsequent arrivals were infected by defiance towards the current order of society and this was bolstered by the general shortage of labour in Port Phillip. Complaints abound of servants refusing employment except for higher wages, demanding short-term rather than yearly contracts and better quality or more abundant rations. A servant girl hired straight off the immigrant ship by William Waterfield got a better offer from the next enquirer and simply did not appear. Even when unemployment was alarmingly high during the depression years, a number of labourers, all married men with children, went on strike against lowered pay. Moreover unemployed men often bluntly rejected offers of work in the bush because conditions there were most uncongenial. Town life was seen as more secure and offering greater chances for work and advancement.[35]

The much vaunted claim that unlike New South Wales and Van Diemen's Land the new settlement had no 'convict stain' helped to create a unifying sense of identity which newcomers quickly absorbed. The fact that, between 1837 and 1839, about 150 convicts were sent from Sydney to work in government service ranging from labour gangs to trade and shop work was generally overlooked. A few also came as assigned servants to early pastoralists, and some convicts who had served their time were taken on as police constables. Other 'expirees' from the older colonies also came looking for a fresh start. Tailor Michael McNamara who stood for election to the Melbourne municipal council in November 1848 was said to have had a convict background. His time in the limelight was brief. Seven months later he vanished from Melbourne 'leaving a wife and many creditors'.[36]

At the census of 1851, only sixty-five men still held tickets of leave and seventy-nine men and two women were still in government or private assignment in Victoria. However, hints of previous bondage were recognized in the 3053 men and 356 women who were categorised as 'other free persons', distinct from the bulk of the population who had either been born in the colony or had 'arrived free'. About one third of these 3409 may have been the 'exiles', who arrived during an otherwise slack period of migration between 1844 and 1848. 'Exiles', or Pentonvillians, were persons convicted of minor crimes in Britain who had served part of their time in the British prisons of Pentonville, Parkhurst and Millbank and who were then released on conditional pardon or ticket-of-leave if they agreed to leave Britain and spend the remainder of their lives in the colonies. About 1700 of such 'exiles' were sent to Port Phillip. Squatters generally welcomed what they regarded as an addition to the labour market, but a vocal section of Melburnians remained hostile, protesting at the dumping of ex-convicts on their free society. They doubted too whether the exiles would go bush any more willingly than other workers.[37]

Well into his old age, the early settler Edmund Finn carried the memory of the town's indignation when, a week after a gang of burglars and 'crooked' professional men arrived on the *Thomas Arbuthnot* in May 1847, a number of skilful and daring robberies took place in Melbourne which defied police solution and probably set up some men with capital for life. But even Finn admitted in 1883 that some exiles had made good. One had been a Melbourne city councillor, but had failed in a bid to become mayor, and at least four others were local magistrates.[38]

The remarkable swelling of Port Phillip's population after 1838, however, was predominantly the result of free and direct migration from Britain.[39] A very small element of diversity was provided by migrants from Switzerland and the German states. According to the admittedly imperfect statistics, more than 90,000 people arrived by sea up to December 1851, including many from the other Australian colonies. Several thousand more probably came overland. Immigration was heaviest between 1839 and 1842, and again after 1848. In the twelve months of 1841 alone, 10,000 people landed, doubling the population in a year.

About one-third of the overseas immigrants were assisted by government bounties, their passages paid for from the proceeds of land sales. While the organisers of the bounty system intended that it would supply the labour considered necessary to the prosperity of the new society, many bounty immigrants seem to have cherished the hope that their term of wage labour would be short. Part of the urge to emigrate was the expectation of bettering oneself so that independence and self-sufficiency were prime goals. Some looked to achieve this in the rural style idealised by John Dunmore Lang in *Phillipsland*. It was published in 1847 as part of his colonial immigration campaign. As an example, Lang glowingly described the McMillan family, who had arrived on the *David Clarke* at the end of 1839 and within seven years had become successful Brighton farmers about to embark on pastoral enterprises.[40]

Publicised success stories of bounty immigrants who followed town lifestyles are rare. Three who made good with relative speed were Richard Heales, his wife Rhoda, and Edmund Ashley. They arrived in 1842 when unemployment was reaching a peak and occasional day labour the only source of work. Yet by 1847 Heales had returned to his trade as coachbuilder, with a business in his own name in Flinders Lane, where Ashley joined him as a partner. In 1850 Heales was elected to the city council as the precursor to a political career in which he led one Victorian ministry and held a major portfolio in another.[41]

Heales came to Melbourne from an established urban background. His father was an inronmonger and he had served his apprenticeship in London. However, the background of the 60,000 immigrants who came *without* assistance from government is harder to determine, because they were generally untrammelled by bureaucratic records. Many must have had similar urban backgrounds and all of them would have brought at least small amounts of capital with which to establish a new lifestyle. One who came unassisted was John O'Shannassy, who led three Victorian ministries between 1857 and 1863 and whose parliamentary career spanned three decades. O'Shannassy's surveyor father had died in Tipperary, Ireland in 1831 when his son was aged thirteen. The boy learnt merchanting in the drapery and wine business, then married in 1839 and left for the colonies. Although he turned first to rural pursuits, the holding which he took up at Western Port did not prosper, because it was too small and there was not enough capital to carry it through the low prices of the depression. Aided by his wife's astute sense of business, he then opened a draper's shop in Collins Street in 1845, and was able to begin his political career by standing in the Melbourne council elections of 1847.[42]

A survey of the occupations of all town councillors between 1842 and 1850[43] show that about two thirds got their main income from urban trade, whether as wholesale merchants, stock agents, retail grocers and drapers, or builders. Single individuals were a saddler, a tailor and a coachmaker. At least a dozen were publicans, brewers, distillers, or wine and spirit merchants—an indication of the unfailing profitability of alcohol. The remaining one-third were professionals, notably journalists, surgeons and lawyers. Some were gentlemen in the sense that their income came from investments and property rather than day-to-day trading. Gentlemen, in the sense of being gently born,[44] were rarely councillors, although several offered themselves as members of the town council's precursor, the Melbourne Market Commission of 1841. At that municipal body's only election, there were eight successful and five unsuccessful candidates of whom only four were engaged in trade. Of these four, a publican and a builder were successful and two merchants were unsuccessful. The rest, many of whom had at least pretensions to gentility, were professionals often with substantial pastoral interests. Their urban focus was perhaps not so singleminded as the broader trading interests which later held sway on the city council. The urbanism of Melbourne in the late 1840s was more intensified.

Men with business interests and 'working men' who had risen to be self-employed or even employers on a small scale were generally recognised to have proved their fitness for municipal office. The European class advantage of gentlemen over tradesmen quickly lost some of its force in the Antipodes. Voting cliques and factions, among ratepayers and on the council itself, were influenced by inherited ethnic and religious groupings and perhaps even more by local lodge and trade associations, which also afforded social outlets for their members.[45] Such clubs and societies are a distinctively urban activity and their proliferation in Melbourne can be traced through the town's newspapers during the 1840s.

Town and out-of-town interests at first united in the separation movement which was under way as early as 1840. Its roots lay partly in the pride and confident self-assertiveness of the earliest immigrants. William Waterfield noted in his diary for instance that in July 1838 a gentleman from 'the Geelong side of the country' had told him that Melbourne's progress was 'far in advance of Swan River [Perth] though the latter was twelve years old'. In November a ship's captain had given him 'a rather unfavourable account of Adelaide', which was confirmed in June 1839 by Joseph Hawdon, fresh from overlanding cattle, who declared that 'Adelaide is not to be compared with Port Phillip'. Five months later Melbourne's social luminary and speculator PW Welsh gave the Yarra settlement just 'seven years to make it equal Sydney'.[46]

People holding such attitudes readily became irritated, even outraged, if they suspected curbs were being placed on their progress. In May 1839 the *Port Phillip Patriot* protested at the district's enforced submission to Sydney authorities and the 'parsimony of the New South Wales Legislative Council'.[47] The sale of land and the disposal of the resultant revenue in promoting the district's interest, whether in obtaining labour or on building public works, was the crux of the problem. From October 1839 when Port Phillip's new superintendent, Charles Joseph La Trobe, arrived, he was the medium through which local agitation for separation and responses from the various governors in Sydney and the Colonial Office in London were channelled. Analysis of these responses has shown that the Colonial Office, La Trobe and the Sydney authorities came to be held in descending order of esteem by the separatists.[48] According to editor Hugh McCrae's note in *Georgiana's Journal*, La Trobe's local fall from grace began at a welcome banquet to Governor Gipps in October 1841 when J P Fawkner among others overheard him declare his willingness to play 'second fiddle' to any tune the Sydney-centred Gipps cared to play.[49]

Melbourne's first separation meetings held in 1840 sought to by-pass Sydney by sending a petition direct to the imperial parliament. Such a destination only served to accentuate the residents' hyperbole:

> It is entirely undeniable that Melbourne possesses natural advantages far superior to any other seaport in Van Diemen's Land or New South Wales . . . From the central position of Melbourne, as well as from the richness of the lands of Australia Felix, the extraordinary influx of stock and population must soon render it one of, if not quite, the most populous of provinces in this Hemisphere.[50]

From its distant, if not to say aloof, perspective the Colonial Office considered that local feelings of isolation from the centre of power would be relieved by Port Phillip's quota of six members, who were to be elected to the New South Wales Legislative Council of 1843. An imperial act of 1842 also made provision for district councils. In fact both measures accentuated the isolation. Few residents were prepared to travel to Sydney for meetings of the Legislative Council particularly as it became apparent that the Port Phillip group was a hopelessly small minority in a council of thirty-six.[51] Furthermore this council blocked the enabling legislation which would have allowed district councils to raise and dispose of local revenue. Governor Gipps did incorporate the district of Bourke and nominated its council but local landholders rejected the notion of paying rates to be used for instance, in policing the district by a force which was wholly under the control of the Sydney government.

In 1844 the separation movement was renewed. At a preliminary meeting in Melbourne on 22 March Archibald Cunninghame, a barrister with pastoral interests, gave the 'speech of the day':

> It is more than time that this fair province should have a Government and Governor of its own, with a Legislature empowered to frame laws suited to the circumstances of a free colony . . . aiding in the development of her vast resources, and in spreading population over these fertile plains . . .[52]

Later in the year a 'separation committee' was appointed largely under the direction of Edward Curr, former manager of The Van Diemen's Land Company who had embarked on a Port Phillip pastoral enterprise with his family. In Melbourne, Geelong and Portland funds were raised to send a delegate to the Westminster Parliament to put the residents' point of view directly. Archibald Cunninghame was chosen and sailed from Port Phillip in January 1846.

To the dismay of town residents, reports then began to filter back that Cunninghame had advocated sending convict labour to Port Phillip and was also proposing a grossly restricted franchise for the local legislative council. At a public meeting in October his 'official misbehaviour' was denounced by all but two of the seven speakers. Urban commercial strength maintained that Cunninghame was simply an agent for the squattocracy, and for that self-interest was prepared to sacrifice 'the whole agricultural commercial and trading interests of the colony'.[53] Those interests certainly strengthened Melbourne's commercial revival after 1846. Cunninghame chose not to return to Port Phillip, and in any event separation came under more serious review at the Colonial Office in the following year.

Evidence of renewed city growth and more diverse industry may be gleaned not only from population counts but also from export statistics after 1846 and especially in 1849-50. Industries which produced soap, candles, leather and tannin accounted for the doubling in processed or manufactured exports from the colony after 1846. Most were located on the Yarra close to the point of export[54] although some soap, possibly produced in a Barwon River works, was exported from Geelong in 1847. Melbourne's strong early commercial base is evident from the census taken on 2 March 1851. Nearly 30 per cent of the city's workforce of 8896 were in commerce trade or manufacturing. Only five per cent were professional people, 17 per cent were domestic servants, 17.5 per cent were skilled mechanics or 'artificers' and nearly 15 per cent were general labourers.

Such was the balance of interests which actively monitored the progress of separation. By 1848 news from London made it clear that separation was to be part of a revised constitution for the colonies, although unsettled British politics was to delay the passing of the Bill even after its introduction in 1849. Predictably the separationists in Melbourne held an indignation meeting on 26 November. It was chaired by the mayor of the city, AFA Greeves, whose amalgam of interests was a mirror of the emergent metropolitan energy. Son of a Yorkshire merchant, he had studied medicine before his migration to Port Phillip in 1840. He continued to practise medicine, being one of the local team which first operated with chloroform in 1848, but he also owned a hotel, edited the *Port Phillip Gazette* for a time, helped found the town's debating society and a branch of the Oddfellows lodge, and was a town councillor from 1843.[55]

Greeves shared the platform at the 1849 indignation meeting with eight other citizens of broad interests. All were either past or current councillors and included merchant George Ward Cole. Two with early pastoral connections were CH Ebden and JL Foster, but both had retired to comfortable outer suburban estates and were active in the public affairs of Melbourne. The meeting drew up a protest petition couched in 'unmincing' terms, and in forwarding it, La Trobe felt bound to convey the local mood by emphasising that 'the longer the meditated separation may be delayed, the more embarrassing the task of governing the district must become'.[56]

A revised Bill was introduced in 1850 and news of its progress through Parliament was monitored in the colony. Although there was always a lapse of several months before news arrived, local confidence was such that a meeting was called in September 1850 to plan 'a scheme of rejoicings' to be held once the news of the Bill's passage was received. A rival 'unofficial' meeting of citizens called for moves that Edmund Finn rather contemptuously described as the 'Politics of the Masses'. Led by temperance hotel owner, John Tankard, the citizens wanted rejoicings to include the immediate construction of a People's Hall, and there was talk of vote by secret ballot and universal suffrage.[57] A year later Geelong also formed a political People's Association so it is evident that Victoria's popular democracy, which is often attributed to the inrush of gold immigrants, grew on ground already prepared in the urban environment.

For the moment, however, both officials and radicals welcomed separation. London newspapers reporting that the Act only awaited Royal Assent were delivered by a ship's captain who arrived in Port Phillip Bay on Monday, 11 November 1850.[58] On the following day there was a formal flag-raising ceremony and gun salute. On Wednesday evening illuminations throughout the town marked the beginning of a two-day holiday. Painted transparencies, either set in windows or mounted outside and lit from behind, played on the themes of Victoria, Loyal, Separate and Free.

Church services of thanksgiving on Thursday morning preceded general street celebrations, which passed off with great gusto and no mishaps, despite exploding firecrackers and lighted tar barrels being rolled about the streets by tipsy revellers.

Friday's street procession drew crowds estimated at 15,000, about three-quarters of Melbourne's population. Masonic and benefit lodge members paraded in jewels and regalia, clubs and societies with banners. A small group of Germans had painted no less than three banners and some of the city's trade associations put on displays for the parade. The highlight was claimed to be the dray, organised by Melbourne's printers, on which a working press was mounted continually throwing off a list drawn up by JP Fawkner of the most important events from 1835 to 1850.[59] The sheets were distributed to the crowds lining the route with a view to fostering the sense of history which some citizens had already developed. The separation revelries reflected Melbourne's unchallenged central position in the new colony of Victoria. This position was enhanced during the even more momentous events of the decades to come.

Notes

[1] See *H.R.V.*, Vol. 1, (Melbourne, 1981), p.24.

[2] *Ibid.*, p.39.

[3] *Ibid.*, p.29.

[4] *Ibid.*, pp.34, 31.

[5] *H.R.V.*, Vol. 3, p.433.

[6] *Ibid.*, p.150.

[7] Census, 1841.

[8] McCrae, Hugh, (ed.), *Georgiana's Journal*, 3rd ed. (Sydney, 1978), pp.67, 114, 226.

[9] Dingle, T. *Settling*, Vol. 2 of *The Victorians*, (Melbourne, 1984), pp.21-28.

[10] Census, 1851.

[11] Boys, R.D. *First Years at Port Phillip 1834-42*, 2nd ed. (Melbourne, 1959).

[12] McGowan, R.M. *A Study of Social Life and Conditions in Early Melbourne*, (M.A. thesis, U.M., 1951) and Priestley, Susan, *Making their Mark*, Vol. 3 of *The Victorians, op.cit.*, pp.45-58, deals with road and sea transport generally.

[13] Wirth, Louis. 'Urbanism as a Way of Life' in *American Journal of Sociology*, XLIV, (July, 1938), pp.1-24.

[14] Cited in McGowan, *op.cit.*, p.22, entry for March, 1847.

[15] *Ibid.*, entry for 23-5-1838, p.15.

[16] *Port Phillip Herald*, 5-3-1841, p.2c.

[17] *Ibid.*, 24-3-1846, p.3c.

[18] 'The History of Melbourne's Water Supply' (in two parts), by Seeger, R.C. in *V.H.M.*, Vol. 19, 1942.

[19] Newspaper descriptions quoted extensively in McGowan, *op.cit.*

[20] McCrae, *Georgiana's Journal, op.cit.*, p.106.

[21] Garryowen. *Chronicles of Early Melbourne*, facsimile ed. (Melbourne, 1977), pp.265-6.

[22] Reminiscences in *V.H.M.*, Vol. 4, 1918, pp.186-9.

[23] *Argus*, 27-6-1850, p.2f.

[24] Sullivan, Martin. *Men and Women of Port Phillip*, (Sydney, 1985), pp.223-4.

[25] *V.H.M.*, 24 (3), 1951, p.92. Childers letter cited in Oldham, J. and Stirling, A. (eds.) *Victoria. A Visitors Book*, 2nd ed. (Melbourne, 1969), pp.28-9.

[26] *Argus*, 16-12-1850, p.2.

[27] Greig, A.W. 'Cabs and Cabstands of the Seventies', *Argus*, 15-6-1929, p.10.

[28] Cited in Strahan, F. 'James Graham: The Counting House Discounted', *V.H.M.*, 36 (2), 1965, p.102.

[29] Linge, G.F.R. *Industrial Awakening*, (Canberra, 1979), p.153.

[30] *Argus*, 8-7-1850, p.2.

[31] *Ibid.*, 3-10-1850, p.2.

[32] *H.R.V.*, Vol. 3, p.505.

[33] *Ibid.*, Vol. 1, pp.36-7.

[34] *Ibid.*, p.82.

[35] See Dingle, *op.cit.*, pp.31-5. Also Sullivan, *op.cit.*

[36] Barrett, B. *The Civic Frontier: the origin of local communities and local government*, (Melbourne, 1979), p.54.

[37] McGowan, pp.80-1 and Sullivan, pp.143-52, *op.cit.*, both review the exiles question.

[38] Garryowen, 'Chronicles', *op.cit.*, pp.519-20.

[39] Broome, R. *Arriving*, Vol. 1 of *The Victorians*, *op.cit.*, p.47ff.

[40] Lang, J.D. *Phillipsland*, (Edinburgh, 1847).

[41] *A.D.B.*, Vol. 4, p.368.

[42] *Ibid.*, Vol. 5, p.378.

[43] Barrett, *op.cit.*, pp.303-5.

[44] de Serville, Paul. *Port Phillip Gentlemen*, (Melbourne, 1980), pp.29-31.

[45] Barrett, *op.cit.*, pp.44-62.

[46] Extracts printed in *H.R.V.*, Vol. 3, p.535ff.

[47] *Port Phillip Patriot*, 6-5-1839, 13-5-1839.

[48] Shaw, A.G.L. 'Agitation for the Separation of the Port Phillip District from the Colony of New South Wales, 1838-1850' in *J.R.A.H.S.*, 68 (1), 1982, pp.1-17.

[49] *Op.cit.*, p.75.

[50] Recorded in Garryowen, 'Chronicles' *op.cit.*, p.906.

[51] Shaw, also Barrett, *op.cit.*, pp.69-71.

[52] Garryowen, *op.cit.*, p.907.

[53] *Ibid.*, pp.908-9.

[54] Linge, *op.cit.*, pp.148-50.

[55] *A.D.B.*, Vol. 4, p.292.

[56] Cited by Shaw, *op.cit.*, p.13.

[57] Garryowen. 'Chronicles' *op.cit.*, pp.909-10.

[58] Serle, Geoffrey, *The Golden Age*, (Melbourne, 1963), p.17.

[59] Garryowen. 'Chronicles' *op.cit.*, pp.912-13.

Brisbane

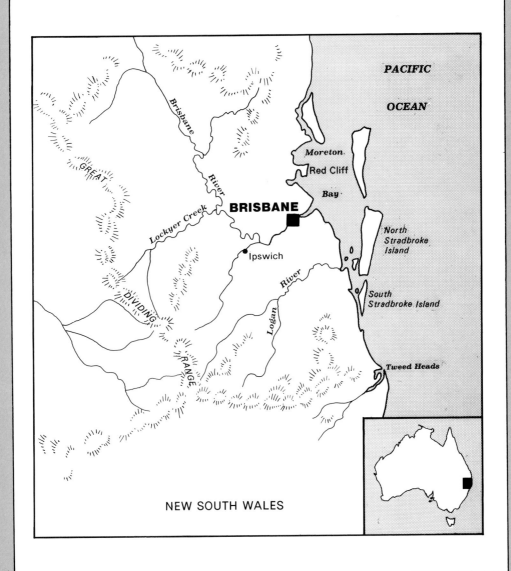

PACIFIC

OCEAN

Brisbane

River

GREAT

Moreton

Red Cliff

Bay

Lockyer Creek

BRISBANE

North
Stradbroke
Island

• Ipswich

Logan River

DIVIDING

South
Stradbroke Island

RANGE

Tweed Heads

NEW SOUTH WALES

BRISBANE.

|JAMES LANG & CO..|

The Leading, Oldest, and Largest House for

Chapter XII

Choosing Brisbane

Ross Johnston and Helen Gregory

'Nature has pointed out that spot as the site of the northern capital of Australia'. So announced *The Australian* on 5 February 1842 in referring to Brisbane Town. This was on the occasion of the authorities in Sydney officially throwing Moreton Bay open to free settlement, thereby ending its days as a penal establishment. But the newspaper was too sanguine about Brisbane's prospects, for it was not until the late 1850s that Brisbane could rest assured that it would become the capital of what was then northern New South Wales.

Indeed, the first spot chosen for a north-eastern settlement was not at Brisbane but at Red Cliff Point on Moreton Bay. One year later, in 1825, the move was made to Brisbane Town on the Brisbane River. At that stage there was no plan to erect a separate northern colony with its own capital; all that was intended was a northern outpost controlled from Sydney. Its role was penal until 1842 but from 1840 private interests began to shape the destiny of these northern lands. Finally, in 1859, a separate colony of Queensland was created with Brisbane as its capital. In the meantime Brisbane was the subject of indecision, criticism, frustration and competition; it was to undergo difficulties in establishment and problems in adjustment; it was neglected and it was threatened with abandonment. Brisbane Town just grew—it was not planned. In a sense it was a capital without a colony for it had to wait more than one generation, for thirty-five years from 1824, to gain that honour. To understand its final emergence as the capital of the colony of Queensland one cannot look at it in isolation: its growth was bound up implicitly with the Moreton Bay region and with the convict system. Without both, Brisbane's cause would not have existed.

The founding of Brisbane Town resulted from the fears of British authorities that the punishment of transportation to New South Wales was not severe enough to deter criminals in the United Kingdom. In 1817 Lord Bathurst, Secretary of State for War and the Colonies, was facing increasing criticism at the domestic level over the rising crime rate in Britain; a phenomenon that was upsetting many respectable people. In the past, the terror of exile had been thought to have had a salutary effect on the crime rate but this was now in question. In April of that year Bathurst told his colleague Viscount Sidmouth at the Home Office:

I have for some time past had under consideration the present state of the settlements in New South Wales principally with a view of satisfying myself whether they are now calculated to answer the object for which they were originally established or whether it might not be expedient to introduce some alteration in the existing system.[1]

In January 1819 John Thomas Bigge was finally commissioned to carry out such an inquiry. Three years later he submitted his first report. In addition to various suggestions for improving the efficiency of the transportation system, as it applied in the existing settlements, Bigge recommended the creation of additional isolated penal establishments where a considerable body of convicts might be separated from the mass of the population and subjected to a regime of stern discipline and constant supervision. Three sites were suggested in the report as likely bases for accommodating the 4000-odd convicts who at the time did not seem to be wanted in New South Wales. All three were in what is now Queensland, and included Port Curtis (now Gladstone), Port Bowen (now Port Clinton) and Moreton Bay which had been named by Cook in 1770.

By the time the report was submitted, and in the following years, the demand for assigned convict labour from private employers had risen markedly and so the numbers in government hands which had disturbed Bigge had quickly fallen. Instead of three additional penal establishments there was need only for the settlement which Bigge had envisioned as a place of secondary punishment 'for convicts sentenced to punishment by the magistrates of . . . the older and settled districts'.[2] Which of the three sites should become this new depot was a matter for further investigation but in general it should be that which was 'found on further examination to possess the fewest recommendations of soil, and to be the least accessible to ships'[3]—appropriate criteria for an isolated gaol but one which hardly augered well for future development.

Bigge had suggested that the place of secondary punishment should hold some 1000 convicts, be administered by sixteen civil officers (including the commandant) and be guarded by seventy-five military men, numbers which in fact were only reached when the settlement was at its peak[4]. Bigge had also set out details on how the establishment should be conducted, with regulations regarding labour, rations, clothing and segregated accommodation. The British government largely approved the severe disciplinary principles underlying Bigge's proposals and the Home Secretary, Sir Robert Peel, echoed them when speaking in Parliament on the 1824 Transportation of Offenders Bill.[5]

The settlement that was eventually made at Moreton Bay was thus essentially a response to the problem of how to control convicts in New South Wales and Van Diemen's Land—and indirectly in Britain. Economic considerations were not paramount, although some concern was given to the productive potential of the area because the penal establishment was expected to become self-supporting as quickly as possible. Strategic concerns also took a secondary place although, as shown in Chapters VI and XIV, Moreton Bay can be seen as part of a wider imperial strategy—to ensure the exclusion of a foreign power from the unclaimed parts of the continent by establishing a ring of outposts. As a result of this policy, however, the New South Wales government found itself lumbered with small settlements and dependencies scattered around the continent—at Newcastle, Port Macquarie, Moreton Bay, Melville Island and Raffles Bay in the north, King George Sound in the west, Western Port in Bass Strait and Norfolk Island,—with the possibility of another settlement at Shark Bay in the middle of the west coast.[6] Then (the early 1820s), the government clearly thought it prudent to have a spread of settlements at strategic points on the coastline, especially in the unoccupied territories to the north, south and west.

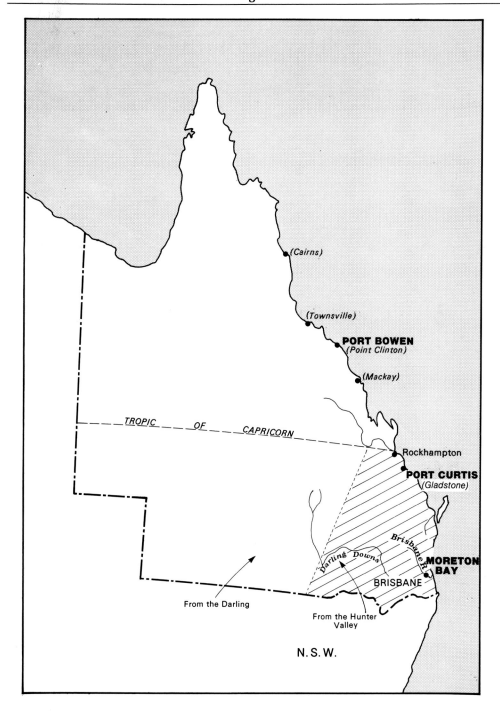

Figure 43: Oxley's three choices—Port Bowen, Port Curtis or Moreton Bay

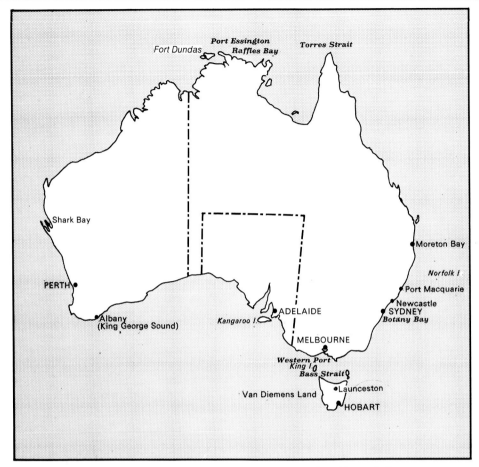

Figure 44: The spread of settlement—actual and intended settlements—circa 1840

Moreton Bay, being on the eastern seaboard and fairly close to the main base, did not take on the same strategic significance.

In September 1822 Lord Bathurst despatched instructions to Sir Thomas Brisbane, the then Governor of New South Wales, to carry out the Bigge proposals regarding penal settlements on the north-east coast and in October 1823 Brisbane sent his surveyor general, John Oxley, to examine the country to which he referred. Three months later, Oxley reported that he had been unable to visit Port Bowen, the most northerly spot suggested by Bigge, because the weather was too unfavourable at that time of the year to make a trip of inspection. He also discounted Bigge's second choice, Port Curtis, after visiting it in the dry season, for he thought the site lacked water, timber for building and was unsuitable for agriculture.[7]

That left the third choice, Moreton Bay, and with this Oxley was impressed—especially after discovering what he considered to be 'by far the largest fresh water river on the Eastern Coast of New South Wales', which he named the Brisbane, and promised would 'be of the utmost importance to the Colony'[8]. The proud and dogmatic Oxley believed that with this discovery he had solved the mystery of the inland rivers. After flowing to the north-west and melting into a swampy morass these waters, he now considered, were drained into the sea by the north-easterly flowing Brisbane River. So, partly in justification of his own theorising, he strongly recommended settlement of the Moreton Bay area. It possessed good grazing and agricultural lands which were well timbered and watered and 'capable of producing the richest productions of the tropics'. He thought that a site on the Brisbane River should be chosen as the permanent base for settlement, but as an interim location for immediate occupation, he nominated the Red Cliff peninsula on the northern shore of Moreton Bay. Here, pursuant to Colonial Office instructions, a small convict force and its minders could establish an outpost of British civilisation. When the settlement moved up the river, this base could become a military post, but meanwhile the peninsula seemed to possess sufficient advantages for a small settlement (water, timber and reasonable soil), a convenient and safe anchorage in the bay with ease of access to the main shipping route.[9]

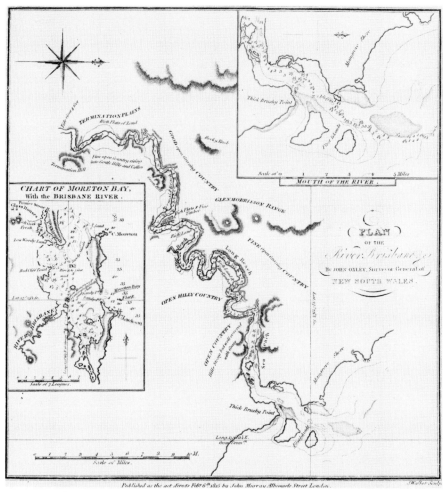

Figure 45: Oxley's chart of the Brisbane River, 1823. From Barron Field's *Geographical Memoires of New South Wales* (1825) (Courtesy of the National Library)

239

In September 1824 the New South Wales government was finally ready to carry out London's instructions and form a penal establishment to the north. Brisbane appointed Lieutenant Henry Miller of the 40th Regiment to take a small party of convicts, with military guards and some professional civilians, to establish a first base. Brisbane issued fairly detailed instructions to Miller, the first commandant, and Surveyor General Oxley who accompanied him. The latter was to choose the actual site—and he was told to consider some of the bay islands as a possible alternative—while the former was to implement settlement.[10] After settling upon the Red Cliff peninsula, rather than a bay island, Oxley indicated a suitable anchorage, located waterholes and marked out where the different buildings should be positioned. Meanwhile his assistant, Robert Hoddle, drew up the maps for the Red Cliff settlement. Allan Cunningham, the botanical collector for the Royal Gardens at Kew, who had accompanied the expedition, attended to the marking out of a garden and its preparation for the sowing of plants and seeds.

The size of the founding party cannot be accurately counted, mainly because of the presence of an unknown number of wives and servants. There was the commandant and his family of three, Lieutenant Butler, a sergeant, corporal and twelve privates from the 40th regiment (plus wives and children); as expert advisers there were Oxley, his assistant surveyor, Hoddle, and Cunningham, as King's botanist. The labour force consisted of twenty-nine convicts. Precisely how these were selected is not known, though most were volunteers, with nine, perhaps more, serving colonial sentences—mainly for escaping from Port Macquarie. In all they provided a variety of useful skills—workers in wood, stone, plaster, bricks, guns, ships and so on. Only three were listed as general labourers so that at least on the surface Miller was supplied with capable hands.[11]

Indeed, in various respects the expedition seemed well prepared. Charles Frazer, the New South Wales botanist, had chosen a wide range of fruiting trees and bushes, grasses, roots, herbs and seeds from the government garden in Sydney. Even a bag of seed cotton was included. Also sent were numbers of goats, sheep, pigs and poultry. Cunningham, in fact, was somewhat critical of the extent of provisioning, 'from which extravagant supply one would infer the new colonists would have nought to do but eat, drink and be merry'.[12] Miller, however, complained that labour was in short supply—as were various tools and implements, medicines, potatoes and seed wheat:

> The grand impediment to preparing the land for the purpose of cultivation arises from the total want of oxen and ploughs . . . A large supply of cattle and grain should be sent in order to enable the settlement to depend in process of time on its own resources.[13]

But this was asking too much. After all, the government's philosophy was that life should not be easy for the convicts. They had to understand the meaning of hard labour; they themselves, and not oxen and ploughs, would have to break up the soil. Miller, in his demands for items such as frying pans and window glass, did not show sufficient resourcefulness or initiative to push the difficult task of initial settlement in a strange environment to a successful conclusion.

Official planning for this new penal base was soon modified. When information about the surrounding territory was supplied from Oxley's trip of 1823, it became clear that the Moreton Bay district was not the uninviting area that had been sought. In July 1824, before Brisbane in Sydney had completed arrangements for the founding convict party, Bathurst in London was noting that the area showed 'a fitness for general colonization' which would be wasted on 'the worst Class of Offenders'.[14] He advised that Norfolk Island should be reopened for that purpose, and that Brisbane should modify the original plan for Moreton Bay. Now it was to be a place of secondary punishment for lesser criminals, such as accomplice bushrangers, runaways from Port Macquarie, and others who had committed minor offences in Australia.[15] Already authorities in both Sydney and London were contemplating free settlement in the area, with convict occupation as only an initial stage of development.

The Red Cliff peninsula quickly proved to have certain disadvantages. The commandant claimed that the area was unhealthy; crops would not grow abundantly, water was short, the timber was not suitable for building, and he was very short of labour. Although Miller may have been complaining too much and perhaps was not the person to cope with the trials of first settlement, progress overall was faltering—and for a variety of reasons. The site was certainly not as good as originally thought, there was trouble from the Aboriginals, mainly in the form of pilfering, and the anchorage could quickly turn dangerous.

In any case it had always been planned to move up the Brisbane River. Probably in May 1825 Miller took his small band seventeen miles upstream to where the present city heart lies. This in fact was exceeding his instructions. Oxley, in 1823 and 1824, as well as Governor Brisbane and Chief Justice Forbes, when they visited the area in November

Figure 46: The site of Brisbane

241

1824, had recommended that a permanent settlement be made at a place called Breakfast Creek further down towards the river mouth. The reason for Miller's choice of location is not known.[16] It is possible that he mistook his instructions to move seventeen miles—from Red Cliff or from the mouth of the river? Alternatively, he may have thought Breakfast Creek too floodprone. At first the new establishment on the Brisbane River was known as the Moreton Bay Settlement, but by 1826 the commandant was signing some of his despatches from Brisbane Town, named after the governor and the river. Confusion over the siting of the town continued during its first year. When Major Edmund Lockyer was sent by the governor in 1825 to further explore the Brisbane River, he sketched a plan of the settlement lower down the river than Miller's designated spot, at a point which would have been in the middle of a flood plain.[17]

After its creation as a penal station, official government interest in Moreton Bay declined, especially in London. The administration in Sydney played a role of superintendence, checking on the efficiency and success of the system in operation, and forever concerned about keeping down costs. Most vital decisions concerning the establishment and its day-to-day routine and management were actually made by the man on the spot—the commandant.

At this stage the British government was primarily interested in the larger issue of convictism itself—how a system of punishment could be most effectively and cheaply operated. As applied to Moreton Bay this became a question of what sort of convict should be sent there and how the settlement should be related to other existing establishments. Even at its inception in 1824 Moreton Bay's original purpose had been changed and, after the decision to reoccupy Norfolk Island, an air of uncertainty prevailed. Despite earlier remarks about the fitness of the bay region for 'general colonization' Brisbane proposed and Bathurst agreed that the Port Macquarie area to the south should be thrown open for that purpose.[18] This left Moreton Bay as the major penal settlement, at least until Norfolk Island could be built up.[19] In 1826 this was done. Moreton Bay was officially proclaimed a penal settlement to receive offenders convicted in New South Wales, though in fact this merely put a legal stamp on what had already been happening.

Brisbane's successor, Governor Darling, was critical of the whole penal system. With outposts scattered around the rim of Australia it was too costly, and, despite Bigge's recommendations, it had been rather loosely administered under the somewhat casual Brisbane. In consequence the 'terror' had been taken out of transportation. Port Macquarie, in particular, seemed to Darling to have been an easy place, but this was also partly true of Moreton Bay. Both were 'radically defective' and needed to be toughened up: 'my own opinion is that every man at the Penal Settlements should be worked in Irons, that the example may deter others from the Commission of crimes; and I shall very soon see whether this cannot be effected'.[20]

In Logan, the new Moreton Bay commandant appointed in 1826, Governor Darling had a like mind: stern discipline, with arduous labour and strict punishment was to be the order of the day. Darling, when visiting the settlement in June 1827, was well pleased with the pattern of control that had been instituted. Floggings were regularly handed out for misbehaviour, and although fifty lashes were the maximum, by regulation, that the commandant could unilaterally impose, this was exceeded in practice by sometimes up to 200 lashes. Most men worked in irons and, following a complaint from Logan that effective control was difficult to secure without the threat of an additional punishment, cells for solitary confinement were erected and a treadmill was installed.[21]

At first, the penal establishment at Moreton Bay grew slowly but in Logan's period (1826 to 1830) the number of convicts increased rapidly. By April 1827 there were 195 convicts guarded by seventy-seven military men at the out-station. During 1828 Moreton Bay, with an average of 553 prisoners, overtook both Port Macquarie and Norfolk Island as the largest repository of re-convicted convicts. By October the following year there were 940 male prisoners, eighteeen women prisoners and 150 military men and their families based at Brisbane Town (when there were only about 200 all told on Norfolk Island). A peak in numbers was reached two years later in 1831 when there was a total of 1140 adult males (1019 of whom were convicts), fifty-eight adult females (including forty convicts) and forty-three children (twenty-nine of whom belonged to military men).[22]

In the 1830s the British government's concern with cost and efficiency led it to consider the question of abandoning the Moreton Bay outpost. The Treasury recommended in 1830 that 'all subordinate settlements . . . should be restricted within certain limits'. Accordingly, the Colonial Office in 1831 issued general instructions to Bourke, the then Governor of New South Wales, to reduce civil establishments.[23] This policy was reinforced by the 1832 House of Commons Select Committee into Secondary Punishment which strongly condemned transportation as an effective means of deterring the rising crime rate. Pursuant to this policy, as enunciated by the Treasury and the Colonial Office, the establishment at Moreton Bay was earmarked for abolition. After mid 1832 Goderich, at the Colonial Office, advised breaking up the Moreton Bay settlement on the grounds that 'it appears . . . a considerable number of convicts are employed in a manner comparatively unproductive'. But neither Goderich nor his successor Glenelg (who wrote in the same vein in 1835) offered Governor Bourke (who followed Darling) any constructive suggestions regarding the future of Moreton Bay.[24]

The saga of abandonment became a protracted and wasting affair. So long as its fate lay undecided the local community were seriously demoralised. At the end of 1832 Bourke began to implement the running down of the establishment but final closure was not yet at hand. By 1834 the number of convicts had declined to just over four hundred. Bourke had changed government policy with respect to secondary offenders who were now to be used locally: 'the number of convicts sentenced to work in irons on the roads has been considerably augmented, by substituting this punishment for transportation for short periods to Norfolk Island and Moreton Bay.' While worst offenders would still be sent to the former, reduced numbers would allow the latter in due course to be closed.[25]

At the end of 1835 Lord Glenelg at the Colonial Office expressed surprise, even dismay, at the slowness of the New South Wales authorities in shutting down Moreton Bay.[26] Late in 1837 Governor Bourke eventually explained why it had taken six years to achieve only a partial abandonment of Moreton Bay. At this stage the settlement housed only about 300 convicts and Bourke could report that it was now not so costly, since it was supplying much of its own food. It had also become secure, with few escapes. If it was closed down, there was the question of what to do with the convict women. More important still was the future of the area itself: should it be thrown open to free settlement? How would it pay for its administration? Major decisions had to be made on these points, and until they were settled it was best, Bourke felt, to keep the penal settlement going. Bourke also argued that he wanted to avoid the problem of an uncontrolled grab for land—something that had already happened when the Port Phillip district was thrown open to free settlement.[27]

Although from the time of his arrival in 1837 Commandant Cotton had been keen to continue the development of the area, the government in Sydney continued its slow run-down until May 1839 when the bulk of the convicts were removed. All the women (fifty-four) were then taken away, and by mid year there was only a maintenance crew of ninety-four males remaining. This action by the new governor, Sir George Gipps, following Bourke's acceptance of the 1835 instructions, effectively spelled the end of the penal settlement.[28]

Government policy as devised in London and Sydney on the role of transportation vitally affected the development of Brisbane as a town. So long as transportation was in favour, through the 1820s, the community and township at Brisbane grew, but from 1831 onwards, when government policy began to take a negative stance, Brisbane Town was left in limbo. Uncertainty as to its future led to stagnation and decline. By 1839 Brisbane Town was taking on a deserted air, and this situation was compounded by the government's failure to make a definite plan for the area's future. It was eventually to be thrown open to free settlement, but no timetable was set. Over the next two years, except for surveying, the Sydney government did nothing to develop the northern districts.

Apart from uncertainty as to the future use of the whole Moreton Bay region, common official reactions to the choice of the site of Brisbane included doubt, disapproval and indecision—at least until 1837 when a sense of resignation and acceptance came to prevail. Thereafter officials appear to have given no further thought to moving the settlement to another spot, although its primacy in the area was not yet fully acknowledged. Throughout the 1840s and 1850s other urban communities attempted to challenge, albeit unsuccessfully, Brisbane's claim to be the main commercial and administrative centre of the northern district of New South Wales. Indeed, it was not until the late 1850s that it became clear that Brisbane would be the capital city of the new colony of Queensland, which gained separation in December 1859.

The short-lived Red Cliff settlement and the overlooked possibility at Breakfast Creek seem to have put a blight on the development of Brisbane Town, as located up river by Miller in mid 1825. His choice of the northern bank meant that a flood-free position was taken for the placement of main buildings, although the lower ground, where gardens could grow, did flood. Across the river, however, was a large, fertile, low flat which could be used for growing crops. Building materials were at hand—with plenty of fine timber nearby and a porphyry stone cliff on the southern bank at Kangaroo Point.

The third commandant, Logan, was particularly dissatisfied with the location of Brisbane Town. His discoveries of the fertile Logan River district seemed to prove to him that the settlement should be moved to a more central position. If the potential of the Logan and the Tweed areas were to be fully realised, a base on Moreton Bay would be far more sensible than one some miles up the Brisbane River. Shoals in the bay and the river bar could make sea travel hazardous and imposed a limitation upon the size of vessels visiting Brisbane Town. So, in 1827, he suggested that the establishment should be moved to Stradbroke Island, where there was a safe anchorage and plenty of water.[29] Governor Darling, after a personal visit to the area, agreed with Logan that the situation of Brisbane Town was 'highly objectionable' because of its difficult access. But, anxious to avoid expense, he suggested an interim solution—that a stores depot be established at Dunwich on Stradbroke Island. This would allow large vessels to turn around quickly, unloading supplies from Sydney and picking up timber and other products from the area. A small vessel could then be kept at Dunwich to ferry commodities to Brisbane Town.[30] This idea became a reality in 1828 with the establishment of a small base at Dunwich.

Further problems with the siting of Brisbane arose in 1829 when John Bowman, head of the medical department, complained that the inadequate and impure water supply was contributing to much sickness, especially among the convicts:

> The only water they now have for use is collected in ponds in wet weather, which being stagnant, soon becomes putrid, and unfit for use, and during the long continued drought last summer the water was not only very deficient in quantity, but bad in quality, and in all probability this was one of the greatest causes of the dysenteric affections which were so prevalent . . .[31]

As a result Darling advised the Colonial Office that he was asking Logan to check whether a more suitable location might be found to which the settlement could be moved. Logan had already suggested opening an agricultural establishment some five miles up the river from Brisbane, at Oxley Creek, with the intention of dispersing Brisbane's population and weakening its centrality. However, the governor argued that such a move would only add to the problem of communication and said he was contemplating transferring the settlement towards the bay.[32] In the end, a convict farm was established down the river at a place named Eagle Farm, and the idea of a total move faded into obscurity. So Brisbane Town survived, as the focal point of a growing number of out-stations.

Dissatisfaction with the siting of Brisbane Town became muted in the early 1830s as official interest switched to the larger question of Moreton Bay's possible abandonment. It was thus not until the arrival of Commandant Cotton in 1837 that any realistic appreciation was given to the situation of the town. Cotton was determined to use the town site to its best advantage and discounted all talk of moving the centre to another location, be it on the bay, upriver or elsewhere. Drawing on a military career with active service in India and Burma, and also on experience acquired as acting-engineer and architect in Hobart Town, he ruled Moreton Bay with a practical efficiency and a desire for success.

Most previous criticism of the town site had related to the difficulties of communication, and during his two years there Cotton reassessed the situation and instead of placing so much reliance on water communication—a common approach taken by British people who had grown up with a tradition of the sea, canals and the waterwheel—gave his attention to land links, perhaps not unusual for a military man.[33] He accepted Brisbane as the focal point of settlement in the area, and urged that roads should span out like the spokes of a wheel. Earlier commandants had seen the rivers as the main routes for products, people and messages, but the Brisbane River carved out such a tortuous passage that it made communication extremely slow and inefficient. Cotton pushed for direct access overland, so that the various out-stations could be brought into rapid contact with the centre of settlement, and was therefore not as concerned with the problem of the bar at the river mouth as other commandants had been. In any case the commissary-general in Sydney was planning that only small vessels, of about eight feet draught, would be used on the Sydney-Brisbane run.

As to the positioning of Brisbane Town, Andrew Petrie, foreman of works, claimed that he and Cotton had checked various sites in 1838 and had decided that the existing site was the most suitable.[34] In hindsight this might seem a little surprising, given that the amount of flat land for settlement on the river point was restricted, that the environs were hilly and provided obstacles to easy access, and that the river at this point was strong-flowing hence making a crossing to the productive lands to the south and west quite hazardous. But the site was never changed, even when the whole area was thrown open to free settlement in 1842 and rival urban groups developed to challenge Brisbane's claim to be the main centre of the Moreton Bay and inland Darling Downs districts. Through the 1840s three communities, at South Brisbane, Kangaroo Point and Fortitude Valley, grew up around the original convict site, so dispersing the urban population of the area—and in addition there were further outlying urban groups such as that at Ipswich.

On the south bank of the river, South Brisbane developed quickly as a rival to the older settlement which became known as North Brisbane. The wily and opportunistic John Williams opened a hotel and store on the south bank in 1841 to supply the squatters moving into the south and west, and to provide accommodation for draymen bringing loads of wool from the hinterland. Soon shipping was turning around at South Brisbane, with the Hunter River Steam Navigation Company taking the lead. In 1845 it built a wharf and storehouses, which had to be extended the following year as business built up. The confidence of this company led to the rise of other businesses in South Brisbane and so a separate township began to grow.

Land was surveyed in South Brisbane in a simple grid pattern with the streets named after Colonial Office officials such as Stanley, Grey, Melbourne, Russell and Glenelg. The first section was sold in July 1842, at the same time as land in North Brisbane. The south side's favourable position for commerce through its easier access pushed along its early development. Although the government placed the same upset price on land in both North and South Brisbane, the growth of the latter for a time outpaced its rival. In several land sales during the mid 1840s, investment in land at South Brisbane exceeded that in North Brisbane and the 1846 census showed that South Brisbane had more wooden houses than its older sister.[35]

Despite apparent commercial and geographical advantages, commercial decisions ended South Brisbane's rise to dominance in the 1850s when several businesses, and especially the Australian Steam Navigation Company, decided to move to the main administrative centre in North Brisbane. In the meantime, however, a second subsidiary town had been developing on the south side, at Kangaroo Point. This was first opened up as suburban land in 1843, but the establishment in that same year of a boiling-down works nearby, and the opening of a second cross-river ferry in 1844, increased the industrial and residential potential of that area and prompted further urbanisation.[36]

The arrival in 1849 of immigrants sponsored by the Reverend Dr J D Lang led to the rise of the third urban cluster at Fortitude Valley, near to but separate from North Brisbane. Earlier it had been expected that Eagle Farm land would sell well after free settlement was declared and that this would create another urban nucleus, but the sale of land there in December 1843 proved disappointing. The dispersal of population in the Brisbane district, and the early struggle for primacy between North and South Brisbane, detracted from the growth of Brisbane Town. But more serious challenges appeared from other areas.

In 1828 the botanists Cunningham and Frazer had realised the significance of the site of the limestone hills west of Brisbane Town on the Bremer River; it had immediate access to the Darling Downs through Cunningham's Gap, and the Bremer and Brisbane Rivers were both suitable for river traffic.[37] The movement of squatters from New England into the Darling Downs in 1840, and then into the West Moreton district, soon promoted urban settlement at a spot first appropriately called Limestone, but renamed Ipswich in 1843. Dray tracks facilitating the handling of supplies and produce were established down the range through to Ipswich and the Bremer. River traffic built up and Ipswich became an obvious supply base for the growing number of stations in the hinterland. The first sale of town land there occurred in 1843.[38]

Throughout the 1840s sales of land at Ipswich were consistently more successful than sales of land in either North or South Brisbane. In the period 1842 to 1849 just over 83 per cent of land offered in Ipswich was sold, compared with 58 per cent of the offering in North Brisbane and 57 per cent in South Brisbane. Although the lower upset price of £8 per acre placed on Ipswich town land (compared with £100 per acre in North and South Brisbane) may have attracted some of the land buyers, many lots at Ipswich reached prices that were higher than those paid for Brisbane land.[39]

Some squatters, notably Francis Bigge, wanted to bypass Brisbane and promote the interests of Ipswich with a separate central port on Moreton Bay. The existence of sandbars at the mouth of the Brisbane River also prompted the surveyor, Robert Dixon, to suggest replacing Brisbane with a port at Cleveland Point on the Bay. From that point a road could be made to Cooper Plains to connect with the road to Ipswich and the interior.[40] A number of interests agreed with this view, arguing that Cleveland would be a suitable discharge port for overseas vessels; and that lighters could then carry cargo to and from Ipswich via the waterways, while from Ipswich it could be distributed to the squatters in the interior. In 1840 Deputy Surveyor General Perry had advised Governor Gipps that he considered the site of Brisbane had been poorly chosen, but went on to add 'as it has been observed before, the chief point of concentration will depend on the disposition of the settlers themselves'.[41]

After visiting the area in 1842 Governor Gipps found Cleveland to be quite an unsuitable alternative because of its surrounding mud flats, but his decision did not stop the issue from reappearing through the 1840s and 1850s. Even when an Admiralty survey by Captain Stanley in 1847 found unfavourably against Cleveland, its advocates would not give in.[42] So a bitter contest was waged in the press and in politics through the early 1850s. It was not until 1855 that the New South Wales government resolved that Brisbane, and not Cleveland, should be the port for the whole Moreton Bay region. Yet although the government then agreed that the Brisbane River should be dredged and a passage cleared through the bar, money for this purpose was not forthcoming before separation in 1859.

Some of the opposition to Brisbane's primacy came from those who were primarily interested in opening up and occupying the vast lands further north. Knowledge about Brisbane's hinterland had been non-existent in the early 1820s and when an Irish medical scientist, McCreight, proposed in London a grand exploration scheme through north and west Queensland, the British authorities considered it premature.[43] It was not until 1845–56 that Ludwig Leichhardt and Surveyor-General Mitchell finally led two separate exploring parties to acquire the knowledge of inland Queensland that McCreight had hoped to gain. The reports of these explorers revealed that a huge potential for development lay to the north of Brisbane and that, because of the distances involved, new centres of government and supply should be created closer to these lands.[44] Such arguments have persisted through to the present day, especially from Townsville and Rockhampton.

In 1837, the Reverend Dr JD Lang had proposed to the House of Commons Select Committee investigating transportation that Brisbane be made the capital of a new colony, stretching from beyond Port Macquarie as far as Cape York.[45] This was the first time that Brisbane had been thought of as such a seat of government. With attention to the tropical geography of the territory, Lang urged the introduction of some southern Europeans for hard labour, although he recommended Scottish Highlanders as the best settlers. By 1852 Lang had formulated another plan involving the subdivision of north-eastern Australia into three colonies, starting at 30 degrees south latitude. These

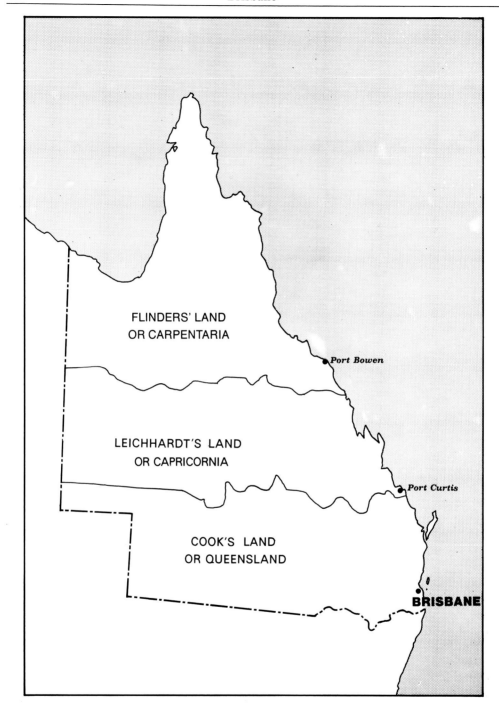

Figure 47: J D Lang's subdivision proposals

were Cook's Land, centring on Brisbane, Leichhardt's land further to the north, and Flinders' Land above that in Cape York peninsula.[46] After the separation of Queensland from New South Wales, Lang proposed yet another three-way division of the north—into Queensland (with its northern boundary at 25 degrees south latitude), Capricornia and Carpentaria.

In 1839 John Mayo proposed a scheme based on imported Indian labour for the colonisation of all northern Australia.[47] Using Moreton Bay as the first step he planned to use English settlers to teach the Indians who would then go out establishing cotton, coffee and sugar plantations along the northern tropical coast, under European supervision. He claimed that his scheme would cost the government nothing but it was turned down as a rather harebrained confidence trick.

Yet another scheme centred on colonisation by chartered companies: this was first proposed by Major Benjamin Sullivan in 1833. Six years later he revised this plan with a prospectus to colonise the north half of eastern Australia, from the Tropic of Capricorn to Cape York.[48] Port Bowen would be the centre of a chartered colony called Victoria. He tried again in 1842 but the Colonial Office was not interested.

The 1830s and 1840s were a time when British imperalists were experimenting with schemes of scientific colonisation. None was implemented in north-eastern Australia although in 1845 Lord Stanley and his successor at the Colonial Office, William Gladstone, proposed a new colony near Port Curtis (now Gladstone), to dispose of an oversupply of pardoned or time-expired convicts in Van Diemen's Land and to provide a home for exiles (pardoned convicts) sent out from the United Kingdom.[49] This scheme was abruptly terminated, however, when the British government had a change of policy with respect to the disposal of convicts and exiles.[50] So, North Australia and the township of Gladstone faded and another possible rival to Brisbane was eliminated.

Brisbane thus survived as the main northern centre more by accident than by determination and planning. Its convict heritage helped, mainly due to the fact that, although a somewhat overlooked penal establishment, its very existence gave Brisbane Town a head start upon any other centre. Local rivals appeared, but failed because they were not clearly or forthrightly promoted, and so Brisbane became Queensland's capital almost by default.

Notes

[1] *C.O.*, 324, Entry books, series 1 (hereafter cited as 'C.O.324'), p.138.

[2] Report of the Commissioner of Inquiry into the state of N.S.W., *Parliamentary Papers*, 1822, No. 448, Australian Facsimile Editions No. 68 (Adelaide, 1966), p.163.

[3] Bigge, J.T. *Report of the Commissioner of Inquiry into the State of the Colony of New South Wales*, (London, 1822), pp.164, 178.

[4] Parliamentary Papers 1822, *Ibid.*, pp.180-6.

[5] *British Parliamentary Debates*, XI (1824), p.1092.

[6] *C.O.*, 202, p.15, (Nos. 16 and 17, and 11-3-1826), *H.R.A.*, I, xi, pp.215-9.

[7] *H.R.A.*, I, xi, pp.215-9.

[8] *Ibid.*

[9] *Ibid.*, p.219-22; *Oxley Field Books*, 3-12-1823, cited in Steele, John, G. *The Explorers of the Moreton Bay District 1770-1830*, (U.Q.P., 1972), p.116; Cunningham, Allan, *Cunningham's Journal*, 13-9-1824, SZ9, *A.O.N.S.W.*

[10] Cunningham, *Ibid.*, 13-9-1824; *C.S.*, (to Moreton Bay), 4/3794, Reel 749, *A.O.N.S.W.* 27-8-1824.

[11] Steele, J.G. *Brisbane Town in Convict Days 1824-1842*, (U.Q.P., 1975), pp.7-9.

[12] *J.D. Lang Papers*, Vol. 6, A2226, M.L., pp.5-12, (20-10-1824).

[13] *C.S.*, (from Moreton Bay), 4/1803, Reel 751, (30-9-1824).

[14] *H.R.A.*, I, xi, p.321, (22-7-1824).

[15] *H.R.A.*, I, xi, p.603, (21-5-1825), *H.R.A.*, I, xi, p.553, (24-3-1825).

[16] *C.S.*, Tasmanian State Archives 1/371/8476, (25-4-1826).

[17] *C.S.*, (from Moreton Bay), *A.O.N.S.W.*, 4/1803, F. 39, Reel 751.

[18] *H.R.A.*, I, xi, p.604, (21-5-1825, 1-4-1826).

[19] *H.R.A.*, I, xii, pp.194, 514, (31-8-1826).

[20] *H.R.A.*, I, xiii, p.106, (10-2-1827); Bonwick, James, *Records Relating to Moreton Bay 1822-49*, I, pp.83-4.

[21] *Logan Letterbook*, entry for 6-4-1827.

[22] Statistics from *H.R.A.*, I, xiii, p.305; xiv, pp.522, 637, 648; Archdeacon Broughton's Report, (29-9-1831), *B.P.P.*, XIX (1837), p.502. O'Keeffe, Mamie, *A Brief Account of the Moreton Bay Penal Settlement 1824-1839*, (Brisbane Library Board, Queensland, 1974), [N.B. p.5, gives lower figures drawing on medical estimates. For further figures see next chapter.]

[23] 'Third Report of Commissioner of inquiry into receipt and expenditure of Colonial revenue: Australia', *B.P.P.*, IV (1830-31), p.77; *H.R.A.*, I, xvi, pp.382-394, (29-9-1831).

[24] *H.R.A.*, I, xvi, p.832, (25-12-1832); I, xvii, p.328, (15-1-1834), I, xviii, p.244, (26-12-1835).

[25] *H.R.A.*, I, xvii, pp.316 and 328, 'Correspondence on the subject of secondary punishment', *B.P.P.*, XLVII (1834), p.298.

[26] *H.R.A.*, I, xviii, p.244, (26-12-1835).

[27] *H.R.A.*, I, xix, p.150, (5-11-1837).

[28] *H.R.A.*, I, xx, p.209. (1-7-1839).

[29] *Logan Letterbook*, entry for 28-7-1827, *C.O.*, 201/183, 26-9-1827.

[30] *C.O.*, *Ibid.*

[31] *Logan Letterbook*, entries for 22-2-1829 and 3-4-1829; Bowman Report (13-6-1829), *C.S.*, *A.O.N.S.W.*, 30/5094.

[32] *Logan Letterbook*, 20-5-1828; *H.R.A.*, I, xv, p.21, (24-6-1829).

[33] *Moreton Bay Correspondence 1824-1859*, A2, J.O.L., Reel 9, (14-2-1837).

[34] Petrie, A. *Address to the Corporation of Brisbane*, c. 1866, Typescript, J.O.L.

[35] Census 1846 *N.S.W.G.G.*, 4-11-1846. For land sales see *N.S.W.G.G.*, 18-2-1845 and 18-8-1846.

[36] *N.S.W.G.G.*, 10-10-1843, 5-4-1844, 12-11-1844.

[37] *C.O.*, 201/200, 16-12-1828, 24-2-1829; Frazer, C. 'Journal of a two months' residence on the banks of the rivers Brisbane and Logan on the east coast of New Holland', *(Hooker's) Botanical Miscellany, 1*, (1830), p.248.

[38] *N.S.W.G.G.*, 15-4-1843.

[39] Gregory, Helen. 'Squatters, selectors and dare I say it speculators', *J.R.H.S.Q.*, XI (1983), pp.76-7.

[40] *Surveyor-General's Correspondence*, 2/1531, *A.O.N.S.W.*, 28-4-1840.

[41] Perry, 'Appendix on progress of survey', *Bonwick, III*, p.415, (February, 1840).

[42] Macgillivray, John, *Narrative of the voyage of H.M.S. Rattlesnake...*, (Libraries Board of South Australia, 1967), II, pp.46-7.

[43] McCreight proposals, *C.O.*, 201/204, 1-5-1829.

[44] Leichhardt, Ludwig, *Journal of an overland expedition in Australia*, (Libraries Board of South Australia, 1964); Mitchell, T.L. *Journal of an expedition into the interior of Tropical Australia ...*, (London, Brown, Green and Longmans, 1848).

[45] Lang, J.D. in 'Report of the Select committee appointed to enquire into the System of Transportation ...', (518), *B.P.P.*, XIX (1837), pp.267-8.

[46] Lang, J.D. *Freedom and Independence for the Golden Lands of Australia*, (London, Longman, Brown, Green and Longmans, 1852), Lang. J.D. *The Coming Event! or Freedom and Independence for the Seven United Provinces of Australia*, (London, Sampson Low, Son and Marston, 1870).

[47] *C.O.*, 201/293, 31-1-1839.

[48] *C.O.*, 201/330, 3-7-1834. Includes *Prospectus for Colonizing the North-Eastern Parts of Australasia under the Appellation of the Colony of Victoria . . .*, (Sydney, 1839).

[49] 'Correspondence Relative to Convict Discipline in Van Diemen's Land', (36), *B.P.P.*, XXIX (1846), pp.304-11, (September, 1845).

[50] For a general history of this settlement, see Hogan J.F. *The Gladstone Colony*, (Sydney, Brooks, 1897).

Chapter XIII

Brisbane: Making it Work

Ross Johnston and Helen Gregory

The founding of any new settlement is beset with problems; for no matter how thorough the planning, unforeseen difficulties arise to frustrate objectives and intentions, and in the case of the Moreton Bay settlement the limited plans that were made in London and Sydney suffered from far too little on-the-spot knowledge. The first difficulty that arose was the choice of a suitable site, as discussed in Chapter XII. The next problem was to make the new settlement work, that is, to establish an economic base. This was very dependent on the quality and quantity of the personnel involved—both commandants and convicts. And it involved a settlement of relations between the original inhabitants and the European newcomers—the latter having ideas about land use which were totally different from the way the Aboriginals viewed the environment. The white intruders wanted to make the land productive, they had to try to find some useful staple and to establish a base of self-sufficiency. Yet they were so unfamiliar with their new environment that they had to undertake many experiments in their quest for success. Finally, as the impetus for development moved in the mid 1840s from the direction and control of the government to the initiative and enterprise of private free settlers, so the appurtenances of 'civilised' nineteenth century living began to appear in the straggling urban centre of Brisbane.

The success of the settlement was partly a factor of the competency of the Europeans involved. In particular, the role of the commandants was important since the Sydney authorities left much of the planning and execution, especially at the particular and daily level, to the man-on-the-spot.

Table 5: Names and dates of commencement as Commandants of Moreton Bay Penal Settlement

Miller, Captain Henry	August 1824
Bishop, Captain Peter	August 1825
Logan, Captain Patrick	March 1826
Clunie, Captain James	October 1830
Fyans, Captain Foster	November 1835
Cotton, Major Sydney	July 1837
Gravatt, Lieutenant George	May 1839
Gorman, Lieutenant Owen	July 1839

Among the commandants, Logan and Cotton were the most effective. Both efficiently oversaw the daily operation of the penal establishment and, more importantly, both also had plans for the future of the area. Other commandants were less satisfactory from a development point of view; they tended to let the system drag along, seeing their role as a set of tasks to be carried out according to official instructions.

As to the convicts, they supplied the labour—the brawn and muscle to clear the land, build shelters and provide the produce for survival. Theirs was a rather unwilling role with labour extracted under duress. They had no plans for the future—except perhaps their own survival.

Table 6: Convicts at Moreton Bay Settlement[1]

Year	Male	Total
1826	145	145
1831	1019	1066
1832	792	836
1839	100	100
1841	131	133

When the free settlers came in the 1840s they saw a glorious future for themselves. Eagerly, rapaciously, they grabbed whatever opportunities presented themselves in this somewhat unregulated territory. They intended to use the vast expanses of land to generate the greatest possible profits so their planning was rather single-minded, with little thought for future generations.

To these three European groups, the Australian Aboriginals were at most an annoyance and a frustration; they were never a serious obstacle. By and large the commandants, convicts and settlers went about their tasks with little regard for these people—and generally with little obstruction. Official instructions with respect to the Aboriginals of Moreton Bay were similar to those issued to government personnel in other parts of Oceania—to establish friendly intercourse. But in this case little attempt was made to come to any real understanding of the Aboriginals, nor was any regard paid to Aboriginal holding of land. The usual approach adopted by convict officials was to keep the Aboriginals at a distance from the settlement—although friendliness was encouraged by the distribution of gifts such as tomahawks, blankets and so on, especially to Aboriginals who were helpful. For example, if they returned a runaway convict they would be rewarded.

Misunderstandings, nevertheless, easily arose and trouble often ensued. At Brisbane Town raids by Aboriginals on the cornfields led to a guard being posted around the clock but, even so, numerous fracas occurred with some shootings and killings. Aboriginals suffered in these incidents far more than Europeans but the latter had to be careful as they could easily be ambushed when some distance from the settlement.[2] European belief in the so-called hostility and ferocity of Aboriginals was whetted at the time by reports of the murders of survivors from shipwrecks in north-eastern Australia. On Stradbroke Island relations between the two races deteriorated considerably, with reports of a 'massacre' of Aboriginals in the mid 1830s.[3]

By the late 1830s a humanitarian concern was arising among officials in London—and then in Sydney—about the welfare of native inhabitants. Major Cotton, when appointed to Moreton Bay, put up a forward-looking plan that the more northerly tribes be visited by a properly equipped party which would slowly progress along the coast, spending about ten days with each group, distributing gifts, indulging in friendly intercourse and gaining their confidence, while at the same time undertaking surveys and so reducing the real cost of the venture.[4] This plan was not put into operation, but an alternative was implemented by the Reverend Dr JD Lang, who installed two Lutheran pastors (with a support group of twenty Germans) at Xions Hill about seven miles north of Brisbane. Although this group eventually began to succeed as a farming community, their religious and 'civilising' work among the Aboriginals was fruitless.[5]

Throughout the 1840s Aboriginal anguish mounted as squatters began making serious inroads into the Brisbane valley and the Moreton Bay region as a whole. In 1842 a nefarious incident occurred at Kilcoy station in the Brisbane valley involving the poisoning of Aboriginals. Already theirs was a lost cause. They could not withstand the pressure of the squatters taking up their land and those around Brisbane were becoming quite dependent on 'handouts'. The Reverend JC Handt noted in the early 1840s that their numbers were dropping; they had become 'rejects' through the failure of the missionaries to convert and 'civilise' them:

> The progress they have made bears . . . an inferior proportion to the time and strength which have been spent upon them: not as much on account of their being in want of faculties, as by reason of their unsettled and fugitive habits.[6]

Only occasionally did the Aboriginals provide casual labour during this early period. As the township grew on the banks of the river they must have been bemused by the scurry of white activity—by convicts, overseers and the commandant. To the Aboriginals this growing urban cluster provided some benefits in the form of handouts, but it also brought frustrations and hardship through lack of acceptance and exclusion from their traditional hunting, fishing and gathering lands. To the convicts the growing township meant hard labour, but also a degree of security. To the commandant the building of Brisbane Town might be either a stepping stone to future personal glory or a dead weight, a backward step.

As noted in the previous chapter, Brisbane Town was not well planned; indeed, its layout arose more by chance than by deliberation. The positioning of the various public buildings, residences and workplaces occurred without long-term development in mind. In the convict settlement, building sites were chosen at random, according to immediate impressions of expediency, convenience and function. Unlike the first settlement at Red Cliff, designed by Oxley, no grid was initially laid-out for the streets of Brisbane, but there was some degree of segregation of buildings according to the social caste of the people concerned.

Commandant Bishop witnessed the first growth of the township. The prefabricated, demountable, commandant's residence was moved from Red Cliff, and another was sent up from Sydney. The residences of those in command were placed on an elevated position near the river, while temporary accommodation was provided for the convicts, the military troops and for stores. Apart from being impatient with the lack of planning, Bishop was critical of the shortage of skilled tradesmen to undertake proper building. Construction work in Brisbane Town was supervised at first by military officers who were appointed as engineers or superintendents of works but who lacked adequate training or qualifications. In fact, it was not until 1837 when a civilian, Andrew Petrie, was appointed foreman of works that a truly competent person took over the task of construction.

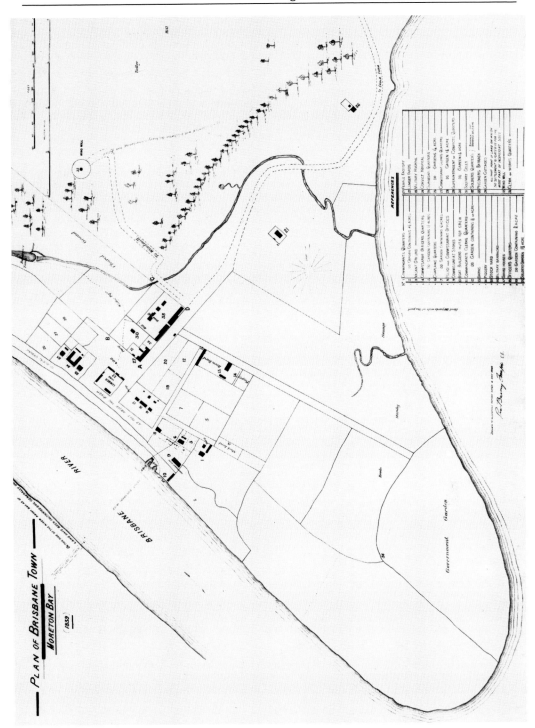

Figure 48: Brisbane Town in 1839 (original) (Courtesy of the Dixson Library)

255

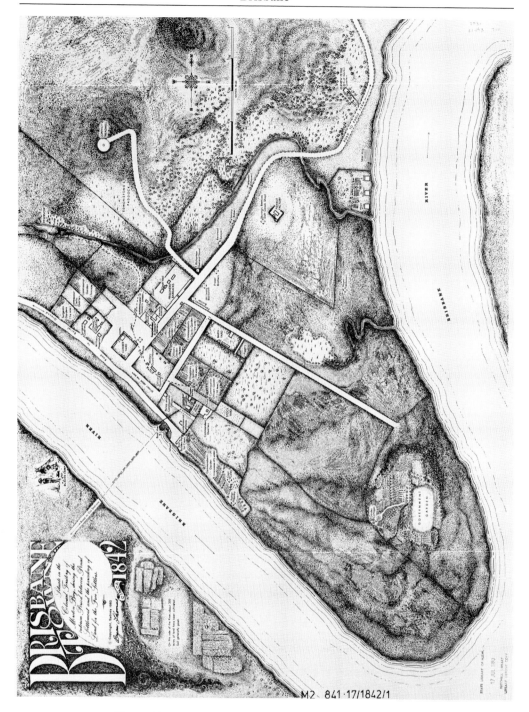

Figure 49: Brisbane Town in 1842 (Courtesy of the Mitchell Library, State Library of New South Wales)

Under Commandant Logan the township began to assume a more definite shape. Plans for buildings and materials were meant to come from offices in Sydney—the chief engineer's office (within the Directorate of Public Works) for plans, and the commissariat for materials. But this system often broke down. Of his own accord Logan went ahead with the building of a permanent prisoners' barrack in stone, rather than in wood as the governor preferred. Also without authority Logan provided for solitary cells in a brick apartment building. Both Bishop and Logan had hoped for a separate gaol, to make punishment more effective, but this was not realised. Administrative inefficiency often arose through conflict between local and New South Wales authorities. For example, confusion arose about the building of the hospital, when plans were prepared in Sydney while plans drawn under Bishop's directions had already been authorised and actual building begun.[7]

Only two buildings remain in Brisbane today from the convict period. These are the stone commissariat store on the river and the windmill on the hill. The years 1827 to 1829 saw considerable building activity, such as the two buildings mentioned above, a female factory (segregated from the men), and smaller residences and buildings.[8] A minor building boom also occurred in 1831, when the size of the convict establishment was at a peak. The permanent military barrack was provided at this time along with more medical facilities.

Public services and utilities in the community were minimal in the convict period. At first the water supply, coming from water holes in the vicinity, was poor in both quality and quantity, a situation that was improved but not totally overcome by the sinking of large tanks in the brickfields in 1828.[9] At one end of the town, on the point of the river, the government garden was set (later becoming the nucleus of the Botanic Garden) and at the other end of the town a burial ground was marked out. Tracks rather than streets grew up at first according to topography and function. The positioning of the prisoners' barrack, however, came to have long-term significance because, being such a large stone building and lying at right angles to the river, it was an immovable object with which the surveyors had to cope when they finally came in 1839. Indeed this building virtually determined the location and direction of what was to become the main thoroughfare of the city—Queen Street.

From this fulcrum of Brisbane Town on the river, with its residences and workplaces for military and convicts, tracks wandered out in various directions: one to the windmill, another to the bridge across Wheat Creek (later Creek Street), and the main path leading to New Farm and Eagle Farm. A track also led from the south side of the river to Emu Point (Cleveland), to connect with Dunwich (on Stradbroke Island) by water. In general, water provided the main means of communication between Brisbane Town and the out-stations, until Cotton began pushing through tracks in 1837.

Most of the buildings of the out-stations—at Amity Point and Dunwich and those at Limestone, Eagle Farm, Redbank, Cooper Plains and Oxley Creek—were temporary, flimsy affairs, usually slab huts. Eagle Farm had the most substantial buildings by the late 1830s with a large compound for women prisoners including a washhouse, hospital and school. Outside the palisade there were residences for the matron of women and the superintendent of agriculture, and huts for the men working the fields. The other camps had more makeshift accommodation—usually one hut for the soldiers and another for the working convicts; sometimes the overseer had a separate hut. At Dunwich there were two permanent buildings, a brick storehouse (within a brick wall) and a brick dwelling. Limestone (later Ipswich) also had one brick building for the military.[10]

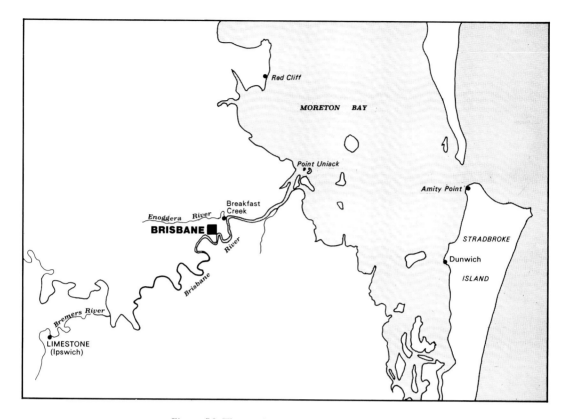

Figure 50: The environs of Brisbane Town

It was while Cotton was commandant that preparations for opening the area to free settlers began to receive proper consideration. Cotton was ably assisted by Andrew Petrie,
both seeming to desire to lay firm foundations for the future, in spite of the New South
Wales government's apparent determination to run the establishment down. In fact three
important developments occurred in 1838-9 with significance for the future shape of the
whole area. First, the German missionaries set up a farming village at Xions Hill (later
Nundah) which was set out on a rudimentary plan with a main street and houses of uniform size and pattern along either side made of slab and plaster. This was perhaps the first
real town planning in the area.[11] Second, as well as building a residence for himself and
family, Petrie prepared an inventory of the government's buildings in Brisbane and surrounds, and drew plans of them,[12] which enabled Major Barney, the colonial engineer in
Sydney, to draw up the first plan of Brisbane Town in May 1839. Third, in that same year,
the government sent up three surveyors: Robert Dixon, James Warner and Granville
Stapylton, to survey the coastal belt east of the range and south to the Richmond River.
Using a theodolite, these surveyors made the first accurate survey in New South Wales;
previous to this time such work had been carried out using compass bearings. In 1840
Governor Gipps issued instructions to map out counties and parishes, to set aside areas

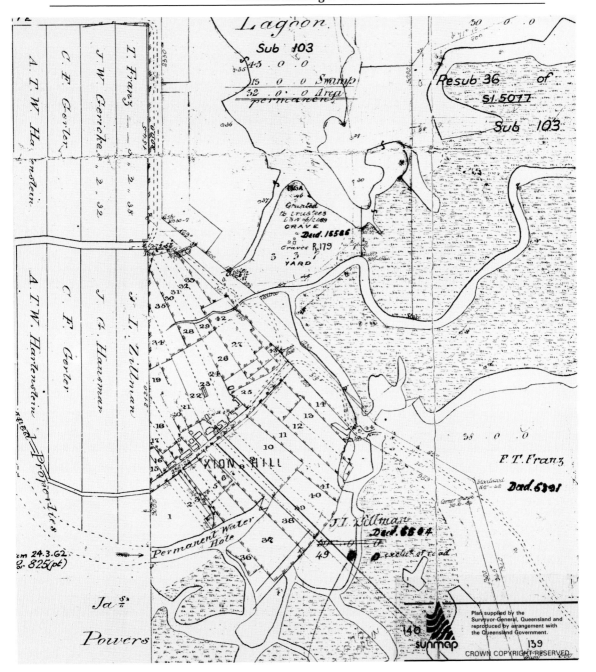

Figure 51: The Xion Hill settlement, Nundah (1862). The long blocks to the left of the township belonged to the German missionaries who established the settlement in 1838 (Crown copyright, supplied by the Surveyor-General, Queensland and reproduced by arrangement with the Queensland Government)

for towns and other public purposes, and to subdivide the land for sale, leaving small allotments for cultivation around each town site.[13]

So, between 1840 and 1842 the proper planning of Brisbane Town was at last undertaken. Dixon prepared the first plan, with large square blocks each ten chains long and streets one chain wide. Subsequent plans were drawn by Henry Wade, who replaced Stapylton. Ultimately a rectangular grid was adopted with Queen Street (in front of the prisoners barrack) providing the main alignment and blocks of ten chains each. Gipps had ordered that all street widths be a narrow one chain wide but Wade somehow arranged for Queen Street to be wider than the rest. The names of the streets were chosen from British royalty: those running to the north-east after queens—Anne, Adelaide, Elizabeth, Charlotte, Mary, Margaret—and those to the north-west after kings (and one Prince Consort)—William, George, Albert and Edward.[14]

The question of street widths may have reflected a belief that Brisbane did not have a

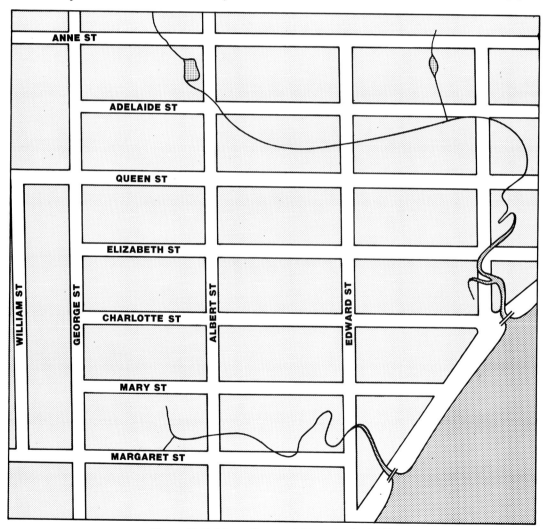

Figure 52: Brisbane Town as laid out in the 1840s

very significant future, but more probably fitted in with contemporary thinking that narrow streets in warm climates provided shade and created draughts. Criticism of the town plan arose not only on this issue but also over the failure to set aside adequate reserve and park lands, and the very limited extent of river frontage that was set aside for public purposes, such as roads, wharves and open public access. Considerable areas of land had been sold before the surveyor, Burnett, was instructed to determine adequate reserves for defences, boat harbours and anchorages and for the preservation of coal and limestone deposits or for any other purpose 'of public convenience, utility, health or enjoyment'.[15] So, in many parts private ownership already ran right down to the river. The issue of waterfrontage reflected the persistence of economic considerations in planning in New South Wales. In order to capitalise on projected demand for riverfront land, the surveyor-general rescinded the existing order that all land within one hundred feet of high water should be reserved, as 'whoever has the Water frontage on any river has the command of all the land in the rear of it.'[16]

The first land was not sold in Brisbane until 14 July 1842, although the surveys had been completed somewhat earlier. This sale, moreover, was by way of auction in Sydney. In the interim, however, the spirit of free enterprise had become firmly established, replacing the regulation of the convict hierarchy. Through 1841 and 1842, following the example of John Williams in South Brisbane, a number of traders and tradesmen had set up shop in North Brisbane, taking leases of convict premises. Soon two hotels were vying for custom.

The first land sale showed keen bidding and high prices were paid: for thirteen and a half acres the average price was £343.10s. per acre.[17] This interest was soon dampened, however, by a commercial crash in Sydney, and many lots were forfeited while others were sold off cheaply.

Gradually North Brisbane gained a commercial and trading ascendancy over other urban centres, often through default in decisions elsewhere and through the passage of time rather than through positive planning. Being the place of first settlement and initial command headquarters gave North Brisbane a start on the others which was reinforced by the failure of rival places to maintain a sustained campaign for primacy. None had outstanding advantages over North Brisbane and each had disadvantages. Government decisions, sometimes made reluctantly, sometimes unwittingly, helped to cement the position of North Brisbane. This was especially true in the case of the siting of the Customs House, which in 1848-9 the government decided should be at North Brisbane, despite the commercial development that had occurred on the south bank due to its easier access for shipping. In consequence wharf and store owners began to transfer their operations from South to North Brisbane. Retail businesses followed in their wake. Financial strength was added by the opening of a branch of the Bank of New South Wales in 1850. Through the 1850s building societies and a savings bank were established by local men, and the building industry expanded. William Pettigrew, for example, set up a steam sawmill in 1852. So, throughout the 1850s North Brisbane kept gaining over its rivals.

By this time Brisbane was large enough to support a number of local industries that replaced previous imports from the south. A soft-drink factory and a brewery were established, for example. This development of commercial, financial and industrial activity, although still small in scale, was a flow-on mainly from the overall economic development of the area and its consequent build-up of trade and shipping.

It was similar with the placement of administrative activity. When free settlement came, buildings already existed in North Brisbane which could be used for civil establishment purposes. So activity continued to centre there; for example, part of the prisoners' barrack served as courtrooms while in 1849 the female factory was opened as a gaol. Lower courts were established in 1843, and the Circuit Court of the Supreme Court opened in 1850. Postal services were offered from the beginning of convict settlement and from 1839 the post office was run from one of the brick apartment buildings in Queen Street. Otherwise, administrative functions in the area were minimal. Land administration was handled from outside Brisbane—from the commissioner's headquarters on the Brisbane to Ipswich road. Shipping safety was obviously centred in the bay area, away from Brisbane. This involved a transfer of pilotage duties from Amity Point to Moreton Island in 1848, and the erection of a lighthouse on that island in 1856.

While administrative functions were gradually expanding in North Brisbane and an economic take-off, based on the pastoral industry, was evidently imminent in the late 1840s, the social development of the area showed increasing signs of vigour. Some religious care had been offered to the penal establishment in 1829 and 1830 and again from 1837. Existing buildings were used for temporary religious purposes until 1848 when the Wesleyans began to build the first permanent church. In 1850 the Roman Catholics opened a 'beautiful' stone church in Elizabeth Street; the Anglican church opened in 1854 and other denominations followed in the later 1850s.

Education was not a high priority in early Brisbane. Nevertheless, from 1826 some tuition was provided for the young, usually at the hands of military men. In Brisbane Town school classes moved to three different premises in the convict period, while in 1836 a new school was planned for the Eagle Farm Female Factory. The German missionaries established their own school at Xions Hill in 1838. By the late 1840s both the Anglicans and the Roman Catholics had opened their own schools in North Brisbane and Fortitude Valley, and throughout the 1850s more private schools were opened in North and South Brisbane reflecting the growing population.[18]

Apart from formal education, self-education and self-improvement were strong characteristics of the rising society of Brisbane in the 1840s. In 1846 the first newspaper, *The Moreton Bay Courier*, was published in the belief that this infant society had already reached 'an advanced state', and accordingly needed 'those beneficial moral influences which have their origins in the Press'.[19] In 1849 a School of Arts was formed and two years later had its own building which incorporated a public hall, library and lecture-debating room. A second newspaper opened in Brisbane in 1850 and after 1855 even Ipswich's interests were advanced by its own newspaper.

In contrast to these cultural facilities, Brisbane was somewhat deficient in the kind of municipal utilities usually found in a nineteenth-century town. Throughout the 1840s and much of the 1850s authorities in Sydney neglected the provision of public amenities for this distant community, and whenever attention was paid to the north it was given to the hinterland—the productive areas. The local population itself was too small to make any major contribution towards providing a proper infrastructure. So the streets of Brisbane were largely unformed dirt tracks, and even when the town plan was implemented and the roads straightened they still remained boggy thoroughfares in wet weather. Two privately leased ferries crossed the river but their operations suffered because the approaches were so poorly maintained. As the 1850s progressed the Sydney government came under increasing local pressure, and eventually it provided more money for streets and bridges out of Brisbane, one being built at Breakfast Creek.

The poor condition of the streets in the growing urban centre was matched by an inadequate and impure water supply, which in the 1840s was still coming from the tanks built for the convict establishment in 1828-9. Recreational areas were also lacking, especially after the government garden was allowed to fall into neglect. In 1855 a trust finally took over its restoration. To some extent, then, when it came to the provision of recreational outlets, private enterprise made up for public neglect. By 1846 horseracing, cricket, rowing and billiards were established sports and in 1847 a vaudeville theatre opened, though only for a while.[20] On the whole, however, diversions were few and families created their own entertainment.

The emergence of a centre of 'civilisation' in the north-east was thus a hesitant affair, pushed ahead by some commandants and free settlers and hindered by the negligence and uninterest of others who failed to make adequate plans, concocted inappropriate development schemes, or did nothing. Where planning was most needed was in economic matters, particularly in the devising of a profitable economic base upon which a flourishing community could exist and expand. The quest for economic survival had been a major problem for the early commandants Bishop and Logan. In 1825-6 their efforts to establish relative self-sufficiency were bedevilled by shortages of labour, and especially skilled labour. Bishop reported only slow progress in clearing land, cultivating and erecting permanent buildings:

> Our present buildings are merely temporary, being constructed of slabs and plastering, for want of proper mechanics to erect others. I can only say I have but two men capable of doing anything . . . and they are in daily expectation of getting tickets of leave. There were ten men sent here some short time ago from Port Macquarie as Mechanics, but there is really not one amongst them.[21]

Nor were sufficient stock or seeds supplied to allow the community to move towards any degree of self sufficiency. Through 1826 the authorities in Sydney began to be more responsive to these complaints and requests from Moreton Bay, partly because a build-up of convict numbers was being planned. More livestock and seed were sent and, among the convicts, more skilled men were selected, especially from the building trades.[22]

Logan was enthusiastic about the economic potential of the area, particularly for tropical produce. But neither he nor the authorities in Sydney in the initial stages looked to much more than establishing self-sufficiency. Moreton Bay was not thought of as having potential as a granary, for instance, except for local use. The growth of tobacco and cotton, on the other hand, was given some encouragement at this stage. It was also thought that the area had an important pastoral potential and another recommended basis for growth was timber.[23]

In 1824 Oxley, Cunningham and Brisbane had been enthusiastic about the species of hoop pine found in the Brisbane Valley. Naval trials, using it for topmasts, were subsequently conducted and satisfaction expressed in Sydney with the results. Officers at the Deptford Yard in England, however, found it to be 'so very inferior as to be totally unfit' for the Royal Navy.[24] Nevertheless it was used widely for buildings and ships in Brisbane Town, Sydney and other parts of the colony. A main supply area for this wood was Oxley Creek (about seven miles upstream from Brisbane), where timber parties cut down the trees and prepared planks in sawpits as well as shingles and other pieces. Although a variety of timber species were cut in the area the most useful were definitely this type of pine and the less abundant red cedar.

In 1830 timber sawing provided employment for twenty-six convicts while others were occupied as builders and as boat builders, a small industry having been developed to supply local needs. Sadly, however, timber resources were indiscriminately plundered in this early period. JD Lang later pointed to the wilful destruction of several valuable species, such as the cypress pine, and the senseless felling of all the native timber on a number of bay islands. He also noted the wastage of timber; for example, hundreds of loads of cedar were left waiting for shipment at Dunwich, only to drift away with the winds and currents. The full extent of this destruction is not known but certainly by 1835, when Sydney authorities asked for an increased number of timber spars, the commandant had to admit there was a shortage of easily available timber.[25]

Two agricultural objectives exercised the minds of early commandants at Moreton Bay: the first was the usual imperial directive to achieve local self-sufficiency as quickly as possible; and the second was to develop tropical products. Certainly the first was the most urgent though it was not easily done, partly because of lack of knowledge of local soils and weather patterns and partly because government planning had failed to provide the necessary men and seeds, either in number or quality. By mid 1827, however, Commandant Logan was optimistic about the future. He already had a twelve-month supply of maize and he claimed that if the New South Wales government quickly sent enough seed he would be able to plant another 150 acres with wheat.[26] Unfortunately, his plans for wheat production were frustrated, for by the end of the following year it was sadly reported to London that crops had totally failed in Moreton Bay owing to 'a long and severe drought'.[27]

Agricultural growth received a distinct boost in 1828. This to some extent reflected Logan's planning and his interest in the future of the area. JS Parker arrived as superintendent of agriculture from Norfolk Island where he had held a similar position. Allan Cunningham visited Moreton Bay for the second time, as did Charles Frazer, Colonial Botanist, who was sent from Sydney to establish botanical gardens. These two indulged in considerable botanical research during their stay, which extended knowledge about the natural potential of the area. In response to medical advice that sickness at the Moreton Bay establishment could be significantly reduced through the supply of fresh vegetables, a gardener was sent from Sydney; in addition four cows were supplied to provide milk for the hospital.[28]

More important were the instructions given in 1828 to extend the amount of land under cultivation to cope with the expanding convict population. Although previously it had been intended to abandon maize cultivation on the south side of the river, this was now continued. At first Logan looked enthusiastically at 5000 acres upstream at Oxley Creek and forecast that in one year the settlement would produce three times the existing annual wheat requirement.[29] But, although given approval to proceed, this idea was dropped. Instead, in 1829, Logan and Frazer chose a 5000-acre site seven miles down stream at Eagle Farm which had good wheat and maize lands.[30]

This establishment started well, with better quality wheat than could be grown at Brisbane Town and such bounteous crops of maize that, early in 1830, Logan could send his surplus maize down to Sydney. But increasingly wheat production was unreliable and the quality of the grain poor in comparison with elsewhere. So the Sydney authorities determined to abandon wheat growing at Brisbane Town and to allow it on only a limited scale at Eagle Farm. The problem had arisen out of ignorance about growing crops in a humid, subtropical climate. Both Logan in 1830 and Commandant Clunie in 1831 proposed growing wheat further inland—on the Bremer—but the authorities refused to entertain such a notion, bearing in mind London's desire to restrict and reduce separate agricultural establishments.[31]

The year 1832 was a good one for maize production and again a large surplus was sent to Sydney.[32] But in subsequent years production slackened as a combined result of dryness, fires, weevils, vermin and government policy. As the convict establishment was allowed to run down, farm labour became scarce. In 1836 Commandant Fyans complained that the crop at New Farm, two miles from Brisbane Town, would be lost because there were not enough convicts to keep the weeds down, and that Eagle Farm had become useless because of reduced numbers.[33] By 1839 maize production was down to 2500 bushels, a far cry from the expansive days of 1831 when Clunie had reported the production of some 65,000 bushels.[34]

The second source of agricultural development lay in tropical products. Explorers were enthusiastic about the potential of the area in this respect. But initiative was slow in coming. This was partly because British knowledge on tropical culture was limited and problems of adaptation had not been faced. There was also some official hindrance. Sugarcane, in particular, was not encouraged, mainly because an experiment at Port Macquarie in 1825 had proved a failure. In Moreton Bay a little sugarcane grew luxuriantly but it was used mainly as a fencing break. The growing of cotton, and some other products, did receive mild official encouragement in convict times. But it was not until the period of free settlement that tropical cultivation began to be properly tried and tested. Even then there was an abortive start, with JD Lang in 1847 trying unsuccessfully to promote the cultivation of cotton in the Moreton Bay region by free British labour.[35] It was not until the 1860s that both cotton and sugarcane were able to establish some kind of viability in the local economy.

The agricultural and especially the subtropical potential of Moreton Bay was thus only slowly tested. This was not surprising since it was purely a penal settlement at first and lacked the entrepreneurial skill to profit from such endeavours. There was, however, a more easily exploitable resource—the broad pasture lands of the district. As overland explorers such as Logan and Cunningham entered into new areas—the Logan, Fassifern and Lockyer valleys and the Darling Downs—the potential for livestock production was immediately realised. The Darling Downs afforded 'a valuable and sound sheep pasturage' wrote Cunningham in 1827.[36] This value was increased even more when in the following year he discovered a pass through to the Richmond River in the south. Brisbane Town then became the obvious heart of the rich river valleys and downlands, so much so that Charles Frazer considered that 'it promises to be, ere long, the emporium of Australia'.[37]

Four pastoral stations were established in the early period, starting with one at Limestone (Ipswich) in 1827. This became a very successful sheep and cattle-run, which led to two other outlying stations being established—at Redbank Plains for sheep and Cowper's (Cooper) Plains for cattle. The agricultural establishment at Eagle Farm also carried stock, while in Brisbane Town itself cattle, sheep and pigs were kept for domestic use. In the 1820s there had been a scarcity of domestic animals—both Dr Bowman and the 1829 convict regulations made this point—and in the next decade more stock was supplied by the government so that herds could be built up. However, by March 1839 there were only 929 cattle and 4638 sheep.[38] Still, livestock breeding was the most successful aspect of economic development in the Moreton Bay district, as evidenced by the fact that production kept increasing through the 1830s even though the convict establishment was running down. Fewer problems were encountered in adjustment to the climate and environment than occurred with agriculture, the biggest problem being the poor quality of siring bulls and rams. Few people commented on the unsuitability of sheep in such a humid, subtropical climate. By and large the stock was healthy and pastures so 'luxuriant' that numbers kept increasing. Moreover the whole operation seemed so efficient in comparison with other aspects of convict activity, for only a corporal and private were required at each station to look after the small band of convicts that tended the government stock.

Brisbane Town emerged then as the centre of a pastoral empire, linked by road to the nearby stations at Eagle Farm (which was also agricultural) and Cooper Plains, and by water to Redbank and Limestone (which after 1837 were also linked by road tracks). Indeed this success in livestocking was to prove an embarrassment to the authorities in Sydney when they decided to close down the penal base at Brisbane Town. The possession of so many government animals meant that a small band of convicts had to be retained to maintain them. London authorities delayed until 1841 in giving the order for disposal by sale, and then the Sydney authorities had to wait until 1846 for a favourable market as the depression of 1843 had seen livestock prices collapse.[39]

One natural product that could have been exploited by the European settlers was fish, but this was confined only to limited local consumption. No serious attempt was made to use this abundant commodity until the 1850s when Dr Cowper began processing dugong oil at a small factory on Dunwich Island. As elsewhere, the building industry stimulated various economic activities. Stone quarries were established at Kangaroo Point and up the Brisbane River beyond Oxley Creek.[40] Lime was first produced from shells taken from the Bay, but the valuable deposits of limestone that were discovered by Logan in 1827 on the Bremer River soon led to a small lime-burning party being stationed there to work the kiln. River transport was used to ferry the lime and stone from their respective works. Brick-making was also an early activity in the settlement, with a kiln erected at Red Cliff and later at Brisbane Town. By 1826 brick-making was in active progress at the latter site.

Coal outcrops on the Brisbane and Bremer rivers were noted by early explorers, such as Lockyer and Logan. These were not exploited until free settlement when, in 1843, John Williams opened the first mine. Six years earlier, however, Commandant Cotton had seen the possibility of exploiting the coal resources to provide a bunkering supply, if the government ever decided to turn to steamers for the carriage of timber and other products from the Moreton Bay region.[41]

Taken overall, the Moreton Bay area had a sufficient variety of economic resources to justify the foundation of a trade centre, but it took considerable experimentation to establish a really viable base. It was fortunate that Brisbane grew initially as a penal establishment, as this provided time and support for the development of tried economic foundations, but it also meant that decisions by the commandants in that period largely shaped the destiny of Brisbane Town and its surrounds. As shown earlier, two of them stand out—Logan and Cotton. Under the former much building took place and under the latter longer term planning began. Both were concerned with the settlement's economic viability and it was on their foundations that the free settlers of the 1840s and 1850s were able to capitalise. The township itself developed initially as a ramshackle and motley collection of buildings, based on the convict past and then added to by freewheeling capitalism.

From the late 1840s Brisbane Town seemed assured of a flourishing future, as entrepreneurs began to tap the wealth of the hinterland and channel it through its port. Throughout the 1850s the separation issue generated considerable heat. A variety of questions were vigorously debated—but the location of the capital was never seriously raised. Brisbane, with its head start, thus gained the title of capital, the administrative centre and seat of government, when Queensland became a separate, self-governing colony in December 1859.

Notes

[1] Main records used were returns of prisoners from Convict Rolls, Peter Spicer's diary, 'Sickness and death at the Moreton Bay Convict Settlement', *Medical Journal of Australia*, II, September, 1963, p.474. For 1831 see *B.P.P.*, XIX, 1837, p.502, for 1841, *N.S.W.G.G.*, (Census). Figures cannot be taken to be fully accurate but do indicate trends.

[2] *C.S.*, 4/1395, (30-5-1827); *Logan Letterbook*, (28-1-1837).

[3] Steele, J.G. *Brisbane Town in Convict Days 1824-1842*. (U.Q.P., 1975), pp.172-6, 231-5.

[4] *Moreton Bay Correspondence 1824-1859*, A2, *J.O.L.*, Reel 9 (10-11-1837).

[5] Sparks, H.J. *Queensland's First Free Settlement 1838-1938*. (Brisbane, Smith and Patterson, 1938).

[6] Handt, J.C. Report on the Aboriginals for 1841, *H.R.A.*, I, xxi, pp.737-9, for 1842, *H.R.A.*, I, xxii, pp.647-8.

[7] Plans of the buildings at Moreton Bay are in the Queensland State Archives, see also Plan of Hospital, 29-8-1826, 4/1917.1, *A.O.N.S.W.*, Reel 751. For Brisbane Town in 1828-9 see Cunningham, A. *List of Buildings*, (30-6-1828), M.S.S. 1374, M.L.; and *Steele, op.cit.*, pp.86-8, 116-8.

[8] *C.S.*, 4/2081, July 1829, *C.S.*, 4/3794, (15-8-1829), *A.O.N.S.W.*

[9] Petrie, Andrew, Return of Government Property at Moreton Bay, (hereafter cited as 'Return of property'), (15-3-1837), *Letters from Moreton Bay 1835-1841*, (A115, J.O.L).

[10] Petrie, A. 'Return of property' *op.cit.*,

[11] Eipper, Christopher, *Statement of the Origin, Condition, and Prospects of the German Mission . . .*, (Sydney, Reading, 1841), p.12.

[12] Petrie, A. 'Return of property', *op.cit.*, (15-3-1839).

[13] *H.R.A.*, I, xx, p.209 1-7-1839; *C.S.*, 4/5429, (10-9-1840). Surveyor-General to Surveyors, *A.O.N.S.W.*

[14] Wade, 1843, MT 8, Plan room, Department of Mapping and Surveying, Brisbane. (Note that Queen Anne's name was misspelt).

[15] *C.S.*, 4/5431, 30-8-1845. *A.O.N.S.W.*

[16] *H.R.A.*, I, xxi, p.110-14, (19-12-1840).

[17] *H.R.A.*, I, xxii, p.148, (15-7-1842).

[18] Wyeth, Ezra, R. *Education in Queensland*, (Melbourne, Australian Council for Educational Research,), pp.40-57.

[19] *Moreton Bay Courier*, 20-6-1846.

[20] Laverty, John, *Development of the Town of Brisbane, 1823-1859*. (B.A. Thesis U.Q., 1955).

[21] *Letters to Moreton Bay*, *C.S.*, 4/1803, (14-3-1826), Reel 751.

[22] *Ibid.*, 4/3794, Reel 749, (8-2-1826 and 12-4-1826).

[23] *Logan Letterbook*, entry for 29-3-1826, *C.S.*, 4/2794. (10-5-1826 and 11-8-1826).

[24] *H.R.A.*, I, xi, p.456, (1-1-1825); *H.R.A.*, I, xii, (5-11-1827), p.621.

[25] Lang, J.D. *An Historical and Statistical Account of New South Wales . . .*, (London, Longmans, 1852), II, pp.255-6; A2, *J.O.L.*, Reel 8, (24-6-1835).

[26] *Logan Letterbook*, entries for 6-4-1827, 20-12-1827.

[27] *H.R.A.*, I, xiv, p.519, (12-12-1828).

[28] *C.S.*, 4/3794, (10-4-1828).

[29] *C.A.*, 4/3794, (3-4-1828, 6-6-1828); *Logan Letterbook*, entry for 20-5-1828.

[30] Steele, *op.cit.*, pp.113-4.

[31] A2 *J.O.L.*, Reel 5, (17-3-1830, 8-7-1831), *C.S.*, 4/3794, (8-6-1831, 30-7-1831).

[32] *Ibid.*, Reel 6, (31-1-1832, 30-6-1832).

[33] *Ibid.*, Reel 8, (6-1-1836).

[34] *C.S.*, 4/2539.2, Reel 751, March 1841.

[35] Backhouse, James. *A Narrative of a Visit to Australian Colonies*, (London, Adams, 1843), p.358; Regulations of 1829, *H.R.A.*, I, xv, p.105; Ross, William. *The Fell Tyrant*, (London, Ward, 1836), p.33; Lang, J.D. *Queensland, Australia*, (London, Stanford, 1861), pp.206-7, 224-5.

[36] Cunningham, A. 'Brief view of the progress of interior discovery in New South Wales', *J.R.G.S.*, II, (1832), pp.112-3.

[37] Frazer, C. 'Journal of a two month's residence on the banks of the rivers Brisbane and Logan, on the east coast of New Holland', (hereafter cited as 'Journal'), *(Hooker's) Botanical Miscellany*, I, (1830), p.265.

[38] *A2, J.O.L.*, Reel 9, 25-8-1837, 14-11-1837; *A115, J.O.L.*, 30-1-1838, and return of livestock 15-3-1839, *Australian*, 15-1-1839.

[39] *H.R.A.*, I, xxx, p.336, (25-4-1841).

[40] Frazer 'Journal', *op.cit.*, p.240; *C.O.*, 201/200, (24-2-1829) and encl.

[41] *A2, J.O.L.*, Reel 9, (14-11-1837).

Darwin

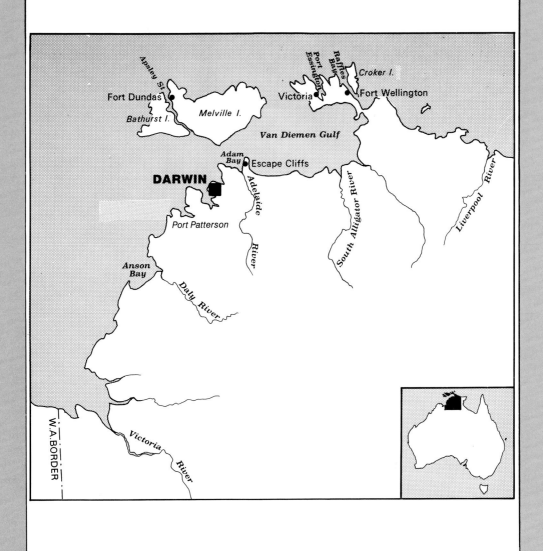

Chapter XIV

The Northern Settlements: Outposts of Empire

James Cameron

The British government made three unsuccessful attempts to establish a permanent presence on Australia's northern coastline between 1824 and 1849. The few historians who
have examined the origins of these settlements—Melville Island (1824-8), Raffles Bay
(1826-9) and Port Essington (1836-49)—have generally concluded that commercial
motives were paramount: these settlements were to be a second Singapore sited to tap the
trade potential of the eastern end of the Indonesian Archipelago.[1] Some historians have
been sceptical of commercial motivations, however, and, building upon Geoffrey
Blainey's observation that 'Britain was more interested in controlling Australian seas than
Australian Land', have argued that occupation of the northern coastline was primarily
strategic.[2]

The view developed here is that these apparently conflicting viewpoints are two dimensions of Britain's imperial impulse in the period following the Napoleonic wars, an
impulse fuelled by the search for raw materials and markets to sustain rapid industrial
growth and by the desire to establish maritime supremacy over its traditional European
rivals. The occupation of northern Australia when viewed in the context of Britain's continuing 'swing to the east' was only a minor act in this much larger drama. Why it should
have been occupied is explained by the increasingly intricate pattern of sea traffic in
neighbouring seas which, in some eyes at least, made it a location of some strategic and
commercial significance.

Before 1813 all areas to the east of the Cape of Good Hope were the exclusive trading
preserve of the British East India Company. However, the company's monopoly had been
gradually eroded by the activities of private traders, particularly from the 1790s when a
few traders were given permission to carry on a local or 'country' trade in the company's
Indian possessions.

The East India Company stoutly resisted the traders' inroads at first but was forced to
make major concessions when its charter was reviewed by parliament in 1813. Henceforth, traders could operate under licence in all areas east of the Cape except Canton.
This legitimised the opening of trading links with the Indonesian archipelago, made possible by its seizure from the Dutch in 1811. Seizure of the Dutch East Indies was made as
much to guarantee access to the heavily trafficked Sunda Strait as it was to punish the
Dutch for their alliance with the French, and was the culmination of a string of strategic

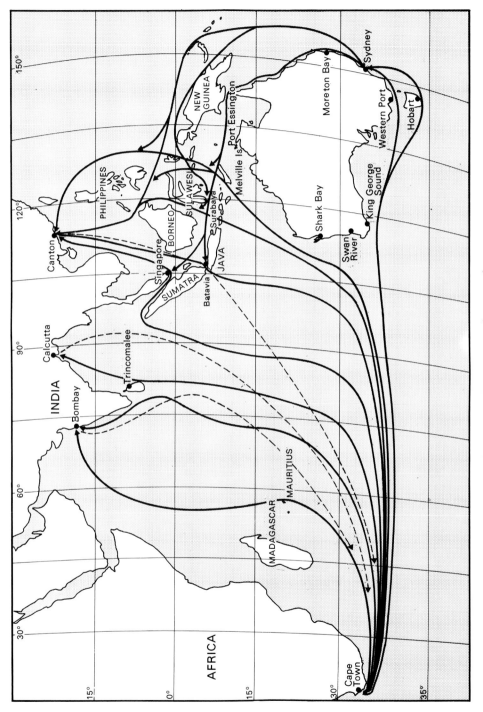

Figure 53: Swing to the east—as European trade centred more on the East and especially on Canton, Australia became more strategically important

seizures which saw the Cape, Mauritius and Trincomalee pass to British control. Trade throughout this enlarged region then increased sharply.[3]

Thus traders and the Admiralty alike viewed with dismay the return of the Indonesian archipelago to the Dutch in 1814, an action fully endorsed by the directors of the East India Company who considered that continued possession would be a major drain on their profits. Dismay turned to strident opposition when the Dutch promptly imposed restrictions on foreign shipping as this was seen as heralding the restoration of their former exclusive trading policies. The traders, therefore, openly welcomed Raffles' establishment of a free port on Singapore Island in January 1819. Located astride the much-used Malacca Strait, Singapore provided a base from which to control the Sunda Strait and from which traders could tap the western section of the archipelago.[4] Their approbation was not shared by the East India Company which feared that Raffles' flagrant breach of his instructions would jeopardise its fragile commercial understandings with the Dutch and could even precipitate war. It was widely rumoured that the company, supported by the Foreign Office, would repudiate Raffles' annexation and readily acquiesce to Dutch demands that the British be ejected. In order to present a united resistance to the Dutch and to gain maximum advantage from a forthcoming parliamentary enquiry into foreign trade, the traders banded together in 1820 in a loose association which became in time the East India Trade Committee. This committee was to play a prominent role in the first occupation of the north on Melville Island.

In July 1823, William Barnes, freshly returned from four years' trading between Sydney and the Moluccas, sought an interview with Lord Bathurst, Secretary for War and the Colonies, to lay before him vital information concerning Dutch involvement in the lucrative trepang fishery in the Gulf of Carpentaria.[5] Although firmly rebuffed, Barnes responded by urging the Colonial Office to establish a trading port in the gulf on the grounds that this would not only seriously curtail the exclusive control of trade which the Dutch currently enjoyed in the eastern part of the Indonesian archipelago but would also ensure direct access to the thirty or forty Macassan proas that came to the gulf each year in search of trepang. Once the port was established, the Macassans would exchange their trepang there for a wide range of British manufactured goods which they would then sell throughout the archipelago.[6] Believing Barnes' proposition to be a commercial rather than a colonial matter, the Colonial Office referred it to the Board of Trade for consideration.[7]

Barnes admitted having received the enthusiastic support of a 'few of the first merchants' for his proposal, but he did not reveal that these merchants constituted the East India Trade Committee, or that he, as an employee of one of the largest trading houses, was acting on their behalf. But the committee, now representing the twenty largest companies involved in the eastern trade, including several with a strong Australian interest, subsequently held informal discussions with Colonial Office officials and with Phillip Parker King. On 13 December 1823, five months after Barnes' first approach, the committee chairman George Larpent urged Bathurst to occupy Port Essington, the place recommended by Phillip Parker King who had just completed his survey of the north Australian coastline.[8] The timing of the request was no mere accident. As the traders were well aware, the final round of protracted Anglo-Dutch negotiations over rival territorial claims was to begin two days later.[9]

Larpent's proposal enhanced the commercial and strategic grounds for occupation which Barnes had outlined earlier. He was certain that Port Essington, as the centre of the trepang trade, would attract Macassan proas and Chinese junks in such numbers that it would become the dominant trading and strategic centre in the region, its influence extending westward to embrace all the islands of the eastern archipelago and eastwards through Torres Strait to eastern Australia, New Zealand and the 'unknown regions' of the Pacific.

Apart from its physical attributes of a capacious, sheltered and easily defended harbour close to fertile land which could support an extensive agricultural population of Chinese and Malays, Port Essington had the further advantage of being located beyond territory currently claimed by the Dutch and outside the jurisdiction of the Board of Control and the East India Company. Any settlement placed there would have to be controlled by the Colonial Office through its administration in New South Wales.

Despite urging the Colonial Office to give as 'little publicity as possible' to these proposals, Larpent's next move was to initiate a series of steps which would inform the Board of Control and thus the Foreign Office of the negotiations between the committee and the Colonial Office. Their purpose was to emphasise the necessity of retaining Singapore.[10] The Board of Control, of course, wrote immediately to Horton, the Parliamentary Undersecretary at the Colonial Office, to ask what intentions the Colonial Office had concerning the northern Australian coast. Horton, perturbed that the Board of Control should know that an approach had been made to the Colonial Office, delayed his reply for five weeks. Much happened in that time, culiminating in a mid January meeting between Bathurst and members of the East India Trade Committee.[11] Persuaded by the committee's proposal and convinced that he needed to act while negotiations with the Dutch were proceeding, Bathurst agreed to take immediate possession of Port Essington or nearby Mountnorris Bay. Accordingly, Larpent's memorial was sent for advice to John Barrow, Second Secretary at the Admiralty who was, as noted in Chapter VI, the recognised government authority on the southern hemisphere. Barrow's reply and subsequent discussion with Horton endorsed occupation but not, as it turned out, at the sites or for the reasons put forward by the traders.

Barrow's involvement added a further dimension to the deliberations and was to shape events associated with northern Australia for the next twenty years. A fervent imperialist, he was an equally fervent advocate of Britain's naval supremacy and a trenchant critic of the East India Company for its concern with profits at the expense of the greater glory of the empire. Pre-eminent among British geographers of his day, Barrow had an unparalleled grasp of imperial geography and was convinced that colonies were essential for maritime supremacy and thus for Britain's security.[12]

Given this, it is perhaps surprising that Barrow's support for the commercial advantages the East India Trade Committee claimed for Port Essington was lukewarm.[13] While the trepang fishery could provide a means of involving Macassans in local trade, and he was not convinced of this, he was certain that the Chinese would not venture so far south. It was imperative, therefore, that Singapore be retained. But the northern Australian coast did hold the key to the eastern passages and should also be occupied.

This assessment, obviously endorsed by Horton, provided the framework for the instructions Barrow prepared for Captain Gordon Bremer, commander of the proposed occupying force.[14] Protection of the eastern passage was to have priority over the formation of a trading base, and Bremer was ordered to take possession of the area encompassed by Bathurst Island and the east side of Cobourg Peninsula before establishing a settlement in Apsley Strait between Melville and Bathurst Islands. If he could obtain more troops at Sydney, a further settlement was to be established at Port Essington. If neither site was suitable, then the garrison was to be formed on the Liverpool River, or, failing that, on the 'nearest convenient situation or situations on the North West extreme of New Holland'.[15]

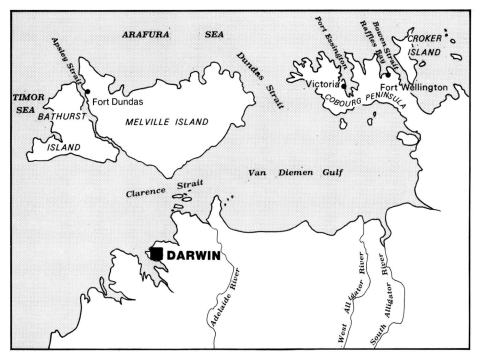

Figure 54: The Melville Island area. The first settlement was at Fort Dundas on Melville Island and the second Fort Wellington on Raffles Bay. The third settlement was at Victoria, Port Essington. Darwin itself was settled much later

Despite these developments, nothing of substance was said to the Board of Control when Horton replied to their queries at the end of January. Copies of material received from the East India Trade Committee were sent but again without reference to Colonial Office intentions.[16] Diplomatic negotiations had now reached a delicate stage. Although Canning, the Foreign Minister, was mainly interested in obtaining unrestricted access for British traders and used Singapore as a bargaining point, the Dutch had virtually conceded the island by mid January. A treaty was concluded on 17 March 1824.[17]

As soon as these negotiations seemed to guarantee the outcomes they wished, the East India Trade Committee all but broke off contact with the Colonial Office. Horton had written to the committee in February seeking details of the ways they planned to support the new colony but, despite several interim meetings,[18] the committee delayed replying until 17 May. Larpent then apprised Horton that, 'anxious to concur in the . . . furtherance of the objects which influenced them in soliciting His Majesty's Government for the establishment of the Settlement in question', 'several' merchants (actually Palmer, Wilson & Company) proposed sending the schooner *Stedcombe* under Barnes' command to open up the archipelago trade.[19] By then, Captain Bremer was well on his way to Sydney with Barrow's instructions.

Unaware that the traders' support would be at best half-hearted, Bremer reached Melville Island on 26 September 1824 with the *Tamar*, the transport *Countess of Harcourt* and the schooner *Lady Nelson* which was to be attached to the settlement. He had already examined Port Essington but, while being rhapsodic about its capacious harbour, rejected it as a potential site because of the shortage of drinking water. In line with Barrow's instructions, priority was given to the construction of a fortified emplacement on Melville Island, named Fort Dundas, on an open and well-watered site towards the middle of Apsley Strait. Progress was rapid and on the eve of his departure on 12 November, Bremer reported that the fort and pier were completed, the garrison of 113 men, including forty-four convicts, was adequately housed, the soils were fertile, the climate was healthy, plants brought from Sydney had transplanted well, and he had discovered fine stands of native cotton, nutmeg and pepper.[20] Despite this, three items buried in the body of his report should have triggered immediate unease: no evidence was found to show that the Macassans visited the site; although the anchorage was sound, the passage leading to it was very difficult to negotiate; and there had been a bloody confrontation on 30 October when some Aboriginals had been fired on and wounded.

Bremer's report reached London on 25 April 1825 by the *Countess of Harcourt* and was greeted with jubilation. Barrow was elated with his choice of site and urged immediate colonisation on a major scale. As he told Horton:

> There never was so promising a spot in a Naval, Commercial and Agricultural point of view, as the two Islands of Melville and Bathurst and the intervening Strait. The soil and climate is so fine that there is not an article either in the Temperate or Torrid zone that might not be raised ... We may here therefore redeem what we have lost by our generosity to the Dutch. And I have no doubt, that in a commercial point of view, it will become another Singapore.[21]

The traders' response was more circumspect but equally favourable. Following a meeting with Horton on 3 May at which the question of colonisation was discussed, they sought the government's reaction three days later to a proposal modelled on the Australian Agricultural Company in which they would undertake to introduce agricultural settlers in return for a charter to the whole area between 129°E and 135°E. This received enthusiastic support but when Horton pressed them for more details, the traders drew back to await further intelligence from the settlement.[22]

When this did reach the Colonial Office in February of the following year the traders were not informed. The news was too bad. According to George Miller, the commissariat clerk at Melville Island, there had been a serious outbreak of scurvy in January which had persisted because the men had been placed on reduced rations which were all but exhausted by the end of March. Greatly alarmed by Miller's news, Robert Hay, recently appointed Permanent Undersecretary to the Colonial Office, instructed Governor Darling to mount an immediate relief expedition.[23]

Meanwhile, however, the Melville Island Commandant, Major Barlow, had sent a very different story to Sydney. In August 1825 Barlow had written a short and cheerful report to let his superiors know that scurvy was under control, no one was on the sick list, fresh supplies had arrived from Sydney and they were hopeful of a regular supply of cattle from Timor or Batavia.[24] But Barnes, now stranded on the island and experiencing Barlow's wrath for interfering with his administration and for supplying the convicts with rum, poured out a litany of woe to Begbie, the secretary of the East India Trade Committee. The settlement, he maintained, was in 'great distress for want of provisions' and the capabilities of this 'miserable hole' were negligible: 'we are too far west, and off the trepang grounds altogether, and it is my firm opinion that if we stay here until the day of resurrection it will be a place of no consequence in the commercial world'.[25]

This news, after Bremer's glowing initial account, was totally unexpected. Begbie wrote a stinging letter to Hay letting him know that the East India Trade Committee took the view that Bremer was culpable in not selecting a better site than Melville Island. The settlement was remote from the main shipping lanes as well as the trepang fishing grounds, and was only accessible through a dangerous channel. It was now completely isolated, 'not even having a boat . . . for fishing'. If a little more time had been given to the examination of the coast to the east, 'a settlement might have been formed in that direction . . . which would have afforded the advantages looked for'.[26]

Hay was equally appalled. He and Barrow, with whom he enjoyed a close personal and professional relationship, were in the midst of an ambitious plan to encircle the Australian continent with further strategic outposts at Moreton Bay, King George Sound and Western Port. He therefore moved quickly to repair any damage that Barnes' outburst might precipitate. After exploring the implications of Begbie's note with Barrow, he informed the committee that the Colonial Office was willing to attempt another settlement further to the east.[27] Simultaneously, Hay instructed the Admiralty to divert the next of its India-bound ships to Timor to collect urgently needed provisions and then to proceed to Melville Island to collect a small detachment of troops who were to use Croker Island as a base from which to explore the adjacent coast 'so that a fit spot can be selected for the formation of a permanent settlement'.[28]

When the *Success*, the ship chosen for this task, was ready to sail, Barrow and Hay had a further discussion.[29] As a consequence, the decision to occupy the new settlement with troops from Melville Island was overruled and Darling was instructed to provide another detachment from New South Wales. In addition, he was to hire or purchase a schooner to maintain communication between the two settlements and, when necessary, to obtain provisions from Timor.[30] They were unaware that Darling had already stationed the *Mermaid* at Melville Island.

The arrival in Sydney of the *Success*, captained by James Stirling, on 28 November 1826 coincided with the return of the *Isabella* from Melville Island bearing reassuring news from Major Campbell, the new commandant who had replaced Barlow in September.[31] Obviously in dread of his government-imposed exile, Campbell had been pleasantly surprised to find the settlement 'in a much more forward state' than he expected, well provisioned, and occupying a fertile, healthy site. As trepang had just been sighted in Apsley Strait, he was confident of attracting the Macassans but would delay doing so for the time being as this would mean sending the *Mermaid* to Port Essington where the Macassans congregated. Of more immediate priority was the use of the *Mermaid* to establish a regular trade with a Mr Bechade at Kupang.[32]

The *Isabella* was reloaded and sent north again but Stirling, now the urgency was over, declared that it would be unwise for the *Success* to follow immediately. This was the wrong season to attempt to form a new settlement and, in any event, his ship could be usefully employed while he waited for drier weather and more favourable winds. With Darling's blessing, Stirling sailed off to examine the Swan River area. As related in Chapter VI he returned to Sydney in April 1827 convinced he had found his 'southern paradise' and anxious to mount his long and forceful campaign to have the Swan River colonised.[33] Thus it was not until 19 May that the *Success* sailed north.

Unknown to either Stirling or Darling, Campbell had now changed his mind about

Melville Island. His optimism had persisted into the beginning of the rainy season despite destructive storms in October, increasing confrontation with the Aboriginals (in which one of his men was killed) and a fresh outbreak of scurvy. He had been hopeful as late as December that Melville Island would become the dominant trading centre in the region,[34] but that hope had vanished by early April.[35] The 'wet' had not yet ended but he had had his fill of it and the island. Scurvy and dysentery were rampant. Some men had been hospitalised three or four times, five men had died and the 'Constitutions of all are much weakened'. Despite the presence of the *Mermaid* and the *Ann* which he had been forced to hire, and despite being reprovisioned by the *Isabella,* it was a constant struggle to maintain adequate supplies. A severe storm, northern Australia's first recorded cyclone, had battered the island on 2-3 April, levelling the gardens which had been extended so assiduously and destroying buildings, the wharf and the settlement's two boats. Moreover, he now realised that the soil was poor, the climate unhealthy, the channel dangerous, the harbour unsafe, the prospect of trade illusory and the Aboriginals increasingly troublesome. Even the grass, which grew luxuriantly and to great height, was not nutritious. In sum, he was now convinced that the island would not 'answer the view of Government'.

On the eve of the *Isabella's* departure on 7 June and still anxiously awaiting Stirling's arrival, Campbell wrote again.[36] Cheered by the return of the dry weather and an improvement in health, and reprovisioned once more from Timor by the *Mermaid* and the *Isabella*, some of his earlier optimism had returned. It now looked as if Mr Bechade would establish a trading link after all. This was most opportune as the crops had been destroyed and mortality among the livestock had reached alarming proportions. As he had been able finally to send Lieutenant Williamson to inspect Port Essington he was confident that Stirling would endorse it as the site for the new settlement as it had a superb anchorage, ample fresh water and was the hub of the trepang fishery.

But Stirling, unaware of these developments and anxious to pursue other plans, had no time to make unnecessary diversions to Melville Island. After a quick and safe passage in which he nevertheless parted company with the *Mary Elizabeth* which carried troops and most of the equipment for the new garrison, he reached Croker Island on 15 June 1827.[37] Rejecting the island as unsafe for shipping, he began an immediate survey of the nearby mainland. Raffles Bay, selected as the site next day, had all the required attributes and Stirling expressed himself to be satisfied 'with the abundance and goodness of Fresh Water, the Security of the anchorage, and all minor advantages of soil, shade, timber, grass and fishing'.[38] Reassured by the commander of the *Amity*, who had been a member of King's earlier survey, that the Macassans fished in the bay, Stirling ordered stores to be landed from the *Lansdowne* which then sailed for Batavia. The *Amity*, bound for King George Sound, was sent to Melville Island with despatches for Major Campbell who promptly wrote to his superiors expressing his deep regret that his settlement was to be retained.[39]

Within a month of its arrival the *Success* was ready to depart. The stockade at Raffles Bay, named Fort Wellington, was 270 feet in circumference and nearing completion, the hostility between soldiers and the Aboriginals seemed to be under control, and the debilitating effects of a severe attack of fever showed signs of declining. The *Mary Elizabeth* finally arrived in mid July, its experiences being a pointer to the confusion surrounding the selection of this new site. After parting company with the *Success* and with inadequate or non-existent charts and 'no instructions where to proceed', her commander Lieutenant Hicks successfully negotiated a way through the Great Barrier Reef to reach Port

Essington safely at the end of June. Fully expecting to find Stirling there, he was astonished to see no sign of either ships or settlement. After waiting a week he had sailed on to Melville Island where Campbell told him about Raffles Bay.[40] Unconcerned by this and the now unseaworthy state of the *Mary Elizabeth*, Stirling set sail for Melville Island on 23 July. Staying only long enough to declare that the *Mermaid* was also unseaworthy, Stirling sailed for Penang on 29 July 1827. Events now moved inexorably towards a major crisis, impelled by the actions of the traders, Stirling and Darling, and by reports of conditions in both settlements.

As long as news was encouraging the traders had been happy to claim credit for the occupation of northern Australia. Once they heard to the contrary they lost all interest. As for Barnes, their representative, he left Melville Island in early May 1826 to go trading throughout the islands.[41] After a brief appearance in Sydney which prompted Darling to describe him as an 'unprincipled adventurer' he vanished from the scene. Darling was forced to conclude that as commercial ventures the northern outposts 'have produced only disappointment and expense, without holding out any prospect of a better result'.[42] About this there could be no dispute.

This conclusion was only a minor element in Darling's increasingly jaundiced perception of the extension of settlement around the coast. Throughout 1827 and into 1828 he asserted with growing candour that not only were these settlements very difficult to sustain and administer because of their remoteness from Sydney, but their very existence also placed the security of the parent colony in jeopardy. More than half the troops allocated to New South Wales were now on detached duty and too far away to be of use if an emergency should erupt. A rapidly expanding fleet of colonial vessels was required to service them. While each outpost might have an important strategic function which justified this situation, Darling felt compelled to ask in May 1827 if any one of them could 'consistently with the views of Government' be dispensed with. His October financial estimates showed an alarming increase in administrative costs and he felt compelled to register his objection to having to man and sustain remote settlements created by the home government for purposes not connected with New South Wales.[43] In this stand he received wide public support in Sydney.[44]

Thus Darling actively sought evidence that bolstered his concern. This was readily forthcoming. When Campbell's damning indictment of Melville Island written in April 1827 reached him in the following October, it was forwarded immediately to London with the observation: 'motives of policy alone can render it desirable to keep Possession of that Settlement, there appearing to be no other inducement whatever to retain it'.[45] This produced a flurry of consultation which built upon earlier discussions concerning Stirling's advocacy of Swan River and ensured that the fate of settlements on the northern and western coasts would thenceforth be intertwined.

As noted in Chapter VI, initial reaction to Stirling's glowing report of Swan River was decidedly chilly. Barrow had acknowledged that the Swan River area contained 'all physical elements required for settlement' but maintained that its occupation should only be countenanced if the outpost at King George Sound was to be retained and then as a separate colony. Moreover such an action was in no way to interfere with the retention of Western Port whose strategic importance Barrow took great pains to stress. He was far more reticent about the retention of Melville Island and Raffles Bay, however, believing that they were likely to succeed as entrepôts only if the government permitted their extensive occupation by Malays and Chinese emulating Raffles' actions in Singapore.

With the arrival of Darling's despatch and its enclosure from Campbell, Barrow's advice was sought once more. So that he could consider again the broad question of coastal settlement as well as the specific issue of whether the Melville Island garrison should be transferred to Raffles Bay, Hay provided him with all relevant reports. To underline the way the political winds were now blowing, Hay stressed that financial considerations now loomed large in Colonial Office thinking.[47]

On the specific issue, Barrow's advice was unequivocal. Independently of the great disadvantages of Melville Island, including the obvious unhealthiness of its climate, it had failed in its primary purpose which was to develop trade with the Malays. Its garrison should be transferred to Raffles Bay. This would enhance rather than weaken their broader purpose. With viable settlements at Western Port, King George Sound and Raffles Bay, and a possible settlement at Swan River, 'we may consider ourselves to be in unmolested possession of the Great Continent of New South Wales'.[48]

Barrow's advice on Melville Island was sent to Darling at the end of May 1828[49] but Darling had already reached a different conclusion three months before. The *Mermaid* limped into Sydney Harbour in late February after a protracted voyage from Melville Island. From the reports it carried, Darling learned that both Campbell at Melville Island and Smyth, the commandant at Raffles Bay, had examined Port Essington personally and deeply regretted that their settlements had not been sited there. Darling intended instructing Smyth to move to Port Essington 'as soon as his people are equal to the undertaking' and recommended the abandonment of Melville Island once more, for the general picture revealed in Smyth's and Campbell's reports was devasting.[50] The condition of the nine seriously ill evacuees on board the *Mermaid*, two others having died at sea, was a sufficient indication of just how grim the situation was.

Writing at the end of October 1827, Smyth recorded that progress at Raffles Bay had been initially rapid following Stirling's departure.[51] Major buildings were completed and several wells were dug to replace the rapidly disappearing surface water, but this progress all but stopped in early August when the first signs of a major outbreak of scurvy made their appearance. Since then forty-two men had become so ill they had to be put into hospital. Only twenty-seven of the settlement's seventy-six inhabitants were now capable of doing any work at all and only ten of these were free of the affliction. Treatment had been inhibited because of the acute shortage of lime juice and other anti-scorbutics. The vegetable garden was yet to be planted. To make matters worse, Cornelius Wood, the settlement's medical officer had attempted to take his own life on three occasions before dying from the effects of a violent fever.

In deep despair over Wood's attempted suicide, Smyth ordered the *Mary Elizabeth*, now partially repaired but too unsafe to send to Timor, to Melville Island on 1 October to request that Dr Gold might be sent to their assistance. It arrived there two days later in 'so very leaky a state' that it had to be beached once more for repairs. Fortunately, repairs to the *Mermaid* were now nearing completion. These were speeded up and Campbell set sail in her with relief stores on 6 October but ran into strong winds. It took him three weeks to reach Raffles Bay and when he did arrive Smyth was deeply grieved to find that he had come without Dr Gold or lime juice. He took some consolation from Campbell's agreeing to take back with him the most serious of the incapacitated including a soldier ambushed and speared by Aboriginals on 28 July.

When Campbell arrived back in Melville Island after his month's absence he was met on the wharf by a distressed Lieutenant Hicks who informed him of the death of his wife and her burial the day before and the murder of Dr Gold and Mr Green, the commissariat clerk, by Aboriginals. With no medical officer in either settlement, Campbell now had no alternative but to evacuate the most seriously ill. As the *Mermaid* prepared for its voyage to Sydney, his despair poured out in the despatch he wrote: 'I need not endeavour, by a long and circumstantial account of the evils that now surround us, to point out to His Excellency our critical situation, and the gloom that hangs over both these settlements.' Scurvy had now appeared among his men, the rains had already started and the vegetable seeds recently sent from Sydney were ruined; Mr Bechade had failed them once more and the yams, which he had been saving for seed and as a hedge against scurvy, were found to be decayed. The *Mary Elizabeth* was in no fit state to sail to Timor for fresh provisions and, for want of food, he was forced to slaughter many of 'our already reduced Herd of Stock and Pigs'. As for himself, 'I have had a complete surfeit on this Island and sincerely hope His Excellency will order me to be immediately relieved'.[52]

Darling's reaction was prompt and predictable. After organising the appointment of a medical officer, replacements for Campbell and his second-in-command and the early despatch of the *Governor Phillip* and the *Phillip Dundas*, he informed the Colonial Office that while the decision to retain or abandon these settlements was not his to make, he was compelled to note that neither place had been visited by trader or trepanger.[53]

In one of these fascinating twists of fate, Darling's views reached London at the same time that Stirling began his personal assault on the Colonial Office. Barrow's advice was sought once again but he was out of town, so it was John Croker, the First Secretary of the Admiralty, who responded. His reply was brief: he *'always* considered the establishments as of very doubtful policy' and was convinced of their 'complete inutility'.[54] Unaware of Croker's recommendation and equally unaware that Stirling was urging the occupation of Swan River as an alternative to the northern outposts, Barrow met Stirling on his return. So impressed was he that he recommended the immediate transfer to Swan River of the outpost at King George Sound as the first stage of its colonisation.[55]

As the two issues were mutually dependent, action on Croker's recommendation was delayed until the outcome of Stirling's negotiations was known. This allowed Barrow time to plead for the retention of Raffles Bay but he could not obtain Hay's support. In fact, Hay told him, with uncharacteristic bluntness, that the only issue now to be resolved was the occupation of Swan River.[56] And that is what turned out. As soon as Stirling convinced the Colonial Office that Swan River could be established at no expense to the government, the order to abandon the northern settlements was given.[57]

This should have ended the matter except that Darling, on receiving Smyth's and Campbell's alarming reports, had sought assistance from Admiral Gage, naval commander of the India Station who responded by diverting the *Satellite*, en route to Sydney, to the north coast.[58] When Laws, the *Satellite's* commander, arrived at the beginning of September 1828, conditions had much improved. He concluded that the commandants had objected to their isolation and had wilfully misrepresented actual conditions. In a stinging indictment he noted that the climate was in fact very healthy and 'infinitely superior' to that in other tropical areas occupied by Britons, and the unproductiveness of the soil was due more to ignorance of tropical agriculture than to infertility. Scurvy had been a problem, certainly, but that was also due to ignorance and a failure to take even basic precautions. As both settlements were now firmly established Laws recommended that both should be retained along with Port Essington because of their potential, particularly now that the Macassans had finally arrived, promising a flourishing trade.[59]

When this report reached London, Barrow was spurred into action once more. He nearly succeeded. Despite Hay's reservations, careful consideration was given to establishing Port Essington as a sub-colony of Swan River with Laws in charge.[60] While this did not eventuate, Laws' imputation that incompetent commandants had deliberately created an illusion of failure guaranteed that the issue did not die, particularly as later reports indicated that Raffles Bay was on the brink of success when it was broken up in August 1828.[61] Reports of possible threats from the French and the Americans and several shipwrecks in Torres Strait kept a small flicker of interest alive, but for the armchair strategists like Barrow and Hay the issue was very simple. A base on the northern coast, complemented as it was by Singapore, would contain the Dutch in a vice-like grip while warding off any foreign incursions.

Thus, Robert Hay, with another about-face, this time induced by his growing interest in the colonisation of New Zealand, told Governor Bourke, Darling's replacement, in January 1832 that abandoning Raffles Bay was both premature and injudicious as outlying settlements were essential for 'the future security and prosperity of our possessions in the Australian seas'.[62] Barrow pursued the same line two years later when alerting readers of the *Quarterly Review* to the implications flowing from the opening of China to private traders. An expected increase in the Britain-China-New South Wales trade would make security of the route through Torres Strait a matter of national concern.[63] This route, as he had earlier and unsuccessfully pointed out to the Colonial Office,[64] was under threat from continued Dutch expansion in the archipelago. With the Colonial Office committed to continuing tight financial control and to a belief that colonies should be self-sustaining, such pleas went unheeded. The locus of concern about northern Australia, such as it was, now moved to the Royal Geographical Society.

This society, formed with the primary aim of promoting geographical discovery, was avowedly imperial in orientation, its dominance by men prominent in government circles ensuring that it had a significant political voice.[65] Australia was of particular interest to its members so it is not surprising that Major Campbell was invited to address the society in May 1834 on the geographical potential of northern Australia.[66] While convinced still that Melville Island was unsuited for extensive settlement, Campbell extolled the attractions of Port Essington. It was a second Singapore.

Seizing the opportunity which his review of TB Wilson's *Voyage Round the World* provided, Barrow built upon Campbell's assessment in the following year.[67] Wilson, a naval surgeon employed on convict transports, had been shipwrecked in Torres Strait and so stayed at Raffles Bay during the last two months of its existence. He deplored the abandonment of the settlement when 'all the difficulties necessarily attending a new settlement had been overcome, and pleasing prospects for future prosperity had opened into view', and urged re-occupation.[68] Barrow, in a skilful highlighting of these observations, particularly Wilson's conclusion that the 'alleged causes of abandonment' were demonstrably false, developed a convincing argument for the importance of the northern coastline from a 'political point of view'.

Although the evidence is circumstantial, it is highly probable that George Windsor Earl, to whom the occupation of Port Essington is generally attributed, first heard the rumours that prompted his April 1836 approach to the Colonial Office from Geographical Society members.[69] He was firmly rebuffed,[70] but responded a month later by submitting a pamphlet, based heavily on Barrow and Wilson, which promoted the commercial and agricultural potential of Port Essington.[71] As Earl had been urged to write on behalf of a 'few friends' it is clear that a favourable attitude towards reoccupation was growing among the merchant community but, as far as the Colonial Office was concerned, he was only going over old ground. Despite the cogency of his argument, he was again rebuffed.[72]

Less than six months later, the situation changed. In November 1836, Barrow, now president of the Geographical Society, was approached by two young army lieutenants, George Grey and Franklin Lushington, who offered their services to go exploring anywhere in Australia that he or the society nominated.[73] Barrow had long been interested in the mystery surrounding the geography of north-western Australia and used this unexpected offer to reopen discussions with the Colonial Office and impress upon it the absolute necessity of ensuring that the whole of northern Australia was again placed firmly under British control. Marshalling the support of the society, he led a deputation consisting of the geologist Roderick Impey Murchison, the naval hydrographer Francis Beaufort, and John Washington the society secretary which met with Lord Glenelg, newly appointed as Colonial Secretary, on 6 December 1836 to seek financial support for the proposed expedition.

Their discussions ranged well beyond consideration of the benefits to geographical knowledge that such an exploration might bring.[74] Should a major river be discovered, for example, the superior advantages of a settlement established at its mouth for the protection of shipping bound to India and China and 'from its power of extension inland by water communication' would be 'incalculable'. Drawing attention to preparations being made by the French and Americans for similar scientific voyages to the area, Barrow felt compelled to again stress the vulnerability of northern Australia to foreign occupation and the likely effect this would have on the Australia-China trade, the growth of which was such that the Admiralty had under consideration a detailed survey of Torres Strait. Barrow and Beaufort were therefore confident that the Admiralty would join the Colonial Office and the society in a joint survey by land and sea. This would reduce the extent of the Colonial Office commitment as the Admiralty would absorb the costs of transporting Grey and Lushington to the north-west. Glenelg, fresh from his presidency of the Board of Control where he had successfully manoeuvred the East India Company into accepting the end of its trading monopoly, was well versed in the issues the deputation raised and, while shying away from the question of reoccupation, undertook to seek Treasury approval for a grant of £1000.

Without waiting for that approval, the Royal Geographical Society pressed on with its planning.[75] Under Barrow's guidance, arrangements for the maritime survey were completed and a detailed set of instructions for the land expedition was prepared. Earl was recruited to the planning committee to assist the Hydrographic Office to update its charts of the Arafura Sea and to advise on the most appropriate season for exploring the coast. This advice, read to the society on 13 February 1837,[76] helped to sustain the air of excitement but, unknown to the planners, Grey had already informed the Colonial Office that he had serious misgivings about his loss of control of the expedition he had initiated.[77] With the sympathetic support of James Stephen, Robert Hay's successor as Permanent Undersecretary, he was able to press his objections forcibly on Glenelg's attention.[78]

Perplexed by Grey's reaction, Glenelg turned to Barrow and Beaufort for advice. The summary of their discussion, dated 10 April 1837, was much more pointed than before:

> Having duly considered the important points on which your Lordship did us the honour of communicating regarding the former settlements in Northern Australia, and other portions of the coast in their vicinity, [we] beg leave . . . to observe that if our information be correct, the

mere act of taking, or resuming formal possession in His Majesty's name of any territory, unaccompanied by actual occupancy, would not be sufficiently valid to prevent any other power from seizing and forming a settlement on such Territory. If original discovery and the act of taking nominal possession constituted sovereignty, the Dutch might claim the larger portion of the Coasts of New Holland and Van Dieman's [sic] Land now occupied by us.[79]

To ensure that the several large rivers and fine ports to the east of Cobourg Peninsula were firmly placed in British control, it would be prudent to claim the whole north coast, particularly Cape York which was the key to Endeavour Passage and Torres Strait. 'If this point, or the adjacent islands, were in the hands of an Enemy the communication with India [from Sydney] by this route would be completely struck out, and consequences must be most pernicious'.[80] To avoid a repetition of earlier difficulties, the settlements should be occupied by marines under the superintendence of a naval officer, for 'naval officers, from their experience of difficulties and practical habits of providing against them, have more resources at their command than most others'.[81]

This summary, prepared with an eye on its eventual submission to the Treasury, was accompanied by a lengthy memorandum on the history of Melville Island and Raffles Bay which Barrow had prepared to show that they had been 'sacrificed' to hasty and unfounded misrepresentations, as evidenced in Laws' damning report.[82]

The complaints from Grey and Lushington were rejected[83] but Grey's continued opposition to Barrow's proposal ensured that his expedition came under the direct supervision of the Colonial Office.[84]

Alerted to these developments, Earl approached the Colonial Office once more. Restating his earlier argument, he strengthened the analogy with Singapore and stressed that the agricultural and commercial attractions of Port Essington were 'so obvious' that it would not remain unoccupied for long.[85] But Earl's pleas were again pushed aside.[86]

Yet, two days earlier Stephen had written to the Admiralty seeking an urgent response to Barrow's and Beaufort's memorandum because Glenelg was 'so fully impressed with the paramount importance of retaining permanent possession of the entire coast of Australia' that no time should be lost in taking the appropriate steps.[87] The Colonial Office had in fact been content to await a more favourable political climate but had been forced to act by a group of Greenock shipowners concerned at the loss of one of their vessels on the east coast of Australia and the 'barbarous' murder of its crew by Aboriginals. The solution they posed was the establishment of a string of protective settlements around the coast from Moreton Bay to Port Essington.[88] After considerable inter-office discussion,[89] the Colonial Office replied to the shipowners on 19 June, that the government was taking active steps to ensure the 'increased security of the lives and property of H.M. Subjects in that quarter of the Globe'.[90]

But it was another six weeks before Treasury approval was sought.[91] The grounds for approval were essentially those advanced by Barrow and Beaufort and included provision for the occupation of Cape York as well as Port Essington but emphasised commercial rather than strategic motives in an attempt to demonstrate that these settlements would be 'inexpensive to form'. Annual expenditure on the salaries of key officers was nevertheless estimated at £1465. Treasury was also notified that an expedition was ready to sail as soon as approval was given but this Spring Rice, the Chancellor of the Exchequer, refused to give. He told Barrow and Glenelg that he was not prepared to seek parliamentary approval at present for the reoccupation of a settlement that had already been abandoned as unsuitable.[92]

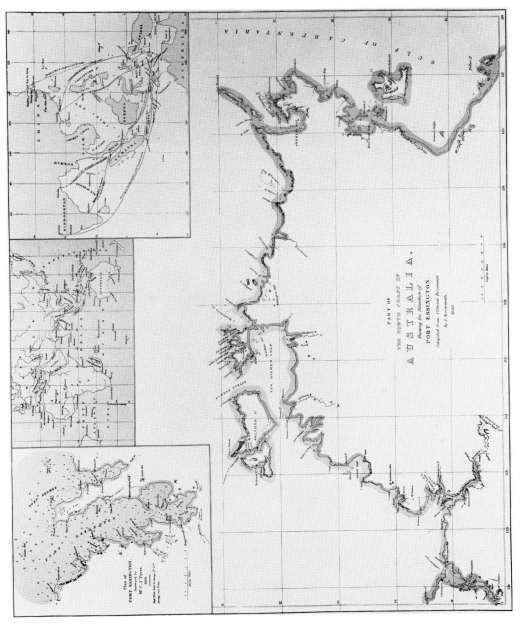

Figure 55: Port Essington in context (Courtesy of the Mitchell Library, State Library of New South Wales)

What happened subsequently cannot be reconstructed precisely because no record exists of the various meetings between Spring Rice, Glenelg and Barrow. Nevertheless, it is clear that, despite strong pressure from Barrow and Earl,[93] Spring Rice refused to alter his stance. Barrow countered by arguing that occupation could be undertaken by a small naval force financed from within the Admiralty's normal budget. As success was inevitable, any opposition would be quashed once occupation had taken place.[94] This proposal was agreed upon by mid October. Earl was finally successful in gaining a government appointment as translator and draughtsman and Barrow proceeded to draft the instructions for the expedition which were submitted for Colonial Office approval in late January 1838.[95] Still with his grand vision of future prospects and quite contrary to agreement, he authorised Bremer, once more selected to command the expedition, to encourage colonisation on an extensive scale. But the Treasury, in reminding the Colonial Office that it was 'not prepared to sanction' such an undertaking, thwarted his plans once more.[96] Alterations to Barrow's draft instructions put an end to any possibility of a major British presence on the north coast. Bremer was not to occupy Cape York, only examine it in case occupation was deemed necessary at some point in the future. He was allowed discretion in fixing the site of a port, to be established 'for the purposes of affording protection to the increasing and beneficial commerce of Her Majesty's Subjects which is carried on through Torres Strait . . . and to afford a secure place of refuge for those who may meet with Disasters in the difficult Navigation in passing the Barrier Reefs'. But he was to 'distinctly understand' that there was to be no 'permanent settlement of Her Majesty's Subjects at the Port selected'.[97]

Bremer reached Port Essington on 27 October 1837 and set to work in much the same way as he had done fourteen years before. Like the other key actors, he had learned little from that earlier experience and the string of shortcomings that emerged had a familiar ring to them: Port Essington was too far south of the main sea lane to attract passing ships; the township of Victoria which Bremer established deep within the harbour was difficult to get to; the entrance was dangerous; all attempts to grow crops and achieve self sufficiency were thwarted, and trade, despite Earl's prodigious efforts, never showed any sign of developing. As a place of refuge for shipwrecked crews, Port Essington was a failure. The need was along the Barrier Reef, 1200 km to the east. After initial interest waned, the infrequent arrival of supply vessels and the survey ships then operating in north Australian waters provided the only break in the monotonous grind of garrison duty insisted upon by the Commandant, Captain John McArthur, a pettifogging martinet. That Port Essington survived until 1849 was due more to oversight than to any hope that it might eventually succeed.[98]

However, the early reports from Bremer at Port Essington had been so encouraging that advice had been sought from the newly appointed Land and Emigration Commissioners on the best means of regularising its status as a crown colony.[99] The commissioners responded enthusiastically. Although it was too early to judge agricultural capabilities, they recommended the immediate release of land for sale and the granting of a loan of £25,000 to enable this.[100] The Colonial Office baulked at approaching Treasury for such a sum[101] but was taking steps to transfer control from the Admiralty when disaster struck. Rumours reached London at the end of 1840 that the settlement had been totally destroyed by a violent hurricane.[102] With this it was determined that until Port Essington's

Opposite: Figure 56: Port Essington, from 1839 survey map (Courtesy of the Mitchell Library, State Library of New South Wales)

286

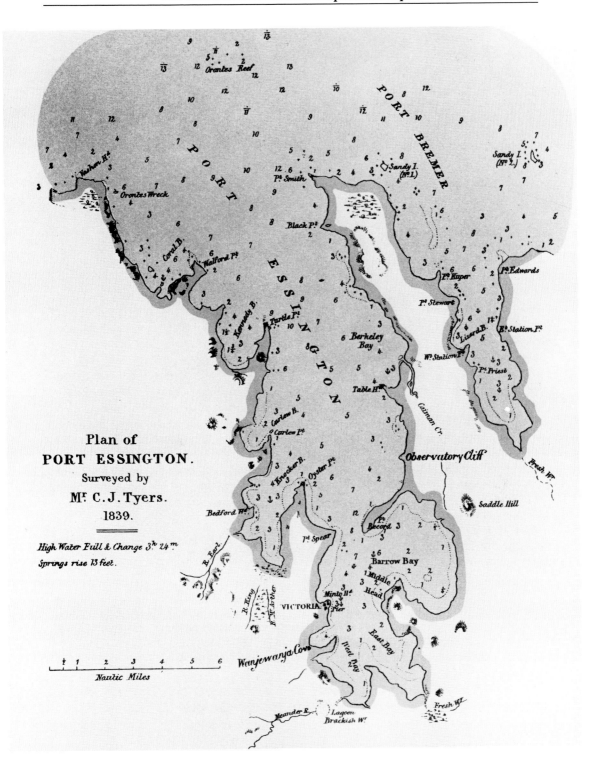

Plan of
PORT ESSINGTON.
Surveyed by
Mr. C. J. Tyers.
1839.

High Water Full & Change 3h. 24m.
Springs rise 13 feet.

Nautic Miles

success was assured, the costs of its administration would continue to be met by the Admiralty which would then be reimbursed by the Colonial Office. In effect, Port Essington would not become a Crown colony but would remain a naval station.[103]

Strenuous lobbying to have this decision reversed and to have the settlement thrown open for colonisation[104] had little effect beyond encouraging a group of London merchants involved in the Australian-Asian trade to propose establishing a trading post at Victoria in April 1843 provided they were given exclusive trading rights for a number of years.[105] Their proposal was immediately referred to the Board of Trade but then disaster struck again. Despite a gentle request for the board's reaction, made in the following February, nothing was heard until 20 November 1844 when a very embarrassed Dalhousie, now retired as president of the board, 'dug up out of one of my boxes' the papers sent to him nineteen months before.[106] Understandably, the merchants' initial enthusiasm had now waned. Equally abortive was a proposal made in early 1849 that Port Essington become a coaling station for the steamship service about to be introduced between India and Australia.[107] When the Admiralty moved soon thereafter to shed its responsibility for the settlement and reclaim its marines for normal duties, Port Essington was abandoned.[108]

As to whether northern Australia was occupied for commercial or strategic reasons, there is no definitive answer. The traders' initial interest was undoubtedly commercial but their actions were prompted by the uncertain status of Singapore. Once that status was resolved satisfactorily, they showed little interest. Certainly they did not object publicly, at least at first, to Barrow's selection of Melville Island which was not known to have any commercial attractions and was chosen for reasons of strategy alone; and while they pressed for the formation of a further settlement more to the east they showed no inclination to exploit the trepang trade as a means of gaining access to China and thus circumventing the East Indies Company's monopoly. Earl claimed considerable commercial support for the occupation of Port Essington but, if the traders' actions are any guide, that was illusory. By then the eastern archipelago was known to have limited potential and the traders had gained legal access to the wealth of China.

While he was inclined to shape his statements to suit the occasion, Barrow had no doubts about why the settlements were formed. As he stated with some pride in 1841 in his masterly review of the progress of the Australian colonies, Port Essington was the last and vital 'stake' in the 'ring fence' erected around Australia to keep out intruders.[109] That this was so and that it was necessary is open to question. The French visited Port Essington in 1839 and sailed away unimpressed.[110] The Dutch had problems enough in managing their dispersed possessions within the archipelago.

What can be said is that the occupation of northern Australia, however ill conceived and poorly carried out, was the product of the spread of empire and that this spread was influenced by a small number of key individuals, one of whom, John Barrow, is one of the most under-recognised figures in the story of Australia's colonisation.

Notes

[1] Howard, D. 'The English Activities on the North Coast of Australia in the First Half of the Nineteenth Century', *Proceedings of the Royal Geographical Society of Australasia*, (South Australian Branch), Vol. 33, pp.21-194. See also Donovan, P.F. *A Land Full of Possibilities*, (St. Lucia, 1981), pp.13-14; Powell, Alan, *Far Country*, (Melbourne, 1982), pp.47-8; Spillett, Peter, *Forsaken Settlement*, (NSW, 1972), pp.12-13.

[2] Blainey, G. *The Tyranny of Distance*, (Melbourne, 1966), p.72. See also Allen, J. 'Port Essington—A Successful Limpet Port', *Historical Studies*, Vol. 15, 1972, pp.341-60, and Graham, G.S. *Great Britain in the Indian Ocean*, (Oxford, 1967), pp.423-4.

[3] Redford, A. *Manchester Merchants and Foreign Trade 1794-1858*, (Manchester, 1934), p.112. See also *H.R.A.*, III, v, pp.755-7.

[4] Marks, H.J. *The First Contest for Singapore 1819-1824*, (The Hague, 1959), pp.1-2; Tarling, N. *Anglo-Dutch Rivalry in the Malay World 1780-1824*, (St. Lucia, 1962), pp.94-7; Wong Lin Ken, 'The Strategic Significance of Singapore in Modern History', *The Great Circle*, Vol. 4, 1982, pp.34-5. See also (John Barrow), 'Raffles History of Java', *Quarterly Review*, Vol. XVIII, April 1817, pp.72-96, and 'The Indian Archipelago', *Quarterly Review*, Vol. XXVIII, October, 1822, pp.111-38.

[5] 'Trepang', derived from Malay, was the name used throughout northern Australian and Indonesian waters for edible holothurians. They were also called sea slugs, sea cucumbers and bêche-de-mer. See Macknight, C.C. *The Voyage to Marege. Macassan Trepangers in Northern Australia*, (Melbourne, 1976), pp.6-7.

[6] *H.R.A.*, III, v, pp.737-41.

[7] *Ibid.*, p.737.

[8] *Ibid.*, pp.743-7.

[9] Tarling, *op.cit.*, p.133.

[10] Larpent to Courtenay, 18-12-1823, *India Office Records*, 1-2-1834, No. 64.

[11] *H.R.A.*, III, v, pp.750-53.

[12] On Barrow's influence see Barrow, John, *An Autobiographical Memoir*, (London, 1847); Lloyd, Christopher, *Mr. Barrow of the Admiralty*, (London, 1970); Varley, D.H. 'Sir John Barrow', in de Kock, W.J. and Kruger, D.W. (eds.), *Dictionary of South African Biography*, (Capetown, 1972), Vol. II, pp.34-6.

[13] *H.R.A.*, III, v, pp.751-3.

[14] When Barrow prepared Bremer's instructions, sent under Bathurst's signature on 17-2-1824, (see *H.R.A.*, III, v, pp.758-60) is unclear. An undated but much worked-over draft is contained in the bundle of Admiralty papers relating to the foundation of Melville Island in the *P.R.O*, at ADM 1/4239, 'Settlement of the NW Coast of New Holland and Sailing Orders for New Holland'.

[15] *H.R.A.*, III, v, pp.760-1.

[16] *C.O.*, 77/63, p.120; p.121; *India Office Records*, 1-2-1832, No. 27.

[17] The full text of the Treaty of Holland is contained in Maxwell, W.G. and Gibson, W.S. (eds.), *Treaties and Engagements Affecting the Malay States and Borneo*, (London, 1924), pp.8-17. See also Marks, *op.cit.*, pp.252-6.

[18] *H.R.A.*, III, v, pp.762-4 and *C.O.*, 201/155, p.37.

[19] *H.R.A.*, III, v, pp.764-5.

[20] *Ibid.*, pp.769-90.

[21] *Ibid.*, p.793.

[22] *H.R.A.*, III, v, p.792; p.793-5; and *C.O.*, 202/13, pp.334-5.

[23] *H.R.A.*, I, xii, p.187.

[24] *H.R.A.*, III, vi, pp.645-9 and pp.641-3.

[25] Cited in Spillett, P. 'From the Other Side: Indonesian Evidence on the Loss of the *Lady Nelson* and *Stedcombe* (1825)', *Great Circle*, Vol. 5, April 1983, p.27.

[26] *H.R.A.*, I, xii, pp.226-7.

[27] *H.R.A.*, III, v, pp.796-7.

[28] *H.R.A.*, I, xii, pp.224-5.

[29] *C.O.*, 201/175, p.27.

[30] *H.R.A.*, I, xii, p.339.

[31] *Ibid.*, p.749.

[32] *H.R.A.*, III, vi, pp.658-77.

[33] For an account of Stirling's examination of Swan River and his subsequent advocacy of its colonisation, see Cameron, J.M.R. *Ambition's Fire: The Agricultural Colonization of Pre-Convict Western Australia*, (Nedlands, 1981), pp.16-47.

[34] *H.R.A.*, III, vi, pp.677-86.

[35] *H.R.A.*, III, v, pp.799-808.

[36] *H.R.A.*, III, vi, pp.687-95.

[37] Stirling's activities are outlined in *H.R.A.*, III, vi, pp.808-11, and pp.811-5.

[38] *H.R.A.*, III, v, p.811.

[39] *H.R.A.*, III, vi, pp.696-8.

[40] *Ibid.*, pp.773-4.

[41] *Ibid.*, pp.659, 666.

[42] *H.R.A.*, I, xiii, p.796.

[43] *Ibid.*, p.110; pp.274-6; pp.301-4; pp.544-5; pp.549-51; pp.793-7; and *H.R.A.*, I, xiv, pp.11-13.

[44] See, for example, *Australian*, 8-11-1826.

[45] *H.R.A.*, I, xiii, p.551.

[46] *C.O.*, 202/20, pp.1-2; and *C.O.*, 201/185, pp.23-5.

[47] *C.O.*, 324/86, pp.73-6.

[48] *C.O.*, 201/195, pp.40-1.

[49] *H.R.A.*, I, xiv, pp.214-5.

[50] *H.R.A.*, I, xiii, pp.793-7.

[51] For conditions at Melville Island and Raffles Bay see *H.R.A.*, III, v, pp.816-20; pp.821-4; *H.R.A.*, III, vi, pp.698-701, pp.701-8; pp.774-81.

[52] *H.R.A.*, III, vi, p.707.

[53] *H.R.A.*, I, xiii, p.795.

[54] *C.O.*, 201/195, p.46.

[55] *C.O.*, 18/1, pp.96-8.

[56] *C.O.*, 324/86, pp.137-9.

[57] *C.O.*, 18/1, pp.67-9; and *H.R.A.*, III, v, pp.410-11.

[58] *P.R.O.*, Documents under ADM 1/193, S65.

[59] *C.O.*, 201/204, pp.15-19.

[60] *C.O.*, 201/204, p.24; *Mitchell Papers*, Vol. 4, pp.312-13, (M.L., A293).

[61] See *H.R.A.*, III, vi, pp.825-27; and p.832.

[62] *H.R.A.*, I, xvi, pp.505-6.

[63] 'Free Trade to China', (John Barrow), *Quarterly Review*, Vol. L (100), January 1834, pp.430 and 448.

[64] *C.O.*, 201/214, pp.9-11; pp.21-29.

[65] As well as Hay and Barrow, the first council included Sir George Murray, John Cam Hobhouse, President of the Board of Control; Mountstuart Elphinstone, a Director of the East India Company and a leading authority on India. The president, Lord Goderich, was Sir George Murray's replacement as Colonial Secretary.

[66] Campbell, J. 'Geographical Memoir on Melville Island and Port Essington', *J.R.G.S.*, Vol. 4, 1834, pp.129-81.

[67] Wilson, T.B. *Narrative of a Voyage Round the World*; (Barrow), *J.R.G.S.*, Vol. 5, 1835, pp.349-54.

[68] Wilson, T.B. *Narrative of a Voyage Round the World*, (London, 1835), pp.83-174.

[69] *C.O.*, 201/257, pp.505-6.

[70] *C.O.*, 202/35, p.16.

[71] *Observations on the Commercial and Agricultural Capabilities of the North Coast of New Holland* (London, 1836), *C.O.*, 201/257, pp.507-32.

[72] *C.O.*, 202/35, p.31.

[73] *Grey and Lushington Papers, Journal MSS Australia 1836, R.G.S.A.*

[74] Council Minutes of the Royal Geographical Society, 12-12-1836; Beaufort, Francis, 'Proposal for a Survey of the NW Coast of Australia', *Grey and Lushington Papers*; 7-12-1836, Barrow, 'Report of the Deputation from the Council of the Royal Geographical Society to the Secretary of State for the Colonies concerning discoveries in New South Wales', *Grey and Lushington Papers'*, 10-12-1836.

[75] *C.O.*, 201/256, p.51.

[76] Earl, George Windsor. 'Opinion on the Best Time for Exploring the Coast of Australia', *R.G.S.A. 'Journal' 1836.*

[77] *C.O.*, 201/266, pp.336-43.

[78] *C.O.*, 201/266, pp.664-45.

[79] *C.O.*, 201/264, p.37.

[80] *Ibid.*, p.41.

[81] *Ibid.*, p.40.

[82] *Ibid.*, pp.43-55.

[83] *Ibid.*, p.42.

[84] *C.O.*, 201/266, pp.664-5; *C.O.*, 202/36, p.70; *Grey and Lushington Papers* letter of 5-6-37.

[85] *C.O.*, 201/266, p.384. His argument was outlined in 'Appendix 1', pp.421-47 of *The Eastern Seas on Voyages and Adventures in the Indian Archipelago in 1832-33-34*, (London, 1837).

[86] *C.O.*, 202/36, p.52.

[87] *Ibid.*, pp.99-100.

[88] *C.O.*, 201/267, pp.113-8.

[89] *Ibid.*, p.115; *C.O.*, 201/264, p.67.

[90] *C.O.*, 202/36, pp.87-9.

[91] *Ibid.*, pp.132-5.

[92] *C.O.*, 201/302, pp.40-1.

[93] *C.O.*, 201/264, p.103 and *C.O.*, 201/265, pp.309-17.

[94] *C.O.*, 201/302, p.144.

[95] *C.O.*, 201/278, p.7-21.

[96] *C.O.*, 201/279, p.43.

[97] *C.O.*, 201/278, pp.12, 13-20.

[98] See Spillett, 'Forsaken Settlement', *op.cit.*

[99] *C.O.*, 385/19, pp.213-5.

[100] *B.P.P. (1840)*, XXXIII, (613), pp.45-50, letter of 18-4-1840.

[101] *C.O.*, 385/19, pp.310-11.

[102] See *C.O.*, 201/302, pp.162-4. The storm was graphically described by Lord Stokes in *The Nautical Magazine and Naval Chronicle*, 1840, pp.738-9.

[103] *C.O.*, 202/42, pp.271-2; pp.293-4.

[104] For example, *C.O.*, 201/327, pp.50-1; pp.99-100; *C.O.*, 201/337, p.21; pp.45-6; *C.O.*, 201/329, pp.35-45; *Board of Trade Records*, 6/278.

[105] *C.O.*, 201/340, p.162, also pp.163-4.

[106] *Board of Trade*, 6/278, (5-2-1844 and 20-11-1844).

[107] *C.O.*, 201/420, p.34; pp.423-4; p.425.

[108] *C.O.*, 201/420, pp.41-2; *C.O.*, 202/57, pp.131-40 and *C.O.*, 201/420, p.424.

[109] (Barrow) 'The Australian Colonies', *op.cit.*, pp.133-4.

[110] See Macknight, C.C. *The Farthest Coast*, (Melbourne, 1969), pp.87-103.

Chapter XV

Palmerston (Darwin): Four Expeditions in Search of a Capital

Robert Reece

No less than four expeditions were despatched by the South Australian government between 1863 and 1868 to choose a capital for its newly acquired Northern Territory and to survey a quarter of a million acres for pastoral use. Palmerston (or Darwin as it was called after 1911 when the Commonwealth took over responsibility) was thus the most elusive and problematical of all capital cities in its initial establishment. The story is a complicated one: lack of first-hand knowledge and poor communications bedevilled the efforts of a series of short-lived colonial governments who, regardless of the original reasons for annexation, became increasingly preoccupied with placating their land-order holders both in Britain and the colonies. Furthermore, from the outset there was a basic conflict between the idea of a capital in close proximity to the pastoral hinterland of the Victoria River near the Western Australian border, and that of an entrepôt port capital at the 'top end', based on mercantile-agricultural settlement. The lack of any agreed purpose for annexation and for the settlement lay at the heart of the problem.

*   *   *

British imperial interest in Northern Australia did not expire with the abandonment of Port Essington in 1849. Although the outpost had not attracted merchants, pastoralists and Indonesian traders in the way that some people had hoped, it had fulfilled its primary role as a garrison settlement, protecting the Torres Strait sea route and deterring French or other European imperialism in northern Australia.[1] By the late 1840s there was no longer the need for what Geoffrey Blainey has called the 'limpet port' strategy,[2] but there was an abiding interest in the economic potential of the north. John Lort Stokes who visited the area in 1839 had painted a favourable picture of the northern harbours and hinterland in his *Discoveries in Australia*,[3] and, like William Barnes and George Windsor Earl before him, campaigned vigorously in Britain in the early 1850s for the establishment of a northern settlement.

The concept of a trading entrepôt still appealed to the London merchants and this, together with interest in the virtually unknown interior and its resources, was sufficient to launch the North Australian Expedition in 1855, sponsored jointly by the Royal Geographical Society and the British government. Stokes was initially as anxious to join the expedition as his old friend Charles Sturt was to lead it. However, the command was given to Augustus Charles Gregory, an English-born surveyor who had migrated to Western Australia with his parents in 1829 and had quickly won the praise of settlers and officials for his expert bushmanship and his ability to follow instructions to the letter. Gregory's subsequent report of having traversed '. . . at least 3,000,000 acres of available grazing land' suitable for sheep in the Victoria River district[4] made a profound impression on pastoralists anxious to find new locations for their stock.

The driving force for South Australia's subsequent annexation of the Northern Territory in 1863 was thus its pastoralists and speculative investors, led by an expansionist governor, Sir Richard MacDonnell, who relinquished his position in 1862 and on his return to London became chairman of the North Australian Company which was to invest so heavily in land orders. However, the initial approach made by MacDonnell in October 1860 to the Secretary of State for Colonies, the Duke of Newcastle, for the extension of South Australia as far as the northern coast was evidently an afterthought, arising from his application to take the western boundary of the colony to the Western Australian border. His main argument was that pastoral occupation was already proceeding apace, thus creating a need to protect life and property. MacDonnell expected that the explorer John McDouall Stuart's northern route would be followed by pastoralists and that South Australia was well placed to provide a police presence 'till a separate settlement can be established at the Victoria River, or some other spot on the north coast . . .'[5]

The official case made by the Executive Council and forwarded to London by MacDonnell's successor, Sir Dominick Daly, in November 1862, focused exclusively on the Victoria River as the 'nucleus' of the territory to be acquired. On the basis of Stuart's reports from his first expedition, it was believed that pastoralists would be able to overland their stock to the Victoria River where the country was 'far superior to any known to be available in this Province.'[6] The Victoria River was also thought to be the 'best point' for the export of horses to India and China, while the 'intermediate settlements' thus established would facilitate the building of a transcontinental telegraph. In its own attached memorandum, however, the South Australian Pastoral Association did not advocate any specific locality.[7] Governor Daly pursued the issue again in a despatch to the Duke of Newcastle in December 1862 on Stuart's return from his second overland trek to Van Diemen Gulf. Ignoring the less favourable remarks made by the naturalist FG Waterhouse who accompanied the explorer,[8] the Governor echoed Stuart's euphoric report of the agricultural potential of the north:

> Arnheim's [sic] Land is described as possessing the advantages of a tropical vegetation, and as being highly adapted to the growth of cotton, whilst its proximity to the immense markets of the East . . . removes one of the greatest obstacles to the successful cultivation of that most valuable plant.[9]

Daly thought that pastoral settlement in the Victoria River area would come first, but he stressed the general importance of opening up 'this vast and magnificent expanse of country . . . where the greatest advantages exist for speedy communication and uninterrupted trade with the East Indies . . .:'[10] As it happened, however, the Duke of Newcastle had already responded favourably to the Executive Council's request[11] and Daly's commercial and agricultural arguments were not needed. Indeed, the imperial government appears to have been only too happy for someone else to bear the cost of supervising what Newcastle had chosen to call 'this addition of back country'.[12]

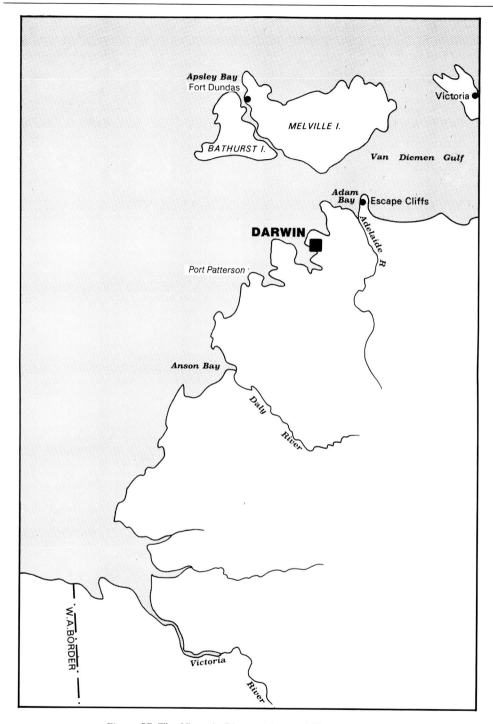

Figure 57: The Victoria River region and Van Diemen Gulf

Although the Executive Council had not stressed these arguments, there was some interest in a northern entrepôt both for exports from the Indonesian archipelago, and for horses and other livestock and tropical crops produced by Asian coolie labour in northern Australia. Indeed, it was this trading and planting view of the north, aired in Britain by Earl in 1836 before the establishment of Port Essington[13] and now revived by Stuart's euphoric account of the agricultural potential of the north, which was to influence the decision on the first site of settlement. Although some of the talk of a 'second Singapore' was probably for the benefit of the imperial and neighbouring colonial governments, who were properly sceptical of fledgling South Australia's ability to manage this huge addition of territory, influential members of the Adelaide parliament were confident that the Territory's economic potential was not just limited to the pastoral industry. Commercial interest was fuelled by newspaper accounts of British cotton manufacturers' need for an alternative source of supply in the light of the American Civil War. The prospect of routing a north-south overland telegraph, and possibly a railway, was also seen as extending South Australia's commercial scope so that it would become the 'leading colony'.

When the Waterhouse government's Northern Territory Bill was being debated in October and November 1863, the assumption was nevertheless that the Victoria River would be the focus of settlement. There was no discussion of location during the debates in both houses, the only real issue being the right of the government to sell land in the provisionally annexed Territory and the quantity and price to be fixed. A call for a select committee which might have dealt with the location and mode of settlement, thereby arousing public interest, was rejected on the grounds that there was an urgent need to proceed. What did emerge was the discrepancy between Waterhouse's original notion of the Territory being taken up by pastoralists on a leasehold basis without official settlement, and Treasurer John Hart's idea that agricultural settlement should be equally stressed. Chief Secretary Ayers stated at the end of the second reading of the debate in the House of Assembly that the first settlement would be made 'in the neighbourhood of the Victoria River' and that it was intended to send the Government Resident and stores there 'to found the settlement.'[14] However, the official government pamphlet on the Northern Territory, published in late November, made no mention of the location of settlement. Instead, it cited Earl's published views on both the Victoria River ('. . . appears to become the site of the first permanent settlement established on the northern coasts of Australia . . .') and Van Diemen Gulf ('. . . the gem of tropical Australia . . . [which] . . . may even compete with the Victoria River as the site of the great northern capital . . .').[15] Noting the pamphlet's failure to specify a definite location, the *Register* rightly pointed out that there were major disparities of climate between the Victoria River and the tropical north and that '. . . capitalists who might buy land for cultivation at the one place would not do so at the other.'[16] For its parliamentary critics, the whole enterprise seemed nothing more than 'a gigantic land speculation', 'something like the South Sea Bubble, and a vent for land jobbing and gambling'.[17]

By the time that Colonel Boyle Travers Finniss, former surveyor and unsuccessful politician, was officially commissioned as the first Northern Government Resident in April 1864,[18] the succeeding Ayers ministry had decided instead on the Adelaide River with Adam Bay at the western end of Van Diemen Gulf as the first destination. Permission had already been obtained from the British government to send the naval vessel *Beatrice* under Captain Hutchison to Van Diemen Gulf to conduct a detailed coastal survey, including the navigability of the Adelaide River.

As PF Donovan has pointed out,[19] what swung the balance in early 1864 was the attitude of the *South Australian Register* and the arrival in Adelaide on 10 February of Earl, former Crown Lands Commissioner at Port Essington, whose advocacy of northern settlement had been partly responsible for the establishment of the garrison in 1838. Earl's knowledge of northern Australia and the Indonesian Archipelago, together with his writings which included a *Handbook for Colonists in Tropical Australia*,[20] lend considerable weight to his memorandum to government advocating Adam Bay.[21] It was at this time, too, that the *South Australian Almanack* for 1864 was making available his 1837 *Observations on the unexplored Parts of North and North-Western Australia*.[22]

In its editorial of 27 February the *Register* reiterated the arguments for the Van Diemen Gulf area, which it had advanced in recent months: its advantages for shipping; its proximity to Indian Ocean winds; its easy access to Java and other places where cheap labour could be obtained, and its overland connection with South Australia by means of Stuart's route. If this were not enough, there were the additional arguments enthusiastically provided by Earl on his arrival: the probability of regular steam communication with India and Europe (thanks to the French in New Caledonia); and the healthiness of the area (thanks to it not being landlocked, like Port Darwin, which was otherwise 'an excellent spot'). 'Salubrity' was of particular importance to Earl whose own health had been broken by malaria contracted at Port Essington, and it may well have been this emphasis which swayed the minds of Ayers and his colleagues. It certainly coloured Earl's memorandum and was reflected in the instructions to Finniss. Adam Bay and Port Patterson further to the west both seemed strong possibilities but the *Register* was unwilling to commit itself to any particular site for a capital:

> It would be impossible . . . to decide satisfactorily upon the best spots within a given distance until the coast had been examined. All that is intended for now, is that the new colony should be in the neighbourhood of Van Diemen's Gulf, and not the Victoria River. This is desirable, not only for trading and maritime purposes, but also because the Gulf country is much cooler than the north-west coast . . .[23]

At this point, then, the commercial and maritime aspects of northern settlement, together with the health requirements of a resident European population were paramount concerns in locating a capital. Furthermore, the matter was urgent because the allocation of rural land was tied to a prior survey of urban land and *The Northern Territory Act* had provided that 'at a date not earlier than 1 September 1864' the Government Resident was to call a meeting of land-order holders and supervise the allocation of town allotments.

There was very little public response to the limited official and editorial discussion of the purpose of northern settlement and the choice of a capital. However, the question of names aroused some interest. One correspondent to the *Register* in early 1864 hoped that 'such appellations as Ayerston, Andrewsborough, Glydeville, Hartchester, or Santocombe' would be set aside in favour of Stuart whose 'indomitable courage, heroic fortitude, and persevering efforts had made South Australia the largest dependency in the British Empire'.[24] Another suggested that in commemoration of the tercentenary of the bard of Avon, it should be called 'Shakspeare' [sic] and its districts and divisions named after his characters. These, he felt, were certainly as euphonious as the names bestowed by Stuart on 'each sandhill, waterhole, rut, or claypan' after 'some Adelaide nobody who shook hands with him on his return'. They would also have the advantage of bringing the new colony to the notice of the old world.[25] All this was too much for a third correspondent who could imagine such shipping notices as 'For Shakespeare-town direct, calling at Much Ado About Nothing . . . '[26] Since Australia already had Queensland and Victoria, he concluded, why not Albertia and Albert-town?

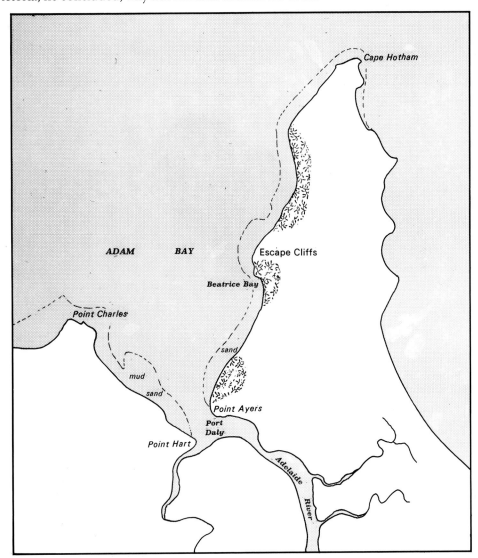

Figure 58: Adam Bay and the settlement at Escape Cliffs

In his instructions to Finniss of 14 April 1864, Chief Secretary Ayers specified Adam Bay, at the western end of Van Diemen Gulf, as the area which would first be considered as a suitable site for settlement.[27] Stokes, who named and surveyed the bay[28] and the Adelaide River in 1839, had described the hinterland favourably and one of his fellow officers, Lieutenant Helpman, had been lavish in its praise. Earl had given Adam Bay his blessing, although confessing that his personal knowledge of the place was 'confined to a passing view' in 1859. It is important to note the criteria that Finniss was required to apply to

297

Adam Bay, particularly in view of the allegations which were subsequently made against him. He was required to find:

> 1. A secure port or harbour, easily navigable, conveniently situated as a port of call for vessels trading to Malaysia and India.
> 2. A healthy site for a capital, at or near the port or harbour, in close proximity to water and timber.[29]

Indeed, 'salubrity' was a quality of 'the utmost importance', the fevers and other diseases experienced at Port Essington being attributed to the *malaria* (literally, bad air) or *miasma* which arose from swamps and land locked waters in the tropics.

From the outset, it was recognised by those in government that capital and port might not be one and the same. In fact, Finniss was told that it might be necessary to select sites for a capital and a riverine town as well as a port. The estuary of the Adelaide River, for example, might have certain advantages over a coastal port. All this reflected the conflicting considerations involved in the push for northern settlement. A port was essential for external communications and the entrepôt trade with south-east Asia, but a riverine settlement would be needed for the collection of inland produce and a capital for reasons of administration and, not least important, South Australian prestige. So optimistic was Earl about the economic potential of the interior that he even suggested in his memorandum that ships might eventually load at the different mouths, making it necessary to establish an inland capital 'in some central position near the sources of all these rivers' in order to reconcile conflicting local interests.[30] In the event of Adam Bay proving unsuitable, Finniss was to examine Port Patterson, the Victoria River, the other inlets of Van Diemen Gulf, and the western side of the Gulf of Carpenteria—in that order. Maritime exploration would be made possible by the government schooner *Yatala* and Finniss was expected to establish a depot for supplies and stock carried by the *Henry Ellis* which was too expensive to keep on charter. Having chosen a site or sites for settlement, Finniss was then to proceed to the all-important task of surveying 250,000 acres of town lots and rural sections 'in such a manner as to place the purchasers in possession with least delay'.[31] Detailed instructions on the method of survey were given to Finniss by Ayers, together with a memorandum from the Surveyor General, GM Goyder, who also urged haste in commencing the survey:

> In a new country—whose settlement is only attempted on the strength of lands applied for and sold prior to the blocks being marked upon the ground—delay in effecting the survey should be carefully avoided . . .[32]

For Finniss's benefit, Goyder also prepared a rough town plan, based on Adelaide's own grid system.[33]

When Finniss landed with his advance party at Escape Cliffs, Adam Bay, on 21 June 1864, he might well have reflected on the unpromising circumstances which had given the place its name: the narrow escape from hostile Aboriginals by members of Stokes' party in 1839.[34] Although the slight escarpment commanded a clear view of the surrounding country and the sea, the land was low-lying and in the wet season would become one vast swamp. The first priority at this time, however, was the livestock which the party had brought with them. One third of the sheep had died on the voyage and Finniss was concerned about the cattle and the horses. When water could not be found at Escape Cliffs, he decided to land the stock at a place forty miles up the Adelaide River which had earlier been located by Captain Hutchison of the *Beatrice*. When this was done, Finniss set out to explore the surrounding country in the hope of finding a site for a permanent camp for the forthcoming wet season, which might even serve as the ultimate settlement. A nearby range of hills seemed promising, but access was made extremely difficult by swamps and Finniss quickly abandoned the idea of an inland depot. Navigation of the Adelaide River had also been found more difficult than was first envisaged, because of obstruction by rocky bars and the need for ships to be towed. Finniss turned his attention once again to Escape Cliffs where a good supply of water was now located. This, together with its healthy location and access to the sea, persuaded him that Escape Cliffs should be the depot. Consequently the *Henry Ellis* was unloaded there and the next month was taken up with recovering the stores and stock from the river depot which had been left in charge of JT Manton, the party's senior surveyor.

On receipt of Finniss' despatch of 16 August from Escape Cliffs, reporting the need to discipline members of his party and the loss of some stores at the Adelaide River depot,[35] Ayers was regretful but expressed the hope that by the time Finniss received his reply the site of the capital, which had by now officially been designated 'Palmerston' after Britain's new Prime Minister, would have been decided and its survey started.[36] As it happened, Finniss had already fixed on Escape Cliffs as the site for the capital and Adam Bay as its seaport. Bearing in mind Ayers's emphasis on the required 'salubrity' of the site, he told the Chief Secretary:

> I do not believe that there is a more healthy and cheerful site for a settlement on the whole of the north coast . . . It is open to the sea breezes of both monsoons, and the soil is dry and well timbered for shade and building purposes.[37]

Adam Bay he described as 'a fine harbour' with shelter from winds at all seasons and where ships would be able to discharge cargo half a mile away when jetties were built. Altogether, Escape Cliffs 'would be as well provided with a harbour in close proximity as most cities in the southern seas . . .' and he had decided to 'make a trial of it' by establishing his depot there.[39] 'It appears to me that we have everything sought for, and certainly more than the Ministry expected' he told Ayers in a private letter of 13 August 1864 . . .[39] However, in deference to Captain Hutchison (who had just sailed for Timor in the *Beatrice* for badly needed supplies), and 'to avoid the imputation of having acted precipitately, and without sufficient information', he was willing to consider Port Darwin and Port Patterson as 'the only other places that can compete with this . . .' before making his final decision.[40] Finniss also announced to Ayers his intention to begin surveying in the neighbourhood of Escape Cliffs as soon as the stores had been recovered from the Adelaide River depot, a task which he expected would take until the beginning of September.

When Hutchison returned in early October, Finniss accompanied him in the *Beatrice* to investigate the potential of Port Darwin and Port Patterson as alternative sites for the capital. Although he did not explore the hinterland of each location, he rapidly concluded that there was '. . . nothing . . . to cause any alteration in my opinion as to the superior advantages of Adam Bay for a place of settlement':

> The superiority of Adam Bay and Escape Cliffs consists in its affording ingress and egress of and from the distant interior by water communication, which will be ultimately navigable by the largest vessels, and which in the meantime will be available for lighters bringing down stock from the interior to the ships' side when anchored either in Adam Bay or Port Daly.[41]

Consequently, he took responsibility for fixing on Escape Cliffs 'for the main part of the town' and on Port Daly (also known as The Narrows), a location he had designated for a river port near the entrance to the Adelaide River, 'for the remainder of the town allotments.' He sent Ayers a sketch map of the site of the town and the river port and informed him that surveying would begin as soon as hands could be spared from the construction of the Escape Cliffs camp.[42]

The work of surveying had not started by early December when the *South Australian* brought Ayers' first despatch of 28 October, but the disembarkation of the reinforcing party 'completely changed the aspect of affairs' and Finniss was now able to tell the Chief Secretary that he expected to make arrangements for the survey of Palmerston at Escape Cliffs, which he continued to believe was 'the best site in the north-west coast . . .'[43] He also went to some pains to discount the Victoria River alternative, which had enthusiastic supporters within his own party, and in so doing no doubt did much to fuel the personal conflicts which blighted his command from the outset. In Finniss's view, navigation of the Victoria River with its huge tides and powerful currents was even more difficult than the Adelaide River where steam tugs would be needed to tow merchant ships. While he did not rule out the possibility of 'new sites of Commerce and new ports' in the future, he believed that to make the first settlement at the Victoria River 'would be a complete and fatal mistake'. Indeed, he had 'never felt more satisfied with any opinion on which I may have acted than with that which I have formed as to the propriety of the site I have selected for Palmerston'.[44] With its outer harbour less than a mile from the landing place and its river port connected by a road of less than six miles, Palmerston could 'safely look to the future in support of its pretensions to be hereafter a flourishing settlement'.[45]

Finniss's first awareness that the Escape Cliffs site would arouse serious opposition in Adelaide had come a few days earlier when he had visited the *South Australian.* Although there was nothing in the official despatches brought from Adelaide to indicate that the site would not be approved by the government, he was given a taste of what was in store. On board the *South Australian* were three land agents, Jefferson Stow, John Stuckey and Jacob Bauer, all of whom strongly supported the Victoria River location. Whatever they may have believed on leaving Adelaide, their meeting en route in Brisbane with Gregory, now Queensland's Surveyor General, seems to have been crucial.[46] Gregory was an ardent advocate of the Victoria River location and was no doubt nettled that his advice had not been acted upon by the South Australian government. Finniss was somewhat taken aback when on their first meeting Stuckey asked him to take them to inspect the Victoria River country at once. 'He almost urged this request as a right; and seemed astonished when I informed him that the site of the capital was already fixed . . .'[47]

At this point the land agents had not yet inspected Escape Cliffs, an experience which was only to strengthen their demand for an examination of the Victoria River and other alternative sites. In a letter to Finniss written after a brief visit ashore, the three men totally condemned Escape Cliffs:

> while the capital of a new settlement required everything to attract, the proposed site of Palmerston has everything about it to repel settlers. It will have neither open country, pastoral land, elevation, agriculture, commerce, surface water nor building materials, and we feel ourselves, after the utmost serious consideration, utterly unable to imagine upon what grounds we could expect the proposed capital to attract population or become a commercial town.[48]

Accordingly, they announced that they would decline to select town allotments if the Escape Cliffs site was adhered to. In view of their influence with the land-order holders, this was no light threat and although Finniss answered many of their objections in his reply to them a few days later,[49] he did not make a full report to Ayers until the following April when it seemed that the land agents were about to make their letters public.[50] The agents' views, however, had already carried the day in Adelaide. On 10 January 1865, shortly after the return of Stuckey and Bauer in the *South Australian*, a public meeting of land order holders and agents was called by HBT Strangways, one of the principal agents for British investors. Although the meeting steered away from outright condemnation of Finniss, it resolved to ask the governor 'not to allow the site of settlement to be decided until a complete examination of the country has been made . . .'[51] Apart from his opposition to the Escape Cliffs site, Strangways was also concerned that dividing the town lots between town and port might allow a group of landholders at the more successful site to divert all the trade to their benefit. In this respect he was no doubt thinking of the British shareholders of the South Australian Company who held more than half the land orders and whose interests were entirely speculative. No doubt another important factor was the series of articles published in the Melbourne *Argus* in early January by a journalist who had been specially despatched on the *South Australian* to report on the progress of northern settlement. These were reprinted in the *Register* of 13 January, and provided further fuel for those land-order holders and others who had always favoured the Victoria River.

Although the government had said nothing to Finniss up to this point to suggest that it would not endorse his choice of Escape Cliffs, its principal concern was to satisfy the land-order holders. Even before the landholders' delegation to the Governor on 18 January 1865 it had been decided not to confirm Finniss' choice of Escape Cliffs until further exploration of the coast and the interior had been completed. According to Ayers, who wrote to Finniss of the decision on 10 February, Escape Cliffs had been 'condemned by everybody, including those resident there . . .'[52] although it could serve as a 'temporary location' and might even become in time a 'subsidiary township':

> the universal feeling is, that it is utterly unfit for the principal town, and certainly, before such a site is selected, situated as it is on a narrow peninsula, far removed from the interior, in the neighbourhood of swamps, not well supplied with fresh water, and deficient in building materials, a thorough examination of the seaboard and interior must be made . . .[53]

Captain Howard had accordingly been despatched in the *Beatrice* to assist Finniss in examining the area 'from Adam Bay to Port Darwin and Port Patterson and if necessary, the Victoria River'.[54]

Ayers told Finniss that he had made his choice of site 'too readily' and without sufficient consideration of the alternatives. He rightly believed that only a cursory examination had been made of Port Darwin and Port Patterson and expressed surprise that there had been no exploration of the country between the Adelaide River and Port Darwin. Examination of this country, together with other parts of the coast and the interior, was now to be of the highest priority and was to be carried out by a small exploring party while the surveyors worked on the survey of rural lands on the Adelaide River. In the catalogue of omissions detailed by Ayers, Finniss' failure to begin surveying either town or rural land loomed large, although it was by no means clear that the Government Resident could have embarked on this without official approval first being given to the site chosen by him. Ayers' concluding remarks, no doubt coloured by the bitter wrangles within Finniss' party which had reflected unfavourably on his leadership, sounded the knell of his recall six months later:

> There appears to have been an absence of that energy, and foresight which are indispensable in the leader of such an enterprise as you have undertaken.[55]

On Captain Howard's arrival in April 1865, Finniss went with him in the *Beatrice* to Port Darwin for a more thorough investigation while another party made its way overland from Escape Cliffs to assess the intervening country. In his detailed report on Port Darwin, Finniss concluded that while it was 'a magnificent harbour, as far as shipping and landing conveniences are concerned,' it was 'greatly inferior' to Escape Cliffs as a site for settlement on account of the unsuitable land and of water being more difficult to obtain. The principal objection, however, was its lack of 'salubrity'. The harbour was landlocked, surrounded by low mangrove shores and 'completely excluded from all breezes of a refreshing character.'[56] Captain Howard was enthusiastic about the area between Point Emery and Fort Point where deep water and a shelving beach made it possible to unload goods from ships at any time. However, while both Port Darwin and Escape Cliffs were equally well endowed with water, 'for coolness and health' he thought the latter was 'far preferable'.[57]

Finniss no doubt hoped that he had disposed of Port Darwin with his report. He told Ayers that he would soon investigate Port Patterson and the coast down to the Victoria River 'as I am sure that no one will be satisfied until I have done so.'[58] In the meantime he would proceed with the town surveys at Escape Cliffs and the Narrows, completing the marking of squares on which sections could subsequently be made. Even before visiting the Victoria River, however, Finniss was determined to answer the case being made for it in Adelaide. In a long despatch to Ayers of 15 April he detailed the case against the Victoria River as the location of settlement, citing Earl, Stokes and Helpman to support his views. He was already becoming defensive about the possibility of Escape Cliffs being passed over and likening himself to Colonel Light whose location of Adelaide he had supported at the time—against bitter criticism:

> the founders of Adelaide were similarly maligned and attacked; but South Australia and its capital have risen and thriven in spite of all early evil prognostication. So it will be with Palmerston and the Northern Settlement; but time with its results, only, can effectually solve this question—Is Palmerston . . . destined to become a great and flourishing commercial emporium?[59]

Not surprisingly, when Finniss finally visited the Victoria River in early August he found it 'one of the worst and most unsafe rivers for navigable purposes on the coast'. Nor was there any land of value, he suggested, until Gregory's Whirlwind Plains. The country there was 'fit for all purposes of settlement' and perhaps a port for inland produce, but not for a capital.[60]

In his despatch of 21 September 1865 recalling Finniss, and appointing the senior surveyor JT Manton in his place, Ayers made it clear that the main accusation against him was his 'delay in taking steps to ascertain the nature and capabilities of the country . . .'[61] In particular, he referred to the 'inaction' of Finniss and his party from the time of the *South Australian's* arrival in December 1864 to the following April and to the 'meagreness' of Finniss' reports. However, it was the survey of land at the head of the Adelaide River which finally discredited Finniss in the eyes of his own party and ultimately the government. With the wet season well advanced, much of the low-lying country surrounding Escape Cliffs became covered with water, thus providing tangible proof of the impracticality of the site. Although this made the work of the surveyors extremely difficult, Finniss would not be persuaded to abandon the effort and expend the party's energy elsewhere.

Two members of the three-man commission set up under Colonel WL O'Halloran in

February 1866 to investigate the charges against Finniss later concluded that, among other things, he had 'prematurely' fixed the site of the capital. While they conceded the possibility that there was no better or healthier location on the coast, they did not believe that this had justified Finniss:

> in fixing upon a locality surrounded with swamps, and so little elevated above the level of the sea, without previous examination of the coast and adjacent country.[62]

O'Halloran himself believed that Finniss had 'faithfully (and almost literally) carried out his instructions in respect to the port and capital' which he believed might prove with the assistance of Asian and Creole labour 'to be the best that offers on the northern coast'.[63] By this time, however, Adam Bay had long been discredited as a site for a capital.

Since the decision to recall Finniss had been based largely on his failure to examine alternative sites thoroughly, notably Port Darwin, Port Patterson and the Victoria River, the government needed someone who would complete this task. To this end, John McKinlay, who had earlier distinguished himself as leader of the South Australian Burke Relief Expedition, was commissioned in September 1865 to explore the country 'thoroughly' and to report on 'the best places for settlement and the most suitable localities for a capital'.[64] In his instructions to McKinlay, however, Ayers gave more emphasis to the location of pastoral land and its economic potential than to possible sites for a capital.[65] McKinlay was specifically directed to examine the country east of the Adelaide River towards the Liverpool River and its mouth, and then to move southward to the Roper River and its mouth, returning to Adam Bay by a different route. Ayers emphasised that his expedition should be made 'with the utmost despatch consistent with the efficient discharge of the undertaking'.[66] In the meantime, Manton had been given temporary charge of Escape Cliffs with instructions to obtain information about the adjacent country (which was not to be traversed by McKinlay) and to survey rural lands.[67] At this stage there was no mention of the Victoria River.

Arriving at Adam Bay in November 1865, McKinlay condemned out of hand the Escape Cliffs site and the 'disorganisation' which he believed had prevented more from being achieved. Describing the situation as 'beyond the power of my pen', he was still able to make this damning judgment:

> A greater scene of desolation and waste cannot be pictured; the whole improvement of the settlement would be much over-estimated at £200, exclusive of the wooden houses forwarded here from Adelaide. As a seaport and city, this place is worthless; the land up the Adelaide I have visited, where the survey parties have been employed, and not one individual land-holder out of every hundred could make a selection upon which he could erect his homestead, without the almost positive certainty of being washed off by floods, that must of a certainty occur nearly every season.[68]

Delayed in his departure from Escape Cliffs until January 1866, McKinlay's progress was greatly impeded by the floods of the wet season. Unable to reach the Liverpool River, he turned north towards the Alligator. After an epic but futile journey down that river on a raft made from saplings and the hides of his horses, he returned with his emaciated party to Adam Bay. When the prudent Manton then refused him permission to use the settlement's only boat to explore the West Alligator River and other localities, McKinlay described him as a 'maniac'.

Not surprisingly, McKinlay's recommendations on a site for settlement were inclusive. Port Darwin, he thought, possessed 'vast advantages' for shipping and healthy sites for a township on either side of the entrance to the port. Of these Talc Head on the western side would command all the useful country in the neighbourhood of the Adelaide River. McKinlay's personal preference, however, seemed to be for Cliffhead even further west in Anson Bay, near the entrance to the Daly River which gave access to the 'best land, as a whole, that was seen during the explorations of the party . . .'[69] However, sandbanks and rocks had made it difficult to navigate the Daly River and McKinlay was unable to give a detailed assessment of the country through which it flowed. Thus the information he supplied could not assist the new Boucaut ministry in making a decision on settlement. The range of alternatives for a capital had been extended, but McKinlay's inland exploration had taken up most of his time and energy and had not resulted in the discovery of the required tracts of suitable pastoral land.

Manton's judgment on McKinlay's expedition must also have helped to negate the effect of the explorer's recommendations. The surveyor, who had been in bitter conflict with McKinlay from the time of the latter's arrival at Adam Bay, told South Australia's Agent-General in London that it had been 'one of the greatest failures ever recorded in the history of exploration'.[70] Writing to Ayers on McKinlay's choice of Anson Bay for a capital, he said that it had been 'generally spoken against by everyone who had visited it'.[71] Port Darwin, by contrast, had been spoken of 'in the highest terms', and was 'said to be scarcely inferior to Sydney Harbour'. In his own opinion it was 'perhaps . . . the most eligible spot to be found anywhere round the north-west coast of this territory for the capital of the first settlement'.[72] However, he felt that he lacked the resources with which to undertake further exploration of Port Darwin and its hinterland. In the meantime he was carrying out Ayers's standing instructions to Finniss by supervising the survey of a township and 14,000 acres of rural land at Adam Bay, although he admitted that the whole exercise had been perfectly useless:

> I regret that it appears to be the universal opinion of everyone that has seen the country that it is not worth surveying, and in this opinion I concur, for, so far as we have been able to examine it, we have found very little else than mud flats and swamps, which are covered with water six months out of twelve, and what is not swamp is worthless land ridges and scrub.[73]

Although the substance of McKinlay's recommendations on Port Darwin could have been made available much earlier, his final report was not received in Adelaide until September 1866 when it raised general doubts about the advisability of persevering with the whole northern venture. By this time three of the five years which the government had given itself to satisfy the land-order holders had elapsed and a decision on the location of settlement was now a matter of some urgency. If JP Boucaut, the new Premier, could have had his way, the entire scheme for the colonisation of the Northern Territory would have been dropped and the land-order holders reimbursed. He believed that the government was legally liable, an opinion which was shared by the Crown Solicitor and upheld by the South Australian Supreme Court and the Privy Council when the British shareholders subsequently sued. Indeed, a temporary hold was anticipated by Governor Daly who wrote to the new Secretary of State for Colonies, Lord Carnarvon, on the day after McKinlay's return to Adelaide that the Adam Bay settlement 'must be considered a complete failure'.[74] Boucaut managed to get four resolutions through the Legislative Council, which would have meant abandoning the scheme and reimbursing the land-order holders,[75] but most of the members of the House of Assembly were determined to see it through and in the end would agree only to the withdrawal of the Adam Bay party.[76]

In late October 1866, the government called tenders for the survey of 300,000 acres of land without specifying any location. Altogether there were eleven responses, but the striking disparity in their estimates of costs suggested that more information was needed. In his report on the tenders, Surveyor General Goyder expressed his belief that the best site for settlement had still not been chosen and recommended that none be accepted, suggesting instead that someone be appointed immediately to select a site after visiting Victoria River, Anson Bay, Port Darwin and Escape Cliffs.[77] Boucaut subsequently decided to authorise another investigation. The British land-order holders were now demanding reimbursement, together with 10 per cent interest, and the embattled Premier attempted to hold them off by announcing that Captain Francis Cadell,[78] the swashbuckling veteran of the Murray River paddle steamers and the Pacific Islands labour trade, had been despatched to the north.

By this time, however, there was considerable scepticism about the wisdom of sending out yet another expedition. In an article some months earlier entitled 'Where is Palmerston?', the editor of *Pasquin* poured scorn on the whole enterprise:

> The Lost City—Palmerston in the mud—sold before it was discovered, lost before it was surveyed, and deserted before it was built. Founded by the people who had ruined their own country, and vainly hoped to make a tremendous mess of another, is represented, at present—on paper—by a plan in our favorite [sic] style of urban inconvenience and ugliness—as a gridiron in a swamp—Adelaide junior . . .[79]

Chief Secretary Blyth's instructions to Cadell of 22 February 1867 made it clear that the question of the capital was now of secondary importance:

> the principal object of your mission . . . is to select, as soon as possible, a favourable site for the survey of 300,000 acres of good land, within a reasonable distance of a secure harbour, easily navigable and conveniently situated as a port of call; with a healthy site for a capital, in close proximity to fresh water and timber . . .[80]

Just as Adam Bay had been designated as the most favoured location in 1864, now it was the Liverpool River district in Arnhem Land which had originally been recommended in 1858 by JS Wilson, the geologist who accompanied Gregory's party. Although he had not actually visited the area, Wilson cited the opinions of Captain PP King who had named the river in 1819 after what he himself called an 'imperfect and hasty examination'.[81] Apart from its access to what Wilson assumed to be suitable pastoral land, the estuary evidently offered good harbourage and was on the direct line of communication between the two oceans.[82] Blyth suggested to Cadell that owing to its geographical position, its fine river entrance and other factors it was, 'par excellence, the site for settlement'.[83] And Cadell himself believed that ' . . . Nature manifestly intended it as civilization's "starting point" for that region of Tropical Australia'.[84] The only questions to be answered, it seemed, were whether there was sufficient land for the government to fulfil its obligations to the land-order holders and whether there was a suitable site for a capital.

The first report telegraphed by Cadell to Chief Secretary Blythe from Burke Town on 26 September seemed to bear out the latter's optimism about the Liverpool River:

> Very good land is to be found on the Liverpool and immediate vicinity, commanding easy water carriage, as it is a fine deep estuary; moderately elevated land as a healthy site for a capital, with wood, water, and stone in abundance; it lies almost dead in the track of all ships coming through Torres Straits; it is exactly equidistant to our Queensland and Western Australian boundary.[85]

This favourable description was incorporated in Cadell's report, written at Bowen on 7 January 1868, in which he added that the site for the capital was fanned by a 'perennial

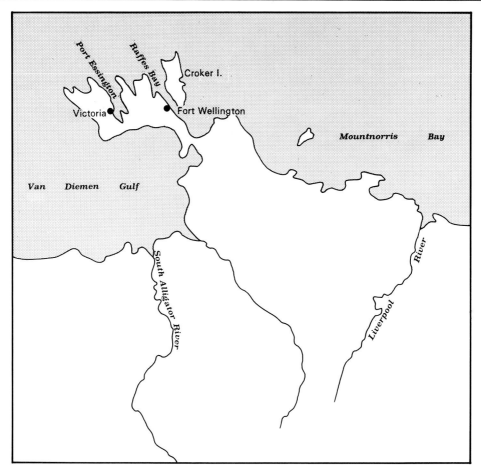

Figure 59: The Liverpool River area

sea breeze from the Arafura Sea'. Its general level of 'salubrity' was good and his party had suffered very little illness. The only disadvantage, as far as he could seen, was mosquitoes. Cadell reported that the interior possessed good soil, was well watered with 'luxurious' feed for cattle and within easy distance of water transport. Altogether, he considered that the Liverpool River location perfectly satisfied the criteria set out in his instructions. 'I therefore unhesitatingly recommend it as the *true base of operations*,' he confidently concluded.[86] He also believed that if it was put out to tender the necessary survey could be completed by the end of the year.

Of the other sites that had been suggested, Cadell had not been able to explore the country of the Victoria River:

> But owing to the numerous dangers of that rapid and shoal-encumbered river, also taking into consideration the 100-mile belt of most wretched, rocky, barren, and waterless country, a perfect Tierra del Fuego, that if the Elysian fields had been beyond I should have felt it to have been a duty to report against its selection.[87]

The Roper River was his second choice, but it did not possess a site for a capital within easy reach of the sea. Adam Bay, while being more suitable than any other site to the west of

Van Diemen Gulf, did not possess a sufficiently good anchorage to make it a 'port of call'. In a separate letter to South Australia's Agent-General in London, however, Cadell emphasised that Finniss' preference for Adam Bay over the Victoria River had been a wise one.[88]

The brevity of Cadell's visit and the speed of his return inevitably aroused suspicion and there was considerable resentment from the outset that his expedition had been commissioned without any reference to Parliament. 'We want to know', wrote the editor of *Pasquin*, 'how this last ministerial spree—this tinkers, "knifegrinders" and "sausage makers" expedition—is going to be paid for.'[89] Although Cadell's report was explicit enough in its recommendations, his subsequent letter to Blyth raised serious doubts about its credibility. He now admitted that it might not be possible to locate more than 300,000 acres in the Liverpool River area and suggested that the block to be surveyed should be 'elongated as to embrace longitudinally the embouchures' of the Liverpool, Blyth and King rivers.[90] This was in spite of his earlier warning about the possibility of 'cataclysmic floods'.

These doubts, together with his weakness for purple prose, brought down on Cadell the ridicule of the Adelaide newspapers. *Pasquin* described his efforts as reminiscent 'of a Yankee novel—very flowing, plenty of long words, and nothing in it.'[91] And the *Register*, referring to Cadell as 'The Ulysses of the Northern Territory', suggested that:

> these reports having been obviously intended for a pure work of art, it would be vandalism to epitomise their syntax, and mere presumption to look for any practical meaning in them.[92]

Believing that this expedition would bring to an end a disastrous and embarrassing experiment, the newspaper proceeded to caricature Cadell and his predecessors:

> Nature seems to have intended the Northern Territory for the scene of a monster harlequinade. No sooner does the foot of a white man touch its enchanted shore than his character is metamorphosed. The shrewd administrator becomes a military martinate. The energetic explorer adopts an amphibious life, and claims kindred with the *deus loci* of the East Alligator River. The man on the quarter deck, abandoning his nautical style of 'yarns', produces a startling compound of Homer and Mrs Braddon.[93]

More importantly, the fall of the Boucaut ministry in May 1867 and unsettled political conditions during most of 1868 had the effect of postponing all decisions on the Northern Territory. Interest was now focused not on the location of settlement but how best to deal with the demands of increasingly vociferous investors before the five years expired in March 1869. The rumours from early 1868 were that the government would relinquish all further attempts to survey land and would pay back the purchase money. However, it was decided instead to offer the land-order holders twice the amount of land originally purchased, on condition that the deadline for selection was extended from five to ten years, and to repay those who refused. At the same time (November 1868), legislation was passed enabling the government to borrow £40,000 with which to repay land-order holders and finance the survey.

After another unsatisfactory bunch of tenders had been received in September, Hart had apparently accepted Goyder's recommendation that a government party should be sent out to make the survey. The surveyor-general's views on settlement and survey of the north were well known and Hart and his successors, Ayers and Strangways, seem to have been happy to leave the entire business, including the site of the capital, in his hands. As Cavenagh, Commissioner for Crown Lands, told Goyder in December 1868:

Your long experience, the frequent communication between the Government and yourself on the subject of the survey of the Northern Territory, and the manner in which you have personally superintended the fitting out of the present expedition with every requisite render it unnecessary to lay down any instructions on points of detail.[94]

Indeed, after three abortive expeditions which had used up practically all the money raised from the land order sales and with litigation now being mounted by the Northern Territory Company, Goyder could set his own conditions. One of these was that Port Darwin should be the site of the capital, a decision which Goyder reached after reading the three earlier reports and Stokes' original account of 1839. No doubt he was also influenced by the opinions of Manton, an experienced surveyor who had strongly advocated Port Darwin. Another condition which nicely reflected Goyder's awareness of the desperate need to have the survey completed was that a bonus of £3000 should be paid into his bank account *before* he left Adelaide.

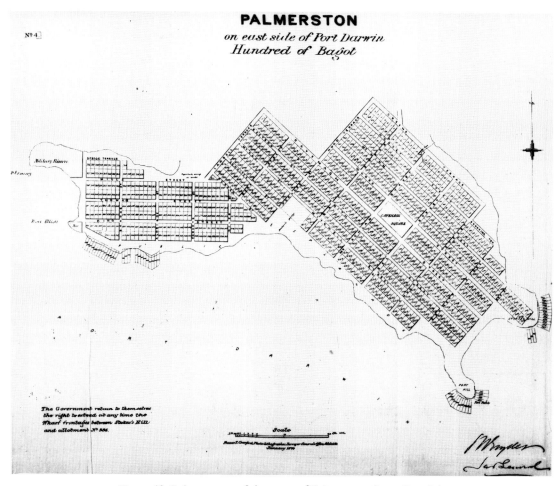

Figure 60: Enlargement of the town of Palmerston (later Darwin) as planned by Goyder, 1870

Goyder and his party disembarked from the *Moonta* at Fort Point in Darwin harbour on 5 February and established a base camp there, finding a good supply of water at nearby Doctor's Gully. Within a month he was reporting that after consultation with members of his party he had chosen Fort Point as the site of the principal township, together with the two other town sites on the East arm and South arm of the harbour.[95] A town plan for Palmerston had already been prepared on board ship by J Brooks,[96] the official photographer to the expedition who was also a township plotter, and this was subsequently modified by Goyder himself in one morning's work in accordance with the local topography. The actual survey of Palmerston was completed within two weeks of the party's arrival and work then began on surveying the other town sites and rural land. All sites were 'healthy and free from swamp', according to Goyder, and he advised that land-order holders could begin immediately to select town lots. Goyder praised the virtues of the harbour and was optimistic about the suitability of the land for livestock and all kinds of agriculture, assuming a supply of island labour. His one regret was that Port Darwin had not been chosen earlier as the site for settlement:

> I am very pleased with what I have seen, and can only express regret that the points and localities referred to . . . had not been more fully examined by the preceding parties, when much trouble and expense, as well as delay, might have been avoided.[97]

Apart from the ever-vigilant editor of *Pasquin*, no one questioned Goyder's authority to pronounce on the pastoral and agricultural capabilities of the area.[98] To the admiring public he was a conquering Caesar, 'little Energy'.

The work of surveying proceeded at a furious pace in order to meet the deadline of 1 October which Goyder had set for himself. At the beginning of May he despatched to Adelaide twenty-six plans and drafts of the townships, together with photographs of the Palmerston site and a diagram of 43,000 acres already surveyed into 160 and 320 acre sections. In fact the actual field survey of almost 600,000 acres was completed by the end of August and after the preparation of final plans and diagrams Goyder was able to leave for Adelaide on 28 September, just eight months after his arrival.[99] 'Energy' had lived up to his sobriquet.

Credit must be given to Goyder for his determined approach to the whole exercise, but the extraordinary speed of his town surveys was partly due to the fact that he did little more than superimpose on the four sites the grid model reflected in Adelaide. Where topography made this difficult, as at Palmerston where the site was a narrow peninsular, he was forced to compromise to some extent. At Virginia, however, he was able to use the square grid model, complete with surrounding parklands on three sides.

One notable feature of Goyder's reports was his appreciation of the Aboriginal reaction to the European presence. Apart from the killing by Aboriginals of one member of his party and their subsequent exclusion from the survey camps, relations with the indigenous owners were reasonably good. Goyder was well aware that 'we were in what to them appeared unauthorised and unwarrantable occupation of their country . . .' and acknowledged that the survey consisted of portions of 'four native districts, viz, the "Woolner", "Woolner-Larakeeyah", "Larakeeyah", and "Warnunger" . . .'[100] Of these, it seemed that he at least wished to retain 'Larakeeyah' as an official name.[101] However, by March 1870 the sub-divisions of the entire surveyed area bore the names of Adelaide politicians such as Ayers, Strangways and Hart—and of Finniss and Goyder—rather than those of the Aboriginal custodians such as 'King' Mira, whose friendship and mediation had evidently

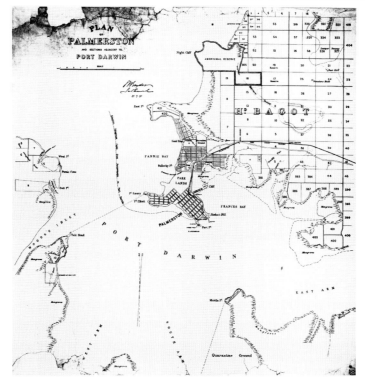

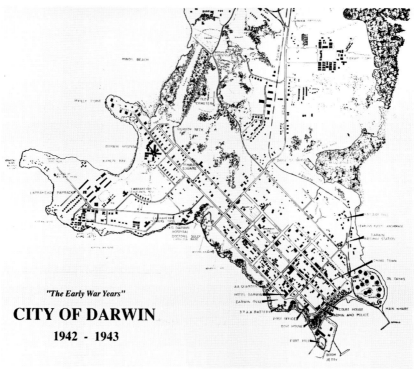

"The Early War Years"

CITY OF DARWIN
1942 - 1943

prevented many conflicts. The streets of Palmerston itself had been named by Goyder before reaching Port Darwin after surveyors and other members of his own party, the only exception being Cavenagh, Commissioner for Crown Lands, who was honoured by the town's only square as well as its principal street.[102]

With the arrival of the new Resident, Captain Bloomfield Douglas, in June 1870, work began on the town's first permanent building, the Residency on the hill facing Fort Hill where Goyder's party had originally planted the Union Jack.[103] The stables erected by Goyder became the first Land Office and it was there that town lots were selected in July 1870. Most of these were acquired for speculative reasons, however, and of the 1019 allocated only forty were actually occupied. This, together with an extreme shortage of durable building materials, meant that Palmerston for the first two decades of its existence bore the appearance of an unplanned shanty town waiting forlornly for 'something to turn up'. Only the handful of government buildings and the headquarters of the British Australia Telegraph Company served as reminders of the grand scheme to settle the north.

*   *   *

The final acceptance of Port Darwin by the South Australian authorities had been dictated more by the need for a quick decision than by any other consideration. British and colonial land-order holders were clamouring for action after five years of delays and uncertainty, exacerbated by deteriorating economic conditions. By this time there was little interest in debating the advantages and disadvantages of the site Goyder had chosen. As it happened, however, his choice was more in keeping with the rationale of earlier British settlements in northern Australia than with the predominantly pastoral purpose of settlement. Port Darwin could certainly be seen as an entrepôt for the trade of eastern Indonesia, but it offered no easy access to the hinterland either by land or by water and could not serve as an outlet for inland produce. The port offered certain military and strategic advantages which would have recommended it to the Admiralty, but by the 1860s the importance of the Torres Strait sea route had been greatly diminished and most ships were taking the southern route. Palmerston, then, was doomed to be an almost entirely administrative capital, geographically isolated from the pastoral and mining industries of the interior and increasingly disposed to view its South-East Asian neighbours as representing the 'menace of colour' to an Anglo-Saxon white Australia. The effective expulsion of the last Macassan trepangers by 1911 brought to an end George Windsor Earl's dream of a second Singapore in the Australian tropics.

Opposite: Figure 61: Palmerston (later Darwin) and surrounds, 1891 (Courtesy of the Mitchell Library, State Library of New South Wales)

Figure 62: War-time map of Darwin, taken after a poster issued by the Northern Territory Lands Department (note how little of Goyder's plan had been fulfilled)

Notes

[1] Allen, J. 'Port Essington: a successful limpet port?', *Historical Studies*, Vol. 14, No. 59, (October, 1972), pp.341-360.

[2] Blainey, G. *The Tyranny of Distance*, (Macmillan, 1975), Ch. 4.

[3] Stokes, J.L. *Discoveries in Australia . . .*, 3 Vols., (London, T. & W. Boone, 1846).

[4] *S.A.P.P.*, 1861, No. 170, See also Gregory's 'Journal of the North Australian Exploring Expedition . . .', *J.R.G.S.*, Vol. 28, (1858), pp.1-135. (NB—There is as yet no full account of the expedition and its significance).

[5] *S.A.P.P.*, 1861, No. 129.

[6] *S.A.P.P.*, 1863, No. 37, p.4.

[7] *Ibid.*

[8] 'Report by F.G. Waterhouse . . .', *S.A.P.P.*, 1863, No. 125.

[9] *S.A.P.P.*, 1863, No. 12, (23-12-1862).

[10] *Ibid.*

[11] *Ibid.* (26-5-1863).

[12] *S.A.P.P.*, 1863, No. 37, (21-9-1862).

[13] Earl, G.W. *Observations on the Commercial and Agricultural Capabilities of the North Coast of New Holland*, (London, Effingham Wilson, 1836).

[14] *Register*, 6-11-1863.

[15] *The Northern Territory of South Australia*, (Adelaide, Government Printer, 1863), pp.21, 28.

[16] *Register*, 26-11-1863.

[17] *Register*, 5-11-1863 and 6-11-1863.

[18] See *A.D.B.*, Vol. 2, pp.377-9; and Manhood, C.H. *The Life of Boyd Travers Finniss* (1807-1893), (M.A. Thesis, U.A., 1965).

[19] Donovan, P.F. *A Land Full of Possibilities: A History of South Australia's Northern Territory*, (U.Q.P., 1981), p.45.

[20] Published in Singapore in early 1864 as the final issue of the *Journal of the Indian Archipelago*, and reprinted in London in 1882 by George Rivers.

[21] 'Memo on the best Site for Preliminary Settlement in the Northern Territory . . .'. (n.d.), (hereafter cited as 'Memo') *S.A.P.P.*, 1865-66, No. 36.

[22] Originally published as an appendix in Earl's *The Eastern Seas, or Voyages and Adventures in the Indian Archipelago*, (London, Allen & Co., 1837).

[23] *Register*, 27-2-1864.

[24] *Register*, 5-3-1864.

[25] *Ibid.*

[26] *Register*, 8-3-1864.

[27] 'Instructions to Boyle Travers Finniss, Esq . . .', (hereafter cited as 'Instructions') *S.A.P.P.*, 1865-66, No. 36.

[28] The bay was named after Vice-Admiral Sir Charles Adam.

[29] 'Instructions . . .', *op.cit.*

[30] 'Memo . . .', *op.cit.*

[31] 'Instructions . . .', *op.cit.*

[32] 'Suggestions by the Surveyor-General relative to the System to be followed in laying out and surveying the Northern Territory' 5-3-1864, *S.A.P.P.*, 1865-66, No. 36.

[33] *Ibid.*

[34] Stokes. *op.cit.*, Vol. 1, pp.413-5. See also the frontispiece of Vol. 2.

[35] *S.A.P.P.*, 1864, No. 163, (16-8-1864).

[36] *S.A.P.P.*, 1864, No. 36A, (28-10-1864).

[37] *S.A.P.P.*, 1865, No. 89, (10-8-1864).

[38] *Ibid.*

[39] *S.A.P.P.*, 1864, No. 163, (13-8-1864).

[40] *Ibid.*

[41] *S.A.P.P.*, No. 64, No. 36A, (28-10-1864).

[42] *Ibid.* This map has not been located.

[43] *S.A.P.P.*, 1865, No. 89, (8-12-1864).

[44] *Ibid.*

[45] *Ibid.*

[46] *S.A.P.P.*, 1865-66, No. 15, (15-4-1865).

[47] *Ibid.*

[48] 16-1-1864, *Ibid.* See also letter of 20-1-1865, *Ibid.*

[49] 19-12-1864, *Ibid.*

[50] 15-4-1886, *Ibid.*

[51] *Register*, 11-1-1865 and 19-1-1865.

[52] *S.A.P.P.*, 1865, No. 189, (10-2-1865).

[53] *Ibid.*

[54] *Ibid.*

[55] *Ibid.*

[56] *S.A.P.P.*, 1865-66, No. 15, (2-5-1865).

[57] *Ibid.*, (1-5-1865).

[58] *Ibid.*, (2-5-1865).

[59] *Ibid.*, (15-4-1865).

[60] *S.A.P.P.*, 1865-66, No. 83, (1-8-1865).

[61] *S.A.P.P.*, 1865-66, No. 15, p.19, (21-8-1865).

[62] Report of Commissioners, *S.A.P.P.*, 1866-67, No. 17, (16-5-1866).

[63] *Ibid.*

[64] *S.A.P.P.*, 1865-66, No. 15, (21-9-1865).

[65] *Ibid.*, p.21, (20-9-1865).

[66] *Ibid.*

[67] *Ibid.*, p.20, (21-9-1865).

[68] *S.A.P.P.*, 1865-66, No. 131, (29-11-1865).

[69] *S.A.P.P.*, 1866-67, No. 82A, (3-10-1866).

[70] *Ibid.*, (18-7-1866).

[71] *Ibid.*, (15-7-1866).

[72] *Ibid.*

[73] *Ibid.*

[74] *S.A.P.P.*, 1866-67, No. 79, (27-8-1866).

[75] *South Australian Parliamentary Debates*, 1866-67, pp.660, 667-72.

[76] *Ibid.*, p.710.

[77] *S.A.P.P.*, 1866-67, No. 188, (12-12-1866).

[78] For a summary of Cadell's colourful career, see *A.D.B.*, Vol. 3, p.324-5.

[79] *Pasquin*, 27-4-1867, pp.5-6.

[80] *S.A.P.P.*, 1868-69, No. 79, (22-2-1869).

[81] King, P.P. *Narrative of a Survey of the Intertropical and Western Coasts of Australia*, 2 Vols. (Adelaide: Libraries Board of South Australia, 1969, first published 1827), Vol. 1, pp.259-60.

[82] Wilson, J.S. 'On the Capabilities of Northern Australia', 1858. M.L., MS C174, pp.20-23.

[83] *S.A.P.P.*, 1868-69, No. 79, (22-2-1867).

[84] *S.A.P.P.*, 1868-69, No. 24, (7-1-1868).

[85] *S.A.P.P.*, 1868-69, No. 79A, (26-8-1867).

[86] *S.A.P.P.*, 1868-69, No. 24, (7-1-1868).

[87] *Ibid.*

[88] *S.A.P.P.*, 1868-69, No. 51, (27-11-1867). This letter was published in *The Times*, 7-2-1868, in an attempt to placate British land-order holders.

[89] *Pasquin*, 28-2-1868.

[90] *S.A.P.P.*, 1868-69, No. 79, (18-2-1868) and the *Register*, 29-2-1868.

[91] *Pasquin*, 28-2-1868.

[92] *Register*, 29-2-1868.

[93] *Ibid.*

[94] *S.A.P.P.*, 1868-69, No. 175, (23-12-1868).

[95] *S.A.P.P.*, 1869-70, No. 31, (2-3-1869).

[96] Kerr, M.G. *The Surveyors: The Story of the Founding of Darwin*, (Adelaide, Rigby, 1971), pp.60, 74.

[97] *S.A.P.P.*, 1869-70, No. 31, (2-3-1869).

[98] *Pasquin*, 2-2-1869, 1-5-1869, 8-5-1869 and 15-5-1869.

[99] *S.A.P.P.*, 1869-70, No. 157, (27-8-1869).

[100] *Ibid.*

[101] 'General Plan showing Natural Features of the Country, Towns, Reserves, Roads & Sectional Lands at, and in the vicinity of Port Darwin . . . November 1869', *S.A.P.P.*, 1868-69, No. 161.

[102] 'General plan of the vicinity of Port Darwin . . . March 1870'. *S.A.P.P.*, 1868-69, No. 204. See Figure X for the map of the town site of Palmerston dated January 1870.

[103] Daly, Mrs D. *Digging, Squatting and Pioneering Life in the Northern Territory of South Australia*, (London, Sampson Low, 1887), p.108.

Canberra

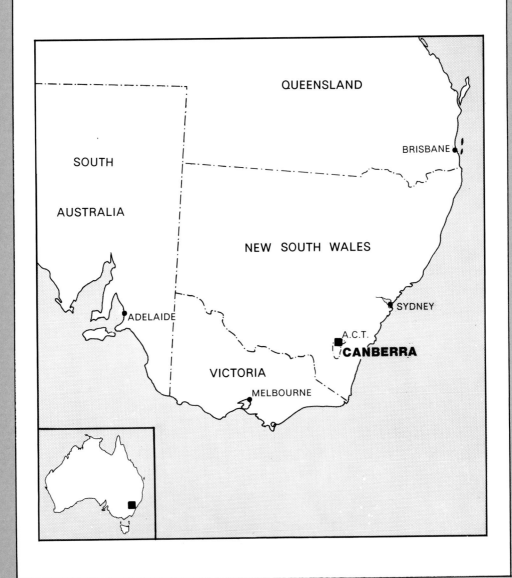

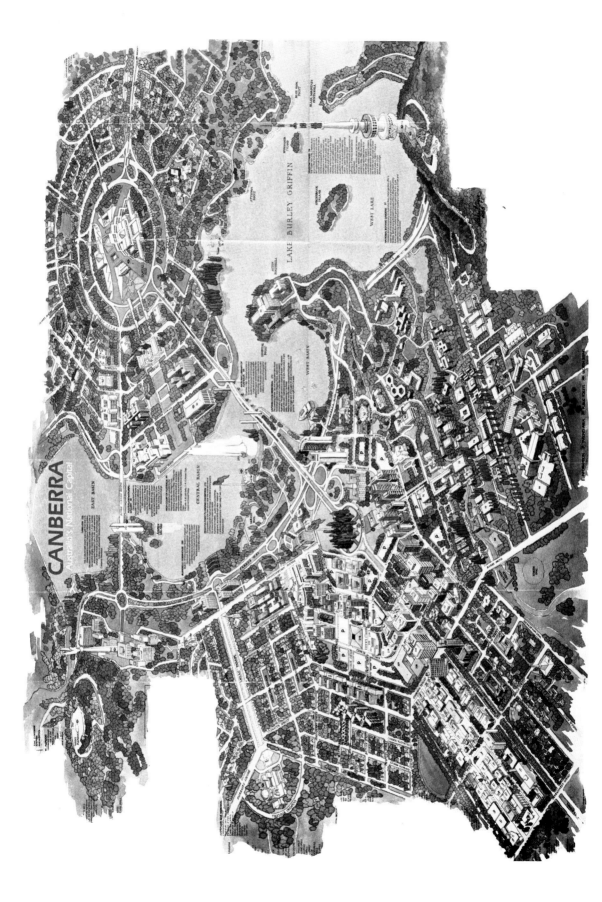

CANBERRA
Australia's National Capital

LAKE BURLEY GRIFFIN

WEST LAKE

WEST BASIN

CENTRAL BASIN

EAST BASIN

Chapter XVI

Canberra: The Bush Capital

Roger Pegrum

Canberra, the capital of the Commonwealth, is the odd-city out in this story of Australia's capital cities. The state capitals owe a great deal to Britain, convicts, trade, defence and geography. Canberra is there because the Australian states needed, or thought they needed, a national city and federal territory free from the political or commercial domination of any one state. New South Wales and Victoria became the principal protagonists in what has become known as 'the battle of the sites', a struggle which occupied most of the first decade of the twentieth century but which was not really settled until the federal Parliament met for the first time in Canberra in 1927. In the middle of the 'battle', the *Sydney Morning Herald* suggested that future generations in Australia would not be impressed by the way the new Commonwealth had handled its first major planning exercise:

> When the history of this business of the capital comes to be written, it is not impossible that the historian will be able to compile some spicy chapters on interstate jealousy and intrigue, and on the slight estimation in which certain fundamental federal obligations have been held.[1]

The background to the federation of the Australian colonies contains the origins of distrust between Sydney, the oldest city, and Melbourne. Interstate rivalries and parochial self-interest overshadowed the larger national issues in this first round of the site struggle and in the following three rounds. Rounds two and three were conducted within the federal Parliament, which was initially unable and unwilling to settle the question, but which in 1904 chose Dalgety in the Snowy Mountains. In the fourth and final round a spirit of compromise prevailed; the remote tablelands site was reassessed and Canberra emerged as an acceptable solution for all interested parties. The site was handed over by New South Wales and accepted by the Commonwealth in 1911. Sixteen years later, after new battles about the layout of the federal city, the Parliament left its temporary home in Melbourne to meet thereafter in Canberra. The location and design of the federal capital were not the most significant matters resolved during the first twenty-five years of the Commonwealth, but they are useful reminders of the difficulties faced by a newly federated Australia.

*   *   *

A federation of the Australian colonies was suggested as early as 1851[2] but the young colonies found it difficult enough to agree from time to time on common tariffs, postal services and railway gauges and they side stepped discussion of a permanent association whenever the question arose. By 1883 Queensland, Victoria, Tasmania, Western Australia and Fiji had formed a Federal Australasian Council to control 'the marine defences of Australia[3] but New South Wales, the oldest and most populated colony, refused to join on the grounds that the council had no power to raise revenue and would therefore be impotent as a political forum. In 1890, when the total population of the colonies had reached almost 3.5 million, New South Wales Premier Henry Parkes invited the colonies to discuss a full 'union of the colonies under one legislative and executive government'.[4] Meeting in Sydney in March 1891, the colonial premiers prepared Australia's first draft Constitution.

The premiers discussed at some length the financial arrangements which would allow a Commonwealth of Australia to assume responsibility for tariffs, customs and defence, and they agreed that the Commonwealth would adopt a Westminster system of government and a bicameral federal parliament. The convention closed after a short but heated debate on where a House of Representatives and a Senate would meet. Washington DC and Ottawa were held up as examples of 'neutral' federal districts, but the New South Wales representatives insisted that Australia should ignore these North American precedents. Sydney, they argued, was the 'mother city' of all the colonies, and it would be an insult to history and to the people of New South Wales if the parliament were to gather in any other place. The Victorian delegation was not amused and New South Wales was unable to convince the other colonies that Sydney should be the federal capital city. It was finally agreed that it should be left to the future parliament to choose the location of its own home. Clause 118 of the draft Constitution said simply that:

> The seat of government of the Commonwealth shall be determined by the Parliament. Until such determination the Parliament shall be summoned to meet at such a place within the Commonwealth as a majority of the Governors of the States, or, in the event of an equal division of opinion amongst the Governors, as the Governor-General shall direct.[5]

Over the next three years, the draft Constitution was debated only lethargically in the colonial parliaments. In New South Wales federation was likened to a teetotaller setting up house with five drunkards,[6] and despite the efforts of Edmond Barton, Alfred Deakin and Federation Leagues in each of the colonies little advance was made towards a general acceptance of the Constitution. When George Reid became Premier of New South Wales in 1894, he promised to restore federation 'to its rightful position of commanding importance and urgency'.[7] Preparations were made for a second convention, but within New South Wales most public debate centred on the 'historical right' of the oldest colony to contain the seat of a federal government. At one stage Reid suggested that a fair solution would be for the parliament to meet in rotation at each of the state capital cities, but public opinion in the colonial capital was more generally behind the proposal that the federal capital 'if not in Sydney, should be on an area to be declared federal within easy distance of the city'.[8] Several country areas were nominated as being 'not unduly exposed to risks of war or invasion',[9] and the ideal qualities of a federal district were seen, at least in the mind of the general public, as 'climate, access and safety'.

Most of what is now Australia's Constitution was written between March 1897 and March 1898 at meetings in Adelaide, Sydney and Melbourne. The delegates, elected by popular vote within each colony, fought hard to protect their own interests in the important financial clauses, the structure of the parliament and the judiciary and the rights of each state to control its own land and rivers. Debate on the location of a federal city was by comparison a very light-hearted affair. When New South Wales again insisted that Sydney should be the capital, the Victorians put up St Kilda and Tasmanian Premier Braddon proposed 'some suitable place in Tasmania'.[10] When the convention ended, the Constitution once more avoided the question, saying only that 'the seat of government of the Commonwealth shall be determined by the Parliament and shall be within territory vested in the Commonwealth'.

Queensland and Western Australia did not participate in the referendums of June 1898, but the Constitution was approved by a majority of electors in each of the other colonies. In New South Wales, however, the affirmative vote fell short of the 80,000 needed for approval, and Premier Reid asked the other colonies to review the Constitution to make it 'more acceptable to New South Wales'.[11] Of particular concern to the people of New South Wales, said Reid, was a constitutional guarantee that the federal parliament would in due course choose a capital site within the 'mother colony'. At Reid's request, the premiers gathered in Melbourne in January 1899, where they agreed to some minor modifications sought by Reid and later issued a memorandum summarising their discussions on the location of a federal capital:

> It is considered that the fixing of the site of the capital is a question which might well be left to the Parliament to decide; but in view of the strong expression of opinion in relation to this matter in New South Wales the Premiers have modified the clause so that while the capital cannot be fixed in Sydney, or in its neighbourhood, provision is made in the Constitution for its establishment in New South Wales at a reasonable distance from the city. Accordingly the request of New South Wales that the capital should be in that colony was granted; but with two conditions which Victoria insisted upon: (1) that it should not be within 100 miles of Sydney; (2) that the Parliament should sit at Melbourne until it could meet at the seat of government.[12]

This decision of the premiers was a reasonable compromise between New South Wales and Victoria, which had between them three-quarters of the total population of the coming Commonwealth. The oldest colony was given the right to contain the capital, but Victoria won two major concessions by ensuring that the capital would be well clear of Sydney and that Melbourne would be the temporary home of the Parliament until a suitable territory had been found in New South Wales. The premiers further agreed that New South Wales would hand over at least a hundred square miles of its land to become a federal territory. At a second referendum, New South Wales and the other colonies, except Western Australia, accepted the revised Constitution, which included as Section 125 the following provisions for the capital of Australia:

> The seat of government of the Commonwealth shall be determined by the Parliament and shall be within territory which shall have been granted to or acquired by the Commonwealth and shall be vested in and belong to the Commonwealth, and shall be in the State of New South Wales, and be distant not less than one hundred miles from Sydney.
>   Such territory shall contain an area of not less than one hundred square miles and such portion thereof as shall consist of crown lands shall be granted to the Commonwealth without any payment therefor.
>   The Parliament shall sit at Melbourne until it meet at the seat of government.

New South Wales began a search for a suitable capital site even as formal arrangements were being made in London for the creation of the Commonwealth. With the election of a federal parliament more than a year away, and with the political make-up of that parliament as yet unknown, it is perhaps not surprising that ideological differences within New South Wales were suspended in favour of a general enthusiasm to find the very best site. But the investigations of 1900 were more than an absorbing diversion for New South

Wales; Section 125 of the Constitution gave New South Wales a glorious opportunity to triumph over the unworthy 'cabbage gardeners' south of the Murray. A 'suitable' site was no longer only a place with a pleasant climate and inland from the coast to provide some chance of freedom from invasion by foreign armies (or naval bombardment); it was now a site which would show Victorians and all the world how rich was the hinterland of Australia's oldest and greatest city and how right and proper it was for those who wrote Australia's Constitution to choose New South Wales as the home for a fine and regal national city.

United perhaps in their patriotism, the people of New South Wales nevertheless divided spectacularly in their support for federal city sites. Sydney interests formed the only cohesive group, pushing with single-minded logic for a site as close as possible to the 100-mile limit and as far as possible from Melbourne. The colonial administrative city of Bathurst became their flag-bearer. It was almost exactly 100 miles from Sydney, with a bracing tableland climate and the advantage, to Sydney that is, of being 400 miles from Melbourne. Bathurst, Orange and nearby Lyndhurst formed into a Western Federal Capital League, and for the next eight years these western sites carried the hopes of the residents and businessmen in or near Sydney. With the notable exception of the *Bulletin*, the Sydney press refused to accept any other district as fit for a federal territory. But to the distress of Sydney, many distant parts of New South Wales claimed an equal right to be considered as capital sites. With the active encouragement of country members of the colonial assembly, they too formed Federal Capital Leagues. By the beginning of 1900, more than sixty such leagues had been established, representing areas as far north as Armidale and Tamworth, all the southern tablelands and western slopes, and all the River-ina district as far south as the Victorian border. The commercial interests of Sydney heaped scorn on 'these Tinpot Creeks' and pushed hard the claims of the peaceful and civilised Bathurst over 'torrid Albury, swamp-bound Wagga Wagga and remote Bombala'.[13]

In November 1899, the New South Wales government arranged for a Royal Commission to investigate the claims of all the Federal Capital Leagues. The Commission was entrusted to Alexander Oliver, then president of the Land Appeal Court, who was authorised to make 'full enquiry as to the suitability . . . of such tracts or areas as you are invited to consider'.[14] Forty-five such areas were nominated. Oliver discarded all sites much north of Sydney as being too remote from the centre of Australia's population, and then divided the remaining sites into three groups. A western group contained the Sydney favourites Bathurst, Orange and Lyndhurst, and a south-western group included those sites south of Goulburn and along the main southern rail line to Melbourne. Goulburn was well promoted, but this group also contained Tumut, Yass, Wagga Wagga and Cootamundra as well as Albury and Corowa on the Victorian border. Oliver's third group, the southern sites, was on the tablelands from Lake George to Cooma, and included Queanbeyan, Braidwood and Bombala. The site proposed by an active Queanbeyan Federal League was in fact the Canberra Valley, west of the town. At the turn of the century it was indeed a pleasant spot, but it would have to wait six more years before it was finally accepted as being not only beautiful but in the right place.

Of the western sites, Oliver found Orange to have all the prerequisites for the construction of a 'beautiful and commodious city' and he placed Orange first in that group. The soil was fertile, the climate of Orange, said Oliver, was superior to that of Bathurst because of its greater elevation, and the gently sloping and lightly timbered country gave

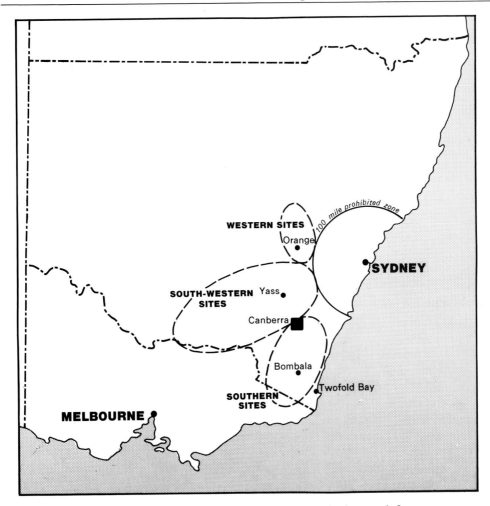

Figure 63: The three main site groups identified in the search for a
National Capital

promise of fine building sites with a background of the Canobolas mountains. Oliver had
greater difficulty with his south-western group, in which a number of sites were considerably closer to Melbourne than they were to Sydney. A study of Section 125 of the Constitution, concluded Oliver, suggested that 'topographical justice' demanded the site be as
near to Sydney as possible. Goulburn was an excellent site, but Oliver settled on Yass,
which had a better climate than Goulburn and cheaper land. The best site of all, said Oliver, was in his southern grouping. The Queanbeyan site had all the needed qualities, but
was overshadowed by the potential of a federal city further south on the plains of
Bombala, which could be easily connected to a federal port at Twofold Bay. In his final
report, tabled in the New South Wales parliament in October 1900 Oliver ranked
Bombala as the best site in New South Wales, with Yass and Orange equal in second place.

The Commonwealth of Australia was inaugurated on New Year's Day 1901 and general
elections in March confirmed Edmund Barton as Prime Minister in a protectionist gov-

ernment. Immediately after the election, the New South Wales government wrote to Barton offering him his choice of Oliver's three sites of Orange, Yass and Bombala, an invitation likened by William Morris Hughes to that of 'a bridal couple returning from their honeymoon to be overwhelmed by enterprising real estate agents'.[15] The federal parliament gathered in Melbourne in May 1901, where its urgent work on legislation for the administration of the country prevented any early debate on the location of a permanent seat of government. The subject was, however, not completely forgotten, particularly by the New South Wales men in the parliament. William Lyne, first federal Minister for Home Affairs, organised the claims of his Riverina constituency which included most of the southern sites from Tumut to the Victorian border; Austin Chapman, the member for Eden-Monaro and the government whip, canvassed his new associates on behalf of Bombala and the Snowy Mountains region; and George Reid became both the leader of the free-trade opposition and the leader of the Sydney interests fighting for a site west of Sydney.

At the end of round one of the battle, New South Wales had managed to find not one but three sites. It was now up to the federal parliament to determine whether any one of these would make a good site for a capital city.

*   *   *

Round two of the battle of the sites began slowly. Government business was being conducted with the support of the Labour members, but party alignments were generally ignored in the matter of a future capital city. The Labour Party announced that it preferred no single site, provided the federal territory was 'vested in the Commonwealth'. Members and senators from New South Wales and Queensland were gathered behind George Reid in his fight for a site near Sydney, the Victorians were naturally keen on Lyne's sites near Albury, and the representatives of the other states argued only for a site that would make their trips to parliament as short and as comfortable as possible. In the first year of federation little was done to resolve the question by formal discussion. Some dismay was nevertheless expressed within the New South Wales parliament at the proposal by Tasmania's King O'Malley that the federal territory should contain 'not less than 1000 square miles, in a good, healthy and fertile situation'.[16] The sudden jump from 100 to 1000 square miles did not however alarm the three principal protagonists, who proclaimed to a number of audiences that each of their districts was 'good, healthy and fertile' and that an area of 1000 square miles could be found easily within the large areas they proudly represented.

By the end of 1901, the lobbying of Lyne, Chapman and Reid had confused rather than clarified the issues in the minds of members of the parliament, a situation made worse by gratuitous advice from a number of architects, town planners and geographers who gave public lectures on the design and location of a 'perfect' capital city.[17] Pressure grew for a tour of the various sites so that members and senators might make up their own minds as to who was telling the truth and who was not. Prime Minister Barton asked his Minister for Home Affairs to organise tours by the parliament, a responsibility William Lyne accepted with enthusiasm. George Reid refused to go on what he called 'Lyne's picnics', but by the middle of 1902 most of the representatives from the more distant states and all but seven of the senators had seen Orange, Yass and Bombala and the majority of the other sites on offer. A party of senators toured New South Wales in March 1902, and a similar tour was undertaken by the lower house in May that year. Neither group saw the sites to their best advantage. New South Wales was by then in its third year of drought; Lake George, once seen as the site for an Australian Venice or Como, had dried up completely, and at Yass the red dust was so thick that one visitor protested that he 'did not want to eat the site, but to see it'.[18] The senators looked over Chapman's southern Monaro district in early autumn and were impressed by the sight of a wide and deep Snowy River. Bombala's stock rose noticeably in the senate, but the mountain sites were less favourably received by the representatives two months later. A piercing winter wind blew all day at Bombala, Dalgety was no more than a 'frozen waste' and the Snowy River had turned into 'liquid ice'.[19] When the tours were over, Lyne seemed to have the support of those representatives who favoured a tableland site with a moderate climate, and he concentrated his efforts on Tumut. Chapman had most of the Senate (except for New South Wales and Queensland) in favour of Bombala, and George Reid relied on the Queenslanders and the Sydney metropolitan members to push for the selection of a site near Bathurst or Orange.

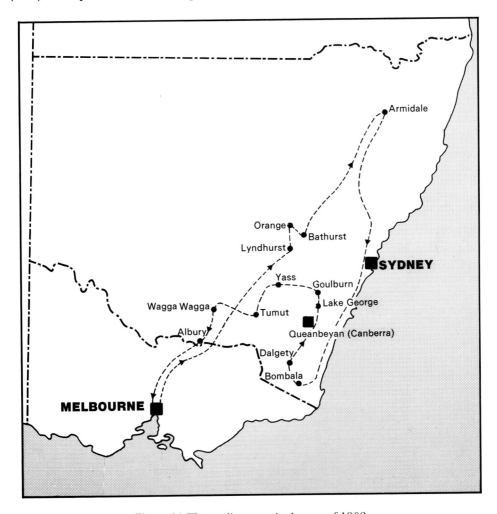

Figure 64: The parliamentarian's tour of 1902

323

All climatic and other information about possible capital sites had to this point been gathered by the New South Wales government, but the federal politicians were now adamant that they needed 'a report of our own'. Barton agreed to the establishment of a Commonwealth Royal Commission to provide an assessment of the most likely sites and in January 1903 John Kirkpatrick, a Sydney architect, Henry Stanley, recently retired as chief engineer of railways in Queensland, Graham Stewart, the superintending surveyor for South Australia and Alfred Howitt, a Victorian magistrate and explorer, were appointed to 'inquire into and examine the sites proposed for the seat of government of the Commonwealth in the following localities—Albury, Armidale, Bathurst, Bombala, Lake George, Lyndhurst, Orange and Tumut.'[20]

The terms of reference of this Commonwealth Royal Commission were more clearly defined than those issued to Alexander Oliver three years earlier. It was hoped that the representation of four of the six states would remove any suggestion of improper influence, and the commissioners were careful to point out that their report was not to be read as a recommendation for any one site but as a guide to assist the parliament in its 'fateful choice which will fix for ever the site of the nation's capital'.[21] Their findings were nevertheless more than a little controversial. After examining the eight sites (and also Dalgety, which was later added to the list at the request of Chapman), the commissioners ranked the sites from first preference to last in each of the six categories—accessibility, water supply, cost, climate, soil productiveness and general suitability. Albury, a Lyne site on the border between New South Wales and Victoria, was placed first in the category of accessibility because it was the only site on the main railway between Sydney and Melbourne, even though it was twice as far from Sydney as Melbourne. Lyndhurst, just south of Bathurst, came second although it was more than twice as far from Melbourne as it was from Sydney. Similarly unusual conclusions were drawn in other categories. Lyne's other competing site at Tumut came first in water supply but was followed by the dried-up Lake George, whereas Bombala and the perpetual waters of the Snowy River could manage no better than a fourth place. Indeed Bombala fared badly in all areas and was placed last in the categories of accessibility, cost, climate and general suitability. Tumut, on the other hand, did very well. It scored four first places and was only once not listed in the top three sites.

The Commonwealth commissioners had not really succeeded in simplifying the issue before the parliament and, although Lyne was obviously delighted with the outcome, the Sydney newspapers greeted the final report with disbelief. They were particularly incensed with the commissioners' choice of Albury as the most 'accessible' site, and the *Telegraph* wrote angrily that Albury was not truly 'within New South Wales as required by section 125 of the Constitution'. If parliament were now to settle on Albury 'it would for all practical purposes mean that a Victorian site had been chosen.'[22] Alexander Oliver was equally upset at the abrupt dismissal of his Bombala district. If proper weight were given to the importance of each of the categories, he said, Bombala would still come first, Orange would be second, Tumut would be third and Albury would be a very poor last.[23]

With Edmund Barton's departure for the High Court in September 1903, Alfred Deakin took over as Prime Minister for the last two months of Australia's first parliament. Under pressure from Lyne, Deakin agreed to allow a full debate on the capital question in the parliament. The Senate rejected all suggestions for a joint house conference and it was therefore agreed that the matter would be debated separately in both the House of Representatives and the Senate as required by the standing orders for normal parliamentary business. The debate opened in the House of Representatives on a hastily drafted *Seat of Government Bill 1903*, which said that the federal capital would be 'at or near _____'. While Lyne, Reid and Chapman lobbied for support for their own districts, the members discussed with considerable feeling how they might vote to fill the blank in the Bill. There was some fear on the opposition benches that the government parties would combine to ensure the early elimination of George Reid's western sites, and William Lyne and his supporters similarly feared that Reid and Chapman might unite their table-land backers to remove all sites on the Riverina and western slopes. It was finally agreed that a series of ballots would be conducted among the sites inspected by the Common-wealth commissioners, each member voting for the site he most preferred, and that the least-favoured site at each ballot would be removed from the list. It was not a perfect sys-tem, but it was probably the only reasonable way to handle such an unusual piece of legislation.[24]

Two days of rather unnecessary debate followed the resolution of a voting method. The member for New England spoke at length on the merits of Armidale, the Labour member for the Goulburn area did the same for the vanished Lake George and King O'Malley, speaking on behalf of the Bombala district, reminded the House that 'cold climates have produced the greatest geniuses'.[25] There was in fact never any doubt but that the real battle would be between Lyne's Tumut, Reid's Lyndhurst and Chapman's Bombala. At 11 o'clock on the evening of Thursday 8 October 1903, the House voted in the first ballot. Bathurst and Dalgety disappeared, quickly followed by Lake George and Orange. The third and fourth rounds of voting saw the end of Armidale and Albury, and Lyndhurst was then leading the field from Tumut and Bombala. At the penultimate ballot Albury's votes went not unexpectedly to Lyne's other site at Tumut. Bombala came last in that round of voting, but at the next and last ballot the Bombala supporters switched to Tumut. Reid's Lyndhurst lost by thirty-six votes to twenty-five and early on Friday morning a victorious William Lyne moved to insert Tumut in the place of the blank in the Bill.[26]

The House of Representatives sent the Bill across to the Senate four days later, just nine days before the parliament was due to be prorogued. From a number of directions, the senators were urged to choose any site except Tumut and thus abort the Bill. Sydney did not want the capital as far away as Tumut, and Melbourne still had hopes for Albury. Newspapers in both state capitals said that it would be wrong to settle on Tumut after only a few days' debate at the 'fag end' of the first parliament; such an important decision should be left to a second parliament, which could consider the matter in its own time. Austin Chapman renewed his efforts for Bombala, the site which had so impressed the touring senators eighteen months before. After two days of parochial debate, the senators chose 'remote Bombala'; some because they wanted the capital in that district, but most because it meant the end of the *Seat of Government Bill 1903*.[27]

The second skirmish in the battle of the sites had not been totally without value. It was now clear that the critical characteristic of a 'suitable' site was not its climate, nor its water supply nor even its topographical beauty, but rather its location. Neither Sydney nor Mel-bourne would willingly allow the selection of a site that could be seen to advantage the other. The first parliament had seen the crystallisation of this historical antagonism; it was now up to the second parliament to find a reasonable compromise.

*   *   *

As the third round of the battle began, the Canberra district was still not a contender. Deakin was returned as Prime Minister, but with a reduced majority, and he re-formed his protectionist government with the support of the Labour party. The capital question was not high on Deakin's list of parliamentary priorities, but he favoured the 'neutral' sites of Bombala and Dalgety, which were almost equidistant from Sydney and Melbourne and, as a Victorian, he recognised that Sydney would find it difficult to influence the workings of a Commonwealth parliament situated so far from the oldest city. Further surveys of the southern Monaro and Tumut were authorised and Deakin was quietly pleased with the advice that 'Dalgety surpasses all of (the other sites) and would attract visitors and tourists from all parts of Australia.'[28]

In April 1904, the Labour members withdrew their support for Deakin. John Watson became Australia's first Labour Prime Minister, backed by Deakin and most of his previous ministry. It was nevertheless a minority government, unlikely to succeed with radical socialist legislation. Watson decided that Section 125 of the Constitution was one matter which could be tackled without prejudice to Labour philosophies. The *Seat of Government Bill 1904* was drafted, once more containing a blank, but stipulating also that the capital would be in a federal territory not less than 900 square miles in area. Because the House of Representatives was busy debating a Bill for a federal arbitration system, the Seat of Government Bill was first given to the Senate for its consideration.

*   *   *

From the beginning of the Senate debate in May 1904, it was apparent that Tumut was out of the question and that the choice lay between Bombala and the even more remote Dalgety. Each had limitless supplies of clear mountain water and ample land for an extensive federal territory. The senators from New South Wales and Queensland argued in vain for a site nearer Sydney. On 3 June 1904 the Senate confirmed the choice of the previous Senate and settled on a site 'within 50 miles of Bombala'.[29] Eight months earlier the Sydney press had encouraged the Senate to pick Bombala, but they had done so then to avoid the selection of Tumut. The same papers were now outraged that the senators should again nominate such a remote site. Public meetings in Sydney talked of New South Wales' secession from the Commonwealth unless Sydney or some site very near to Sydney were made the federal capital district. A capital in the far south of the state, it was said, would for most of the year be a place of 'magnificent distances and deadly dullness [where] melancholy lunatics could live and thrive.'[30] In London, *The Times* gently disagreed, writing that 'a bush capital is both the simplest and cheapest way out of Australia's present difficulty and, being in the Constitution, it is the only possible one.'[31]

Prime Minister Watson represented a Sydney city electorate, but his support for the southern Monaro district indicated that, at this stage at least, he was placing the national interests above those of his own state and its capital. When the matter was brought before the House of Representatives, Watson agreed that the Senate choice of Bombala should be pitted against Lyne's southern sites and Reid's western district. Watson was confident that Bombala would win, but Lyne lobbied the new and old members of the House in support of Tumut or a nearby site, and Reid sought the votes of members for a site near Sydney, on the grounds that life in the far south of the state compared most unfavourably with current conditions in civilised Melbourne. By the time that the House was ready to vote again, battle lines were drawn exactly as before, except that this time Austin Chapman was

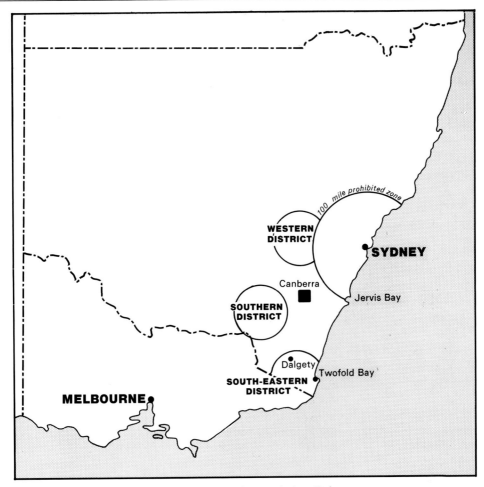

Figure 65: In 1904 they settled on Dalgety

a marginal favourite, armed with a Senate decision for Bombala and a backup site at Dalgety.

Only two rounds of balloting were necessary to see the end of the hopes of Lyne and Reid. At the first vote, Lyndhurst topped the poll with twenty-five votes, the Bombala district came next with twenty-two, and Lyne's southern district scored twenty-one. Lyne and two of his supporters transferred their votes to Lyndhurst, but the other southern votes moved over the mountains to Bombala. In the second ballot, Bombala defeated Lyndhurst by thirty-nine votes to twenty-eight. With a decision for the southern Monaro district confirmed, the House debated the relative merits of Bombala and Dalgety. A desire to show independence from the Senate led inevitably to a decision for Dalgety, and it was agreed to draw a circle around Dalgety with a radius of seventeen miles, giving a national federal territory of a little more than nine hundred square miles. It was further agreed that the future federal city should have 'access to the sea'.[32]

The next day the Senate took less than an hour to agree to the amendments of the lower House, and to approve of Dalgety instead of Bombala. That afternoon the Bill went back to the Representatives, was read a third time and became the *Seat of Government Act 1904* on 15 August 1904. Needless to say, the Sydney newspapers were furious, writing that 'the interests of this State were made a plaything between Mr Chapman and Sir William Lyne.'[33] It was now necessary for the Commonwealth government to negotiate with New South Wales for the handing over of land around Dalgety. From the outset, communication between Melbourne and Sydney on the capital question had been terse and uncompromising; for three years from 1904 it became both voluminous and acrimonious. In charge in Sydney was Premier Joseph Carruthers. His adversaries in Melbourne were George Reid, Prime Minister following the fall of the Watson Government in August 1904, and Alfred Deakin, Prime Minister from July 1905 to November 1908.

Carruthers wrote first to Reid. It was the opinion of the New South Wales government, he said, that the Seat of Government Act was 'premature'[34] because the Dalgety site had never been offered to the Commonwealth. Rather more importantly, New South Wales did not consider the choice of Dalgety as a 'reasonable interpretation' of the 100-mile limit in Section 125, nor was a 900-square mile federal territory a fair extension of the 100 square miles provided for in the Constitution. New South Wales was prepared, however, to offer the Commonwealth an area of between 100 and 200 square miles 'at or near Tumut, Lyndhurst or Yass.'[35] Meetings between Reid and Carruthers brought no resolution of the conflict and, when Deakin once more became Prime Minister, Carruthers suggested that the matter be referred to the High Court. Amongst other things, the court could be asked for an opinion as to whether land 'within a radius of 17 miles from Dalgety' could be seen as 'reasonably near to the 100 mile limit from Sydney.'[36]

It was clear to Deakin that the New South Wales objection to Dalgety could be sustained indefinitely. There was also a reluctant admission from the federal politicians in Melbourne that Dalgety, which had no direct rail connection to the southern states, would prove to be inconvenient from the point of view of accessibility and that its harsh winter climate would make it an unattractive place in which to live and work. Both sides searched for a compromise site, free from historical associations with any of the major factions. By early 1906, responding in part to a new surge of lobbying by businessmen in the Queanbeyan district, the focus of both groups had narrowed to a triangular area between Goulburn, Yass and Queanbeyan. At the southern tip of the triangle lay the Canberra Valley, 140 miles from Sydney but only seven miles from the railhead at Queanbeyan and with a bracing but bearable climate. A government surveyor described the valley as 'situated in an amphitheatre of picturesque hills [offering] almost perfect conditions for city building purposes'.[37] By September, even Deakin was showing a disinclination to press on with the claims of Dalgety. In a letter to Carruthers, Deakin said that the new sites 'including the Canberra site, in respect of which a good deal of interest has been displayed',[38] had persuaded him to leave any further action until more details were available.

And so it was that the 'battle of the sites' entered its final phase with Canberra the possible choice of both State and Commonwealth governments. Canberra had the apparent advantage of being a 'new site'. It had been favourably reviewed by Oliver in 1900 and had been inspected by some of the touring politicians in 1902, but since that time it had slipped into obscurity, overshadowed by the main fighting between Lyne and Chapman. However, the selection of Canberra as the site for the national capital city was still far from certain, and it would be another three years before the parliament was convinced that this was indeed the place for Australia's capital city.

* * *

Canberra in 1906 was no more than a scatter of settlements north and south of the Molongo River. Several parties of parliamentarians visited the valley that year, returning with generally enthusiastic reports of its topographical charm. Sir John Forrest, famous for his early explorations of Western Australia, inspected the district at Deakin's request in June 1907. Forrest concluded that Canberra possessed 'nothing of particular importance in either scenery or great natural features',[39] but he was outnumbered by many positive opinions, the most influential of which came surprisingly from John Watson. Watson said it was unfortunate that the 1902 tours of inspection had failed to reveal the true advantages of the Canberra district. Had he been able to assess the site at that time, he confesses, 'I should never have voted for any other'.[40]

Charles Wade succeeded Carruthers as Premier of New South Wales in October 1907. In a letter to Deakin that month, Wade sought an assurance that the seat of government issue would be resolved during the current session of the federal parliament, promising that such an undertaking 'would tend greatly to improve the relationship between the Commonwealth and this State'.[41] Deakin was in a difficult position after three years of fruitless correspondence. There was a growing pressure to reopen the matter, but Deakin could see no simple way to do this without first repealing the 1904 Act which named Dalgety, and to do that could lay him open to accusations of succumbing to the arguments of New South Wales. By April 1908, Deakin had found a solution to his dilemma. A Bill was introduced into the House of Representatives 'to determine more definitely the seat of government of the Commonwealth in the neighbourhood of Dalgety'. Deakin told the House that 'the supremacy of Dalgety is unchallenged and unchallengable,'[42] but if the House were now to vote to remove the word 'Dalgety' from the Bill, his government would support any move from a new ballot of the sites.

The House entered enthusiastically into a new debate on the meaning of Section 125 of the Constitution and the relative merits of all the likely sites. George Reid reminded the House that the final form of Section 125 had been settled in his presence and at his request. He had gone to Melbourne in 1899 to insist that the federal capital be within New South Wales and as close as possible to Sydney. In the memorandum issued later by the Premiers, the words 'at a reasonable distance *from* that city' were used to indicate that, while the capital could not be within 100 miles of Sydney, the Premiers had agreed that it should be 'within a reasonable distance *of* that city.' Such an agreement, said Reid, 'rises to the highest degree of sanctity.' It was no longer possible to ignore the spirit of Section 125, he said. If the parliament did not now favour the Dalgety district it should choose a spot near Bathurst or near Canberra, each of which would comply with both the letter and the spirit of the Constitution that Reid had helped to write.[43]

Debate on the second reading of the Dalgety Bill ended when the Parliament rose for the winter recess. The House resumed its discussion on 23 September 1908, to the warning from the *Sydney Morning Herald* that 'Dalgety is impossible and the sooner that position is accepted the better it will be for everybody.'[44] For six days the representatives argued the whole question anew. Canberra, it was said, was in a 'suitable position', and its location would confirm a general impression in Sydney in 1899 that the capital city would be 'within a three hours rail journey of Sydney'. Dalgety, on the other hand, was an 'outlandish, freezing place' and the members were assured that 'if we go to Dalgety, the climate will kill half the older men in Parliament.' Sir John Forrest said that the House should make up its mind once and for all on a site 'because federation will never be complete so long as we are visitors in the capital city of one or another of the States'. But it

329

was apparent that neither Dalgety nor Canberra was a clear favourite, and that the will of the House could be determined only by yet another vote.[45]

On the evening of 1 October 1908, the House of Representatives agreed to conduct a new ballot. In Sydney the decision was greeted with some caution. The *Telegraph* hoped that the House 'will surprise us by rising to what is really a great occasion'[46] and the *Sydney Morning Herald* urged the members to think very carefully indeed before they cast their ballots—'the selection of Dalgety yet again, after proofs of its geographic and climatic unsuitability, and with the knowledge that it is unacceptable to New South Wales, will be a cynical and contemptuous move.'[47]

Lobbying for the various sites reached a new level of seriousness. Lyne nominated Albury, Tumut and a new site called Tooma. Reid put up both Bathurst and Lyndhurst. Unfortunately for Dalgety, Austin Chapman was taken ill with a stroke that left him partly paralysed. Following an electoral redistribution in 1906, Chapman found himself representing not only Dalgety and Bombala but also Canberra. This clash of interests boded ill for Canberra; Watson and other Sydney members therefore nominated a composite site called Yass-Canberra. It was a clever tactical move. As the better known sites fell by the wayside, many members switched their votes to the large and loosely defined new site rather than join one of the established factions. In the final ballot, when the choice lay between one site, Dalgety, which might favour Melbourne, and a site at Yass-Canberra which clearly would not favour Melbourne, the mystery site nearer Sydney won the day.

The representatives' final ballot in the 'battle of the sites' was held on 8 October 1908 and was all over in less than three hours. As Watson had predicted, Canberra received only token support and was removed at the fourth ballot, but the numbers for Yass-Canberra grew steadily and on the ninth and last ballot Yass-Canberra defeated Dalgety by 39 votes to 33.[48] The Sydney press hailed the decision. The *Telegraph* wrote that federation had been 'rehabilitated'[49] and Premier Wade was reported as satisfied, saying that 'although Dalgety had some attractions, it was absolutely unfitted as a place of residence the whole year round.'[50] In Melbourne the *Age* hinted darkly that 'no one should be surprised if the whole thing drags on.'[51] Deakin was still in an awkward situation. It was probable, but by no means certain, that the Senate would agree with the lower House. Until the Senate had voted, Deakin could do nothing with Watson's Dalgety Act.

Three weeks later, the matter was brought before the Senate. The senators from New South Wales and Queensland argued for Yass-Canberra, but those from Victoria and South Australia spoke generally against the new moves, and the West Australians and Tasmanians seemed equally divided in their preferences for Dalgety and Yass-Canberra, the Sydney men made vague promises of a federal seaport at Jervis Bay and suggested that the New South Wales government would be generous in the size of a federal territory in the Yass-Canberra district. Supporters of Dalgety made a head count and realised that Dalgety could not win. They decided instead to rally all opponents of Yass-Canberra around Tumut; if successful this would bring about the selection of Dalgety through the 1904 Act. On 6 November 1908 the Senate voted and the entire thirty-six votes were split evenly between Yass-Canberra and Tumut.[52]

This unusual result caused an uproar in the Senate. Tumut's supporters argued that the tied vote meant that the Senate wished to stay with its earlier choice of Dalgety, but the President ruled that a second ballot should be taken. In the first vote, only one Victorian had chosen Yass-Canberra; in the second ballot James McColl, one of the other five Victorians, changed sides and Yass-Canberra beat Tumut by nineteen votes to seventeen. The

Age was furious with its turncoat senator and said he had 'ratted' on Victoria.[53] McColl replied that at the first ballot he had been manipulated to support Tumut merely to bring about a disagreement with the House of Representatives. To the jeers of Melbourne and the cheers of Sydney, McColl announced that 'I am satisfied with my actions, and would do the same thing again if circumstances demanded it'.[54]

* * *

The last steps in the search for a capital city site were conducted by Andrew Fisher, who formed Australia's second Labour government in November 1908. A Seat of Government (Yass-Canberra) Bill was introduced into Parliament the following month, repealing the 1904 Act naming Dalgety. After its swift passage through both Houses, a determined Dalgety supporter proposed that its name be changed to the 'Seat of Government and Surrender to Sydney Influence Act',[55] but the decision was now irreversible. Fisher began at once the search for the best city site. A survey was made of the Yass-Lake George-Canberra district, and a New South Wales surveyor, Charles Scrivener, was instructed to find a site 'for a beautiful city, occupying a commanding position with extensive views and embracing distinctive features which will lend themselves to the evolution of a design worthy of the object, not only for the present, but for all time.'[56]

Scrivener reported in February 1909 that he had inspected all likely capital sites in the triangle. It was, he said, critical to ensure an ample supply of good water to the city and only at Canberra could such a condition be guaranteed. Those Queanbeyan businessmen who had maintained their ambitions for Canberra for ten lonely years must have been delighted when Scrivener described their site in glowing terms. Canberra, said Scrivener, 'approaches nearer to what is required than any other I have inspected in the Yass-Canberra district', and he concluded with a vision of a federal city which would be both beautiful and practical:

> A city could be located at Canberra that would be visible on approach for many miles; streets with easy gradients would be readily designed, while prominent hills of moderate altitude present suitable sites for the principal public buildings. The capital would probably lie in an amphitheatre of hills with an outlook towards the north and north-east, well-sheltered from both southerly and westerly winds, and in the immediate vicinity of the capital there are large areas of gently undulating country that would be suitable for the evolutions of large bodies of troops.[57]

By October the Commonwealth and state governments had agreed on the present borders of a federal territory of about 912 square miles and had further agreed to transfer in due course land at Jervis Bay for use as a federal port. Acceptance and Surrender Bills passed easily through both Houses and by the start of 1910, the 'battle of the sites' was over.[58] Deakin, once more Prime Minister, was unsure what to do with his large new territory, but elections in April restored a Labour government and Andrew Fisher set to work at once to plan a city worthy of its splendid site.

With the passage of a Seat of Government Administration Bill, the federal capital territory was officially handed over to the Commonwealth on New Year's Day 1911, exactly ten years after the pomp and ceremony of federation in Sydney's Centennial Park. By April, Fisher had authorised a worldwide design competition for the city. It was not a well-run event. King O'Malley, now Minister for Home Affairs, declared that he would be the final judge of the submitted designs, a stand which antagonised many architects and

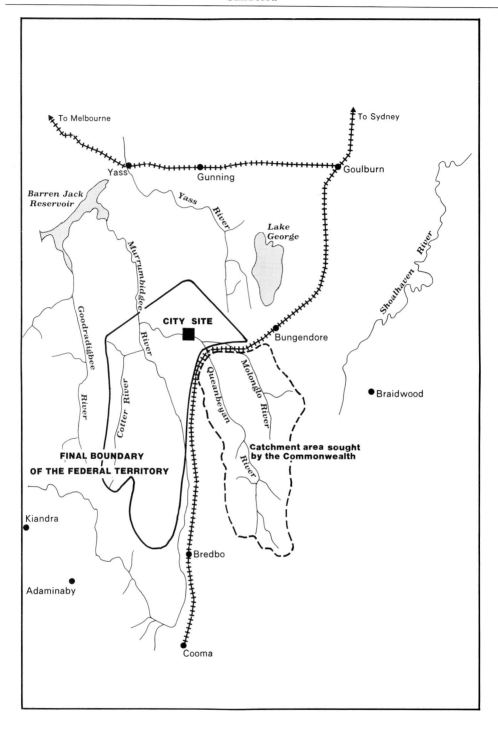

Figure 66: The final boundaries of the Australian Capital Territory

townplanners and caused a boycott of the competition by the Royal Institute of British Architects. The boycott was only partly successful, and by the close of the competition in February 1912 no fewer than 137 entries had been received in Melbourne. At stake was a prize of £1750 and the rare opportunity to design the capital city of a continent.[59]

In May 1912, King O'Malley announced that the winning design had been prepared by Walter Burley Griffin of Chicago.[60] Griffin's submission, beautifully drawn and coloured by his wife Marion Mahony, fitted the city into the gentle topography of the Canberra Valley, and drew broad avenues converging on a Capital Hill and forming an ornamental lake below a parliamentary triangle.[61] It was a simple and splendid concept, designed by a landscape architect of great skill and understanding, but it was attacked from many directions for its apparent extravagance. By June public criticism forced O'Malley to refer the design to a departmental board for their opinion. The board advised that it was unable to accept Griffin's plan or any of the other premiated designs. Instead, the members prepared their own design, borrowing here and there from Griffin and the other plans. The departmental board plan, 'concocted on the combination salad principle,'[62] was a ghastly thing, likened to a 'third rate Luna Park'. But the government accepted it and Griffin was told he could keep his prize money but that his design would never be built. Fortunately for Australia, Griffin would one day come to Australia to oversee the beginnings of his grand plan.

In February 1913, King O'Malley drove a survey peg into the northern slopes of Capital Hill to mark the start of construction of Australia's bush capital. Three weeks later, on 12 March, a grand ceremony was held to name the city. 'Canberra' was a sentimental favourite and a logical choice. In various forms it had been in common use in the district for more than three-quarters of a century; the people of Australia nevertheless responded with imagination and good humour to a government invitation for a suitable name for their future capital. Cookaburra, Fisherburra, Wheatwoolgold, Eucalypta and Kangaremu headed a list of Australiana which also included the strange Meladneyperbane and Sydmelperadbrisho. Politics brought forward Swindleville, Gonebroke, Revenuelia, Caucus City and Liberalism; and from the anglophiles came Cromwell, Gladstone, Shakespeare and Victoria Deferenda Defender.[63] As the christening day drew near, the chances of the names were discussed in the daily press 'with the same zest and in much the same spirit as sporting writers weigh the chances of candidates for the Melbourne Cup.'[64] It was a relief to most observers when at noon Lady Denman, wife of the Governor-General, mounted a crimson draped platform and declared in a clear English voice 'I name the capital of Australia, Canberra'.

At an official banquet that day, most of the speakers seemed relieved that more than a decade of wrangling was over and that Australia was about to build its capital city. As to the 'battle of the sites' that had so absorbed the new Commonwealth, Sir Robert Garran suggested that no better selection than Canberra could have been made by 'a committee of disinterested archangels'.[65] That first battle was nevertheless followed by an equally strenuous 'battle of the plans' which began almost as soon as the visitors left Canberra that day. The departmental board plan was certainly a messy compromise and, although there were many within the government service who pressed for its immediate implementation, there were as many others who resented the debasement of Griffin's wonderful scheme. O'Malley rejected Griffin's request to be 'on the ground in consultation with your Board,'[66] but an election only two months later saw the defeat of Fisher's Labour government and the formation of a 'fusion' anti-Labour ministry led by Joseph Cook. The new

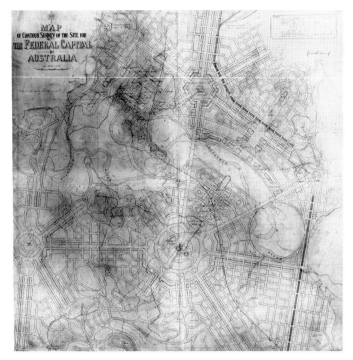

Figure 67: Griffin's 1913 plan for Canberra (Courtesy of the
National Capital Development Commission and the National
Archives, Canberra, A.A., CRS, A710 36-7)

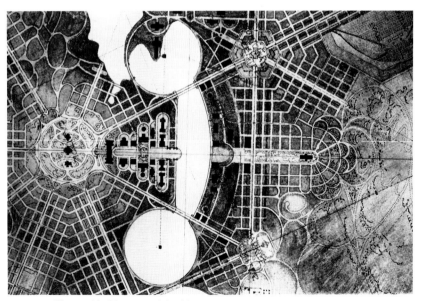

Figure 68: Closeup of Griffin's 1913 plan of the Parliamentary
Triangle (Courtesy of the National Capital Development
Commission and the National Archives, Canberra, A.A., CRS,
A710 36-8)

Figure 69: Mrs Griffin's sketch of future Canberra (Courtesy of the National Capital Development Commission and the National Archives, Canberra, A.A. CRS A710, 49)

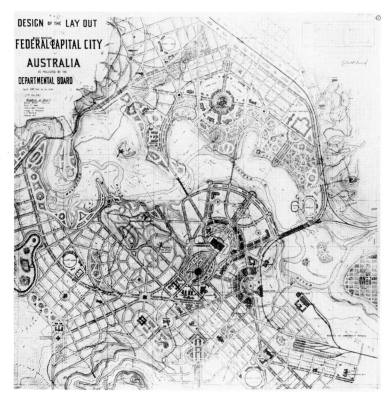

Figure 70: The Department's plan (Courtesy of the National Capital Development Commission and the National Archives, Canberra, A.A. CRS A761, 1)

335

Cabinet decided to 'bring out the author of the premiated design to confer with the gentlemen who have charge of the matter,'[67] and on 19 August 1913 Griffin saw the Canberra Valley for the first time. He looked over the site for a week and then met in Melbourne with the Board. His meetings were predictably profitless and on 15 October the Assistant Minister for Home Affairs, W H Kelly, 'called the members of the Board before him, thanked them for their labours and disbanded them'.[68] The same day, Kelly was full of praise for Griffin in a speech in the House of Representatives, saying that 'since we have seen Mr Griffin we have realised that in him we have an authority on town planning such as we have certainly never seen before in Australia.'[69] This did not prevent the sacked board members from undermining Griffin's every effort to lay out his plan, nor did it stop others from ridiculing what they saw as the 'grand theorising, moonshine and dreaming'[70] of the quiet American landscape architect.

On 18 October 1913, Griffin was appointed Federal Capital Director of Design and Construction for a three-year term, and the fighting began in earnest. Colonel Percy Owen, the Director-General of Works and one of the dismissed board members, told the minister that the basic infrastructure of the new city should properly be his responsibility and not that of Griffin. The Griffin design, said Owen and others, violated essential principles of planning and engineering, and funds could not be released from Owen's budget to lay out the Griffin plan. For three years Griffin could build nothing, his work was obstructed and funds unavailable. A Royal Commission looked for six months into the conflict between Griffin and his public service opponents. The commissioner's findings in March 1917 were in favour of Griffin, 'necessary information and assistance were withheld from him . . . he and his office were ignored . . . members of the Departmental Board endeavoured to set aside his design for the capital city.'[71] But, although Griffin was reappointed to a second term, his first three years had shown that he lacked the confidence and ability needed to coordinate the authorities and individuals at work in Canberra. It was only a matter of time before the organised forces of bureaucracy prevailed.

After release of the findings of the Royal Commission, the unrepentant Owen was removed from direct involvement in Canberra, but Griffin failed again to attract support and the necessary money to move ahead with construction. The war on the other side of the world forced abandonment of his plans for an international competition for a parliament house. He laid out some of the major avenues of his plan, but the general lack of funds for non-essential work prevented all but minor maintenance work elsewhere. With the end of the war came moves to speed up the work by means of a coordinating committee. Griffin was asked to join the committee but refused. In December 1920 his position was abolished and Griffin left Canberra to concentrate on his work in Sydney and Melbourne. His place was taken by a new Federal Capital Advisory Committee under the chairmanship of Sydney architect and planner John Sulman. Early moves by the committee to alter the Griffin design were fortunately resisted, and in 1925 the Griffin plan was gazetted as the official road layout, so that thenceforth, and still today, any changes must first be approved by parliament. This might have been little consolation for Griffin, but it certainly has allowed Canberra to grow into today's splendid city without excessive tinkering by later 'experts'.

The final stages of Canberra's transformation from bush to federal city were organised by Sulman's Advisory Committee and, from 1925, by a new Federal Capital Commission. With the aim of moving the parliament to Canberra as soon as possible, the government began construction of houses and schools on both sides of the river to accommodate the first move of some 600 public officials and their families. Land on long leases was sold to private enterprise for business purposes, the railway was extended from Queanbeyan, and work started on a 'provisional' parliament, sadly not where Griffin had placed it but some 200 metres to the north. As the day of transfer drew near, a memorials committee split the Canberra valley into twenty-three districts and set about naming suburbs, streets and parks.[72] Some traditional names bestowed by the first European property owners in the area—Ainslie in the north, Duntroon in the east, Narrabundah and Pialligo in the south—were retained, but for the majority of suburbs the committee listed those colonials most closely associated with the movement for federation of which Canberra would be the symbol—Barton, Braddon, Deakin, Dickson, Forrest, Fysh, Griffith, Kingston, Lyne, O'Connor, Parkes, Reid, Symon and Turner. To Parkes was given the honour of the central parliamentary triangle, the sides of which were then named for the King, the Commonwealth and the Constitution. As Griffin had earlier suggested, the avenues radiating from his Capital Hill were then named after the state capitals in whose directions they vaguely ran. The four circular roads around the hill were called State, National, Dominion and Empire as their distance from the centre grew. Suburban streets and parks, most no more than lines on a plan, were named after explorers, past governors, local settlers, Aboriginal tribes and botanical species until, by early 1927, the Canberra valley was ready, in spirit at least, to assume its national role.

By the beginning of that year, the 'smokeless, dustless, mudless, odourless and slumless' Canberra[73] had cost Australia £12 million and its inauguration on 9 May was an event of worldwide interest. The London *Morning Post* called it a 'notable enterprise in the wilderness . . . a horde of officials and politicians will have to trek into the unknown, but with characteristic Australian courage they will make the best of the circumstances',[74] and on its following pages the *Post* displayed advertisements inviting British workers and their families to migrate and see it all for themselves. Just before noon on a sunny autumn day, Nellie Melba sang 'God Save the King', the doors of the new Parliament House were unlocked with a golden key and the battles for location and possession were ended. In its editorial the following day, the Melbourne *Argus* hinted at the past bitterness and showed some insight into what lay ahead for Australia's bush capital:

Figure 71: The opening of Parliament House, 1927 (Courtesy of the National Library)

The point so frequently made about a young city for a young country has really not so much in it when examined. There may be many youths of 12 to 16 years of age who will make excellent Prime Ministers in time, but no one thinks of selecting the most likely of the young fellows to be Prime Minister and waiting till he grows up. The application of that illustration is that, apart from the capital cities altogether, apart from the blasted hopes of Sydney and the ravening ambition of Melbourne, there were many cities in existence and growing on their own diet, which would have been fit for a federal capital . . . The new capital is remote, and many profess to believe that it will be better for its remoteness. Arguing thus, they will provide money for communications until the capital is no longer remote and for buildings until it is no longer simple. When it has been made, at much expense, much like any other city of moderate size, then the wonder will be why the city once remote and now convenient, once simple and now complex, was specially created to add to the number of ordinary cities more or less convenient and more or less complex.[75]

Questions of remoteness and convenience aside, Canberra is now a far from ordinary city by Australian or any other definition. By its circumstances of siting, creation and timing, it is not surprisingly totally different from the older state capitals on the coast. Its consolidation over the past sixty years has been hindered by economic indifference or antagonism. But its future is assured and its beauty undeniable. The filling of the lake in 1964 gave it a cohesion it had not enjoyed before, and the new Parliament House surmounts the valley at a scale appropriate to the land it celebrates. What was once called 'a handful of hovels in a howling wilderness' has become a fine capital city for Australia.

Notes

1. *Sydney Morning Herald*, 24-5-1904.
2. Wigmore, Lionel, *The Long View*, (Melbourne, 1963), p.27.
3. Quick, John and Garran, Robert Randolph, *The Annotated Constitution of the Australian Commonwealth*, (Sydney, 1901), pp.109-15.
4. Parkes, Sir Henry, *Fifty Years in the making of Australian History*, (London, 1892), p.336.
5. Official Record of the Proceedings and Debates of the National Australian Convention, *N.S.W. (LA) V&P*, 1891, p.133 ff.
6. Quick and Garran, *op.cit.*, p.145.
7. *N.S.W. (LA) V&P*, 13-11-1894, p.188.
8. *Telegraph*, (Sydney), 5-2-1897.
9. Griffith, Sir Samuel, *Notes on Australian Federation: Its nature and probable effects*, (paper presented to the Government of Queensland and published by authority, 1896), p.21.
10. Quick and Garran, *op.cit.*, p.204.
11. Correspondence printed under Report No. 1, *N.S.W. (LA) V&P*, September, 1898.
12. La Nauze, J.A. *The Making of the Australian Constitution*, (Melbourne, 1972), pp.239-47.
13. *Telegraph*, (Sydney), 22-2-1899.
14. Oliver, Alexander. *Report of the Commissioner on Sites for the Seat of Government of the Commonwealth*, N.S.W. (LA) *P.P.* 425 of 1900.
15. Wigmore, *op.cit.*, p.35.
16. *Commonwealth Parliamentary Debates*, (hereafter cited as 'C.P.D.'), 19-7-1901, p.2807.
17. Knibbs, G.H. 'The Theory of City Design', read to the *R.S.N.S.W.*, 4-9-1901 and Gipps, F.B. 'Lake George (New South Wales) as a site for the federal capital of Australia', read to the *R.G.S.Aust.*, 22-4-1901.
18. Fitzhardinge, L.F. 'William Hughes in Search of a federal capital' in *J.R.A.H.S.*, Vol. 51, March 1965, pp.88-9.
19. *Ibid.*, pp.90-1.
20. Oliver, A. *Royal Commission on sites for the seat of government of the Commonwealth: Report of the Commissioners*, *C.P.P.*, 23 of 1903.

[21] *Ibid.*, p.3.

[22] *Telegraph*, (Sydney), 21-7-1903.

[23] Oliver, A. *A short review of the contents of the Report of the Commonwealth Commissioners on Sites for the Seat of Government of the Commonwealth*, N.S.W. (LA) *P.P.* 177 of 1903.

[24] 'C.P.D.', 30-9-1903 and 6,7,8-10-1903. The various voting systems are discussed in Pegrum, Roger, *The Bush Capital*, (Sydney, 1983), pp.92-4.

[25] 'C.P.D.', 8-10-1903, pp.5933-4.

[26] *Ibid.*, pp.5935-6. Tables printed in the *Sydney Morning Herald*, 10-10-1903 give the votes cast in sequence showing also the States represented by each member.

[27] 'C.P.D.', 13-10-1903, p.6000 (First Reading); p.6047 ff. (Second Reading) and p.6051 ('fag end'); also pp.6269-313. (NB—The Melbourne *Age*, 10-10-1903, wrote that the 'Commonwealth may now thank Heaven it has a Senate powerful enough to check the indecent rush for a bush capital').

[28] *Papers presented to Parliament and ordered to be Printed*, 1904, Vol. II, pp.483-511; *C.P.P.* 18, (Scrivener reporting on southern Monaro), *C.P.P.* 19 (Chesterman reporting on Tumut); *C.P.P.* 14 (Forrest reporting on southern Monaro and Tumut).

[29] 'C.P.D.', 3-6-1904, p.1953.

[30] 'C.P.D.', 20-7-1904, p.3413.

[31] *The Times*, 20-7-1904.

[32] 'C.P.D.', 9-8-1904, p.3936. (The tables give the votes recorded by each representative in the two ballots).

[33] *Sydney Morning Herald*, 13-12-1904.

[34] N.S.W. LA. 'Seat of government of the Commonwealth (Opinions of Mr. C.G. Wade (Attorney-General) and Sir Julian Salomons and Mr C.B. Stephen as to whether the Seat of Government Act 1904 (Commonwealth Act No. 7, 1904) is binding on New South Wales)'. Ordered to be printed 22-11-1904, *P.P.* 242 of 1904, pp.1-2.

[35] *N.S.W. (LA) V&P* 14-12-1904, p.219.

[36] Correspondence between the Prime Minister and the Premier of N.S.W. re draft Bill to expedite settlement of the federal capital site, *C.P.P.* 38, 41, 50, 51, 55 of 1905.

[37] Reports representing proposed sites at Mahkoolma, Canberra and other sites in the Yass (Lake George) district, *C.P.P.* 29 of 1906, p.9.

[38] Deakin to Carruthers, 18-9-1906, *C.P.P.* 100 of 1906. (NB—*Morning Post*, 13-2-1906, recorded Deakin as saying that Dalgety was 'inconvenient, its winter climate severe, its position not easily accessible'). See also Sherington, G.E. 'The selection of Canberra, as Australia's National Capital,' in *J.R.A.H.S.*, Vol. 56, June 1970, p.137.

[39] Federal Capital: Proposed Sites—Minute by the Rt Hon. Sir John Forrest . . . on the suggested site for the seat of government of the Commonwealth at Canberra, near Queanbeyan, in New South Wales., *C.P.P.* 5 of 1907. Also Gale, J. 'The federal capital: Dalgety or Canberra: Which?', paper read at a public meeting in Queanbeyan, 24-7-1907.

[40] 'C.P.D.', 10-7-1907, p.300.

[41] *C.P.P.*, 153 of 1907-8, (31-10-1907).

[42] 'C.P.D.', 2-12-1908, p.2539.

[43] 'C.P.D.', 8-4-1908, pp.10313-316.

[44] *Sydney Morning Herald*, 24-9-1908.

[45] 'C.P.D.', 29-9-1908, pp.495-583.

[46] *Telegraph*, (Sydney), 6-10-1908.

[47] *Sydney Morning Herald*, 26-9-1908.

[48] 'C.P.D.', 8-10-1908, pp.936-40. (Tables give the votes of each member in the nine ballots).

[49] *Telegraph*, (Sydney), 10-10-1908.

[50] *Ibid.*, 9-10-1908.

[51] *Age*, (Melbourne), 9-10-1908.

[52] 'C.P.D.', 6-10-1908, pp.2100-8. (Tables give the votes of each senator in the two ballots).

[53] *Age*, (Melbourne), 9-11-1908.

[54] *Argus*, (Melbourne), 9-11-1908.

[55] 'C.P.D.', 8-12-1908, p.2823.

[56] Watson, F. *A Brief History of Canberra*, (Canberra, 1927), p.124ff.

[57] Report on *Federal Capital Site, Papers and Plans etc.*, N.S.W. (LA) *P.P.* 66 of 1909.

[58] 'C.P.D.', 8-10-1909, pp.4297-310; 13-10-1909, pp.4417-27; 20-10-1909, pp.4701-20; 21-10-1909, pp.4791-818; 22-10-1909, pp.4910-24; 27-10-1909, pp.5004-28.

[59] 'Information, conditions and particulars for guidance in the preparation of competitive designs for the federal capital city of the Commonwealth of Australia'. Report for the Department of Home Affairs, 30-4-1911. Reprinted as Appendix A, pp.85-92 in Senate, *Report from the select committee appointed to inquire into and report upon the development of Canberra*, September, 1955.

[60] *Federal capital city: Report of Board appointed to investigate and report to the Minister for Home Affairs in regard to competitive designs*, (Government Printer, Melbourne, 1912).

[61] Griffin's original report accompanying his drawings was reprinted as Appendix B, pp.93-102 in 'Report from the select committee' (1955), *op.cit.*

[62] Wigmore, *op.cit.*, p.52.

[63] Daly, C.S. 'Canberra Nomenclature' in Selth, P.A. (ed.), *Canberra Collection*, (Kilmore, 1976), pp.4-6.

[64] Speech by Lord Denman quoted in King O'Malley, *Concerning Canberra: The christening and dedication of Australia's national capital, 12 March 1913, and its dire neglect*, (Melbourne, 1936).

[65] Garran, R.R. *Prosper the Commonwealth*, (Sydney, 1958), p.283.

[66] Letter from Griffin to O'Malley, 21-1-1913, in Report of the Royal Commission (1) Issues relating to Mr Griffin, *C.P.P.*, 378 of 1914-17, p.7.

[67] Letter from Miller to the Minister for Home Affairs in 'Federal Capital—Design for layout of federal capital city—correspondence and papers: progress plan etc.', *C.P.P.*, 153 of 1914-15, p.21.

[68] *C.P.P.*, 378 of 1914-17, p.9.

[69] 'C.D.P.', 15-10-1913, p.2124.

[70] Brennan, Frank, *Canberra in Crisis: A history of land tenure and leasehold administration*, (Canberra 1971), p.40.

[71] *C.P.P.*, 378 of 1914-17, pp.45-46.

[72] Daley, C.S. *op.cit.*, pp.8-16.

[73] *Daily News*, (London), 9-5-1927.

[74] *Morning Post* (London), 9-5-1927.

[75] *Argus*, 10-5-1927.

INDEX

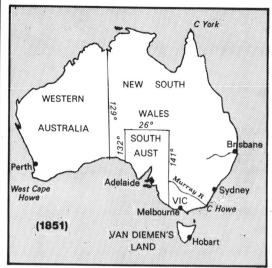

(1851)

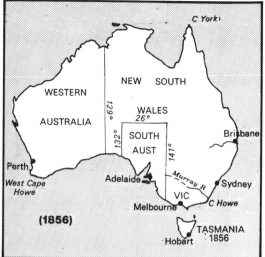

(1856)

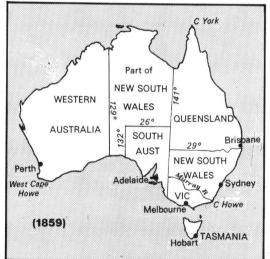

(1859)

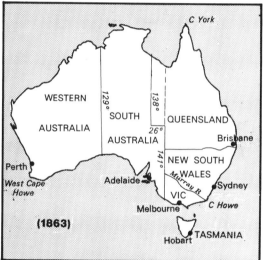

(1863)

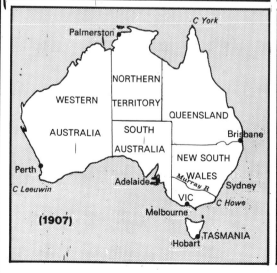

(1907)

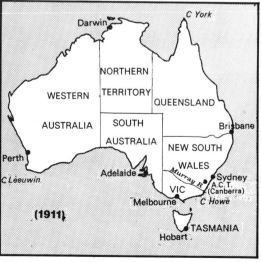

(1911)